Student Solutions Manual

Doreen Kelly

Mesa Community College

Elementary Algebra
for College Students

■ Seventh Edition

Allen R.
Angel

PEARSON
Prentice Hall

Upper Saddle River, NJ 07458

Vice President and Editorial Director, Mathematics: Christine Hoag
Executive Editor: Paul Murphy
Project Manager: Dawn Nuttall
Editorial Assistant: Georgina Brown
Senior Managing Editor: Linda Behrens
Assistant Managing Editor: Lynn Savino Wendel
Production Editor: Ashley M. Booth
Supplement Cover Manager: Paul Gourhan
Supplement Cover Designer: Victoria Colotta
Manufacturing Buyer: Ilene Kahn
Associate Director of Operations: Alexis Heydt-Long

© 2007 Pearson Education, Inc.
Pearson Prentice Hall
Pearson Education, Inc.
Upper Saddle River, NJ 07458

Printed in the United States of America

10 9 8 7 6 5 4 3 2 1

ISBN 13:   978-0-13-199458-4   Standalone
ISBN 10:   0-13-199458-1   Standalone
ISBN 13:   978-0-13-199469-0   Student Study Pack Component
ISBN 10:   0-13-199469-7   Student Study Pack Component

Pearson Education Ltd., *London*
Pearson Education Australia Pty. Ltd., *Sydney*
Pearson Education Singapore, Pte. Ltd.
Pearson Education North Asia Ltd., *Hong Kong*
Pearson Education Canada, Inc., *Toronto*
Pearson Educación de Mexico, S.A. de C.V.
Pearson Education—Japan, *Tokyo*
Pearson Education Malaysia, Pte. Ltd.

Table of Contents

Chapter 1

Exercise Set 1.1

1.-10. Answers will vary.

11. To prepare properly for this class, you need to do all the homework carefully and completely; preview the new material that is to be covered in class.

13. At least 2 hours of study and homework time for each hour of class time is generally recommended.

15.a. You need to do the homework in order to practice what was presented in class.

  b. When you miss class, you miss important information. Therefore it is important that you attend class regularly.

17. Answers will vary.

Exercise Set 1.2

1. understand, translate, calculate, check, state answer

3. when a number has been rounded

5. Rank the data. The median is the value in the middle.

7. Divide the sum of the data by the number of pieces of data.

9. A mean average of 80 corresponds to a total of 800 points for the 10 quizzes. Walter's mean average of 79 corresponds to a total of 790 points for the 10 quizzes. Thus, he actually missed a B by 10 points.

11.a. $\dfrac{78 + 97 + 59 + 74 + 74}{5} = \dfrac{382}{5} = 76.4$

The mean grade is 76.4.

  b. 59, 74, 74, 78, 97
The middle value is 74.
The median grade is 74.

13.a. $\dfrac{96.56 + 108.78 + 87.23 + 85.90 + 79.55 + 65.88}{6} = \dfrac{523.90}{6} \approx 87.32$

The mean bill is about \$87.32.

  b. \$65.88, \$79.55, \$85.90, \$87.23, \$96.56, \$108.78
The middle values are \$85.90 and \$87.23.
$\dfrac{85.90 + 87.23}{2} = \dfrac{173.13}{2} = 86.57$
The median bill is about \$86.57.

15.a. $\dfrac{10.63 + 10.67 + 10.68 + 10.83 + 11.6 + 11.76 + 11.87 + 12.18 + 12.8 + 12.91}{10}$

$= \dfrac{115.93}{10} = 11.593$

The mean inches for rainfall for the 10 years is 11.593.

  b. 10.63, 10.67, 10.68, 10.83, 11.6, 11.76, 11.87, 12.18, 12.8, 12.91
The middle values are 11.6 and 11.76.

$\dfrac{11.6 + 11.76}{2} = \dfrac{23.36}{2} = 11.68$

The median inches for rainfall for the 10 years is 11.68.

17.   Barbara's earnings = 5% of sales
       Barbara's earnings = 0.05(9400)
                     = 470
       Her week's earnings were $470.

19.a. sales tax = 8% of price
       sales tax = 0.08(16,700)
                 = 1336
       The sales tax was $1,336.

   b. Total cost = price + tax
       Total cost = 16,700 + 1,336
                  = 18,036
       The total cost was $18,036.

21. operations performed = (number of operations in billions)(amount of time in seconds)
                         = (2.3)(0.7)
                         = 1.61 billion
     In 0.7 seconds, 1,610,000,000 operations can be performed.

23.a. time to use energy = $\dfrac{\text{kJ in hamburger}}{\text{kJ/min running}}$

                         $= \dfrac{1550}{80}$

                         $= 19.375$

       It takes 19.375 minutes to use up the energy from a hamburger by running.

   b. time to use energy = $\dfrac{\text{kJ in milkshake}}{\text{kJ/min walking}}$

                         $= \dfrac{2200}{25}$

                         $= 88$

       It takes 88 minutes to use up the energy from a chocolate milkshake by walking.

   c. time to use energy = $\dfrac{\text{kJ in glass of skim milk}}{\text{kJ/min cycling}}$

                         $= \dfrac{350}{35}$

                         $= 10$

       It takes 10 minutes to use up the energy from a glass of skim milk by cycling.

25. miles per gallon = $\dfrac{\text{number of miles}}{\text{number of gallons}}$

                     $= \dfrac{16,935.4 - 16,741.3}{10.5}$

                     $= \dfrac{194.1}{10.5}$

                     ≈ 18.49

     His car gets about 18.49 miles per gallon.

27.   savings = local cost − mail order cost
       local cost = $425 + (0.08)(425)$
                  = 425 + 34
                  = 459
       mail cost = $4(62.30 + 6.20 + 8)$
                 = $4(76.50)$
                 = 306
       savings = 459 − 306
               = 153
       Eric saved $153.

29. A single green block should be placed on the 3 on the right.

31.a. gallons per year = 365(gallons per day)
       gallons per year = 365(11.25 gallons)
                        = 4106.25
       There are 4106.25 gallons of water wasted each year.

2

b. additional money spent = (cost)(gallons wasted)

$$= \frac{5.20}{1000 \text{ gallons}} \cdot 4106.25 \text{ gallons}$$

$$\approx 21.35$$

About $21.35 extra is spent because of the wasted water.

33.a. cost = deductible + 20% (doctor bill − deductible)

$$= 150 + 0.20(365 - 150)$$

$$= 150 + 0.20(215)$$

$$= 150 + 43$$

$$= 193$$

Mel will be responsible for $193.

b. The insurance company would be responsible for the remainder of the bill which would be $365 - 193 = \$172$.

35.a. Hong Kong-China; 550

b. Mexico;

c. $550 - 385 = 165$

37.a. 1992: 275,000; 2004: 1,050,000

b. $1,050,000 - 275,000 = 775,000$

c. $\dfrac{1,050,000}{275,000} \approx 3.818$

$$\approx 3.82 \text{ times greater}$$

39.a. 82% of 1.7 million $= 0.82(1.7 \text{ million})$

$$= 1.394 \text{ million}$$

b. 15% of 1.7 million $= 0.15(1.7 \text{ million})$

$$= 0.255 \text{ million}$$

c. 3% of 1.7 million $= = 0.03(1.7 \text{ million})$

$$= 0.051 \text{ million}$$

41. $\text{mean} = \dfrac{\text{sum of grades}}{\text{number of exams}}$

$$60 = \frac{50 + 59 + 67 + 80 + 56 + \text{ last}}{6}$$

$$360 = 312 + \text{last}$$

$$\text{last} = 360 - 312$$

$$= 48$$

Lamond needs at least a 48 on the last exam.

b. $70 = \dfrac{312 + \text{ last}}{6}$

$$420 = 312 + \text{ last}$$

$$\text{last} = 420 - 312$$

$$= 108$$

Lamond would need 108 points on the last exam, so he cannot get a C.

43. bachelor's degree

$$\frac{49,900}{21,600} \approx 2.3$$

45. Answers will vary.
One possible solution is:
50, 60, 70, 80, 90

$$\text{mean} = \frac{50 + 60 + 70 + 80 + 90}{5}$$

$$= \frac{350}{5}$$

$$= 70$$

Exercise Set 1.3

1.a. Variables are letters that represent numbers.

b. Letters often used to represent variables are x, y, and z.

3.a. The top number is the numerator.

b. The bottom number is the denominator.

5. Divide out factors that are common to both the numerator and the denominator.

7. **a.** The least common denominator is the smallest number divisible by the two denominators.
   b. Answers will vary.

9. Part b) shows simplifying a fraction. In part a) common factors are divided out of two fractions.

11. Part a) is incorrect because you cannot divide out common factors when adding.

13. c) $\frac{4}{5} \cdot \frac{1}{4} = \frac{1}{5} \cdot \frac{1}{1} = \frac{1}{5}$. Divide out the common factor, 4. This process can be used only when multiplying fractions and so cannot be used for a) or b). Part d) becomes $\frac{4}{5} \cdot \frac{4}{1}$ so no common factor can be divided out.

15. Multiply numerators and multiply denominators.

17. Write fractions with a common denominator, add or subtract numerators, keep the common denominator.

19. Yes, it is simplified because the greatest common divisor of the numerator and denominator is 1.

21. Yes, it can be written as a mixed number.
    $\frac{13}{5} = \frac{10}{5} + \frac{3}{5} = 2\frac{3}{5}$

23. The greatest common factor of 10 and 15 is 5.
    $\frac{10}{15} = \frac{10 \div 5}{15 \div 5} = \frac{2}{3}$

25. The greatest common factor of 3 and 12 is 3.
    $\frac{3}{12} = \frac{3 \div 3}{12 \div 3} = \frac{1}{4}$

27. The greatest common factor of 36 and 76 is 4.
    $\frac{36}{76} = \frac{36 \div 4}{76 \div 4} = \frac{9}{19}$

29. The greatest common factor of 9 and 21 is 3.
    $\frac{9}{21} = \frac{9 \div 3}{21 \div 3} = \frac{3}{7}$

31. 18 and 49 have no common factors other than 1. Therefore, the fraction is already simplified.

33. 12 and 25 have no common factors other than 1. Therefore, the fraction is already simplified.

35. $2\frac{13}{15} = \frac{30 + 13}{15} = \frac{43}{15}$

37. $7\frac{2}{3} = \frac{21 + 2}{3} = \frac{23}{3}$

39. $3\frac{5}{18} = \frac{54 + 5}{18} = \frac{59}{18}$

41. $9\frac{6}{17} = \frac{153 + 6}{17} = \frac{159}{17}$

43. $\frac{7}{4} = 1\frac{3}{4}$ because $7 \div 4 = 1$ R3

45. $\frac{13}{4} = 3\frac{1}{4}$ because $13 \div 4 = 3$ R 1

47. $\frac{32}{7} = 4\frac{4}{7}$ because $32 \div 7 = 4$ R 4

49. $\frac{86}{14} = 6\frac{2}{14} = 6\frac{1}{7}$ because $86 \div 14 = 6$ R 2

51. $\frac{2}{3} \cdot \frac{4}{5} = \frac{2 \cdot 4}{3 \cdot 5} = \frac{8}{15}$

53. $\frac{5}{12} \cdot \frac{4}{15} = \frac{\cancel{5}^{1}}{\cancel{12}_{3}} \cdot \frac{\cancel{4}^{1}}{\cancel{15}_{3}} = \frac{1 \cdot 1}{3 \cdot 3} = \frac{1}{9}$

55. $\frac{3}{4} \div \frac{1}{2} = \frac{3}{\cancel{4}_{2}} \cdot \frac{\cancel{2}^{1}}{1} = \frac{3}{2} \cdot \frac{1}{1} = \frac{3}{2}$ or $1\frac{1}{2}$

57. $\frac{3}{8} \div \frac{3}{4} = \frac{\cancel{3}^{1}}{\cancel{8}_{2}} \cdot \frac{\cancel{4}^{1}}{\cancel{3}_{1}} = \frac{1 \cdot 1}{2 \cdot 1} = \frac{1}{2}$

59. $\frac{10}{3} \div \frac{5}{9} = \frac{\cancel{10}^{2}}{\cancel{3}_{1}} \cdot \frac{\cancel{9}^{3}}{\cancel{5}_{1}} = \frac{2 \cdot 3}{1 \cdot 1} = \frac{6}{1} = 6$

61. $\frac{15}{4} \cdot \frac{2}{3} = \frac{\cancel{15}^{5}}{\cancel{4}_{2}} \cdot \frac{\cancel{2}^{1}}{\cancel{3}_{1}} = \frac{5 \cdot 1}{2 \cdot 1} = \frac{5}{2}$ or $2\frac{1}{2}$

63. $5\frac{3}{8} \div 1\frac{1}{4}$
    $5\frac{3}{8} = \frac{40 + 3}{8} = \frac{43}{8}$
    $1\frac{1}{4} = \frac{4 + 1}{4} = \frac{5}{4}$
    $5\frac{3}{8} \div 1\frac{1}{4} = \frac{43}{8} \div \frac{5}{4}$
    $= \frac{43}{\cancel{8}_{2}} \cdot \frac{\cancel{4}^{1}}{5}$

$$= \frac{43 \cdot 1}{2 \cdot 5}$$

$$= \frac{43}{10} \text{ or } 4\frac{3}{10}$$

65. $\frac{28}{13} \cdot \frac{2}{7} = \frac{\overset{4}{\cancel{28}}}{13} \cdot \frac{2}{\underset{1}{\cancel{7}}} = \frac{4 \cdot 2}{13 \cdot 1} = \frac{8}{13}$

67. $\frac{3}{8} + \frac{2}{8} = \frac{3+2}{8} = \frac{5}{8}$

69. $\frac{3}{14} - \frac{1}{14} = \frac{3-1}{14} = \frac{2}{14} = \frac{1}{7}$

71. $\frac{4}{5} + \frac{6}{15}$

$$\frac{4}{5} = \frac{4}{5} \cdot \frac{3}{3} = \frac{12}{15}$$

$$\frac{4}{5} + \frac{6}{15} = \frac{12}{15} + \frac{6}{15} = \frac{12+6}{15} = \frac{18}{15} = \frac{6}{5} \text{ or } 1\frac{1}{5}$$

73. $\frac{8}{17} + \frac{2}{34}$

$$\frac{8}{17} = \frac{8}{17} \cdot \frac{2}{2} = \frac{16}{34}$$

$$\frac{8}{17} + \frac{2}{34} = \frac{16}{34} + \frac{2}{34} = \frac{16+2}{34} = \frac{18}{34} = \frac{9}{17}$$

75. $\frac{1}{3} + \frac{1}{4}$

$$\frac{1}{3} = \frac{1}{3} \cdot \frac{4}{4} = \frac{4}{12}$$

$$\frac{1}{4} = \frac{1}{4} \cdot \frac{3}{3} = \frac{3}{12}$$

$$\frac{1}{3} + \frac{1}{4} = \frac{4}{12} + \frac{3}{12} = \frac{4+3}{12} = \frac{7}{12}$$

77. $\frac{7}{12} - \frac{2}{9}$

$$\frac{7}{12} = \frac{7}{12} \cdot \frac{3}{3} = \frac{21}{36}$$

$$\frac{2}{9} = \frac{2}{9} \cdot \frac{4}{4} = \frac{8}{36}$$

$$\frac{7}{12} - \frac{2}{9} = \frac{21}{36} - \frac{8}{36} = \frac{21-8}{36} = \frac{13}{36}$$

79. $3\frac{1}{8} - \frac{5}{12}$

$$3\frac{1}{8} = \frac{24+1}{8} = \frac{25}{8} \cdot \frac{3}{3} = \frac{75}{24}$$

$$\frac{5}{12} = \frac{5}{12} \cdot \frac{2}{2} = \frac{10}{24}$$

$$3\frac{1}{8} - \frac{5}{12} = \frac{75}{24} - \frac{10}{24} = \frac{75-10}{24} = \frac{65}{24} \text{ or } 2\frac{17}{24}$$

81. $6\frac{1}{3} - 3\frac{1}{2}$

$$6\frac{1}{3} = \frac{18+1}{3} = \frac{19}{3} \cdot \frac{2}{2} = \frac{38}{6}$$

$$3\frac{1}{2} = \frac{6+1}{2} = \frac{7}{2} \cdot \frac{3}{3} = \frac{21}{6}$$

$$6\frac{1}{3} - 3\frac{1}{2} = \frac{38}{6} - \frac{21}{6} = \frac{38-21}{6} = \frac{17}{6} \text{ or } 2\frac{5}{6}$$

83. $9\frac{2}{5} - 6\frac{1}{2}$

$$9\frac{2}{5} = \frac{45+2}{5} = \frac{47}{5} \cdot \frac{2}{2} = \frac{94}{10}$$

$$6\frac{1}{2} = \frac{12+1}{2} = \frac{13}{2} \cdot \frac{5}{5} = \frac{65}{10}$$

$$9\frac{2}{5} - 6\frac{1}{2} = \frac{94}{10} - \frac{65}{10} = \frac{94-65}{10} = \frac{29}{10} \text{ or } 2\frac{9}{10}$$

85. $5\frac{9}{10} + 3\frac{1}{3}$

$$5\frac{9}{10} = \frac{50+9}{10} = \frac{59}{10} \cdot \frac{3}{3} = \frac{177}{30}$$

$$3\frac{1}{3} = \frac{9+1}{3} = \frac{10}{3} \cdot \frac{10}{10} = \frac{100}{30}$$

$$5\frac{9}{10} + 3\frac{1}{3} = \frac{177}{30} + \frac{100}{30} = \frac{177+100}{30} = \frac{277}{30} \text{ or } 9\frac{7}{30}$$

87. $\frac{5}{6} - \frac{3}{8}$

$$\frac{5}{6} \cdot \frac{4}{4} = \frac{20}{24}$$

$$\frac{3}{8} \cdot \frac{3}{3} = \frac{9}{24}$$

$$\frac{5}{6} - \frac{3}{8} = \frac{20}{24} - \frac{9}{24} = \frac{20-9}{24} = \frac{11}{24}$$

It is $\frac{11}{24}$ mile larger.

89. $55\dfrac{3}{16} - 46\dfrac{1}{4}$

$$55\dfrac{3}{16} = \dfrac{880+3}{16} = \dfrac{883}{16}$$

$$46\dfrac{1}{4} = \dfrac{184+1}{4} = \dfrac{185}{4} = \dfrac{185}{4}\cdot\dfrac{4}{4} = \dfrac{740}{16}$$

$$53\dfrac{3}{16} - 46\dfrac{1}{4} = \dfrac{883}{16} - \dfrac{740}{16} = \dfrac{143}{16} = 8\dfrac{5}{16}$$

Rebecca has grown $8\dfrac{5}{16}$ inches.

91. $1 - \dfrac{31}{50} = \dfrac{50}{50} - \dfrac{31}{50} = \dfrac{50-31}{50} = \dfrac{19}{50}$

The fraction of putts not made were $\dfrac{19}{50}$.

93. $1 - \dfrac{37}{40} = \dfrac{40}{40} - \dfrac{37}{40} = \dfrac{40-37}{40} = \dfrac{3}{40}$

There were $\dfrac{3}{40}$ people unemployed.

95. 15 feet $2\dfrac{1}{2}$ in. $-$ 3 feet $3\dfrac{1}{4}$ in.

$= 14$ feet $14\dfrac{2}{4}$ in. $-$ 3 feet $3\dfrac{1}{4}$ in.

$= 11$ feet $11\dfrac{1}{4}$ in.

Now convert to inches,

$11(12) + 11\dfrac{1}{4} = 132 + 11\dfrac{1}{4} = 143\dfrac{1}{4}$ in.

Now convert to feet.

$143\dfrac{1}{4} \div 12 = \dfrac{572+1}{4}\cdot\dfrac{1}{12} = \dfrac{573}{48} \approx 11.94$ ft.

97. $10\dfrac{1}{2} - 8\dfrac{2}{5} =$

$10\dfrac{1}{2} = \dfrac{21}{2}\cdot\dfrac{5}{5} = \dfrac{105}{10}$

$8\dfrac{2}{5} = \dfrac{42}{5}\cdot\dfrac{2}{2} = \dfrac{84}{10}$

$\dfrac{105}{10} - \dfrac{84}{10} = \dfrac{105-84}{10} = \dfrac{21}{10} = 2\dfrac{1}{10}$

She improved by $2\dfrac{1}{10}$ minutes.

99. $3\dfrac{1}{8} = \dfrac{24+1}{8} = \dfrac{25}{8}$

$3\dfrac{1}{8} \div 2 = 3\dfrac{1}{8} \div \dfrac{2}{1} = \dfrac{25}{8}\cdot\dfrac{1}{2} = \dfrac{25}{16}$ or $1\dfrac{9}{16}$

Each piece is $\dfrac{25}{16}$ or $1\dfrac{9}{16}$ inches long.

101. $\dfrac{1}{16}\cdot 80 = \dfrac{1}{16}\cdot\dfrac{80}{1} = \dfrac{1}{1}\cdot\dfrac{5}{1} = 5$

Mr. Krisanda should be given 5 milligrams of the drug.

103. $15 \div \dfrac{3}{8} = \dfrac{15}{1}\cdot\dfrac{8}{3} = \dfrac{5}{1}\cdot\dfrac{8}{1} = \dfrac{5\cdot 8}{1\cdot 1} = \dfrac{40}{1} = 40$

Tierra can wash her hair 40 times.

105. $\dfrac{1}{4} + \dfrac{1}{4} + 1 = \dfrac{1}{4} + \dfrac{1}{4} + \dfrac{4}{4} = \dfrac{6}{4} = \dfrac{3}{2}$ or $1\dfrac{1}{2}$

The total thickness is $1\dfrac{1}{2}$ inches.

107. $4\dfrac{2}{3} = \dfrac{12+2}{3} = \dfrac{14}{3}$

$28 \div \dfrac{14}{3} = \dfrac{28}{1}\cdot\dfrac{3}{14} = \dfrac{2}{1}\cdot\dfrac{3}{1} = \dfrac{6}{1} = 6$

There will be 6 whole strips of wood.

109.a. Total height of computer + monitor

$= 7\dfrac{1}{2}$ in. $+ 14\dfrac{3}{8}$ in.

$7\dfrac{1}{2} = \dfrac{15}{2} = \dfrac{15}{2}\cdot\dfrac{4}{4} = \dfrac{60}{8}$

$14\dfrac{3}{8} = \dfrac{112+3}{8} = \dfrac{115}{8}$

$7\dfrac{1}{2} + 14\dfrac{3}{8} = \dfrac{60}{8} + \dfrac{115}{8} = \dfrac{175}{8}$ or $21\dfrac{7}{8}$

Total height of computer and monitor is $\dfrac{175}{8}$ or $21\dfrac{7}{8}$ inches, so there is sufficient room.

b. $22\dfrac{1}{2} = \dfrac{44+1}{2} = \dfrac{45}{2} = \dfrac{45}{2}\cdot\dfrac{4}{4} = \dfrac{180}{8}$

$22\dfrac{1}{2} - 21\dfrac{7}{8} = \dfrac{180}{8} - \dfrac{175}{8} = \dfrac{5}{8}$

There will be $\dfrac{5}{8}$ inch of extra height.

c. $22\dfrac{1}{2} = \dfrac{44+1}{2} = \dfrac{45}{2} = \dfrac{45}{2}\cdot\dfrac{2}{2} = \dfrac{90}{4}$

$26\dfrac{1}{2} = \dfrac{52+1}{2} = \dfrac{53}{2} = \dfrac{53}{2}\cdot\dfrac{2}{2} = \dfrac{106}{4}$

$$2\frac{1}{2} = \frac{4+1}{2} = \frac{5}{2} = \frac{5}{2} \cdot \frac{2}{2} = \frac{10}{4}$$

$$1\frac{1}{4} = \frac{4+1}{4} = \frac{5}{4}$$

$$22\frac{1}{2} + 26\frac{1}{2} + 2\frac{1}{2} + 1\frac{1}{4}$$

$$= \frac{90}{4} + \frac{106}{4} + \frac{10}{4} + \frac{5}{4}$$

$$= \frac{211}{4} \text{ or } 52\frac{3}{4}$$

The height of the desk is $52\frac{3}{4}$ in.

111. a. $\dfrac{*}{a} + \dfrac{?}{a} = \dfrac{*+?}{a}$

   b. $\dfrac{\odot}{?} - \dfrac{\square}{?} = \dfrac{\odot - \square}{?}$

   c. $\dfrac{\Delta}{\square} + \dfrac{4}{\square} = \dfrac{\Delta + 4}{\square}$

   d. $\dfrac{x}{3} - \dfrac{2}{3} = \dfrac{x-2}{3}$

   e. $\dfrac{12}{x} - \dfrac{4}{x} = \dfrac{12-4}{x} = \dfrac{8}{x}$

113. number of pills

$$= \frac{(\text{mg per day})(\text{days per month})(\text{number of months})}{\text{mg per pill}}$$

$$\text{number of pills} = \frac{(450)(30)(6)}{300} = 270$$

Dr. Muechler should prescribe 270 pills

115. Answers will vary.

116. $\dfrac{9+8+15+32+16}{5} = \dfrac{80}{5} = 16$

The mean is 16.

117. In order, the values are: 8, 9, 15, 16, 32.
The median is 15.

118. Variables are letters used to represent numbers.

Exercise Set 1.4

1. A set is a collection of elements.

3. Answers will vary. One possible answer is the set of all natural numbers less than 0.

5. The set of whole numbers contains the natural numbers and zero, which is not a natural number.

7. a. The natural number 7 is a whole number because it is a member of the set $\{0, 1, 2, 3, \ldots\}$.

   b. The natural number 7 is a rational number because it can be written as the quotient of two integers, $\dfrac{7}{1}$.

   c. All natural numbers are real numbers.

9. a. yes   **c.** no

   b. no   **d.** yes

11. The integers are $\{\ldots, -3, -2, -1, 0, 1, 2, 3, \ldots\}$.

13. The whole numbers are $\{0, 1, 2, \ldots\}$.

15. The negative integers are $\{\ldots, -3, -2, -1\}$.

17. True; the whole numbers are $\{0, 1, 2, \ldots\}$.

19. True; any number that can be represented on a real number line is a real number.

21. False; the integers are $\{\ldots, -2, -1, 0, 1, 2, \ldots\}$.

23. False; $\sqrt{2}$ cannot be expressed as the quotient of two integers.

25. True; $-\dfrac{1}{5}$ is a quotient of two integers, $\dfrac{-1}{5}$.

27. True; 0 can be expressed as a quotient of two integers, $\dfrac{0}{1}$.

29. False; $4\dfrac{5}{8}$ is rational since it can be expressed as a quotient of two integers.

31. True; $-\sqrt{5}$ is irrational since it cannot be expressed exactly as a decimal number.

33. True, either $\varnothing$ or $\{\ \}$ is used.

35. False; irrational numbers are real but not rational.

37. True; any rational number can be represented on a real number line and is therefore real.

39. True; irrational numbers are real numbers which are not rational.

41. False; any negative irrational number is a counterexample.

43. True; the symbol $\mathbb{R}$ represents the set of real numbers.

45. False; every number greater than zero is positive but not necessarily an integer.

47. True; the integers are

$$\left\{ \underbrace{\ldots, -2, -1,}_{\text{negative integers}} \underbrace{0}_{\text{zero}}, \underbrace{1, 2, \ldots}_{\text{positive integers}} \right\}.$$

49. a. 13 is a positive integer.
  b. –2 and 13 are rational numbers.
  c. –2 and 13 are real numbers.
  d. 13 is a whole number.

51. a. 3 and 77 are positive integers.

  b. 0, 3, and 77 are whole numbers

  c. 0, –2, 3, and 77 are integers.

  d. $-\dfrac{5}{7}$, 0, – 2, 3, $6\dfrac{1}{4}$, 1.63, and 77
     are rational numbers.

  e. $\sqrt{7}$ and $-\sqrt{3}$ are irrational numbers.

  f. $-\dfrac{5}{7}$, 0, – 2, 3, $6\dfrac{1}{4}$, $\sqrt{7}$, $-\sqrt{3}$, 1.63, and
     77 are real numbers.

For Exercises 53–63, answers will vary. One possible answer is given.

53. 0, 1, 2

55. $-\sqrt{2},\ -\sqrt{3},\ -\sqrt{7}$

57. $-\dfrac{2}{3},\ \dfrac{1}{2},\ 6.3$

59. –13, –5, –1

61. $\sqrt{2},\ \sqrt{3},\ -\sqrt{5}$

63. –7, 1, 5

65. {8, 9, 10, 11, ..., 94}
  $94 - 8 + 1 = 86 + 1 = 87$
  The set has 87 elements.

67. a. $A = \{1, 3, 4, 5, 8\}$

  b. $B = \{2, 5, 6, 7, 8\}$

  c. A and $B = \{5, 8\}$

  d. A or $B = \{1, 2, 3, 4, 5, 6, 7, 8\}$

69. a. Set B continues beyond 4.

  b. Set A has 4 elements.

c. Set B has an infinite number of elements.

d. Set B is an infinite set.

71. a. There are an infinite number of fractions between any 2 numbers.

  b. There are an infinite number of fractions between any 2 numbers.

73. $5\dfrac{2}{5} = \dfrac{5 \cdot 5 + 2}{5} = \dfrac{25 + 2}{5} = \dfrac{27}{5}$

74. $\dfrac{16}{3} = 5\dfrac{1}{3}$ because $16 \div 3 = 5$ R 1

75. $\dfrac{7}{8} - \dfrac{2}{3}$

$$\dfrac{7}{8} = \dfrac{7}{8} \cdot \dfrac{3}{3} = \dfrac{21}{24}$$
$$\dfrac{2}{3} = \dfrac{2}{3} \cdot \dfrac{8}{8} = \dfrac{16}{24}$$
$$\dfrac{7}{8} - \dfrac{2}{3} = \dfrac{21}{24} - \dfrac{16}{24} = \dfrac{21 - 16}{24} = \dfrac{5}{24}$$

76. $\dfrac{3}{5} \div 6\dfrac{3}{4}$

$$6\dfrac{3}{4} = \dfrac{24 + 3}{4} = \dfrac{27}{4}$$

$$\dfrac{3}{5} \div 6\dfrac{3}{4} = \dfrac{3}{5} \div \dfrac{27}{4} = \dfrac{\overset{1}{\cancel{3}}}{5} \cdot \dfrac{4}{\underset{9}{\cancel{27}}} = \dfrac{1 \cdot 4}{5 \cdot 9} = \dfrac{4}{45}$$

Exercise Set 1.5

1. a.

  b.

  c. –2 is greater than –4 because it is farther to the right on the number line.

  d. $-4 < -2$

  e. $-2 > -4$

3. a. 4 is 4 units from 0 on a number line.

  b. –4 is 4 units from 0 on a number line.

  c. 0 is 0 units from 0 on a number line.

5. Yes; for example, 5 > 3 and 3 < 5. Also, –2 > –5 and –5 < –2.

7. No, $-4 < -3$ but $|-4| > |-3|$.

9. No, $|-3| < |-4|$ but $-3 > -4$.

11. $|7| = 7$

13. $|-15| = 15$

15. $-|0| = 0$

17. $-|-5| = -(5) = -5$

19. $-|21| = -(21) = -21$

21. $6 > 2$; 6 is to the right of 2 on a number line.

23. $-4 < 0$; -4 is to the left of 0 on a number line.

25. $\dfrac{1}{2} > -\dfrac{2}{3}$; $\dfrac{1}{2}$ is to the right of $-\dfrac{2}{3}$ on a number line.

27. $0.7 < 0.8$; 0.7 is to the left of 0.8 on a number line.

29. $-\dfrac{1}{2} > -1$; $-\dfrac{1}{2}$ is to the right of -1 on a number line.

31. $-5 < 5$; -5 is to the left of 5 on a number line.

33. $-2.1 < -2$; -2.1 is to the left of -2 on a number line.

35. $\dfrac{4}{5} > -\dfrac{4}{5}$; $\dfrac{4}{5}$ is to the right of $-\dfrac{4}{5}$ on a number line.

37. $-\dfrac{3}{8} < \dfrac{3}{8}$; $-\dfrac{3}{8}$ is to the left of $\dfrac{3}{8}$ on a number line.

39. $0.49 > 0.43$; 0.49 is to the right of 0.43 on a number line.

41. $5 > -7$; 5 is to the right of -7 on a number line.

43. $0.001 < 0.002$; 0.001 is to the left of 0.002 on a number line.

45. $\dfrac{5}{8} > 0.6$ because $\dfrac{5}{8} = 0.625$ and 0.625 is to the right of 0.6 on a number line.

47. $-\dfrac{4}{3} < -\dfrac{1}{3}$; $-\dfrac{4}{3}$ is to the left of $-\dfrac{1}{3}$ on a number line.

49. $-0.8 < -\dfrac{3}{5}$; -0.8 is to the left of -0.6 on a number line.

51. $0.3 < \dfrac{1}{3}$; 0.3 is to the left of $.333...$ on a number line.

53. $-\dfrac{17}{30} > -\dfrac{16}{20}$; $-\dfrac{34}{60}$ is to the right of $-\dfrac{48}{60}$ on a number line.

55. $-(-6) > -(-5)$; 6 is to the right of 5 on a number line.

57. $5 > |-2|$ since $|-2| = 2$

59. $\dfrac{3}{4} < |-4|$ since $|-4| = 4$

61. $|0| < |-4|$ since $|0| = 0$ and $|-4| = 4$

63. $4 < \left|-\dfrac{9}{2}\right|$ since $\left|-\dfrac{9}{2}\right| = \dfrac{9}{2}$ or $4\dfrac{1}{2}$

65. $\left|-\dfrac{4}{5}\right| < \left|-\dfrac{5}{4}\right|$ since $\left|-\dfrac{4}{5}\right| = \dfrac{4}{5} = \dfrac{16}{20}$ and $\left|-\dfrac{5}{4}\right| = \dfrac{5}{4} = \dfrac{25}{20}$

67. $|-4.6| = \left|-\dfrac{23}{5}\right|$ since $|-4.6| = 4.6$ and $\left|-\dfrac{23}{5}\right| = \dfrac{23}{5} = 4.6$

69. $\dfrac{2}{3} + \dfrac{2}{3} + \dfrac{2}{3} + \dfrac{2}{3} = 4 \cdot \dfrac{2}{3}$ since $\dfrac{2}{3} + \dfrac{2}{3} + \dfrac{2}{3} + \dfrac{2}{3} = \dfrac{2+2+2+2}{3} = \dfrac{8}{3}$ and $4 \cdot \dfrac{2}{3} = \dfrac{4}{1} \cdot \dfrac{2}{3} = \dfrac{8}{3}$

71. $\dfrac{1}{2} \cdot \dfrac{1}{2} < \dfrac{1}{2} \div \dfrac{1}{2}$ since $\dfrac{1}{2} \cdot \dfrac{1}{2} = \dfrac{1 \cdot 1}{2 \cdot 2} = \dfrac{1}{4}$ and $\dfrac{1}{2} \div \dfrac{1}{2} = \dfrac{1}{2} \cdot \dfrac{2}{1} = \dfrac{1}{1} \cdot \dfrac{1}{1} = 1$

73. $\dfrac{5}{8} - \dfrac{1}{2} < \dfrac{5}{8} \div \dfrac{1}{2}$ since $\dfrac{5}{8} - \dfrac{1}{2} = \dfrac{5}{8} - \dfrac{4}{8} = \dfrac{1}{8}$ and $\dfrac{5}{8} \div \dfrac{1}{2} = \dfrac{5}{8} \cdot \dfrac{2}{1} = \dfrac{10}{8}$

75. $-|-1|, \dfrac{3}{7}, \dfrac{4}{9}, 0.46, |-5|$ because $-|-1| = -1$, $\dfrac{3}{7} \approx 0.429$, $\dfrac{4}{9} = 0.444...$, and $|-5| = 5$.

77. $\dfrac{5}{12}$, 0.6, $\dfrac{2}{3}$, $\dfrac{19}{25}$, $|-2.6|$ because

$\dfrac{5}{12} = 0.416416...$, $\dfrac{2}{3} = 0.666...$,

$\dfrac{19}{25} = 0.76$ and $|-2.6| = 2.6$.

79. 4 and -4 since $|4| = |-4| = 4$

For Exercises 81-87, answers will vary. One possible answer is given.

81. There are no real numbers that are less than 4 and greater than 6.

83. Three numbers less than -2 and greater than -6 are $-3, -4, -5$.

85. Three numbers greater than -3 and greater than 3 are 4, 5, 6.

87. Three numbers greater than $|-2|$ and less than $|-6|$ are 3, 4, 5.

89.a. Between does not include endpoints.

b. Three real numbers between 4 and 6 are 4.1, 5, and $5\dfrac{1}{2}$.

c. No, 4 is an endpoint.

d. Yes, 5 is greater than 4 and less than 6.

e. True

91.a. dietary fiber and thiamin

b. vitamin E, niacin, and riboflavin

93. The result of dividing a number by itself is 1. Thus, the result of dividing a number between 0 and 1 by itself is a number, 1, which is greater than the original number.

95. No, an absolute value of a number cannot be negative.

97.

98. $2\dfrac{3}{5} + 3\dfrac{1}{3}$

$2\dfrac{3}{5} = \dfrac{10+3}{5} = \dfrac{13}{5} \cdot \dfrac{3}{3} = \dfrac{39}{15}$

$3\dfrac{1}{3} = \dfrac{9+1}{3} = \dfrac{10}{3} \cdot \dfrac{5}{5} = \dfrac{50}{15}$

$2\dfrac{3}{5} + 3\dfrac{1}{3} = \dfrac{39}{15} + \dfrac{50}{15} = \dfrac{39+50}{15} = \dfrac{89}{15} = 5\dfrac{14}{15}$

99. The set of integer numbers is $\{..., -3, -2, -1, 0, 1, 2, 3, ...\}$.

100. The set of whole numbers is $\{0, 1, 2, 3, ...\}$.

101. a. 5 is a natural number.

b. 5 and 0 are whole numbers.

c. 5, -2, and 0 are integers.

d. 5, -2, 0, $\dfrac{1}{3}$, $-\dfrac{5}{9}$, and 2.3 are rational numbers.

e. $\sqrt{3}$ is an irrational number.

f. 5, -2, 0, $\dfrac{1}{3}$, $\sqrt{3}$, $-\dfrac{5}{9}$, and 2.3 are real numbers.

Mid-Chapter Test: Sections 1.1-1.5

1. At least two hours of study and homework for each hour of class time is generally recommended.

2. a. The mean is

$\dfrac{78.83 + 96.57 + 62.23 + 88.79 + 101.75 + 55.62}{6}$

$= \dfrac{483.78}{6} = \$80.63$.

b. To find the median place the numbers in order: 55.62, 62.23, 78.83, 88.79, 96.57, 101.75. Since there are an even amount of numbers, take the two in the middle and take their mean.

$\dfrac{78.83 + 88.79}{2} = \dfrac{167.62}{2} = \$83.81$.

3. New balance = Old balance + Deposits − Purchases

New balance = $652.70 + 230.75 - 3(19.62)$
$= 652.70 + 230.75 - 58.86$
$= 824.59$

Her new balance is $824.59.

4. a. Rental cost from Natwora's
$= 7.50$(each 15-minute increment)
$= 7.5(16)$
$= 120$

Rental cost for Gurney's
$= 18$(each 30-minute increment)
$= 18(8)$
$= 144$

Natwora's is the better deal.

b. 144–120 = 24
   You will save $24.

5. We must find out how many 1000 gallons was
   used. $\dfrac{33,700}{1000} = 33.7$
   Water Bill = 1.85(number of 1000 gallons used)
   = 1.85(33.7)
   ≈ 62.345
   The water bill would be $62.35.

6. $\dfrac{3}{7} \cdot \dfrac{7}{18} = \dfrac{\cancel{3}^{1}}{\cancel{7}_{1}} \cdot \dfrac{\cancel{7}^{1}}{\cancel{18}_{6}} = \dfrac{1 \cdot 1}{1 \cdot 6} = \dfrac{1}{6}$

7. $\dfrac{9}{16} \div \dfrac{12}{13} = \dfrac{\cancel{9}^{3}}{16} \cdot \dfrac{13}{\cancel{12}_{4}} = \dfrac{3 \cdot 13}{16 \cdot 4} = \dfrac{39}{64}$

8. $\dfrac{5}{8} + \dfrac{3}{5}$

   $\dfrac{5}{8} \cdot \dfrac{5}{5} = \dfrac{25}{40}$

   $\dfrac{3}{5} \cdot \dfrac{8}{8} = \dfrac{24}{40}$

   $\dfrac{5}{8} + \dfrac{3}{5} = \dfrac{25}{40} + \dfrac{24}{40} = \dfrac{25+24}{40} = \dfrac{49}{40} = 1\dfrac{9}{40}$

9. $6\dfrac{1}{4} - 3\dfrac{1}{5}$

   $6\dfrac{1}{4} = \dfrac{24+1}{4} = \dfrac{25}{4} \cdot \dfrac{5}{5} = \dfrac{125}{20}$

   $3\dfrac{1}{5} = \dfrac{15+1}{5} = \dfrac{16}{5} \cdot \dfrac{4}{4} = \dfrac{64}{20}$

   $6\dfrac{1}{4} - 3\dfrac{1}{5} = \dfrac{125}{20} - \dfrac{64}{20} = \dfrac{125-64}{20} = \dfrac{61}{20} = 3\dfrac{1}{20}$

10. $p = 2l + 2w$

   $= 2\left(14\dfrac{2}{3}\right) + 2\left(12\dfrac{1}{2}\right)$

   $= 2\left(\dfrac{44}{3}\right) + 2\left(\dfrac{25}{2}\right)$

   $= \dfrac{88}{3} + \dfrac{50}{2}$

   $= \left(\dfrac{88}{3} \cdot \dfrac{2}{2}\right) + \left(\dfrac{50}{2} \cdot \dfrac{3}{3}\right)$

$= \dfrac{176}{6} + \dfrac{150}{6}$

$= \dfrac{326}{6} = 54\dfrac{2}{6} = 54\dfrac{1}{3}$

He will need $54\dfrac{1}{3}$ feet of fencing.

11. False   **12.** True

13. False   **14.** True

15. False   **16.** $-\left|-\dfrac{7}{10}\right| = -\dfrac{7}{10}$

17. –0.005 > –0.006 because –0.005 is to the right of –0.006 on the number line.

18. $\dfrac{7}{8} > \dfrac{5}{6}$ because

   $\dfrac{7}{8} = \dfrac{7}{8} \cdot \dfrac{3}{3} = \dfrac{21}{24}$ and $\dfrac{5}{6} = \dfrac{5}{6} \cdot \dfrac{4}{4} = \dfrac{20}{24}$.

19. $|-9| < |-12|$ because $|-9| = 9$ and $|-12| = 12$.

20. $\left|-\dfrac{3}{8}\right| = |-0.375|$ because $\left|-\dfrac{3}{8}\right| = \dfrac{3}{8} = 0.375$
   and $|-0.375| = 0.375$.

Exercise Set 1.6

1. The 4 basic operations of arithmetic are addition, subtraction, multiplication, and division.

3.a. No; $-\dfrac{2}{3} + \dfrac{3}{2}$ does not sum to 0.

b. The opposite of $-\dfrac{2}{3}$ is $\dfrac{2}{3}$ because $-\dfrac{2}{3} + \dfrac{2}{3} = 0$.

5. If we add two negative numbers, the sum is negative. When two numbers have the same sign, their sum also has the same sign.

7. Answers will vary.

9.a. He owed 162, a negative, and then paid a positive amount, 85, toward his debt. This would translate to –162 + 85.

b. –162 + 85
   The numbers have different signs so find the difference between the absolute values.
   $|-162| - |85| = 162 - 85 = 77$

$|-162|$ is greater so sum is negative.
$-162 + 85 = -77$

c. Since this is a negative amount, it is considered a debt.

11. Yes, it is correct.

13. The opposite of 9 is –9 since $9 + (-9) = 0$.

15. The opposite of –28 is 28 since $-28 + 28 = 0$.

17. The opposite of 0 is 0 since $0 + 0 = 0$.

19. The opposite of $\dfrac{5}{3}$ is $-\dfrac{5}{3}$ since $\dfrac{5}{3} + \left(-\dfrac{5}{3}\right) = 0$.

21. The opposite of $2\dfrac{3}{5}$ is $-2\dfrac{3}{5}$

since $2\dfrac{3}{5} + \left(-2\dfrac{3}{5}\right) = 0$.

23. The opposite of 3.72 is –3.72 since $3.72 + (-3.72) = 0$.

25. Numbers have same sign, so add absolute values.
$|5| + |6| = 5 + 6 = 11$
Numbers are positive so sum is positive.
$5 + 6 = 11$

27. Numbers have different signs so find difference between larger and smaller absolute values.
$|4| - |-3| = 4 - 3 = 1$. $|4|$ is greater than $|-3|$ so the sum is positive.
$4 + (-3) = 1$

29. Numbers have same sign, so add absolute values.
$|-4| + |-2| = 4 + 2 = 6$.
Numbers are negative, so sum is negative.
$-4 + (-2) = -6$

31. Numbers have different signs, so find difference between absolute values.
$|6| - |-6| = 6 - 6 = 0$
$6 + (-6) = 0$

33. Numbers have different signs, so find difference between absolute values.
$|-4| - |4| = 4 - 4 = 0$
$-4 + 4 = 0$

35. Numbers have same sign, so add absolute values. $|-8| + |-2| = 8 + 2 = 10$. Numbers are negative, so sum is negative.
$-8 + (-2) = -10$

37. Numbers have different signs, so take difference between larger and smaller absolute values. $|-7| - |3| = 7 - 3 = 4$. $|-7|$ is greater than $|3|$ so sum is negative.
$-7 + 3 = -4$

39. Numbers have same sign, so add absolute values.
$|-8| + |-5| = 8 + 5 = 13$
Numbers are negative, so sum is negative.
$-8 + (-5) = -13$

41. $0 + 0 = 0$

43. $-6 + 0 = -6$

45. Numbers have different signs, so find difference between larger and smaller absolute values. $|18| - |-9| = 18 - 9 = 9$. $|18|$ is greater than $|-9|$ so sum is positive.
$18 + (-9) = 9$

47. Numbers have same sign, so add absolute values.
$|-33| + |-31| = 33 + 31 = 64$
Numbers are negative, so sum is negative.
$-33 + (-31) = -64$

49. Numbers have same sign, so add absolute values.
$|7| + |9| = 7 + 9 = 16$.
Numbers are positive, so sum is positive.
$7 + 9 = 16$

51. Numbers have same sign, so add absolute values.
$|-8| + |-4| = 8 + 4 = 12$
Numbers are negative, so sum is negative.
$-8 + (-4) = -12$

53. Numbers have different signs, so find difference between larger and smaller absolute values. $|6| - |-3| = 6 - 3 = 3$. $|6|$ is greater than $|-3|$ so sum is positive.
$6 + (-3) = 3$

55. Numbers have different signs, so take difference between larger and smaller absolute values. $|-19| + |13| = 19 - 13 = 6$. $|-19|$ is greater than $|13|$ so sum is negative.
$13 + (-19) = -6$

57. Numbers have different signs, so find difference between larger and smaller absolute values. $|-200| - |180| = 200 - 180 = 20$. $|-200|$ is greater than $|180|$ so sum is negative.
$180 + (-200) = -20$

59. Numbers have same sign, so add absolute values. $|-11| + |-20| = 11 + 20 = 31$. Numbers are negative, so sum is negative.
$-11 + (-20) = -31$

61. Numbers have different signs, so find difference between larger and smaller absolute values. $|-67| - |28| = 67 - 28 = 39$. $|-67|$ is greater than $|28|$ so sum is negative.
$-67 + 28 = -39$

63. Numbers have different signs, so find difference between larger and smaller absolute values. $|184| - |-93| = 184 - 93 = 91$. $|184|$ is greater than $|-93|$ so sum is positive.
$184 + (-93) = 91$

65. Numbers have different signs, so find difference between larger and smaller absolute values. $|-90.4| - |80.5| = 90.4 - 80.5 = 9.9$. $|-90.4|$ is greater than $|80.5|$ so sum is negative.
$80.5 + (-90.4) = -9.9$

67. Numbers have same sign, so add absolute values. $|-124.7| + |-19.3| = 124.7 + 19.3 = 144.0$. Numbers are negative, so sum is negative.
$-124.7 + (-19.3) = -144.0$

69. Numbers have same sign, so add absolute values. $|-123.56| + |-18.35| = 123.56 + 18.35 = 141.91$. Numbers are negative, so sum is negative.
$-123.56 + (-18.35) = -141.91$

71. Numbers have different signs, so take difference between larger and smaller absolute values. $|-99.36| - |45.71| = 99.36 - 45.71 = 53.65$. $|-99.36|$ is greater than $|45.71|$ so sum is negative.
$-99.36 + 45.71 = -53.65$

73. $\dfrac{3}{5} + \dfrac{1}{7} = \dfrac{21}{35} + \dfrac{5}{35} = \dfrac{21 + 5}{35} = \dfrac{26}{35}$

75. $\dfrac{5}{12} + \dfrac{6}{7} = \dfrac{35}{84} + \dfrac{72}{84} = \dfrac{35 + 72}{84} = \dfrac{107}{84}$

77. Numbers have different signs, so find difference between larger and smaller absolute values.
$-\dfrac{8}{11} + \dfrac{4}{5} = -\dfrac{40}{55} + \dfrac{44}{55} = \left|\dfrac{44}{55}\right| - \left|-\dfrac{40}{55}\right| = \dfrac{44}{55} - \dfrac{40}{55} = \dfrac{4}{55}$

$\left|\dfrac{44}{55}\right|$ is greater than $\left|-\dfrac{40}{55}\right|$ so sum is positive.
$-\dfrac{8}{11} + \dfrac{4}{5} = \dfrac{4}{55}$

79. Numbers have different signs, so find difference between larger and smaller absolute values.
$-\dfrac{7}{10} + \dfrac{11}{90} = \left|-\dfrac{63}{90}\right| - \left|\dfrac{11}{90}\right| = \dfrac{63}{90} - \dfrac{11}{90} = \dfrac{63 - 11}{90} = \dfrac{52}{90} = \dfrac{26}{45}$

$\left|-\dfrac{63}{90}\right|$ is greater than $\left|\dfrac{11}{90}\right|$ so sum is negative.
$-\dfrac{7}{10} + \dfrac{11}{90} = -\dfrac{26}{45}$

81. Numbers have same sign, so add absolute values.
$-\dfrac{7}{30} + \left(-\dfrac{5}{6}\right) = \left|-\dfrac{7}{30}\right| + \left|-\dfrac{25}{30}\right| = \dfrac{7}{30} + \dfrac{25}{30} = \dfrac{7 + 25}{30} = \dfrac{32}{30} = \dfrac{16}{15}$

Numbers are negative so sum is negative.
$-\dfrac{7}{30} + \left(-\dfrac{5}{6}\right) = -\dfrac{16}{15}$

83. Numbers have different signs, so find difference between larger and smaller absolute values
$\dfrac{9}{25} + \left(-\dfrac{3}{50}\right) = \left|\dfrac{18}{50}\right| - \left|-\dfrac{3}{50}\right| = \dfrac{18}{50} - \dfrac{3}{50} = \dfrac{18 - 3}{50} = \dfrac{15}{50} = \dfrac{3}{10}$

$\left|\dfrac{18}{50}\right|$ is greater than $\left|-\dfrac{3}{50}\right|$ so sum is positive.
$\dfrac{9}{25} + \left(-\dfrac{3}{50}\right) = \dfrac{3}{10}$

85. Numbers have same sign, so add absolute values.
$-\dfrac{4}{5} + \left(-\dfrac{5}{75}\right) = \left|-\dfrac{60}{75}\right| + \left|-\dfrac{5}{75}\right| = \dfrac{60}{75} + \dfrac{5}{75} = \dfrac{60 + 5}{75} = \dfrac{65}{75} = \dfrac{13}{15}$

Numbers are negative so sum is negative.
$-\dfrac{4}{5} + \left(-\dfrac{5}{75}\right) = -\dfrac{13}{15}$

87. Numbers have different signs, so find difference between larger and smaller absolute values.
$-\dfrac{9}{24} + \dfrac{5}{7} = -\dfrac{63}{168} + \dfrac{120}{168} = \left|\dfrac{120}{168}\right| - \left|-\dfrac{63}{168}\right| = \dfrac{120}{168} - \dfrac{63}{168} = \dfrac{120 - 63}{168} = \dfrac{57}{168} = \dfrac{19}{56}$

$\left|\dfrac{120}{168}\right|$ is greater than $\left|-\dfrac{63}{168}\right|$ so sum is positive.

$$-\dfrac{9}{24}+\dfrac{5}{7}=\dfrac{19}{56}$$

89. Numbers have same sign, so add absolute values.

$$-\dfrac{5}{12}+\left(-\dfrac{3}{10}\right)=-\dfrac{25}{60}+\left(-\dfrac{18}{60}\right)=-\left|\dfrac{25}{60}\right|+\left|-\dfrac{18}{60}\right|=$$

$$\dfrac{25}{60}+\dfrac{18}{60}=\dfrac{43}{60}$$

Numbers are negative so sum is negative.

$$-\dfrac{5}{12}+\left(-\dfrac{3}{10}\right)=-\dfrac{43}{60}$$

91. Numbers have same sign, so add absolute values.

$$-\dfrac{13}{14}+\left(-\dfrac{7}{42}\right)=-\dfrac{39}{42}+\left(-\dfrac{7}{42}\right)=-\left|\dfrac{39}{42}\right|+\left|-\dfrac{7}{42}\right|=$$

$$\dfrac{39}{42}+\dfrac{7}{42}=\dfrac{39+7}{42}=\dfrac{46}{42}=\dfrac{23}{21}$$

Numbers are negative so sum is negative.

$$-\dfrac{13}{14}+\left(-\dfrac{7}{42}\right)=-\dfrac{23}{21}$$

93.a. Positive; |587| is greater than $\left|-197\right|$ so sum will be positive.

  b. $587+(-197)=390$

  c. Yes; By part a) we expect a positive sum. The magnitude of the sum is the difference between the larger and smaller absolute values.

95.a. Negative; the sum of 2 negative numbers is always negative.

  b. $-84+(-289)=-373$

  c. Yes; the sum of 2 negative numbers should be (and is) a larger negative number.

97.a. Negative; $\left|-947\right|$ is greater than $\left|495\right|$ so sum will be negative.

  b. $-947+495=-452$

  c. Yes; by part a) we expect a negative sum. Magnitude of sum is the difference between the larger and smaller absolute values.

99.a. Negative; the sum of 2 negative numbers is always negative.

  b. $-496+(-804)=-1300$

  c. Yes; the sum of 2 negative numbers should be (and is) a larger negative number.

101.a. Negative; |–375| is greater than $\left|263\right|$ so sum will be negative.

  b. $-375+263=-112$

  c. Yes; by part a) we expect a negative sum. The magnitude of the sum is the difference between the larger and smaller absolute values.

103.a. Negative; the sum of 2 negative numbers is always negative.

  b. $-1833+(-2047)=-3880$

  c. Yes; The sum of 2 negative numbers should be (and is) a larger negative number.

105.a. Positive; |3124| is greater than $\left|-2013\right|$ so sum will be positive.

  b. $3124+(-2013)=1111$

  c. Yes; by part a) we expect a positive sum. Magnitude of sum is difference between larger and smaller absolute values.

107.a. Negative; the sum of 2 negative numbers is always negative.

  b. $-1025+(-1025)=-2050$

  c. Yes; the sum of 2 negative numbers should be (and is) a larger negative number.

109. True; the sum of two negative numbers is always negative.

111. True; the sum of two positive numbers is always positive.

113. False; the sum has the sign of the number with the larger absolute value.

115. David's balance was –$94. His new balance can be found by adding. $-94+(-183)=-277$ David owes the bank $277.

117. Total loss can be represented as $-18+(-3)$. $\left|-18\right|+\left|-3\right|=18+3=21$. The total loss in yardage is 21 yards.

119. The depth of the well can be found by adding $-27+(-34)=-61$. The well is 61 feet deep.

121. The height of the mountain peak above sea level can be found by adding $33,480 + (-19,684) = 13,796$. The mountain peak is 13,796 feet above sea level.

123.a. -12 million

The deficit is $12 million.

b. 1999: -20 million; 2000; 8 million; 2001; 17 million

$-20 + 8 + 17 = 5$

From 1999-2001, there was a surplus of $5 million.

125. $(-4) + (-6) + (-12) = (-10) + (-12) = -22$

127. $29 + (-46) + 37 = (-17) + 37 = 20$

129. $(-12) + (-10) + 25 + (-3) = (-22) + 25 + (-3)$
$$= 3 + (-3)$$
$$= 0$$

131. $\dfrac{1}{2} + \left(-\dfrac{1}{3}\right) + \dfrac{1}{5} = \left(\dfrac{3}{6} - \dfrac{2}{6}\right) + \dfrac{1}{5}$
$$= \dfrac{1}{6} + \dfrac{1}{5}$$
$$= \dfrac{5}{30} + \dfrac{6}{30}$$
$$= \dfrac{11}{30}$$

133. $1 + 2 + 3 + \cdots + 10 = (1 + 10) + (2 + 9) \cdots + (5 + 6)$
$$= (5)(11)$$
$$= 55$$

135. $2\dfrac{3}{8} = \dfrac{16 + 3}{8} = \dfrac{19}{8}$

$\left(\dfrac{4}{7}\right)\left(2\dfrac{3}{8}\right) = \dfrac{\overset{1}{\cancel{4}}}{7} \cdot \dfrac{19}{\underset{2}{\cancel{8}}} = \dfrac{1 \cdot 19}{7 \cdot 2}$

$= \dfrac{19}{14} = 1\dfrac{5}{14}$

136. $3 = \dfrac{3}{1} \cdot \dfrac{16}{16} = \dfrac{48}{16}$

$3 - \dfrac{5}{16} = \dfrac{48}{16} - \dfrac{5}{16} = \dfrac{48 - 5}{16} = \dfrac{43}{16} = 2\dfrac{11}{16}$

137. False, -0.25 is less than zero and not an integer.

138. $|-3| > 2$ since $|-3| = 3$

139. $8 < |-12|$ since $|-12| = 12$

Exercise Set 1.7

1. $2 - 7$

3. $\odot - ?$

5. a. to subtract b from a, add the opposite of b to a.

b. $5 + (-14)$

c. $5 + (-14) = -9$

7. a. $a - (-b) = a + b$

b. $-4 - (-12) = -4 + 12$

c. $-4 + 12 = 8$

9. a. $3 - (-6) + (-5) = 3 + 6 - 5$

b. $3 + 6 - 5 = 9 - 5 = 4$

11. Yes it is correct.

13. $8 - (+2) = 8 + (-2) = 6$

15. $12 - 5 = 12 + (-5) = 7$

17. $8 - 9 = 8 + (-9) = -1$

19. $9 - (-3) = 9 + 3 = 12$

21. $-6 - 6 = -6 + (-6) = -12$

23. $0 - 7 = 0 + (-7) = -7$

25. $8 - 8 = 8 + (-8) = 0$

27. $-3 - 1 = -3 + (-1) = -4$

29. $-8 - (-5) = -8 + 5 = -3$

31. $6 - (-3) = 6 + 3 = 9$

33. $-9 - 11 = -9 + (-11) = -20$

35. $0 - (-9.8) = 0 + 9.8 = 9.8$

37. $-4.8 - (-5.1) = -4.8 + 5.1 = 0.3$

39. $14 - 7 = 14 + (-7) = 7$

41. $-8 - (-12) = -8 + 12 = 4$

43. $18 - (-4) = 18 + 4 = 22$

45. $-9 - 2 = -9 + (-2) = -11$

47. $-90.7 - 40.3 = -90.7 + (-40.3) = -131.0$

49. $-45 - 37 = -45 + (-37) = -82$

51. $70 - (-70) = 70 + 70 = 140$

53. $42.3 - 49.7 = 42.3 + (-49.7) = -7.4$

55. $-7.85 - (-3.92) = -7.85 + 3.92 = -3.93$

57. $4 - 15 = 4 + (-15) = -11$

59. $21 - 21 = 21 + (-21) = 0$

61. $-6.3 - (-12.4) = -6.3 + 12.4 = 6.1$

63. $10.3 - (-7.9) = 10.3 + 7.9 = 18.2$

65. $13 - 24 = 13 + (-24) = -11$

67. $-10.3 - 7.8 = -10.3 + (-7.8) = -18.1$

69.
$$\frac{5}{9} - \frac{3}{8} = \frac{5}{9} + \left(-\frac{3}{8}\right)$$
$$= \frac{40}{72} + \left(-\frac{27}{72}\right)$$
$$= \frac{40 + (-27)}{72}$$
$$= \frac{13}{72}$$

71.
$$\frac{8}{15} - \frac{7}{45} = \frac{8}{15} + \left(-\frac{7}{45}\right)$$
$$= \frac{24}{45} + \left(-\frac{7}{45}\right)$$
$$= \frac{24 + (-7)}{45}$$
$$= \frac{17}{45}$$

73.
$$-\frac{7}{10} - \frac{5}{12} = -\frac{7}{10} + \left(-\frac{5}{12}\right)$$
$$= -\frac{42}{60} + \left(-\frac{25}{60}\right)$$
$$= \frac{-42 + (-25)}{60}$$
$$= -\frac{67}{60}$$

75.
$$-\frac{4}{15} - \frac{3}{20} = -\frac{4}{15} + \left(-\frac{3}{20}\right)$$
$$= -\frac{16}{60} + \left(-\frac{9}{60}\right)$$
$$= \frac{-16 + (-9)}{60}$$
$$= -\frac{25}{60} = -\frac{5}{12}$$

77.
$$-\frac{7}{12} - \frac{5}{40} = -\frac{7}{12} + \left(-\frac{5}{40}\right)$$
$$= -\frac{70}{120} + \left(-\frac{15}{120}\right)$$
$$= \frac{-70 + (-15)}{120}$$
$$= -\frac{85}{120} = -\frac{17}{24}$$

79.
$$\frac{3}{8} - \frac{6}{48} = \frac{3}{8} + \left(-\frac{6}{48}\right)$$
$$= \frac{18}{48} + \left(-\frac{6}{48}\right)$$
$$= \frac{18 + (-6)}{48}$$
$$= \frac{12}{48} = \frac{1}{4}$$

81.
$$-\frac{4}{9} - \left(-\frac{3}{5}\right) = -\frac{4}{9} + \frac{3}{5}$$
$$= -\frac{20}{45} + \frac{27}{45}$$
$$= \frac{-20 + 27}{45}$$
$$= \frac{7}{45}$$

83.
$$\frac{3}{16} - \left(-\frac{5}{8}\right) = \frac{3}{16} + \frac{5}{8}$$
$$= \frac{3}{16} + \frac{10}{16}$$
$$= \frac{3 + 10}{16}$$
$$= \frac{13}{16}$$

85. $\dfrac{4}{7} - \dfrac{7}{9} = \dfrac{4}{7} + \left(-\dfrac{7}{9}\right)$

$= \dfrac{36}{63} + \left(-\dfrac{49}{63}\right)$

$= \dfrac{36 + (-49)}{63}$

$= -\dfrac{13}{63}$

87. $-\dfrac{5}{12} - \left(-\dfrac{3}{10}\right) = -\dfrac{5}{12} + \dfrac{3}{10}$

$= -\dfrac{25}{60} + \dfrac{18}{60}$

$= \dfrac{-25 + 18}{60}$

$= -\dfrac{7}{60}$

89. a. Positive; $378 - 279 = 378 + (-279)$
|378| is greater than |−279| so the sum will be positive.

b. $378 + (-279) = 99$

c. Yes; by part a) we expect a positive sum. The size of the sum is the difference between the absolute values of the 2 numbers.

91. a. Negative; $-482 - 137 = -482 + (-137)$
The sum of 2 negative numbers is always negative.

b. $-482 + (-137) = -619$

c. Yes; the sum of two negative numbers should be (and is) a larger negative number.

93. a. Positive; $843 - (-745) = 843 + 745$.
The sum of 2 positive numbers is always positive.

b. $843 + 745 = 1588$

c. Yes; by part a) we expect a positive answer. The size of the sum is the sum of the absolute values of the numbers.

95. a. Positive; $-408 - (-604) = -408 + 604$.
|604| is greater than |−408| so the sum will be positive.

b. $-408 + 604 = 196$

c. Yes; by part a) we expect a positive answer. The size of the answer is the difference

between the larger and smaller absolute values.

97. a. Negative; $-1024 - (-576) = -1024 + 576$.
|−1024| is greater than |576| so the sum will be negative.

b. $-1024 + 576 = -448$

c. Yes; by part a) we expect a negative answer. The size of the answer is the difference between the larger and the smaller absolute values.

99. a. Positive; $165.7 - 49.6 = 165.7 + (-49.6)$.
|165.7| is greater than |−49.6| so the sum will be positive.

b. $165.7 + (-49.6) = 116.1$

c. Yes; by part a) we expect a negative answer. The size of the answer is the difference between the larger and the smaller absolute values.

101. a. Negative; $295 - 364 = 295 + (-364)$.
Since |−364| is greater than |295| the answer will be negative.

b. $295 + (-364) = -69$

c. Yes; by part a) we expect a negative answer. The size of the answer is the difference between the larger and the smaller absolute values.

103. a. Negative; $-1023 - 647 = -1023 + (-647)$.
The sum of two negative numbers is always negative.

b. $-1023 + (-647) = -1670$

c. Yes; the sum of two negative numbers should be (and is) a larger negative number.

105. a. Zero; $-7.62 - (-7.62) = -7.62 + 7.62$.
The sum of two opposite numbers is always zero.

b. $-7.62 + 7.62 = 0$

c. Yes; by part a) we expect zero.

107. $7 + 5 - (+8) = 7 + 5 + (-8) = 12 + (-8) = 4$

109. $-6 + (-6) + 6 = -12 + 6 = -6$

111. $-13 - (+5) + 3 = -13 + (-5) + 3 = -18 + 3 = -15$

113. $-9-(-3)+4=-9+3+4=-6+4=-2$

115. $5-(-9)+(-1)=5+9+(-1)=14+(-1)=13$

117. $17+(-8)-(+14)=17+(-8)+(-14)$
$$=9+(-14)$$
$$=-5$$

119. $-36-5+9=-36+(-5)+9=-41+9=-32$

121. $-2+7-9=-2+7+(-9)=5+(-9)=-4$

123. $25-19+3=25+(-19)+3=6+3=9$

125. $(-4)+(-6)+5-7=(-4)+(-6)+5+(-7)$
$$=-10+5+(-7)$$
$$=-5+(-7)$$
$$=-12$$

127. $17+(-3)-9-(-7)=17+(-3)+(-9)+7$
$$=14+(-9)+7$$
$$=5+7$$
$$=12$$

129. $-9+(-7)+(-5)-(-3)=-9+(-7)+(-5)+3$
$$=-16+(-5)+3$$
$$=-21+3$$
$$=-18$$

131. a. $300-343=300+(-343)=-43$
They had 43 sweaters on back order.

b. $43+100=143$
They would need to order 143 sweaters.

133. $2\dfrac{1}{4}-\dfrac{3}{8}=2\dfrac{1}{4}+\left(-\dfrac{3}{8}\right)$
$$=\dfrac{9}{4}+\left(-\dfrac{3}{8}\right)$$
$$=\dfrac{18}{8}+\left(-\dfrac{3}{8}\right)$$
$$=\dfrac{18+(-3)}{8}$$
$$=\dfrac{15}{8}=1\dfrac{7}{8}$$

After the second day $1\dfrac{7}{8}$ inches of water remains.

135. $44-(-56)=44+56=100$
Thus the temperature dropped 100°F.

137. a. $288+(-7)=281$
In 2006, his score was 281.

b. $-5-(-2)=5+2=-3$
T. Clark had 3 less strokes than S. Cink.

139. $1-2+3-4+5-6+7-8+9-10$
$$=(1-2)+(3-4)+(5-6)+(7-8)+(9-10)$$
$$=(-1)+(-1)+(-1)+(-1)+(-1)$$
$$=-5$$

141. a. 8 units

b. $-3-(-11)=-3+11=8$

143. a. $3+2+2+1+1=9$
The ball travels 9 feet vertically.

b. $-3+2+(-2)+1+(-1)=-3$
The net distance is –3 feet.

144. The counting numbers are $\{1, 2, 3, ...\}$.

145. The set of rational numbers together with the set of irrational numbers forms the set of real numbers.

146. $|-3| > -5$ since $|-3| = 3$

147. $-|-9| < -|-5|$ since $-|-9| = -9$ and $-|-5| = -5$

148. $\dfrac{5}{6}-\dfrac{7}{8}=\dfrac{5}{6}+\left(-\dfrac{7}{8}\right)$
$$=\dfrac{20}{24}+\left(-\dfrac{21}{24}\right)$$
$$=\dfrac{20+(-21)}{24}$$
$$=-\dfrac{1}{24}$$

Exercise Set 1.8

1. Like signs: product is positive. Unlike signs: product is negative.

3. When multiplying 3 or more real numbers, the product is positive if there is an even number of negative numbers and the product is negative if there is an odd number.

5. a. When a is a nonzero real number, $\dfrac{0}{a}=0$.

b. When a is a nonzero real number, $\dfrac{a}{0}$ is undefined.

7. a. With $3 - 5$ you subtract, but with $3(-5)$ you multiply.

   b. $3 - 5 = 3 + (-5) = -2$

9. a. With $x - y$ you subtract, but with $x(-y)$ you multiply.

   b. $x - y = 5 - (-2) = 5 + 2 = 7$

   c. $x(-y) = [-(-2)] = 5(2) = 10$

   d. $-x - y = -5 - (-2) = -5 + 2 = -3$

11. The product $(8)(4)(-5)$ is negative since there is an odd number (1) of negatives

13. The product $(-102)(-16)(24)(19)$ is positive since there is an even number of negatives.

15. The product $(-40)(-16)(30)(50)(-13)$ is negative since there is an odd number (3) of negatives.

17. Since the numbers have like signs, the product is positive. $(-5)(-4) = 20$

19. Since the number have unlike signs, the product is negative. $6(-3) = -18$

21. Since the numbers have like signs, the product is positive. $(-8)(-10) = 80$

23. Since the numbers have unlike signs, the product is negative. $-2.1(6) = -12.6$

25. Since the numbers have like signs, the product is positive. $6(7) = 42$

27. Since the numbers have unlike signs, the product is negative. $9(-9) = -81$

29. Since the numbers have like signs, the product is positive. $(-5)(-6) = 30$

31. Zero multiplied by any real number equals zero. $(-9(0)(-6) = 0(-6) = 0$

33. Since there is one negative number (an odd number), the product will be negative.
$(21)(-1)(4) = (-21)(4) = -84$

35. Since there are three negative numbers (an odd number), the product will be negative.
$-1(-3)(3)(-8) = 3(3)(-8) = 9(-8) = -72$

37. Since there are two negative numbers (an even number), the product will be positive.
$(-4)(5)(-7)(1) = (-20)(-7)(1) = (140)(1) = 140$

39. Zero multiplied by any real number equals zero.
$(-1)(3)(0)(-7) = (-3)(0)(-7) = 0(-7) = 0$

41. $\left(\dfrac{-1}{2}\right)\left(\dfrac{3}{5}\right) = \dfrac{(-1)(3)}{2 \cdot 5} = \dfrac{-3}{10} = -\dfrac{3}{10}$

43. $\left(\dfrac{-5}{9}\right)\left(\dfrac{-7}{15}\right) = \left(\dfrac{-\cancel{5}^{1}}{9}\right)\left(\dfrac{-7}{\cancel{15}_{3}}\right) = \dfrac{(-1)(-7)}{9 \cdot 3} = \dfrac{7}{27}$

45. $\left(\dfrac{6}{-3}\right)\left(\dfrac{4}{-2}\right) = (-2)(-2) = 4$

47. $\left(\dfrac{3}{4}\right)\left(\dfrac{-2}{15}\right) = \left(\dfrac{^{1}\cancel{3}}{_{2}\cancel{4}}\right)\left(\dfrac{-\cancel{2}^{1}}{\cancel{15}_{5}}\right)$

            $= \dfrac{(1)(-1)}{(2)(5)}$

            $= \dfrac{-1}{10} = -\dfrac{1}{10}$

49. Since the numbers have like signs, the quotient is positive. $\dfrac{42}{6} = 7$

51. Since the numbers have like signs, the quotient is positive. $-16 \div (-4) = \dfrac{-16}{-4} = 4$

53. Since the numbers have like signs, the quotient is positive. $\dfrac{-36}{-9} = 4$

55. Since the numbers have unlike signs, the quotient is negative. $\dfrac{36}{-2} = -18$

57. Since the numbers have like signs, the quotient is positive. $\dfrac{-19.8}{-2} = 9.9$

59. Since the numbers have unlike signs, the quotient is negative. $40/(-4) = \dfrac{40}{-4} = -10$

61. Since the numbers have unlike signs, the quotient is negative. $\dfrac{-66}{11} = -6$

63. Since the numbers have unlike signs, the quotient is negative. $\dfrac{48}{-6} = -8$

65. Since the numbers have like signs, the quotient is positive. $-64.8 \div (-4) = \dfrac{-64.8}{-4} = 16.2$

67. Zero divided by any nonzero number is zero. $\dfrac{0}{4} = 0$

69. Since the numbers have unlike signs, the quotient is negative. $\dfrac{30.8}{-5.6} = -5.5$

71. Since the numbers have like signs, the quotient is positive. $\dfrac{-30}{-5} = 6$

73. $\dfrac{3}{12} \div \left(\dfrac{-5}{8} \right) = \dfrac{3}{12} \cdot \left(\dfrac{8}{-5} \right)$

$= \dfrac{1}{{}_1\cancel{4}} \cdot \left(\dfrac{\cancel{8}^2}{-5} \right)$

$= \dfrac{1 \cdot 2}{1(-5)}$

$= \dfrac{2}{-5} = -\dfrac{2}{5}$

75. $\dfrac{-5}{12} \div (-3) = \dfrac{-5}{12} \cdot \dfrac{1}{-3} = \dfrac{-5(1)}{12(-3)} = \dfrac{-5}{-36} = \dfrac{5}{36}$

77. $\dfrac{-15}{21} \div \left(\dfrac{-15}{21} \right) = \dfrac{-\cancel{15}^{1}}{{}_1\cancel{21}} \cdot \dfrac{\cancel{21}^{1}}{-\cancel{15}_{1}}$

$= \dfrac{(-1)(1)}{(1)(-1)}$

$= \dfrac{-1}{-1}$

$= 1$

79. $-12 \div \dfrac{5}{12} = \dfrac{-12}{1} \cdot \dfrac{12}{5}$

$= \dfrac{(-12)(12)}{(1)(5)}$

$= \dfrac{-144}{5}$

$= -\dfrac{144}{5}$

81. Since the numbers have unlike signs, the product is negative. $-4(8) = -32$

83. Since the numbers have like signs, the quotient is positive. $\dfrac{-100}{-5} = 20$

85. Since the numbers have unlike signs, the product is negative. $-7(2) = -14$

87. Since the numbers have unlike signs, the quotient is negative. $27.9 \div (-3) = \dfrac{27.9}{-3} = -9.3$

89. Since the numbers have unlike signs, the quotient is negative. $\dfrac{-100}{5} = -20$

91. Since the numbers have like signs, the quotient is positive. $\dfrac{-90}{-90} = 1$

93. Zero divided by any nonzero number is zero. $0 \div 8.6 = \dfrac{0}{8.6} = 0$

95. Any nonzero number divided by zero is undefined. $\dfrac{5}{0}$ is undefined.

97. Zero divided by any nonzero number is zero. $0 \div (-7) = \dfrac{0}{-7} = 0$

99. Any nonzero number divided by zero is undefined. $\dfrac{8}{0}$ is undefined.

101. a. Since the numbers have unlike signs, the product will be negative.

   b. $92(-38) = -3496$

c. Yes; as expected the product is negative.

103. **a.** Since the numbers have unlike signs, the quotient will be negative.

  b. $-240 / 15 = \dfrac{-240}{15} = -16$

  c. Yes; as expected the quotient is negative.

105. **a.** Since the numbers have unlike signs, the quotient will be negative.

  b. $243 \div (-27) = \dfrac{243}{-27} = -9$

  c. Yes; as expected the quotient is negative.

107. **a.** Since the numbers have like signs, the product will be positive.

  b. $(-49)(-126) = 6174$

  c. Yes; as expected the product is positive.

109. **a.** The quotient will be zero; zero divided by any nonzero number is zero.

  b. $\dfrac{0}{5335} = 0$

  c. Yes; as expected the answer is zero.

111. **a.** Undefined; any nonzero number divided by 0 is undefined.

  b. $7.2 \div 0 = \dfrac{7.2}{0}$ is undefined

  c. Yes; as expected the quotient is undefined.

113. **a.** Since the numbers have like signs, the quotient will be positive.

  b. $8 \div 2.5 = \dfrac{8}{2.5} = 3.2$

  c. Yes; as expected the quotient is positive.

115. **a.** Since there are two negative numbers (an even number), the product will be positive.

  b. $(-3.0)(4.2)(-18) = 226.8$

  c. Yes; as expected the product is positive.

117. False; the product of two numbers with like signs is a positive number

119. False; the quotient of two numbers with unlike signs is a negative number.

121. True; the quotient of two numbers with like signs is a positive number.

123. True

125. False; zero divided by 1 is zero.

127. True; any nonzero number divided by zero is undefined.

129. $3(-15) = -45$
The total loss was 45 yards.

131. **a.** $\dfrac{1}{5}(520) = \dfrac{520}{5} = 104$
  She paid back $104.

  b. $-520 + 104 = -416$
  Her new balance is –$416.

133. Find out how much is left after giving the husbands each
$50. $775.40 - (4 \cdot 50) = 775.40 - 200 = 575.40$
Now take the remainder and divide it by 4.
$\dfrac{575.40}{4} = 143.85$
Each woman receives $143.85.

135. **a.** $5(-4) = -20$
  Josue lost 20 points.

  b. $100 - 20 = 80$
  His test score is 80.

137. **a.** $220 - 50 = 170$
  60% of $170 = 0.6(170) = 102$
  75% of $170 = 0.75(170) = 127.5$
  Target heart rate is 102 to 128 beats per minute.

  b. Answers will vary.

139. $(-5)^3 = (-5)(-5)(-5) = 25(-5) = -125$

141. $1^{100} = 1$

143. The product $(-1)(-2)(-3)(-4)\cdots(-10)$ will be positive because there are an even number (10) of negative numbers.

144. The product will be negative since there are an odd number (17) of negatives.

145. The country will start with D. Most students will select Denmark. They will most likely select kangaroo which leads to orange.

146. $|-3.6| > |-2.7|$

147. $-\dfrac{7}{12} + \left(-\dfrac{1}{10}\right) = -\dfrac{35}{60} + \left(-\dfrac{6}{60}\right)$

$$= \dfrac{-35 + (-6)}{60}$$

$$= -\dfrac{41}{60}$$

148. $-20 - (-18) = -20 + 18 = -2$

149. $6 - 3 - 4 - 2 = 3 - 4 - 2 = -1 - 2 = -3$

150. $5 - (-2) + 3 - 7 = 5 + 2 + 3 - 7$

$$= 7 + 3 - 7$$

$$= 10 - 7$$

$$= 3$$

Exercise Set 1.9

1. In the expression a^b, a is the base and b is the exponent.

3. a. Every number has an understood exponent of 1.

  b. In $5x^3 y^2 z$, 5 has exponent of 1, x has an exponent of 3, y has an exponent of 2, and z has an exponent of 1.

5. a. $y + y + y + y = 4y$

  b. $y \cdot y \cdot y \cdot y = y^4$

7. The order of operations are parentheses, exponents, multiplication or division, then addition or subtraction.

9. No; $4 + 5 \times 2 = 4 + 10 = 14$, on a scientific calculator.

11. a. $15 - 10 \div 5 = 15 - 2 = 13$

  b. $(15 - 10) \div 5 = 5 \div 5 = 1$

  c. The keystrokes in b) are used since the fraction bar is a grouping symbol.

13. b. $\left[10 - (16 \div 4)\right]^2 - 6^3 = \left[10 - 4\right]^2 - 6^3$

$$= 6^2 - 6^3$$

$$= 36 - 216$$

$$= -180$$

15. b. When $x = 5$:

$$-4x^2 + 3x - 6 = -4(5)^2 + 3(5) - 6$$

$$= -4(25) + 3(5) - 6$$

$$= -100 + 15 - 6$$

$$= -85 - 6$$

$$= -91$$

17. $5^2 = 5 \cdot 5 = 25$

19. $1^7 = 1 \cdot 1 \cdot 1 \cdot 1 \cdot 1 \cdot 1 \cdot 1 = 1$

21. $-8^2 = -(8)(8) = -64$

23. $(-3)^2 = (-3)(-3) = 9$

25. $(-1)^3 = (-1)(-1)(-1) = -1$

27. $-10^2 = -(10)(10) = -100$

28. $5^3 = 5 \cdot 5 \cdot 5 = 125$

29. $(-9)^2 = (-9)(-9) = 81$

31. $3^3 = 3 \cdot 3 \cdot 3 = 27$

33. $(-4)^4 = (-4)(-4)(-4)(-4) = 256$

35. $-2^4 = -(2)(2)(2)(2) = -16$

37. $\left(\dfrac{3}{4}\right)^2 = \dfrac{3}{4} \cdot \dfrac{3}{4} = \dfrac{9}{16}$

39. $\left(-\dfrac{1}{2}\right)^5 = \left(-\dfrac{1}{2}\right)\left(-\dfrac{1}{2}\right)\left(-\dfrac{1}{2}\right)\left(-\dfrac{1}{2}\right)\left(-\dfrac{1}{2}\right)$

$$= -\dfrac{1}{32}$$

41. $5^2 \cdot 3^2 = 5 \cdot 5 \cdot 3 \cdot 3 = 225$

43. $4^3 \cdot 3^2 = 4 \cdot 4 \cdot 4 \cdot 3 \cdot 3 = 576$

45. a. Positive; a positive number raised to any power is positive.

    b. $7^3 = 343$

    c.   Yes; as expected the answer is positive.

47. a.   Positive; a positive number raised to any power is positive.

    b. $6^4 = 1296$

    c.   Yes; as expected the answer is positive.

49. a.   Negative; a negative number raised to an odd power is negative.

    b. $(-3)^5 = -243$

    c.   Yes; as expected the answer is negative.

51. a.   Positive; a negative number raised to an even power is positive.

    b. $(-5)^4 = 625$

    c.   Yes; as expected the answer is positive.

53. a.   Negative; the opposite of a positive number is negative..

    b. $-(-9)^2 = -(-9)(-9) = -81$

    c.   Yes; as expected the answer is negative.

55. a.   Negative; $\left(\dfrac{3}{8}\right)^2$ is positive therefore,

         $-\left(\dfrac{3}{8}\right)^2$ is negative.

    b. $-\left(\dfrac{3}{8}\right)^2 = -0.140625$

    c.   Yes; as expected the answer is negative.

57. $3 + 2 \cdot 6 = 3 + 12 = 15$

59. $6 - 6 + 8 = 0 + 8 = 8$

61. $-7 + 2 \cdot 6^2 - 8 = -7 + 2 \cdot 36 - 8$
$$= -7 + 72 - 8$$
$$= 65 - 8$$
$$= 57$$

63. $-3^3 + 27 = -27 + 27 = 0$

65. $(4 - 3) \cdot (5 - 1)^2 = (1) \cdot (4)^2 = 1 \cdot 16 = 16$

67. $3 \cdot 7 + 4 \cdot 2 = 21 + 8 = 29$

69. $5 - 2(7 + 5) = 5 - 2(12) = 5 - 24 = -19$

71. $-32 - 5(7 - 10)^2 = -32 - 5(-3)^2$
$$= -32 - 5(9)$$
$$= -32 - 45$$
$$= -77$$

73. $\dfrac{3}{4} + 2\left(\dfrac{1}{5}\right)^2 = \dfrac{3}{4} + 2\left(\dfrac{1}{25}\right)$
$$= \dfrac{3}{4} + \dfrac{2}{25}$$
$$= \dfrac{75}{100} + \dfrac{8}{100}$$
$$= \dfrac{83}{100}$$

75. $-4 + 3\left[-1 + \left(12 \div 2^2\right)\right] = -4 + 3\left[-1 + \left(12 \div 4\right)\right]$
$$= -4 + 3[-1 + 3]$$
$$= -4 + 3[2]$$
$$= -4 + 6$$
$$= 2$$

77. $(6 \div 3)^3 + 4^2 \div 8 = (2)^3 + 4^2 \div 8$
$$= 8 + 16 \div 8$$
$$= 8 + 2$$
$$= 10$$

79. $-7 - 48 \div 6 \cdot 2^2 + 5 = -7 - 48 \div 6 \cdot 4 + 5$
$$= -7 - 8 \cdot 4 + 5$$
$$= -7 - 32 + 5$$
$$= -39 + 5$$
$$= -34$$

81. $(9 \div 3) + 4(7 - 2)^2 = (9 \div 3) + 4(5)^2$
$$= (9 \div 3) + 4(25)$$
$$= 3 + 100$$
$$= 103$$

83. $[4 + ((5 - 2)^2 \div 3)^2]^2 = [4 + ((3)^2 \div 3)^2]^2$
$$= [4 + (9 \div 3)^2]^2$$
$$= [4 + (3)^2]^2$$
$$= [4 + 9]^2$$
$$= (13)^2$$
$$= 169$$

85. $(-3)^2 + 8 \div 2 = 9 + 8 \div 2$
$$= 9 + 4$$
$$= 13$$

87. $2\left[1.55 + 5(3.7)\right] - 3.35 = 2\left[1.55 + 18.5\right] - 3.35$
$$= 2(20.05) - 3.35$$
$$= 40.1 - 3.35$$
$$= 36.75$$

89. $\left(\dfrac{2}{5} + \dfrac{3}{8}\right) - \dfrac{3}{20} = \left(\dfrac{16}{40} + \dfrac{15}{40}\right) - \dfrac{3}{20}$
$$= \dfrac{31}{40} - \dfrac{3}{20}$$
$$= \dfrac{31}{40} - \dfrac{6}{40}$$
$$= \dfrac{25}{40} = \dfrac{5}{8}$$

91. $\dfrac{3}{4} - 4 \cdot \dfrac{5}{40} = \dfrac{3}{4} - \dfrac{4}{1} \cdot \dfrac{5}{40} = \dfrac{3}{4} - \dfrac{4}{8} = \dfrac{3}{4} - \dfrac{2}{4} = \dfrac{1}{4}$

93. $\dfrac{4}{5} + \dfrac{3}{4} \div \dfrac{1}{2} - \dfrac{2}{3} = \dfrac{4}{5} + \dfrac{3}{4} \cdot \dfrac{2}{1} - \dfrac{2}{3}$
$$= \dfrac{4}{5} + \dfrac{3}{2} - \dfrac{2}{3}$$
$$= \dfrac{24}{30} + \dfrac{45}{30} - \dfrac{20}{30}$$
$$= \dfrac{49}{30}$$

95. $\dfrac{-4 - \left[2(9 \div 3) - 5\right]}{6^2 - 3^2 \cdot 7} = \dfrac{-4 - \left[2(3) - 5\right]}{36 - 9 \cdot 7}$
$$= \dfrac{-4 - \lfloor 6 - 5 \rfloor}{36 - 63}$$
$$= \dfrac{-4 - 1}{-27}$$
$$= \dfrac{-5}{-27} = \dfrac{5}{27}$$

97. $\dfrac{-[4 - (6 - 12)^2]}{\left[(9 \div 3) + 4\right]^2 + 2^2} = \dfrac{-[4 - (-6)^2]}{(3 + 4)^2 + 4}$
$$= \dfrac{-[4 - 36]}{7^2 + 4}$$
$$= \dfrac{-(-32)}{49 + 4}$$
$$= \dfrac{32}{53}$$

99. $\left\{5 - 2\left[4 - (6 \div 2)\right]^2\right\}^2 = \left\{5 - 2\left[4 - 3\right]^2\right\}^2$
$$= \left\{5 - 2(1)^2\right\}^2$$
$$= \left\{5 - 2(1)\right\}^2$$
$$= \left\{5 - 2\right\}^2$$
$$= (3)^2$$
$$= 9$$

101. $-\left\{4 - \left[-3 - (2 - 5)\right]^2\right\} = -\left\{4 - \left[-3 - (-3)\right]^2\right\}$
$$= -\left\{4 - \left[-3 + 3\right]^2\right\}$$
$$= -\left\{4 - \left[0\right]^2\right\}$$
$$= -\left\{4 - 0\right\}$$
$$= -(4)$$
$$= -4$$

103. $\left\{4 - 3\left[2 - (9 \div 3)\right]^2\right\}^2 = \left\{4 - 3\left[2 - 3\right]^2\right\}^2$
$$= \left\{4 - 3\left[-1\right]^2\right\}^2$$
$$= \left\{4 - 3\left[1\right]\right\}^2$$
$$= \left\{4 - 3\right\}^2$$
$$= 1^2$$
$$= 1$$

105. Substitute 5 for x

    a. $x^2 = 5^2 = 5 \cdot 5 = 25$

    b. $-x^2 = -5^2 = -(5)(5) = -25$

    c. $(-5)^2 = (-5)^2 = (-5)(-5) = 25$

107. Substitute -2 for x

    a. $x^2 = (-2)^2 = (-2)(-2) = 4$

    b. $-x^2 = -(-2)^2 = -(-2)(-2) = -(4) = -4$

    c. $(-x)^2 = 2^2 = 2 \cdot 2 = 4$

109. Substitute 6 for x

    a. $x^2 = 6^2 = 6 \cdot 6 = 36$

    b. $-x^2 = -6^2 = -(6 \cdot 6) = -36$

    c. $(-x)^2 = (-6)^2 = (-6)(-6) = 36$

111. Substitute $-\dfrac{1}{3}$ for x.

   a. $x^2 = \left(-\dfrac{1}{3}\right)^2 = \left(-\dfrac{1}{3}\right)\left(-\dfrac{1}{3}\right) = \dfrac{1}{9}$

   b. $-x^2 = -\left(-\dfrac{1}{3}\right)^2 = -\left(-\dfrac{1}{3}\right)\left(-\dfrac{1}{3}\right) = -\dfrac{1}{9}$

   c. $(-x)^2 = \left(\dfrac{1}{3}\right)^2 = \left(\dfrac{1}{3}\right)\left(\dfrac{1}{3}\right) = \dfrac{1}{9}$

113. Substitute -2 for x in the expression.
$x + 6 = -2 + 6 = 4$

115. Substitute 6 for z in the expression.
$-7z - 3 = -7(6) - 3 = -42 - 3 = -45$

117. Substitute -3 for a in the expression.
$a^2 - 6 = (-3)^2 - 6 = 9 - 6 = 3$

119. Substitute 2 for each p in the expression.
$$
\begin{aligned}
3p^2 - 6p - 4 &= 3(2)^2 - 6(2) - 4 \\
&= 3(4) - 12 - 4 \\
&= 12 - 12 - 4 \\
&= 0 - 4 \\
&= -4
\end{aligned}
$$

121. Substitute -1 for each x in the expression.
$$
\begin{aligned}
-4x^2 - 2x + 1 &= -4(-1)^2 - 2(-1) + 1 \\
&= -4(1) - 2(-1) + 1 \\
&= -4 + 2 + 1 \\
&= -2 + 1 \\
&= -1
\end{aligned}
$$

123. Substitute $\dfrac{1}{2}$ for each x in the expression.
$$
\begin{aligned}
-x^2 - 2x + 5 &= -(\tfrac{1}{2})^2 - 2(\tfrac{1}{2}) + 5 \\
&= -\dfrac{1}{4} - 1 + 5 \\
&= -\dfrac{1}{4} - \dfrac{4}{4} + \dfrac{20}{4} \\
&= -\dfrac{5}{4} + \dfrac{20}{4} \\
&= \dfrac{15}{4}
\end{aligned}
$$

125. Substitute 5 for each x in the expression.
$$
\begin{aligned}
4(3x + 1)^2 - 6x &= 4(3(5) + 1)^2 - 6(5) \\
&= 4(15 + 1)^2 - 30 \\
&= 4(16)^2 - 30 \\
&= 4(256) - 30 \\
&= 1024 - 30 \\
&= 994
\end{aligned}
$$

127. Substitute -2 for r and -3 for s in the expression.
$r^2 - s^2 = (-2)^2 - (-3)^2 = 4 - 9 = -5$

129. Substitute 1 for x and -5 for y in the expression.
$$
\begin{aligned}
5(x - 6y) + 3x - 7y &= 5(1 - 6(-5)) + 3(1) - 7(-5) \\
&= 5(1 - (-30)) + 3 + 35 \\
&= 5(31) + 3 + 35 \\
&= 155 + 3 + 35 \\
&= 158 + 35 \\
&= 193
\end{aligned}
$$

131. Substitute -1 for x and -2 for y in the expression.
$$
\begin{aligned}
3(x - 4)^2 - (3y - 4)^2 &= 3(-1 - 4)^2 - [3(-2) - 4]^2 \\
&= 3(-5)^2 - (-6 - 4)^2 \\
&= 3(-5)^2 - (-10)^2 \\
&= 3(25) - 100 \\
&= 75 - 100 \\
&= -25
\end{aligned}
$$

133. $6 \cdot 3$ Multiply 6 by 3
$(6 \cdot 3) - 4$ Subtract 4 from the product
$[(6 \cdot 3) - 4] - 2$ Subtract 2 from the difference
Evaluate:
$[(6 \cdot 3) - 4] - 2 = [18 - 4] - 2 = 14 - 2 = 12$

135. $10 \cdot 4$ Multiply 10 by 4
$(10 \cdot 4) + 9$ Add 9 to the product
$[(10 \cdot 4) + 9] - 6$ Subtract 6 from the sum
$\{[(10 \cdot 4) + 9] - 6\} \div 7$ Divide the difference
                                   by 7
Evaluate:
$$
\begin{aligned}
\{[(10 \cdot 4) + 9] - 6\} \div 7 &= \{[40 + 9] - 6\} \div 7 \\
&= \{49 - 6\} \div 7 \\
&= 43 \div 7 \\
&= \dfrac{43}{7}
\end{aligned}
$$

137. $\dfrac{4}{5}+\dfrac{3}{7}$ Add $\dfrac{4}{5}$ to $\dfrac{3}{7}$

$\left(\dfrac{4}{5}+\dfrac{3}{7}\right)\cdot\dfrac{2}{3}$ Multiply the sum by $\dfrac{2}{3}$

Evaluate:

$$\left(\dfrac{4}{5}+\dfrac{3}{7}\right)\cdot\dfrac{2}{3}=\left(\dfrac{28}{35}+\dfrac{15}{35}\right)\cdot\dfrac{2}{3}$$

$$=\left(\dfrac{43}{35}\right)\cdot\left(\dfrac{2}{3}\right)$$

$$=\dfrac{86}{105}$$

139. $-\left(x^2\right)=-x^2$ is true for all real numbers.

141. When $t=2.5$, $65t=65(2.5)=162.5$

The car travels 162.5 miles.

143. When $t=2$,

$$-16t^2+48t+70=-16(2)^2+48(2)+70$$

$$=-16(4)+48(2)+70$$

$$=-64+96+70$$

$$=32+70$$

$$=102$$

After 2 seconds the height will be 102 feet.

145. a. $2\div5^2=2\div25=0.08$

b. $(2\div5)^2=(0.4)^2=0.16$

147. When $R=2$ and $T=70$,

$$0.2R^2+0.003RT+0.0001T^2$$

$$=0.02(2)^2+0.003(2)(70)+0.0001(70)^2$$

$$=0.2(4)+0.003(2)(70)+0.0001(4900)$$

$$=0.8+0.42+0.49=1.71$$

The growth is 1.71 inches.

149. $12-(4-6)+10=24$

151. a. $2^2\cdot2^3=2\cdot2\cdot2\cdot2\cdot2=2^5$

b. $3^2\cdot3^3=3\cdot3\cdot3\cdot3\cdot3=3^5$

c. $2^3\cdot2^4=2\cdot2\cdot2\cdot2\cdot2\cdot2\cdot2=2^7$

d. $x^m\cdot x^n=x^{m+n}$

153. a. $\left(2^3\right)^2=2^3\cdot2^3=2\cdot2\cdot2\cdot2\cdot2\cdot2=2^6$

b. $\left(3^3\right)^2=3^3\cdot3^3=3\cdot3\cdot3\cdot3\cdot3\cdot3=3^6$

c. $\left(4^2\right)^2=4^2\cdot4^2=4\cdot4\cdot4\cdot4=4^4$

d. $\left(x^m\right)^n=x^{mn}$

155. a. There are 3 houses with 2 dogs.

b.

Dogs	Number of Houses
0	4
1	5
2	3
3	1
4	1

c. $4(1)+3(1)+2(3)+1(5)+0(4)$

$=4+3+6+5+0$

$=7+6+5$

$=13+5$

$=18$

There are 18 dogs in all.

d. Number of dogs $=18$

$$\text{mean}=\dfrac{\text{number of dogs}}{\text{number of houses}}=\dfrac{18}{14}\approx1.29$$

There is a mean of 1.29 dogs per house.

156. $3=\dfrac{6}{2}=\dfrac{1}{2}+\dfrac{5}{2}=\dfrac{1}{2}+\dfrac{20}{8}$

Cost

$=\$2.40+20(0.20)=\$2.40+\$4.00=\$6.40$

157. $-\dfrac{7}{12}+\dfrac{4}{9}=\dfrac{-21}{36}+\dfrac{16}{36}=\dfrac{-21+16}{36}=-\dfrac{5}{36}$

158. $\left(\dfrac{-5}{7}\right)\div\left(\dfrac{-3}{14}\right)=\left(\dfrac{-5}{\underset{1}{\cancel{7}}}\right)\cdot\left(\dfrac{\overset{2}{\cancel{14}}}{-3}\right)$

$$=\dfrac{-5}{1}\cdot\dfrac{2}{-3}$$

$$=\dfrac{(-5)(2)}{(1)(-3)}$$

$$=\dfrac{10}{3}\text{ or }3\dfrac{1}{3}$$

Exercise Set 1.10

1. The commutative property of addition states that the sum of two numbers is the same regardless of the order in which they are added. One possible example is $3+4=4+3$.

3. The associative property of addition states that the sum of 3 numbers is the same regardless of the way the numbers are grouped. One possible example is $(2+3)+4 = 2+(3+4)$.

5. **a.** In $x+(y+z)$ the sum of y and z is added to x whereas in $x(y+z)$, x is multiplied by the sum.

    b. When $x = 4$, $y = 5$, and $z = 6$, $x+(y+z) = 4+(5+6) = 4+11 = 15$.

    c. When $x = 4$, $y = 5$, and $z = 6$, $x(y+z) = 4(5+6) = 4(11) = 44$.

7. The associative property involves changing parentheses with one operation whereas the distributive property involves distributing a multiplication over an addition.

9. 0

11. **a.** -6 **b.** $\dfrac{1}{6}$

13. **a.** 3 **b.** $-\dfrac{1}{3}$

15. **a.** $-x$ **b.** $\dfrac{1}{x}$

17. **a.** -1.6 **b.** $\dfrac{1}{1.6}$ or 0.625

19. **a.** $-\dfrac{1}{5}$ **b.** 5

21. **a.** $\dfrac{5}{6}$ **b.** $-\dfrac{6}{5}$

23. Distributive property

25. Associative property of addition

27. Commutative property of multiplication

29. Associative property of multiplication

31. Distributive property

33. Identity property for multiplication

35. Inverse property for multiplication

37. $1+(-4)$

39. $(-6 \cdot 4) \cdot 2$

41. $-2x - 2y$

43. $y \cdot x$

45. $3y + 4x$

47. $a+(b+3)$

49. $3x+(4+6)$

51. $(m+n)3$

53. $4x+4y+12$

55. 0

57. $\dfrac{5}{2}n$

59. Yes; the order does not affect the outcome so the process is commutative.

61. Yes; the order does not affect the outcome so the process is commutative.

63. No; the order affects the outcome, so the process is not commutative.

65. Yes; the outcome is not affected by whether you do the first two items first or the last two first, so the process is associative.

67. No; the outcome is affected by whether you do the first two items first or the last two first, so the process is not associative.

69. No; the outcome is affected by whether you do the first two items first or the last two first, so the process is not associative.

71. In $(3+4)+x = x+(3+4)$ the $(3+4)$ is treated as one value.

73. This illustrates the commutative property of addition because the change is $3 + 5 = 5 + 3$.

75. No; it illustrates the associative property of addition since the grouping is changed.

77. $2\dfrac{3}{5}+\dfrac{2}{3}$

$2\dfrac{3}{5} = \dfrac{13}{5} = \dfrac{3}{3} \cdot \dfrac{13}{5} = \dfrac{39}{15}$

$\dfrac{2}{3} = \dfrac{2}{3} \cdot \dfrac{5}{5} = \dfrac{10}{15}$

$2\dfrac{3}{5}+\dfrac{2}{3} = \dfrac{39}{15}+\dfrac{10}{15} = \dfrac{49}{15}$ or $3\dfrac{4}{15}$

78. $3\dfrac{5}{8}-2\dfrac{3}{16}$

$3\dfrac{5}{8} = \dfrac{29}{8} = \dfrac{2}{2} \cdot \dfrac{29}{8} = \dfrac{58}{16}$

$$2\frac{3}{16} = \frac{35}{16}$$

$$3\frac{5}{8} - 2\frac{3}{16} = \frac{58}{16} - \frac{35}{16} = \frac{23}{16} \text{ or } 1\frac{7}{16}$$

79. $102.7 + (-113.9) = -11.2$

80. $-\dfrac{7}{8}$

Review Exercises

1. $13(12) - (32 + 29 + 36 + 31) = 156 - 128$
$$= 28$$
He had 28 doughnuts left over.

2. $1.05\big[1.05(500.00)\big] = 1.05[525] = 551.25$
In 2 years the goods will cost \$551.25.

3. a. $899.99(.0825) = 74.25$
The sales tax is \$74.25.

　b. total cost = cost of laptop + sales tax
　total cost $= 899.99 + 74.25$
$$= 974.24$$
The total cost of the laptop is \$974.24.

4. $\big[30 + 12(25)\big] - 300 = [30 + 300] - 300$
$$= 330 - 300$$
$$= 30$$
She can save \$30.

5. a. mean $= \dfrac{75 + 79 + 86 + 88 + 64}{5}$
$$= \dfrac{392}{5}$$
$$= 78.4$$
The mean grade is 78.4.

　b. 64, 75, 79, 86, 88
　The middle number is 79. The median grade is 79.

6. a. mean $= \dfrac{21 + 3 + 17 + 10 + 9 + 6}{6} = \dfrac{66}{6} = 11$
The mean is 11.

　b. 3, 6, 9, 10, 17, 21
　The middle numbers are 9 and 10. Their average is $\dfrac{9 + 10}{2} = \dfrac{19}{2} = 9.5$. The median is 9.5.

7. a. 28.5 minutes

　b. 27.0 minutes

8. a. $1.6(0.637) = 1.0192$
In 1967, 1.0192 million freshman applied to two or fewer colleges.

　b. $2.1(0.247) = 0.5187$
In 2003, 0.5187 million freshman applied to six or more colleges.

9. $\dfrac{3}{5} \cdot \dfrac{5}{6} = \dfrac{\cancel{3}^{1}}{\cancel{5}} \cdot \dfrac{\cancel{5}^{1}}{\cancel{6}_{2}} = \dfrac{1 \cdot 1}{1 \cdot 2} = \dfrac{1}{2}$

10. $3\dfrac{5}{7} + 2\dfrac{1}{3} = \dfrac{26}{7} + \dfrac{7}{3}$
$$= \dfrac{26}{7} \cdot \dfrac{3}{3} + \dfrac{7}{3} \cdot \dfrac{7}{7}$$
$$= \dfrac{78}{21} + \dfrac{49}{21}$$
$$= \dfrac{78 + 49}{21}$$
$$= \dfrac{127}{21} \text{ or } 6\dfrac{1}{21}$$

11. $\dfrac{5}{12} \div \dfrac{3}{5} = \dfrac{5}{12} \cdot \dfrac{5}{3} = \dfrac{5 \cdot 5}{12 \cdot 3} = \dfrac{25}{36}$

12. $\dfrac{5}{6} + \dfrac{1}{3} = \dfrac{5}{6} + \dfrac{1}{3} \cdot \dfrac{2}{2} = \dfrac{5}{6} + \dfrac{2}{6} = \dfrac{7}{6} \text{ or } 1\dfrac{1}{6}$

13. $3\dfrac{1}{6} - 1\dfrac{1}{4} = \dfrac{19}{6} - \dfrac{5}{4}$
$$= \dfrac{19}{6} \cdot \dfrac{2}{2} - \dfrac{5}{4} \cdot \dfrac{3}{3}$$
$$= \dfrac{38}{12} - \dfrac{15}{12}$$
$$= \dfrac{38 - 15}{12}$$
$$= \dfrac{23}{12} \text{ or } 1\dfrac{11}{12}$$

14. $7\dfrac{3}{8} \div \dfrac{5}{12} = 7\dfrac{3}{8} \cdot \dfrac{12}{5}$
$$= \dfrac{59}{\cancel{8}_{2}} \cdot \dfrac{\cancel{12}^{3}}{5}$$
$$= \dfrac{59 \cdot 3}{2 \cdot 5}$$
$$= \dfrac{177}{10} \text{ or } 17\dfrac{7}{10}$$

15. The natural numbers are $\{1, 2, 3, \ldots\}$.

16. The whole numbers are $\{0, 1, 2, 3, \ldots\}$.

17. The integers are $\{\ldots, -3, -2, -1, 0, 1, 2, \ldots\}$.

18. The set of rational numbers is the set of all numbers which can be expressed as the quotient of two integers, denominator not zero.

19. a. 3 and 426 are positive integers.

   b. 3, 0, and 426 are whole numbers.

   c. $3, -5, -12, 0$, and 426 are integers.

   d. $3, -5, -12, 0, \frac{1}{2}, -0.62, 426$, and $-3\frac{1}{4}$ are rational numbers.

   e. $\sqrt{7}$ is an irrational number.

   f. $3, -5, -12, 0, \frac{1}{2}, -0.62, \sqrt{7}, 426$, and $-3\frac{1}{4}$ are real numbers.

20. a. 1 is a natural number.

   b. 1 is a whole number.

   c. -8 and -9 are negative numbers.

   d. $-8, -9$, and 1 are integers.

   e. $-2.3, -8, -9, 1\frac{1}{2}, 1$, and $-\frac{3}{17}$ are rational numbers.

   f. $-2.3, -8, -9, 1\frac{1}{2}, \sqrt{2}, -\sqrt{2}, 1$, and $-\frac{3}{17}$ are real numbers.

21. $-7 < -5$; -7 is to the left of -5 on a number line.

22. $-2.6 > -3.6$; -2.6 is to the right of -3.6 on a number line.

23. $0.50 < 0.509$; 0.50 is to the left 0.509 on a number line.

24. $4.6 > 4.06$; 4.6 is to the right of 4.06 on a number line.

25. $-6.3 < -6.03$; -6.3 is to the left of -6.03 on a number line.

26. $5 > |-3|$ since $|-3|$ equals 3.

27. $\left|-\frac{9}{2}\right| = |-4.5|$ since $\left|-\frac{9}{2}\right| = |-4.5| = 4.5$.

28. $|-10| > |-7|$ since $|-10|$ equals 10 and $|-7|$ equals 7.

29. $-9 + (5) = -14$

30. $-6 + 6 = 0$

31. $0 + (-3) = -3$

32. $-10 + 4 = -6$

33. $-8 - (-2) = -8 + 2 = -6$

34. $-2 - (-4) = -2 + 4 = 2$

35. $4 - (-4) = 4 + 4 = 8$

36. $12 - 12 = 12 + (-12) = 0$

37. $2 - 7 = 2 + (-7) = -5$

38. $7 - (-7) = 7 + 7 = 14$

39. $0 - (-4) = 0 + 4 = 4$

40. $-7 - 5 = -7 + (-5) = -12$

41. $\dfrac{4}{3} - \dfrac{3}{4} = \dfrac{16}{12} - \dfrac{9}{12} = \dfrac{16 - 9}{12} = \dfrac{7}{12}$

42. $\dfrac{1}{2} + \dfrac{3}{5} = \dfrac{5}{10} + \dfrac{6}{10} = \dfrac{5 + 6}{10} = \dfrac{11}{10}$

43. $\dfrac{5}{9} - \dfrac{3}{4} = \dfrac{20}{36} - \dfrac{27}{36} = \dfrac{20 - 27}{36} = -\dfrac{7}{36}$

44. $-\dfrac{5}{7} + \dfrac{3}{8} = -\dfrac{40}{56} + \dfrac{21}{56} = \dfrac{-40 + 21}{56} = -\dfrac{19}{56}$

45. $-\dfrac{5}{12} - \dfrac{5}{6} = -\dfrac{5}{12} - \dfrac{10}{12} = \dfrac{-5 - 10}{12} = -\dfrac{15}{12} = -\dfrac{5}{4}$

46. $-\dfrac{6}{7} + \dfrac{5}{12} = -\dfrac{72}{84} + \dfrac{35}{84} = \dfrac{-72 + 35}{84} = -\dfrac{37}{84}$

47. $\dfrac{2}{9} - \dfrac{3}{10} = \dfrac{20}{90} - \dfrac{27}{90} = \dfrac{20 - 27}{90} = -\dfrac{7}{90}$

48. $\dfrac{5}{12} - \left(-\dfrac{3}{5}\right) = \dfrac{25}{60} + \dfrac{36}{60} = \dfrac{25 + 36}{60} = \dfrac{61}{60}$ or $1\dfrac{1}{60}$

49. $9 - 4 + 3 = 5 + 3 = 8$

50. $-8 - 9 + 4 = -17 + 4 = -13$

51. $-5 - 4 - 3 = -9 - 3 = -12$

52. $-2 + (-3) - 2 = -5 - 2 = -7$

53. $7 - (+4) - (-3) = 7 - 4 + 3 = 3 + 3 = 6$

54. $6 - (-2) + 3 = 6 + 2 + 3 = 8 + 3 = 11$

55. Since the numbers have unlike signs, the product is negative; $7(-9) = -63$

56. Since the numbers have like signs, the product is positive; $(-8.2)(-3.1) = 25.42$

57. Since there are an odd number (3) of negatives the product is negative;
$$(-4)(-5)(-6) = (20)(-6) = -120$$

58. $\left(\dfrac{3}{5}\right)\left(\dfrac{-2}{7}\right) = \dfrac{3(-2)}{5 \cdot 7} = \dfrac{-6}{35} = -\dfrac{6}{35}$

59. $\left(\dfrac{10}{11}\right)\left(\dfrac{3}{-5}\right) = \dfrac{2}{11} \cdot \dfrac{3}{-1} = \dfrac{2 \cdot 3}{(11)(-1)} = \dfrac{6}{-11} = -\dfrac{6}{11}$

60. $\left(\dfrac{-5}{8}\right)\left(\dfrac{-3}{7}\right) = \dfrac{(-5)(-3)}{8 \cdot 7} = \dfrac{15}{56}$

61. Zero multiplied by any real number is zero.
$$0 \cdot \dfrac{4}{9} = 0$$

62. Since there are four negative numbers (an even number), the product is positive.
$$(-4)(-6)(-2)(-3) = (24)(-2)(-3)$$
$$= (-48)(-3)$$
$$= 144$$

63. Since the numbers have unlike signs, the quotient is negative; $15 \div (-3) = \dfrac{15}{-3} = -5$

64. Since the numbers have unlike signs, the quotient is negative.
$$12 \div (-2) = \dfrac{12}{-2} = -6$$

65. Since the numbers have unlike signs, the quotient is negative;
$$-14.72 \div 4.6 = \dfrac{-14.72}{4.6} = -3.2$$

66. Since the numbers have like signs, the quotient is positive: $-37.41 \div (-8.7) = 4.3$

67. Since the numbers have like signs, the quotient is positive: $-88 \div (-11) = 8$

68. $-4 \div \left(\dfrac{-4}{9}\right) = \dfrac{-4}{1} \cdot \dfrac{9}{-4} = \dfrac{-1}{1} \cdot \dfrac{9}{-1} = \dfrac{-9}{-1} = 9$

69. $\dfrac{28}{-3} \div \left(\dfrac{9}{-2}\right) = \left(\dfrac{28}{-3}\right) \cdot \left(\dfrac{-2}{9}\right) = \dfrac{-56}{-27} = \dfrac{56}{27}$

70. $\dfrac{14}{3} \div \left(\dfrac{-6}{5}\right) = \dfrac{7\cancel{14}}{3} \cdot \left(\dfrac{5}{-\cancel{6}_3}\right)$
$$= \dfrac{7(5)}{3(-3)}$$
$$= \dfrac{35}{-9} = -\dfrac{35}{9}$$

71. Zero divided by any nonzero number is zero;
$$0 \div 5 = \dfrac{0}{5} = 0$$

72. Zero divided by any nonzero number is zero;
$$0 \div (-6) = \dfrac{0}{-6} = 0$$

73. Any real number divided by zero is undefined;
$$-4 \div 0 = \dfrac{-4}{0} \text{ is undefined.}$$

74. Any real number divided by zero is undefined;
$$-4 \div 0 = \dfrac{-4}{0} \text{ is undefined.}$$

75. Any real number divided by zero is undefined;
$$\dfrac{8.3}{0} \text{ is undefined}$$

76. Zero divided by any nonzero number is zero;
$$\dfrac{0}{-9.8} = 0$$

77. $-5(3 - 8) = -5(-5) = 25$

78. $2(4 - 8) = 2(-4) = -8$

79. $(3 - 6) + 4 = -3 + 4 = 1$

80. $(-4 + 3) - (2 - 6) = (-1) - (-4) = -1 + 4 = 3$

81. $[6 + 3(-2)] - 6 = [6 + (-6)] - 6 = 0 - 6 = -6$

82. $(-5 - 3)(4) = (-5 + (-3))(4) = (-8)(4) = -32$

83. $[12 + (-4)] + (6 - 8) = 8 + (-2) = 6$

84. $9[3 + (-4)] + 5 = 9(-1) + 5 = -9 + 5 = -4$

85. $-4(-3) + [4 \div (-2)] = (12) + (-2) = 10$

86. $(-3 \cdot 4) \div (-2 \cdot 6) = -12 \div (-12) = 1$

87. $(-3)(-4) + 6 - 3 = 12 + 6 - 3 = 18 - 3 = 15$

88. $[-2(3) + 6] - 4 = [-6 + 6] - 4 = 0 - 4 = -4$

89. $-6^2 = -(6)(6) = -36$

90. $(-6)^2 = (-6)(-6) = 36$

91. $2^4 = (2)(2)(2)(2) = 16$

92. $(-3)^3 = (-3)(-3)(-3) = -27$

93. $(-1)^9 = (-1)(-1)(-1)(-1)(-1)(-1)(-1)(-1)(-1)$
$\qquad = -1$

94. $(-2)^5 = (-2)(-2)(-2)(-2)(-2) = -32$

95. $\left(\dfrac{-4}{5}\right)^2 = \left(\dfrac{-4}{5}\right)\left(\dfrac{-4}{5}\right) = \dfrac{16}{25}$

96. $\left(\dfrac{2}{5}\right)^3 = \left(\dfrac{2}{5}\right)\left(\dfrac{2}{5}\right)\left(\dfrac{2}{5}\right) = \dfrac{8}{125}$

97. $5^3 \cdot (-2)^2 = (5)(5)(5)(-2)(-2) = 500$

98. $(-2)^4 \left(\dfrac{1}{2}\right)^2 = (-2)(-2)(-2)(-2)\left(\dfrac{1}{2}\right)\left(\dfrac{1}{2}\right) = 4$

99. $\left(-\dfrac{2}{3}\right)^2 \cdot 3^3 = \left(-\dfrac{2}{3}\right)\left(-\dfrac{2}{3}\right)(3)(3)(3) = 12$

100. $(-4)^3 (-2)^2 = (-4)(-4)(-4)(-2)(-2) = -256$

101. $-5 + 3 \cdot 4 = -5 + 12 = 7$

102. $4 \cdot 6 + 4 \cdot 2 = 24 + 8 = 32$

103. $(3.7 - 4.1)^2 + 6.2 = (-0.4)^2 + 6.2$
$\qquad = 0.16 + 6.2$
$\qquad = 6.36$

104. $10 - 36 \div 4 \cdot 3 = 10 - 9 \cdot 3 = 10 - 27 = -17$

105. $6 - 3^2 \cdot 5 = 6 - 9 \cdot 5 = 6 - 45 = -39$

106. $\left[6.9 - (3 \cdot 5)\right] + 5.8 = \left[6.9 - 15\right] + 5.8$
$\qquad = -8.1 + 5.8$
$\qquad = -2.3$

107. $\dfrac{6^2 - 4 \cdot 3^2}{-\left[6 - (3 - 4)\right]} = \dfrac{36 - 4 \cdot 9}{-\left[6 - (-1)\right]}$
$\qquad = \dfrac{36 - 36}{-7}$
$\qquad = \dfrac{0}{-7} = 0$

108. $\dfrac{4 + 5^2 \div 5}{6 - (-3 + 2)} = \dfrac{4 + 25 \div 5}{6 - (-1)} = \dfrac{4 + 5}{7} = \dfrac{9}{7}$

109. $3[9(4^2 + 3)] \cdot 2 = 3[9 - (16 + 3)] \cdot 2$
$\qquad = 3[9 - 19] \cdot 2$
$\qquad = 3 \cdot (-10) \cdot 2$
$\qquad = -30 \cdot 2$
$\qquad = -60$

110. $(-3^2 + 4^2) + (3^2 \div 3) = (-9 + 16) + (9 \div 3)$
$\qquad = (7) + (3)$
$\qquad = 10$

111. $2^3 \div 4 + 6 \cdot 3 = 8 \div 4 + 6 \cdot 3 = 2 + 18 = 20$

112. $(4 \div 2)^4 + 4^2 \div 2^2 = (2)^4 + 16 \div 4$
$\qquad = 16 + 16 \div 4$
$\qquad = 16 + 4$
$\qquad = 20$

113. $\left(8 - 2^2\right)^2 - 4 \cdot 3 + 10 = (8 - 4)^2 - 4 \cdot 3 + 10$
$\qquad = (4)^2 - 4 \cdot 3 + 10$
$\qquad = 16 - 4 \cdot 3 + 10$
$\qquad = 16 - 12 + 10$
$\qquad = 4 + 10$
$\qquad = 14$

114. $4^3 \div 4^2 - 5(2 - 7) \div 5 = 64 \div 16 - 5(-5) \div 5$
$\qquad = 4 - (-25) \div 5$
$\qquad = 4 - (-5)$
$\qquad = 4 + 5$
$\qquad = 9$

115. $-\left\{-4\left[27 \div 3^2 - 2(4 - 2)\right]\right\}$
$\qquad = -\left\{-4\left[27 \div 9 - 2(2)\right]\right\}$
$\qquad = -\left\{-4\left[3 - 4\right]\right\}$
$\qquad = -\left\{-4\left[-1\right]\right\}$
$\qquad = -\left\{4\right\}$
$\qquad -4$

116. $2\left\{4^3 - 6\left[4 - (2 - 4)\right] - 3\right\}$
$\qquad = 2\left\{64 - 6\left[4 - (2 - 4)\right] - 3\right\}$
$\qquad = 2\left\{64 - 6\left[4 - (-2)\right] - 3\right\}$
$\qquad = 2\left\{64 - 6[6] - 3\right\}$

$$= 2\{64 - 36 - 3\}$$
$$= 2\{25\}$$
$$= 50$$

117. Substitute 4 for x;
$$3x - 7 = 3(4) - 7 = 12 - 7 = 5$$

118. Substitute –5 for x;
$$6 - 4x = 6 - 4(-5) = 6 - (-20) = 6 + 20 = 26$$

119. Substitute 6 for x;
$$2x^2 - 5x + 3 = 2(6)^2 - 5(6) + 3$$
$$= 2(36) - 30 + 3$$
$$= 72 - 30 + 3$$
$$= 42 + 3$$
$$= 45$$

120. Substitute –1 for y;
$$5y^2 + 3y - 2 = 5(-1)^2 + 3(-1) - 2$$
$$= 5(1) - 3 - 2$$
$$= 5 - 3 - 2$$
$$= 2 - 2$$
$$= 0$$

121. Substitute –2 for x;
$$-x^2 + 2x - 3 = -(-2)^2 + 2(-2) - 3$$
$$= -4 + (-4) - 3$$
$$= -8 - 3$$
$$= -11$$

122. Substitute 2 for x;
$$-x^2 + 2x - 3 = -2^2 + 2(2) - 3$$
$$= -4 + 4 - 3$$
$$= 0 - 3$$
$$= -3$$

123. Substitute 1 for x;
$$-3x^2 - 5x + 5 = -3(1)^2 - 5(1) + 5$$
$$= -3(1) - 5 + 5$$
$$= -3 - 5 + 5$$
$$= -8 + 5$$
$$= -3$$

124. Substitute –3 for x and –2 for y;
$$-x^2 - 8x - 12y = -(-3)^2 - 8(-3) - 12(-2)$$
$$= -9 - (-24) + 24$$
$$= -9 + 24 + 24$$
$$= 15 + 24$$
$$= 39$$

125. a. $278 + (-493) = -215$

b. $|-493|$ is greater than $|278|$ so the sum should be (and is) negative.

126. a. $324 - (-29.6) = 324 + 29.6 = 353.6$

b. The sum of two positive numbers is always positive. As expected, the answer is positive.

127. a. $\dfrac{-17.28}{6} = -2.88$

b. Since the numbers have unlike signs, the quotient is negative, as expected.

128. a. $(-62)(-1.9) = 117.8$

b. Since the numbers have like signs, the product is positive, as expected.

129. a. $(-4)^8 = 65,536$

b. A negative number raised to an even power is positive. As expected, the answer is positive.

130. a. $-(4.2)^3 = -74.088$

b. Since $(4.2)^3$ is positive, $-(4.2)^3$ should be (and is) negative.

131. Associative property of addition

132. Distributive property

133. Commutative property of addition

134. Commutative property of multiplication

135. Distributive property

136. Associative property of addition

137. Identity property of multiplication

138. Inverse property of addition

Practice Test

1. a. $2(1.30) + 4.75 + 3(1.10)$
$$= 2.60 + 4.75 + 3.30$$
$$= 7.35 + 3.30$$
$$= 10.65$$
The bill is $10.65 before tax.

b. $0.07(3.30) \approx 0.23$
The tax on the soda is $0.23.

c. $10.65 + 0.23 = 10.88$
The total bill is $10.88.

d. $50 - 10.88 = 39.12$
Her change will be $39.12.

2. $\dfrac{1,600,000}{643,500} \approx 2.48$

The price was about 2.5 times greater in the twelfth year compared to the first year.

3. a. $13.0 - 5.1 = 7.9$

About 7.9 million listened to WRAB at this time.

b. During this specific time, half the time KFUN had more than 8.8 million listeners and half the time KFUN had less than 8.8 million listeners.

4. a. 42 is a natural number.

b. 42 and 0 are whole numbers.

c. $-6, 42, 0, -7,$ and -1 are integers.

d. $-6, 42, -3\dfrac{1}{2}, 0, 6.52, \dfrac{5}{9}, -7,$ and -1 are rational numbers.

e. $\sqrt{5}$ is an irrational number.

f. $-6, 42, -3\dfrac{1}{2}, 0, 6.52, \sqrt{5}, \dfrac{5}{9}, -7,$ and -1 are real numbers.

5. $-9.9 < -9.09$; -9.9 is to the left of -9.09 on a number line.

6. $|-3| > |-2|$ since $|-3| = 3$ and $|-2| = 2$.

7. $-7 + (-8) = -15$

8. $-6 - 5 = -6 + (-5) = -11$

9. $15 - 12 - 17 = 3 - 17 = -14$

10. $(-4 + 6) - 3(-2) = (2) - (-6) = 2 + 6 = 8$

11. $(-4)(-3)(2)(-1) = (12)(2)(-1)$
$= (24)(-1)$
$= -24$

12. $\left(\dfrac{-2}{9}\right) \div \left(\dfrac{-7}{8}\right) = \dfrac{-2}{9} \cdot \dfrac{8}{-7} = \dfrac{-16}{-63} = \dfrac{16}{63}$

13. $\left(-18 \cdot \dfrac{1}{2}\right) \div 3 = \left(\dfrac{-\overset{9}{\cancel{18}}}{1} \cdot \dfrac{1}{\cancel{2}_1}\right) \div 3$

$= \left(\dfrac{-9 \cdot 1}{1 \cdot 1}\right) \div 3$

$= -9 \div 3$

$= -3$

14. $-\dfrac{3}{8} - \dfrac{4}{7} = -\dfrac{21}{56} - \dfrac{32}{56} = \dfrac{-21 - 32}{56} = -\dfrac{53}{56}$

15. $-6(-2 - 3) \div 5 \cdot 2 = -6(-5) \div 5 \cdot 2$
$= 30 \div 5 \cdot 2$
$= 6 \cdot 2$
$= 12$

16. $\left(-\dfrac{2}{3}\right)^5 = \left(-\dfrac{2}{3}\right)\left(-\dfrac{2}{3}\right)\left(-\dfrac{2}{3}\right)\left(-\dfrac{2}{3}\right)\left(-\dfrac{2}{3}\right)$
$= -\dfrac{32}{243}$

17. $2 \cdot 2 \cdot 5 \cdot 5 \cdot yyzzz = 2^2 5^2 y^2 z^3$

18. $2^2 3^3 x^4 y^2 = 2 \cdot 2 \cdot 3 \cdot 3 \cdot 3xxxxyy$

19. Substitute -3 for x;
$5x^2 - 8 = 5(-3)^2 - 8 = 5(9) - 8 = 45 - 8 = 37$

20. Substitute 3 for x and -2 for y;
$6x - 3y^2 + 4 = 6(3) - 3(-2)^2 + 4$
$= 6(3) - 3(4) + 4$
$= 18 - 12 + 4$
$= 6 + 4$
$= 10$

21. Substitute -2 for each x;
$-x^2 - 6x + 3 = -(-2)^2 - 6(-2) + 3$
$= -4 - (-12) + 3$
$= -4 + 12 + 3$
$= 8 + 3$
$= 11$

22. Substitute 1 for x and -2 for y;
$-x^2 + xy + y^2 = -(1)^2 + (1)(-2) + (-2)^2$
$= -1 + (-2) + 4$
$= -3 + 4$
$= 1$

23. Commutative property of addition

24. Distributive property

25. Associative property of addition

Chapter 2

Exercise Set 2.1

1. a. The terms of an expression are the parts that are added.

   b. The terms of $3x - 4y - 5$ are $3x$, $-4y$, and -5.

   c. The terms of $6xy + 3x - y - 9$ are $6xy$, $3x$, $-y$, and -9.

3. a. In $2x - 5$, the x is called the variable.

   b. In $2x - 5$, the -5 is called the constant.

   c. In $2x - 5$, the 2 is called the coefficient.

5. a. Yes, $5x$ and $-7x$ are like terms because they have the same variable with the same exponent.

   b. No, $7y$ and 2 are not like terms because the 2 does not have a y variable.

   c. Yes, $-3(t + 2)$ and $6(t + 2)$ are like terms because they have the same variable with the same exponent.

   d. Yes, $4pq$ and $-9pq$ are like terms because they have the same variables with the same exponents

7. a. The signs of all the terms inside the parentheses are changed when the parentheses are removed.

   b. $-(x - 8) = -x + 8$

9. $6x + 3x = 9x$

11. There are no like terms.
$3x + 6$

13. $y + 3 + 4y = y + 4y + 3$
$$= 5y + 3$$

15. $\dfrac{3}{4} - \dfrac{6}{11} = \dfrac{33}{44} - \dfrac{24}{44} = \dfrac{9}{44}$
$\dfrac{3}{4}a - \dfrac{6}{11}a = \dfrac{9}{44}a$

17. $2 - 6x + 5 = -6x + 2 + 5$
$$= -6x + 7$$

19. $-2w - 3w + 5 = -5w + 5$

21. $-x + 2 - x - 2 = -x - x + 2 - 2$
$$= -2x$$

23. $3 + 6x - 3 - 6x = 6x - 6x + 3 - 3 = 0$

25. $5 + 2x - 4x + 6 = 2x - 4x + 5 + 6$
$$= -2x + 11$$

27. $4r - 6 - 6r - 2 = -4r - 6r - 6 - 2$
$$= -2r - 8$$

29. $3x^2 - 9y^2 + 7x^2 - 5 - y^2 - 2$
$$= 3x^2 + 7x^2 - 9y^2 - y^2 - 5 - 2$$
$$= 10y^2 - 10y^2 - 7$$

31. $-2x + 4x - 3 = 2x - 3$

33. $b + 4 + \dfrac{3}{5} = b + \dfrac{20}{5} + \dfrac{3}{5}$
$$= b + \dfrac{23}{5}$$

35. $5.1n + 6.42 - 4.3n = 5.1n - 4.3n + 6.42$
$$= 0.8n + 6.42$$

37. There are no like terms.
$\dfrac{1}{2}a + 3b + 1$

39. $13.4x + 1.2x + 8.3 = 14.6x + 8.3$

41. $-x^2 + 2x^2 + y = x^2 + y$

43. $2x - 7y - 5x + 2y = 2x - 5x - 7y + 2y$
$$= -3x - 5y$$

45. $4 - 3n^2 + 9 - 2n = -3n^2 - 2n + 4 + 9$
$$= -3n^2 - 2n + 13$$

47. $-19.36 + 40.02x + 12.25 - 18.3x$
$$= 40.02x - 18.3x - 19.36 + 12.25$$
$$= 21.72x - 7.11$$

49. $\dfrac{3}{5}x - 3 - \dfrac{7}{4}x - 2 = \dfrac{3}{5}x - \dfrac{7}{4}x - 3 - 2$
$$= \dfrac{12}{20}x - \dfrac{35}{20}x - 5$$
$$= -\dfrac{23}{20}x - 5$$

51. There are no like terms.
$5w^3 + 2w^2 + w + 3$

53. $2z - 5z^3 - 2z^3 - z^2 = -5z^3 - 2z^3 - z^2 + 2z$
$$= -7z^3 - z^2 + 2z$$

55. There are no like terms.
$6x^2 - 6xy + 3y^2$

57. $4a^2 - 3ab + 6ab + b^2 = 4a^2 + 3ab + b^2$

59. $5(x+2) = 5x + 5(2)$
$$= 5x + 10$$

61. $5(x+4) = 5x + 5(4)$
$$= 5x + 20$$

63. $3(x - 6) = 3x + 3(-6) = 3x - 18$

65. $-\dfrac{1}{2}(2x - 4) = -\dfrac{1}{2}[2x + (-4)]$
$$= -\dfrac{1}{2}(2x) + \left(-\dfrac{1}{2}\right)(-4)$$
$$= -x + 2$$

67. $1(-4 + x) = 1(-4) + 1(x)$
$$= -4 + x$$
$$= x - 4$$

69. $\dfrac{4}{5}(s - 5) = \dfrac{4}{5}s - \dfrac{4}{5}(5)$
$$= \dfrac{4}{5}s - 4$$

71. $-0.3(3x + 5) = -0.3(3x) + (-0.3)(5)$
$$= -0.9x + (-1.5)$$
$$= -0.9x - 1.5$$

73. $-\dfrac{1}{3}(3r - 12) = -\dfrac{1}{3}(3r) + \left(-\dfrac{1}{3}\right)(-12)$
$$= -r + 4$$

75. $0.7(2x + 0.5) = 0.7(2x) + 0.7(0.5)$
$$= 1.4x + 0.35$$

77. $-(-x + y) = -1(-x + y)$
$$= -1(-x) + (-1)(y)$$
$$= x + (-y)$$
$$= x - y$$

79. $-(2x + 4y - 8) = -1[2x + 4y + (-8)]$
$$= -1(2x) + (-1)(4y) + (-1)(-8)$$
$$= -2x - 4y + 8$$
$$= -2x - 4y + 8$$

81. $1.1(3.1x - 5.2y + 2.8)$
$$= 1.1[3.1x + (-5.2y) + 2.8]$$
$$= (1.1)(3.1x) + (1.1)(-5.2y) + (1.1)(2.8)$$
$$= 3.41x + (-5.72y) + 3.08$$
$$= 3.41x - 5.72y + 3.08$$

83. $(2x - 9y)5 = (2x)5 + (-9y)5$
$$= 10x - 45y$$

85. $(x + 3y - 9) = 1[x + 3y + (-9)]$
$$= 1(x) + 1(3y) + (1)(-9)$$
$$= x + 3y + (-9) = x + 3y - 9$$

87. $-3(-x + 2y + 4) = -3(-x) + (-3)(2y) + (-3)(4)$
$$= 3x + (-6y) + (-12)$$
$$= 3x - 6y - 12$$

89. $5 - (3x + 4) = 5 - 3x - 4$
$$= -3x + 5 - 4$$
$$= -3x + 1$$

91. $-2(3 - x) + 7 = -6 + 2x + 7$
$$= 2x - 6 + 7$$
$$= 2x + 1$$

93. $6x + 2(4x + 9) = 6x + 8x + 18$
$$= 14x + 18$$

95. $2(x - y) + 2x + 3 = 2x - 2y + 2x + 3$
$$= 2x + 2x - 2y + 3$$
$$= 4x - 2y + 3$$

97. $4(2c - 3) - 3(c - 4) = 8c - 12 - 3c + 12$
$$= 8c - 3c - 12 + 12$$
$$= 5c$$

99. $8x - (x - 3) = 8x - x + 3$
$$= 7x + 3$$

101. $-\left(\dfrac{3}{4}x - \dfrac{1}{3}\right) + 2x = -\dfrac{3}{4}x + \dfrac{1}{3} + 2x$
$$= -\dfrac{3}{4}x + 2x + \dfrac{1}{3}$$
$$= -\dfrac{3}{4}x + \dfrac{8}{4}x + \dfrac{1}{3}$$
$$= \dfrac{5}{4}x + \dfrac{1}{3}$$

103. $\dfrac{2}{3}x + \dfrac{1}{2}(5x-4) = \dfrac{2}{3}x + \dfrac{5}{2}x - 2$

$$= \dfrac{4}{6}x + \dfrac{15}{6}x - 2$$

$$= \dfrac{19}{6}x - 2$$

105. $-(3s+4) - (s+2) = -3s - 4 - s - 2$

$$= -3s - s - 4 - 2$$

$$= -4s - 6$$

107. $4(x-1) + 2(3-x) - 4 = 4x - 4(1) + 2(3) - 2x - 4$

$$= 4x - 4 + 6 - 2x - 4$$

$$= 4x - 2x - 4 + 6 - 4$$

$$= 2x - 2$$

109. $4(m+3) - 4m - 12 = 4m + 4(3) - 4m - 12$

$$= 4m + 12 - 4m - 12$$

$$= 4m - 4m + 12 - 12$$

$$= 0$$

111. $0.4 - (y+5) + 0.6 - 2 = 0.4 - y - 5 + 0.6 - 2$

$$= -y + 0.4 - 5 + 0.6 - 2$$

$$= -y - 6$$

113. $4 + (3x-4) - 5 = 4 + 3x - 4 - 5$

$$= 3x + 4 - 4 - 5$$

$$= 3x - 5$$

115. $4(x+2) - 3(x-4) - 5$

$$= 4x + 4(2) - 3x - 3(-4) - 5$$

$$= 4x + 8 - 3x + 12 - 5$$

$$= 4x - 3x + 8 + 12 - 5$$

$$= x + 15$$

117. $-0.2(6-x) - 4(y+0.4)$

$$= -0.2(6) - 0.2(-x) - 4y - 4(0.4)$$

$$= -1.2 + 0.2x - 4y - 1.6$$

$$= 0.2x - 4y - 1.2 - 1.6$$

$$= 0.2x - 4y - 2.8$$

119. $-6x + 7y - (3+x) + (x+3)$

$$= -6x + 7y - 3 - x + x + 3$$

$$= -6x - x + x + 7y - 3 + 3$$

$$= -6x + 7y$$

121. $\dfrac{1}{2}(x+3) + \dfrac{1}{3}(3x+6) = \dfrac{1}{2}x + \dfrac{3}{2} + \dfrac{3}{3}x + \dfrac{6}{3}$

$$= \dfrac{1}{2}x + \dfrac{3}{2} + x + 2$$

$$= \dfrac{1}{2}x + x + \dfrac{3}{2} + 2$$

$$= \dfrac{1}{2}x + \dfrac{2}{2}x + \dfrac{3}{2} + \dfrac{4}{2}$$

$$= \dfrac{3}{2}x + \dfrac{7}{2}$$

123. $\square + \ominus + \ominus + \square + \ominus = 2\square + 3\ominus$

125. $x + y + \Delta + \Delta + x + y + y$

$$= x + x + y + y + y + \Delta + \Delta$$

$$= 2x + 3y + 2\Delta$$

127. $3\Delta + 5\square - \Delta - 3\square = 3\Delta - \Delta + 5\square - 3\square$

$$= 2\Delta + 2\square$$

129. $1 \cdot 18,\; 2 \cdot 9,\; 3 \cdot 6$

positive factors: $1, 2, 3, 6, 9, 18$

131. $4x^2 + 5y^2 + 6(3x^2 - 5y^2) - 4x + 3$

$$= 4x^2 + 5y^2 + 18x^2 - 30y^2 - 4x + 3$$

$$= 4x^2 + 18x^2 - 4x + 5y^2 - 30y^2 + 3$$

$$= 22x^2 - 25y^2 - 4x + 3$$

133. $2[3 + 4(x-5)] - [2 - (x-3)]$

$$= 2[3 + 4x - 20] - [2 - x + 3]$$

$$= 6 + 8x - 40 - 2 + x - 3$$

$$= 8x + x + 6 - 40 - 2 - 3$$

$$= 9x - 39$$

135. $|-7| = 7$

136. $-|-16| = -(16) = -16$

137. $-4 - 3 - (-6) = -4 - 3 + 6$

$$= -7 + 6$$

$$= -1$$

138. Answers will vary. The answer should include that the order is parentheses, exponents, multiplication and division from left to right, and addition and subtraction from left to right.

139. Substitute –1 for each x in the expression.
$$-x^2 + 5x - 6 = -(-1)^2 + 5(-1) - 6$$
$$= -1 + (-5) - 6$$
$$= -6 - 6$$
$$= -12$$

Exercise Set 2.2

1. An equation is a statement that shows two algebraic expressions are equal.

3. A solution to an equation may be checked by substituting the value in the equation and determining if it results in a true statement.

5. Equivalent equations are two or more equations with the same solution.

7. Subtract 2 from both sides of the equation to isolate the variable.

9. One example is $x + 2 = 1$.

11. All 3 equations have $x = 1$ as their solution.

13. Substitute 2 for $x = 2$.
$$4x - 3 = 5$$
$$4(2) - 3 = 5$$
$$8 - 3 = 5$$
$$5 = 5 \quad \text{True}$$
Since we obtain true statement, 2 is a solution.

15. Substitute –3 for x, $x = -3$.
$$2x - 5 = 5(x + 2)$$
$$2(-3) - 5 = 5[(-3) + 2]$$
$$-6 - 5 = 5(-1)$$
$$-11 = -5 \text{ False}$$
Since we obtain a false statement, –3 is not a solution.

17. Substitute –15 for p, $p = -15$.
$$2p - 5(p + 7) = 10$$
$$2(-15) - 5(-15 + 7) = 10$$
$$-30 - 5(-8) = 10$$
$$-30 + 40 = 10$$
$$10 = 10 \quad \text{True}$$
Since we obtain a true statement, –15 is a solution.

19. Substitute 3.4 for x, $x = 3.4$.
$$3(x + 2) - 3(x - 1) = 9$$
$$3(3.4 + 2) - 3(3.4 - 1) = 9$$
$$3(5.4) - 3(2.4) = 9$$
$$16.2 - 7.2 = 9$$
$$9 = 9 \quad \text{True}$$
Since we obtain a true statement, 3.4 is a solution.

21. Substitute $\frac{1}{2}$ for x, $x = \frac{1}{2}$.
$$4x - 4 = 2x - 2$$
$$4\left(\frac{1}{2}\right) - 4 = 2\left(\frac{1}{2}\right) - 2$$
$$2 - 4 = 1 - 2$$
$$-2 = -1 \text{ False}$$
Since we obtain a false statement, $\frac{1}{2}$ is not a solution.

23. Substitute $\frac{11}{2}$ for x, $x = \frac{11}{2}$.
$$3(x + 2) = 5(x - 1)$$
$$3\left(\frac{11}{2} + 2\right) = 5\left(\frac{11}{2} - 1\right)$$
$$3\left(\frac{15}{2}\right) = 5\left(\frac{9}{2}\right)$$
$$\frac{45}{2} = \frac{45}{2} \quad \text{True}$$
Since we obtain a true statement, $\frac{11}{2}$ is a solution.

25. $x + 2 = 7$
$$x + 2 - 2 = 7 - 2$$
$$x + 0 = 5$$
$$x = 5$$
Check: $x + 2 = 7$
$$5 + 2 = 7$$
$$7 = 7 \quad \text{True}$$

27. $x + 1 = -6$
$$x + 1 - 1 = -6 - 1$$
$$x + 0 = -7$$
$$x = -7$$
Check: $x + 1 = -6$
$$-7 + 1 = -6$$
$$-6 = -6 \quad \text{True}$$

29. $x - 4 = -8$
$x - 4 + 4 = -8 + 4$
$x + 0 = -4$
$x = -4$
Check: $x - 4 = 8$
$-4 - 4 = -8$
$-8 = -8$ True

31. $x + 9 = 52$
$x + 9 - 9 = 52 - 9$
$x + 0 = 43$
$x = 43$
Check: $x + 9 = 52$
$43 + 9 = 52$
$52 = 52$ True

33. $-6 + w = 9$
$-6 + 6 + w = 9 + 6$
$0 + w = 15$
$w = 15$
Check: $-6 + w = 9$
$-6 + 15 = 9$
$9 = 9$ True

35. $27 = x + 16$
$27 - 16 = x + 16 - 16$
$11 = x + 0$
$11 = x$
Check: $27 = x + 16$
$27 = 11 + 16$
$27 = 27$ True

37. $-18 = x - 14$
$-18 + 14 = x - 14 + 14$
$-4 = x + 0$
$-4 = x$
Check: $-18 = x - 14$
$-18 = -4 - 14$
$-18 = -18$ True

39. $9 + x = 4$
$9 - 9 + x = 4 - 9$
$0 + x = -5$
$x = -5$
Check: $9 + x = 4$
$9 + (-5) = 4$
$4 = 4$ True

41. $4 + x = -9$
$4 - 4 + x = -9 - 4$
$0 + x = -13$
$x = -13$
Check: $4 + x = -9$
$4 + (-13) = -9$
$-9 = -9$ True

43. $7 + r = -23$
$7 + r = -23$
$7 - 7 + r = -23 - 7$
$0 + r = -30$
$r = -30$
Check: $7 + r = -23$
$7 + (-30) = -23$
$-23 = -23$ True

45. $8 = 8 + v$
$8 - 8 = 8 - 8 + v$
$0 = 0 + v$
$0 = v$
Check: $8 = 8 + v$
$8 = 8 + 0$
$8 = 8$ True

47. $7 + x = -50$
$7 - 7 + x = -50 - 7$
$0 + x = -57$
$x = -57$
Check: $7 + x = -50$
$7 + (-57) = -50$
$-50 = -50$ True

49. $12 = 16 + x$
$12 - 16 = 16 - 16 + x$
$-4 = 0 + x$
$-4 = x$
Check: $12 = 16 + x$
$12 = 16 + (-4)$
$12 = 12$ True

51. $15 + x = -5$
$15 - 15 + x = -5 - 15$
$0 + x = -20$
$x = -20$
Check: $15 + x = -5$
$15 + (-20) = -5$
$-5 = -5$ True

53. $-15 + x = -15$

$-15 + 15 + x = -15 + 15$

$0 + x = 0$

$x = 0$

Check: $-15 + x = -15$

$-15 + 0 = -15$

$-15 = -15$ True

55. $5 = x - 12$

$5 + 12 = x - 12 + 12$

$17 = x + 0$

$17 = x$

Check: $5 = x - 12$

$5 = 17 - 12$

$5 = 5$ True

57. $-50 = x - 24$

$-50 + 24 = x - 24 + 24$

$-26 = x + 0$

$-26 = x$

Check: $-50 = x - 24$

$-50 = -26 - 24$

$-50 = -50$ True

59. $43 = 15 + p$

$43 - 15 = 15 - 15 + p$

$28 = 0 + p$

$28 = p$

Check: $43 = 15 + p$

$43 = 15 + 28$

$43 = 43$ True

61. $40.2 + x = -5.9$

$40.2 - 40.2 + x = -5.9 - 40.2$

$0 + x = -46.1$

$x = -46.1$

Check: $40.2 + x = -5.9$

$40.2 + (-46.1) = -5.9$

$-5.9 = -5.9$ True

63. $-37 + x = 9.5$

$-37 + 37 + x = 9.5 + 37$

$0 + x = 46.5$

$x = 46.5$

Check: $-37 + x = 9.5$

$-37 + 46.5 = 9.5$

$9.5 = 9.5$ True

65. $x - 8.77 = -17$

$x - 8.77 + 8.77 = -17 + 8.77$

$x + 0 = -8.23$

$x = -8.23$

Check: $x - 8.77 = -17$

$-8.23 - 8.77 = -17$

$-17 = -17$ True

67. $9.32 = x + 3.75$

$9.32 - 3.75 = x + 3.75 - 3.75$

$5.57 = x + 0$

$5.57 = x$

Check: $9.32 = x + 3.75$

$9.32 = 5.57 + 3.75$

$9.32 = 9.32$ True

69. No; there are no real numbers that can make $x + 1 = x + 2$.

71. $x - \Delta = \square$

$x - \Delta + \Delta = \square + \Delta$

$x = \square + \Delta$

73. $\odot = \square + \Delta$

$\odot - \Delta = \square + \Delta - \Delta$

$\odot - \Delta = \square$

75. a. yes   **b.** yes   **c.** yes

d. yes   **e.** Since the left side of the equation is equal to the right side of the equation, $2x + 6 = 2x + 6$, the solution is all real numbers.

76. $-\dfrac{7}{15} + \dfrac{5}{6} = -\dfrac{14}{30} + \dfrac{25}{30} = \dfrac{-14 + 25}{30} = \dfrac{11}{30}$

77. $-\dfrac{11}{12} + \left(-\dfrac{3}{8}\right) = -\dfrac{22}{24} + \left(-\dfrac{9}{24}\right)$

$= \dfrac{-22 + (-9)}{24} = -\dfrac{31}{24}$

78. $4x + 3(x - 2) - 5x - 7 = 4x + 3x - 6 - 5x - 7$

$= 4x + 3x - 5x - 6 - 7$

$= 2x - 13$

79. $-(2t + 4) + 3(4t - 5) - 3t = -2t - 4 + 12t - 15 - 3t$

$= -2t + 12t - 3t - 4 - 15$

$= 7t - 19$

Exercise Set 2.3

1. Answers will vary. Answer should include that both sides of an equation can be multiplied by the same nonzero number without changing the solution to the equation.

3. a.
$$-x = a$$
$$-1x = a$$
$$(-1)(-1x) = (-1)a$$
$$1x = -a$$
$$x = -a$$

b.
$$-x = 5$$
$$-1x = 5$$
$$(-1)(-1x) = (-1)5$$
$$1x = -5$$
$$x = -5$$

c.
$$-x = -5$$
$$-1x = -5$$
$$(-1)(-1x) = (-1)(-5)$$
$$1x = 5$$
$$x = 5$$

5. Divide by 3 to isolate the variable.

7. Multiply both sides by 2 because $2 \cdot \dfrac{x}{2} = x$.

9.
$$4x = 12$$
$$\frac{4x}{4} = \frac{12}{4}$$
$$x = 3$$
Check: $4x = 12$
$$4(3) = 12$$
$$12 = 12 \text{ True}$$

11.
$$\frac{x}{3} = 7$$
$$3\left(\frac{x}{3}\right) = 3(7)$$
$$x = 21$$
Check: $\dfrac{x}{3} = 7$
$$\frac{21}{3} = 7$$
$$7 = 7 \text{ True}$$

13.
$$-4x = 12$$
$$\frac{-4x}{-4} = \frac{12}{-4}$$
$$x = -3$$
Check: $-4x = 12$
$$-4(-3) = 12$$
$$12 = 12 \text{ True}$$

15.
$$\frac{x}{4} = -2$$
$$4\left(\frac{x}{4}\right) = 4(-2)$$
$$x = 4(-2)$$
$$x = -8$$
Check: $\dfrac{x}{4} = -2$
$$\frac{-8}{4} = -2$$
$$-2 = -2 \text{ True}$$

17.
$$\frac{x}{5} = 1$$
$$5\left(\frac{x}{5}\right) = 5(1)$$
$$x = 5$$
Check: $\dfrac{x}{5} = 1$
$$\frac{5}{5} = 1$$
$$1 = 1 \text{ True}$$

19.
$$-27n = 81$$
$$\frac{-27n}{-27} = \frac{81}{-27}$$
$$n = -3$$
Check: $-27n = 81$
$$-27(-3) = 81$$
$$81 = 81 \text{ True}$$

21.
$$-7 = 3r$$
$$\frac{-7}{3} = \frac{3r}{3}$$
$$-\frac{7}{3} = r$$
Check: $-7 = 3r$
$$-7 = 3\left(-\frac{7}{3}\right)$$
$$-7 = -7 \text{ True}$$

23.

$$-x = 13$$
$$-1x = 13$$
$$(-1)(-1x) = (-1)(13)$$
$$1x = -13$$
$$x = -13$$

Check: $-x = 13$
$$-(-13) = 13$$
$$13 = 13 \text{ True}$$

25.

$$-x = -8$$
$$-1x = -8$$
$$(-1)(-1x) = (-1)(-8)$$
$$1x = 8$$
$$x = 8$$

Check: $-x = -8$
$$-8 = -8 \text{ True}$$

27.

$$-\frac{w}{3} = -13$$
$$\frac{w}{-3} = -13$$
$$(-3)\left(\frac{w}{-3}\right) = (-3)(-13)$$
$$w = 39$$

Check: $-\frac{w}{3} = -13$
$$-\frac{39}{3} = -13$$
$$-13 = -13 \text{ True}$$

29.

$$4 = -12x$$
$$\frac{4}{-12} = \frac{-12x}{-12}$$
$$-\frac{1}{3} = x$$

Check: $4 = -12x$
$$4 = -12\left(-\frac{1}{3}\right)$$
$$4 = 4 \text{ True}$$

31.

$$-\frac{x}{3} = -2$$
$$\frac{x}{-3} = -2$$
$$(-3)\left(\frac{x}{-3}\right) = (-3)(-2)$$
$$x = 6$$

Check: $-\frac{x}{3} = -2$
$$-\frac{6}{3} = -2$$
$$-2 = -2 \text{ True}$$

33.

$$43t = 26$$
$$\frac{43t}{43} = \frac{26}{43}$$
$$t = \frac{26}{43}$$

Check: $43t = 26$
$$43\left(\frac{26}{43}\right) = 26$$
$$26 = 26 \text{ True}$$

35.

$$-4.2x = -8.4$$
$$\frac{-4.2x}{-4.2} = \frac{-8.4}{-4.2}$$
$$x = 2$$

Check: $-4.2x = -8.4$
$$-4.2(2) = -8.4$$
$$-8.4 = -8.4 \text{ True}$$

37.

$$3x = \frac{3}{5}$$
$$\frac{1}{3} \cdot 3x = \frac{1}{3} \cdot \frac{3}{5}$$
$$x = \frac{1}{1} \cdot \frac{1}{5}$$
$$x = \frac{1 \cdot 1}{1 \cdot 5}$$
$$x = \frac{1}{5}$$

Check: $3x = \frac{3}{5}$
$$3\left(\frac{1}{5}\right) = \frac{3}{5}$$
$$\frac{3}{5} = \frac{3}{5} \text{ True}$$

39. $5x = -\dfrac{3}{8}$

$\dfrac{1}{5} \cdot 5x = \left(\dfrac{1}{5}\right) \cdot \left(-\dfrac{3}{8}\right)$

$x = \dfrac{1(-3)}{5(8)}$

$x = -\dfrac{3}{40}$

Check: $5x = -\dfrac{3}{8}$

$5\left(-\dfrac{3}{40}\right) = -\dfrac{3}{8}$

$-\dfrac{3}{8} = -\dfrac{3}{8}$ True

41. $15 = -\dfrac{x}{4}$

$15 = \dfrac{x}{-4}$

$(-4)(15) = (-4) \cdot \left(\dfrac{x}{-4}\right)$

$-60 = x$

Check: $15 = -\dfrac{x}{4}$

$15 = -\dfrac{(-60)}{4}$

$15 = 15$ True

43. $-\dfrac{b}{4} = -60$

$\dfrac{b}{-4} = -60$

$-4\left(\dfrac{b}{-4}\right) = (-4)(-60)$

$b = 240$

Check: $-\dfrac{b}{4} = -60$

$-\dfrac{240}{4} = -60$

$-60 = -60$ True

45. $\dfrac{x}{5} = -7$

$5\left(\dfrac{x}{5}\right) = 5(-7)$

$x = -35$

Check: $\dfrac{x}{5} = -7$

$\dfrac{-35}{5} = -7$

$-7 = -7$ True

47. $5 = \dfrac{x}{4}$

$4 \cdot 5 = 4\left(\dfrac{x}{4}\right)$

$20 = x$

Check: $5 = \dfrac{x}{4}$

$5 = \dfrac{20}{4}$

$5 = 5$ True

49. $\dfrac{3}{5}d = -30$

$\dfrac{5}{3} \cdot \dfrac{3}{5}d = \dfrac{5}{3}(-30)$

$d = -50$

Check: $\dfrac{3}{5}d = -30$

$\dfrac{3}{5}(-50) = -30$

$-30 = -30$ True

51. $\dfrac{y}{-2} = 0$

$(-2)\left(\dfrac{y}{-2}\right) = (-2)(0)$

$y = 0$

Check: $\dfrac{y}{-2} = 0$

$\dfrac{0}{-2} = 0$

$0 = 0$ True

53. $\dfrac{-7}{8}w = 0$

$$\dfrac{8}{-7}\left(\dfrac{-7}{8}w\right) = \dfrac{8}{-7}\cdot 0$$

$$w = 0$$

Check: $\dfrac{-7}{8}w = 0$

$$\dfrac{-7}{8}(0) = 0$$

$$0 = 0 \ \text{True}$$

55. $\dfrac{1}{5}x = 4.5$

$$5\left(\dfrac{1}{5}x\right) = 5(4.5)$$

$$x = 22.5$$

Check: $\dfrac{1}{5}x = 4.5$

$$\dfrac{1}{5}(22.5) = 4.5$$

$$4.5 = 4.5 \ \text{True}$$

57. $-4 = -\dfrac{2}{3}z$

$$\left(-\dfrac{3}{2}\right)(-4) = \left(-\dfrac{3}{2}\right)\left(-\dfrac{2}{3}\right)z$$

$$6 = z$$

Check: $-4 = -\dfrac{2}{3}z$

$$-4 = -\dfrac{2}{3}\cdot 6$$

$$-4 = -4 \ \text{True}$$

59. $-1.4x = 28.28$

$$\dfrac{-1.4x}{-1.4} = \dfrac{28.28}{-1.4}$$

$$x = -20.2$$

Check: $-1.4x = 28.28$

$$-1.4(-20.2) = 28.28$$

$$28.28 = 28.28 \ \text{True}$$

61. $-8x = -56$

$$x = \dfrac{-56}{-8}$$

$$x = 7$$

Check: $-8x = -56$

$$-8(7) = -56$$

$$-56 = -56 \ \text{True}$$

63. $\dfrac{2}{3}x = 6$

$$x = \dfrac{3}{2}\cdot 6$$

$$x = 9$$

Check: $\dfrac{2}{3}x = 6$

$$\dfrac{2}{3}(9) = 6$$

$$6 = 6 \ \text{True}$$

65. a. In $5 + x = 10$, 5 is added to the variable, whereas in $5x = 10$, 5 is multiplied by the variable.

b. $\qquad 5x = 10$

$$5 + x - 5 = 10 - 5$$

$$x = 5$$

c. $5x = 10$

$$\dfrac{5x}{5} = \dfrac{10}{5}$$

$$x = 2$$

67. Multiplying by $\dfrac{3}{2}$ is easier because the equation involves fractions.

$$\dfrac{2}{3}x = 4$$

$$\left(\dfrac{3}{2}\right)\left(\dfrac{2}{3}\right)x = \left(\dfrac{3}{2}\right)\left(\dfrac{4}{1}\right)$$

$$x = \dfrac{12}{2}$$

$$x = 6$$

69. Multiplying by $\dfrac{7}{3}$ is easier because the equation involves fractions.

$$\dfrac{3}{7}x = \dfrac{4}{5}$$

$$\left(\dfrac{7}{3}\right)\dfrac{3}{7}x = \left(\dfrac{7}{3}\right)\dfrac{4}{5}$$

$$x = \dfrac{28}{15}$$

71. a. $\boxdot$

b. Divide both sides of the equation by $\triangle$.

c. $\boxdot = \dfrac{\smiley}{\triangle}$

73. $-8 - (-4) = -8 + 4$
$= -4$

74. $(-3)(-2)(5)(-1) = 6(5)(-1)$
$= 30(-1)$
$= -30$

75. $4^2 - 2^3 \cdot 6 \div 3 + 6 = 16 - 8 \cdot 6 \div 3 + 6$
$= 16 - 48 \div 3 + 6$
$= 16 - 16 + 6$
$= 0 + 6$
$= 6$

76. Associative property of addition

77. $-48 = x + 9$
$-48 - 9 = x + 9 - 9$
$-57 = x + 0$
$-57 = x$

Exercise Set 2.4

1. No; the variable x is on both sides of the equal sign.

3. $x = \dfrac{1}{3}$ because $1x = x$.

5. $x = -\dfrac{1}{2}$ because $-x = -1x$.

7. $x = \dfrac{4}{9}$ because $-x = -1x$.

9. You evaluate an expression. An expression cannot be solved. It is not true or false for given values; instead, it has a numerical value.

11. a. Answers will vary.

b. Answers will vary.

13. a. Use the distributive property.
Subtract 8 from both sides of the equation.
Divide both sides of the equation by 6.

b. $2(3x + 4) = -4$
$6x + 8 = -4$
$6x + 8 - 8 = -4 - 8$
$6x = -12$
$\dfrac{6x}{6} = -\dfrac{12}{6}$
$x = -2$

15. $5x - 6 = 19$
$5x - 6 + 6 = 19 + 6$
$5x = 25$
$\dfrac{5x}{5} = \dfrac{25}{5}$
$x = 5$

17. $-4w - 5 = 11$
$-4w - 5 + 5 = 11 + 5$
$-4w = 16$
$\dfrac{-4w}{-4} = \dfrac{16}{-4}$
$w = -4$

19. $3x + 6 = 12$
$3x + 6 - 6 = 12 - 6$
$3x = 6$
$\dfrac{3x}{3} = \dfrac{6}{3}$
$x = 2$

21. $5x - 2 = 10$
$5x - 2 + 2 = 10 + 2$
$5x = 12$
$\dfrac{5x}{5} = \dfrac{12}{5}$
$x = \dfrac{12}{5}$

23. $-5k - 4 = -19$
$-5k - 4 + 4 = -19 + 4$
$-5k = -15$
$\dfrac{-5k}{-5} = \dfrac{-15}{-5}$
$k = 3$

25. $12 - x = 9$
$12 - 12 - x = 9 - 12$
$-x = -3$
$(-1)(-x) = (-1)(-3)$
$x = 3$

27.
$$8 + 3x = 19$$
$$8 - 8 + 3x = 19 - 8$$
$$3x = 11$$
$$\frac{3x}{3} = \frac{11}{3}$$
$$x = \frac{11}{3}$$

29.
$$16x + 5 = -14$$
$$16x + 5 - 5 = -14 - 5$$
$$16x = -19$$
$$\frac{16x}{16} = \frac{-19}{16}$$
$$x = -\frac{19}{16}$$

31.
$$-4.2 = 3x + 25.8$$
$$-4.2 - 25.8 = 3x + 25.8 - 25.8$$
$$-30 = 3x$$
$$\frac{-30}{3} = \frac{3x}{3}$$
$$-10 = x$$

33.
$$7r - 16 = -2$$
$$7r - 16 + 16 = -2 + 16$$
$$7r = 14$$
$$\frac{7r}{7} = \frac{14}{7}$$
$$r = 2$$

35.
$$60 = -5s + 9$$
$$60 - 9 = -5s + 9 - 9$$
$$51 = -5s$$
$$\frac{51}{-5} = \frac{-5s}{-5}$$
$$-\frac{51}{5} = s$$

37.
$$14 = 5x + 8 - 3x$$
$$14 = 5x - 3x + 8$$
$$14 = 2x + 8$$
$$14 - 8 = 2x + 8 - 8$$
$$6 = 2x$$
$$\frac{6}{2} = \frac{2x}{2}$$
$$3 = x$$

39.
$$2.3x - 9.34 = 6.3$$
$$2.3x - 9.34 + 9.34 = 6.3 + 9.34$$
$$2.3x = 15.64$$
$$\frac{2.3x}{2.3} = \frac{15.64}{2.3}$$
$$x = 6.8$$

41.
$$0.91y + 2.25 - 0.01y = 5.85$$
$$0.91y - 0.01y + 2.25 = 5.85$$
$$0.90y + 2.25 = 5.85$$
$$0.90y + 2.25 - 2.25 = 5.85 - 2.25$$
$$0.90y = 3.60$$
$$\frac{0.90y}{0.90} = \frac{3.60}{0.90}$$
$$y = 4$$

43.
$$28.8 = x + 1.40x$$
$$28.8 = 2.40x$$
$$\frac{28.8}{2.40} = \frac{2.40x}{2.40}$$
$$12 = x$$

45.
$$\frac{1}{7}(x + 6) = 4$$
$$7\left[\frac{1}{7}(x + 6)\right] = 7(4)$$
$$x + 6 = 28$$
$$x + 6 - 6 = 28 - 6$$
$$x = 22$$

47.
$$\frac{d + 3}{7} = 9$$
$$7\left(\frac{d + 3}{7}\right) = 7(9)$$
$$d + 3 = 63$$
$$d + 3 - 3 = 63 - 3$$
$$d = 60$$

49.
$$\frac{1}{3}(t - 5) = -6$$
$$3\left[\frac{1}{3}(t - 5)\right] = 3(-6)$$
$$t - 5 = -18$$
$$t - 5 + 5 = -18 + 5$$
$$t = -13$$

51. $\dfrac{3}{4}(x-5)=-12$

$$\dfrac{4}{3}\left[\dfrac{3}{4}(x-5)\right]=\dfrac{4}{3}(-12)$$

$$x-5=-16$$

$$x-5+5=-16+5$$

$$x=-11$$

53. $\dfrac{x+4}{7}=\dfrac{3}{7}$

$$7\left(\dfrac{x+4}{7}\right)=7\left(\dfrac{3}{7}\right)$$

$$x+4=3$$

$$x+4-4=3-4$$

$$x=-1$$

55. $\dfrac{3}{4}=\dfrac{4m-5}{6}$

$$12\left(\dfrac{3}{4}\right)=12\left(\dfrac{4m-5}{6}\right)$$

$$9=2(4m-5)$$

$$9=8m-10$$

$$9+10=8m-10+10$$

$$19=8m$$

$$\dfrac{19}{8}=\dfrac{8m}{8}$$

$$\dfrac{19}{8}=m$$

57. $4(n+2)=8$

$$4n+8=8$$

$$4n+8-8=8-8$$

$$4n=0$$

$$\dfrac{4n}{4}=\dfrac{0}{4}$$

$$n=0$$

59. $-2(x-3)=26$

$$-2x+6=26$$

$$-2x+6-6=26-6$$

$$-2x=20$$

$$\dfrac{-2x}{-2}=\dfrac{20}{-2}$$

$$x=-10$$

61. $-4=-(x+5)$

$$-4=-x-5$$

$$-4+5=-x-5+5$$

$$1=-x$$

$$(-1)(1)=(-1)(-x)$$

$$-1=x$$

63. $12=4(x-3)$

$$12=4x-12$$

$$12+12=4x-12+12$$

$$24=4x$$

$$\dfrac{24}{4}=\dfrac{4x}{4}$$

$$6=x$$

65. $2x-3(x+5)=6$

$$2x-3x-15=6$$

$$-x-15=6$$

$$-x-15+15=6+15$$

$$-x=21$$

$$x=-21$$

67. $-3r-4(r+2)=11$

$$-3r-4r-8=11$$

$$-7r-8=11$$

$$-7r-8+8=11+8$$

$$-7r=19$$

$$\dfrac{-7r}{-7}=\dfrac{19}{-7}$$

$$r=-\dfrac{19}{7}$$

69. $x-3(2x+3)=11$

$$x-6x-9=11$$

$$-5x-9=11$$

$$-5x-9+9=11+9$$

$$-5x=20$$

$$\dfrac{-5x}{-5}=\dfrac{20}{-5}$$

$$x=-4$$

71. $5x + 3x - 4x - 7 = 9$

$$4x - 7 = 9$$
$$4x - 7 + 7 = 9 + 7$$
$$4x = 16$$
$$\frac{4x}{4} = \frac{16}{4}$$
$$x = 4$$

73. $\qquad 0.7(x - 3) = 1.4$

$$0.7x - 2.1 = 1.4$$
$$0.7x - 2.1 + 2.1 = 1.4 + 2.1$$
$$0.7x = 3.5$$
$$\frac{0.7x}{0.7} = \frac{3.5}{0.7}$$
$$x = 5$$

75. $\qquad 2.5(4q - 3) = 0.5$

$$10q - 7.5 = 0.5$$
$$10q - 7.5 + 7.5 = 0.5 + 7.5$$
$$10q = 8$$
$$\frac{10q}{10} = \frac{8}{10}$$
$$q = 0.8$$

77. $3 - 2(x + 3) + 2 = 1$

$$3 - 2x - 6 + 2 = 1$$
$$-2x + 3 - 6 + 2 = 1$$
$$-2x - 1 = 1$$
$$-2x - 1 + 1 = 1 + 1$$
$$-2x = 2$$
$$\frac{-2x}{-2} = \frac{2}{-2}$$
$$x = -1$$

79. $1 + (x + 3) + 6x = 6$

$$1 + x + 3 + 6x = 6$$
$$x + 6x + 1 + 3 = 6$$
$$7x + 4 = 6$$
$$7x + 4 - 4 = 6 - 4$$
$$7x = 2$$
$$\frac{7x}{7} = \frac{2}{7}$$
$$x = \frac{2}{7}$$

81. $\qquad 4.85 - 6.4x + 1.11 = 22.6$

$$-6.4x + 4.85 + 1.11 = 22.6$$
$$-6.4x + 5.96 = 22.6$$
$$-6.4x + 5.96 - 5.96 = 22.6 - 5.96$$
$$-6.4x = 16.64$$
$$\frac{-6.4x}{-6.4} = \frac{16.64}{-6.4}$$
$$x = -2.6$$

83. $\qquad 7 = 8 - 5(m + 3)$

$$7 = 8 - 5m - 15$$
$$7 = -5m - 7$$
$$7 + 7 = -5m - 7 + 7$$
$$14 = -5m$$
$$\frac{14}{-5} = \frac{-5m}{-5}$$
$$-\frac{14}{5} = m$$

85. $\qquad 10 = \frac{2s + 4}{5}$

$$5(10) = 5\left(\frac{2s + 4}{5}\right)$$
$$50 = 2s + 4$$
$$50 - 4 = 2s + 4 - 4$$
$$46 = 2s$$
$$\frac{46}{2} = \frac{2s}{2}$$
$$23 = s$$

87. $\qquad x + \frac{2}{3} = \frac{3}{5}$

$$15\left(x + \frac{2}{3}\right) = 15\left(\frac{3}{5}\right)$$
$$15x + 10 = 9$$
$$15x + 10 - 10 = 9 - 10$$
$$15x = -1$$
$$\frac{15x}{15} = \frac{-1}{15}$$
$$x = -\frac{1}{15}$$

89. $\dfrac{r}{3} + 2r = 7$

$3\left(\dfrac{r}{3} + 2r\right) = 3(7)$

$r + 6r = 21$

$7r = 21$

$\dfrac{7r}{7} = \dfrac{21}{7}$

$r = 3$

91. $\dfrac{3}{7} = \dfrac{3t}{4} + 1$

$28\left(\dfrac{3}{7}\right) = 28\left(\dfrac{3t}{4} + 1\right)$

$12 = 21t + 28$

$12 - 28 = 21t + 28 - 28$

$-16 = 21t$

$\dfrac{-16}{21} = \dfrac{21t}{21}$

$-\dfrac{16}{21} = t$

93. $\dfrac{1}{2}r + \dfrac{1}{5}r = 7$

$10\left(\dfrac{1}{2}r + \dfrac{1}{5}r\right) = 10(7)$

$5r + 2r = 70$

$7r = 70$

$\dfrac{7r}{7} = \dfrac{70}{7}$

$r = 10$

95. $\dfrac{2}{8} + \dfrac{3}{4} = \dfrac{w}{5}$

$\dfrac{1}{4} + \dfrac{3}{4} = \dfrac{w}{5}$

$\dfrac{4}{4} = \dfrac{w}{5}$

$1 = \dfrac{w}{5}$

$5(1) = 5\left(\dfrac{w}{5}\right)$

$5 = w$

97. $\dfrac{1}{2}x + 4 = \dfrac{1}{6}$

$6\left(\dfrac{1}{2}x + 4\right) = 6\left(\dfrac{1}{6}\right)$

$3x + 24 = 1$

$3x + 24 - 24 = 1 - 24$

$3x = -23$

$\dfrac{3x}{3} = \dfrac{-23}{3}$

$x = -\dfrac{23}{3}$

99. $\dfrac{4}{5}s - \dfrac{3}{4}s = \dfrac{1}{10}$

$20\left(\dfrac{4}{5}s - \dfrac{3}{4}s\right) = 20\left(\dfrac{1}{10}\right)$

$16s - 15s = 2$

$s = 2$

101. $\dfrac{4}{9} = \dfrac{1}{3}(n - 7)$

$\dfrac{4}{9} = \dfrac{1}{3}n - \dfrac{7}{3}$

$9\left(\dfrac{4}{9}\right) = 9\left(\dfrac{1}{3}n - \dfrac{7}{3}\right)$

$4 = 3n - 21$

$4 + 21 = 3n - 21 + 21$

$25 = 3n$

$\dfrac{25}{3} = \dfrac{3n}{3}$

$\dfrac{25}{3} = n$

103. $-\dfrac{3}{5} = -\dfrac{1}{9} - \dfrac{3}{4}x$

$180\left(-\dfrac{3}{5}\right) = 180\left(-\dfrac{1}{9} - \dfrac{3}{4}x\right)$

$-108 = -20 - 135x$

$-108 + 20 = -20 + 20 - 135x$

$-88 = -135x$

$\dfrac{-88}{-135} = \dfrac{-135x}{-135}$

$\dfrac{88}{135} = x$

105. a. By subtracting first, you will not have to work with fractions.

b.
$$3x + 2 = 11$$
$$3x + 2 - 2 = 11 - 2$$
$$3x = 9$$
$$\frac{3x}{3} = \frac{9}{3}$$
$$x = 3$$

107. $3(x-2) - (x+5) - 2(3-2x) = 18$
$$3x - 6 - x - 5 - 6 + 4x = 18$$
$$3x - x + 4x - 6 - 5 - 6 = 18$$
$$6x - 17 = 18$$
$$6x - 17 + 17 = 18 + 17$$
$$6x = 35$$
$$\frac{6x}{6} = \frac{35}{6}$$
$$x = \frac{35}{6}$$

109. $4[3 - 2(x+4)] - (x+3) = 13$
$$4(3 - 2x - 8) - x - 3 = 13$$
$$4(-2x - 5) - x - 3 = 13$$
$$-8x - 20 - x - 3 = 13$$
$$-9x - 23 = 13$$
$$-9x - 23 + 23 = 13 + 23$$
$$-9x = 36$$
$$\frac{-9x}{-9} = \frac{36}{-9}$$
$$x = -4$$

111. a. Let x = cost of one box of stationery
$$3x + 6 = 42$$

b.
$$3x + 6 = 42$$
$$3x + 6 - 6 = 42 - 6$$
$$3x = 36$$
$$x = 12$$
A box of stationery costs $12.00.

113. False. $\sqrt{2}$ is a real number but is irrational.

114. $\left[5(2-6) + 3(8 \div 4)^2\right]^2 = \left[5(-4) + 3(2)^2\right]^2$
$$= \left[-20 + 3(4)\right]^2$$
$$= \left[-20 + 12\right]^2$$
$$= \left[-8\right]^2$$
$$= 64$$

115. To solve an equation, we need to isolate the variable on one side of the equation.

116. To solve the equation, we divide both sides of the equation by –4.

Mid-Chapter Test: Sections 2.1 – 2.4

1. $5x - 9y - 12 + 4y - 7x + 6$
$$= 5x - 7x - 9y + 4y - 12 + 6$$
$$= -2x - 5y - 6$$

2. $\frac{2}{5}x - 8 - \frac{3}{4}x + \frac{1}{2} = \frac{2}{5}x - \frac{3}{4}x - 8 + \frac{1}{2}$
$$= \frac{8}{20}x - \frac{15}{20}x - \frac{16}{2} + \frac{1}{2}$$
$$= -\frac{7}{20}x - \frac{15}{2}$$

3. $-4(2a - 3b + 6) = -8a + 12b - 24$

4. $1.6(2.1x - 3.4y - 5.2) = 3.36x - 5.44y - 8.32$

5. $5(t-3) - 3(t+7) - 2 = 5t - 15 - 3t - 21 - 2$
$$= 5t - 3t - 15 - 21 - 2$$
$$= 2t - 38$$

6. Substitute 2 for x in the following equation .
$$3(x-4) = -2(x+1)$$
$$3(2-4) = -2(2+1)$$
$$3(-2) = -2(3)$$
$$-6 = -6 \text{ True}$$
Since we obtained a true statement, 2 is a solution.

7. Substitute $\frac{2}{5}$ for p in the following equation .
$$7p - 3 = 2p - 5$$
$$7\left(\frac{2}{5}\right) - 3 = 2\left(\frac{2}{5}\right) - 5$$
$$\frac{14}{5} - \frac{15}{5} = \frac{4}{5} - \frac{25}{5}$$
$$-\frac{9}{5} = -\frac{21}{5} \text{ False}$$

Since we obtained a false statement, $\frac{2}{5}$ is not a solution.

8.
$$x - 5 = -9 \qquad \text{Check: } x - 5 = -9$$
$$x - 5 + 5 = -9 + 5 \qquad -4 - 5 = -9$$
$$x = -4 \qquad -9 = -9 \text{ True}$$

9. $12 + x = -4$ Check: $12 + x = -4$
$12 - 12 + x = -4 - 12$ $12 + (-16) = -4$
$x = -16$ $-4 = -4$

10. $-16 = 7 + y$ Check: $-16 = 7 + y$
$-16 - 7 = 7 - 7 + y$ $-16 = 7 + (-23)$
$-23 = y$ $-16 = -16$ True

11. Multiply both sides by 4.

12. $6 = 12y$ Check: $6 = 12y$
$\dfrac{6}{12} = \dfrac{12y}{12}$ $6 = 12\left(\dfrac{1}{2}\right)$
$\dfrac{1}{2} = y$ $6 = 6$ True

13. $\dfrac{x}{8} = 3$ Check: $\dfrac{x}{8} = 3$
$8\left(\dfrac{x}{8}\right) = 8(3)$ $\dfrac{24}{8} = 3$
$x = 24$ $3 = 3$ True

14. $-\dfrac{x}{5} = -2$ Check: $-\dfrac{x}{5} = -2$
$\dfrac{x}{-5} = -2$ $-\dfrac{10}{5} = -2$
$-5\left(\dfrac{x}{-5}\right) = -5(-2)$ $-2 = -2$ True
$x = 10$

15. $-x = \dfrac{3}{7}$ Check: $-x = \dfrac{3}{7}$
$-1x = \dfrac{3}{7}$ $-\left(-\dfrac{3}{7}\right) = \dfrac{3}{7}$
$-1(-1x) = -1\left(\dfrac{3}{7}\right)$ $\dfrac{3}{7} = \dfrac{3}{7}$
$x = -\dfrac{3}{7}$

16. $6x - 3 = 12$
$6x = 15$
$x = \dfrac{15}{6}$
$x = \dfrac{5}{2}$

17. $-4 = -2w - 7$
$3 = -2w$
$-\dfrac{3}{2} = w$

18. $\dfrac{3}{4} = \dfrac{4n - 1}{6}$
$12\left(\dfrac{3}{4}\right) = 12\left(\dfrac{4n - 1}{6}\right)$
$9 = 2(4n - 1)$
$9 = 8n - 2$
$11 = 8n$
$\dfrac{11}{8} = n$

19. $-5(x + 4) - 7 = 3$
$-5x - 20 - 7 = 3$
$-5x - 27 = 3$
$-5x = 30$
$x = -6$

20. $8 - 9(y + 4) + 6 = -2$
$8 - 9y - 36 + 6 = -2$
$-9y + 8 - 36 + 6 = -2$
$-9y - 22 = -2$
$-9y = 20$
$y = -\dfrac{20}{9}$

Exercise Set 2.5

1. Answers will vary.

3. a. An identity is an equation that is true for infinitely many values of the variable.

  b. The solution is all real numbers.

5. The equation is an identity because both sides of the equation are identical.

7. An equation has no solution if it simplifies to a false statement.

9. a. Use the distributive property.
  Combine like terms.
  Subtract $5x$ from both sides of the equation.
  Subtract 6 from both sides of the equation.
  Divide both sides of the equation by 2.

  b. $4x + 3(x + 2) = 5x - 10$
  $4x + 3x + 6 = 5x - 10$
  $7x + 6 = 5x - 10$
  $2x + 6 = -10$
  $2x = -16$
  $x = -8$

11. $3x = -2x + 15$
$3x + 2x = -2x + 2x + 15$
$5x = 15$
$\dfrac{5x}{5} = \dfrac{15}{5}$
$x = 3$

13.
$$-4x + 10 = 6x$$
$$-4x + 4x + 10 = 6x + 4x$$
$$10 = 10x$$
$$\frac{10}{10} = \frac{10x}{10}$$
$$1 = x$$

15.
$$5x + 3 = 6$$
$$5x + 3 - 3 = 6 - 3$$
$$5x = 3$$
$$\frac{5x}{5} = \frac{3}{5}$$
$$x = \frac{3}{5}$$

17.
$$21 - 6p = 3p - 2p$$
$$21 - 6p = p$$
$$21 - 6p + 6p = p + 6p$$
$$21 = 7p$$
$$\frac{21}{7} = \frac{7p}{7}$$
$$3 = p$$

19.
$$2x - 4 = 3x - 6$$
$$2x - 2x - 4 = 3x - 2x - 6$$
$$-4 = x - 6$$
$$-4 + 6 = x - 6 + 6$$
$$2 = x$$

21.
$$6 - 2y = 9 - 8y + 6y$$
$$6 - 2y = 9 - 2y$$
$$6 - 2y + 2y = 9 - 2y + 2y$$
$$6 = 9 \quad \text{False}$$
Since a false statement is obtained, there is no solution.

23.
$$124.8 - 9.4x = 4.8x + 32.5$$
$$124.8 - 9.4x + 9.4x = 4.8x + 9.4x + 32.5$$
$$124.8 = 14.2x + 32.5$$
$$124.8 - 32.5 = 14.2x + 32.5 - 32.5$$
$$92.3 = 14.2x$$
$$\frac{92.3}{14.2} = \frac{14.2x}{14.2}$$
$$6.5 = x$$

25.
$$0.62x - .065 = 9.75 - 2.63x$$
$$0.62x + 2.63x - 0.65 = 9.75 - 2.63x + 2.63x$$
$$3.25x - 0.65 = 9.75$$
$$3.25x - 0.65 + 0.65 = 9.75 + 0.65$$
$$3.25x = 10.4$$
$$\frac{3.25x}{3.25} = \frac{10.4}{3.25}$$
$$x = 3.2$$

27.
$$5x + 3 = 2(x + 6)$$
$$5x + 3 = 2x + 12$$
$$5x - 2x + 3 = 2x - 2x + 12$$
$$3x + 3 = 12$$
$$3x + 3 - 3 = 12 - 3$$
$$3x = 9$$
$$\frac{3x}{3} = \frac{9}{3}$$
$$x = 3$$

29.
$$4y - 2 - 8y = 19 + 5y - 3$$
$$4y - 8y - 2 = 5y + 19 - 3$$
$$-4y - 2 = 5y + 16$$
$$-4y + 4y - 2 = 5y + 4y + 16$$
$$-2 = 9y - 16$$
$$-2 - 16 = 9y + 16 - 16$$
$$-18 = 9y$$
$$\frac{-18}{9} = \frac{9y}{9}$$
$$-2 = y$$

31.
$$2(x - 2) = 4x - 6 - 2x$$
$$2x - 4 = 2x - 6$$
$$2x - 2x - 4 = 2x - 2x - 6$$
$$-4 = -6 \quad \text{False}$$
Since a false statement is obtained, there is no solution.

33. $-(w+2) = -6w + 32$

$\qquad -w - 2 = -6w + 32$

$\qquad -w + w - 2 = -6w + w + 32$

$\qquad\qquad -2 = -5w + 32$

$\qquad -2 - 32 = -5w + 32 - 32$

$\qquad\qquad -34 = -5w$

$\qquad\qquad \dfrac{-34}{-5} = \dfrac{-5w}{-5}$

$\qquad\qquad \dfrac{34}{5} = w$

35. $-3(2t - 5) + 5 = 3t + 13$

$\qquad -6t + 15 + 5 = 3t + 13$

$\qquad\qquad -6t + 20 = 3t + 13$

$\qquad -6t + 6t + 20 = 3t + 6t + 13$

$\qquad\qquad 20 = 9t + 13$

$\qquad 20 - 13 = 9t + 13 - 13$

$\qquad\qquad 7 = 9t$

$\qquad\qquad \dfrac{7}{9} = \dfrac{9t}{9}$

$\qquad\qquad \dfrac{7}{9} = t$

37. $\dfrac{a}{5} = \dfrac{a-3}{2}$

$\qquad 10\left(\dfrac{a}{5}\right) = 10\left(\dfrac{a-3}{2}\right)$

$\qquad\qquad 2a = 5(a-3)$

$\qquad\qquad 2a = 5a - 15$

$\qquad 2a - 5a = 5a - 5a - 15$

$\qquad\qquad -3a = -15$

$\qquad\qquad \dfrac{-3a}{-3} = \dfrac{-15}{-3}$

$\qquad\qquad a = 5$

39. $\dfrac{n}{10} = 9 - \dfrac{n}{5}$

$\qquad 10\left(\dfrac{n}{10}\right) = 10\left(9 - \dfrac{n}{5}\right)$

$\qquad\qquad n = 90 - 2n$

$\qquad n + 2n = 90 - 2n + 2n$

$\qquad\qquad 3n = 90$

$\qquad\qquad \dfrac{3n}{3} = \dfrac{90}{3}$

$\qquad\qquad n = 30$

41. $\dfrac{5}{2} - \dfrac{x}{3} = 3x$

$\qquad 6\left(\dfrac{5}{2} - \dfrac{x}{3}\right) = 6(3x)$

$\qquad\qquad 15 - 2x = 18x$

$\qquad 15 - 2x + 2x = 18x + 2x$

$\qquad\qquad 15 = 20x$

$\qquad\qquad \dfrac{15}{20} = \dfrac{20x}{20}$

$\qquad\qquad \dfrac{15}{20} = x$

$\qquad\qquad \dfrac{3}{4} = x$

43. $\dfrac{5}{8} + \dfrac{1}{4}a = \dfrac{1}{2}a$

$\qquad 8\left(\dfrac{5}{8} + \dfrac{1}{4}a\right) = 8\left(\dfrac{1}{2}a\right)$

$\qquad\qquad 5 + 2a = 4a$

$\qquad 5 + 2a - 2a = 4a - 2a$

$\qquad\qquad 5 = 2a$

$\qquad\qquad \dfrac{5}{2} = \dfrac{2a}{2}$

$\qquad\qquad \dfrac{5}{2} = a$

45. $0.1(x + 10) = 0.3x - 4$

$\qquad 0.1x + 1 = 0.3x - 4$

$\qquad 0.1x - 0.1x + 1 = 0.3x - 0.1x - 4$

$\qquad 1 + 4 = 0.2x - 4 + 4$

$\qquad\qquad 5 = 0.2x$

$\qquad\qquad \dfrac{5}{0.2} = \dfrac{0.2x}{0.2}$

$\qquad\qquad 25 = x$

47. $2(x + 4) = 4x + 3 - 2x + 5$

$\qquad 2x + 8 = 4x + 3 - 2x + 5$

$\qquad 2x + 8 = 2x + 8$

Since the left side of the equation is identical to the right side, the equation is true for all values of x. Thus the solution is all real numbers.

49.
$$5(3n+3) = 2(5n-4)+6n$$
$$15n+15 = 10n-8+6n$$
$$15n+15 = 16n-8$$
$$15n-15n+15 = 16n-15n-8$$
$$15 = n-8$$
$$15+8 = n-8+8$$
$$23 = n$$

51.
$$-(3-p) = -(2p+3)$$
$$-3+p = -2p-3$$
$$-3+p+2p = -2p+2p-3$$
$$-3+3p = -3$$
$$-3+3+3p = -3+3$$
$$3p = 0$$
$$\frac{3p}{3} = \frac{0}{3}$$
$$p = 0$$

53. $-(x+4)+5 = 4x+1-5x$
$$-x-4+5 = 4x+1-5x$$
$$-x+1 = -x+1$$

Since the left side of the equation is identical to the right side, the equation is true for all values of x. Thus the solution is all real numbers.

55.
$$35(2x-1) = 7(x+4)+3x$$
$$70x-35 = 7x+28+3x$$
$$70x-35 = 10x+28$$
$$70x-10x-35 = 10x-10x+28$$
$$60x-35 = 28$$
$$60x-35+35 = 28+35$$
$$60x = 63$$
$$\frac{60x}{60} = \frac{63}{60}$$
$$x = \frac{21}{20}$$

57.
$$0.4(x+0.7) = 0.6(x-4.2)$$
$$0.4x+0.28 = 0.6x-2.52$$
$$0.4x-0.4x+0.28 = 0.6x-0.4x-2.52$$
$$0.28 = 0.2x-2.52$$
$$0.28+2.52 = 0.2x-2.52+2.52$$
$$2.8 = 0.2x$$
$$\frac{2.8}{0.2} = \frac{0.2x}{0.2}$$
$$14 = x$$

59.
$$\frac{3}{5}x-2 = x+\frac{1}{3}$$
$$15\left(\frac{3}{5}x-2\right) = 15\left(x+\frac{1}{3}\right)$$
$$9x-30 = 15x+5$$
$$9x-9x-30 = 15x-9x+5$$
$$-30 = 6x+5$$
$$-30-5 = 6x+5-5$$
$$-35 = 6x$$
$$\frac{-35}{6} = \frac{6x}{6}$$
$$-\frac{35}{6} = x$$

61.
$$\frac{y}{5}+2 = 3(y-4)$$
$$\frac{y}{5}+2 = 3y-12$$
$$\frac{y}{5}+2-2 = 3y-12-2$$
$$\frac{y}{5} = 3y-14$$
$$5\left(\frac{y}{5}\right) = 5(3y-14)$$
$$y = 15y-70$$
$$y-15y = 15y-15y-70$$
$$-14y = -70$$
$$\frac{-14y}{-14} = \frac{-70}{-14}$$
$$y = 5$$

63. $12-3x+7x = -2(-5x+6)$
$$12+4x = 10x-12$$
$$12+4x-4x = 10x-4x-12$$
$$12 = 6x-12$$
$$12+12 = 6x-12+12$$
$$24 = 6x$$
$$\frac{24}{6} = \frac{6x}{6}$$
$$4 = x$$

65. $3(x-6)-4(3x+1)=x-22$

$3x-18-12x-4=x-22$

$-9x-22=x-22$

$-9x+9x-22=x+9x-22$

$-22=10x-22$

$-22+22=10x-22+22$

$0=10x$

$\dfrac{0}{10}=\dfrac{10x}{10}$

$0=x$

67. $5+2x=6(x+1)-5(x-3)$

$5+2x=6x+6-5x+15$

$5+2x=x+21$

$5+2x-x=x-x+21$

$5+x=21$

$5-5+x=21-5$

$x=16$

69. $7-(-y-5)=2(y+3)-6(y+1)$

$7+y+5=2y+6-6y-6$

$12+y=-4y$

$12+y-y=-4y-y$

$12=-5y$

$\dfrac{12}{-5}=\dfrac{-5y}{-5}$

$-\dfrac{12}{5}=y$

71. $\dfrac{3}{5}(x-6)=\dfrac{2}{3}(3x-5)$

$\dfrac{3}{5}x-\dfrac{18}{5}=2x-\dfrac{10}{3}$

$15\left(\dfrac{3}{5}x-\dfrac{18}{5}\right)=15\left(2x-\dfrac{10}{3}\right)$

$9x-54=30x-50$

$9x-9x-54=30x-9x-50$

$-54=21x-50$

$-54+50=21x-50+50$

$-4=21x$

$\dfrac{-4}{21}=\dfrac{21x}{21}$

$-\dfrac{4}{21}=x$

73. $\dfrac{3(2r-5)}{5}=\dfrac{3r-6}{4}$

$\dfrac{6r-15}{5}=\dfrac{3r-6}{4}$

$20\left(\dfrac{6r-15}{5}\right)=20\left(\dfrac{3r-6}{4}\right)$

$4(6r-15)=5(3r-6)$

$24r-60=15r-30$

$24r-15r-60=15r-15r-30$

$9r-60=-30$

$9r-60+60=-30+60$

$9r=30$

$\dfrac{9r}{9}=\dfrac{30}{9}$

$r=\dfrac{30}{9}=\dfrac{10}{3}$

75. $\dfrac{2}{7}(5x+4)=\dfrac{1}{2}(3x-4)+1$

$\dfrac{10x}{7}+\dfrac{8}{7}=\dfrac{3x}{2}-2+1$

$\dfrac{10x}{7}+\dfrac{8}{7}=\dfrac{3x}{2}-1$

$14\left(\dfrac{10x}{7}+\dfrac{8}{7}\right)=14\left(\dfrac{3x}{2}-1\right)$

$20x+16=21x-14$

$20x-20x+16=21x-20x-14$

$16=x-14$

$16+14=x-14+14$

$30=x$

77. $\dfrac{a-5}{2}=\dfrac{3a}{4}+\dfrac{a-25}{6}$

$12\left(\dfrac{a-5}{2}\right)=12\left(\dfrac{3a}{4}+\dfrac{a-25}{6}\right)$

$6(a-5)=9a+2(a-25)$

$6a-30=9a+2a-50$

$6a-30=11a-50$

$6a-6a-30=11a-6a-50$

$-30=5a-50$

$-30+50=5a-50+50$

$20=5a$

$\dfrac{20}{5}=\dfrac{5a}{5}$

$4=a$

79. a. One example is $x + x + 1 = x + 2$.

  b. It has a single solution.

  c. Answers will vary. For equation given in part **a)**:

$$x + x + 1 = x + 2$$
$$2x + 1 = x + 2$$
$$2x - x + 1 = x - x + 2$$
$$x + 1 = 2$$
$$x + 1 - 1 = 2 - 1$$
$$x = 1$$

81. a. One example is $x + x + 1 = 2x + 1$.

  b. Both sides simplify to the same expression.

  c. The solution is all real numbers.

83. a. One example is $x + x + 1 = 2x + 2$.

  b. It simplifies to a false statement.

  c. The solution is that there is no solution.

85.
$$5 * -1 = 4 * + 5 *$$
$$5 * -5 * -1 = 9 * -5 *$$
$$-1 = 4 *$$
$$\frac{-1}{4} = \frac{4 *}{4}$$
$$-\frac{1}{4} = *$$

87. $3 ☺ - 5 = 2 ☺ - 5 + ☺$
$$3 ☺ - 5 = 3 ☺ - 5$$
The left side of the equation is identical to the right side. The solution is all real numbers.

89. $4 - \left[5 - 3(x + 2) \right] = x - 3$
$$4 - (5 - 3x - 6) = x - 3$$
$$4 - 5 + 3x + 6 = x - 3$$
$$3x + 5 = x - 3$$
$$3x - x + 5 = x - x - 3$$
$$2x + 5 = -3$$
$$2x + 5 - 5 = -3 - 5$$
$$2x = -8$$
$$\frac{2x}{2} = \frac{-8}{2}$$
$$x = -4$$

91. a. $|4| = 4$

  b. $|-7| = 7$

  c. $|0| = 0$

92. $\left(\dfrac{2}{3} \right)^5 \approx 0.131687243$

93. Factors are expressions that are multiplied together; terms are expressions that are added together.

94. $2(x - 3) + 4x - (4 - x) = 2x - 6 + 4x - 4 + x$
$$= 7x - 10$$

95. $2(x - 3) + 4x - (4 - x) = 0$
$$2x - 6 + 4x - 4 + x = 0$$
$$7x - 10 = 0$$
$$7x - 10 + 10 = 0 + 10$$
$$7x = 10$$
$$\frac{7x}{7} = \frac{10}{7}$$
$$x = \frac{10}{7}$$

96. $(x + 4) - (4x - 3) = 16$
$$x + 4 - 4x + 3 = 16$$
$$-3x + 7 = 16$$
$$-3x + 7 - 7 = 16 - 7$$
$$-3x = 9$$
$$\frac{-3x}{-3} = \frac{9}{-3}$$
$$x = -3$$

Exercise Set 2.6

1. A formula is an equation used to express a relationship mathematically.

3. The simple interest formula is:
$i = prt$ where i is interest, p is principle, r is the interest rate, and t is time.

5. $d = rt$; d represents distance, r represents rate and t represents time

7. No, π is an irrational number that is approximately equal to 3.14, but not exactly.

  b. Area is the total surface within the figure boundaries.

9. When you multiply a unit by the same unit, you get a square unit.

11. Substitute 60 for r and 4 for t.
$$d = rt$$
$$d = 60(4) = 240$$

13. Substitute 12 for l and 8 for w.
$$A = lw$$
$$A = 12(8) = 96$$

15. Substitute 2000 for p, 0.06 for r, and 3 for t.
$$i = prt$$
$$i = 2000(0.06)(3)$$
$$i = 360$$

17. Substitute 8 for l and 5 for w.
$$P = 2l + 2w$$
$$P = 2(8) + 2(5)$$
$$P = 16 + 10$$
$$P = 26$$

19. Substitute 5 for r.
$$A = \pi r^2$$
$$A = \pi(5)^2$$
$$A = 25\pi \approx 78.54$$

21. Substitute 72 for a, 81 for b, and 93 for c.
$$A = \frac{a+b+c}{3}$$
$$A = \frac{72+81+93}{3}$$
$$A = \frac{246}{3}$$
$$A = 82$$

23. Substitute 100 for x, 80 for m, and 10 for s.
$$z = \frac{x-m}{s}$$
$$z = \frac{100-80}{10}$$
$$z = \frac{20}{10} = 2$$

25. Substitute 28 for P and 6 for w.
$$P = 2l + 2w$$
$$28 = 2l + 2(6)$$
$$28 = 2l + 12$$
$$28 - 12 = 2l + 12 - 12$$
$$16 = 2l$$
$$\frac{16}{2} = \frac{2l}{2}$$
$$8 = l$$

27. Substitute 678.24 for V, and 6 for r.
$$V = \pi r^2 h$$
$$678.24 = \pi(6)^2 h$$
$$678.24 = 36\pi h$$
$$\frac{678.24}{36\pi} = \frac{36\pi h}{36\pi}$$
$$\frac{678.24}{36\pi} = h$$
$$6.00 \approx h$$

29. Substitute 24 for B and 61 for h.
$$B = \frac{703w}{h^2}$$
$$24 = \frac{703w}{(61)^2}$$
$$24(61)^2 = \frac{703w}{61^2}(61)^2$$
$$89,304 = 703w$$
$$\frac{89,304}{703} = \frac{703w}{703}$$
$$127.03 \approx w$$

31. Substitute 8 for r.
$$A = \pi r^2$$
$$A = \pi(4^2)$$
$$A = 16\pi \approx 50.27 \text{ft}^2$$

33. Substitute 3 for h, 4 for b and 7 for d.
$$A = \frac{1}{2}h(b+d)$$
$$A = \frac{1}{2}(3)(4+7)$$
$$A = \frac{1}{2}(3)(11)$$
$$A = \frac{1}{2}(33)$$
$$A = 16.5 \text{ ft}^2$$

35. Substitute 4 for r and 9 for h.
$$V = \pi r^2 h$$
$$V = \pi(4)^2(9)$$
$$V = \pi(16)(9)$$
$$V = 144\pi \approx 452.39 \text{ cm}^3$$

37. Substitute 50 for *F*.

$$C = \frac{5}{9}(F - 32)$$

$$C = \frac{5}{9}(50 - 32)$$

$$= \frac{5}{9}(18)$$

$$= 10$$

The equivalent temperature is 10°C.

39. Substitute 25 for *C*.

$$F = \frac{9}{5}C + 32$$

$$F = \frac{9}{5}(25) + 32$$

$$= 45 + 32$$

$$= 77$$

The equivalent temperature is 77°F.

41. $P = \dfrac{KT}{V}$

$$P = \frac{(2)(20)}{1} = \frac{40}{1} = 40$$

43. $P = \dfrac{KT}{V}$

$$3 = \frac{(0.5)(30)}{V}$$

$$3 = \frac{15}{V}$$

$$3V = 15$$

$$V = \frac{15}{3} = 5$$

45. $A = lw$

$$\frac{A}{l} = \frac{lw}{l}$$

$$\frac{A}{l} = w$$

47. $d = rt$

$$\frac{d}{r} = \frac{rt}{r}$$

$$\frac{d}{r} = t$$

49. $\quad i = prt$

$$\frac{i}{pr} = \frac{prt}{pr}$$

$$\frac{i}{pr} = t$$

51. $\quad A = \dfrac{1}{2}bh$

$$2A = 2\left(\frac{1}{2}bh\right)$$

$$2A = bh$$

$$\frac{2A}{h} = \frac{bh}{h}$$

$$\frac{2A}{h} = b$$

53. $\quad P = 2l + 2w$

$$P - 2l = 2l - 2l + 2w$$

$$P - 2l = 2w$$

$$\frac{P - 2l}{2} = \frac{2w}{2}$$

$$\frac{P - 2l}{2} = w$$

55. $\quad 3 - 2r = n$

$$3 - 3 - 2r = n - 3$$

$$-2r = n - 3$$

$$\frac{-2r}{-2} = \frac{n - 3}{-2}$$

$$r = \frac{n - 3}{-2} = \frac{3 - n}{2}$$

57. $\quad y = mx + b$

$$y - mx = mx - mx + b$$

$$y - mx = b$$

59. $\quad d = a + b + c$

$$d - a = a - a + b + c$$

$$d - a = b + c$$

$$d - a - c = b + c - c$$

$$d - a - c = b$$

61.
$$ax + by + c = 0$$
$$ax - ax + by + c = -ax$$
$$by + c = -ax$$
$$by + c - c = -ax - c$$
$$by = -ax - c$$
$$\frac{by}{b} = \frac{-ax - c}{b}$$
$$y = \frac{-ax - c}{b}$$

63.
$$V = \frac{1}{3}\pi r^2 h$$
$$3V = 3\left(\frac{1}{3}\pi r^2 h\right)$$
$$3V = \pi r^2 h$$
$$\frac{3V}{\pi r^2} = \frac{\pi r^2 h}{\pi r^2}$$
$$\frac{3V}{\pi r^2} = h$$

65.
$$A = \frac{m + d}{2}$$
$$2A = 2\left(\frac{m + d}{2}\right)$$
$$2A = m + d$$
$$2A - d = m + d - d$$
$$2A - d = m$$

67.
$$2x + y = 5$$
$$2x - 2x + y = -2x + 5$$
$$y = -2x + 5$$

69.
$$-3x + 3y = -15$$
$$-3x + 3x + 3y = 3x - 15$$
$$3y = 3x - 15$$
$$\frac{3y}{3} = \frac{3x - 15}{3}$$
$$y = \frac{3x}{3} + \frac{-15}{3}$$
$$y = x - 5$$

71.
$$4x = 6y - 8$$
$$4x + 8 = 6y - 8 + 8$$
$$4x + 8 = 6y$$
$$\frac{4x + 8}{6} = \frac{6y}{6}$$
$$\frac{4x}{6} + \frac{8}{6} = y$$
$$\frac{2}{3}x + \frac{4}{3} = y$$
$$y = \frac{2}{3}x + \frac{4}{3}$$

73.
$$5y = -10 + 3x$$
$$\frac{5y}{5} = \frac{-10 + 3x}{5}$$
$$y = \frac{-10}{5} + \frac{3x}{5}$$
$$y = -2 + \frac{3}{5}x$$
$$y = \frac{3}{5}x - 2$$

75.
$$15 - 3x = -6y$$
$$\frac{15 - 3x}{-6} = \frac{-6y}{-6}$$
$$\frac{15}{-6} + \frac{-3x}{-6} = y$$
$$-\frac{5}{2} + \frac{1}{2}x = y$$
$$y = \frac{1}{2}x - \frac{5}{2}$$

77.
$$-8 = -x - 2y$$
$$x - 8 = x - x - 2y$$
$$x - 8 = -2y$$
$$\frac{x - 8}{-2} = \frac{-2y}{-2}$$
$$\frac{-x}{2} + \frac{-8}{-2} = y$$
$$-\frac{1}{2}x + 4 = y$$
$$y = -\frac{1}{2}x + 4$$

79. $y + 3 = -\dfrac{1}{3}(x - 4)$

$y + 3 = -\dfrac{1}{3}x + \dfrac{4}{3}$

$y + 3 - 3 = -\dfrac{1}{3}x + \dfrac{4}{3} - 3$

$y = -\dfrac{1}{3}x + \dfrac{4}{3} - \dfrac{9}{3}$

$y = -\dfrac{1}{3}x - \dfrac{5}{3}$

81. $y - \dfrac{1}{5} = 2\left(x + \dfrac{1}{3}\right)$

$y - \dfrac{1}{5} = 2x + \dfrac{2}{3}$

$y - \dfrac{1}{5} + \dfrac{1}{5} = 2x + \dfrac{2}{3} + \dfrac{1}{5}$

$y = 2x + \dfrac{10}{15} + \dfrac{3}{15}$

$y = 2x + \dfrac{13}{15}$

83. $d = rt$

$d = (2r)\left(\dfrac{1}{2}t\right)$

$d = 2 \cdot \dfrac{1}{2}rt$

$d = rt$

The distance remains the same.

85. $A = s^2$

$A = (2s)^2 = 4s^2$

The area is 4 times as large as the original area.

87.   Substitute $\dfrac{1}{2}s$ for r in the area formula.

$A_{circle} = \pi r^2$

$= \pi \left(\dfrac{1}{2}s\right)^2$

$= \dfrac{1}{4}\pi s^2$

$= \dfrac{1}{4}(3.14)s^2$

$= 0.785s^2$

$A_{square} = s^2$

The area of a square is larger because
$1s^2 > 0.785s^2$.

89. $i = prt$

$i = (6000)(0.08)(3) = 1440$

He will pay $1440 interest.

91. $i = prt$

$450 = p(0.03)(3)$

$450 = 0.09p$

$\dfrac{450}{0.09} = \dfrac{0.09p}{0.09}$

$5000 = p$

She placed $5000 in the savings account.

93. $d = rt$

$150 = r(3)$

$50 = r$

Her average speed was 50 mph.

95. $d = rt$

$d = (763.2)(0.01)$

$d = 7.632$

The car traveled 7.632 mi.

97. $A = lw$

$A = (8)(6)$

$A = 48$

The area of the screen is 48 sq. in.

99. $A = \dfrac{1}{2}bh$

$A = \dfrac{1}{2}(36)(31) = 558$

The area is 558 sq. in.

101. $C = 2\pi r$

$C = 2\pi(12)$

$C = 24\pi \approx 75.40$

The circumference of the pool is about 75.40 ft.

103.   Total area = Area of top triangle + area of
bottom triangle
Total Area = $0.5b_1\,h_1 + 0.5b_2\,h_2$
Total Area = $0.5(2)(1) + 0.5(2)(2)$
Total Area = $1 + 2 = 3$
The area of the kite is 3 square feet.

105. $A = \dfrac{1}{2}h(b+d)$

$A = \dfrac{1}{2}(2)(4+3)$

$= \dfrac{1}{2}(2)(7)$

$= (1)7$

$= 7$

The area of the sign is 7 sq. ft.

107. $\quad C = 2\pi r$

$390 = 2\pi(r)$

$390 = 2\pi r$

$\dfrac{390}{2\pi} = \dfrac{2\pi r}{2\pi}$

$62.07 \approx r$

The radius of the roots is about 62.07 feet.

The diameter is twice the radius, so
$d = 2(62.07) = 124.14$
The diameter is about 124.1 ft.

109. The radius is half the diameter.

$V = \dfrac{4}{3}\pi r^3$

$V = \dfrac{4}{3}\pi\left(\dfrac{9}{2}\right)^3$

$V \approx 381.7$

The volume of the basketball is about 381.7 cu. in.

111. a. $B = \dfrac{703w}{h^2}$

　b. 5 feet 3 inches $= 5(12) + 3$

$= 60 + 3$

$= 63$ inches

$B = \dfrac{703(135)}{(63)^2} = \dfrac{94{,}905}{3969} \approx 23.91$

113. a. $V = lwh$

$V = (3x)(x)(6x-1)$

$= 3x^2(6x-1)$

$= 18x^3 - 3x^2$

　b. $V = 18x^3 - 3x^2$

$V = 18(7)^3 - 3(7)^2$

$= 6174 - 147$

$= 6027$

Volume is 6027 cm^3.

c. $S = 2lw + 2lh + 2wh$

$S = 2(3x)(x) + 2(3x)(6x-1)$

$\qquad + 2(x)(6x-1)$

$= 6x^2 + 36x^2 - 6x + 12x^2 - 2x$

$= 54x^2 - 8x$

d. $S = 54x^2 - 8x$

$S = 54(7)^2 - 8(7)$

$= 2646 - 56$

$= 2590$

Surface area is 2590 cm^2.

115. $-\dfrac{4}{15} + \dfrac{2}{5} = -\dfrac{4}{15} + \dfrac{6}{15} = \dfrac{2}{15}$

116. $-6 + 7 - 4 - 3 = 1 - 4 - 3 = -3 - 3 = -6$

117. $\left[4\left(12 \div 2^2 - 3\right)^2\right]^2 = \left[4\left(12 \div 4 - 3\right)^2\right]^2$

$= \left[4(3-3)^2\right]^2$

$= \left[4(0)^2\right]^2$

$= [0]^2$

$= 0$

118. $\quad \dfrac{r}{2} + 2r = 20$

$2\left(\dfrac{r}{2} + 2r\right) = 2(20)$

$r + 4r = 40$

$5r = 40$

$r = 8$

Exercise Set 2.7

1. A ratio is a quotient of two quantities.

3. The ratio of c to d can be written as c to d, $c{:}d$, and $\dfrac{c}{d}$.

5. To set up and solve a proportion, we need a given ratio and one of the two parts of a second ratio.

7. Yes, similar figures have the same shape but not necessarily the same size.

9. Yes; the terms in each ratio are in the same order.

11. No; The terms in each ratio are not in the same order.

13. $6:9 = 2:3$

15. $3:6 = 1:2$

17. Total grades $= 6 + 4 + 9 + 3 + 2 = 24$
Ratio of total grades to D's $= 24 : 3 = 8 : 1$

19. $7:4$

21. $5:15 = 1:3$

23. 3 hours $= 3 \times 60 = 180$ minutes
Ratio is $\dfrac{180}{30} = \dfrac{6}{1}$ or $6:1$.

25. 12 nickels is $12 \cdot \left(\dfrac{1}{2}\right) = 6$ dimes

Ratio is $7:6$.

27. Gear ratio $= \dfrac{\text{number of teeth on driving gear}}{\text{number of teeth on driven gear}}$

$\qquad = \dfrac{40}{5} = \dfrac{8}{1}$

Gear ratio is $8:1$.

29. a. $50:23$

   b. Since $50 \div 23 \approx 2.17$, $50:23 \approx 2.17:1$.

31. a. $5.15:3.35$

   b. Since $5.15 \div 3.35 \approx 1.54$, $5.15:3.35 \approx 1.54:1$.

33. a. $19.2:2.2$ or $9.6:1.1$

   b. $6.7:3.1$

35. a. $40:32$ or $5:4$

   b. $15:11$

37. $\dfrac{x}{3} = \dfrac{20}{5}$

$x \cdot 5 = 3 \cdot 20$

$5x = 60$

$\dfrac{5x}{5} = \dfrac{60}{5}$

$x = 12$

39. $\dfrac{5}{3} = \dfrac{75}{a}$

$5 \cdot a = 3 \cdot 75$

$5a = 225$

$\dfrac{5a}{5} = \dfrac{225}{5}$

$a = 45$

41. $\dfrac{-7}{3} = \dfrac{21}{p}$

$-7 \cdot p = 3 \cdot 21$

$-7p = 63$

$\dfrac{-7p}{-7} = \dfrac{63}{-7}$

$p = -9$

43. $\dfrac{15}{45} = \dfrac{x}{-6}$

$15 \cdot -6 = 45 \cdot x$

$-90 = 45x$

$\dfrac{-90}{45} = \dfrac{45x}{45}$

$-2 = x$

45. $\dfrac{3}{z} = \dfrac{-1.5}{27}$

$3 \cdot 27 = z \cdot -1.5$

$81 = -1.5z$

$\dfrac{81}{-1.5} = \dfrac{-1.5z}{-1.5}$

$-54 = z$

47. $\dfrac{9}{12} = \dfrac{x}{8}$

$9 \cdot 8 = 12 \cdot x$

$72 = 12x$

$\dfrac{72}{12} = \dfrac{12x}{12}$

$6 = x$

49. $\dfrac{3}{12} = \dfrac{8}{x}$

$3x = 12 \cdot 8$

$3x = 96$

$\dfrac{3x}{3} = \dfrac{96}{3}$

$x = 32$

Thus the side is 32 inches in length.

51. $\dfrac{4}{7} = \dfrac{9}{x}$

$4x = 7 \cdot 9$

$4x = 63$

$\dfrac{4x}{4} = \dfrac{63}{4}$

$x = 15.75$

Thus the side is 15.75 inches in length.

53. $\dfrac{16}{12} = \dfrac{26}{x}$

$16x = (12)(26)$

$16x = 312$

$\dfrac{16x}{16} = \dfrac{312}{16}$

$x = 19.5$

Thus the side is 19.5 inches in length.

55. Let $x =$ number of loads one bottle can do.

$\dfrac{4 \text{ fl ounces}}{1 \text{ load}} = \dfrac{100 \text{ fl ounces}}{x \text{ loads}}$

$\dfrac{4}{1} = \dfrac{100}{x}$

$4x = 100$

$x = 25$

One bottle can do 25 loads.

57. Let $x =$ number of miles that can be driven with a full tank.

$$\frac{19 \text{ miles}}{1 \text{ gallon}} = \frac{x}{14.2 \text{ gallons}}$$

$$\frac{19}{1} = \frac{x}{14.2}$$

$$x = (19)(14.2)$$

$$x = 269.8$$

It can travel 269.8 miles on a full tank.

59. Let x = length of model in feet.

$$\frac{1 \text{ foot model}}{20 \text{ foot train}} = \frac{x \text{ foot model}}{30 \text{ foot train}}$$

$$\frac{1}{20} = \frac{x}{30}$$

$$20x = 30$$

$$x = 1.5$$

The model should be 1.5 feet long.

61. Let x = number of teaspoons needed for sprayer.

$$\frac{3 \text{ teaspoons}}{1 \text{ gallon water}} = \frac{x \text{ teaspoons}}{8 \text{ gallons water}}$$

$$\frac{3}{1} = \frac{x}{8}$$

$$3 \cdot 8 = 1 \cdot x$$

$$24 = x$$

Thus 24 teaspoons are needed for the sprayer.

63. Let x = length of beak of blue heron in inches.

$$\frac{3.5 \text{ inches in photo}}{3.75 \text{ feet}} = \frac{0.4 \text{ inches in photo}}{x \text{ feet}}$$

$$\frac{3.5}{3.75} = \frac{0.4}{x}$$

$$3.5x = 3.75 \cdot 0.4$$

$$3.5x = 1.5$$

$$x \approx 0.43$$

It's beak is about 0.43 feet long.

65. Let x = number of cups needed.

$$\frac{1\frac{1}{2} \text{ cups}}{6 \text{ servings}} = \frac{x \text{ cups}}{15 \text{ servings}}$$

$$\frac{\frac{3}{2}}{6} = \frac{x}{15}$$

$$6x = 15 \cdot \frac{3}{2}$$

$$6x = 22.5$$

$$x = 3.75$$

3.75 cups of onions are needed.

67. Let x = length of the model bull in feet.

$$\frac{2.95 \text{ feet metal bull}}{1 \text{ feet real bull}} = \frac{28 \text{ feet metal bull}}{x \text{ feet real bull}}$$

$$\frac{2.95}{1} = \frac{28}{x}$$

$$2.95 \cdot x = 1 \cdot 28$$

$$2.95x = 28$$

$$x \approx 9.49$$

The model bull is about 9.49 feet long.

69. Let x = number of milliliters to be given.

$$\frac{1 \text{ milliliter}}{400 \text{ micrograms}} = \frac{x \text{ milliliter}}{220 \text{ micrograms}}$$

$$\frac{1}{400} = \frac{x}{220}$$

$$1 \cdot 220 = 400 \cdot x$$

$$220 = 400x$$

$$\frac{220}{400} = x$$

$$0.55 = x$$

Thus 0.55 milliliter should be given.

71. Let x = number of minutes to read entire book.

$$\frac{40 \text{ pages}}{30 \text{ minutes}} = \frac{760 \text{ pages}}{x \text{ minutes}}$$

$$\frac{40}{30} = \frac{760}{x}$$

$$40x = (30)(760)$$

$$40x = 22,800$$

$$x = \frac{22,800}{40} = 570$$

Thus it will take her 570 minutes or
9 hours 30 minutes to read the entire book.

73. Let x = number of children born with Prader-Willi Syndrome.

$$\frac{12,000 \text{ births}}{1 \text{ baby with syndrome}} = \frac{4,063,000 \text{ births}}{x \text{ babies with syndrome}}$$

$$\frac{12,000}{1} = \frac{4,063,000}{x}$$

$$12,000x = 4,063,000$$

$$x = \frac{4,063,000}{12,000} \approx 339$$

Thus, about 339 children were born with Prader-Willi Syndrome.

75. $\dfrac{12 \text{ inches}}{1 \text{ foot}} = \dfrac{78 \text{ inches}}{x \text{ feet}}$

$$\frac{12}{1} = \frac{78}{x}$$

$$12x = 78$$

$$x = \frac{78}{12} = 6.5$$

Thus 42 inches equals 6.5 feet.

77. $\dfrac{9 \text{ square feet}}{1 \text{ square yard}} = \dfrac{26.1 \text{ square feet}}{x \text{ square yards}}$

$$\frac{9}{1} = \frac{26.1}{x}$$

$$9x = 26.1$$

$$x = \frac{26.1}{9} = 2.9$$

Thus 26.1 square feet equals 2.9 square yards.

79. $\dfrac{2.54 \text{ cm}}{1 \text{ inch}} = \dfrac{50.8 \text{ cm}}{x \text{ inches}}$

$$\frac{2.54}{1} = \frac{50.8}{x}$$

$$2.54x = 50.8$$

$$x = \frac{50.8}{2.54} = 20$$

Thus the length of the newborn is 20 inches.

81. Let x = number of home runs needed to break Bonds' record

$$\frac{73 \text{ home runs}}{162 \text{ games}} = \frac{x}{50 \text{ games}}$$

$$\frac{73}{162} = \frac{x}{50}$$

$$162 \cdot x = 73 \cdot 50$$

$$162x = 3650$$

$$x = \frac{3650}{162} \approx 22.53$$

A player would need to hit 23 home runs.

83. Let x = amount of interest Jim would earn after 500 days.

$$\frac{\$110.52 \text{ interest}}{180 \text{ days}} = \frac{\$x \text{ interest}}{500 \text{ days}}$$

$$\frac{110.52}{180} = \frac{x}{500}$$

$$180x = 55,260$$

$$x = \frac{55,260}{180} = 307$$

He would earn $307 in interest.

Thus the cost per grain is $0.85.

85. Let x = the number of pesos she would receive in return for U.S. dollars.

$$\frac{\$1.00 \text{ U.S.}}{10.567 \text{ pesos}} = \frac{\$200 \text{ U.S.}}{x \text{ pesos}}$$

$$\frac{1}{10.567} = \frac{200}{x}$$

$$x = 2113.4$$

She will receive 2113.4 pesos.

87. The ratio of Mrs. Ruff's low density to high density cholesterol is $\dfrac{127}{60}$. If we divide 127 by 60 we obtain approximately 2.12. Thus Mrs. Ruff's ratio is approximately equivalent to 2.12:1. Therefore her ratio is less than the desired 4:1 ratio.

89. In $\dfrac{a}{b} = \dfrac{c}{d}$, if b and d remain the same while a increases, then c increases because $ad=bc$. If a increases ad increases so bc must increase by increasing c.

91. Let x = number of miles remaining on the life of each tire.
Inches remaining on the life of each tire:
$$0.31 - 0.06 = 0.25$$

$$\frac{0.03 \text{ inches}}{5000 \text{ miles}} = \frac{0.25 \text{ miles}}{x \text{ miles}}$$

$$\frac{0.03}{5000} = \frac{0.25}{x}$$

$$0.03x = 5000 \cdot 0.25$$

$$0.03x = 1250$$

$$x = \frac{1250}{0.03}$$

$$x \approx 41,667$$

The tires will last about 41,667 more miles.

93. Let x = number of cubic centimeters of fluid needed.

$$\frac{1}{40} = \frac{x}{25}$$

$$40x = 25$$

$$x = \frac{25}{40}$$

$$x = 0.625$$

0.625 cubic centimeters of fluid should be drawn up into a syringe.

95. Answers will vary.

96. Commutative property of addition

97. Associative property of multiplication

98. Distributive property

99.
$$3(4x-3)=6(2x+1)-15$$
$$12x-9=12x+6-15$$
$$12x-9=12x-9$$
$$12x-12x-9=12x-12x-9$$
$$-9=-9 \quad \text{True}$$

Since a true statement is obtained, the solution is all real numbers.

100.
$$y=mx+b$$
$$y-b=mx+b-b$$
$$y-b=mx$$
$$\frac{y-b}{x}=\frac{mx}{x}$$
$$\frac{y-b}{x}=m$$

Exercise Set 2.8

1. >: is greater than;
≥: is greater than or equal to;
<: is less than;
≤: is less than or equal to

3. a. $3>3$ is false because 3 is not greater than 3.

b. $3\ge 3$ is true because 3 is greater than or equal to 3.

5. The direction of the inequality symbol is changed when multiplying or dividing by a negative number.

7. Since 3 is always less than 5, the solution is all real numbers.

9. a.
$$-7<3$$
$$-4(-7)>-4(3)$$
$$28>-12$$

b.
$$-7<3$$
$$\frac{-7}{-4}>\frac{3}{-4}$$
$$\frac{7}{4}>-\frac{3}{4}$$

11.
$$x+2>6$$
$$x+2-2>6-2$$
$$x>4$$

13.
$$x-5>-1$$
$$x-5+5>-1+5$$
$$x>4$$

15.
$$-x+3<8$$
$$-x+3-3<8-3$$
$$-x<5$$
$$(-1)(-x)>(-1)(5)$$
$$x>-5$$

17.
$$8\le 2-r$$
$$8-2\le 2-r-2$$
$$6\le -r$$
$$(-1)(6)\ge(-1)(-r)$$
$$-6\ge r$$
$$r\le -6$$

19. $-2x<3$
$$\frac{-2x}{-2}>\frac{3}{-2}$$
$$x>-\frac{3}{2}$$

21. $2x + 3 \le 5$

$2x + 3 - 3 \le 5 - 3$

$2x \le 2$

$\dfrac{2x}{2} \le \dfrac{2}{2}$

$x \le 1$

23. $-4x - 3 > 5$

$-4x - 3 + 3 > 5 + 3$

$-4x > 8$

$\dfrac{-4x}{-4} < \dfrac{8}{-4}$

$x < -2$

25. $4 - 6x > -5$

$4 - 4 - 6x > -5 - 4$

$-6x > -9$

$\dfrac{-6x}{-6} < \dfrac{-9}{-6}$

$x < \dfrac{3}{2}$

27. $15 > -9x + 50$

$9x + 15 > -9x + 9x + 50$

$9x + 15 > 50$

$9x + 15 - 15 > 50 - 15$

$9x > 35$

$\dfrac{9x}{9} > \dfrac{35}{9}$

$x > \dfrac{35}{9}$

29. $7 > 2x + 10$

$7 - 10 > 2x + 10 - 10$

$-3 > 2x$

$\dfrac{-3}{2} > \dfrac{2x}{2}$

$-\dfrac{3}{2} > x$

$x < -\dfrac{3}{2}$

31. $6s + 2 \le 6s - 9$

$6s + 2 - 2 \le 6s - 9 - 2$

$6s \le 6x - 11$

$6s - 6s \le 6s - 6s - 11$

$0 \le -11 \quad$ False

Since a false statement is obtained, there is no solution.

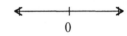

33. $x - 4 \le 3x + 8$

$x - 4 - 8 \le 3x + 8 - 8$

$x - 12 \le 3x$

$x - x - 12 \le 3x - x$

$-12 \le 2x$

$\dfrac{-12}{2} \le \dfrac{2x}{2}$

$-6 \le x$

$x \ge -6$

35. $-x + 4 < -3x + 6$

$-x + 4 - 4 \le -3x + 6 - 4$

$-x < -3x + 2$

$-x + 3x < -3x + 3x + 2$

$2x < 2$

$\dfrac{2x}{2} < \dfrac{2}{2}$

$x < 1$

37.
$$6(2m-4) \geq 2(6m-12)$$
$$12m - 24 \geq 12m - 24$$
$$12m - 12m - 24 \geq 12m - 12m - 24$$
$$-24 \geq -24 \quad \text{True}$$

Since a true statement is obtained, the solution is all real numbers.

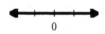

39.
$$x + 3 < x + 4$$
$$x - x + 3 < x - x + 4$$
$$3 < 4$$

Since 3 is always less than 4, the solution is all real numbers.

41.
$$6(3-x) < 2x + 12$$
$$18 - 6x < 2x + 12$$
$$18 - 12 - 6x < 2x + 12 - 12$$
$$6 - 6x < 2x$$
$$6 - 6x + 6x < 2x + 6x$$
$$6 < 8x$$
$$\frac{6}{8} < \frac{8x}{8}$$
$$\frac{3}{4} < x$$
$$x > \frac{3}{4}$$

43.
$$4x - 4 < 4(x-5)$$
$$4x - 4 < 4x - 20$$
$$4x - 4x - 4 < 4x - 4x - 20$$
$$-4 < -20$$

Since –4 is never less than –20, there is no solution.

45.
$$5(2x+3) \geq 6 + (x+2) - 2x$$
$$10x + 15 \geq 6 + x + 2 - 2x$$
$$10x + 15 \geq 8 - x$$
$$10x + 15 - 15 \geq 8 - 15 - x$$
$$10x \geq -7 - x$$
$$10x + x \geq -7 - x + x$$
$$11x \geq -7$$
$$\frac{11x}{11} \geq \frac{-7}{11}$$
$$x \geq -\frac{7}{11}$$

47.
$$1.2x + 3.1 < 3.5x - 3.8$$
$$1.2x - 1.2x + 3.1 < 3.5x - 1.2x - 3.8$$
$$3.1 < 2.3x - 3.8$$
$$3.1 + 3.8 < 2.3x - 3.8 + 3.8$$
$$6.9 < 2.3x$$
$$\frac{6.9}{2.3} < \frac{2.3x}{2.3}$$
$$3 < x$$
$$x > 3$$

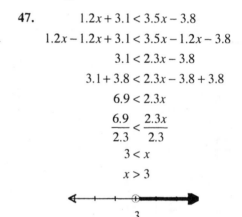

49.
$$1.2(m-3) \geq 4.6(2-m) + 1.7$$
$$1.2m - 3.6 \geq 9.2 - 4.6m + 1.7$$
$$1.2m - 3.6 \geq 10.9 - 4.6m$$
$$1.2m + 4.6m - 3.6 \geq 10.9 - 4.6m + 4.6m$$
$$5.8m - 3.6 \geq 10.9$$
$$5.8m - 3.6 + 3.6 \geq 10.9 + 3.6$$
$$5.8m \geq 14.5$$
$$\frac{5.8m}{5.8} \geq \frac{14.5}{5.8}$$
$$m \geq 2.5$$

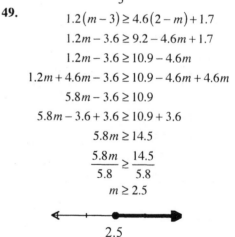

51. $\dfrac{x}{2} \geq \dfrac{x}{3} + 5$

$6\left(\dfrac{x}{2}\right) \geq 6\left(\dfrac{x}{3} + 5\right)$

$3x \geq 2x + 30$

$3x - 2x \geq 2x - 2x + 30$

$x \geq 30$

30

53. $t + \dfrac{1}{6} > \dfrac{2}{3}t$

$6\left(t + \dfrac{1}{6}\right) > 6\left(\dfrac{2}{3}t\right)$

$6t + 1 > 4t$

$6t - 6t + 1 > 4t - 6t$

$1 > -2t$

$\dfrac{1}{-2} < \dfrac{-2t}{-2}$

$-\dfrac{1}{2} < t$

$t > -\dfrac{1}{2}$

$-\dfrac{1}{2}$

55. $\dfrac{1}{8}(4 - r) \leq \dfrac{1}{4}$

$\dfrac{4}{8} - \dfrac{1}{8}r \leq \dfrac{1}{4}$

$8\left(\dfrac{4}{8} - \dfrac{1}{8}r\right) \leq 8\left(\dfrac{1}{4}\right)$

$4 - r \leq 2$

$4 - 4 - r \leq 2 - 4$

$-r \leq -2$

$(-1)(-r) \geq (-1)(-2)$

$r \geq 2$

2

57. $\dfrac{2}{3}(t + 2) \leq \dfrac{1}{4}(2t - 6)$

$\dfrac{2}{3}t + \dfrac{4}{3} \leq \dfrac{1}{2}t - \dfrac{3}{2}$

$6\left(\dfrac{2}{3}t + \dfrac{4}{3}\right) \leq 6\left(\dfrac{1}{2}t - \dfrac{3}{2}\right)$

$4t + 8 \leq 3t - 9$

$4t - 3t + 8 \leq 3t - 3t - 9$

$t + 8 \leq -9$

$t + 8 - 8 \leq -9 - 8$

$t \leq -17$

-17

59. a. The average high temperature was greater than 65°F in May, June, July, August, and September.

   b. The average high temperature was less than or equal to 59°F in January, February, March, April, November, and December.

   c. The average low temperature was less than 29°F in January, February, and December.

   d. The average low temperature was greater than or equal to 58°F in June, July, and August.

61. $\neq$

63. We cannot divide both sides of an inequality by y because we do not know that y is positive. If y is negative, we must reverse the sign of the inequality.

65. $6x - 6 > -4(x + 3) + 5(x + 6) - x$

$6x - 6 > -4x - 12 + 5x + 30 - x$

$6x - 6 > 18$

$6x - 6 + 6 > 18 + 6$

$6x > 24$

$\dfrac{6x}{6} > \dfrac{24}{6}$

$x > 4$

66. Substitute 3 for x.

$-x^2 = -(3)^2$

$ = -(3)(3)$

$ = -9$

67. Substitute –5 for x.
$$-x^2 = -(-5)^2$$
$$= -(-5)(-5)$$
$$= -25$$

68.
$$4 - 3(2x - 4) = 5 - (x + 3)$$
$$4 - 6x + 12 = 5 - x - 3$$
$$-6x + 16 = 2 - x$$
$$-6x + 6x + 16 = 2 - x + 6x$$
$$16 = 2 + 5x$$
$$16 - 2 = 2 - 2 + 5x$$
$$14 = 5x$$
$$\frac{14}{5} = \frac{5x}{5}$$
$$\frac{14}{5} = x$$
$$x = \frac{14}{5} \text{ or } 2\frac{4}{5}$$

69. Let x = number of kilowatt-hours of electricity used.
$$\frac{\$0.174}{1 \text{ kilowatt-hour}} = \frac{\$87}{x \text{ kilowatt-hours}}$$
$$\frac{0.174}{1} = \frac{87}{x}$$
$$0.174x = 87$$
$$x = \frac{87}{0.174} = 500$$
Thus the Vega's used 500 kilowatt-hours of electricity in July.

Review Exercises

1. $3(x + 4) = 3x + 3(4)$
$$= 3x + 12$$

2. $5(x - 2) = 5[x + (-2)]$
$$= 5x + 5(-2)$$
$$= 5x + (-10)$$
$$= 5x - 10$$

3. $-2(x + 4) = -2x + (-2)(4)$
$$= -2x + (-8)$$
$$= -2x - 8$$

4. $-(x + 2) = -1(x + 2)$
$$= (-1)(x) + (-1)(2)$$
$$= -x + (-2)$$
$$= -x - 2$$

5. $-(m + 3) = -1(m + 3)$
$$= (-1)(m) + (-1)(3)$$
$$= -m - 3$$

6. $-4(4 - x) = -4[4 + (-x)]$
$$= (-4)(4) + (-4)(-x)$$
$$= -16 + 4x$$

7. $5(5 - p) = 5[5 + (-p)]$
$$= 5(5) + 5(-p)$$
$$= 25 + (-5p)$$
$$= 25 - 5p$$

8. $6(4x - 5) = 6(4x) - 6(5)$
$$= 24x - 30$$

9. $-5(5x - 5) = -5[5x + (-5)]$
$$= -5(5x) + (-5)(-5)$$
$$= -25x + 25$$

10. $4(-x + 3) = 4(-x) + 4(3)$
$$= -4x + 12$$

11. $\frac{1}{2}(2x + 4) = \left(\frac{1}{2}\right)(2x) + \left(\frac{1}{2}\right)(4)$
$$= x + 2$$

12. $-\frac{1}{3}(3 + 6y) = \left(-\frac{1}{3}\right)(3) + \left(-\frac{1}{3}\right)(6y)$
$$= -1 + (-2y)$$
$$= -1 - 2y$$

13. $-(x + 2y - z) = -1[x + 2y + (-z)]$
$$= -1(x) + (-1)(2y) + (-1)(-z)$$
$$= -x + (-2y) + z$$
$$= -x - 2y + z$$

14.
$$-3(2a - 5b + 7) = -3\left[2a + (-5b) + 7\right]$$
$$= -3(2a) + (-3)(-5b) + (-3)(7)$$
$$= -6a + 15b + (-21)$$
$$= -6a + 15b - 21$$

15. $7x - 3x = 4x$

16.
$$5 - 3y + 3 = -3y + 5 + 3$$
$$= -3y + 8$$

17.
$$1 + 3x + 2x = 1 + 5x$$
$$= 5x + 1$$

18. $-2x - x + 3y = -3x + 3y$

19.
$$4m + 2n + 4m + 6n = 4m + 4m + 2n + 6n$$
$$= 8m + 8n$$

20. There are no like terms.
$9x + 3y + 2$ cannot be further simplified.

21. $6x - 2x + 3y + 6 = 4x + 3y + 6$

22.
$$x + 8x - 9x + 3 = 9x - 9x + 3$$
$$= 3$$

23. $-4x^2 - 8x^2 + 3 = -12x^2 + 3$

24.
$$-2(3a^2 - 4) + 6a^2 - 8 = -6a^2 + 8 + 6a^2 - 8$$
$$= -6a^2 + 6a^2 + 8 - 8$$
$$= 0$$

25.
$$2x + 3(x + 4) - 5 = 2x + 3x + 12 - 5$$
$$= 5x + 7$$

26.
$$-4 + 2(3 - 2b) - b = -4 + 6 - 4b - b$$
$$= 2 - 5b$$
$$= -5b + 2$$

27.
$$6 - (-7x + 6) - 7x = 6 + 7x - 6 - 7x$$
$$= 7x - 7x + 6 - 6$$
$$= 0$$

28.
$$2(2x + 5) - 10 - 4 = 4x + 10 - 10 - 4$$
$$= 4x - 4$$

29.
$$-6(4 - 3x) - 18 + 4x = -24 + 18x - 18 + 4x$$
$$= 18x + 4x - 24 - 18$$
$$= 22x - 42$$

30.
$$4y - 3(x + y) + 6x^2 = 4y - 3x - 3y + 6x^2$$
$$= 6x^2 - 3x + 4y - 3y$$
$$= 6x^2 - 3x + y$$

31.
$$\frac{1}{4}d + 2 - \frac{3}{5}d + 5 = \frac{1}{4}d - \frac{3}{5}d + 2 + 5$$
$$= \frac{5}{20}d - \frac{12}{20}d + 7$$
$$= -\frac{7}{20}d + 7$$

32.
$$3 - (x - y) + (x - y) = 3 - x + y + x - y$$
$$= -x + x + y - y + 3$$
$$= 3$$

33.
$$\frac{5}{6}x - \frac{1}{3}(2x - 6) = \frac{5}{6}x - \frac{2}{3}x + 2$$
$$= \frac{5}{6}x - \frac{4}{6}x + 2$$
$$= \frac{1}{6}x + 2$$

34.
$$\frac{2}{3} - \frac{1}{4}n - \frac{1}{3}(n + 2) = \frac{2}{3} - \frac{1}{4}n - \frac{1}{3}n - \frac{2}{3}$$
$$= -\frac{1}{4}n - \frac{1}{3}n + \frac{2}{3} - \frac{2}{3}$$
$$= -\frac{3}{12}n - \frac{4}{12}n + 0$$
$$= -\frac{7}{12}n$$

35.
$$-3x = -3$$
$$\frac{-3x}{-3} = \frac{-3}{-3}$$
$$x = 1$$

36.
$$x + 6 = -7$$
$$x + 6 - 6 = -7 - 6$$
$$x = -13$$

37.
$$x - 4 = 7$$
$$x - 4 + 4 = 7 + 4$$
$$x = 11$$

38.
$$\frac{x}{3} = -9$$
$$3\left(\frac{x}{3}\right) = 3(-9)$$
$$x = -27$$

39.
$$5x + 1 = 12$$
$$5x + 1 - 1 = 12 - 1$$
$$5x = 11$$
$$\frac{5x}{5} = \frac{11}{5}$$
$$x = \frac{11}{5}$$

40.
$$14 = 3 + 2x$$
$$14 - 3 = 3 - 3 + 2x$$
$$11 = 2x$$
$$\frac{11}{2} = \frac{2x}{2}$$
$$\frac{11}{2} = x$$

41.
$$4c + 3 = -21$$
$$4c + 3 - 3 = -21 - 3$$
$$4c = -24$$
$$\frac{4c}{4} = \frac{-24}{4}$$
$$c = -6$$

42.
$$9 - 2a = 15$$
$$9 - 9 - 2a = 15 - 9$$
$$-2a = 6$$
$$\frac{-2a}{-2} = \frac{6}{-2}$$
$$a = -3$$

43.
$$-x = -12$$
$$-1x = -12$$
$$(-1)(-1x) = (-1)(-12)$$
$$1x = 12$$
$$x = 12$$

44.
$$3(x - 2) = 6$$
$$3x - 6 = 6$$
$$3x - 6 + 6 = 6 + 6$$
$$3x = 12$$
$$\frac{3x}{3} = \frac{12}{3}$$
$$x = 4$$

45.
$$-12 = 3(2x - 8)$$
$$-12 = 6x - 24$$
$$-12 + 24 = 6x - 24 + 24$$
$$12 = 6x$$
$$\frac{12}{6} = \frac{6x}{6}$$
$$2 = x$$

46.
$$4(6 + 2x) = 0$$
$$24 + 8x = 0$$
$$24 - 24 + 8x = 0 - 24$$
$$8x = -24$$
$$\frac{8x}{8} = \frac{-24}{8}$$
$$x = -3$$

47.
$$-6n + 2n + 6 = 0$$
$$-4n + 6 = 0$$
$$-4n + 6 - 6 = 0 - 6$$
$$-4n = -6$$
$$\frac{-4n}{-4} = \frac{-6}{-4}$$
$$n = \frac{6}{4} = \frac{3}{2}$$

48.
$$-3 = 3w - (4w + 6)$$
$$-3 = 3w - 4w - 6$$
$$-3 = -1w - 6$$
$$-3 + 6 = -1w - 6 + 6$$
$$3 = -1w$$
$$\frac{3}{-1} = \frac{-1w}{-1}$$
$$-3 = w$$

49.
$$6 - (2n + 3) - 4n = 6$$
$$6 - 2n - 3 - 4n = 6$$
$$6 - 3 - 2n - 4n = 6$$
$$3 - 6n = 6$$
$$3 - 3 - 6n = 6 - 3$$
$$-6n = 3$$
$$\frac{-6n}{-6} = \frac{3}{-6}$$
$$n = -\frac{3}{6} = -\frac{1}{2}$$

50.
$$4x + 6 - 7x + 9 = 18$$
$$-3x + 15 = 18$$
$$-3x + 15 - 15 = 18 - 15$$
$$-3x = 3$$
$$\frac{-3x}{-3} = \frac{3}{-3}$$
$$x = -1$$

51.
$$5 + 3(x - 1) = 3(x + 1) - 1$$
$$5 + 3x - 3 = 3x + 3 - 1$$
$$3x + 2 = 3x + 2$$
$$3x - 3x + 2 = 3x - 3x + 2$$
$$2 = 2 \text{ True}$$
The solution is all real numbers.

52.
$$8.4r - 6.3 = 6.3 + 2.1r$$
$$8.4r - 2.1r - 6.3 = 6.3 + 2.1r - 2.1r$$
$$6.3r - 6.3 = 6.3$$
$$6.3r - 6.3 + 6.3 = 6.3 + 6.3$$
$$6.3r = 12.6$$
$$\frac{6.3r}{6.3} = \frac{12.6}{6.3}$$
$$r = 2$$

53.
$$19.6 - 21.3t = 80.1 - 9.2t$$
$$19.6 - 21.3t + 21.3t = 80.1 - 9.2t + 21.3t$$
$$19.6 = 80.1 + 12.1t$$
$$19.6 - 80.1 = 80.1 - 80.1 + 12.1t$$
$$-60.5 = 12.1t$$
$$\frac{-60.5}{12.1} = \frac{12.1t}{12.1}$$
$$-5 = t$$

54.
$$0.35(c - 5) = 0.45(c + 4)$$
$$0.35c - 1.75 = 0.45c + 1.8$$
$$0.35c - 0.35c - 1.75 = 0.45c - 0.35c + 1.8$$
$$-1.75 = 0.10c + 1.8$$
$$-1.75 - 1.8 = 0.10c + 1.8 - 1.8$$
$$-3.55 = 0.10c$$
$$\frac{-3.55}{0.10} = \frac{0.10c}{0.10}$$
$$-35.5 = c$$

55.
$$0.2(x + 6) = -0.3(2x - 1)$$
$$0.2x + 1.2 = -0.6x + 0.3$$
$$0.2x + 0.6x + 1.2 = -0.6x + 0.6x + 0.3$$
$$0.8x + 1.2 = 0.3$$
$$0.8x + 1.2 - 1.2 = 0.3 - 1.2$$
$$0.8x = -0.9$$
$$\frac{0.8x}{0.8} = \frac{-0.9}{0.8}$$
$$x = -1.125$$

56.
$$-2.3(x - 8) = 3.7(x + 4)$$
$$-2.3x + 18.4 = 3.7x + 14.8$$
$$-2.3x + 2.3x + 18.4 = 3.7x + 2.3x + 14.8$$
$$18.4 = 6.0x + 14.8$$
$$18.4 - 14.8 = 6.0x + 14.8 - 14.8$$
$$3.6 = 6.0x$$
$$\frac{3.6}{6.0} = \frac{6.0x}{6.0}$$
$$0.6 = x$$

57.
$$\frac{p}{3} + 2 = \frac{1}{4}$$
$$12\left(\frac{p}{3} + 2\right) = 12\left(\frac{1}{4}\right)$$
$$4p + 24 = 3$$
$$4p + 24 - 24 = 3 - 24$$
$$4p = -21$$
$$\frac{4p}{4} = \frac{-21}{4}$$
$$p = -\frac{21}{4}$$

58.
$$\frac{d}{6} + \frac{1}{7} = 2$$
$$42\left(\frac{d}{6} + \frac{1}{7}\right) = 42(2)$$
$$7d + 6 = 84$$
$$7d + 6 - 6 = 84 - 6$$
$$7d = 78$$
$$\frac{7d}{7} = \frac{78}{7}$$
$$d = \frac{78}{7}$$

59. $\dfrac{3}{5}(r-6) = 3r$

$\dfrac{3}{5}r - \dfrac{18}{5} = 3r$

$5\left(\dfrac{3}{5}r - \dfrac{18}{5}\right) = 5(3r)$

$3r - 18 = 15r$

$3r - 3r - 18 = 15r - 3r$

$-18 = 12r$

$\dfrac{-18}{12} = \dfrac{12r}{12}$

$-\dfrac{18}{12} = r$

$-\dfrac{3}{2} = r$

60. $\dfrac{2}{3}w = \dfrac{1}{7}(w-2)$

$\dfrac{2}{3}w = \dfrac{1}{7}w - \dfrac{2}{7}$

$21\left(\dfrac{2}{3}w\right) = 21\left(\dfrac{1}{7}w - \dfrac{2}{7}\right)$

$14w = 3w - 6$

$14w - 3w = 3w - 3w - 6$

$11w = -6$

$\dfrac{11w}{11} = \dfrac{-6}{11}$

$w = -\dfrac{6}{11}$

61. $8x - 5 = -4x + 19$

$8x + 4x - 5 = -4x + 4x + 19$

$12x - 5 = 19$

$12x - 5 + 5 = 19 + 5$

$12x = 24$

$\dfrac{12x}{12} = \dfrac{24}{12}$

$x = 2$

62. $-(w+2) = 2(3w-6)$

$-w - 2 = 6w - 12$

$-w - 2 + 12 = 6w - 12 + 12$

$-w + 10 = 6w$

$-w + w + 10 = 6w + w$

$10 = 7w$

$\dfrac{10}{7} = \dfrac{7w}{7}$

$\dfrac{10}{7} = w$

63. $2x + 6 = 3x + 9 - 3$

$2x + 6 = 3x + 6$

$2x - 2x + 6 = 3x - 2x + 6$

$6 = x + 6$

$6 - 6 = x + 6 - 6$

$0 = x$

64. $-5a + 3 = 2a + 10$

$-5a + 3 - 10 = 2a + 10 - 10$

$-5a - 7 = 2a$

$-5a + 5a - 7 = 2a + 5a$

$-7 = 7a$

$\dfrac{-7}{7} = \dfrac{7a}{7}$

$-1 = a$

65. $5p - 2 = -2(-3p + 6)$

$5p - 2 = 6p - 12$

$5p - 5p - 2 = 6p - 5p - 12$

$-2 = p - 12$

$-2 + 12 = p - 12 + 12$

$10 = p$

66. $3x - 12x = 24 - 9x$

$-9x = 24 - 9x$

$-9x + 9x = 24 - 9x + 9x$

$0 = 24$ False

Since a false statement is obtained, there is no solution.

67. $4(2x - 3) + 4 = 8x - 8$

$8x - 12 + 4 = 8x - 8$

$8x - 8 = 8x - 8$

Since the equation is true for all values of x, the solution is all real numbers.

68. $4 - c - 2(4 - 3c) = 3(c - 4)$

$4 - c - 8 + 6c = 3c - 12$

$5c - 4 = 3c - 12$

$5c - 3c - 4 = 3c - 3c - 12$

$2c - 4 = -12$

$2c - 4 + 4 = -12 + 4$

$2c = -8$

$\dfrac{2c}{2} = \dfrac{-8}{2}$

$c = -4$

69. $2(x + 7) = 6x + 9 - 4x$

$2x + 14 = 6x + 9 - 4x$

$2x + 14 = 2x + 9$

$2x - 2x + 14 = 2x - 2x + 9$

$14 = 9$ False

Since a false statement is obtained, there is no solution.

70. $-5(3 - 4x) = -6 + 20x - 9$

$-15 + 20x = -6 + 20x - 9$

$-15 + 20x = -15 + 20x$

The statement is true for all values of x, thus the solution is all real numbers.

71. $4(x - 3) - (x + 5) = 0$

$4x - 12 - x - 5 = 0$

$3x - 17 = 0$

$3x - 17 + 17 = 0 + 17$

$3x = 17$

$\dfrac{3x}{3} = \dfrac{17}{3}$

$x = \dfrac{17}{3}$

72. $-2(4 - x) = 6(x + 2) + 3x$

$-8 + 2x = 6x + 12 + 3x$

$-8 + 2x = 9x + 12$

$-8 - 12 + 2x = 9x + 12 - 12$

$-20 + 2x = 9x$

$-20 + 2x - 2x = 9x - 2x$

$-20 = 7x$

$\dfrac{-20}{7} = \dfrac{7x}{7}$

$-\dfrac{20}{7} = x$

73. $\dfrac{x + 3}{2} = \dfrac{x}{2}$

$2(x + 3) = 2x$

$2x + 6 = 2x$

$2x - 2x + 6 = 2x - 2x$

$6 = 0$ False

Since a false statement is obtained, there is no solution.

74. $\dfrac{x}{6} = \dfrac{x - 4}{2}$

$2 \cdot x = 6(x - 4)$

$2x = 6x - 24$

$2x - 6x = 6x - 6x - 24$

$-4x = -24$

$\dfrac{-4x}{-4} = \dfrac{-24}{-4}$

$x = 6$

75. $\dfrac{1}{5}(3s + 4) = \dfrac{1}{3}(2s - 8)$

$\dfrac{3}{5}s + \dfrac{4}{5} = \dfrac{2}{3}s - \dfrac{8}{3}$

$15\left(\dfrac{3}{5}s + \dfrac{4}{5}\right) = 15\left(\dfrac{2}{3}s - \dfrac{8}{3}\right)$

$9s + 12 = 10s - 40$

$9s - 9s + 12 = 10s - 9s - 40$

$12 = s - 40$

$12 + 40 = s - 40 + 40$

$52 = s$

76. $\dfrac{2(2t - 4)}{5} = \dfrac{3t + 6}{4} - \dfrac{3}{2}$

$\dfrac{4t - 8}{5} = \dfrac{3t + 6}{4} - \dfrac{3}{2}$

$20\left(\dfrac{4t - 8}{5}\right) = 20\left(\dfrac{3t + 6}{4} - \dfrac{3}{2}\right)$

$4(4t - 8) = 5(3t + 6) - 30$

$16t - 32 = 15t + 30 - 30$

$16t - 32 = 15t + 0$

$16t - 16t - 32 = 15t - 16t$

$-32 = -1t$

$\dfrac{-32}{-1} = \dfrac{-1t}{-1}$

$32 = t$

77. $\frac{2}{5}(2-x)=\frac{1}{6}(-2x+2)$

$$\frac{4}{5}-\frac{2}{5}x=-\frac{2}{6}x+\frac{2}{6}$$

$$\frac{4}{5}-\frac{2}{5}x=-\frac{1}{3}x+\frac{1}{3}$$

$$15\left(\frac{4}{5}-\frac{2}{5}x\right)=15\left(-\frac{1}{3}x+\frac{1}{3}\right)$$

$$12-6x=-5x+5$$

$$12-6x+6x=-5x+6x+5$$

$$12=x+5$$

$$12-5=x+5-5$$

$$7=x$$

78. $\frac{x}{4}+\frac{x}{6}=\frac{1}{2}(x+3)$

$$\frac{x}{4}+\frac{x}{6}=\frac{x}{2}+\frac{3}{2}$$

$$12\left(\frac{x}{4}+\frac{x}{6}\right)=12\left(\frac{x}{2}+\frac{3}{2}\right)$$

$$3x+2x=6x+18$$

$$5x=6x+18$$

$$5x-6x=6x-6x+18$$

$$-1x=18$$

$$\frac{-1x}{-1}=\frac{18}{-1}$$

$$x=-18$$

79. Substitute 7 for y, 2 for x, and 1 for b. Then solve for m.

$$y=mx+b$$

$$7=m(2)+1$$

$$7=2m+1$$

$$7-1=2m+1-1$$

$$6=2m$$

$$\frac{6}{2}=\frac{2m}{2}$$

$$3=m$$

80. Substitute 12 for h, 3 for b, and 5 for d. Then solve for A.

$$A=\frac{1}{2}h(b+d)$$

$$A=\frac{1}{2}(12)(3+5)$$

$$A=\frac{1}{2}(12)(8)$$

$$A=48$$

81. $A=\frac{1}{2}bh$

$$A=\frac{1}{2}(8)(3)$$

$$A=12\text{ cm}^2$$

82. $V=\frac{4}{3}\pi r^3$

$$V=\frac{4}{3}\pi(2)^3$$

$$V=\frac{4}{3}\pi(8)$$

$$V=\frac{32}{3}\pi\approx 33.51\text{ in.}^3$$

83. $P=2l+2w$

$$P-2w=2l+2w-2w$$

$$P-2w=2l$$

$$\frac{P-2w}{2}=\frac{2l}{2}$$

$$\frac{P-2w}{2}=l$$

84. $y-y_1=m(x-x_1)$

$$\frac{y-y_1}{x-x_1}=\frac{m(x-x_1)}{(x-x_1)}$$

$$\frac{y-y_1}{x-x_1}=m$$

85. $-x+3y=2$

$$-x+x+3y=2+x$$

$$3y=x+2$$

$$\frac{3y}{3}=\frac{x+2}{3}$$

$$y=\frac{x}{3}+\frac{2}{3}$$

$$y=\frac{1}{3}x+\frac{2}{3}$$

86. $d = rt$

$d = (61.7)(5)$

$d = 308.5$

He traveled 308.5 miles.

87. $A = lw$

$A = (20)(12)$

$A = 240$

The area of the flower garden is 240 sq. ft.

88. $V = \pi r^2 h$

$V = \pi (2)^2 (2)$

$V = 8\pi \approx 25.13$ in.^{3}

89. $12 : 20 = 3 : 5$

90. 80 ounces $= \dfrac{80}{16} = 5$ pounds

The ratio of 80 ounces to 12 pounds is thus 5:12.

91. 4 minutes = 240 seconds

The ratio of 4 minutes to 40 seconds is $\dfrac{240}{40} = \dfrac{6}{1}$.

The ratio is 6:1.

92. $\dfrac{x}{4} = \dfrac{8}{16}$

$16 \cdot x = 8 \cdot 4$

$16x = 32$

$x = \dfrac{32}{16} = 2$

93. $\dfrac{5}{20} = \dfrac{x}{80}$

$20 \cdot x = 80 \cdot 5$

$20x = 400$

$x = \dfrac{400}{20} = 20$

94. $\dfrac{3}{x} = \dfrac{15}{45}$

$3 \cdot 45 = 15 \cdot x$

$135 = 15x$

$\dfrac{135}{15} = x$

$9 = x$

95. $\dfrac{20}{45} = \dfrac{15}{x}$

$20 \cdot x = 15 \cdot 45$

$20x = 675$

$x = \dfrac{675}{20} = \dfrac{135}{4}$

96. $\dfrac{6}{5} = \dfrac{-12}{x}$

$6 \cdot x = -12 \cdot 5$

$6x = -60$

$x = \dfrac{-60}{6} = -10$

97. $\dfrac{b}{6} = \dfrac{8}{-3}$

$-3 \cdot b = 6 \cdot 8$

$-3b = 48$

$x = \dfrac{48}{-3} = -16$

98. $\dfrac{-7}{9} = \dfrac{-12}{y}$

$-7 \cdot y = -12 \cdot 9$

$-7y = -108$

$y = \dfrac{-108}{-7}$

$y = \dfrac{108}{7}$

99. $\dfrac{x}{-15} = \dfrac{30}{-5}$

$-5 \cdot x = -15 \cdot 30$

$-5x = -450$

$x = \dfrac{-450}{-5} = 90$

100. $\dfrac{6}{8} = \dfrac{30}{x}$

$6 \cdot x = 8 \cdot 30$

$6x = 240$

$x = \dfrac{240}{6} = 40$

The length of the side is thus 40 in.

101. $\dfrac{7}{3.5} = \dfrac{2}{x}$

$7 \cdot x = 2 \cdot 3.5$

$7x = 7$

$x = \dfrac{7}{7} = 1$

The length of the side is thus 1 ft.

102. $3x + 4 \geq 10$

$3x + 4 - 4 \geq 10 - 4$

$3x \geq 6$

$\dfrac{3x}{3} \geq \dfrac{6}{3}$

$x \geq 2$

103. $-4a - 6 > 4a - 14$

$-4a + 4a - 6 > 4a + 4a - 14$

$-6 > 8a - 14$

$-6 + 14 > 8a - 14 + 14$

$8 > 8a$

$\dfrac{8}{8} > \dfrac{8a}{8}$

$1 > a$

$a < 1$

104. $5 - 3r \leq 2r + 15$

$5 - 15 - 3r \leq 2r + 15 - 15$

$-10 - 3r \leq 2r$

$-10 - 3r + 3r \leq 2r + 3r$

$-10 \leq 5r$

$\dfrac{-10}{5} \leq \dfrac{5r}{5}$

$-2 \leq r$

$r \geq -2$

105. $2(x + 4) \leq 2x - 5$

$2x + 8 \leq 2x - 5$

$2x - 2x + 8 \leq 2x - 2x - 5$

$8 \leq -5$

Since 8 is never less than or equal to –5, there is

no solution.

106. $2(x + 3) > 6x - 4x + 4$

$2x + 6 > 6x - 4x + 4$

$2x + 6 > 2x + 4$

$2x - 2x + 6 > 2x - 2x + 4$

$6 > 4$

Since 6 is always greater than 4, the answer is all real numbers.

107. $x + 6 > 9x + 30$

$x + 6 - 30 > 9x + 30 - 30$

$x - 24 > 9x$

$x - x - 24 > 9x - x$

$-24 > 8x$

$\dfrac{-24}{8} > \dfrac{8x}{8}$

$-3 > x$

$x < -3$

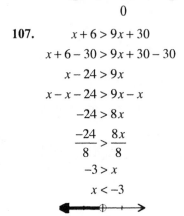

108. $x - 8 \leq -3x + 9$

$x + 3x - 8 \leq -3x + 3x + 9$

$4x - 8 \leq 9$

$4x - 8 + 8 \leq 9 + 8$

$4x \leq 17$

$\dfrac{4x}{4} \leq \dfrac{17}{4}$

$x \leq \dfrac{17}{4}$

109.

$$-(x+2) < -2(-2x+5)$$
$$-x-2 < 4x-10$$
$$-x-2+10 < 4x-10+10$$
$$-x+8 < 4x$$
$$-x+x+8 < 4x+x$$
$$8 < 5x$$
$$\frac{8}{5} < \frac{5x}{5}$$
$$\frac{8}{5} < x$$
$$x > \frac{8}{5}$$

110.

$$\frac{x}{2} < \frac{2}{3}(x+3)$$
$$\frac{x}{2} < \frac{2}{3}x+2$$
$$6\left(\frac{x}{2}\right) < 6\left(\frac{2}{3}x+2\right)$$
$$3x < 4x+12$$
$$3x-4x < 4x-4x+12$$
$$-1x < 12$$
$$\frac{-1x}{-1} > \frac{12}{-1}$$
$$x > -12$$

111.

$$\frac{3}{10}(t-2) \le \frac{3}{4}(4+2t)$$
$$\frac{3}{10}t - \frac{6}{10} \le 3 + \frac{6}{4}t$$
$$20\left(\frac{3}{10}t - \frac{6}{10}\right) \le 20\left(3 + \frac{6}{4}t\right)$$
$$6t-12 \le 60+30t$$
$$6t-6t-12 \le 60+30t-6t$$
$$-12 \le 60+24t$$
$$-12-60 \le 60-60+24t$$
$$-72 \le 24t$$
$$\frac{-72}{24} \le \frac{24t}{24}$$
$$-3 \le t$$
$$t \ge -3$$

112. Let t = the time it will take in hours to make the boat trip.

$$\frac{40 \text{ miles}}{1.8 \text{ hours}} = \frac{140 \text{ miles}}{t \text{ hours}}$$
$$\frac{40}{1.8} = \frac{140}{t}$$
$$40 \cdot t = 1.8 \cdot 140$$
$$40t = 252$$
$$\frac{40t}{40} = \frac{252}{40}$$
$$t = 6.3$$

It will take the boat 6.3 hours to travel 140 miles.

113. Let x = number of dishes he can wash in 21 minutes.

$$\frac{12 \text{ dishes}}{3.5 \text{ minutes}} = \frac{x \text{ dishes}}{21 \text{ minutes}}$$
$$\frac{12}{3.5} = \frac{x}{21}$$
$$12 \cdot 21 = 3.5 \cdot x$$
$$252 = 3.5x$$
$$\frac{252}{3.5} = \frac{3.5x}{3.5}$$
$$72 = x$$

He can wash 72 dishes in 21 minutes.

114. Let x = number of pages that can be copied in 22 minutes.

$$\frac{1 \text{ minutes}}{20 \text{ pages}} = \frac{22 \text{ minutes}}{x \text{ pages}}$$

$$\frac{1}{20} = \frac{22}{x}$$

$$1 \cdot x = 22 \cdot 20$$

$$x = 440$$

440 pages can be copied in 22 minutes.

115. Let x = number of inches representing 380 miles.

$$\frac{60 \text{ miles}}{1 \text{ inch}} = \frac{380 \text{ miles}}{x \text{ inches}}$$

$$\frac{60}{1} = \frac{380}{x}$$

$$60 \cdot x = 380 \cdot 1$$

$$60x = 380$$

$$x = \frac{380}{60} = 6\frac{1}{3}$$

$6\frac{1}{3}$ inches on the map represent 380 miles.

116. Let x = size of actual car in feet

$$\frac{1 \text{ inch}}{1.5 \text{ feet}} = \frac{10.5 \text{ inches}}{x \text{ feet}}$$

$$\frac{1}{1.5} = \frac{10.5}{x}$$

$$1 \cdot x = 1.5 \cdot 10.5$$

$$x = 15.75$$

The size of the actual car is 15.75 ft.

117. Let x = the value of 1 peso in terms of U.S. dollars.

$$\frac{\$1 \text{ U.S.}}{9.165 \text{ pesos}} = \frac{x \text{ dollars}}{1 \text{ peso}}$$

$$\frac{1}{9.165} = \frac{x}{1}$$

$$9.165 \cdot x = 1 \cdot 1$$

$$9.165x = 1$$

$$x = \frac{1}{9.165} \approx 0.109$$

1 peso equals about $0.109.

118. Let x = number of bottles the machine can fill and cap in 2 minutes.

2 minutes = 120 seconds

$$\frac{50 \text{ seconds}}{80 \text{ bottles}} = \frac{120 \text{ seconds}}{x \text{ bottles}}$$

$$\frac{50}{80} = \frac{120}{x}$$

$$50 \cdot x = 80 \cdot 120$$

$$50x = 9600$$

$$x = \frac{9600}{50} = 192$$

The machine can fill and cap 192 bottles in 2 minutes.

Practice Test

1. $-3(4 - 2x) = -3[4 + (-2x)]$

$$= -3(4) + (-3)(-2x)$$

$$= -12 + 6x \text{ or } 6x - 12$$

2. $-(x + 3y - 4) = -[x + 3y + (-4)]$

$$= -1[x + 3y + (-4)]$$

$$= (-1)(x) + (-1)(3y) + (-1)(-4)$$

$$= -x + (-3y) + 4$$

$$= -x - 3y + 4$$

3. $5x - 8x + 4 = -3x + 4$

4. $4 + 2x - 3x + 6 = 2x - 3x + 4 + 6$

$$= -x + 10$$

5. $-y - x - 4x - 6 = -x - 4x - y - 6$

$$= -5x - y - 6$$

6. $a - 2b + 6a - 6b - 3 = a + 6a - 2b - 6b - 3$

$$= 7a - 8b - 3$$

7. $2x^2 + 3 + 2(3x - 2) = 2x^2 + 3 + 6x - 4$

$$= 2x^2 + 6x + 3 - 4$$

$$= 2x^2 + 6x - 1$$

8.

$$2.4x - 3.9 = 3.3$$

$$2.4x - 3.9 + 3.9 = 3.3 + 3.9$$

$$2.4x = 7.2$$

$$\frac{2.4x}{2.4} = \frac{7.2}{2.4}$$

$$x = 3$$

9.
$$\frac{5}{6}(x-2) = x - 3$$
$$\frac{5}{6}x - \frac{10}{6} = x - 3$$
$$6\left(\frac{5}{6}x - \frac{10}{6}\right) = 6(x - 3)$$
$$5x - 10 = 6x - 18$$
$$5x - 5x - 10 = 6x - 5x - 18$$
$$-10 = x - 18$$
$$-10 + 18 = x - 18 + 18$$
$$8 = x$$

10.
$$2x - 3(-2x + 4) = -13 + x$$
$$2x + 6x - 12 = -13 + x$$
$$8x - 12 = -13 + x$$
$$8x - 12 + 12 = -13 + 12 + x$$
$$8x = -1 + x$$
$$8x - x = -1 + x - x$$
$$7x = -1$$
$$\frac{7x}{7} = \frac{-1}{7}$$
$$x = -\frac{1}{7}$$

11.
$$3x - 4 - x = 2(x + 5)$$
$$3x - 4 - x = 2x + 10$$
$$2x - 4 = 2x + 10$$
$$2x - 2x - 4 = 2x - 2x + 10$$
$$-4 = 10 \quad \text{False}$$
Since a false statement is obtained, there is no solution.

12.
$$-3(2x + 3) = -2(3x + 1) - 7$$
$$-6x - 9 = -6x - 2 - 7$$
$$-6x - 9 = -6x - 9$$
Since the equation is true for all values of x, the solution is all real numbers.

13.
$$ax + by + c = 0$$
$$ax + by - by + c = 0 - by$$
$$ax + c = -by$$
$$ax + c - c = -by - c$$
$$ax = -by - c$$
$$\frac{ax}{a} = \frac{-by - c}{a}$$
$$x = \frac{-by - c}{a}$$

14.
$$-6x + 5y = -2$$
$$-6x + 6x + 5y = -2 + 6x$$
$$5y = 6x - 2$$
$$\frac{5y}{5} = \frac{6x - 2}{5}$$
$$y = \frac{6x}{5} - \frac{2}{5}$$
$$y = \frac{6}{5}x - \frac{2}{5}$$

15.
$$\frac{1}{7}(2x - 5) = \frac{3}{8}x - \frac{5}{7}$$
$$\frac{2}{7}x - \frac{5}{7} = \frac{3}{8}x - \frac{5}{7}$$
$$56\left(\frac{2}{7}x - \frac{5}{7}\right) = 56\left(\frac{3}{8}x - \frac{5}{7}\right)$$
$$16x - 40 = 21x - 40$$
$$16x - 16x - 40 = 21x - 16x - 40$$
$$-40 = 5x - 40$$
$$-40 + 40 = 5x - 40 + 40$$
$$0 = 5x$$
$$\frac{0}{5} = \frac{5x}{5}$$
$$0 = x$$

16.
$$\frac{9}{x} = \frac{3}{-15}$$
$$9(-15) = 3x$$
$$-135 = 3x$$
$$\frac{-135}{3} = x$$
$$-45 = x$$

17. a. An equation that has exactly one solution is a conditional equation.

   b. An equation that has no solution is a contradiction.

   c. An equation that has all real numbers as its solution is an identity.

18.
$$2x - 4 < 4x + 10$$
$$2x - 4 - 10 < 4x + 10 - 10$$
$$2x - 14 < 4x$$
$$2x - 2x - 14 < 4x - 2x$$
$$-14 < 2x$$
$$\frac{-14}{2} < \frac{2x}{2}$$
$$-7 < x$$
$$x > -7$$

19.
$$3(x + 4) \geq 5x - 12$$
$$3x + 12 \geq 5x - 12$$
$$3x + 12 + 12 \geq 5x - 12 + 12$$
$$3x + 24 \geq 5x$$
$$3x - 3x + 24 \geq 5x - 3x$$
$$24 \geq 2x$$
$$\frac{24}{2} \geq \frac{2x}{2}$$
$$12 \geq x$$
$$x \leq 12$$

20.
$$4(x + 3) + 2x < 6x - 3$$
$$4x + 12 + 2x < 6x - 3$$
$$6x + 12 < 6x - 3$$
$$6x - 6x + 12 < 6x - 6x - 3$$
$$12 < -3$$
Since 12 is never less than −3, the answer is no solution.

21.
$$-(x - 2) - 3x = 4(1 - x) - 2$$
$$-x + 2 - 3x = 4 - 4x - 2$$
$$-4x + 2 = -4x + 2 \quad \text{True}$$
This equation is true for all real numbers.

22.
$$\frac{3}{4} = \frac{8}{x}$$
$$3x = 4 \cdot 8$$
$$3x = 32$$
$$x = \frac{32}{3}$$
The length of side x is $\frac{32}{3}$ feet or $10\frac{2}{3}$ feet.

23. Let r = the simple interest rate.
$$i = prt$$
$$80 = 2000 \cdot r \cdot 1$$
$$80 = 2000r$$
$$\frac{80}{2000} = \frac{2000r}{2000}$$
$$0.04 = r$$
The interest rate was 4%.

24. Let C = the circumference of the pie.
$$C = 2\pi r$$
$$C = 2\pi(4.5)$$
$$C = 9\pi \approx 28.27$$
The circumference of the pie is 28.27 in.

25. Let x = number of minutes it will take.
$$\frac{25 \text{ miles}}{35 \text{ minutes}} = \frac{125 \text{ miles}}{x \text{ minutes}}$$
$$\frac{25}{35} = \frac{125}{x}$$
$$25x = 35 \cdot 125$$
$$25x = 4375$$
$$x = \frac{4375}{25} = 175$$
It would take 175 minutes or 2 hours 55 minutes.

Cumulative Review Test

1.
$$\frac{52}{15} \cdot \frac{10}{13} = \frac{\overset{4}{\cancel{52}}}{\underset{3}{\cancel{15}}} \cdot \frac{\overset{2}{\cancel{10}}}{\cancel{13}_{1}}$$
$$= \frac{4 \cdot 2}{3 \cdot 1}$$
$$= \frac{8}{3}$$

2. $\dfrac{5}{24} \div \dfrac{2}{9} = \dfrac{5}{24} \cdot \dfrac{9}{2}$

$= \dfrac{5}{8} \cdot \dfrac{3}{2}$

$= \dfrac{5 \cdot 3}{8 \cdot 2}$

$= \dfrac{15}{16}$

3. $|-2| > 1$ since $|-2| = 2$ and $2 > 1$.

4. $-5 - (-4) + 12 - 8 = -5 + 4 + 12 - 8$

$= -1 + 12 - 8$

$= 11 - 8$

$= 3$

5. $-7 - (-6) = -7 + 6$

$= -1$

6. $20 - 6 \div 3 \cdot 2 = 20 - 2 \cdot 2$

$= 20 - 4$

$= 16$

7. $3\left[6 - \left(4 - 3^2\right)\right] - 30 = 3\left[6 - (4 - 9)\right] - 30$

$= 3\left[6 - (-5)\right] - 30$

$= 3[6 + 5] - 30$

$= 3(11) - 30$

$= 33 - 30$

$= 3$

8. Substitute -2 for each x.

$-2x^2 - 6x + 8 = -2(-2)^2 - 6(-2) + 8$

$= -2(4) - (-12) + 8$

$= -8 + 12 + 8$

$= 4 + 8$

$= 12$

9. Distributive property

10. $8x + 2y + 4x - y = 8x + 4x + 2y - y$

$= 12x + y$

11. $9 - \dfrac{2}{3}x + 16 + \dfrac{3}{4}x = \dfrac{3}{4}x - \dfrac{2}{3}x + 9 + 16$

$= \dfrac{9}{12}x - \dfrac{8}{12}x + 25$

$= \dfrac{1}{12}x + 25$

12. $7x + 3 = -4$

$7x + 3 - 3 = -4 - 3$

$7x = -7$

$\dfrac{7x}{7} = \dfrac{-7}{7}$

$x = -1$

13. $4(x - 2) = 5(x - 1) + 3x + 2$

$4x - 8 = 5x - 5 + 3x + 2$

$4x - 8 = 5x + 3x - 5 + 2$

$4x - 8 = 8x - 3$

$4x - 4x - 8 = 8x - 4x - 3$

$-8 = 4x - 3$

$-8 + 3 = 4x - 3 + 3$

$-5 = 4x$

$\dfrac{-5}{4} = \dfrac{4x}{4}$

$-\dfrac{5}{4} = x$

14. $\dfrac{3}{4}n - \dfrac{1}{5} = \dfrac{2}{3}n$

$60\left(\dfrac{3}{4}n - \dfrac{1}{5}\right) = 60\left(\dfrac{2}{3}n\right)$

$45n - 12 = 40n$

$45n - 45n - 12 = 40n - 45n$

$-12 = -5n$

$\dfrac{-12}{-5} = \dfrac{-5n}{-5}$

$\dfrac{12}{5} = n$

15. $A = \dfrac{a + b + c}{3}$

$3 \cdot A = 3 \cdot \left(\dfrac{a + b + c}{3}\right)$

$3A = a + b + c$

$3A - a = a - a + b + c$

$3A - a = b + c$

$3A - a - c = b + c - c$

$3A - a - c = b$

16. $\dfrac{40}{30} = \dfrac{3}{x}$

$40 \cdot x = 30 \cdot 3$

$40x = 90$

$\dfrac{40x}{40} = \dfrac{90}{40}$

$x = \dfrac{90}{40} = \dfrac{9}{4}$ or 2.25

17. $x - 3 > 7$

$x - 3 + 3 > 7 + 3$

$x > 10$

10

18. $2x - 7 \le 3x + 5$

$2x - 7 - 5 \le 3x + 5 - 5$

$2x - 12 \le 3x$

$2x - 2x - 12 \le 3x - 2x$

$-12 \le x$

$x \ge -12$

-12

19. Let A = the area of the trampoline.

$A = \pi r^2$

$A = \pi (11)^2$

$A = 122\pi \approx 380.13$

The area of the trampoline is 380.13 sq. ft.

20. Let x = amount he earns after 8 hours.

$\dfrac{2 \text{ hours}}{\$10.50} = \dfrac{8 \text{ hours}}{x \text{ dollars}}$

$\dfrac{2}{10.5} = \dfrac{8}{x}$

$2x = (10.5)(8)$

$2x = 84$

$x = \dfrac{84}{2} = 42$

He earns $42 after 8 hours.

Chapter 3

Exercise Set 3.1

1. Added to, more than, increased by, and sum indicate the operation of addition.

3. Multiplied by, product of, twice, and three times indicate the operation of multiplication.

5. The cost is increased by 25% of the cost, so the expression needs to be $c + 0.25c$.

7. $25 - x$

9. Answers will vary.

11. $h + 4$

13. $a - 5$

15. $5h$

17. $2d$

19. $\frac{1}{2}a$

21. $r - 5$

23. $8 - m$

25. $2w + 8$

27. $5a - 4$

29. $\frac{1}{3}w - 7$

31. $x =$ Sonya's height

33. $x =$ the length of Jones Beach

35. $x =$ the number of medals Finland won

37. $x =$ the cost of the Chevy

39. $x =$ Teri's grade

41. $x =$ the amount that Kristen receives or $x =$ the amount Yvonne receives

43. $x =$ Don's weight of $x =$ Angela's weight

45. If $c =$ the cost of the chair, then $3c$ is the cost of the table.

47. If $a =$ the area of the kitchen, then $2a + 20 =$ the area of the living room.

49. If $w =$ the width of the rectangle, then $5w - 2 =$ the length of the rectangle.

51. If $w =$ the number of medals won by Sweden, then $38 - w =$ the number of medals won by Brazil.
If $w =$ the number of medals won by Brazil, then $38 - w =$ the number of medals won by Sweden.

53. If $g =$ George's age, then $\frac{1}{2}g + 2 =$ Mike's age.

55. If $m =$ the number of miles Jan walked, then $6.4 - m =$ the number of miles Edward walked.
If $m =$ the number of miles Edward walked, then $6.4 - m =$ the number of miles Jan walked.

57. $n + 8$

59. $\frac{1}{2}x$ or $\frac{x}{2}$

61. $2a - 1$

63. $2t - 30$

65. $1.2p + 20$

67. $80,000 - m$

69. $2r - 673$

71. $10x$

73. $100d$

75. $45 + 0.40x$

77. $s + 0.20s$

79. $e - 0.12e$

81. $c + 0.07c$

83. $m - 0.313m$

85. If $f =$ Frieda's weight, then $(f + 15) =$ Jennifer's weight. The sum of their weights is $f + (f + 15)$.

87. If $l =$ Luis' height, then $(2l - 1)$ is Armando's height. The difference in their heights is $(2l - 1) - l$.

89. If $n =$ the larger number, then $(3n - 40) =$ the smaller number. Their difference is $n - (3n - 40)$.

91. If $w =$ the younger child's weight, then $(2w - 3)$ = the weight of the older child. The sum of their weights is $w + (2w - 3)$.

93. If $r =$ the area of Rhode Island, then $(479r + 462)$ = the area of Alaska. The sum of their areas is $r + (479r + 462)$.

95. If $n =$ the cost of the bank stock, then $(n + 0.06n)$ = the price of Apple stock. Their sum is $n + (n + 0.06n)$.

97. If $a =$ the assets of the bank in 2005, then $(a - 0.023a) =$ the assets of the bank in 2006. Their difference in assets is $a - (a - 0.023a)$.

99. Let $x =$ one number, then $4x =$ second number. First number + second number = 20
$x + 4x = 20$

101. Let $x =$ smaller integer, then $x + 1 =$ larger consecutive integer. Smaller + larger $= 41$
$x + (x + 1) = 41$

103. Let x = the number.
Twice the number decreased by 8 is 12.
$2x - 8 = 12$

105. Let x = the number.
One-fifth of the sum of the number and 10 is 150.
$\frac{1}{5}(x + 10) = 150$

107. Let x = smaller consecutive even integer.
Then $x + 2$ = larger consecutive even integer.

smaller + twice larger = 22
$x + 2(x + 2) = 22$

109. $12.50h = 150$

111. $2.99x = 17.94$

113. $25q = 175$

115. Let a = Julie's age.
Then Darla's age = $2a + 1$
Julie's age + Darla's age = 52
$a + (2a + 1) = 52$

117. Let s = the number of cards Saul owns.
Then $(2s + 300)$ = the number of cards Jakob owns.
Their difference is equal to 420.
$(2s + 300) - s = 420$

119. Let s = the distance traveled by the Southern Pacific train.
Then $(2s - 4)$ = the distance traveled by the Amtrak train.
Their sum is equal to 890.
$s + (2s - 4) = 890$

121. Let m = the number of miles Malik walked.
Then $(3m - 2)$ = the number of miles Donna walked.
Their sum is equal to 12.6

$m + (3m - 2) = 12.6$

123. Let c = the cost of the car.
The new price is $89,900 after a 2.3% increase.
$c + 0.023c = 89,900$

125. Let p = the population of the town.
The town decreased by 1.9% to 12,087.
$p - 0.019p = 12,087$

127. Let c = the cost of the car.
When 7% sales tax was added the car increased in price to $32,600.
$c + 0.07c = 32,600$

129. Let c = the cost of the meal.
When the 15% tip was added the price increased to $42.50.
$c + 0.15c = 42.50$

131. a. 1 minute = 60 seconds
1 hour = 60 minutes = 3600 seconds
1 day = 24 hours
$\phantom{1 \text{ day}} = 1440$ minutes
$\phantom{1 \text{ day}} = 86{,}400$ seconds
$86{,}400d + 3600h + 60m + s$

b. $86{,}400d + 3600h + 60m + s$
$= 86{,}400(4) + 3600(6) + 60(15) + 25$
$= 368{,}125$ seconds

133. Let s = amount of weekly sales.
$200 + 0.05s = 100 + 0.08s$

134. $3\left[(4 - 16) \div 2\right] + 5^2 - 3$
$= 3\left[(-12) \div 2\right] + 25 - 3$
$= 3(-6) + 25 - 3$
$= -18 + 25 - 3$
$= 7 - 3$
$= 4$

135. Substitute 40 for P and 5 for w.
$P = 2l + 2w$
$40 = 2l + 2(5)$
$40 = 2l + 10$
$30 = 2l$
$15 = l$

136. $3x - 2y = 6$
$3x - 3x - 2y = -3x + 6$
$-2y = -3x + 6$
$\dfrac{-2y}{-2} = \dfrac{-3x + 6}{-2}$
$y = \dfrac{3x - 6}{2}$
$y = \dfrac{3}{2}x - 3$

137. $\dfrac{3.6}{x} = \dfrac{10}{7}$
$3.6 \cdot 7 = 10 \cdot x$
$25.2 = 10x$
$\dfrac{25.2}{10} = \dfrac{10x}{10}$
$2.52 = x$

138.
$$2x - 4 > 3$$
$$2x - 4 + 4 > 3 + 4$$
$$2x > 7$$
$$\frac{2x}{2} > \frac{7}{2}$$
$$x > \frac{7}{2}$$

Exercise Set 3.2

1. Answers will vary.

3. Let n = a number
$$4n - 3 = 17$$
$$4n = 20$$
$$n = 5$$
The number is 5.

5. Let x = smaller integer, then
$x + 1$ = next consecutive integer.
Smaller number + larger number = 87.
$$x + (x + 1) = 87$$
$$2x + 1 = 87$$
$$2x = 86$$
$$x = 43$$
Smaller number = 43
Larger number = $x + 1 = 43 + 1 = 44$

7. Let x = smaller odd integer, then
$x + 2$ = next consecutive odd integer.
Sum of integers = 96.
$$x + (x + 2) = 96$$
$$2x + 2 = 96$$
$$2x = 94$$
$$x = 47$$
Smaller integer = 47
Larger integer = 47 + 2 = 49

9. Let x = one number.
Then $2x + 3$ = second number.
First number + second number = 27
$$x + (2x + 3) = 27$$
$$3x + 3 = 27$$
$$3x = 24$$
$$x = 8$$
First number = 8
Second number = $2x + 3 = 2(8) + 3 = 19$

11. Let x = the smaller number.
Then the larger number = $5x - 4$.
Larger number – smaller number = 4
$$(5x - 4) - x = 4$$
$$5x - 4 - x = 4$$
$$4x - 4 = 4$$
$$4x = 8$$
$$x = 2$$
The smaller number is 2 and the larger number is $5(2) - 4 = 6$.

13. Let x = smaller integer, then
larger integer = $2x - 8$.
Larger integer – Smaller integer = 17
$$(2x - 8) - x = 17$$
$$2x - 8 - x = 17$$
$$x - 8 = 17$$
$$x = 25$$
Smaller number = 25
Larger number $= 2x - 8 = 2(25) - 8 = 42$

15. Let x = the number of baseball cards given to Richey, then $3x$ = number of baseball cards given to Erin.
Number of cards given to Richey + Number of cards given to Erin = 260
$$x + 3x = 260$$
$$4x = 260$$
$$4x = 260$$
$$x = 65$$
Grandma gave 65 baseball cards to Richey.

17. Let x = the number of hours it takes to build a horse, then $(2x + 1.4)$ = the number of hours it takes to attach the gloves to the horse.
Time to build horse + Time to attach gloves to horse = 32.6
$$x + (2x + 1.4) = 32.6$$
$$3x + 1.4 = 32.6$$
$$3x = 31.2$$
$$x = 10.4$$
$2x + 1.4 = 2(10.4) + 1.4 = 22.3$
It took him 22.2 hours to attach the gloves to the horse.

19. Let x = the number of weeks, then $6x$ = the amount she wishes to add to her collection over x weeks.
Amount started with in collection + Amount added each week to the collection over x weeks = Total number in collection
$$422 + 6x = 500$$
$$6x = 78$$

$x = 13$

It will take her about 13 weeks to get 500 frogs in her collection.

21. Let x = the number of years, then $250x$ = the number of employees retiring after x years.
Current amount of employees – Employees retiring after x years = Future total employees
$4600 - 250x = 2200$

$$-250x = -2400$$

$$x = 9.6$$

In 9.6 years the total employment will be 2200.

23. Let x = the average number of tornados in December, then $(11x - 16)$ = the average number of tornados in June.
Number of tornados in June – Number of tornados in December = 204

$$(11x - 16) - x = 204$$
$$11x - 16 - x = 204$$
$$10x - 16 = 204$$
$$10x = 220$$
$$x = 22$$

There was an average of 22 tornados in December and $11(22) - 16 = 226$ in June.

25. Let x = the average hourly wage paid to housekeepers in New Orleans, then $(2x + 1.46)$ = the average hourly wage paid to housekeepers in New York City.
Wage of housekeepers in New York – Wage of housekeepers in New Orleans = 8.10

$$(2x + 1.46) - x = 8.10$$
$$2x + 1.46 - x = 8.10$$
$$x + 1.46 = 8.10$$
$$x = 6.64$$

The average hourly wages paid to a housekeeper in New York City is $2(6.64) + 1.46 = \$14.74$.

27. Let x = the cost to produce a shirt in Northern China, then $(3x - 0.16)$ = the cost to produce a shirt in Mexico.

Cost to produce a shirt in Northern China + the cost to produce a shirt in Mexico = 3.28
$$x + (3x - 0.16) = 3.28$$
$$x + 3x - 0.16 = 3.28$$
$$4x - 0.16 = 3.28$$
$$4x = 3.44$$
$$x = 0.86$$

The cost to produce a shirt in Northern China is

$0.86 and the cost to produce a shirt in Mexico is $3(0.86) + 0.16 = \$2.42$.

29. Let x = number of gallons of gasoline that Luis can purchase.
(Cost per gallon) (Price per gallon) = Total cost
$3.20x = 48$

$$x = 15$$

Luis can purchase 15 gallons of gasoline.

31. Let x the number of copies made, then $0.02x$ = the cost to make x number of copies.
Cost of machine + Cost of copies made = Total cost
$2100 + 0.02x = 2462$
$$0.02x = 362$$
$$x = 18,100$$

In one year, 18,100 copies were made.

33. Let x = the number of On Demand movies watched, then $3.95x$ = the cost to watch x On Demand movies.
Cost for Cable + Additional fee for On Demand movies = 96.38
$72.68 + 3.95x = 96.38$
$$3.95x = 23.70$$
$$x = 6$$

He watched 6 movies.

35. Let x = number of miles driven, then $20 + 0.25x$ = American rental fee and $35 + 0.15x$ = SavMor rental fee.
American rental fee = SavMor rental fee
$20 + 0.25x = 35 + 0.15x$
$$20 + 0.10x = 35$$
$$0.10x = 15$$
$$x = 150$$

Driving 150 miles would result in both plans having the same total cost.

37. Let x = number of years until the salaries are the same
yearly salary = base salary + (yearly increase) · (number of years)
yearly salary at Data Tech. = yearly salary at Nuteck
$40,000 + 2400x = 49,600 + 800x$
$$40,000 + 1600x = 49,600$$
$$1600x = 9600$$
$$x = 6$$

It will take 6 years for the two salaries to be the same.

39. Let x = the number of pages, then $0.06x$ = the cost of printing x pages on the HP and $0.08x$ = the cost of printing x pages on the Lexmark.
Cost of the HP printer + Cost of printing x pages on the

HP = Cost of the Lexmark printer + Cost of printing x pages on the Lexmark
$$499 + 0.06x = 419 + 0.08x$$
$$499 = 419 + 0.02x$$
$$80 = 0.02x$$
$$4000 = x$$
For the two printers to have the same cost, 4000 pages would have to be printed.

41. Let x = the number of envelopes used, then $0.39x$ = the mailing cost.
Printing cost + Mailing cost = Total cost
$$600 + 0.39x = 1380$$
$$0.39x = 780$$
$$x = 2000$$
There were 2000 newsletters mailed.

43. Let x = the cost of the flight before tax, then $0.07x$ = the sales tax on the flight.
Cost of flight before tax + Sales tax on flight = Total cost
$$x + 0.07x = 280$$
$$1.07x = 280$$
$$x = 261.68$$
The cost of the flight before taxes was $261.68.

45. Let x = Zhen's present salary, then $x + 0.30x$ = Zhen's salary at his new job.
New salary = 30,200
$$x + 0.30x = 30,200$$
$$1.3x = 30,200$$
$$x = 23230.77$$
Zhen's present salary is $23,230.77.

47. Let x = the number of bushels of oysters harvested in 2001, then $x - 0.93x$ = the number of bushels of oysters harvested in 2004.
The number of bushels of oysters harvested in 2004 = 26,000
$$x - 0.93x = 26,000$$
$$0.07x = 26,000$$
$$x \approx 371,428.57$$
About 371 thousand bushels were harvested in 2001.

49. Let x = total amount collected at door;
3000 + 3% of admission fees = total amount received.
$$3000 + 0.03x = 3750$$
$$0.03x = 750$$
$$x = \frac{7.50}{0.03} = 25,000$$
The total amount collected at the door was $25,000.

51. Let x = average salary before wage cut.
(average salary before cut) – (decrease in salary) = average salary after wage cut
$$x - 0.02x = 38,600$$
$$0.98x = 38,600$$
$$x \approx 39,387.76$$
The average salary before the wage cut was $39,387.76.

53. Let x = the average salary of a graduate with a Bachelor's degree, then $x - 0.246x$ = the average salary of a graduate with an Associate's degree.
Average salary of a graduate with an Associate's degree = 37,600
$$x - 0.246x = 37,600$$
$$0.754x = 37,600$$
$$x \approx 49,867.374$$
The average salary of a graduate with a Bachelor's degree is about $49,867.

55. Let x = the amount of sales in dollars, then $600 + 0.02x$ = Plan 1 salary and $0.10x$ = Plan 2 salary.
Plan 1 salary = Plan 2 salary
$$600 + 0.02x = 0.10x$$
$$600 = 0.08x$$
$$7500 = x$$
Sales of $7,500 will result in the same salary from both plans.

57. Let x = the number of pages in the second edition, then $x - 0.04x$ = the number of pages in the third edition.
Number of pages in the third edition = 480
$$x - 0.04x = 480$$
$$0.96x = 480$$
$$x = 500$$
There were 500 pages in the second edition.

59. Let x = the amount of sales in dollars, then $400 + 0.02x$ = Plan 1 salary and $250 + 0.16x$ = Plan 2 salary.
Plan 1 salary = Plan 2 salary
$$400 + 0.02x = 250 + 0.16x$$
$$400 = 250 + 0.14x$$
$$150 = 0.14x$$
$$1071.43 = x$$
Sales of $1071.43 will result in the same salary from both plans.

61. Let x = maximum price of meal she can afford, then amount of tax = $0.07x$ and amount of tip = $0.15x$.
Price of meal + tax + tip = 30
$$x + 0.07x + 0.15x = 30$$

$$1.22x = 30$$
$$x \approx 24.59$$
The maximum price she can afford for a meal is $24.59.

63. Let x = the amount in dollars Phil's daughter receives, then $x + 0.25x$ = amount in dollars Phil's wife receives.
Daughter's share + Wife's share = $140,000
$$x + (x + 0.25x) = 140,000$$
$$2x + 0.25x = 140,000$$
$$2,25x = 140,000$$
$$x = 62,222.22$$
$$x + 0.25x = 62,222.22 + (0.25)(62,222.22)$$
$$= 77,777.78$$
Phil's wife will receive $77,777.78.

65. a. $\dfrac{74 + 88 + 76 + x}{4} = 80$

b. $\dfrac{74 + 88 + 76 + x}{4} = 80$
$$74 + 88 + 76 + x = 320$$
$$238 + x = 320$$
$$x = 82$$
Paul must receive an 82 on his fourth exam.

67. $4\left[(4-6) \div 2\right] + 3^2 - 1$
$$= 4\left[(-2) \div 2\right] + 9 - 1$$
$$= 4\left[-1\right] + 9 - 1$$
$$= -4 + 9 - 1$$
$$= 4$$

68. Commutative property of addition

69. $A = \dfrac{1}{2}bh$
$$2A = 2\left(\dfrac{1}{2}bh\right)$$
$$2A = bh$$
$$\dfrac{2A}{b} = \dfrac{bh}{b}$$
$$\dfrac{2A}{b} = h$$

70. $\dfrac{4.5}{6} = \dfrac{9}{x}$
$$4.5 \cdot x = 6 \cdot 9$$
$$4.5x = 54$$
$$x = 12$$

Mid-Chapter Test: Sections 3.1-3.2

1. $6w$

2. $3h + 5$

3. $c + 0.20c$

4. Let m = number of miles driven, then $0.25m$ = total mileage cost. The total rental cost is $(40 + 0.25m)$.

5. $50n$

6. $25 - x$

7. $(c - 25)$ would be the cost of the item minus $25. The cost of an item at a 25% off sale would be $(c - 0.25c)$.

8. x = the length of the Poison Dart frog

9. If p = the distance Pedro traveled, then $(4p + 6)$ = the distance Mary traveled.

10. Let v = the value of a car in 2006, then $(v - 0.18v)$ = the value of the car in 2005. Car value in 2006 − Car value in 2005 = $v - (v - 0.18v)$.

11. Let p = the original population of Cedar Oaks, then $0.12p$ = the amount of increase in the population.
Original population + the increase in population = 38,619
$$p + 0.12p = 38,619$$

12. Let x = the smaller integer and $(x + 2)$ = the larger consecutive odd integer.
Smaller integer + 3 times the larger is 26.
$$x + 3(x + 2) = 26$$

13. Let x = the smaller integer, then $(x + 1)$ = the larger consecutive integer.
Smaller integer + Larger integer = 93
$$x + (x + 1) = 93$$
$$x + x + 1 = 93$$
$$2x + 1 = 93$$
$$2x = 92$$
$$x = 46$$
The smaller integer is 46 and the larger is $(46 + 1) = 47$.

14. Let x = the smaller integer, then $(3x - 1)$ = the larger integer.
Larger integer − Smaller integer = 7

$$(3x-1)-x=7$$
$$3x-1-x=7$$
$$2x-1=7$$
$$2x=8$$
$$x=4$$

The smaller number is 4 and the larger is $3(4) - 1 = 11$.

15. Let x = the number of days of production, then $20x$ = the increased production.
Original production + Increase = 600
$$240+20x=600$$
$$20x=360$$
$$x=18$$
It will take 18 days for production to reach 600 boxes daily.

16. Let h = the number of hours tennis is played, then $4h$ = the court cost at Dale's and $8h$ = the court cost at Abel's.
Total cost at Dale's = Total cost at Abel's
$$90+4h=30+8h$$
$$90=30+4h$$
$$60=4h$$
$$15=h$$
Kristina would have to play 15 hours of tennis a month for the total cost to be the same at both clubs.

17. Let c = the cost of the television, then $0.07c$ = the amount of sales tax.
Cost of the television + Sales tax = Total cost
$$c+0.07c=749$$
$$1.07c=749$$
$$c=700$$
The cost of the television before sales tax was $700.

18. Let c = the number of clients that Betty has, then $(2c + 12)$ = the number of clients that Anita has.
Clients of Betty + Clients of Anita = 600
$$c+(2c+12)=600$$
$$c+2c+12=600$$
$$3c+12=600$$
$$3c=588$$
$$c=196$$
Betty has 196 clients and Anita has $2(196) + 12 = 404$ clients.

19. Let m = the number of miles driven, then $0.18m$ = the mileage cost.
Truck cost + Mileage cost = Total cost

$$36+0.18m=45.36$$
$$0.18m=9.36$$
$$m=52$$
There were 52 miles driven that day.

20. Let s = the amount of sales, then $0.08s$ = the commission from Plan 1 and $0.06s$ = the commission from Plan 2.
Total salary from Plan 1 = Total salary from Plan 2
$$200+0.08s=300+0.06s$$
$$200+0.02s=300$$
$$0.02s=100$$
$$s=5000$$
He must make $5,000 in sales per week for the two plans to have the same total salary.

Exercise Set 3.3

1. $A=(2l)\cdot\left(\dfrac{w}{2}\right)=lw$

The area remains the same

3. $V=2l\cdot 2w\cdot 2h=8(lwh)$
The volume is eight times as great.

5. $A=\pi r^2=\pi(3r)^2=\pi(9r^2)=9\pi r^2$
The area is nine times as great.

7. An isosceles triangle is a triangle with 2 equal sides.

9. The sum of the measures of the angles in a triangle is 180°.

11. Let x = the measure of the two equal angles, then $x + 42$ = the measure of the third angle.
Sum of the three angles = 180°
$$x+x+(x+42)=180$$
$$3x+42=180$$
$$3x=138$$
$$x=46$$
The two equal angles are each 46°. The third angle is $x + 42° = 46° + 42° = 88°$.

13. Let x = length of each side of the triangle, then $P = x + x + x = 3x$.
Perimeter = 34.5
$$3x=34.5$$
$$x=11.5$$
The length of each side is 11.5 inches.

15. Let x = measure of angle B. Then
$2x + 21$ = measure of angle A.
Sum of the 2 angles = 90
$$x + (2x + 21) = 90$$
$$3x + 21 = 90$$
$$3x = 69$$
$$x = 23$$
Measure of angle $A = 2(23) + 21 = 67°$
Measure of angle $B = 23°$

17. Let x = measure of angle A, then
$3x - 8$ = measure of angle B.
Sum of the 2 angles = 180
$$x + (3x - 8) = 180$$
$$4x - 8 = 180$$
$$4x = 188$$
$$x = \frac{188}{4} = 47$$
Measure of angle $A = 47°$
Measure of angle $B = 3(47) - 8 = 141 - 8 = 133°$

19. The two angles have equal measures.
$$2x + 50 = 4x + 12$$
$$38 = 2x$$
$$19 = x$$
$2x + 50 = 2(19) + 50 = 38 + 50 = 88°$
$4x + 12 = 4(19) + 12 = 76 + 12 = 88°$
Each angle measures 88°.

21. Let x = measure of smallest angle. Then second
angle = $x + 10$ and third angle = $2x - 30$.
Sum of the 3 angles = 180
$$x + (x + 10) + (2x - 30) = 180$$
$$4x - 20 = 180$$
$$4x = 200$$
$$x = 50$$
The first angle is 50°.
The second angle is 50 + 10 = 60°.
The third angle is 2(50) − 30 = 70°.

23. Let x = width of rectangle. Then $x + 6$ = length
of rectangle.
$$P = 2l + 2w$$
$$44 = 2(x + 6) + 2x$$
$$44 = 2x + 12 + 2x$$
$$44 = 4x + 12$$
$$32 = 4x$$
$$8 = x$$
Width is 8 feet and length is 8 + 6 = 14 feet.

25. Let x = width of tennis court.
Then $2x + 6$ = length of tennis court.
$$P = 2l + 2w$$
$$228 = 2(2x + 6) + 2x$$
$$228 = 4x + 12 + 2x$$
$$228 = 6x + 12$$
$$216 = 6x$$
$$36 = x$$
The width is 36 feet and the length is
$2(36) + 6 = 78$ feet.

27. Let x = measure of each smaller angle.
Then $3x - 20$ = measure of each larger angle.
(measure of the two smaller angles) + (measure
of the two larger angles) = 360°
$$x + x + (3x - 20) + (3x - 20) = 360$$
$$8x - 40 = 360$$
$$8x = 400$$
$$x = 50$$
Each smaller angle is 50°. Each larger angle is
$3(50) - 20 = 130°$.

29. Let x = measure of each smaller angle, then $5x$ =
measure of each larger angle.
(measure of the two smaller angles) + (measure
of the two larger angles) = 360°
$$x + x + 5x + 5x = 360$$
$$12x = 360$$
$$x = 30$$
Each smaller angle is 30°.
Each larger angle is 5(30) = 150°.

31. Let x = measure of the smallest angle.
Then $x + 10$ = measure of the second angle,
$2x + 14$ = measure of third angle, and
$x + 21$ = measure of fourth angle.
Sum of the four angles = 360°
$$x + (x + 10) + (2x + 14) + (x + 21) = 360$$
$$5x + 45 = 360$$
$$5x = 315$$
$$x = 63$$
Thus the angles are 63°, 63 + 10 = 73°
2(63) + 14 = 140° and 63 + 21 = 84°.

33. Let x = width of bookcase shelf.
Then $x + 3$ = height of bookcase.
4 shelves + 2 sides = total lumber available.

$$4x + 2(x + 3) = 30$$
$$4x + 2x + 6 = 30$$
$$6x + 6 = 30$$
$$6x = 24$$
$$x = 4$$

The width of each shelf is 4 feet and the height is $4 + 3 = 7$ feet.

35. Let x = length of a shelf.
Then $2x$ = height of bookcase.
4 shelves + 2 sides = total lumber available
$$4x + 2(2x) = 20$$
$$4x + 4x = 20$$
$$8x = 20$$
$$x = \frac{20}{8} = 2.5$$

The width of the bookcase is 2.5 feet. The height of the bookcase is $2(2.5) = 5$ feet.

37. Let x = width of fenced in area.
Then $x + 5$ = length of fenced in area
Five "widths" + one "length" = total fencing
$$5x + (x + 5) = 71$$
$$6x + 5 = 71$$
$$6x = 66$$
$$x = 11$$
Width is 11 feet and length is $11 + 5 = 16$ feet.

39. $ac + ad + bc + bd$

41. $-|-6| < |-4|$ since $-|-6| = -6$ and $|-4| = 4$

42. $|-3| > -|3|$ since $|-3| = 3$ and $-|3| = -3$

43. $-8 - (-2) + (-4) = -8 + 2 + (-4)$
$$= -6 + (-4)$$
$$= -10$$

44. $-7y + x - 3(x - 2) + 2y$
$$= -7y + x - 3x + 6 + 2y$$
$$= x - 3x - 7y + 2y + 6$$
$$= -2x - 5y + 6$$

45. $6x + 3y = 9$
$$6x - 6x + 3y = -6x + 9$$
$$3y = -6x + 9$$
$$\frac{3y}{3} = \frac{-6x + 9}{3}$$
$$y = \frac{-6x + 9}{3} \text{ or } y = -2x + 3$$

Exercise Set 3.4

1. Let t = time in hours it will take the ferries to be 6 miles apart.

Ferry	Rate	Time	Distance
Cat	34	t	$34t$
Bird	28	t	$28t$

$$34t - 28t = 6$$
$$6t = 6$$
$$t = 1$$

In 1 hour the two ferries will be 6 miles apart.

3. Let r = Abe's rate of speed..

Person	Rate	Time	Distance
Jodi	8	2	16
Abe	r	2	$2r$

$$16 - 2r = 4$$
$$-2r = -12$$
$$r = 6$$

Abe was traveling at 6 mph.

5. Let t be the time it takes for the planes to pass each other.

Plane	Rate	Time	Distance
Jet Blue	560	t	$560t$
SW	580	t	$580t$

$$560t + 580t = 821$$
$$1140t = 821$$
$$t \approx 0.72$$

It will take about 0.72 hours for the planes to pass each other.

7. Let t be the time it takes for Willie and Shanna to be 16.8 miles apart.

Person	Rate	Time	Distance
Willie	3	t	$3t$
Shanna	4	t	$4t$

$$3t + 4t = 16.8$$
$$7t = 16.8$$
$$t = 2.4$$

It will take 2.4 hours.

9. Let r be the second rate of the machine.

Machine	Rate	Time	Distance
First	60	7.2	432
Second	r	6.8	$6.8r$

$$432 + 6.8r = 908$$
$$6.8r = 476$$
$$r = 70$$

The second speed the machine was set at was 70 miles per hour.

11. Let t be the time it takes for the waves to be 80 miles apart.

Wave	Rate	Time	Distance
p-wave	3.6	t	$3.6t$
s-wave	1.8	t	$1.8t$

$$3.6t - 1.8t = 80$$
$$1.8t = 80$$
$$t \approx 44.4$$

It will take approximately 44.4 seconds.

13. Let r be the speed of the cutter coming from the east (westbound). Then $r + 5$ is the speed of the cutter coming from the west (eastbound).

Cutter	Rate	Time	Distance
Eastbound	$r + 5$	3	$3(r + 5)$
Westbound	r	3	$3r$

$$3(r + 5) + 3r = 225$$
$$3r + 15 + 3r = 225$$
$$6r = 210$$
$$r = 35$$

The speed of the westbound cutter is 35 mph and the speed of the eastbound cutter is 40 mph.

15. Let t be amount of time Samia walked for before she turned around.

Trip	Rate	Time	Distance
In	4	t	$4t$
Out	3.2	$t + 0.5$	$3.2(t + 0.5)$

$$4t + 3.2(t + 0.5) = 6$$
$$4t + 3.2t + 1.6 = 6$$
$$7.2t = 4.4$$
$$t \approx 0.61$$

Samia walked 0.61 hours before she turned around.

17. Let r be the rate of the slower crew. Then $r + 0.75$ is the rate of the faster crew.

Crew	Rate	Ti•e	Distance
Slow	r	3.2	$3.2r$
Fast	$r + 0.75$	3.2	$3.2(r + 0.75)$

$$3.2r + 3.2(r + 0.75) = 12$$
$$3.2r + 3.2r + 2.4 = 12$$
$$6.4r = 9.6$$
$$r = 1.5$$

One crew works at a rate of 1.5 miles/day, and the other crew works at a rate of 2.25 miles/day.

19. Let r be the rate of *Apollo*. Then $r + 4$ is the rate of *Pythagoras*.

Boat	Rate	Time	Distance
Apollo	r	0.7	$0.7r$
Pythagoras	$r + 4$	0.7	$0.7(r + 4)$

$$0.7r + 0.7(r + 4) = 9.8$$
$$0.7r + 0.7r + 2.8 = 9.8$$
$$1.4r = 7$$
$$r = 5$$

The speed of *Apollo* is 5 mph, and the speed of *Pythagoras* is 9 mph.

21. Let t = time, in hours, Betty was traveling at 50 mph.

Speed	Rate	Time	Distance
Faster	70 mph	$t - 0.5$	$70(t - 0.5)$
Slower	50 mph	t	$50t$

$$50t - 70t + 35 = 5$$
$$-20t = -30$$
$$t = 1.5$$

Betty traveled for 1.5 hours at 50 mph.

23. a. Distance = rate × time = $(2.31)(1.04) \approx 2.4$ miles

   b. Distance = rate × time = $(23.0)(4.87) \approx 112.0$ miles

   c. Distance = rate × time = $(8.45)(3.1) \approx 26.2$ miles

   d. $2.4 + 112.0 + 26.2 = 140.6$ miles

   e. $1.04 + 4.87 + 3.10 = 9.01$ hours

25. Let x be the amount invested at 5%. Then $12,000 - x$ is the amount invested at 7%.

Principal	Rate	Time	Interest
x	5%	1	$0.05x$
$12,000 - x$	7%	1	$0.07(12,000 - x)$

$$0.05x + 0.07(12,000 - x) = 800$$
$$0.05x + 840 - 0.07x = 800$$
$$-0.02x = -40$$
$$x = 2000$$

They invested $2000 at 5% and $10,000 at 7%.

27. Let x be the amount invested at 6%. Then $6000 - x$ is the amount invested at 4%.

Principal	Rate	Time	Interest
x	6%	1	$0.06x$
$6000 - x$	4%	1	$0.04(6000 - x)$

$$0.06x = 0.04(6000 - x)$$
$$0.06x = 240 - 0.04x$$
$$0.10x = 240$$
$$x = 2400$$

She invested $2400 at 6% and $3600 at 4%.

29. Let x be the amount invested at 4%. Then $10,000 - x$ is the amount invested at 5%.

Principal	Rate	Time	Interest
x	4%	1	$0.04x$
$10,000 - x$	5%	1	$0.05(10,000 - x)$

$$0.05(10,000 - x) - 0.04x = 320$$
$$500 - 0.05x - 0.04x = 320$$
$$-0.09x = -180$$
$$x = 2000$$

She invested $2000 at 4% and $8000 at 5%.

31. Let t be the time, in months, during which Patricia paid $17.10 per month. Then $12 - t$ is the time during which she paid $18.40 per month.

Rate	Time	Amount
17.10	t	$17.10t$
18.40	$12 - t$	$18.40(12 - t)$

$$17.10t + 18.40(12 - t) = 207.80$$
$$17.10t + 220.80 - 18.40t = 207.80$$
$$-1.30t = -13$$
$$t = 10$$

She paid $17.10 for the first 10 months of the year, and paid $18.40 for the remainder of the year. The rate increase took effect in November.

33. Let x be the number of hours worked at Home Depot ($6.50 per hour). Then $18 - x$ is the number of hours worked at the veterinary clinic ($7.00 per hour).

Rate	Hours	Total
$6.50	x	$6.5x$
$7.00	$18 - x$	$7(18 - x)$

$$6.5x + 7(18 - x) = 122$$
$$6.5x + 126 - 7x = 122$$
$$-0.5x = -4$$
$$x = 8$$

Mihály worked 8 hours at Home Depot and 10 hours at the clinic.

35. Let x be the number of adults who went to the Baseball Hall of Fame. Then $2100 - x$ is the number of children who attended.

	Price	Number	Total
Adults	14.50	x	$14.50x$
Children	5.00	$2100 - x$	$5.00(2100 - x)$

$$14.5x + 5(2100 - x) = 21,900$$
$$14.5x + 10,500 - 5x = 21,900$$
$$9.5x = 11,400$$
$$x = 1200$$

So, there were 1200 adults at the Baseball Hall of Fame.

37. a. Let x be the number of shares of Nike. Then $5x$ is the number of shares of Kellogg.

Stock	Price	Shares	Total
Nike	78	x	$78x$
Kellogg	33	$5x$	$33(5)x$

$$78x + 33(5x) = 10,000$$
$$78x + 165x = 10,000$$
$$244x = 10,000$$
$$x \approx 40.98$$

Since only whole shares can be purchased, he will purchase 41 shares of Nike and 205 shares of Kellogg.

  b. Mike spent $41(78) + 205(33) = \$9963$.
He has $\$10,000 - \$9963 = \$37$ left over.

39. Let x be the number of pounds of almonds. Then $30 - x$ is the number of pounds of walnuts.

Nut	Cost	Pounds	Total
Almond	6.40	x	$6.40x$
Walnut	6.80	$30 - x$	$6.8(30 - x)$
Mixture	6.65	30	199.50

$$6.4x + 6.8(30 - x) = 199.50$$
$$6.4x + 204 - 6.8x = 199.50$$
$$-0.4x = -4.5$$
$$x = 11.25$$

So, 11.25 pounds of almonds should be mixed with 18.75 pounds of walnuts.

41. Let x be the amount of topsoil in cubic yards.

Soil Type	Cost	Amount	Total
Strained	160	x	$160x$
Unstrained	120	$8 - x$	$120(8 - x)$
Mixture	150	8	$150(8)$

$$160x + 120(8 - x) = 150(8)$$
$$160x + 960 - 120x = 1200$$
$$40x + 960 = 1200$$
$$40x = 240$$
$$x = 6$$

He should mix 6 cubic yards of the strained with 2 cubic yards of the unstrained.

43. Let x be the cost per pound of the mixture.

Type	Cost	Pounds	Total
Good & Plenty	2.49	3	$2.49(3)$
Sweet Treats	2.89	5	$2.89(5)$
Mixture	x	8	$8x$

$$2.49(3) + 2.89(5) = 8x$$
$$7.47 + 14.45 = 8x$$
$$21.92 = 8x$$
$$2.74 = x$$

The mixture should sell for $2.74 per pound.

45. Let x be the percentage of alcohol in the mixture.

Percentage	Liters	Amount of Alcohol
12%	5	0.6
9%	2	0.18
$x\%$	7	$\left(\frac{x}{100}\right) \cdot 7$

$$\left(\frac{x}{100}\right) \cdot 7 = 0.6 + 0.18$$
$$0.07x = 0.78$$
$$x \approx 11.1$$

The alcohol content of the mixture is about 11.1%.

47. Let x be the amount of 12% sulfuric acid solution.

Solution	Strength	Liters	Amount
20%	0.20	1	0.20
12%	0.12	x	$0.12x$
Mixture	0.15	$x+1$	$0.15(x+1)$

$$0.20 + 0.12x = 0.15(x+1)$$
$$0.20 + 0.12x = 0.15x + 0.15$$
$$-0.03x = -0.05$$
$$x = \frac{5}{3}$$

$1\frac{2}{3}$ liters of 12% sulfuric acid should be used.

49. Let x be the percentage of alcohol in the mixture.

Brand	Percentage	Ounces	Amount
Listerine	21.6%	6	$(0.216)\cdot 6$
Scope	15%	4	$(0.15)\cdot 4$
Mixture	$x\%$	10	$\left(\frac{x}{100}\right)\cdot 10$

$$(0.216)\cdot 6 + (0.15)\cdot 4 = \left(\frac{x}{100}\right)\cdot 10$$
$$1.296 + 0.6 = \frac{x}{10}$$
$$1.896 = \frac{x}{10}$$
$$18.96 = x$$

The mixture has an 18.96% alcohol content.

51. Let x be the percent of orange juice in the new mixture.

Percent	Quarts	Orange Juice
12%	6	0.72
x	$6\frac{1}{2}$	$\frac{13}{2}x$

$$\frac{13}{2}x = 0.72$$
$$x \approx 0.111$$

The new mixture consists of about 11.1% orange juice.

53. Let x be the percentage of pure juice before mixing.

Solution	Percentage	Amount of Solution	Amt. of Juice
Concentrate	x	12	$12\left(\frac{x}{100}\right)$
Mixture	10%	48	4.8

$$12\left(\frac{x}{100}\right) = 4.8$$
$$0.12x = 4.8$$
$$x = 40$$

40% of the concentrate is pure juice.

55. Let x be the amount of the Clorox to be added to a 6 cups of of water.

Product	Percentage	Cups	Amount
Clorox	5.25%	x	$(0.0525)x$
Shock Treatment	10.5%	$6-x$	$0.105(6-x)$
Mixture	7.2%	6	$0.072(6)$

$$0.0525x + 0.105(6-x) = 0.072(6)$$
$$0.0525x + 0.63 - 0.105x = 0.432$$
$$-0.0525x = -0.198$$
$$x \approx 3.77$$

The mixture needs about 3.77 cups Clorox and $6 - 3.77 = 2.23$ cups of shock treatment.

57. Let x be the number of pints of 12% alcohol.

Type	Percentage	Pints	Amount
12% concen.	12%	x	$0.12x$
5% concen.	5%	15	$0.05(15)$
Mixture	8%	$x+15$	$0.08(x+15)$

$$0.12x + 0.05(15) = 0.08(x+15)$$
$$0.12x + 0.75 = 0.08x + 1.2$$
$$0.04x + 0.75 = 1.2$$
$$0.04x = 0.45$$
$$x = 11.25$$

The mixture should consist of 11.25 pints of the 12% alcohol.

59. The time it takes for the transport to make the trip is:

$$\text{Time} = \frac{\text{Distance}}{\text{Rate}} = \frac{1720}{370} \approx 4.65 \text{ hours}$$

The time it takes for the Hornets to make the trip is: $\text{Time} = \frac{\text{Distance}}{\text{Rate}} = \frac{1720}{900} \approx 1.91$ hours

It takes the transport $4.65 - 1.91 = 2.74$ hours longer to make the trip. Since it needs to arrive 3 hours before the Hornets, it should leave about $2.74 + 3 = 5.74$ hours before them.

61. We must find the time it takes for the car to travel 100 feet.

$$d = rt$$
$$100 = 5.88t$$
$$17 = t$$

It takes the car 17 seconds to go 100 feet. This will allow us to find out how fast the garage door needs to open.

$$d = rt$$
$$6 = r(17)$$
$$0.35 \approx r$$

It must open at 0.35 feet per second.

62. a. $2\frac{3}{4} \div 1\frac{5}{8} = \frac{11}{4} \div \frac{13}{8}$

$$= \frac{11}{4} \cdot \frac{8}{13}$$

$$= \frac{22}{13} \text{ or } 1\frac{9}{13}$$

b. $2\frac{3}{4} + 1\frac{5}{8} = \frac{11}{4} + \frac{13}{8}$

$$= \frac{22}{8} + \frac{13}{8}$$

$$= \frac{35}{8} \text{ or } 4\frac{3}{8}$$

63. $6(x - 3) = 4x - 18 + 2x$

$$6x - 18 = 6x - 18$$

All real numbers are solutions.

64. $\frac{6}{x} = \frac{72}{9}$

$$6 \cdot 9 = 72x$$

$$54 = 72x$$

$$x = \frac{54}{72} = \frac{3}{4} \text{ or } 0.75$$

65. $3x - 4 \le -4x + 3(x - 1)$

$$3x - 4 \le -4x + 3x - 3$$

$$3x - 4 \le -x - 3$$

$$4x \le 1$$

$$x \le \frac{1}{4}$$

Review Exercises

1. $3n + 7$

2. $1.2g$

3. $d - 0.25d$

4. $16y$

5. $200 - x$

6. Let $d = $ Dino's age, then $7d + 6 = $ Mario's age.

7. Let c be the number of robberies in 2005, then $(c - 0.12c)$ is the amount of robberies in 2006. The difference between the robberies is $c - (c - 0.12c)$.

8. Let n be the larger number, then $(3n - 24)$ is the smaller number. Their difference is 8. The equation is $n - (3n - 24) = 8$.

9. Let $x = $ the smaller number.
Then $x + 8 = $ the larger number.
Smaller number + larger number = 74
$$x + (x + 8) = 74$$
$$2x + 8 = 74$$
$$2x = 66$$
$$x = 33$$
The smaller number is 33 and the larger number is $33 + 8 = 41$.

10. Let $x = $ smaller integer.
Then $x + 1 = $ next consecutive integer.
Smaller number + larger number = 237
$$x + (x + 1) = 237$$
$$2x + 1 = 237$$
$$2x = 236$$
$$x = 118$$
The smaller number is 118 and the larger number is $118 + 1 = 119$.

11. Let $x = $ the smaller integer.
Then $5x + 3 = $ the larger integer
Larger number – smaller number = 31

$$(5x+3)-x=31$$
$$4x+3=31$$
$$4x=28$$
$$x=7$$

The smaller number is 7 and the larger number is $5(7)+3=38$.

12. Let x = cost of car before tax.
Then $0.07x$ = amount of tax.
Cost of car before tax + tax on car
= cost of car after tax
$$x+0.07x=23,260$$
$$1.07x=23,260$$
$$x=\frac{23,260}{1.07}=21,738.32$$
The cost of the car before tax is $21,738.32.

13. Let x = the number of months, then $20x$ = the increase in production of bagels over x months.
Current production + Increase in production =
Future production
$$520+20x=900$$
$$20x=380$$
$$x=19$$
It will take 19 months.

14. Let x = weekly dollar sales that would make total salaries from both companies the same.
The commission at present company
$= 0.03x$ and commission at new company =
$0.08x$
Salary + commission for present company
= salary + commission for new company
$$600+0.03x=500+0.08x$$
$$100+0.03x=0.08x$$
$$100=0.05x$$
$$2000=x$$
Irene's weekly sales would have to be $2000 for the total salaries from both companies to be the same.

15. Let x = original price of camcorder. Then $0.20x$ = reduction.
Original price –reduction = sale price
$$x-0.20x=495$$
$$0.8x=495$$
$$x=618.75$$
The original price of the camcorder was $618.75.

16. Let h = the number of hours for both landscapers to charge the same price.
Two Brothers Nursery = ABC Nursery

$$400+45h=200+65h$$
$$400=200+20h$$
$$200=20h$$
$$10=h$$
It would take 10 hours of labor before the costs from both landscapers would be the same.

17. Let x be the median cost of a house in 2003.
Then $0.117x$ would be the amount of increase.
Median price in 2003 + Amount of increase =
Median price in 2005
$$x+0.117x=191,000$$
$$1.117x=191,000$$
$$x=170,993.73$$
The median cost in 2003 was about $171,000.

18. Let x be the average annual refund in 1980.
Then $4x-282$ is the average annual refund in 2004.
$$4x-282=2454$$
$$4x=2736$$
$$x=684$$
The average annual refund in 1980 was $684.

19. Let x = measure of the smallest angle. Then $x+10$ = measure of second angle and $2x-10$ = measure of third angle.
Sum of the three angles = 180°
$$x+(x+10)+(2x-10)=180$$
$$4x=180$$
$$x=45$$
The angles are 45°, $45+10=55°$, and $2(45)-10=80°$.

20. Let x = measure of the smallest angle. Then $x+10$ = measure of second angle,
$5x$ = measure of third angle,
$4x+20$ = measure of the fourth angle.
Sum of the four angles = 360°
$$x+(x+10)+5x+(4x+20)=360$$
$$11x+30=360$$
$$11x=330$$
$$x=\frac{330}{11}=30$$
The angles are 30°, $30+10=40°$.
$5(30)=150°$, and $4(30)+20=140°$.

21. Let w = width of garden. Then
$w+4$ = length of garden.
$$P=2l+2w$$

$$70 = 2(w+4) + 2w$$
$$70 = 4w + 8$$
$$62 = 4w$$
$$15.5 = w$$

The width is 15.5 feet and the length is
$15.5 + 4 = 19.5$ feet.

22. Let x = the width of the room. Then
$x + 30$ = the length of the room. The amount of
string used is the perimeter of the room plus the
wall separating the two rooms.

$$P = 2l + 2w + w$$
$$P = 2l + 3w$$
$$310 = 2(x+30) + 3x$$
$$310 = 2x + 60 + 3x$$
$$310 = 5x + 60$$
$$250 = 5x$$
$$50 = x$$

The width of the room is 50 feet and the length is
$50 + 30 = 80$ feet.

23. Let a be the measure of each of the two smaller
angles. Then each of the two larger angles is $3a$.

$$a + a + 3a + 3a = 360$$
$$8a = 360$$
$$a = 45$$

The angles measure 45°, 45°, and 3(45) = 135°
and 135°.

24. Let h be the height of the bookcase. Then $2h$
would be its length.

Amount of lumber for 4 shelves + Amount of
lumber for the sides = 20

$$4(2h) + 2h = 20$$
$$8h + 2h = 20$$
$$10h = 20$$
$$h = 2$$

The height of the bookcase is 2 feet and the
length is 4 feet.

25. Let t be the time it takes for the joggers to be 4
kilometers apart.

Jogger	Rate	Time	Distance
Harold	8	t	$8t$
Susan	6	t	$6t$

$$8t - 6t = 4$$
$$2t = 4$$
$$t = 2$$

It takes the joggers 2 hours to be 4 kilometers
apart.

26. Let t be the amount of time it takes for the trains
to be 440 miles apart.

Train	Rate	Time	Distance
First	50	t	$50t$
Second	60	t	$60t$

$$50t + 60t = 440$$
$$110t = 440$$
$$t = 4$$

After 4 hours, the two trains will be 440 miles
apart.

27. Rate $= \dfrac{\text{Distance}}{\text{Time}} = \dfrac{200 \text{ feet}}{22.73 \text{ seconds}} \approx 8.8$ ft/sec

The cars travel at about 8.8 ft/sec.

28. Let x be the amount invested at 8%. Then
$12,000 - x$ is the amount invested at $7\frac{1}{4}$%.

Principal	Rate	Tim	Interest
x	8%	1	$0.08x$
$12,000 - x$	$7\frac{1}{4}$%	1	$0.0725(12,000 - x)$

$$0.08x + 0.0725(12,000 - x) = 900$$
$$0.08x + 870 - 0.0725x = 900$$
$$0.0075x = 30$$
$$x = 4000$$

Tatiana should invest $4000 at 8% and $8000 at
$7\frac{1}{4}$%.

29. Let x be the amount invested at 3%. Then
$4,000 - x$ is the amount invested at 3.5%.

Principal	Rate	Tim	Interest
x	3%	1	$0.03x$
$4,000 - x$	3.5%	1	$0.035(4,000 - x)$

$$0.03x + 94.50 = 0.035(4,000 - x)$$
$$0.03x + 94.50 = 140 - .035x$$
$$0.065x = 45.5$$
$$x = 700$$

Aimee invested $700 in the 3% account and $3300 in the 3.5% account.

30. Let x be the number of gallons of pure punch. Then $2 - x$ is the number of liters of the 5% acid solution.

Punch Solution	Strength	Gallons	Amount
98%	0.98	2	0.98(2)
100%	1	x	$1x$
98.5%	0.985	$x + 2$	$0.985(x + 2)$

$$1.96 + x = 0.985(x + 2)$$
$$1.96 + x = 0.985x + 1.97$$
$$0.015x = 0.01$$
$$x \approx 0.67$$

Marcie should add about 0.67 gallons of pure punch.

31. Let x be the number of small wind chimes sold..

Type	Price	Number Sold	Amount
Small	$8	x	$8x$
Large	$20	30 - x	$20(30 - x)$

$$8x + 20(30 - x) = 492$$
$$8x + 600 - 20x = 492$$
$$-12x = -108$$
$$x = 9$$

He sold 9 small and 21 large wind chimes

32. Let x be the number of liters of the 10% solution. Then $2 - x$ is the number of liters of the 5% acid solution.

Solution	Strength	Liters	Amount
10%	0.10	x	$0.10x$
5%	0.05	$2 - x$	$0.05(2 - x)$
Mixture	0.08	2	0.16

$$0.10x + 0.05(2 - x) = 0.16$$
$$0.10x + 0.10 - 0.05x = 0.16$$
$$0.05x = 0.06$$
$$x = 1.2$$

The chemist should mix 1.2 liters of 10% solution with 0.8 liters of 5% solution.

33. Let x = smaller odd integer. Then $x + 2$ = next consecutive odd integer. Smaller number + larger number = 208
$$x + (x + 2) = 208$$
$$2x + 2 = 208$$
$$2x = 206$$
$$x = 103$$

The smaller number is 103 and the larger number is 103 + 2 = 105.

34. Let x = cost of television before tax. Then amount of tax = $0.06x$. Cost of television before tax + tax on television = cost of television after tax.
$$x + 0.06x = 477$$
$$1.06x = 477$$
$$x = \frac{477}{1.06} = 450$$

The cost of the television before tax is $450.

35. Let x = his dollar sales. Then $0.05x$ = amount of commission. Salary + commission = 900
$$300 + 0.05x = 900$$
$$0.05x = 600$$
$$x = \frac{600}{0.05} = 12,000$$

His sales last week were $12,000.

36. Let x = measure of the smallest angle. Then $x + 8$ = measure of second angle and $2x + 4$ = measure of third angle. Sum of the three angles = 180°
$$x + (x + 8) + (2x + 4) = 180$$
$$4x + 12 = 180$$
$$4x = 168$$
$$x = 42$$

The angles are 42°, 42 + 8 = 50°, and $2(42) + 4 = 88°$.

37. Let t = number of years. Then $25t$ = increase in employees over t years Present number of employees + increase in employees = future number of employees

$$427 + 25t = 627$$
$$25t = 200$$
$$t = \frac{200}{25} = 8$$

It will take 8 years before they reach 627 employees.

38. Let x = measure of each smaller angle. Then $x + 40$ = measure of each larger angle (measure of the two smaller angles) +(measure of the two larger angles) = 360°
$$x + x + (x + 40) + (x + 40) = 360$$
$$4x + 80 = 360$$
$$4x = 280$$
$$x = 70$$

Each of the smaller angles is 70° and each of the two larger angles is $70 + 40 = 110$°.

39. Let x = number of copies that would result in both centers charging the same. Then charge for copies at Copy King = 0.04x and charge for copies at King Kopie = 0.03x
Monthly fee + charge for copies at Copy King = monthly fee + charge for copies at King Kopie.
$$20 + 0.04x = 25 + 0.03x$$
$$0.04x = 5 + 0.03x$$
$$0.01x = 5$$
$$x = \frac{5}{0.01} = 500$$

500 copies would result in both centers charging the same.

40. Let r = Jim's swim rate.

Person	Rate	Time	Distance
Rita	1	0.5	0.5
Jim	r	0.5	0.5r

$$0.5 - 0.5r = 0.2$$
$$-0.5r = -0.3$$
$$r = 0.6$$

Jim swims at 0.6 mph.

41. Let x be the amount of $3.50 per pound ground beef. Then $80 - x$ is the amount of $4.10 per pound of ground beef.

Ground Beef	Price	Amount	Total
$3.50	3.50	x	3.50x
$4.10	4.10	$80 - x$	$4.10(80 - x)$
Mixture	3.65	80	292

$$3.50x + 4.10(80 - x) = 292$$
$$3.50x + 328 - 4.10x = 292$$
$$-0.60x = -36$$
$$x = 60$$

The butcher mixed 60 lbs of $3.50 per pound ground beef with 20 lbs of $4.10 per pound ground beef.

42. Let x = the rate the older brother travels. Then $x + 5$ = the rate the younger brother travels.

Brother	Rate	Time	Distance
Younger	$x + 5$	2	$2(x + 5)$
Older	x	2	2x

Younger brother's distance + older brother's distance = 230 miles.
$$2(x + 5) + 2x = 230$$
$$2x + 10 + 2x = 230$$
$$4x + 10 = 230$$
$$4x = 220$$
$$x = 55$$

The older brother travels at 55 miles per hour and the younger brother travels at $55 + 5 = 60$ miles per hour.

43. Let x = the number of liters of 30% solution.

Percent	Liters	Amount
30%	x	0.30x
12%	2	(0.12)(2)
15%	$x + 2$	0.15($x + 2$)

$$0.30x + (0.12)(2) = 0.15(x + 2)$$
$$0.30x + 0.24 = 0.15x + 0.30$$
$$0.15x + 0.24 = 0.30$$
$$0.15x = 0.06$$
$$x = 0.4$$

0.4 liters of the 30% acid solution need to be added.

44. Let w be the width of the yard. Then $1.5w$ would be the width of the yard.

3 widths + 2 lengths = 96

$$3w + 2(1.5w) = 96$$
$$3w + 3w = 96$$
$$6w = 96$$
$$w = 16$$

The width of the yard is 16 ft. and the length is $1.5(16) = 24$ ft.

45. Let x be the number of liters of 8% solution.

Percent	Liters	Amount
3%	6	0.03(6)
8%	x	0.08x
4%	$6 + x$	0.04($6 + x$)

$$0.03(6) + 0.08x = 0.04(6 + x)$$
$$0.18 + 0.08x = 0.24 + 0.04x$$
$$0.18 + 0.04x = 0.24$$
$$0.04x = 0.06$$
$$x = 1.5$$

There was 1.5 liters of the 8% solution used in the mixture.

Practice Test

1. $500 - n$

2. $2w + 6000$

3. $60t$

4. $c + 0.06c$

5. If n = the number of packages of orange, then $7n - 105$ = number of packages of peppermint.

6. If x = the number of men, then $600 - x$ = the number of women.
If x = the number of women, then $600 - x$ = the number of men.

7. If n = the smaller number, then $2n - 1$ is the larger number. The larger number minus the smaller number can be represented by $(2n - 1) - n$.

8. If n = the smaller bottle, then $n + 18$ is the larger bottle. The sum of the amounts can be represented by $n + (n + 18)$.

9. Let c = the cost of the peanuts, then $c + 0.84c$ is the cost of the deluxe can. Their difference is $(c + 0.84c) - c$.

10. Let x = smaller integer.
Then $2x - 10$ = larger integer.
Smaller number + larger number = 158

$$x + (2x - 10) = 158$$
$$3x - 10 = 158$$
$$3x = 168$$
$$x = 56$$

The smaller number is 56 and the larger number is $2(56) - 10 = 102$

11. Let x = smallest integer.
Then $x + 2$ is the consecutive odd integer.
Sum of the two integers = 33

$$x + 4(x + 2) = 33$$
$$x + 4x + 8 = 33$$
$$5x + 8 = 33$$
$$5x = 25$$
$$x = 5$$

The integers are 5 and $5 + 2 = 7$

12. Let x = one number.
Then $5x - 12$ is the other number.
Sum of the two numbers = 42

$$x + (5x - 12) = 42$$
$$x + 5x - 12 = 42$$
$$6x - 12 = 42$$
$$6x = 54$$
$$x = 9$$

The integers are 9 and $5(9) - 12 = 33$.

13. Let c = the cost of the furniture before tax
Tax amount = (cost) · (tax rate) = $0.06c$
Total cost = cost before tax + tax amount

$$2650 = c + 0.06c$$
$$2640 = 1.06c$$
$$\frac{2650}{1.06} = \frac{1.06c}{1.06}$$
$$2500 = c$$

The cost of the furniture before tax was $2500.

14. Let x = price of most expensive meal he can order. Then $0.15x$ = amount of the tip.

$$x + 0.15x = 40$$
$$1.15x = 40$$
$$x = 34.78$$

The price of the most expensive meal he can order is $34.78.

15. Let x = the amount of money Peter invested.
Then $2x$ = the amount of money Julie invested.
Then $2x$ = the amount of profit Julie receives.
Peter's profit + Julie's profit = Total profit

$x + 2x = 120,000$

$3x = 120,000$

$x = 40,000$

Peter will receive $40,000 and Julie receives 2($40,000) = $80,000.

16. Let x = the number of times the plow is needed for the costs to be equal.
Elizabeth's charge = $80 + 5x$
Jan charge = $50 + 10x$
The charges are equal when:

$80 + 5x = 50 + 10x$

$30 + 5x = 10x$

$30 = 5x$

$6 = x$

The snow would need to be plowed 6 times for the costs to be the same.

17. Let x = number of pages to be printed for the total cost of both printers to be equal.
Then $0.01x$ = cost of printing x pages on the Upson printer,
and $0.03x$ = cost of printing x pages on the TexMar printer.
Upson = TexMar

$499 + 0.01x = 350 + 0.03x$

$499 = 0.02x + 350$

$149 = 0.02x$

$7450 = x$

It would take about 7450 pages to be printed for the costs to be the same.

18. Let x = length of smallest side.
Then $x + 15$ = length of second side and $2x$ = length of third side.
Sum of the three sides = perimeter

$x + (x + 15) + 2x = 75$

$4x + 15 = 75$

$4x = 60$

$x = 15$

The three sides are 15 inches,
15 + 15 = 30 inches, and 2(15) = 30 inches.

19. Let w = width of flag
Then $2w - 4$ = length of flag.
$2l + 2w$ = perimeter

$2(2w - 4) + 2w = 28$

$4w - 8 + 2w = 28$

$6w - 8 = 28$

$6w = 36$

$w = 6$

The width is 6 feet and the length is 8 feet.

20. Let x = the measure of the two smaller angles, then $(2x + 3)$ = the measure of the two larger angles.

$x + x + (2x + 3) + (2x + 3) = 360$

$x + x + 2x + 3 + 2x + 3 = 360$

$6x + 6 = 360$

$6x = 354$

$x = 59$

The angles measure 59°, 59°, 2(59) + 3 = 121°, 121°.

21. Let x = the rate Harlene digs.
Then $x + 0.2$ is the rate Ellis digs.

Name	Rate	Time	Distance
Harlene	x	84	$84x$
Ellis	$x + 0.2$	84	$84(x + 0.2)$

Distance Harlene digs + distance Ellis digs = total length of trench

$84x + 84(x + 0.2) = 67.2$

$84x + 84x + 16.8 = 67.2$

$168x = 50.4$

$x = 0.3$

Harlene digs at 0.3 feet per minute and Ellis digs at 0.3 + 2 = 0.5 feet per minute.

22. Let x = the rate Bonnie is running.

Name	Rate	Time	Distance
Alice	8	2	16
Bonnie	x	2	$2x$

$16 - 2x = 4$

$-2x = -12$

$x = 6$

Bonnie is running at 6 mph.

23. Let x be the number of pounds of Jelly Belly candy. Then $3 - x$ is the number of pounds of Kit candy.

Type	Cost	Pounds	Total
Jelly Belly	$2.20	x	$2.20(x)$
Kits	$2.75	$3 - x$	$2.75(3 - x)$
Mixture	$2.40	3	$2.40(3)$

$$2.20x + 2.75(3 - x) = 2.40(3)$$
$$2.2x + 8.25 - 2.75x = 7.2$$
$$-0.55x + 8.25 = 7.2$$
$$-0.55x = -1.05$$
$$x \approx 1.91$$

The mixture should contain about 1.91 pounds of Jelly Belly candy and about 1.09 pounds of Kits candy.

24. Let x = amount of 20% salt solution to be added.

Percent	Liters	Amount
20%	x	$0.20x$
40%	60	$(0.40)(60)$
35%	$x + 60$	$0.35(x + 60)$

$$0.20x + (0.40)(60) = 0.35(x + 60)$$
$$0.20x + 24 = 0.35x + 21$$
$$-0.15x + 24 = 21$$
$$-0.15x = -3$$
$$x = 20$$

20 liters of 20% solution must be added.

25. Let x = number of liters of 8% solution.

Percent	Liters	Amount
8%	x	$0.08x$
5%	$3 - x$	$0.05(3 - x)$
6%	3	$0.06(3)$

$$0.08x + 0.05(3 - x) = 0.06(3)$$
$$0.08x + 0.15 - 0.05x = 0.18$$
$$0.03x + 0.15 = 0.18$$
$$0.03x = 0.03$$
$$x = 1$$

There will be 1 liter of 8% solution and $3 - 1 = 2$ liters of 5% solution.

Cumulative Review Test

1. 40% of $40,000 per year
$$(0.40)(40,000) = 16,000$$
Emily receives $16,000 in social security.

2. a. $38.7\% - 4.7\% = 34.0\%$

    b. 4.7% of 1.3 million
$$(0.047)(1.3) \approx 0.06 \text{ million or } 60,000$$

3. a. $\dfrac{5 + 6 + 8 + 12 + 5}{5} = 7.2$

    The mean level was 7.2 parts per million.

    b. Carbon dioxide levels in order: 5, 5, 6, 8, 12
    The median is 6 parts per million.

4. $\dfrac{5}{12} \div \dfrac{3}{4} = \dfrac{5}{12} \cdot \dfrac{4}{3} = \dfrac{20}{36} = \dfrac{5}{9}$

5. $\dfrac{2}{3} - \dfrac{1}{8} = \dfrac{2 \cdot 8}{3 \cdot 8} - \dfrac{1 \cdot 3}{8 \cdot 3} = \dfrac{16}{24} - \dfrac{3}{24} = \dfrac{13}{24}$

    $\dfrac{2}{3}$ inch is $\dfrac{13}{24}$ of an inch greater than $\dfrac{1}{8}$ inch.

6. a. $\{1, 2, 3, 4, \ldots\}$

    b. $\{0, 1, 2, 3, \ldots\}$

    c. A rational number is a quotient of two integers, denominator not 0.

7. a. $|-4| = 4$

    b. $|-5| = 5$ and $|-3| = 3$. Since $5 > 3$, $|-5| > |-3|$.

8. $2 - 6^2 \div 2 \cdot 2 = 2 - 36 \div 2 \cdot 2$
$$= 2 - 18 \cdot 2$$
$$= 2 - 36$$
$$= -34$$

9. $4(2x - 3) - 2(3x + 5) - 6$
$$= 8x - 12 - 6x - 10 - 6$$
$$= 2x - 28$$

10. $\qquad 5x - 6 = x + 14$
$$5x - 6 - x = x - x + 14$$
$$4x - 6 = 14$$
$$4x - 6 + 6 = 14 + 6$$
$$4x = 20$$
$$\dfrac{4x}{4} = \dfrac{20}{4}$$
$$x = 5$$

11.
$$6r = 2(r+3) - (r+5)$$
$$6r = 2r + 6 - r - 5$$
$$6r = r + 1$$
$$6r - r = r - r + 1$$
$$5r = 1$$
$$\frac{5r}{5} = \frac{1}{5}$$
$$r = \frac{1}{5}$$

12.
$$2(x+5) = 3(2x-4) - 4x$$
$$2x + 10 = 6x - 12 - 4x$$
$$2x + 10 = 2x - 12$$
$$2x - 2x + 10 = 2x - 2x - 12$$
$$10 = -12 \quad \text{False}$$
The equation has no solution.

13. Substitute 6 for r.
$$A = \pi r^2$$
$$A = \pi(6)^2 = 36\pi \approx 113.10$$

14. a.
$$4x + 8y = 16$$
$$4x - 4x + 8y = 16 - 4x$$
$$8y = 16 - 4x$$
$$\frac{8y}{8} = \frac{16 - 4x}{8}$$
$$y = \frac{16}{8} - \frac{4x}{8}$$
$$y = 2 - \frac{1}{2}x$$
$$y = -\frac{1}{2}x + 2$$

b. Substitute –4 for x.
$$y = -\frac{1}{2}(-4) + 2 = 2 + 2 = 4$$

15.
$$P = 2l + 2w$$
$$P - 2l = 2l - 2l + 2w$$
$$P - 2l = 2w$$
$$\frac{P - 2l}{2} = \frac{2w}{2}$$
$$\frac{P - 2l}{2} = w$$

16.
$$\frac{50 \text{ miles}}{2 \text{ gallons}} = \frac{225 \text{ miles}}{x \text{ gallons}}$$
$$\frac{50}{2} = \frac{225}{x}$$
$$50x = 450$$
$$x = 9$$
It will need 9 gallons.

17.
$$3x - 4 \le -1$$
$$3x - 4 + 4 \le -1 + 4$$
$$3x \le 3$$
$$\frac{3x}{3} \le \frac{3}{3}$$
$$x \le 1$$

18. Let x = number of minutes for the two plans to have the same cost.
Cost for Plan A = $19.95 + 0.35x$
Cost for Plan B = $29.95 + 0.10x$
The costs will be equal when the cost for Plan A = cost for Plan B.
$$19.95 + 0.35x = 29.95 + 0.10x$$
$$0.35x = 10 + 0.10x$$
$$0.25x = 10$$
$$x = 40$$
Lori would need to talk 40 minutes in a month for the plans to have the same cost.

19. Let x = smaller number.
Then $2x + 11$ = larger number.
smaller number + larger number = 29
$$x + (2x + 11) = 29$$
$$3x + 11 = 29$$
$$3x = 18$$
$$x = 6$$
The smaller number is 6 and the larger number is $2(6) + 11 = 23$.

20. Let x = smallest angle. Then $x + 5$ = second angle, $x + 50$ = third angle, and $4x + 25$ = fourth angle. Sum of the angle measures = 360°
$$x + (x+5) + (x+50) + (4x+25) = 360$$
$$7x + 80 = 360$$
$$7x = 280$$
$$x = 40$$
The angle measures are 40°, 40 + 5 = 45°, 40 + 50 = 90°, and 4(40) + 25 = 185°.

Chapter 4

Exercise Set 4.1

1. In the expression t^p, t is the base, p is the exponent.

3. a. $\dfrac{x^m}{x^n} = x^{m-n}$, $x \neq 0$

    b. Answers will vary. One possible answer is that to divide terms with like bases, subtract the exponents.

5. a. $\left(x^m\right)^n = x^{m \cdot n}$

    b. Answers will vary. One possible answer is that to raise a power to a power, multiply the powers.

7. $a^2 b^5$

9. Answers will vary. See #5 above.

11. $x^5 \cdot x^4 = x^{5+4} = x^9$

13. $-z^4 \cdot z = -z^{4+1} = -z^5$

15. $y^3 \cdot y^2 = y^{3+2} = y^5$

17. $3^2 \cdot 3^3 = 3^{2+3} = 3^5 = 243$

19. $z^3 \cdot z^5 = z^{3+5} = z^8$

21. $\dfrac{6^2}{6} = \dfrac{6^2}{6^1} = 6^{2-1} = 6^1 = 6$

23. $\dfrac{x^{10}}{x^3} = x^{10-3} = x^7$

25. $\dfrac{3^6}{3^2} = 3^{6-2} = 3^4 = 81$

27. $\dfrac{y^4}{y^6} = \dfrac{y^4}{y^4 \cdot y^2} = \dfrac{1}{1 \cdot y^2} = \dfrac{1}{y^2}$

29. $\dfrac{c^4}{c^4} = c^{4-4} = c^0 = 1$

31. $\dfrac{a^3}{a^9} = \dfrac{a^3}{a^3 \cdot a^6} = \dfrac{1}{1 \cdot a^6} = \dfrac{1}{a^6}$

33. $x^0 = 1$

35. $3x^0 = 3 \cdot 1 = 3$

37. $4\left(5d\right)^0 = 4\left(5^0 d^0\right) = 4(1 \cdot 1) = 4 \cdot 1 = 4$

39. $-9\left(-4x\right)^0 = -9(-4)^0 \cdot x^0$
$$= -9(1 \cdot 1)$$
$$= -9(1)$$
$$= -9$$

41. $6x^3 y^2 z^0 = 6x^3 y^2 (1) = 6x^3 y^2$

43. $-8r(st)^0 = -8rs^0 t^0 = -8r \cdot 1 \cdot 1 = -8r$

45. $\left(x^4\right)^2 = x^{4 \cdot 2} = x^8$

47. $\left(x^5\right)^5 = x^{5 \cdot 5} = x^{25}$

49. $\left(x^3\right)^1 = x^{3 \cdot 1} = x^3$

51. $\left(x^4\right)^3 = x^{4 \cdot 3} = x^{12}$

53. $\left(n^6\right)^3 = n^{6 \cdot 3} = n^{18}$

55. $\left(-2w^2\right)^3 = (-2)^3 w^{2 \cdot 3} = -8w^6$

57. $\left(-3x^3\right)^3 = (-3)^3 x^{3 \cdot 3} = (-27)x^9$

59. $\left(4x^3 y^2\right)^3 = 4^3 \cdot x^{3 \cdot 3} y^{2 \cdot 3} = 64x^9 y^6$

61. $\left(\dfrac{x}{3}\right)^2 = \dfrac{x^2}{3^2} = \dfrac{x^2}{9}$

63. $\left(\dfrac{y}{x}\right)^4 = \dfrac{y^4}{x^4}$

65. $\left(\dfrac{-6}{x}\right)^3 = \dfrac{(-6)^3}{x^3} = \dfrac{-216}{x^3} = -\dfrac{216}{x^3}$

67. $\left(\dfrac{2x}{y}\right)^3 = \dfrac{2^3 x^3}{y^3} = \dfrac{8x^3}{y^3}$

69. $\left(\dfrac{4p}{5}\right)^2 = \dfrac{4^2 p^2}{5^2} = \dfrac{16p^2}{25}$

71. $\left(\dfrac{3x^4}{y}\right)^3 = \dfrac{3^3 x^{4\cdot 3}}{y^3} = \dfrac{27x^{12}}{y^3}$

73. $\dfrac{a^8 b}{ab^4} = \dfrac{a \cdot a^7 \cdot b}{a \cdot b \cdot b^3} = \dfrac{a^7}{b^3}$

75. $\dfrac{5x^{12}y^2}{10xy^9} = \dfrac{5 \cdot x \cdot x^{11} \cdot y^2}{2 \cdot 5 \cdot x \cdot y^2 \cdot y^7} = \dfrac{x^{11}}{2y^7}$

77. $\dfrac{30y^5 z^3}{5yz^6} = \dfrac{5 \cdot 6 \cdot y \cdot y^4 \cdot z^3}{5 \cdot y \cdot z^3 \cdot z^3} = \dfrac{6y^4}{z^3}$

79. $\dfrac{35x^4 y^9}{15x^9 y^{12}} = \dfrac{5 \cdot 7 \cdot x^4 \cdot y^9}{5 \cdot 3 \cdot x^4 \cdot x^5 \cdot y^9 \cdot y^3} = \dfrac{7}{3x^5 y^3}$

81. $\dfrac{-36xy^7 z}{12x^4 y^5 z} = -\dfrac{3 \cdot 12 \cdot x \cdot y^5 \cdot y^2 \cdot z}{12 \cdot x \cdot x^3 \cdot y^5 \cdot z} = -\dfrac{3y^2}{x^3}$

83. $-\dfrac{6x^2 y^7 z}{3x^5 y^9 z^6} = -\dfrac{2 \cdot 3 \cdot x^2 \cdot y^7 \cdot z}{3 \cdot x^2 \cdot x^3 \cdot y^7 \cdot y^2 \cdot z \cdot z^5}$

$$= -\dfrac{2}{x^3 y^2 z^5}$$

85. $\left(\dfrac{10x^4}{5x^6}\right)^3 = \left(\dfrac{10}{5} \cdot \dfrac{x^4}{x^6}\right)^3$

$$= \left(\dfrac{2}{x^2}\right)^3$$

$$= \dfrac{2^3}{x^{2\cdot 3}}$$

$$= \dfrac{8}{x^6}$$

87. $\left(\dfrac{6y^6}{2y^3}\right)^3 = \left(\dfrac{6}{2} \cdot \dfrac{y^6}{y^3}\right)^3$

$$= \left(3y^3\right)^3$$

$$= 3^3 y^{3\cdot 3}$$

$$= 27y^9$$

89. $\left(\dfrac{6a^2 b^4}{3a^2 b^9}\right)^0 = 1$

91. $\left(\dfrac{x^4 y^3}{x^2 y^5}\right)^2 = \left(\dfrac{x^4}{x^2} \cdot \dfrac{y^3}{y^5}\right)^2$

$$= \left(\dfrac{x^2}{y^2}\right)^2$$

$$= \dfrac{x^{2\cdot 2}}{y^{2\cdot 2}}$$

$$= \dfrac{x^4}{y^4}$$

93. $\left(\dfrac{9y^2 z^7}{18y^9 z}\right)^4 = \left(\dfrac{9}{18} \cdot \dfrac{y^2}{y^9} \cdot \dfrac{z^7}{z}\right)^4$

$$= \left(\dfrac{z^6}{2y^7}\right)^4$$

$$= \dfrac{z^{6\cdot 4}}{2^4 y^{7\cdot 4}}$$

$$= \dfrac{z^{24}}{16y^{28}}$$

95. $\left(\dfrac{25s^4 t}{5s^6 t^4}\right)^3 = \left(\dfrac{25}{5} \cdot \dfrac{s^4}{s^6} \cdot \dfrac{t}{t^4}\right)^3$

$$= \left(\dfrac{5}{s^2 t^3}\right)^3$$

$$= \dfrac{5^3}{s^{2\cdot 3} \cdot t^{3\cdot 3}}$$

$$= \dfrac{125}{s^6 t^9}$$

97. $\left(3xy^4\right)^2 = 3^2 x^2 y^{4\cdot 2} = 9x^2 y^8$

99. $\left(5ab^3\right)(b) = 5a\left(b^{3+1}\right) = 5ab^4$

101. $(-2xy)(3xy) = (-2 \cdot 3)\left(x^{1+1}\right)\left(y^{1+1}\right)$

$$= -6x^2 y^2$$

103. $\left(5x^2 y\right)\left(3xy^5\right) = (5 \cdot 3)\left(x^{2+1}\right)\left(y^{1+5}\right) = 15x^3 y^6$

105. $\left(-3p^2 q\right)^2 (-pq) = [(-3)^2 p^{2\cdot 2} q^2](-p^2 q)$

$$= (9p^4 q^2)(-pq)$$

$$= (9 \cdot -1)(p^{4+2})(q^{2+1})$$

$$= -9p^6 q^3$$

107. $\left(7r^3 s^2\right)^2 \left(9r^3 s^4\right)^0 = (7^2 \cdot r^{3\cdot 2} s^{2\cdot 2})(1) = 49r^6 s^4$

109. $(-x)^2 = (-x)(-x) = x^2$

111. $\left(\dfrac{x^5 y^5}{xy^5}\right)^3 = \left(\dfrac{x^5}{x} \cdot \dfrac{y^5}{y^5}\right)^3$

$\qquad = \left(x^4 \cdot 1\right)^3$

$\qquad = \left(x^4\right)^3$

$\qquad = x^{4\cdot3} = x^{12}$

113. $\left(2.5x^3\right)^2 = 2.5^2 \cdot x^{3\cdot2} = 6.25x^6$

115. $\dfrac{x^9 y^3}{x^2 y^7} = \dfrac{x^9}{x^2} \cdot \dfrac{y^3}{y^7} = \dfrac{x^7}{y^4}$

117. $\left(\dfrac{-m^4}{n^3}\right)^3 = \dfrac{(-1)^3 m^{4\cdot3}}{n^{3\cdot3}} = -\dfrac{m^{12}}{n^9}$

119. $\left(-6x^3 y^2\right)^3 = (-6)^3 x^{3\cdot3} y^{2\cdot3} = -216x^9 y^6$

121. $\left(-2x^4 y^2 z\right)^3 = (-2)^3 x^{4\cdot3} y^{2\cdot3} z^{1\cdot3} = -8x^{12} y^6 z^3$

123. $\left(9r^4 s^5\right)^3 = 9^3 \cdot r^{4\cdot3} \cdot s^{5\cdot3} = 729r^{12} s^{15}$

125. $\left(4x^2 y\right)\left(3xy^2\right)^3 = \left(4x^2 y\right)\left(3^3 x^3 y^{2\cdot3}\right)$

$\qquad = \left(4x^2 y\right)\left(27x^3 y^6\right)$

$\qquad = 4 \cdot 27 x^{2+3} y^{1+6}$

$\qquad = 108x^5 y^7$

127. $\left(7.3x^2 y^4\right)^2 = 7.3^2 x^{2\cdot2} y^{4\cdot2} = 53.29x^4 y^8$

129. $\left(x^7 y^5\right)\left(xy^2\right)^4 = \left(x^7 y^5\right)\left(x^{1\cdot4} y^{2\cdot4}\right)$

$\qquad = \left(x^7 y^5\right)\left(x^4 y^8\right)$

$\qquad = x^{7+4} y^{5+8}$

$\qquad = x^{11} y^{13}$

131. $\left(\dfrac{-x^4 z^7}{x^2 z^5}\right)^4 = \left(-1 \cdot \dfrac{x^4}{x^2} \cdot \dfrac{z^7}{z^5}\right)^4$

$\qquad = \left(-x^2 z^2\right)^4$

$\qquad = (-1)^4 x^{2\cdot4} z^{2\cdot4}$

$\qquad = x^8 z^8$

133. $\dfrac{a+b}{b}$ cannot be simplified.

135. $\dfrac{y^2 + 3}{y}$ cannot be simplified.

137. $\dfrac{6yz^4}{yz^2} = 6y^{1-1} \cdot z^{4-2} = 6z^2$

139. $\dfrac{a^2 + b^2}{a^2}$ cannot be simplified.

141. $a^3 b = 2^3 \cdot 5 = 8 \cdot 5 = 40$

143. $(xy)^0 = (-5 \cdot 3)^0 = (-15)^0 = 1$

145. The sign will be positive because a negative number with an even number for an exponent will be positive. This is because $(-1)^m = 1$ when m is even.

147. Area = Length × Width = $8x \cdot x = 8x^2$

149. Area = (Area of Top) + (Area of Middle)

$\qquad\qquad$ + (Area of Bottom)

$\qquad = (a \cdot b) + (a \cdot a) + (b \cdot b)$

$\qquad = ab + a^2 + b^2$

151. $\left(3yz^2\right)^2 \left(\dfrac{2y^3 z^5}{10y^6 z^4}\right)^0 \left(4y^2 z^3\right)^3$

$\qquad = \left(3^2 y^{1\cdot2} z^{2\cdot2}\right) \cdot 1 \cdot \left(4^3 y^{2\cdot3} z^{3\cdot3}\right)$

$\qquad = \left(9y^2 z^4\right)\left(64y^6 z^9\right)$

$\qquad = 9 \cdot 64 y^{2+6} z^{4+9}$

$\qquad = 576y^8 z^{13}$

153. a. $\dfrac{3^2}{3^3} = \dfrac{3 \cdot \cancel{3}}{3 \cdot 3 \cdot \cancel{3}} = \dfrac{3}{9} = \dfrac{1}{3}$

b. $\dfrac{3^2}{3^3} = 3^{2-3} = 3^{-1}$

c. $\dfrac{1}{3} = 3^{-1}$

d. $\dfrac{2^3}{2^4} = \dfrac{2 \cdot \cancel{2} \cdot \cancel{2}}{2 \cdot 2 \cdot \cancel{2} \cdot \cancel{2}} = \dfrac{2}{4} = \dfrac{1}{2}$

$\qquad \dfrac{2^3}{2^4} = 2^{3-4} = 2^{-1}$

$\qquad \dfrac{1}{2} = 2^{-1}$

e. $\dfrac{1}{x^m} = x^{-m}$

154. $3^4 \div 3^3 - (5-8) + 7 = 81 \div 27 - (-3) + 7$

$\qquad\qquad = 3 - (-3) + 7$

$\qquad\qquad = 6 + 7$

$\qquad\qquad = 13$

155. $-4(x-3) + 5x - 2 = -4x + 12 + 5x - 2$

$\qquad\qquad\qquad = -4x + 5x + 12 - 2$

$\qquad\qquad\qquad = x + 10$

156. $2(x+4) - 3 = 5x + 4 - 3x + 1$

$\quad 2x + 8 - 3 = 2x + 5$

$\qquad 2x + 5 = 2x + 5$ True

All real numbers are solutions to this equation.

157. a. $\quad P = 2l + 2w$

$\qquad 26 = 2(x+5) + 2(x)$

$\qquad 26 = 2x + 10 + 2x$

$\qquad 26 = 4x + 10$

$\qquad 16 = 4x$

$\qquad 4 = x$

$\quad x + 5 = 4 + 5 = 9$

The sides are 4 and 9 inches long.

b. $\qquad P = 2l + 2w$

$\qquad P - 2l = 2l + 2w - 2l$

$\qquad P - 2l = 2w$

$\qquad \dfrac{P - 2l}{2} = w$

Exercise Set 4.2

1. When a variable or number is raised to a negative exponent, the expression may be written as 1 divided by the variable or number raised to that positive exponent.

3. No, it is not simplified because of the negative exponent.

$x^5 y^{-3} = \dfrac{x^5}{y^3}$

5. The given simplification is not correct since $5^{-2} = \dfrac{1}{5^2} = \dfrac{1}{25}$.

7. a. The numerator has one term, $x^5 y^2$.

b. The factors of the numerator are x^5 and y^2.

9. The sign of the exponent changes when a factor is moved from the denominator to the numerator of a fraction.

11. $x^{-6} = \dfrac{1}{x^6}$

13. $5^{-1} = \dfrac{1}{5}$

15. $\dfrac{1}{x^{-3}} = x^3$

17. $\dfrac{1}{a^{-1}} = a^1 = a$

19. $\dfrac{1}{6^{-2}} = 6^2 = 36$

21. $\left(x^{-2}\right)^3 = x^{-2 \cdot 3} = x^{-6} = \dfrac{1}{x^6}$

23. $\left(y^{-5}\right)^4 = y^{-5 \cdot 4} = y^{-20} = \dfrac{1}{y^{20}}$

25. $\left(x^4\right)^{-2} = x^{4(-2)} = x^{-8} = \dfrac{1}{x^8}$

27. $\left(3^{-2}\right)^{-1} = 3^{(-2)(-1)} = 3^2 = 9$

29. $y^4 \cdot y^{-2} = y^{4 + (-2)} = y^2$

31. $x^7 \cdot x^{-5} = x^{7-5} = x^2$

33. $3^{-2} \cdot 3^4 = 3^{-2+4} = 3^2 = 9$

35. $\dfrac{r^5}{r^6} = r^{5-6} = r^{-1} = \dfrac{1}{r}$

37. $\dfrac{p^0}{p^{-3}} = p^{0-(-3)} = p^3$

39. $\dfrac{x^{-7}}{x^{-3}} = x^{-7-(-3)} = x^{-4} = \dfrac{1}{x^4}$

41. $\dfrac{3^2}{3^{-1}} = 3^{2-(-1)} = 3^3 = 27$

43. $5^{-3} = \dfrac{1}{5^3} = \dfrac{1}{125}$

45. $\dfrac{1}{z^{-9}} = z^9$

47. $\left(p^{-4}\right)^{-6} = p^{-4(-6)} = p^{24}$

49. $\left(y^{-2}\right)^{-3} = y^{(-2)(-3)} = y^6$

51. $x^3 \cdot x^{-7} = x^{3-7} = x^{-4} = \dfrac{1}{x^4}$

53. $x^{-8} \cdot x^{-7} = x^{-8-7} = x^{-15} = \dfrac{1}{x^{15}}$

55. $-4^{-2} = -\dfrac{1}{4^2} = -\dfrac{1}{16}$

57. $-(-4)^{-2} = -\dfrac{1}{(-4)^2} = -\dfrac{1}{16}$

59. $(-2)^{-3} = \dfrac{1}{(-2)^3} = -\dfrac{1}{8}$

61. $(-6)^{-2} = \dfrac{1}{(-6)^2} = \dfrac{1}{36}$

63. $\dfrac{x^{-5}}{x^5} = x^{-5-5} = x^{-10} = \dfrac{1}{x^{10}}$

65. $\dfrac{n^{-5}}{n^{-7}} = n^{-5-(-7)} = n^2$

67. $\dfrac{9^{-3}}{9^{-3}} = 9^{-3-(-3)} = 9^0 = 1$

69. $\left(2^{-1} + 3^{-1}\right)^0 = 1$

71. $\dfrac{2}{2^{-5}} = 2^{1-(-5)} = 2^6 = 64$

73. $\left(x^{-4}\right)^{-2} = x^{(-4)(-2)} = x^8$

75. $\left(x^0\right)^{-2} = (1)^{-2} = 1$

77. $2^{-3} \cdot 2 = 2^{-3+1} = 2^{-2} = \dfrac{1}{2^2} = \dfrac{1}{4}$

79. $7^{-5} \cdot 7^3 = 7^{-5+3} = 7^{-2} = \dfrac{1}{7^2} = \dfrac{1}{49}$

81. $\dfrac{x^{-1}}{x^{-4}} = x^{-1-(-4)} = x^3$

83. $\left(4^2\right)^{-1} = 4^{2 \cdot -1} = 4^{-2} = \dfrac{1}{4^2} = \dfrac{1}{16}$

85. $\dfrac{5}{5^{-2}} = 5^{1-(-2)} = 5^3 = 125$

87. $\dfrac{3^{-4}}{3^{-2}} = 3^{-4-(-2)} = 3^{-2} = \dfrac{1}{3^2} = \dfrac{1}{9}$

89. $\dfrac{8^{-1}}{8^{-1}} = 8^{-1-(-1)} = 8^0 = 1$

91. $\left(-6x^2\right)^{-2}$

$\quad = (-6)^{-2} x^{2(-2)} = (-6)^{-2} x^{-4} = \dfrac{1}{(-6)^2 x^4} = \dfrac{1}{36x^4}$

93. $3x^{-2}y^2 = 3 \cdot \dfrac{1}{x^2} \cdot y^2 = \dfrac{3y^2}{x^2}$

95. $\left(\dfrac{1}{2}\right)^{-2} = \left(\dfrac{2}{1}\right)^2 = 2^2 = 4$

97. $\left(\dfrac{5}{4}\right)^{-3} = \left(\dfrac{4}{5}\right)^3 = \dfrac{4^3}{5^3} = \dfrac{64}{125}$

99. $\left(\dfrac{c^4}{d^2}\right)^{-2} = \left(\dfrac{d^2}{c^4}\right)^2 = \dfrac{d^{2 \cdot 2}}{c^{4 \cdot 2}} = \dfrac{d^4}{c^8}$

101. $-\left(\dfrac{r^4}{s}\right)^{-4} = -\left(\dfrac{s}{r^4}\right)^4 = -\dfrac{s^4}{r^{4 \cdot 4}} = -\dfrac{s^4}{r^{16}}$

103. $-7a^{-3}b^{-4} = -7 \cdot \dfrac{1}{a^3} \cdot \dfrac{1}{b^4} = -\dfrac{7}{a^3b^4}$

105. $\left(4x^5y^{-3}\right)^{-3}$

$\quad = 4^{-3} x^{5(-3)} y^{(-3)(-3)} = 4^{-3} x^{-15} y^9 = \dfrac{y^9}{4^3 x^{15}} = \dfrac{y^9}{64x^{15}}$

107. $\left(3z^{-4}\right)\left(6z^{-5}\right) = 3 \cdot 6 \cdot z^{-4} \cdot z^{-5} = 18z^{-9} = \dfrac{18}{z^9}$

109. $4x^4\left(-2x^{-4}\right) = 4 \cdot (-2) \cdot x^4 \cdot x^{-4} = -8x^0 = -8$

111. $\left(4x^2y\right)\left(3x^3y^{-1}\right) = 4 \cdot 3 \cdot x^2 \cdot x^3 \cdot y \cdot y^{-1} = 12x^5$

113. $\left(-5y^2\right)\left(4y^{-3}z^5\right) = -5 \cdot 4 \cdot y^2 \cdot y^{-3} \cdot z^5$

$\quad = -20y^{-1}z^5$

$\quad = -\dfrac{20z^5}{y}$

115. $\dfrac{24d^{12}}{3d^8} = \dfrac{24}{3} \cdot d^{12-8} = 8d^4$

117. $\dfrac{36x^{-4}}{9x^{-2}} = \dfrac{36}{4} \cdot \dfrac{x^{-4}}{x^{-2}} = 4 \cdot \dfrac{1}{x^2} = \dfrac{4}{x^2}$

119. $\dfrac{3x^4y^{-2}}{6y^3} = \dfrac{3}{6} \cdot x^4 \cdot \dfrac{y^{-2}}{y^3} = \dfrac{1}{2} \cdot x^4 \cdot \dfrac{1}{y^5} = \dfrac{x^4}{2y^5}$

121. $\dfrac{32x^4y^{-2}}{4x^{-2}y^0} = \left(\dfrac{32}{4}\right)x^{4-(-2)}y^{-2-0}$

$$= 8x^6y^{-2}$$

$$= \dfrac{8x^6}{y^2}$$

123. $\left(\dfrac{5x^4y^{-7}}{z^3}\right)^{-2} = \left(\dfrac{z^3}{5x^4y^{-7}}\right)^2$

$$= \dfrac{z^{3\cdot2}}{5^2x^{4\cdot2}y^{-7\cdot2}}$$

$$= \dfrac{z^6}{25x^8y^{-14}}$$

$$= \dfrac{y^{14}z^6}{25x^8}$$

125. $\left(\dfrac{2r^{-5}s^9}{t^{12}}\right)^{-4} = \left(\dfrac{t^{12}}{2r^{-5}s^9}\right)^4$

$$= \dfrac{t^{12\cdot4}}{2^4r^{-5\cdot4}s^{9\cdot4}}$$

$$= \dfrac{t^{48}}{16r^{-20}s^{36}}$$

$$= \dfrac{r^{20}t^{48}}{16s^{36}}$$

127. $\left(\dfrac{x^3y^{-4}z}{y^{-2}}\right)^{-6} = \left(\dfrac{y^{-2}}{x^3y^{-4}z}\right)^6$

$$= \dfrac{y^{-2\cdot6}}{x^{3\cdot6}y^{-4\cdot6}z^6}$$

$$= \dfrac{y^{-12}}{x^{18}y^{-24}z^6}$$

$$= \dfrac{y^{-12-(-24)}}{x^{18}z^6}$$

$$= \dfrac{y^{12}}{x^{18}z^6}$$

129. $\left(\dfrac{p^6q^{-3}}{4p^8}\right)^2 = \left(\dfrac{p^{6-8}q^{-3}}{4}\right)^2$

$$= \left(\dfrac{p^{-2}q^{-3}}{4}\right)^2$$

$$= \dfrac{p^{-2\cdot2}q^{-3\cdot2}}{4^2}$$

$$= \dfrac{p^{-4}q^{-6}}{16}$$

$$= \dfrac{1}{16p^4q^6}$$

131. a. Yes, $p^{-1}q^{-1} = \dfrac{1}{p}\cdot\dfrac{1}{q} = \dfrac{1}{pq}$.

     b. No, $p^{-1} + q^{-1} = \dfrac{1}{p}+\dfrac{1}{q} \neq \dfrac{1}{p+q}$.

133. $4^2 + 4^{-2} = 16 + \dfrac{1}{4^2} = 16 + \dfrac{1}{16} = 16\dfrac{1}{16}$

135. $5^3 + 5^{-3} = 125 + \dfrac{1}{5^3} = 125 + \dfrac{1}{125} = 125\dfrac{1}{125}$

137. $5^0 - 3^{-1} = 1 - \dfrac{1}{3^1} = 1 - \dfrac{1}{3} = \dfrac{2}{3}$

139. $2^{-3} - 2^3 \cdot 2^{-3} = 2^{-3} - 2^{3-3}$

$$= \dfrac{1}{2^3} - 2^0$$

$$= \dfrac{1}{8} - 1$$

$$= -\dfrac{7}{8}$$

141. $2\cdot4^{-1} - 4\cdot3^{-1} = 2\cdot\dfrac{1}{4} - 4\cdot\dfrac{1}{3}$

$$= \dfrac{2}{4} - \dfrac{4}{3}$$

$$= \dfrac{6}{12} - \dfrac{16}{12}$$

$$= -\dfrac{10}{12} = -\dfrac{5}{6}$$

143. $3 \cdot 5^0 - 5 \cdot 3^{-2} = 3 \cdot 1 - 5 \cdot \dfrac{1}{3^2}$

$$= 3 - 5 \cdot \dfrac{1}{9}$$

$$= 3 - \dfrac{5}{9}$$

$$= \dfrac{27}{9} - \dfrac{5}{9}$$

$$= \dfrac{22}{9}$$

145. The missing number is –2 since

$3^{-2} = \dfrac{1}{3^2} = \dfrac{1}{9}$.

147. The missing number is –3 since

$\dfrac{1}{6^{-3}} = 6^3 = 216$.

149. The missing number is –2 since

$(x^{-2})^{-2} = x^{(-2)(-2)} = x^4$.

151. The missing coefficient is 2 since $2^3 = 8$.

The missing exponent is –3 since

$(x^{-3})^3 = x^{(-3)(3)} = x^{-9} = \dfrac{1}{x^9}$.

153. The product rule is $(xy)^m = x^m y^m$ not $(x + y)^m$.

155. Let x = the number of miles.

$\dfrac{104 \text{ miles}}{52 \text{ minutes}} = \dfrac{x}{93 \text{ minutes}}$

$\dfrac{104}{52} = \dfrac{x}{93}$

$52x = 9672$

$x = 186$

It will travel 186 miles.

156. Let x = the first integer.

Then $x + 2$ = the second integer.

$x + (x + 2) = 190$

$x + x + 2 = 190$

$2x + 2 = 190$

$2x = 188$

$x = 94$

The numbers are 94 and 94 + 2 = 96.

157. Let w = width of the shed.

Then $2w - 8$ = length of the shed.

$P = 2l + 2w$

$56 = 2(2w - 8) + 2w$

$56 = 4w - 16 + 2w$

$56 = 6w - 16$

$72 = 6w$

$12 = w$

The width is 12 ft and the length is 2(12) – 8 = 16 ft.

158. Let x = the amount invested at 3%.

Then $9000 - x$ = the amount invested at 4%.

Principal	Rate	Time	Interest
x	3%	1	$0.03x$
$9000 - x$	4%	1	$0.04(9000 - x)$

$0.03x - 0.04(9000 - x) = 32$

$0.03x - 360 + 0.04x = 32$

$0.07x - 360 = 32$

$0.07x = 392$

$x = 5600$

$5600 was invested at 3% and 9000 – 5600 = $3400 invested at 4%.

Exercise Set 4.3

1. A number in scientific notation is written as a number greater than or equal to 1 and less than 10 that is multiplied by some power of 10.

3. a. Answers will vary.

   b. 0.0000723 in scientific notation is 7.23×10^{-5}.

5. You will move the decimal point 6 places to the right.

7. The exponent will be positive when the number is 10 or greater.

9. The exponent will be negative since 0.00734 < 1.

11. $0.000001 = 1 \times 10^{-6}$

13. $350,000 = 3.5 \times 10^5$

15. $7950 = 7.95 \times 10^3$

17. $0.053 = 5.3 \times 10^{-2}$

19. $.000726 = 7.26 \times 10^{-4}$

21. $5,260,000,000 = 5.26 \times 10^9$

23. $0.00000914 = 9.14 \times 10^{-6}$

25. $220,300 = 2.203 \times 10^5$

27. $.005104 = 5.104 \times 10^{-3}$

29. $4.3 \times 10^4 = 43,000$

31. $9.32 \times 10^{-6} = 0.00000932$

33. $2.13 \times 10^{-5} = 0.0000213$

35. $6.25 \times 10^5 = 625,000$

37. $9.0 \times 10^6 = 9,000,000$

39. $5.35 \times 10^2 = 535$

41. $7.73 \times 10^{-7} = 0.000000773$

43. $1.0 \times 10^4 = 10,000$

45. 8 micrometers = $8 \times 10^{-6} = 0.000008$ meters

47. 125 gigawatts = $125 \times 10^9 = 125,000,000,000$ watts

49. 15.3 km = $15.3 \times 10^3 = 15,300$ meters

51. 48.2 mm = $48.2 \times 10^{-3} = 0.0482$ meters

53. $\left(2.0 \times 10^2\right)\left(3.0 \times 10^5\right) = \left(2.0 \times 3.0\right)\left(10^2 \times 10^5\right)$
$$= 6.0 \times 10^7$$
$$= 60,000,000$$

55. $\left(2.7 \times 10^{-6}\right)\left(9.0 \times 10^4\right)$
$$= \left(2.7 \times 9.0\right)\left(10^{-6} \times 10^4\right)$$
$$= 24.3 \times 10^{-2}$$
$$= 0.243$$

57. $\left(1.6 \times 10^{-2}\right)\left(4.0 \times 10^{-3}\right)$
$$= \left(1.6 \times 4.0\right)\left(10^{-2} \times 10^{-3}\right)$$
$$= 6.4 \times 10^{-5}$$
$$= 0.000064$$

59. $\dfrac{3.9 \times 10^{-5}}{3.0 \times 10^{-2}} = \left(\dfrac{3.9}{3.0}\right)\left(\dfrac{10^{-5}}{10^{-2}}\right)$
$$= 1.3 \times 10^{-3}$$
$$= 0.0013$$

61. $\dfrac{7.5 \times 10^6}{3.0 \times 10^3} = \left(\dfrac{7.5}{3.0}\right)\left(\dfrac{10^6}{10^3}\right) = 2.5 \times 10^3 = 2500$

63. $\dfrac{2.0 \times 10^4}{8.0 \times 10^{-2}} = \left(\dfrac{2.0}{8.0}\right)\left(\dfrac{10^4}{10^{-2}}\right)$
$$= 0.25 \times 10^6$$
$$= 250,000$$

65. $\left(700,000\right)\left(6,000,000\right) = \left(7 \times 10^5\right)\left(6 \times 10^6\right)$
$$= \left(7 \times 6\right)\left(10^5 \times 10^6\right)$$
$$= 42 \times 10^{11}$$
$$= 4.2 \times 10^{12}$$

67. $\left(0.0004\right)\left(320\right) = \left(4.0 \times 10^{-4}\right)\left(3.2 \times 10^2\right)$
$$= \left(4.0 \times 3.2\right)\left(10^{-4} \times 10^2\right)$$
$$= 12.8 \times 10^{-2}$$
$$= 1.28 \times 10^{-1}$$

69. $\dfrac{5,600,000}{8000} = \dfrac{5.6 \times 10^6}{8.0 \times 10^3}$
$$= \left(\dfrac{5.6}{8.0}\right)\left(\dfrac{10^6}{10^3}\right)$$
$$= 0.7 \times 10^3$$
$$= 7.0 \times 10^2$$

71. $\dfrac{0.00035}{0.000002} = \dfrac{3.5 \times 10^{-4}}{2.0 \times 10^{-6}}$
$$= \left(\dfrac{3.5}{2.0}\right)\left(\dfrac{10^{-4}}{10^{-6}}\right)$$
$$= 1.75 \times 10^2$$

73. $3.3 \times 10^{-4}, 5.3, 7.3 \times 10^2, 1.75 \times 10^6$

75. a. $\left(6.55 \times 10^9\right) - \left(2.99 \times 10^8\right)$
$$= \left(65.5 \times 10^8\right) - \left(2.99 \times 10^8\right)$$
$$= \left(65.5 - 2.99\right) \times 10^8$$
$$= 62.51 \times 10^8$$
$$\approx 6,251,000,000$$
The people that live outside the U.S. total about 6,251,000,000.

b. $\dfrac{6.55 \times 10^9}{2.99 \times 10^8} = \left(\dfrac{6.55}{2.99}\right)\left(\dfrac{10^9}{10^8}\right)$
$$\approx 2.19 \times 10$$
$$\approx 21.9$$
The world is about 21.9 times greater than the U.S. population.

77. Minimum volume

$$= \left(\frac{100,000 \text{ ft}^3 \text{sec}}{\text{sec}} \right) \left(\frac{60 \text{ sec}}{\text{min}} \right) \left(\frac{60 \text{ min}}{\text{hr}} \right) (24 \text{ hrs})$$

$$= \left(1.0 \times 10^5 \right) \left(6.0 \times 10^1 \right) \left(6.0 \times 10^1 \right) \left(2.4 \times 10^1 \right) \text{ft}^3$$

$$= \left(1 \times 6 \times 6 \times 2.4 \right) \left(10^5 \times 10^1 \times 10^1 \times 10^1 \right) \text{ft}^3$$

$$= 86.4 \times 10^8 \text{ ft}^3$$

$$= 8,640,000,000 \text{ ft}^3$$

79. $\left(2 \times 10^{-6} \right) \times \left(8 \times 10^{12} \right) = (2 \times 8) \left(10^{-6} \times 10^{12} \right)$

$$= 16 \times 10^6$$

$$= 1.6 \times 10^7$$

It would take 1.6×10^7 seconds.

81. a. $\left(6.01 \times 10^8 \right) - \left(4.33 \times 10^8 \right)$

$$= (6.01 - 4.33) \times 10^8$$

$$= 1.68 \times 10^8$$

Titanic grossed $\$1.68 \times 10^8$ more than *E.T.*

b. $\dfrac{6.01 \times 10^8}{4.33 \times 10^8} = \left(\dfrac{6.01}{4.33} \right) \left(\dfrac{10^8}{10^8} \right)$

$$\approx 1.39(1)$$

$$\approx 1.39$$

The gross ticket sales of *Titanic* was about 1.39 times greater than *E.T.*

83. a. $\left(4.65 \times 10^{10} \right) - \left(9.9 \times 10^9 \right)$

$$= \left(46.5 \times 10^9 \right) - \left(9.9 \times 10^9 \right)$$

$$= (46.5 - 9.9) \times 10^9$$

$$= 36.6 \times 10^9$$

$$= 36,600,000,000$$

Bill Gates was $\$36,600,000,000$ richer than Pierre Omidyar.

b. $\dfrac{4.65 \times 10^{10}}{9.9 \times 10^9} = \left(\dfrac{4.65}{9.9} \right) \left(\dfrac{10^{10}}{10^9} \right)$

$$\approx 0.47 \times 10$$

$$\approx 4.7$$

Bill Gates was worth 4.7 times greater than Pierre Omidyar.

85. a. Earth: 5.794×10^{24} metric tons

Moon: 7.34×10^{19} metric tons

Jupiter: 1.899×10^{27} metric tons

b. $\dfrac{5.794 \times 10^{24}}{7.340 \times 10^{19}} = \left(\dfrac{5.794}{7.340} \right) \left(\dfrac{10^{24}}{10^{19}} \right)$

$$\approx 0.789 \times 10^5$$

$$\approx 7.89 \times 10^4$$

c. $\dfrac{1.899 \times 10^{27}}{5.794 \times 10^{24}} = \left(\dfrac{1.899}{5.794} \right) \left(\dfrac{10^{27}}{10^{24}} \right)$

$$\approx 0.328 \times 10^3$$

$$\succ 3.28 \times 10^2$$

87. 47% of 2,800,000,000

$$0.47(2,800,000,000)$$

$$= \left(4.7 \times 10^{-1} \right) \left(2.8 \times 10^9 \right)$$

$$= (4.7 \times 2.8) \left(10^{-1} \times 10^9 \right)$$

$$= 13.16 \times 10^8$$

$$= 1.316 \times 10^9$$

There was $\$1.316 \times 10^9$ revenue from digital products and services.

89. a. $55 - 59 : 200,000 = 2.0 \times 10^5$

$$20 - 24 : 48,000 = 4.8 \times 10^4$$

b. $\left(2.0 \times 10^5 \right) + \left(4.8 \times 10^4 \right)$

$$= \left(20 \times 10^4 \right) + \left(4.8 \times 10^4 \right)$$

$$= (20.0 + 4.8) \times 10^4$$

$$= 24.8 \times 10^4$$

$$= 2.48 \times 10^5$$

c. $\left(2.0 \times 10^5 \right) - \left(4.8 \times 10^4 \right)$

$$= \left(20 \times 10^4 \right) - \left(4.8 \times 10^4 \right)$$

$$= (20.0 - 4.8) \times 10^4$$

$$= 15.2 \times 10^4$$

$$= 1.52 \times 10^5$$

91. $10^{-18} = 0.00000000000000001$

Thus, there are 17 zeros after the decimal.

93. Answers will vary.

95. $\dfrac{10^{-12}}{10^{-18}} = 10^{-12-(-18)}$

$\qquad = 10^6$

$\qquad = 1,000,000$ times greater

97. a. $1,000,000 = 1.0 \times 10^6$

$1,000,000,000 = 1.0 \times 10^9$

$1,000,000,000,000 = 1.0 \times 10^{12}$

b. $\dfrac{1,000,000}{1000} = \dfrac{1.0 \times 10^6}{1.0 \times 10^3}$

$\qquad = 1.0\left(\dfrac{10^6}{10^3}\right)$

$\qquad = 1.0\left(10^3\right)$

$\qquad = 1000$ days

c. $\dfrac{1,000,000,000}{1000} = \dfrac{1.0 \times 10^9}{1.0 \times 10^3}$

$\qquad = 1.0\left(\dfrac{10^9}{10^3}\right)$

$\qquad = 1.0\left(10^6\right)$

$\qquad = 1,000,000$ days

d. $\dfrac{1,000,000,000,000}{1000} = \dfrac{1.0 \times 10^{12}}{1.0 \times 10^3}$

$\qquad = 1.0\left(\dfrac{10^{12}}{10^3}\right)$

$\qquad = 1.0\left(10^9\right)$

$\qquad = 1,000,000,000$ days

e. $\dfrac{1,000,000,000}{1,000,000} = \dfrac{1.0 \times 10^9}{1.0 \times 10^6}$

$\qquad = 1.0\left(\dfrac{10^9}{10^6}\right)$

$\qquad = 1.0 \times 10^3$

$\qquad = 1,000$

It is 1000 times greater.

98. $4x^2 + 3x + \dfrac{x}{2} = 4 \cdot 0^2 + 3 \cdot 0 + \dfrac{0}{2}$

$\qquad = 0 + 0 + 0$

$\qquad = 0$

99. a. If $-x = -\dfrac{3}{2}$, then $x = \dfrac{3}{2}$.

b. If $5x = 0$, then $x = 0$.

100. $2x - 3(x - 2) = x + 2$

$2x - 3x + 6 = x + 2$

$-x + 6 = x + 2$

$4 = 2x$

$2 = x$

101. $\left(-\dfrac{2x^5 y^7}{8x^8 y^3}\right)^3 = \left(\dfrac{-2}{8} \cdot \dfrac{x^5}{x^8} \cdot \dfrac{y^7}{y^3}\right)^3$

$\qquad = \left(\dfrac{-1}{4} \cdot \dfrac{1}{x^3} \cdot y^4\right)^3$

$\qquad = \left(-\dfrac{y^4}{4x^3}\right)^3$

$\qquad = \dfrac{(-1)^3 y^{4 \cdot 3}}{4^3 x^{3 \cdot 3}}$

$\qquad = -\dfrac{y^{12}}{64x^9}$

Mid-Chapter Test: Sections 4.1-4.3

1. $y^{11} \cdot y^2 = y^{11+2} = y^{13}$

2. $\dfrac{x^{13}}{x^{10}} = x^{13-10} = x^3$

3. $\left(-3x^5 y^7\right)\left(-2xy^6\right) = (-3)(-2)x^{5+1} y^{7+6}$

$\qquad = 6x^6 y^{13}$

4. $\dfrac{6a^{12} b^8}{9a^7 b^2} = \dfrac{6}{9} a^{12-7} b^{8-2} = \dfrac{2}{3} a^5 b^6 = \dfrac{2a^5 b^6}{3}$

5. $\left(-4x^2 y^4\right)^3 = (-4)^3 x^{2 \cdot 3} y^{4 \cdot 3} = -64x^6 y^{12}$

6. $\left(\dfrac{-5s^4 t^6}{10s^6 t^3}\right)^2 = \left(\dfrac{-5}{10} s^{4-6} t^{6-3}\right)^2$

$\qquad = \left(-\dfrac{1}{2} s^{-2} t^3\right)^2$

$\qquad = \left(-\dfrac{1}{2}\right)^2 s^{-2 \cdot 2} t^{3 \cdot 2}$

$\qquad = \dfrac{t^6}{4s^4}$

7. $(7x^9y^5)(-3xy^4)^2 = (7x^9y^5)\left[(-3)^2 x^2 y^{4\cdot2}\right]$

$\qquad = (7x^9y^5)(9x^2y^8)$

$\qquad = (7)(9)x^{9+2}y^{5+8}$

$\qquad = 63x^{11}y^{13}$

8. $\dfrac{p^{-3}}{p^5} = p^{-3-5} = p^{-8} = \dfrac{1}{p^8}$

9. $x^{-4} \cdot x^{-6} = x^{-4+(-6)} = x^{-10} = \dfrac{1}{x^{10}}$

10. $\left(3^{-1} + 5^2\right)^0 = 1$

11. $\left(\dfrac{3}{7}\right)^{-2} = \left(\dfrac{7}{3}\right)^2 = \dfrac{49}{9}$

12. $(8x^{-2}y^5)(4x^3y^{-6}) = (8)(4)x^{-2+3}y^{5-6}$

$\qquad = 32xy^{-1}$

$\qquad = \dfrac{32x}{y}$

13. $\dfrac{6m^{-4}n^{-7}}{2m^0n^{-1}} = \dfrac{6}{2}m^{-4-0}n^{-7-(-1)} = 3m^{-4}n^{-6} = \dfrac{3}{m^4n^6}$

14. $\left(\dfrac{2x^{-3}y^{-4}}{x^3yz^{-2}}\right)^{-2} = \left(2x^{-3-3}y^{-4-1}z^2\right)^{-2}$

$\qquad = \left(2x^{-6}y^{-5}z^2\right)^{-2}$

$\qquad = 2^{-2}x^{-6\cdot(-2)}y^{-5\cdot(-2)}z^{2\cdot(-2)}$

$\qquad = \dfrac{1}{4}x^{12}y^{10}z^{-4}$

$\qquad = \dfrac{x^{12}y^{10}}{4z^4}$

15. a. Answers will vary.

   b. Answers will vary.

16. 6.54×10^9

17. 0.0000327

18. $18.9 \times 10^3 = 18,900$ meters

19. $(3.4 \times 10^{-6})(7.0 \times 10^3)$

$\qquad = (3.4 \times 7.0)(10^{-6} \times 10^3)$

$\qquad = 23.8 \times 10^{-6+3}$

$\qquad = 23.8 \times 10^{-3}$

$\qquad = 0.0238$

20. $\dfrac{0.00006}{200} = \dfrac{6 \times 10^{-5}}{2 \times 10^2} = \dfrac{6}{2} \times 10^{-5-2} = 3.0 \times 10^{-7}$

Exercise Set 4.4

1. A polynomial is an expression containing the sum of a finite number of terms of the form ax^n where a is a real number and n is a whole number.

3. No, it contains a negative exponent.

5. a. A monomial is a one-termed polynomial.

   b. A binomial is a two-termed polynomial.

   c. A trinomial is a three-termed polynomial.

7. Answers will vary.

9. b. and c. If you add the exponents on the variables, the sum is 4.

11. Write with exponents on the variable decreasing from left to right.

13. To add polynomials, combine like terms.

15. To subtract polynomials, use the distributive property to remove parentheses and then combine like terms.

17. fifth

19. eighth

21. third

23. tenth

25. ninth

27. trinomial

29. monomial

31. binomial

33. monomial

35. not a polynomial

37. polynomial

39. trinomial

41. not a polynomial

43. Already in descending order, 0 degree

45. $x^2 - 2x - 4$, second

47. $3x^2 + x - 8$, second

49. Already in descending order, first

51. Already in descending order, second

53. $4x^3 - 3x^2 + x - 4$, third

55. $-2x^4 + 3x^2 + 5x - 6$, fourth

57. $(9x - 2) + (x - 7) = 9x - 2 + x - 7$

$\qquad = 9x + x - 2 - 7$

$\qquad = 10x - 9$

59. $(-3x+8)+(2x+3)=-3x+8+2x+3$
$$=-3x+2x+8+3$$
$$=-x+11$$

61. $(t+7)+(-3t-8)=t-3t+7-8$
$$=-2t-1$$

63. $(x^2+2.6x-3)+(4x+3.8)$
$$=x^2+2.6x-3+4x+3.8$$
$$=x^2+2.6x+4x-3+3.8$$
$$=x^2+6.6x+0.8$$

65. $(4m-3)+(5m^2-4m+7)$
$$=4m-3+5m^2-4m+7$$
$$=5m^2+4m-4m-3+7$$
$$=5m^2+4$$

67. $(2x^2-3x+5)+(-x^2+6x-8)$
$$=2x^2-3x+5-x^2+6x-8$$
$$=2x^2-x^2+6x-3x+5-8$$
$$=x^2+3x-3$$

69. $(-x^2-4x+8)+\left(5x-2x^2+\dfrac{1}{2}\right)$
$$=-x^2-4x+8+5x-2x^2+\dfrac{1}{2}$$
$$=-x^2-2x^2-4x+5x+8+\dfrac{1}{2}$$
$$=-3x^2+x+\dfrac{17}{2}$$

71. $(5.2n^2-6n+1.7)+(3n^2+1.2n-2.3)$
$$=5.2n^2-6n+1.7+3n^2+1.2n-2.3$$
$$=5.2n^2+3n^2-6n+1.2n+1.7-2.3$$
$$=8.2n^2-4.8n-0.6$$

73. $(-7x^3-3x^2+4)+(4x+5x^3-7)$
$$=-7x^3-3x^2+4+4x+5x^3-7$$
$$=-7x^3+5x^3-3x^2+4x+4-7$$
$$=-2x^3-3x^2+4x-3$$

75. $(8x^2+2x-y)+(3x^2-9x+5)$
$$=8x^2+2x-y+3x^2-9x+5$$
$$=8x^2+3x^2+2x-9x-y+5$$
$$=11x^2-7x-y+5$$

77. $(2x^2y+2x-3)+(3x^2y-5x+5)$
$$=2x^2y+2x-3+3x^2y-5x+5$$
$$=2x^2y+3x^2y+2x-5x-3+5$$
$$=5x^2y-3x+2$$

79. $8x-7$
$\underline{3x+4}$
$11x-3$

81. $4y^2-2y+4$
$\underline{3y^2+1}$
$7y^2-2y+5$

83. $-x^2-3x+3$
$\underline{5x^2+5x-7}$
$4x^2+2x-4$

85. $2x^3+3x^2+6x-9$
$\underline{-4x^2+7}$
$2x^3-x^2+6x-2$

87. $4n^3-5n^2+n-6$
$\underline{-n^3-6n^2-2n+8}$
$3n^3-11n^2-n+2$

89. $(4x-4)-(2x+2)=4x-4-2x-2$
$$=4x-2x-4-2$$
$$=2x-6$$

91. $(-2x-3)-(-5x-7)=-2x-3+5x+7$
$$=-2x+5x-3+7$$
$$=3x+4$$

93. $(-r+5)-(2r+5)=-r+5-2r-5$
$$=-r-2r+5-5$$
$$=-3r$$

95. $(-y^2+4y-5.2)-(5y^2+2.1y+7.5)$
$$=-y^2+4y-5.2-5y^2-2.1y-7.5$$
$$=-y^2-5y^2+4y-2.1y-5.2-7.5$$
$$=-6y^2+1.9y-12.7$$

97. $(5x^2-x-1)-(-3x^2-2x-5)$
$$=5x^2-x-1+3x^2+2x+5$$
$$=5x^2+3x^2-x+2x-1+5$$
$$=8x^2+x+4$$

99. $(-4.1n^2-3n)-(2.3n^2-9n+7.6)$
$$=-4.1n^2-3n-2.3n^2+9n-7.6$$
$$=-4.1n^2-2.3n^2-3n+9n-7.6$$
$$=-6.4n^2+6n-7.6$$

101. $\left(8x^3 - 2x^2 - 4x + 5\right) - \left(5x^2 + 8\right)$

$= 8x^3 - 2x^2 - 4x + 5 - 5x^2 - 8$

$= 8x^3 - 2x^2 - 5x^2 - 4x - 8 + 5$

$= 8x^3 - 7x^2 - 4x - 3$

103. $\left(2x^3 - 4x^2 + 5x - 7\right) - \left(3x + \dfrac{3}{5}x^2 - 5\right)$

$= 2x^3 - 4x^2 + 5x - 7 - 3x - \dfrac{3}{5}x^2 + 5$

$= 2x^3 - 4x^2 - \dfrac{3}{5}x^2 + 5x - 3x - 7 + 5$

$= 2x^3 - \dfrac{23}{5}x^2 + 2x - 2$

105. $\left(8x + 2\right) - \left(7x + 4\right) = 8x + 2 - 7x - 4$

$= 8x - 7x + 2 - 4$

$= x - 2$

107. $\left(2x^2 - 4x + 8\right) - \left(5x - 6\right)$

$= 2x^2 - 4x + 8 - 5x + 6$

$= 2x^2 - 4x - 5x + 8 + 6$

$= 2x^2 - 9x + 14$

109. $\left(-5c^3 - 6c^2 + 7\right) - \left(-2c^2 + 7c - 7\right)$

$= -5c^3 - 6c^2 + 7 + 2c^2 - 7c + 7$

$= -5c^3 - 6c^2 + 2c^2 - 7c + 7 + 7$

$= -5c^3 - 4c^2 - 7c + 14$

111.
$$
\begin{array}{l}
6x + 5 \text{ or} \quad 6x + 5 \\
\underline{-(3x - 3)} \quad \underline{-3x + 3} \\
3x + 8
\end{array}
$$

113.
$$
\begin{array}{l}
5a^2 - 13a + 19 \quad \text{or} \quad 5a^2 - 13a + 19 \\
\underline{-\left(2a^2 + 3a - 9\right)} \quad \underline{-2a^2 - 3a + 9} \\
\phantom{-(2a^2+3a-9)\text{or}-}3a^2 - 16a + 28
\end{array}
$$

115.
$$
\begin{array}{l}
7x^2 - 3x - 4 \qquad 7x^2 - 3x - 4 \\
\underline{-(6x^2 - 1)} \quad \underline{-6x^2 + 0x + 1} \\
\text{or} \qquad x^2 - 3x - 3
\end{array}
$$

117.
$$
\begin{array}{l}
x^2 + 4 \qquad x^2 + 4 \\
\underline{-(5x^2 + 4)} \quad \text{or} \quad \underline{-5x^2 - 4} \\
\phantom{-(5x^2+4)\text{or}}-4x^2
\end{array}
$$

119.
$$
\begin{array}{l}
4x^3 - 6x^2 + 7x - 9 \quad \text{or} \quad 4x^3 - 6x^2 + 7x - 9 \\
\underline{-\left(x^2 + 6x - 7\right)} \quad \underline{-x^2 - 6x + 7} \\
4x^3 - 7x^2 + x - 2
\end{array}
$$

121. Answers will vary.

123. Answers will vary.

125. Sometimes

127. Sometimes

129. Answers will vary; one example is: $x^4 - 2x^3 + x$

131. No, all three terms must have degree 4 or 1.

133. $a^2 + 2ab + b^2$

135. $4x^2 + 3xy$

137. $\left(3x^2 - 6x + 3\right) - \left(2x^2 - x - 6\right) - \left(x^2 + 7x - 9\right) = 3x^2 - 6x + 3 - 2x^2 + x + 6 - x^2 - 7x + 9$

$ = \left(3x^2 - 2x^2 - x^2\right) + \left(-6x + x - 7x\right) + \left(3 + 6 + 9\right)$

$ = -12x + 18$

139. $4\left(x^2 + 2x - 3\right) - 6\left(2 - 4x - x^2\right) - 2x\left(x + 2\right) = 4x^2 + 8x - 12 - 12 + 24x + 6x^2 - 2x^2 - 4x$

$ = \left(4x^2 + 6x^2 - 2x^2\right) + \left(8x + 24x - 4x\right) + \left(-12 - 12\right)$

$ = 8x^2 + 28x - 24$

141. $|-9| > |-6|$ since $|-9| = 9$ and $|-6| = 6$.

142. True

143. True

144. False

145. False

146. $\left(\dfrac{b^3 c^{-4}}{2b^{-1}}\right)^{-2} = \left(\dfrac{b^4 c^{-4}}{2}\right)^{-2}$

$= \dfrac{b^{4(-2)} c^{-4(-2)}}{2^{-2}}$

$= \dfrac{b^{-8} c^8}{2^{-2}}$

$= \dfrac{2^2 c^8}{b^8}$

$= \dfrac{4c^8}{b^8}$

Exercise Set 4.5

1. To multiply two monomials, multiply their coefficients and use the product rule for exponents to determine the exponents on the variables.

3. First, Outer, Inner, Last

5. Yes, FOIL is simply a way to remember the procedure.

7. $(a+b)^2 = a^2 + 2ab + b^2$

$(a-b)^2 = a^2 - 2ab + b^2$

9. No, $(x-2)^2 = x^2 - 4x + 4$

11. Answers will vary.

13. Answers will vary.

15. $(3x^4)(-8x^2) = 3 \cdot (-8) x^{4+2} = -24x^6$

17. $5x^3 y^5 (4x^2 y) = (5 \cdot 4) x^{3+2} y^{5+1} = 20x^5 y^6$

19. $4xy^6 (-7x^2 y^9) = -28x^{1+2} y^{6+9} = -28x^3 y^{15}$

21. $9xy^6 (6x^5 y^8) = 9 \cdot 6 x^{1+5} y^{6+8} = 54x^6 y^{14}$

23. $(6x^2 y)\left(\dfrac{1}{2} x^4\right) = 6 \cdot \dfrac{1}{2} x^{2+4} y = 3x^6 y$

25. $(3.3x^4)(1.8x^4 y^3) = (3.3 \cdot 1.8) x^{4+4} y^3 = 5.94x^8 y^3$

27. $9(x-5) = (9)(x) + (9)(-5) = 9x - 45$

29. $-3x(2x-2) = (-3x)(2x) + (-3x)(-2)$

$\qquad = -6x^2 + 6x$

31. $-2(8y+5) = (-2)(8y) + (-2)(5) = -16y - 10$

33. $-2x(x^2 - 2x + 5)$

$= (-2x)(x^2) + (-2x)(-2x) + (-2x)(5)$

$= -2x^3 + 4x^2 - 10x$

35. $5x(-4x^2 + 6x - 4)$

$= (5x)(-4x^2) + (5x)(6x) + (5x)(-4)$

$= -20x^3 + 30x^2 - 20x$

37. $0.5x^2 (x^3 - 6x^2 - 1)$

$= (0.5x^2)(x^3) + (0.5x^2)(-6x^2) + (0.5x^2)(-1)$

$= 0.5x^5 - 3x^4 - 0.5x^2$

39. $0.3x(2xy + 5x - 6y)$

$= (0.3x)(2xy) + (0.3x)(5x) + (0.3x)(-6y)$

$= 0.6x^2 y + 1.5x^2 - 1.8xy$

41. $(x^2 - 4y^3 - 3)y^4$

$= (x^2)(y^4) + (-4y^3)(y^4) + (-3)(y^4)$

$= x^2 y^4 - 4y^7 - 3y^4$

43. $(5x-2)(x+4)$

$= (5x)(x) + (5x)(4) + (-2)(x) + (-2)(4)$

$= 5x^2 + 20x - 2x - 8$

$= 5x^2 + 18x - 8$

45. $(2x+5)(3x-6)$

$= (2x)(3x) + (2x)(-6) + (5)(3x) + (5)(-6)$

$= 6x^2 - 12x + 15x - 30$

$= 6x^2 + 3x - 30$

47. $(2x-4)(2x+4)$

$= (2x)(2x) + (2x)(4) + (-4)(2x) + (-4)(4)$

$= 4x^2 + 8x - 8x - 16$

$= 4x^2 - 16$

49. $(8-5x)(6+x)$

$= (8)(6) + (8)(x) + (-5x)(6) + (-5x)(x)$

$= 48 + 8x - 30x - 5x^2$

$= 48 - 22x - 5x^2$

$= -5x^2 - 22x + 48$

51. $(6x-1)(-2x+5)$

$= (6x)(-2x)+(6x)(5)+(-1)(-2x)+(-1)(5)$

$= -12x^2+30x+2x-5$

$= -12x^2+32x-5$

53. $(x-2)(4x-2)$

$= (x)(4x)+(x)(-2)+(-2)(4x)+(-2)(-2)$

$= 4x^2-2x-8x+4$

$= 4x^2-10x+4$

55. $(3k-6)(4k-2)$

$= (3k)(4k)+(3k)(-2)+(-6)(4k)+(-6)(-2)$

$= 12k^2-6k-24k+12$

$= 12k^2-30k+12$

57. $(x-2)(x+2)$

$= (x)(x)+(x)(2)+(-2)(x)+(-2)(2)$

$= x^2+2x-2x-4$

$= x^2-4$

59. $(2x-3)(2x-3)$

$= (2x)(2x)+(2x)(-3)+(-3)(2x)+(-3)(-3)$

$= 4x^2-6x-6x+9$

$= 4x^2-12x+9$

61. $(6z-4)(7-z)$

$= (6z)(7)+(6z)(-z)+(-4)(7)+(-4)(-z)$

$= 42z-6z^2-28+4z$

$= -6z^2+46z-28$

63. $(9-2x)(7-4x)$

$= (9)(7)+(9)(-4x)+(-2x)(7)+(-2x)(-4x)$

$= 63-36x-14x+8x^2$

$= 8x^2-50x+63$

65. $(x+7)(y-3)=x(y)+(x)(-3)+7(y)+7(-3)$

$= xy-3x+7y-21$

67. $(2x-3y)(3x+2y)$

$= (2x)(3x)+(2x)(2y)+(-3y)(3x)+(-3y)(2y)$

$= 6x^2+4xy-9xy-6y^2$

$= 6x^2-5xy-6y^2$

69. $(9x+y)(4-3x)$

$= (9x)(4)+(9x)(-3x)+y(4)+y(-3x)$

$= 36x-27x^2+4y-3xy$

$= -27x^2-3xy+36x+4y$

71. $(x+0.6)(x+0.3)$

$= x(x)+x(0.3)+(0.6)x+(0.6)(0.3)$

$= x^2+0.3x+0.6x+0.18$

$= x^2+0.9x+0.18$

73. $(x+4)\left(x-\dfrac{1}{2}\right)$

$= x(x)+x\left(-\dfrac{1}{2}\right)+4(x)+4\left(-\dfrac{1}{2}\right)$

$= x^2-\dfrac{1}{2}x+4x-2$

$= x^2+\dfrac{7}{2}x-2$

75. $(x+6)(x-6)=x^2-6^2$

$\qquad\qquad\qquad = x^2-36$

77. $(3x-8)(3x+8)=(3x)^2-8^2=9x^2-64$

79. $(x+y)^2=(x)^2+2(x)(y)+(y)^2$

$\qquad\qquad = x^2+2xy+y^2$

81. $(x-0.2)^2=(x)^2-2(x)(0.2)+(0.2)^2$

$\qquad\qquad = x^2-0.4x+0.04$

83. $(4x+5)(4x+5)=(4x)^2+2(4x)(5)+(5)^2$

$\qquad\qquad\qquad = 16x^2+40x+25$

85. $(0.4x+y)^2=(0.4x)^2+2(0.4x)(y)+(y)^2$

$\qquad\qquad = 0.16x^2+0.8xy+y^2$

87. $(4c-5d)(4c+5d)=(4c)^2-(5d)^2$

$\qquad\qquad\qquad = 16c^2-25d^2$

89. $(-2x+6)(-2x-6)=(-2x)^2-6^2=4x^2-36$

91. $(7s-3t)^2=(7s)^2-2(7s)(3t)+(3t)^2$

$\qquad\qquad = 49s^2-42st+9t^2$

93. $(4m+3)(4m^2-5m+6)$

$= 4m(4m^2-5m+6)+3(4m^2-5m+6)$

$= 16m^3-20m^2+24m+12m^2-15m+18$

$= 16m^3-8m^2+9m+18$

95. $(3x+2)(4x^2-x+5)$

$= (3x)(4x^2-x+5)+2(4x^2-x+5)$

$= 12x^3-3x^2+15x+8x^2-2x+10$

$= 12x^3+5x^2+13x+10$

97. $(-2x^2-4x+1)(7x-3)$

$= -2x^2(7x-3)-4x(7x-3)+1(7x-3)$

$= -14x^3+6x^2-28x^2+12x+7x-3$

$= -14x^3-22x^2+19x-3$

99. $(a+b)(a^2-ab+b^2)$

$= a(a^2-ab+b^2)+b(a^2-ab+b^2)$

$= a^3-a^2b+ab^2+a^2b-ab^2+b^3$

$= a^3+b^3$

101. $(3x^2-2x+4)(2x^2+3x+1)$

$= 3x^2(2x^2+3x+1)-2x(2x^2+3x+1)$

$\quad +4(2x^2+3x+1)$

$= 6x^4+9x^3+3x^2-4x^3-6x^2-2x$

$\quad +8x^2+12x+4$

$= 6x^4+5x^3+5x^2+10x+4$

103. $(x^2-x+3)(x^2-2x)$

$= x^2(x^2-2x)-x(x^2-2x)+3(x^2-2x)$

$= x^4-2x^3-x^3+2x^2+3x^2-6x$

$= x^4-3x^3+5x^2-6x$

105. $(2x^3-6x^2+x-3)(x^2+4x)$

$= 2x^3(x^2+4x)-6x^2(x^2+4x)+x(x^2+4x)$

$\quad -3(x^2+4x)$

$= 2x^5+8x^4-6x^4-24x^3+x^3+4x^2-3x^2-12x$

$= 2x^5+2x^4-23x^3+x^2-12x$

107. $(b-1)^3 = (b-1)(b-1)^2$

$= (b-1)(b^2-2b+1)$

$= b(b^2-2b+1)-1(b^2-2b+1)$

$= b^3-2b^2+b-b^2+2b-1$

$= b^3-3b^2+3b-1$

109. $(3a-5)^3$

$= (3a-5)(3a-5)^2$

$= (3a-5)(9a^2-30a+25)$

$= 3a(9a^2-30a+25)-5(9a^2-30a+25)$

$= 27a^3-90a^2+75a-45a^2+150a-125$

$= 27a^3-135a^2+225a-125$

111. Yes, it will always be a monomial.

113. No, it could have 2 or 4 terms.

115. The missing exponents are 6, 3, and 1 since
$$3x^2(2x^6-5x^3+3x^1) = 3x^2(2x^6)-3x^2(5x^3)+3x^2(3x^1)$$
$$= 6x^8-15x^5+9x^3$$

117. a. $A = (x+2)(2x+1)$

$= x(2x)+x\cdot1+2\cdot2x+2\cdot1$

$= 2x^2+x+4x+2$

$= 2x^2+5x+2$

b. If $x=4$, $A = 2\cdot4^2+5\cdot4+2 = 54$.
The area is 54 square feet.

c. For the rectangle to be a square, all sides must have the same length. Thus,
$x+2 = 2x+1$.

$x+2 = 2x+1$

$2 = x+1$

$1 = x$

The rectangle is a square when $x=1$ foot.

119. a. Area of base $= (x+5)(3x+4)$

$= 3x^2+4x+15x+20$

$= 3x^2+19x+20$

b. Volume = height $\times$ Area

$= (2x-2)(3x^2+19x+20)$

$= 6x^3+38x^2+40x-6x^2-38x-40$

$= 6x^3+32x^2+2x-40$

c. $6x^3 + 32x^2 + 2x - 40$

$= 6(4)^3 + 32(4)^2 + 2 \cdot 4 - 40$

$= 6 \cdot 64 + 32 \cdot 16 + 8 - 40$

$= 384 + 512 - 32$

$= 864$

The volume is 864 cubic feet.

d. $(x+5)(3x+4)(2x-2)$

$= (4+5)(3 \cdot 4 + 4)(2 \cdot 4 - 2)$

$= 9(12+4)(8-2)$

$= 9 \cdot 16 \cdot 6$

$= 864$

The volume is 864 cubic feet.

e.   The volumes are the same.

121. $\left(\dfrac{1}{2}x + \dfrac{2}{3}\right)\left(\dfrac{2}{3}x - \dfrac{2}{5}\right)$

$= \left(\dfrac{1}{2}x\right)\left(\dfrac{2}{3}x\right) + \left(\dfrac{1}{2}x\right)\left(-\dfrac{2}{5}\right) + \left(\dfrac{2}{3}\right)\left(\dfrac{2}{3}x\right)$

$ + \left(\dfrac{2}{3}\right)\left(-\dfrac{2}{5}\right)$

$= \dfrac{1}{3}x^2 - \dfrac{1}{5}x + \dfrac{4}{9}x - \dfrac{4}{15}$

$= \dfrac{1}{3}x^2 - \dfrac{11}{45}x - \dfrac{4}{15}$

123. $3(x+7) - 5 = 3x - 17$

$3x + 21 - 5 = 3x - 17$

$3x + 16 = 3x - 17$ False

Since this is false, there is no solution.

124.   Let x = measure of angle C

Then $x - 16$ = measure of angle D

$x + (x - 16) = 90$

$2x - 16 = 90$

$2x = 106$

$x = 53$

Angle C measures 53° and angle D measures $53 - 16 = 37°$.

125. $\left(\dfrac{3xy^4}{6y^6}\right)^4 = \left(\dfrac{3}{6} \cdot x \cdot \dfrac{y^4}{y^6}\right)^4$

$= \left(\dfrac{1}{2} \cdot x \cdot \dfrac{1}{y^2}\right)^4$

$= \left(\dfrac{x}{2y^2}\right)^4$

$= \dfrac{x^4}{2^4 y^{2 \cdot 4}}$

$= \dfrac{x^4}{16y^8}$

126. a. $-6^3 = -\left(6^3\right) = -216$

    b. $6^{-3} = \dfrac{1}{6^3} = \dfrac{1}{216}$

127. $\left(-x^2 - 6x + 5\right) - \left(4x^2 - 4x - 9\right)$

$= -x^2 - 6x + 5 - 4x^2 + 4x + 9$

$= -x^2 - 4x^2 - 6x + 4x + 5 + 9$

$= -5x^2 - 2x + 14$

Exercise Set 4.6

1.   To divide a polynomial by a monomial, divide each term in the polynomial by the monomial.

3. $\dfrac{2x+8}{2} = \dfrac{2x}{2} + \dfrac{8}{2} = x + 4$

5.   Terms should be listed in descending order.

7. $\dfrac{x^2 - 7}{x - 2} = \dfrac{x^2 + 0x - 7}{x - 2}$

9. $(x+5)(x-3) - 2 = x^2 + 2x - 15 - 2$

$= x^2 + 2x - 17$

11. $\dfrac{x^2 - x - 42}{x - 7} = x + 6$ or $\dfrac{x^2 - x - 42}{x + 6} = x - 7$

13. $\dfrac{2x^2 + 5x + 3}{2x + 3} = x + 1$ or $\dfrac{2x^2 + 5x + 3}{x + 1} = 2x + 3$

15. $\dfrac{4x^2 - 9}{2x + 3} = 2x - 3$ or $\dfrac{4x^2 - 9}{2x - 3} = 2x + 3$

17. $\dfrac{3x+6}{3} = \dfrac{3x}{3} + \dfrac{6}{3} = x + 2$

19. $\dfrac{4n+10}{2} = \dfrac{4n}{2} + \dfrac{10}{2} = 2n + 5$

21. $\dfrac{7x+6}{3} = \dfrac{7x}{3} + \dfrac{6}{3} = \dfrac{7}{3}x + 2$

23. $\dfrac{-6x+4}{2} = \dfrac{-6x}{2} + \dfrac{4}{2} = -3x + 2$

25. $\dfrac{-9x-3}{-3} = 3x + 1$

27. $\dfrac{2x+16}{4} = \dfrac{2x}{4} + \dfrac{16}{4} = \dfrac{x}{2} + 4$

29. $\dfrac{4-10w}{-4} = \dfrac{(-1)(4-10w)}{(-1)(-4)}$

$\qquad = \dfrac{-4+10w}{4}$

$\qquad = -\dfrac{4}{4} + \dfrac{10w}{4}$

$\qquad = -1 + \dfrac{5}{2}w$

31. $(4x^2 + 8x - 12) \div 4x^2 = \dfrac{4x^2 + 8x - 12}{4x^2}$

$\qquad = \dfrac{4x^2}{4x^2} + \dfrac{8x}{4x^2} + \dfrac{-12}{4x^2}$

$\qquad = 1 + \dfrac{2}{x} - \dfrac{3}{x^2}$

33. $\dfrac{-4x^5 + 6x + 8}{2x^2} = \dfrac{-4x^5}{2x^2} + \dfrac{6x}{2x^2} + \dfrac{8}{2x^2}$

$\qquad = -2x^3 + \dfrac{3}{x} + \dfrac{4}{x^2}$

35. $(x^5 + 3x^4 - 3) \div x^3 = \dfrac{x^5 + 3x^4 - 3}{x^3}$

$\qquad = \dfrac{x^5}{x^3} + \dfrac{3x^4}{x^3} + \dfrac{-3}{x^3}$

$\qquad = x^2 + 3x - \dfrac{3}{x^3}$

37. $\dfrac{6x^5 - 4x^4 + 12x^3 - 5x^2}{2x^3}$

$\qquad = \dfrac{6x^5}{2x^3} - \dfrac{4x^4}{2x^3} + \dfrac{12x^3}{2x^3} - \dfrac{5x^2}{2x^3}$

$\qquad = 3x^2 - 2x + 6 - \dfrac{5}{2x}$

39. $\dfrac{8k^3 + 6k^2 - 8}{-4k} = \dfrac{(-1)\left(8k^3 + 6k^2 - 8\right)}{(-1)(-4k)}$

$\qquad = \dfrac{-8k^3 - 6k^2 + 8}{4k}$

$\qquad = \dfrac{-8k^3}{4k} - \dfrac{6k^2}{4k} + \dfrac{8}{4k}$

$\qquad = -2k^2 - \dfrac{3}{2}k + \dfrac{2}{k}$

41. $\dfrac{12x^5 + 3x^4 - 10x^2 - 9}{-3x^2}$

$\qquad = \dfrac{12x^5}{-3x^2} + \dfrac{3x^4}{-3x^2} - \dfrac{10x^2}{-3x^2} - \dfrac{9}{-3x^2}$

$\qquad = -4x^3 - x^2 + \dfrac{10}{3} + \dfrac{3}{x^2}$

43.
$$x+1\overline{)x^2 + 4x + 3}$$
quotient: $x + 3$

$\qquad \underline{x^2 + x}$

$\qquad\qquad 3x + 3$

$\qquad\qquad \underline{3x + 3}$

$\qquad\qquad\qquad 0$

$\dfrac{x^2 + 4x + 3}{x+1} = x + 3$

45.
$$y-7\overline{)5y^2 - 34y - 7}$$
quotient: $5y + 1$

$\qquad \underline{5y^2 - 35y}$

$\qquad\qquad y - 7$

$\qquad\qquad \underline{y - 7}$

$\qquad\qquad\quad 0$

$\dfrac{5y^2 - 34y - 7}{y-7} = 5y + 1$

47.
$$3x+2\overline{)6x^2 + 16x + 8}$$
quotient: $2x + 4$

$\qquad \underline{6x^2 + 4x}$

$\qquad\qquad 12x + 8$

$\qquad\qquad \underline{12x + 8}$

$\qquad\qquad\qquad 0$

$\dfrac{6x^2 + 16x + 8}{3x+2} = 2x + 4$

49. $\dfrac{x^2 - 16}{-4 + x} = \dfrac{x^2 + 0x - 16}{x - 4}$

$$
\begin{array}{r}
x+4 \\
x-4{\overline{\smash{\big)}\,x^2+0x-16}} \\
\underline{x^2-4x} \\
4x-16 \\
\underline{4x-16} \\
0
\end{array}
$$

$$\frac{x^2-16}{-4+x}=x+4$$

51.
$$
\begin{array}{r}
x+5 \\
2x-3{\overline{\smash{\big)}\,2x^2+7x-18}} \\
\underline{2x^2-3x} \\
10x-18 \\
\underline{10x-15} \\
-3
\end{array}
$$

$$(2x^2+7x-18)\div(2x-3)=x+5-\frac{3}{2x-3}$$

53. $\dfrac{x^2-36}{x-6}=\dfrac{x^2+0x-36}{x-6}$

$$
\begin{array}{r}
x+6 \\
x-6{\overline{\smash{\big)}\,x^2+0x-36}} \\
\underline{x^2-6x} \\
6x-36 \\
\underline{6x-36} \\
0
\end{array}
$$

$$\frac{x^2-36}{x-6}=x+6$$

55. $\dfrac{-x+9x^3-16}{3x-4}=\dfrac{9x^3-x-16}{3x-4}$

$$
\begin{array}{r}
3x^2+4x+5 \\
3x-4{\overline{\smash{\big)}\,9x^3+0x^2-x-16}} \\
\underline{9x^2-12x^2} \\
12x^2-x-16 \\
\underline{12x^2-16x} \\
15x-16 \\
\underline{15x-20} \\
4
\end{array}
$$

$$\frac{9x^3-x-16}{3x-4}=3x^2+4x+5+\frac{4}{3x-4}$$

57. $\dfrac{6x+8x^2-12}{2x+3}=\dfrac{8x^2+6x-12}{2x+3}$

$$
\begin{array}{r}
4x-3 \\
2x+3{\overline{\smash{\big)}\,8x^2+6x-12}} \\
\underline{8x^2+12x} \\
-6x-12 \\
\underline{-6x-9} \\
-3
\end{array}
$$

$$\frac{6x+8x^2-12}{2x+3}=4x-3-\frac{3}{2x+3}$$

59.
$$
\begin{array}{r}
7x^2-5 \\
x+4{\overline{\smash{\big)}\,7x^3+28x^2-5x-20}} \\
\underline{7x^3+28x^2} \\
-5x-20 \\
\underline{-5x-20} \\
0
\end{array}
$$

$$\frac{7x^3+28x^2-5x-20}{x+4}=7x^2-5$$

61. $\dfrac{2x^3-4x^2+12}{x-2}=\dfrac{2x^3-4x^2+0x+12}{x-2}$

$$
\begin{array}{r}
2x \\
x-2{\overline{\smash{\big)}\,2x^3-4x^2+0x+12}} \\
\underline{2x^3-4x^2} \\
12
\end{array}
$$

$$\frac{2x^3-4x^2+12}{x-2}=2x^2+\frac{12}{x-2}$$

63. $\left(w^3-8\right)\div(w-3)$

$$=(w^3+0w^2+0w-8)\div(w-3)$$

$$
\begin{array}{r}
w^2+3w+9 \\
w-3{\overline{\smash{\big)}\,w^3+0w^2+0w-8}} \\
\underline{w^3-3w^2} \\
3w^2+0w \\
\underline{3w^2-9w} \\
9w-8 \\
\underline{9w-27} \\
19
\end{array}
$$

$$(w^3-8)\div(w-3)=w^2+3w+9+\frac{19}{w-3}$$

65. $\dfrac{x^3-27}{x-3}=\dfrac{x^3+0x^2+0x-27}{x-3}$

$$\begin{array}{r} x^2+3x+9 \\ x-3\overline{\smash{\big)}\,x^3+0x^2+0x-27} \\ \underline{x^3-3x^2} \\ 3x^2+0x \\ \underline{3x^2-9x} \\ 9x-27 \\ \underline{9x-27} \\ 0 \end{array}$$

$\dfrac{x^3-27}{x-3}=x^2+3x+9$

67. $\dfrac{4x^3-5x}{2x-1}=\dfrac{4x^3+0x^2-5x+0}{2x-1}$

$$\begin{array}{r} 2x^2+x-2 \\ 2x-1\overline{\smash{\big)}\,4x^3+0x^2-5x+0} \\ \underline{4x^3-2x^2} \\ 2x^2-5x \\ \underline{2x^2-\ x} \\ -4x+0 \\ \underline{4x+2} \\ -2 \end{array}$$

$\dfrac{4x^3-5x}{2x-1}=2x^2+x-2-\dfrac{2}{2x-1}$

69.
$$\begin{array}{r} -m^2-7m-5 \\ m-1\overline{\smash{\big)}\,-m^3-6m^2+2m-3} \\ \underline{-m^3+\ m^2} \\ -7m^2+2m \\ \underline{-7m^2+7m} \\ -5m-3 \\ \underline{-5m+5} \\ -8 \end{array}$$

$\dfrac{-m^3-6m^2+2m-3}{m-1}=-m^2-7m-5-\dfrac{8}{m-1}$

71. $\dfrac{4t^3-t+4}{t+2}=\dfrac{4t^3+0t^2-t+4}{t+2}$

$$\begin{array}{r} 4t^2-8t+15 \\ t+2\overline{\smash{\big)}\,4t^3+0t^2-\ t+4} \\ \underline{4t^3+8t^2} \\ -8t^2-\ t \\ \underline{-8t^2-16t} \\ 15t+\ 4 \\ \underline{15t+30} \\ -26 \end{array}$$

$\dfrac{4t^3-t+4}{t+2}=4t^2-8t+15-\dfrac{26}{t+2}$

73. No, $\dfrac{2x+1}{x^2}=\dfrac{2x}{x^2}+\dfrac{1}{x^2}=\dfrac{2}{x}+\dfrac{1}{x^2}$

75. $(x+4)(2x+3)+4=2x^2+3x+8x+12+4$
$$=2x^2+11x+16$$

77. Third Degree

79. It has to be $4x$ since that is what must be multiplied with $4x^3$ in the quotient to get $16x^4$ in the dividend.

81. When dividing by $2x^2$, each exponent will decrease by two. So, the shaded areas must be 5, 3, 2, 1, respectively.

83. $\dfrac{3x^3-5}{3x-2}=\dfrac{3x^3+0x^2+0x-5}{3x-2}$

$$\begin{array}{r} x^2+\frac{2}{3}x+\frac{4}{9} \\ 3x-2\overline{\smash{\big)}\,3x^3+0x^2+0x-5} \\ \underline{3x^3-2x^2} \\ 2x^2+0x \\ \underline{2x^2-\frac{4}{3}x} \\ \frac{4}{3}x-5 \\ \underline{\frac{4}{3}x-\frac{8}{9}} \\ -\frac{37}{9} \end{array}$$

$\dfrac{3x^3-5}{3x-2}=x^2+\dfrac{2}{3}x+\dfrac{4}{9}-\dfrac{37}{9(3x-2)}$

85.

$$-x-3\overline{\smash{\big)}\,3x^2+6x-10} \quad \substack{-3x+3}$$

$$\underline{3x^2+9x}$$
$$-3x-10$$
$$\underline{-3x-\ 9}$$
$$-1$$

$$\frac{3x^2+6x-10}{-x-3}=-3x+3+\frac{1}{x+3}$$

87. $(x+1)(x+3)-1=x^2+4x+3-1$
$$=x^2+4x+2$$

88. a. 2 is a natural number.

   b. 2 and 0 are whole numbers.

   c. $2, -5, 0, \dfrac{2}{5}, -6.3,$ and $-\dfrac{23}{34}$ are rational numbers.

   d. $\sqrt{7}$ and $\sqrt{3}$ are irrational numbers.

   e. All of the numbers are real numbers.

89. a. $\dfrac{0}{1}=0$

   b. $\dfrac{1}{0}$ is undefined

90. Evaluate expressions in parentheses first, then exponents, followed by multiplications and divisions from left to right, and finally additions and subtractions from left to right.

91. $2(x+3)+2x=x+4$
$$2x+6+2x=x+4$$
$$4x+6=x+4$$
$$4x=x-2$$
$$3x=-2$$
$$x=-\frac{2}{3}$$

92. Let p = the purchase price of the sweater, then $0.30p$ = the amount saved on the sweater.
$$p-0.30p=27.65$$
$$0.7p=27.65$$
$$p=\frac{27.65}{0.7}$$
$$p=39.5$$
The regular price of the sweater is \$39.50.

93. $\dfrac{x^9}{x^{-4}}=x^{9-(-4)}=x^{9+4}=x^{13}$

Review Exercises

1. $x^5\cdot x^2=x^{5+2}=x^7$

2. $x^2\cdot x^4=x^{2+4}=x^6$

3. $3^2\cdot 3^3=3^{2+3}=3^5=243$

4. $2^4\cdot 2=2^{4+1}=2^5=32$

5. $\dfrac{x^4}{x}=x^{4-1}=x^3$

6. $\dfrac{a^5}{a^5}=a^{5-5}=a^0=1$

7. $\dfrac{5^5}{5^3}=5^{5-3}=5^2=25$

8. $\dfrac{4^4}{4}=4^{4-1}=4^3=64$

9. $\dfrac{x^6}{x^8}=\dfrac{1}{x^{8-6}}=\dfrac{1}{x^2}$

10. $\dfrac{y^4}{y}=y^{4-1}=y^3$

11. $x^0=1$

12. $7y^0=7\cdot 1=7$

13. $(-6z)^0=1$

14. $6^0=1$

15. $(5x)^2=5^2x^2=25x^2$

16. $(3a)^3=3^3a^3=27a^3$

17. $(-3x)^3=(-3)^3x^3=-27x^3$

18. $(6s)^3=6^3s^3=216s^3$

19. $(2x^2)^4=2^4x^{2\cdot4}=16x^8$

20. $(-x^4)^6=(-1)^6x^{4\cdot6}=x^{24}$

21. $(-p^8)^4=(-1)^4p^{8\cdot4}=p^{32}$

22. $\left(-\dfrac{2x^3}{y}\right)^2=\dfrac{(-2)^2x^{3\cdot2}}{y^2}=\dfrac{4x^6}{y^2}$

23. $\left(\dfrac{5y^2}{2b}\right)^2 = \dfrac{(-5)^2 \, y^{2 \cdot 2}}{2^2 b^2} = \dfrac{25y^4}{4b^2}$

24. $6x^2 \cdot 4x^3 = 6 \cdot 4x^{2+3} = 24x^5$

25. $\dfrac{16x^2 y}{4xy^2} = \dfrac{16}{4} \cdot \dfrac{x^2}{x} \cdot \dfrac{y}{y^2}$

$\qquad = 4x\dfrac{1}{y}$

$\qquad = \dfrac{4x}{y}$

26. $2x(3xy^3)^3 = 2x(3^3 x^3 y^{3 \cdot 3})$

$\qquad\qquad = 2x(27x^3 y^9)$

$\qquad\qquad = 2 \cdot 27x^{1+3} y^9$

$\qquad\qquad = 54x^4 y^9$

27. $\left(\dfrac{9x^2 y}{3xy}\right)^2 = \left(\dfrac{9}{3} \cdot \dfrac{x^2}{x} \cdot \dfrac{y}{y}\right)^2$

$\qquad\qquad = (3x)^2$

$\qquad\qquad = 3^2 x^2$

$\qquad\qquad = 9x^2$

28. $(2x^2 y)^3 (3xy^4) = (2^3 x^{2 \cdot 3} y^3)(3xy^4)$

$\qquad\qquad\quad = (8x^6 y^3)(3xy^4)$

$\qquad\qquad\quad = 8 \cdot 3x^{6+1} y^{3+4}$

$\qquad\qquad\quad = 24x^7 y^7$

29. $4x^2 y^3 \left(2x^3 y^4\right)^2 = 4x^2 y^3 \left(2^2 x^{3 \cdot 2} y^{4 \cdot 2}\right)$

$\qquad\qquad\qquad = 4x^2 y^3 \left(4x^6 y^8\right)$

$\qquad\qquad\qquad = 4 \cdot 4x^{2+6} y^{3+8}$

$\qquad\qquad\qquad = 16x^8 y^{11}$

30. $3c^2(2c^4 d^3) = 3 \cdot 2 \cdot c^{2+4} \cdot d^3 = 6c^6 d^3$

31. $\left(\dfrac{9a^3 b^2}{3ab^7}\right)^3 = \left(\dfrac{9}{3} \cdot \dfrac{a^3}{a} \cdot \dfrac{b^2}{b^7}\right)^3$

$\qquad\qquad = \left(3a^{3-1} \cdot \dfrac{1}{b^5}\right)^3$

$\qquad\qquad = \left(\dfrac{3a^2}{b^5}\right)^3$

$\qquad\qquad = \dfrac{3^3 a^{2 \cdot 3}}{b^{5 \cdot 3}}$

$\qquad\qquad = \dfrac{27a^6}{b^{15}}$

32. $\left(\dfrac{21x^4 y^3}{7y^2}\right)^3 = \left(\dfrac{21}{7} \cdot x^4 \cdot \dfrac{y^3}{y^2}\right)^3$

$\qquad\qquad = \left(3x^4 y\right)^3$

$\qquad\qquad = 3^3 x^{4 \cdot 3} y^3$

$\qquad\qquad = 27x^{12} y^3$

33. $b^{-9} = \dfrac{1}{b^9}$

34. $3^{-3} = \dfrac{1}{3^3} = \dfrac{1}{27}$

35. $5^{-2} = \dfrac{1}{5^2} = \dfrac{1}{25}$

36. $\dfrac{1}{z^{-2}} = z^2$

37. $\dfrac{1}{x^{-7}} = x^7$

38. $\dfrac{1}{4^{-2}} = 4^2 = 16$

39. $y^5 \cdot y^{-8} = y^{5-8} = y^{-3} = \dfrac{1}{y^3}$

40. $x^{-2} \cdot x^{-3} = x^{-2-3} = x^{-5} = \dfrac{1}{x^5}$

41. $p^{-6} \cdot p^4 = p^{-6+4} = p^{-2} = \dfrac{1}{p^2}$

42. $a^{-2} \cdot a^{-3} = a^{-2+(-3)} = a^{-5} = \dfrac{1}{a^5}$

43. $\dfrac{m^5}{m^{-5}} = m^{5-(-5)} = m^{10}$

44. $\dfrac{x^5}{x^{-2}} = x^{5-(-2)} = x^7$

45. $\dfrac{x^{-3}}{x^3} = \dfrac{1}{x^{3+3}} = \dfrac{1}{x^6}$

46. $\left(3x^4\right)^{-2} = 3^{-2}x^{4(-2)}$

$\qquad = 3^{-2}x^{-8}$

$\qquad = \dfrac{1}{3^2 x^8}$

$\qquad = \dfrac{1}{9x^8}$

47. $\left(4x^{-3}y\right)^{-3} = 4^{-3}x^{(-3)(-3)}y^{-3}$

$\qquad = 4^{-3}x^9 y^{-3}$

$\qquad = \dfrac{x^9}{4^3 y^3}$

$\qquad = \dfrac{x^9}{64 y^3}$

48. $\left(-2m^{-3}n\right)^2 = (-2)^2 m^{-3\cdot 2}n^{1\cdot 2}$

$\qquad = 4m^{-6}n^2$

$\qquad = \dfrac{4n^2}{m^6}$

49. $6y^{-2}\cdot 2y^4 = 6\cdot 2y^{-2+4} = 12y^2$

50. $\left(-5y^{-3}z\right)^3 = (-1)^3 5^3 y^{(-3)3}z^3$

$\qquad = -125y^{-9}z^3$

$\qquad = -\dfrac{125z^3}{y^9}$

51. $\left(-4x^{-2}y^3\right)^{-2} = (-1)^{-2}\,4^{-2}x^{(-2)(-2)}y^{3(-2)}$

$\qquad = 4^{-2}x^4 y^{-6}$

$\qquad = \dfrac{x^4}{(-1)^2\,4^2 y^6}$

$\qquad = \dfrac{x^4}{16 y^6}$

52. $2x\left(3x^{-2}\right) = 2\cdot 3x^{1-2} = 6x^{-1} = \dfrac{6}{x}$

53. $\left(5x^{-2}y\right)\left(2x^4 y\right) = 5\cdot 2x^{-2+4}y^{1+1} = 10x^2 y^2$

54. $4y^{-2}\left(3x^2 y\right) = 4\cdot 3x^2 y^{-2+1}$

$\qquad = 12x^2 y^{-1}$

$\qquad = \dfrac{12x^2}{y}$

55. $4x^5\left(6x^{-7}y^2\right) = 4\cdot 6x^{5-7}y^2$

$\qquad = 24x^{-2}y^2$

$\qquad = \dfrac{24y^2}{x^2}$

56. $\dfrac{6xy^4}{2xy^{-1}} = \dfrac{6}{2}\cdot\dfrac{x}{x}\cdot\dfrac{y^4}{y^{-1}} = 3y^5$

57. $\dfrac{12x^{-2}y^3}{3xy^2} = \dfrac{12}{3}\cdot\dfrac{x^{-2}}{x}\cdot\dfrac{y^3}{y^2}$

$\qquad = 4\cdot\dfrac{1}{x^3}\cdot y$

$\qquad = \dfrac{4y}{x^3}$

58. $\dfrac{49x^2 y^{-3}}{7x^{-3}y} = \dfrac{49}{7}\cdot\dfrac{x^2}{x^{-3}}\cdot\dfrac{y^{-3}}{y}$

$\qquad = \left(\dfrac{49}{7}\right)x^{2-(-3)}y^{-3-1}$

$\qquad = 7x^5 y^{-4}$

$\qquad = \dfrac{7x^5}{y^4}$

59. $\dfrac{4x^8 y^{-2}}{8x^7 y^3} = \dfrac{4}{8}\cdot\dfrac{x^8}{x^7}\cdot\dfrac{y^{-2}}{y^3}$

$\qquad = \dfrac{1}{2}\cdot x\cdot\dfrac{1}{y^5}$

$\qquad = \dfrac{x}{2y^5}$

60. $\dfrac{36x^4 y^7}{9x^5 y^{-3}} = \dfrac{36}{9}\cdot\dfrac{x^4}{x^5}\cdot\dfrac{y^7}{y^{-3}}$

$\qquad = 4\cdot\dfrac{1}{x}\cdot y^{10}$

$\qquad = \dfrac{4y^{10}}{x}$

61. $1,720,000 = 1.72\times 10^6$

62. $0.153 = 1.53\times 10^{-1}$

63. $0.00763 = 7.63\times 10^{-3}$

64. $47,000 = 4.7 \times 10^4$

65. $5,760 = 5.76 \times 10^3$

66. $0.000314 = 3.14 \times 10^{-4}$

67. $7.5 \times 10^{-3} = 0.0075$

68. $6.52 \times 10^{-4} = 0.000652$

69. $8.9 \times 10^6 = 8,900,000$

70. $5.12 \times 10^4 = 51,200$

71. $3.14 \times 10^{-5} = 0.0000314$

72. $1.103 \times 10^7 = 11,030,000$

73. 92 milliliters $= 92 \times 10^{-3} = 0.092$ liters

74. 6 gigameters $= 6 \times 10^9 = 6,000,000,000$ meters

75. 12.8 micrograms $= 12.8 \times 10^{-6}$
$$= 0.0000128 \text{ grams}$$

76. 19.2 kilograms $= 19.2 \times 10^3 = 19,200$ grams

77. $\left(2.5 \times 10^2\right)\left(3.4 \times 10^{-4}\right) = (2.5 \times 3.4)\left(10^2 \times 10^{-4}\right)$
$$= 8.5 \times 10^{-2}$$
$$= 0.085$$

78. $\left(4.2 \times 10^{-3}\right)\left(3.0 \times 10^5\right) = (4.2 \times 3)\left(10^{-3} \times 10^5\right)$
$$= 12.6 \times 10^2$$
$$= 1260$$

79. $\left(3.5 \times 10^{-2}\right)\left(7.0 \times 10^3\right) = (3.5 \times 7.0)\left(10^{-2} \times 10^3\right)$
$$= 24.5 \times 10^1$$
$$= 245$$

80. $\dfrac{7.94 \times 10^6}{2.0 \times 10^{-2}} = \left(\dfrac{7.94}{2.0}\right)\left(\dfrac{10^6}{10^{-2}}\right)$
$$= 3.97 \times 10^8$$
$$= 397,000,000$$

81. $\dfrac{1.5 \times 10^{-2}}{5.0 \times 10^2} = \left(\dfrac{1.5}{5}\right)\left(\dfrac{10^{-2}}{10^2}\right)$
$$= 0.3 \times 10^{-4}$$
$$= 0.00003$$

82. $\dfrac{6.5 \times 10^4}{2.0 \times 10^6} = \left(\dfrac{6.5}{2.0}\right)\left(\dfrac{10^4}{10^6}\right)$
$$= 3.25 \times 10^{-2}$$
$$= 0.0325$$

83. $(14,000)(260,000) = \left(1.4 \times 10^4\right)\left(2.6 \times 10^5\right)$
$$= (1.4 \times 2.6)\left(10^4 \times 10^5\right)$$
$$= 3.64 \times 10^9$$

84. $(0.00053)(40,000) = \left(5.3 \times 10^{-4}\right)\left(4 \times 10^4\right)$
$$= (5.3 \times 4)\left(10^{-4} \times 10^4\right)$$
$$= 21.2 \times 10^0$$
$$= 2.12 \times 10^1$$

85. $(12,500)(400,000) = \left(1.25 \times 10^4\right)\left(4.0 \times 10^5\right)$
$$= (1.25 \times 4.0)\left(10^4 \times 10^5\right)$$
$$= 5.0 \times 10^9$$

86. $\dfrac{250}{500,000} = \dfrac{2.5 \times 10^2}{5.0 \times 10^5}$
$$= \left(\dfrac{2.5}{5.0}\right)\left(\dfrac{10^2}{10^5}\right)$$
$$= 0.5 \times 10^{-3}$$
$$= 5.0 \times 10^{-4}$$

87. $\dfrac{0.000068}{0.02} = \dfrac{6.8 \times 10^{-5}}{2 \times 10^{-2}}$
$$= \left(\dfrac{6.8}{2}\right)\left(\dfrac{10^{-5}}{10^{-2}}\right)$$
$$= 3.4 \times 10^{-3}$$

88. $\dfrac{850,000}{0.025} = \dfrac{8.5 \times 10^5}{2.5 \times 10^{-2}}$
$$= \left(\dfrac{8.50}{2.50}\right)\left(\dfrac{10^5}{10^{-2}}\right)$$
$$= 3.40 \times 10^7$$

89. $\dfrac{6.4 \times 10^6}{1.28 \times 10^2} = \left(\dfrac{6.4}{1.28}\right)\left(\dfrac{10^6}{10^2}\right)$
$$= 5 \times 10^4$$
$$= 50,000 \text{ gallons}$$

The milk tank holds 50,000 gallons.

90. a. $1,500,000,000,000

b. $0.075\left(1.5\times10^{12}\right)=\left(7.5\times10^{-2}\right)\left(1.5\times10^{12}\right)$

$$=\left(7.5\times1.5\right)\left(10^{-2}\times10^{12}\right)$$

$$=11.25\times10^{10}$$

$$=\$1.125\times10^{11}$$

91. Not a polynomial

92. monomial, zero degree

93. x^2+3x-4, trinomial, second degree

94. $4x^2-x-3$, trinomial, second degree

95. Not a polynomial

96. $13x^3-4$, binomial, third degree

97. $-4x^2+x$, binomial, second degree

98. Not a polynomial

99. $2x^3+4x^2-3x-7$, polynomial, third degree

100. $(x+8)+(4x-11)=x+8+4x-11$

$$=x+4x+8-11$$

$$=5x-3$$

101. $(2d-3)+(5d+7)=2d-3+5d+7$

$$=2d+5d-3+7$$

$$=7d+4$$

102. $(-x-10)+(-2x+5)=-x-10-2x+5$

$$=-x-2x-10+5$$

$$=-3x-5$$

103. $\left(-3x^2+9x+5\right)+\left(-x^2+2x-12\right)$

$$=-3x^2+9x+5-x^2+2x-12$$

$$=-3x^2-x^2+9x+2x+5-12$$

$$=-4x^2+11x-7$$

104. $\left(-m^2+5m-8\right)+\left(6m^2-5m-2\right)$

$$=-m^2+6m^2+5m-5m-8-2$$

$$=5m^2-10$$

105. $\left(6.2p-4.3\right)+\left(1.9p+7.1\right)$

$$=6.2p+1.9p-4.3+7.1$$

$$=8.1p+2.8$$

106. $(-6y-7)-(-3y+8)=-6y-7+3y-8$

$$=-6y+3y-7-8$$

$$=-3y-15$$

107. $\left(4x^2-9x\right)-\left(3x+15\right)=4x^2-9x-3x-15$

$$=4x^2-12x-15$$

108. $\left(5a^2-6a-9\right)-\left(2a^2-a+12\right)$

$$=5a^2-6a-9-2a^2+a-12$$

$$=5a^2-2a^2-6a+a-9-12$$

$$=3a^2-5a-21$$

109. $\left(x^2+7x-3\right)-\left(x^2+3x-5\right)$

$$=x^2+7x-3-x^2-3x+5$$

$$=x^2-x^2+7x-3x-3+5$$

$$=4x+2$$

110. $\left(-2x^2+8x-7\right)-\left(3x^2+12\right)$

$$=-2x^2+8x-7-3x^2-12$$

$$=-2x^2-3x^2+8x-7-12$$

$$=-5x^2+8x-19$$

111. $\dfrac{1}{7}x(21x+21)=\dfrac{1}{7}x(21x)+\dfrac{1}{7}x(21)$

$$=\dfrac{21}{7}x^2+\dfrac{21}{7}x$$

$$=3x^2+3x$$

112. $-3x(5x+4)=-3x\cdot5x+(-3x)4$

$$=-15x^2-12x$$

113. $3x\left(2x^2-4x+7\right)=3x\left(2x^2\right)+3x(-4x)+3x(7)$

$$=6x^3-12x^2+21x$$

114. $-c\left(2c^2-3c+5\right)$

$$=(-c)\left(2c^2\right)+(-c)(-3c)+(-c)(5)$$

$$=-2c^3+3c^2-5c$$

115. $-7b\left(-4b^2-3b-5\right)$

$$=(-7b)\left(-4b^2\right)+(-7b)(-3b)+(-7b)(-5)$$

$$=28b^3+21b^2+35b$$

116. $(x+4)(x+5)=x\cdot x+x\cdot5+4\cdot x+4\cdot5$

$$=x^2+5x+4x+20$$

$$=x^2+9x+20$$

117. $(3x+6)(-4x+1)$

$$=3x(-4x)+3x(1)+6(-4x)+6(1)$$

$$=-12x^2+3x-24x+6$$

$$=-12x^2-21x+6$$

118. $(-5x+3)^2 = (-5x)^2 + 2(-5x)(3) + (3)^2$
$$= 25x^2 - 30x + 9$$

119. $(6-2x)(2+3x)$
$$= 6 \cdot 2 + 6 \cdot 3x + (-2x)(2) + (-2x)(3x)$$
$$= 12 + 18x - 4x - 6x^2$$
$$= 12 + 14x - 6x^2$$
$$= -6x^2 + 14x + 12$$

120. $(r+5)(r-5) = (r)^2 - (5)^2$
$$= r^2 - 25$$

121. $(x-1)(3x^2 + 4x - 6)$
$$= x(3x^2 + 4x - 6) - 1(3x^2 + 4x - 6)$$
$$= 3x^3 + 4x^2 - 6x - 3x^2 - 4x + 6$$
$$= 3x^3 + x^2 - 10x + 6$$

122. $(3x+1)(x^2 + 2x + 4)$
$$= 3x(x^2 + 2x + 4) + 1(x^2 + 2x + 4)$$
$$= 3x^3 + 6x^2 + 12x + x^2 + 2x + 4$$
$$= 3x^3 + 7x^2 + 14x + 4$$

123. $(-4x+2)(3x^2 - x + 7)$
$$= -4x(3x^2 - x + 7) + 2(3x^2 - x + 7)$$
$$= -12x^3 + 4x^2 - 28x + 6x^2 - 2x + 14$$
$$= -12x^3 + 10x^2 - 30x + 14$$

124. $\dfrac{2x+4}{2} = \dfrac{2x}{2} + \dfrac{4}{2} = x + 2$

125. $\dfrac{12y+18}{3} = \dfrac{12y}{3} + \dfrac{18}{3} = 4y + 6$

126. $\dfrac{8x^2 + 4x}{x} = \dfrac{8x^2}{x} + \dfrac{4x}{x}$
$$= 8x + 4$$

127. $\dfrac{6x^2 + 9x - 4}{3} = \dfrac{6x^2}{3} + \dfrac{9x}{3} - \dfrac{4}{3}$
$$= 2x^2 + 3x - \dfrac{4}{3}$$

128. $\dfrac{6w^2 - 5w + 3}{3w} = \dfrac{6w^2}{3w} - \dfrac{5w}{3w} + \dfrac{3}{3w}$
$$= 2w - \dfrac{5}{3} + \dfrac{1}{w}$$

129. $\dfrac{16x^6 - 8x^5 - 3x^3 + 1}{4x} = \dfrac{16x^6}{4x} - \dfrac{8x^5}{4x} - \dfrac{3x^3}{4x} + \dfrac{1}{4x}$
$$= 4x^5 - 2x^4 - \dfrac{3}{4}x^2 + \dfrac{1}{4x}$$

130. $\dfrac{8m-4}{-2} = \dfrac{(-1)(8m-4)}{(-1)(-2)}$
$$= \dfrac{-8m+4}{2}$$
$$= \dfrac{-8m}{2} + \dfrac{4}{2}$$
$$= -4m + 2$$

131. $\dfrac{5x^3 + 10x + 2}{2x^2} = \dfrac{5x^3}{2x^2} + \dfrac{10x}{2x^2} + \dfrac{2}{2x^2}$
$$= \dfrac{5x}{2} + \dfrac{5}{x} + \dfrac{1}{x^2}$$

132. $\dfrac{5x^2 - 6x + 15}{3x} = \dfrac{5x^2}{3x} - \dfrac{6x}{3x} + \dfrac{15}{3x}$
$$= \dfrac{5x}{3} - 2 + \dfrac{5}{x}$$

133.
$$
\require{enclose}
\begin{array}{r}
x+4 \\
x-3 \enclose{longdiv}{x^2 + x - 12} \\
\underline{x^2 - 3x} \\
4x - 12 \\
\underline{4x - 12} \\
0
\end{array}
$$

$\dfrac{x^2 + x - 12}{x-3} = x + 4$

134.
$$
\begin{array}{r}
5x - 2 \\
x+6 \enclose{longdiv}{5x^2 + 28x - 10} \\
\underline{5x^2 + 30x} \\
-2x - 10 \\
\underline{-2x - 12} \\
2
\end{array}
$$

$\dfrac{5x^2 + 28x - 10}{x+6} = 5x - 2 + \dfrac{2}{x+6}$

135.

$$6n+1 \overline{\smash{\big)}\, 6n^2 + 19n + 3} \quad \underset{\displaystyle n+3}{}$$

$$\underline{6n^2 + n}$$
$$18n + 3$$
$$\underline{18n + 3}$$
$$0$$

$$\frac{6n^2 + 19n + 3}{6n + 1} = n + 3$$

136.

$$2x+3 \overline{\smash{\big)}\, 4x^3 + 12x^2 + x - 12} \quad \underset{\displaystyle 2x^2 + 3x - 4}{}$$

$$\underline{4x^3 + 6x^2}$$
$$6x^2 + x$$
$$\underline{6x^2 + 9x}$$
$$-8x - 12$$
$$\underline{-8x - 12}$$
$$0$$

$$\frac{4x^3 + 12x^2 + x - 12}{2x + 3} = 2x^2 + 3x - 4$$

137.

$$2x-3 \overline{\smash{\big)}\, 4x^2 - 12x + 9} \quad \underset{\displaystyle 2x - 3}{}$$

$$\underline{4x^2 - 6x}$$
$$-6x + 9$$
$$\underline{-6x + 9}$$
$$0$$

$$\frac{4x^2 - 12x + 9}{2x - 3} = 2x - 3$$

Practice Test

1. $5x^4 \cdot 3x^2 = 5 \cdot 3x^{4+2} = 15x^6$

2. $\left(3xy^2\right)^3 = 3^3 x^3 y^{2 \cdot 3} = 27x^3 y^6$

3. $\dfrac{24p^7}{3p^2} = \dfrac{24}{3} p^{7-2} = 8p^5$

4. $\left(\dfrac{3x^2 y}{6xy^3}\right)^3 = \left(\dfrac{3}{6} \cdot \dfrac{x^2}{x} \cdot \dfrac{y}{y^3}\right)^3$

$$= \left(\frac{1}{2} \cdot x \cdot \frac{1}{y^2}\right)^3$$
$$= \left(\frac{x}{2y^2}\right)^3$$
$$= \frac{x^3}{2^3 y^{2 \cdot 3}}$$
$$= \frac{x^3}{8y^6}$$

5. $\left(2x^3 y^{-2}\right)^{-2} = 2^{-2} x^{3(-2)} y^{(-2)(-2)}$

$$= 2^{-2} x^{-6} y^4$$
$$= \frac{y^4}{2^2 x^6}$$
$$= \frac{y^4}{4x^6}$$

6. $\left(4x^0\right)\left(3x^2\right)^0 = \left(4 \cdot 1\right) \cdot 1 = 4$

7. $\dfrac{30x^6 y^2}{45x^{-1} y} = \dfrac{30}{45} x^{6-(-1)} y^{2-1}$

$$= \frac{2}{3} x^7 y$$
$$= \frac{2x^7 y}{3}$$

8. $(285,000)(50,000) = \left(2.85 \times 10^5\right)\left(5.0 \times 10^4\right)$

$$= \left(2.85 \times 5.0\right)\left(10^5 \times 10^4\right)$$
$$= 14.25 \times 10^9$$
$$= 1.425 \times 10^{10}$$

9. $\dfrac{0.0008}{4000} = \dfrac{8.0 \times 10^{-4}}{4.0 \times 10^3}$

$$= \left(\frac{8.0}{4.0}\right)\left(\frac{10^{-4}}{10^3}\right)$$
$$= 2.0 \times 10^{-7}$$

10. $4x$ is a monomial

11. $-8c + 5$, binomial

12. $x^{-2} + 4$, not a polynomial

13. $-5 + 6x^3 - 2x^2 + 5x = 6x^3 - 2x^2 + 5x - 5$, third degree

14. $(6x - 4) + (2x^2 - 5x - 3) = 6x - 4 + 2x^2 - 5x - 3$

$\qquad\qquad\qquad\qquad = 2x^2 + 6x - 5x - 4 - 3$

$\qquad\qquad\qquad\qquad = 2x^2 + x - 7$

15. $(y^2 - 7y + 3) - (4y^2 - 5y - 2)$

$\qquad = y^2 - 7y + 3 - 4y^2 + 5y + 2$

$\qquad = y^2 - 4y^2 - 7y + 5y + 3 + 2$

$\qquad = -3y^2 - 2y + 5$

16. $(4x^2 - 5) - (x^2 + x - 8) = 4x^2 - 5 - x^2 - x + 8$

$\qquad\qquad\qquad\qquad = 4x^2 - x^2 - x - 5 + 8$

$\qquad\qquad\qquad\qquad = 3x^2 - x + 3$

17. $-5d(-3d + 8) = -5d(-3d) - 5d(8)$

$\qquad\qquad\qquad = 15d^2 - 40d$

18. $(5x + 8)(3x - 4)$

$\qquad = (5x)(3x) + (5x)(-4) + 8(3x) + 8(-4)$

$\qquad = 15x^2 - 20x + 24x - 32$

$\qquad = 15x^2 + 4x - 32$

19. $(9 - 4c)(5 + 3c)$

$\qquad = 9 \cdot 5 + 9(3c) + (-4c) \cdot 5 + (-4c)(3c)$

$\qquad = 45 + 27c - 20c - 12c^2$

$\qquad = -12c^2 + 7c + 45$

20. $(3x - 5)(2x^2 + 4x - 5)$

$\qquad = 3x(2x^2 + 4x - 5) - 5(2x^2 + 4x - 5)$

$\qquad = 3x \cdot 2x^2 + 3x \cdot 4x - 3x \cdot 5 - 5 \cdot 2x^2 - 5 \cdot 4x - 5(-5)$

$\qquad = 6x^3 + 12x^2 - 15x - 10x^2 - 20x + 25$

$\qquad = 6x^3 + 2x^2 - 35x + 25$

21. $\dfrac{16x^2 + 8x - 4}{4} = \dfrac{16x^2}{4} + \dfrac{8x}{4} - \dfrac{4}{4}$

$\qquad\qquad\qquad\quad = 4x^2 + 2x - 1$

22. $\dfrac{-12x^2 - 6x + 5}{-3x} = \dfrac{(-1)(-12x^2 - 6x + 5)}{(-1)(-3x)}$

$\qquad\qquad\qquad = \dfrac{12x^2 + 6x - 5}{3x}$

$\qquad\qquad\qquad = \dfrac{12x^2}{3x} + \dfrac{6x}{3x} - \dfrac{5}{3x}$

$\qquad\qquad\qquad = 4x + 2 - \dfrac{5}{3x}$

23.

$$\begin{array}{r} 4x + 5 \\ 2x - 3 \overline{)\; 8x^2 - 2x - 15} \\ \underline{8x^2 - 12x} \\ 10x - 15 \\ \underline{10x - 15} \\ 0 \end{array}$$

$\dfrac{8x^2 - 2x - 15}{2x - 3} = 4x + 5$

24.

$$\begin{array}{r} 3x - 2 \\ 4x + 5 \overline{)\; 12x^2 + 7x - 12} \\ \underline{12x^2 + 15x} \\ -8x - 12 \\ \underline{-8x - 10} \\ -2 \end{array}$$

$\dfrac{12x^2 + 7x - 12}{4x + 5} = 3x - 2 - \dfrac{2}{4x + 5}$

25. a. $5730 = 5.73 \times 10^3$

b. $\dfrac{4.46 \times 10^9}{5.73 \times 10^3} = \left(\dfrac{4.46}{5.73}\right)\left(\dfrac{10^9}{10^3}\right)$

$\qquad\qquad\qquad \approx 0.778 \times 10^6$

$\qquad\qquad\qquad \approx 7.78 \times 10^5$

Cumulative Review Test

1. $12 + 8 \div 2^2 + 3 = 12 + 8 \div 4 + 3$

$\qquad\qquad\qquad = 12 + 2 + 3$

$\qquad\qquad\qquad = 17$

2. $7 - (2x - 3) + 2x - 8(1 - x)$

$\quad = 7 - 2x + 3 + 2x - 8 + 8x$

$\quad = 7 + 3 - 8 - 2x + 2x + 8x$

$\quad = 2 + 8x$

$\quad = 8x + 2$

3. $-4x^2 + x - 7 = -4(-2)^2 + (-2) - 7$

$\qquad\qquad\qquad = -4(4) - 2 - 7$

$\qquad\qquad\qquad = -16 - 2 - 7$

$\qquad\qquad\qquad = -18 - 7$

$\qquad\qquad\qquad = -25$

4. a. Associative property of addition

$\quad$ **b.** Commutative property of multiplication

$\quad$ **c.** Commutative property of multiplication

5. $5y + 7 = 2(y - 3)$

$\quad 5y + 7 = 2y - 6$

$\qquad 3y = -13$

$\qquad y = -\dfrac{13}{3}$

6. $3(x + 2) + 3x - 5 = 4x + 1$

$\quad 3x + 6 + 3x - 5 = 4x + 1$

$\qquad\quad 6x + 1 = 4x + 1$

$\qquad\qquad 2x = 0$

$\qquad\qquad x = 0$

7. $3x - 11 < 5x - 2$

$\quad -11 + 2 < 5x - 3x$

$\qquad -9 < 2x$

$\qquad -\dfrac{9}{2} < x$

$\qquad\quad x > -\dfrac{9}{2}$

8. $3x - 2 = y - 7$

$\quad y - 7 = 3x - 2$

$\qquad y = 3x - 2 + 7$

$\qquad y = 3x + 5$

9. $\qquad 7x - 3y = 21$

$\quad 7x - 3y - 7x = -7x + 21$

$\qquad\qquad -3y = -7x + 21$

$\qquad\qquad y = \dfrac{-7x + 21}{-3}$

$\qquad\qquad y = \dfrac{7x - 21}{3}$

Substitute 6 for x.

$\quad y = \dfrac{7(6) - 21}{3} = \dfrac{42 - 21}{3} = \dfrac{21}{3} = 7$

10. $\left(\dfrac{5xy^{-3}}{x^{-2}y^5}\right)^2 = \left(5x^{1-(-2)}y^{-3-5}\right)^2$

$\qquad\qquad\quad = \left(5x^3 y^{-8}\right)^2$

$\qquad\qquad\quad = 5^2 x^{3 \cdot 2} y^{-8 \cdot 2}$

$\qquad\qquad\quad = \dfrac{25x^6}{y^{16}}$

11. $-5x + 2 - 7x^2 = -7x^2 - 5x + 2$

second degree

12. $\left(x^2 + 4x - 3\right) + \left(2x^2 + 5x + 1\right)$

$\quad = x^2 + 4x - 3 + 2x^2 + 5x + 1$

$\quad = x^2 + 2x^2 + 4x + 5x - 3 + 1$

$\quad = 3x^2 + 9x - 2$

13. $\left(6a^2 + 3a + 2\right) - \left(a^2 - 3a - 3\right)$

$\quad = 6a^2 + 3a + 2 - a^2 + 3a + 3$

$\quad = 6a^2 - a^2 + 3a + 3a + 2 + 3$

$\quad = 5a^2 + 6a + 5$

14. $\left(5t - 3\right)\left(2t - 1\right)$

$\quad = 5t \cdot 2t + 5t \cdot (-1) - 3 \cdot 2t - 3 \cdot (-1)$

$\quad = 10t^2 - 5t - 6t + 3$

$\quad = 10t^2 - 11t + 3$

15. $\left(2x - 1\right)\left(3x^2 - 5x + 2\right)$

$\quad = 2x\left(3x^2 - 5x + 2\right) - 1\left(3x^2 - 5x + 2\right)$

$\quad = 6x^3 - 10x^2 + 4x - 3x^2 + 5x - 2$

$\quad = 6x^3 - 13x^2 + 9x - 2$

16. $\dfrac{10d^2 + 12d - 8}{4d} = \dfrac{10d^2}{4d} + \dfrac{12d}{4d} - \dfrac{8}{4d}$

$\qquad\qquad\qquad = \dfrac{5}{2}d + 3 - \dfrac{2}{d}$

17.

$$\begin{array}{r} 2x + 5 \\ 3x - 2 \overline{\smash{\big)}\, 6x^2 + 11x - 10} \\ \underline{6x^2 - 4x} \\ 15x - 10 \\ \underline{15x - 10} \\ 0 \end{array}$$

$$\frac{6x^2 + 11x - 10}{3x - 2} = 2x + 5$$

18. $\dfrac{x}{8} = \dfrac{1.25}{3}$

$3x = 8(1.25)$

$3x = 10$

$x = \dfrac{10}{3} \approx 3.33$

Eight cans of soup cost $3.33.

19. Let b = Bob's average speed.
Then $b + 7$ = Nick's average speed.
$d = r \cdot t$. Both Bob and Nick drove for 0.5 hour
and the total distance they covered was 60 miles.
$0.5b + 0.5(b + 7) = 60$

$0.5b + 0.5b + 3.5 = 60$

$b = 56.5$

Bob's average speed was 56.5 miles per hour and
Nick's average speed was $56.5 + 7 = 63.5$ miles
per hour.

20. Let x = the width of the rectangle. Then $3x - 2$ =
the length of the rectangle.
$P = 2l + 2w$

$28 = 2(3x - 2) + 2x$

$28 = 6x - 4 + 2x$

$32 = 8x$

$4 = x$

The width of the rectangle is 4 feet and the
length is $3(4) - 2 = 10$ feet.

Chapter 5

Exercise Set 5.1

1. To factor an expression means to write the expression as the product of factors.

3. A composite number is a positive integer, other than 1, that is not a prime number.

5. The greatest common factor of two or more numbers is the greatest number that divides into all the numbers.

7. $1, 2, 4, x, 2x, 4x, x^2, 2x^2, 4x^2$ and the opposites of these factors.

9. $56 = 8 \cdot 7$
$ = 2 \cdot 4 \cdot 7$
$ = 2 \cdot 2 \cdot 2 \cdot 7$
$ = 2^3 \cdot 7$

11. $90 = 9 \cdot 10$
$ = 3 \cdot 3 \cdot 2 \cdot 5$
$ = 2 \cdot 3^2 \cdot 5$

13. $248 = 4 \cdot 62$
$ = 2 \cdot 2 \cdot 2 \cdot 31$
$ = 2^3 \cdot 31$

15. $20 = 2^2 \cdot 5$, $24 = 2^3 \cdot 3$, so the greatest common factor is 2^2 or 4.

17. $70 = 2 \cdot 5 \cdot 7$, $98 = 2 \cdot 7^2$, so the greatest common factor is $2 \cdot 7$ or 14.

19. $80 = 2^4 \cdot 5$, $126 = 2 \cdot 3^2 \cdot 7$,
so the greatest common factor is 2.

21. The greatest common factor is x.

23. The greatest common factor is $3x$.

25. The greatest common factor is a.

27. The greatest common factor is qr.

29. The greatest common factor is $x^3 y^5$.

31. The greatest common factor is 1.

33. The greatest common factor is $x^2 y^2$.

35. The greatest common factor is x.

37. The greatest common factor is $x - 4$.

39. The greatest common factor is $2x - 3$.

41. The greatest common factor is $3w + 5$.

43. The greatest common factor is $x - 4$.

45. The greatest common factor is $x - 1$.

47. The greatest common factor is $x - 9$.

49. The greatest common factor is 4.
$4x - 8 = 4 \cdot x - 4 \cdot 2$
$ = 4(x - 2)$

51. The greatest common factor is 5.
$15x - 5 = 5 \cdot 3x - 5 \cdot 1$
$ = 5(3x - 1)$

53. The greatest common factor is 7.
$7q + 28 = 7 \cdot q + 7 \cdot 4$
$ = 7(q + 4)$

55. The greatest common factor is $3x$.
$9x^2 - 12x = 3x \cdot 3x - 3x \cdot 4$
$ = 3x(3x - 4)$

57. The greatest common factor is x^4.
$7x^5 - 9x^4 = x^4 \cdot 7x - x^4 \cdot 9$
$ = x^4(7x - 9)$

59. The greatest common factor is $3x^2$.
$3x^5 - 12x^2 = 3x^2 \cdot x^3 - 3x^2 \cdot 4$
$ = 3x^2(x^3 - 4)$

61. The greatest common factor is $12x^8$.
$36x^{12} + 24x^8 = 12x^8 \cdot 3x^4 + 12x^8 \cdot 2$
$\phantom{36x^{12} + 24x^8} = 12x^8(3x^4 + 2)$

63. The greatest common factor is $9y^3$.
$27y^{15} - 9y^3 = 9y^3 \cdot 3y^{12} - 9y^3 \cdot 1$
$\phantom{27y^{15} - 9y^3} = 9y^3(3y^{12} - 1)$

65. The greatest common factor is y.
$y + 6x^3 y = y \cdot 1 + y \cdot 6x^3$
$ = y(1 + 6x^3)$

67. The greatest common factor is a^2.
$$7a^4 + 3a^2 = a^2 \cdot 7a^2 + a^2 \cdot 3$$
$$= a^2\left(7a^2 + 3\right)$$

69. The greatest common factor is $4xy$.
$$16xy^2z + 4x^3y = 4xy \cdot 4yz + 4xy \cdot x^2$$
$$= 4xy\left(4yz + x^2\right)$$

71. The greatest common factor is $4x^2yz^3$.
$$80x^5y^3z^4 - 36x^2yz^3$$
$$= 4x^2yz^3 \cdot 20x^3y^2z - 4x^2yz^3 \cdot 9$$
$$= 4x^2yz^3\left(20x^3y^2z - 9\right)$$

73. The greatest common factor is $25x^2yz$.
$$25x^2yz^3 + 25x^3yz = 25x^2yz \cdot z^2 + 25x^2yz \cdot x$$
$$= 25x^2yz\left(z^2 + x\right)$$

75. The greatest common factor is $x^4y^3z^9$.
$$19x^4y^{12}z^{13} - 8x^5y^3z^9$$
$$= x^4y^3z^9 \cdot 19y^9z^4 - x^4y^3z^9 \cdot 8x$$
$$= x^4y^3z^9\left(19y^9z^4 - 8x\right)$$

77. The greatest common factor is 4.
$$8c^2 - 4c - 32 = 4 \cdot 2c^2 - 4 \cdot c - 4 \cdot 8$$
$$= 4\left(2c^2 - c - 8\right)$$

79. The greatest common factor is 3.
$$9x^2 + 18x + 3 = 3 \cdot 3x^2 + 3 \cdot 6x + 3 \cdot 1$$
$$= 3\left(3x^2 + 6x + 1\right)$$

81. The greatest common factor is $4x$.
$$4x^3 - 8x^2 + 12x = 4x \cdot x^2 - 4x \cdot 2x + 4x \cdot 3$$
$$= 4x\left(x^2 - 2x + 3\right)$$

83. The greatest common factor is 8.
$$40b^2 - 48c + 24 = 8 \cdot 5b^2 - 8 \cdot 6c + 8 \cdot 3$$
$$= 8\left(5b^2 - 6c + 3\right)$$

85. The greatest common factor is 3.
$$15p^2 - 6p + 9 = 3 \cdot 5p^2 - 3 \cdot 2p + 3 \cdot 3$$
$$= 3\left(5p^2 - 2p + 3\right)$$

87. The greatest common factor is $3a$.
$$9a^4 - 6a^3 + 3ab = 3a \cdot 3a^3 - 3a \cdot 2a^2 + 3a \cdot b$$
$$= 3a\left(3a^3 - 2a^2 + b\right)$$

89. The greatest common factor is xy.
$$8x^2y + 12xy^2 + 5xy = xy \cdot 8x + xy \cdot 12y + xy \cdot 5$$
$$= xy\left(8x + 12y + 5\right)$$

91. The greatest common factor is $x - 7$.
$$x(x-7) + 6(x-7) = (x-7)(x+6)$$

93. The greatest common factor is $a - 2$.
$$3b(a-2) - 4(a-2) = (a-2)(3b-4)$$

95. The greatest common factor is $2x + 1$.
$$4x(2x+1) + 1(2x+1) = (2x+1)(4x+1)$$

97. The greatest common factor is $2x + 1$.
$$5x(2x+1) + 2x + 1 = 5x(2x+1) + 1(2x+1)$$
$$= (2x+1)(5x+1)$$

99. The greatest common factor is $6c + 7$.
$$3c(6c+7) - 2(6c+7) = (6c+7)(3c-2)$$

101. $12\nabla - 6\nabla^2 = 6\nabla \cdot 2 - 6\nabla \cdot \nabla$
$$= 6\nabla\left(2 - \nabla\right)$$

103. $12\square^3 - 4\square^2 + 4\square$
$$= 4\square \cdot 3\square^2 - 4\square \cdot \square + 4\square \cdot 1$$
$$= 4\square\left(3\square^2 - \square + 1\right)$$

105. The greatest common factor is $2x^2(2x+7)$.
$$6x^5(2x+7) + 4x^3(2x+7) - 2x^2(2x+7)$$
$$= 2x^2(2x+7) \cdot 3x^3 + 2x^2(2x+7) \cdot 2x$$
$$+ 2x^2(2x+7) \cdot (-1)$$
$$= 2x^2(2x+7)\left(3x^3 + 2x - 1\right)$$

107. $x^2 + 2x + 3x + 6$
$$= x \cdot x + x \cdot 2 + 3 \cdot x + 3 \cdot 2$$
$$= x(x+2) + 3(x+2)$$
$$= (x+2)(x+3)$$

108. $2x - (x-5) + 4(3-x) = 2x - x + 5 + 12 - 4x$
$$= x - 4x + 17$$
$$= -3x + 17$$

109. $4 + 3(x-8) = x - 4(x+2)$
$$4 + 3x - 24 = x - 4x - 8$$
$$3x - 20 = -3x - 8$$
$$6x = 12$$
$$x = 2$$

110. $4x - 5y = 20$

$$-5y = -4x + 20$$

$$y = -\frac{-4x + 20}{-5}$$

$$y = \frac{4}{5}x - 4$$

111. $V = \frac{1}{3}\pi r^2 h$

$$= \frac{1}{3}\pi(4)^2(12)$$

$$= \frac{1}{3}\pi(16)(12)$$

$$= 64\pi \text{ in.}^3 \text{ or } 201.06 \text{ in.}^3$$

112. Let x = smaller number, then $2x - 1$ = the larger number.

$$x + (2x - 1) = 41$$

$$x + 2x - 1 = 41$$

$$3x - 1 = 41$$

$$3x = 42$$

$$x = 14$$

$$2x - 1 = 2(14) - 1 = 28 - 1 = 27$$

The numbers are 14 and 27.

113. $\left(\dfrac{3x^2 y^3}{2x^5 y^2}\right)^2 = \left(\dfrac{3y}{2x^3}\right)^2$

$$= \frac{(3y)^2}{(2x^3)^2}$$

$$= \frac{3^2 y^2}{2^2 (x^3)^2}$$

$$= \frac{9y^2}{4x^6}$$

Exercise Set 5.2

1. The first step in any factoring by grouping problem is to factor out a common factor, if one exists.

3. If you multiply $(x - 2y)(x - 3)$ using the FOIL method, you get the polynomial $x^2 - 3x - 2xy + 6y$

5. The number that changes the sign of each term in an expression when factored from each term is -1.

7. $x^2 + 3x + 2x + 6 = x(x + 3) + 2(x + 3)$

$$= (x + 3)(x + 2)$$

9. $x^2 + 5x + 4x + 20 = x(x + 5) + 4(x + 5)$

$$= (x + 5)(x + 4)$$

11. $x^2 + 2x + 5x + 10 = x(x + 2) + 5(x + 2)$

$$= (x + 2)(x + 5)$$

13. $c^2 - 4c + 7c - 28 = c(c - 4) + 7(c - 4)$

$$= (c - 4)(c + 7)$$

15. $4x^2 - 6x + 6x - 9 = 2x(2x - 3) + 3(2x - 3)$

$$= (2x - 3)(2x + 3)$$

17. $3x^2 + 9x + x + 3 = 3x(x + 3) + 1(x + 3)$

$$= (x + 3)(3x + 1)$$

19. $6x^2 + 3x - 2x - 1 = 3x(2x + 1) - 1(2x + 1)$

$$= (2x + 1)(3x - 1)$$

21. $8x^2 + 32x + x + 4 = 8x(x + 4) + 1(x + 4)$

$$= (x + 4)(8x + 1)$$

23. $12t^2 - 8t - 3t + 2$

$$= 4t(3t - 2) - 1(3t - 2)$$

$$= (3t - 2)(4t - 1)$$

25. $x^2 + 9x - x - 9 = x(x + 9) - 1(x + 9)$

$$= (x + 9)(x - 1)$$

27. $6p^2 + 15p - 4p - 10$

$$= 3p(2p + 5) - 2(2p + 5)$$

$$= (2p + 5)(3p - 2)$$

29. $x^2 + 2xy - 3xy - 6y^2$

$$= x(x + 2y) - 3y(x + 2y)$$

$$= (x + 2y)(x - 3y)$$

31. $3x^2 + 2xy - 9xy - 6y^2$

$$= x(3x + 2y) - 3y(3x + 2y)$$

$$= (3x + 2y)(x - 3y)$$

33. $10x^2 - 12xy - 25xy + 30y^2$

$$= 2x(5x - 6y) - 5y(5x - 6y)$$

$$= (5x - 6y)(2x - 5y)$$

35. $x^2 - bx - ax + ab$
$= x(x - b) - a(x - b)$
$= (x - b)(x - a)$

37. $xy + 9x - 5y - 45 = x(y + 9) - 5(y + 9)$
$= (y + 9)(x - 5)$

39. $a^2 + 3a + ab + 3b = a(a + 3) + b(a + 3)$
$= (a + 3)(a + b)$

41. $xy - x + 5y - 5 = x(y - 1) + 5(y - 1)$
$= (y - 1)(x + 5)$

43. $12 + 8y - 3x - 2xy = 4(3 + 2y) - x(3 + 2y)$
$= (3 + 2y)(4 - x)$

45. $z^3 + 5z^2 + z + 5 = z^2(z + 5) + 1(z + 5)$
$= (z + 5)(z^2 + 1)$

47. $x^3 - 5x^2 + 8x - 40 = x^2(x - 5) + 8(x - 5)$
$= (x - 5)(x^2 + 8)$

49. $2x^2 - 12x + 8x - 48$
$= 2 \cdot x^2 - 2 \cdot 6x + 2 \cdot 4x - 2 \cdot 24$
$= 2(x^2 - 6x + 4x - 24)$
$= 2[x(x - 6) + 4(x - 6)]$
$= 2(x - 6)(x + 4)$

51. $4x^2 + 8x + 8x + 16$
$= 4 \cdot x^2 + 4 \cdot 2x + 4 \cdot 2x + 4 \cdot 4$
$= 4(x^2 + 2x + 2x + 4)$
$= 4[x(x + 2) + 2(x + 2)]$
$= 4(x + 2)(x + 2)$
$= 4(x + 2)^2$

53. $6x^3 + 9x^2 - 2x^2 - 3x$
$= x \cdot 6x^2 + x \cdot 9x - x \cdot 2x - x \cdot 3$
$= x(6x^2 + 9x - 2x - 3)$
$= x[3x(2x + 3) - 1(2x + 3)]$
$= x(2x + 3)(3x - 1)$

55. $p^3 - 6p^2 q + 2p^2 q - 12pq^2$
$= p \cdot p^2 - p \cdot 6pq + p \cdot 2pq - p \cdot 12q^2$
$= p(p^2 - 6pq + 2pq - 12q^2)$
$= p[p(p - 6q) + 2q(p - 6q)]$
$= p(p - 6q)(p + 2q)$

57. $5x + 3y + xy + 15 = xy + 5x + 3y + 15$
$= x(y + 5) + 3(y + 5)$
$= (y + 5)(x + 3)$

59. $6x + 5y + xy + 30 = 6x + xy + 5y + 30$
$= x(6 + y) + 5(y + 6)$
$= (x + 5)(y + 6)$

61. $ax + by + ay + bx = ax + ay + bx + by$
$= a(x + y) + b(x + y)$
$= (a + b)(x + y)$

63. $rs - 42 + 6s - 7r$
$= rs - 7r + 6s - 42$
$= r(s - 7) + 6(s - 7)$
$= (s - 7)(r + 6)$

65. $dc + 3c - ad - 3a = c(d + 3) - a(d + 3)$
$= (d + 3)(c - a)$

67.   Not *any* arrangement of the terms of a polynomial is factorable by grouping. $xy + 2x + 5y + 10$ is factorable but $xy + 10 + 2x + 5y$ is not factorable in this arrangement.

69. $\odot^2 + 3\odot - 5\odot - 15 = \odot(\odot + 3) - 5(\odot + 3)$
$= (\odot + 3)(\odot - 5)$

71. a. $2x^2 - 11x + 15 = 2x^2 - 5x - 6x + 15$

    b. $2x^2 - 5x - 6x + 15 = x(2x - 5) - 3(2x - 5)$
$= (x - 3)(2x - 5)$

73. a. $2x^2 - 11x + 15 = 2x^2 - 6x - 5x + 15$

    b. $2x^2 - 6x - 5x + 15$
$= 2x(x - 3) - 5(x - 3)$
$= (x - 3)(2x - 5)$

75. a. $4x^2 - 17x - 15 = 4x^2 + 3x - 20x - 15$

b. $4x^2 + 3x - 20x - 15 = x(4x+3) - 5(4x+3)$
$$= (x-5)(4x+3)$$

77. $\star\odot + 3\star + 2\odot + 6 = \star(\odot + 3) + 2(\odot + 3)$
$$= (\odot + 3)(\star + 2)$$

79. $5 - 3(2x - 7) = 4(x + 5) - 6$
$$5 - 6x + 21 = 4x + 20 - 6$$
$$-6x + 26 = 4x + 14$$
$$12 = 10x$$
$$\frac{12}{10} = x$$
$$\frac{6}{5} = x$$

80. Let x = the number of pounds of jelly beans and $(50 - x)$ = the number of pounds of gumdrops.

Item	Price per pound	Quantity	Cost
Jellybeans	6.25	x	$6.25x$
Gumdrops	2.50	$50 - x$	$2.50(50 - x)$
Mixture	4.75	50	4.75(50)

$$6.25x + 2.50(50 - x) = 4.75(50)$$
$$6.25x + 125 - 2.50x = 237.5$$
$$3.75x + 125 = 237.5$$
$$3.75x = 112.5$$
$$x = 30$$

They should mix 30 pounds of jelly beans with 20 pounds of gumdrops.

81. $\dfrac{15x^3 - 6x^2 - 9x + 5}{3x} = \dfrac{15x^3}{3x} - \dfrac{6x^2}{3x} - \dfrac{9x}{3x} + \dfrac{5}{3x}$
$$= 5x^2 - 2x - 3 + \frac{5}{3x}$$

82. $a+4\overline{\smash{)}a^2 - 16} \quad \overset{\textstyle a-4}{}$
$$\underline{a^2 + 4a}$$
$$-4a - 16$$
$$\underline{-4a - 16}$$
$$0$$

$$\frac{a^2 - 16}{a+4} = a - 4$$

Exercise Set 5.3

1. Since 960 is positive, both signs will be the same. Since 92 is positive, both signs will be positive.

3. Since –1500 is negative, one sign will be positive, the other will be negative.

5. Since 8000 is positive, both signs will be the same. Since 240 is negative, both signs will be negative.

7. The trinomial $x^2 - 11x + 24$ is obtained by multiplying the factors using the FOIL method.

9. The trinomial $2x^2 - 8xy - 10y^2$ is obtained by multiplying all the factors and combining like terms.

11. The answer is not fully factored. A 2 can be factored from $(2x - 4)$.

13. A trinomial factoring problem can be checked by multiplying the factors to see if the product is the same as the original expression.

15. $x^2 - 7x + 10 = (x - 5)(x - 2)$

17. $x^2 + 6x + 8 = (x + 4)(x + 2)$

19. $x^2 + 5x - 24 = (x + 8)(x - 3)$

21. $x^2 + 4x - 6$ is prime.

23. $y^2 - 13y + 12 = (y - 12)(y - 1)$

25. $a^2 - 2a - 8 = (a - 4)(x + 2)$

27. $r^2 - 2r - 15 = (r - 5)(r + 3)$

29. $b^2 - 11b + 18 = (b - 9)(b - 2)$

31. $x^2 - 8x - 15$ is prime.

33. $q^2 + 4q - 45 = (q + 9)(q - 5)$

35. $x^2 - 7x - 30 = (x - 10)(x + 3)$

37. $x^2 + 4x + 4 = (x + 2)(x + 2)$
$$= (x + 2)^2$$

39. $s^2 - 8s + 16 = (s - 4)(s - 4)$
$$= (s - 4)^2$$

41. $p^2 - 12p + 36 = (p - 6)(p - 6)$
$$= (p - 6)^2$$

43. $-18w + w^2 + 45$

$= w^2 - 18w + 45$

$= (w - 15)(w - 3)$

45. $10x - 39 + x^2$

$= x^2 + 10x - 39$

$= (x + 13)(x - 3)$

47. $x^2 - x - 20 = (x - 5)(x + 4)$

49. $y^2 + 13y + 40 = (y + 5)(y + 8)$

51. $x^2 + 12x - 64 = (x + 16)(x - 4)$

53. $s^2 + 14s - 24$ is prime.

54. $x^2 - 13x + 36 = (x - 4)(x - 9)$

55. $x^2 - 20x + 64 = (x - 16)(x - 4)$

56. $x^2 + 19x + 48 = (x + 3)(x + 16)$

57. $a^2 - 20a + 99 = (a - 11)(a - 9)$

58. $x^2 + 5x - 24 = (x - 3)(x + 8)$

59. $x^2 + 2 + 3x = x^2 + 3x + 2$

$= (x + 1)(x + 2)$

61. $7w - 18 + w^2 = w^2 + 7w - 18$

$= (w + 9)(w - 2)$

63. $x^2 - 8xy + 15y^2 = (x - 3y)(x - 5y)$

65. $m^2 - 6mn + 9n^2 = (m - 3n)(m - 3n)$

$= (m - 3n)^2$

67. $x^2 + 8xy + 12y^2 = (x + 6y)(x + 2y)$

69. $m^2 - 5mn - 24n^2 = (m - 8n)(m + 3n)$

71. $6x^2 - 30x + 24 = 6(x^2 - 5x + 4)$

$= 6(x - 4)(x - 1)$

73. $5x^2 + 20x + 15 = 5(x^2 + 4x + 3)$

$= 5(x + 1)(x + 3)$

75. $2x^2 - 18x + 40 = 2(x^2 - 9x + 20)$

$= 2(x - 5)(x - 4)$

77. $b^3 - 7b^2 + 10b = b(b^2 - 7b + 10)$

$= b(b - 5)(b - 2)$

79. $3z^3 - 21z^2 - 54z = 3z(z^2 - 7z - 18)$

$= 3z(z - 9)(z + 2)$

81. $x^3 + 8x^2 + 16x = x(x^2 + 8x + 16)$

$= x(x + 4)(x + 4)$

$= x(x + 4)^2$

83. $7a^2 - 35ab + 42b^2 = 7(a^2 - 5ab + 6b^2)$

$= 7(a - 3b)(a - 2b)$

85. $3r^3 + 6r^2t - 24rt^2 = 3r(r^2 + 2rt - 8t^2)$

$= 3r(r + 4t)(r - 2t)$

87. $x^4 - 4x^3 - 21x^2 = x^2(x^2 - 4x - 21)$

$= x^2(x - 7)(x + 3)$

89.

Sign of Coefficient of x-term	Sign of Constant of Trinomial	Signs of Constant Terms in the Binomial Factors
$-$	$+$	both negative
$-$	$-$	one positive and one negative
$+$	$-$	one positive and one negative
$+$	$+$	both positive

91. $x^2 - 12x + 32 = (x-8)(x-4)$

93. $x^2 - 2x - 35 = (x-7)(x+5)$

95. $x^2 + 0.6x + 0.08 = (x+0.4)(x+0.2)$

97. $x^2 + \dfrac{2}{5}x + \dfrac{1}{25} = \left(x + \dfrac{1}{5}\right)\left(x + \dfrac{1}{5}\right)$

$$= \left(x + \dfrac{1}{5}\right)^2$$

99. $x^2 - 24x - 256 = (x+8)(x-32)$

101.

$$4(2x-4) = 5x + 11$$
$$8x - 16 = 5x + 11$$
$$8x - 5x - 16 = 5x - 5x + 11$$
$$3x - 16 = 11$$
$$3x - 16 + 16 = 11 + 16$$
$$3x = 27$$
$$x = 9$$

102. Let x be the percent of acid in the mixture.

Solution	Strength	Liters	Amount
18%	0.18	4	0.72
26%	0.26	1	0.26
Mixture	$\dfrac{x}{100}$	5	$\dfrac{5x}{100}$

$$0.72 + 0.26 = \dfrac{5x}{100}$$
$$0.98 = \dfrac{x}{20}$$
$$19.6 = x$$

The mixture is a 19.6% acid solution.

103. $\left(2x^2 + 5x - 6\right)(x-2)$

$$= 2x^2(x-2) + 5x(x-2) - 6(x-2)$$
$$= 2x^3 - 4x^2 + 5x^2 - 10x - 6x + 12$$
$$= 2x^3 + x^2 - 16x + 12$$

104.

$$\begin{array}{r} 3x + 2 \\ x-4\overline{)\,3x^2 - 10x - 10} \\ \underline{3x^2 - 12x} \\ 2x - 10 \\ \underline{2x - 8} \\ -2 \end{array}$$

$$\dfrac{3x^2 - 10x - 10}{x-4} = 3x + 2 - \dfrac{2}{x-4}$$

105. $20x^2 + 8x - 15x - 6 = 4x(5x+2) - 3(5x+2)$

$$= (5x+2)(4x-3)$$

Exercise Set 5.4

1. Factoring trinomials is the reverse process of multiplying binomials.

3. When factoring a trinomial of the form $ax^2 + bx + c$, the product of the first terms of the binomial factors must equal the first term of the trinomial, ax^2.

5. $2x^2 + 11x + 5 = (2x+1)(x+5)$

7. $3x^2 + 14x + 8 = (3x+2)(x+4)$

9. $5x^2 - 9x - 2 = (5x+1)(x-2)$

11. $3r^2 + 13r - 10 = (3r-2)(r+5)$

13. $4z^2 - 12z + 9 = (2z-3)(2z-3)$

$$= (2z-3)^2$$

15. $6z^2 + z - 12 = (2z+3)(3z-4)$

17. $5a^2 - 12a + 6$ is prime.

19. $8x^2 + 19x + 6 = (8x+3)(x+2)$

21. $3x^2 + 11x + 4$ is prime.

23. $5y^2 - 16y + 3 = (5y-1)(y-3)$

25. $7x^2 + 43x + 6 = (7x+1)(x+6)$

27. $4x^2 + 4x - 15 = (2x+5)(2x-3)$

29. $49t^2 - 14t + 1 = (7t-1)(7t-1)$

$$= (7t-1)^2$$

31. $5z^2 - 6z - 8 = (5z+4)(z-2)$

33. $4y^2 + 5y - 6 = (4y-3)(y+2)$

35. $10x^2 - 27x + 5 = (5x-1)(2x-5)$

37. $10d^2 - 7d - 12 = (5d+4)(2d-3)$

39. $8x^2 - 46x - 12 = 2 \cdot 4x^2 - 2 \cdot 23x - 2 \cdot 6$
$$= 2(4x^2 - 23x - 6)$$
$$= 2(4x+1)(x-6)$$

41. $10t + 3 + 7t^2 = 7t^2 + 10t + 3$
$$= (7t+3)(t+1)$$

43. $6x^2 + 16x + 10 = 2 \cdot 3x^2 + 2 \cdot 8x + 2 \cdot 5$
$$= 2(3x^2 + 8x + 5)$$
$$= 2(3x+5)(x+1)$$

45. $6x^3 - 5x^2 - 4x = x \cdot 6x^2 - x \cdot 5x - x \cdot 4$
$$= x(6x^2 - 5x - 4)$$
$$= x(2x+1)(3x-4)$$

47. $12x^3 + 28x^2 + 8x = 4x \cdot 3x^2 + 4x \cdot 7x + 4x \cdot 2$
$$= 4x(3x^2 + 7x + 2)$$
$$= 4x(3x+1)(x+2)$$

49. $4x^3 - 2x^2 - 12x = 2x \cdot 2x^2 - 2x \cdot x - 2x \cdot 6$
$$= 2x(2x^2 - x - 6)$$
$$= 2x(2x+3)(x-2)$$

51. $48c^2 + 8c - 16 = 8 \cdot 6c^2 + 8 \cdot c - 8 \cdot 2$
$$= 8(6c^2 + 8c - 2)$$
$$= 8(2c-1)(3c+2)$$

53. $4p - 12 + 8p^2 = 8p^2 + 4p - 12$
$$= 4 \cdot 2p^2 + 4 \cdot p - 4 \cdot 3$
$$= 4(2p^2 + p - 3)$$
$$= 4(2p+3)(p-1)$$

55. $8c^2 + 41cd + 5d^2 = (8c+d)(c+5d)$

57. $15x^2 - xy - 6y^2 = (5x+3y)(3x-2y)$

59. $12x^2 + 10xy - 8y^2 = 2 \cdot 6x^2 + 2 \cdot 5xy - 2 \cdot 4y^2$
$$= 2(6x^2 + 5xy - 4y^2)$$
$$= 2(2x-y)(3x+4y)$$

61. $7p^2 + 13pq + 6q^2 = (7p+6q)(p+q)$

63. $6m^2 - mn - 2n^2 = (3m-2n)(2m+n)$

65. $8x^3 + 10x^2y + 3xy^2 = x \cdot 8x^2 + x \cdot 10xy + x \cdot 3y^2$
$$= x(8x^2 + 10xy + 3y^2)$$
$$= x(4x+3y)(2x+y)$$

67. $4x^4 + 8x^3y + 3x^2y^2$
$$= x^2 \cdot 4x^2 + x^2 \cdot 8xy + x^2 \cdot 3y^2$$
$$= x^2(4x^2 + 8xy + 3y^2)$$
$$= x^2(2x+y)(2x+3y)$$

69. $3x^2 - 20x - 7$. This polynomial was obtained by multiplying the factors.

71. $10x^2 + 35x + 15$. This polynomial was obtained by multiplying the factors.

73. $3t^4 + 11t^3 - 4t^2$. This polynomial was obtained by multiplying the factors.

75. a. The second factor can be found by dividing the trinomial by the binomial.

b.
$$\begin{array}{r} 6x+11 \\ 3x+10{\overline{\smash{\big)}\,18x^2 + 93x + 110}} \\ \underline{18x^2 + 60x} \\ 33x + 110 \\ \underline{33x + 110} \\ 0 \end{array}$$

The other factor is $6x + 11$.

77. $18x^2 + 9x - 20 = (6x-5)(3x+4)$

79. $15x^2 - 124x + 160 = (5x-8)(3x-20)$

81. $105a^2 - 220a - 160$
$$= 5 \cdot 21a^2 - 5 \cdot 44a - 5 \cdot 32$$
$$= 5(21a^2 - 44a - 32)$$
$$= 5(3a-8)(7a+4)$$

83. The other factor is $2x + 45$. The product of the three first terms must equal $6x^3$, and the product of the constants must equal $2250x$.

85. $-x^2 - 4(y+3) + 2y^2$
$$= -(-3)^2 - 4(-5+3) + 2(-5)^2$$
$$= -9 - 4(-2) + 2(25)$$
$$= -9 + 8 + 50$$
$$= 49$$

86. $\dfrac{507.5}{3.56} \approx 142.56$

His average speed was about 142.56 miles per hour.

87. $36x^4y^3 - 12xy^2 + 24x^5y^6$
$= 12xy^2 \cdot 3x^3y - 12xy^2 \cdot 1 + 12xy^2 \cdot 2x^4y^4$
$= 12xy^2\left(3x^3y - 1 + 2x^4y^4\right)$

88. $b^2 + 4b - 96 = (b+12)(b-8)$

Mid-Chapter Test: Sections 5.1 – 5.4

1. Any factoring problem can be checked by multiplying the factors.

2. $18xy^2 : 2 \cdot 3^2 \cdot xy^2$
$27x^3y^4 : 3^3 \cdot x^3y^4$
$12x^2y^3 : 2^2 \cdot 3 \cdot x^2y^3$
GCF: $3 \cdot x \cdot y^2 = 3xy^2$

3. $4a^2b^3 - 24a^3b = 4a^2b \cdot b^2 - 4a^2b \cdot 6a$
$= 4a^2b\left(b^2 - 6a\right)$

4. $5c(d-6) - 3(d-6) = (d-6)(5c-3)$

5. $7x(2x+9) + 2x + 9$
$= 7x(2x+9) + 1(2x+9)$
$= (2x+9)(7x+1)$

6. $x^2 + 4x + 7x + 28$
$= x(x+4) + 7(x+4)$
$= (x+4)(x+7)$

7. $x^2 + 5x - 3x - 15$
$= x(x+5) - 3(x+5)$
$= (x+5)(x-3)$

8. $6a^2 + 15ab - 2ab - 5b^2$
$= 3a(2a+5b) - b(2a+5b)$
$= (2a+5b)(3a-b)$

9. $5x^2 - 2xy - 45x + 18y$
$= x(5x-2y) - 9(5x-2y)$
$= (5x-2y)(x-9)$

10. $8x^3 + 4x^2 - 48x^2 - 24x$
$= 4x\left(2x^2 + x - 12x - 6\right)$
$= 4x\left[x(2x+1) - 6(2x+1)\right]$
$= 4x(2x+1)(x-6)$

11. $x^2 - 10x + 21 = (x-3)(x-7)$

12. $t^2 + 9t + 20 = (t+5)(t+4)$

13. $p^2 - 3p - 8$ is prime

14. $x^2 + 16x + 64 = (x+8)(x+8)$
$= (x+8)^2$

15. $m^2 - 4mn - 45n^2 = (m+5n)(m-9n)$

16. $3x^2 + 17x + 10 = (3x+2)(x+5)$

17. $4z^2 - 11z + 6 = (4z-3)(z-2)$

18. $3y^2 + 13y + 6$ is prime

19. $9x^2 - 6x + 1 = (3x-1)(3x-1)$
$= (3x-1)^2$

20. $6a^2 + 3ab - 3b^2 = 3\left(2a^2 + ab - b^2\right)$
$= 3(2a-b)(a+b)$

Exercise Set 5.5

1. a. $a^2 - b^2 = (a+b)(a-b)$

b. Answers will vary.

3. a. $a^3 + b^3 = (a+b)\left(a^2 - ab + b^2\right)$

b. Answers will vary.

5. No, there is no special formula for factoring the sum of two squares.

7. $x^2 + 9$ is prime

9. $3b^2 + 48 = 3\left(b^2 + 16\right)$

11. $16m^2 + 36n^2 = 4\left(4m^2 + 9n^2\right)$

13. $y^2 - 25 = y^2 - 5^2 = (y+5)(y-5)$

15. $81 - z^2 = 9^2 - z^2$
$$= (9 + z)(9 - z)$$

17. $x^2 - 49 = x^2 - 7^2$
$$= (x + 7)(x - 7)$$

19. $x^2 - y^2 = (x + y)(x - y)$

21. $9y^2 - 25z^2 = (3y)^2 - (5z)^2$
$$= (3y + 5z)(3y - 5z)$$

23. $64a^2 - 36b^2 = 4(16a^2 - 9b^2)$
$$= 4\left[(4a)^2 - (3b)^2\right]$$
$$= 4(4a + 3b)(4a - 3b)$$

25. $36 - 49x^2 = 6^2 - (7x)^2$
$$= (6 + 7x)(6 - 7x)$$

27. $z^4 - 81x^2 = (z^2)^2 - (9x)^2$
$$= (z^2 + 9x)(z^2 - 9x)$$

29. $25x^4 - 49y^4 = (5x^2)^2 - (7y^2)^2$
$$= (5x^2 + 7y^2)(5x^2 - 7y^2)$$

31. $36m^4 - 49n^2 = (6m^2)^2 - (7n)^2$
$$= (6m^2 + 7n)(6m^2 - 7n)$$

33. $2x^4 - 50y^2 = 2(x^4 - 25y^2)$
$$= 2\left[(x^2)^2 - (5y)^2\right]$$
$$= 2(x^2 + 5y)(x^2 - 5y)$$

35. $x^4 - 81 = (x^2)^2 - 9^2$
$$= (x^2 + 9)(x^2 - 9)$$
$$= (x^2 + 9)(x^2 - 3^2)$$
$$= (x^2 + 9)(x + 3)(x - 3)$$

37. $x^3 + y^3 = (x + y)(x^2 - xy + y^2)$

39. $x^3 - y^3 = (x - y)(x^2 + xy + y^2)$

41. $x^3 + 64 = x^3 + 4^3$
$$= (x + 4)(x^2 - 4x + 16)$$

43. $x^3 - 27 = x^3 - 3^3$
$$= (x - 3)(x^2 + 3x + 9)$$

45. $a^3 + 1 = a^3 + 1^3$
$$= (a + 1)(a^2 - a + 1)$$

47. $27x^3 - 1 = (3x)^3 - 1^3$
$$= (3x - 1)(9x^2 + 3x + 1)$$

49. $27a^3 - 125 = (3a)^3 - 5^3$
$$= (3a - 5)(9a^2 + 15a + 25)$$

51. $27 - 8y^3 = 3^3 - (2y)^3$
$$= (3 - 2y)(9 + 6y + 4y^2)$$

53. $64m^3 + 27n^3 = (4m)^3 + (3n)^3$
$$= (4m + 3n)(16m^2 - 12mn + 9n^2)$$

55. $8a^3 - 27b^3 = (2a)^3 - (3b)^3$
$$= (2a - 3b)(4a^2 + 6ab + 9b^2)$$

57. $4x^2 - 24x + 36 = 4(x^2 - 6x + 9)$
$$= 2(x - 3)^2$$

59. $50x^2 - 10x - 12 = 2(25x^2 - 5x - 6)$
$$= 2(5x + 2)(5x - 3)$$

61. $2d^2 + 16d + 32 = 2(d^2 + 8d + 16)$
$$= 2(d + 4)^2$$

63. $5x^2 - 10x - 15 = 5(x^2 - 2x - 3)$
$$= 5(x - 3)(x + 1)$$

65. $5x^2 - 20 = 5(x^2 - 4)$
$$= 5(x^2 - 2^2)$$
$$= 5(x + 2)(x - 2)$$

67. $2x^2 - 50 = 2(x^2 - 25)$
$$= 2(x^2 - 5^2)$$
$$= 2(x + 5)(x - 5)$$

69. $2x^2y - 18y = 2y(x^2 - 9)$
$$= 2y(x^2 - 3^2)$$
$$= 2y(x + 3)(x - 3)$$

71. $3x^3y^2 + 3y^2 = 3y^2(x^3 + 1)$

$\qquad = 3y^2(x^3 + 1^3)$

$\qquad = 3y^2(x+1)(x^2 - x + 1)$

73. $2x^3 - 16 = 2(x^3 - 8)$

$\qquad = 2(x^3 - 2^3)$

$\qquad = 2(x-2)(x^2 + 2x + 4)$

75. $18x^2 - 50 = 2(9x^2 - 25)$

$\qquad = 2((3x)^2 - 5^2)$

$\qquad = 2(3x+5)(3x-5)$

77. $6t^2r - 15tr + 21r = 3r(2t^2 - 5t + 7)$

79. $6x^2 - 4x + 24x - 16$

$\qquad = 2(3x^2 - 2x + 12x - 8)$

$\qquad = 2[x(3x-2) + 4(3x-2)]$

$\qquad = 2(3x-2)(x+4)$

81. $2rs^2 - 10rs - 48r = 2r(s^2 - 5s - 24)$

$\qquad = 2r(s+3)(s-8)$

83. $4x^2 + 5x - 6 = (x+2)(4x-3)$

85. $25b^2 - 100 = 25(b^2 - 4)$

$\qquad = 25(b^2 - 2^2)$

$\qquad = 25(b+2)(b-2)$

87. $a^5b^2 - 4a^3b^4 = a^3b^2(a^2 - 4b^2)$

$\qquad = a^3b^2[a^2 - (2b)^2]$

$\qquad = a^3b^2(a+2b)(a-2b)$

89. $5x^4 + 10x^3 + 5x^2 = 5x^2(x^2 + 2x + 1)$

$\qquad = 5x^2(x+1)^2$

91. $x^3 + 25x = x(x^2 + 25)$

93. $y^4 - 16 = (y^2)^2 - 4^2$

$\qquad = (y^2 + 4)(y^2 - 4)$

$\qquad = (y^2 + 4)(y^2 - 2^2)$

$\qquad = (y^2 + 4)(y+2)(y-2)$

95. $16m^3 + 250 = 2(8m^3 + 125)$

$\qquad = 2[(2m)^3 + 5^3]$

$\qquad = 2(2m+5)(4m^2 - 10m + 25)$

97. $ac + 2a + bc + 2b = a(c+2) + b(c+2)$

$\qquad = (a+b)(c+2)$

99. $9 - 9y^4 = 9(1 - y^4)$

$\qquad = 9[1^2 - (y^2)^2]$

$\qquad = 9(1 + y^2)(1 - y^2)$

$\qquad = 9(1 + y^2)(1^2 - y^2)$

$\qquad = 9(1 + y^2)(1 + y)(1 - y)$

101. You cannot divide both sides of the equation by $(a - b)$, because it equals 0.

103. $2\blacklozenge^6 + 4\blacklozenge^4 \text{\ding{58}}^2$

$\qquad = 2\blacklozenge^4(\blacklozenge^2 + 2\text{\ding{58}}^2)$

105. $x^6 - 27y^9 = (x^2)^3 - (3y^3)^3$

$\qquad = (x^2 - 3y^3)(x^4 + 3x^2y^3 + 9y^6)$

107. $x^2 - 6x + 9 - 4y^2 = (x-3)^2 - (2y)^2$

$\qquad = (x-3+2y)(x-3-2y)$

109. $x^2 + 10x + 25 - y^2 + 4y - 4$

$\qquad = (x+5)^2 - (y^2 - 4y + 4)$

$\qquad = (x+5)^2 - (y-2)^2$

$\qquad = [(x+5) + (y-2)][(x+5) - (y-2)]$

$\qquad = (x+y+3)(x-y+7)$

110. $3x - 2(x+4) \geq 2x - 9$

$\qquad 3x - 2x - 8 \geq 2x - 9$

$\qquad x - 8 \geq 2x - 9$

$\qquad 1 \geq x$

111. Substitute 36 for A, 6 for b, and 12 for d.

$$A = \frac{1}{2}h(b+d)$$

$$36 = \frac{1}{2}h(6+12)$$

$$36 = \frac{1}{2}h(18)$$

$$36 = 9h$$

$$4 = h$$

The height is 4 inches.

112. $-9\left(a^3b^2c^6\right)^0 = -9(1) = -9$

113. $\left(\dfrac{4x^4y}{6xy^5}\right)^3 = \left(\dfrac{4}{6} \cdot \dfrac{x^4}{x} \cdot \dfrac{y}{y^5}\right)^3$

$$= \left(\frac{2}{3} \cdot x^3 \cdot \frac{1}{y^4}\right)^3$$

$$= \left(\frac{2x^3}{3y^4}\right)^3$$

$$= \frac{2^3 x^{3 \cdot 3}}{3^3 y^{4 \cdot 3}}$$

$$= \frac{8x^9}{27y^{12}}$$

114. $a^{-4}a^{-7} = a^{-4-7}$

$$= a^{-11}$$

$$= \frac{1}{a^{11}}$$

Exercise Set 5.6

1. Answers will vary.

3. The standard form of a quadratic equation is $ax^2 + bx + c = 0$, $a \neq 0$.

5. a. The zero-factor property may only be used when one side of the equation is equal to 0.

b. $(x+1)(x-2) = 4$

$$x^2 - 2x + x - 2 = 4$$

$$x^2 - x - 6 = 0$$

$$(x-3)(x+2) = 0$$

$$x-3 = 0 \quad \text{or} \quad x+2 = 0$$

$$x = 3 \qquad\qquad x = -2$$

7. $(x+6)(x-7) = 0$

$$x+6 = 0 \quad \text{or} \quad x-7 = 0$$

$$x = -6 \qquad\qquad x = 7$$

9. $7x(x-8) = 0$

$$x = 0 \quad \text{or} \quad x-8 = 0$$

$$x = 8$$

11. $(3x+7)(2x-11) = 0$

$$3x+7 = 0 \quad \text{or} \quad 2x-11 = 0$$

$$3x = -7 \qquad\qquad 2x = 11$$

$$x = -\frac{7}{3} \qquad\qquad x = \frac{11}{2}$$

13. $\qquad x^2 - 16 = 0$

$$(x+4)(x-4) = 0$$

$$x+4 = 0 \quad \text{or} \quad x-4 = 0$$

$$x = -4 \qquad\qquad x = 4$$

15. $\quad x^2 - 12x = 0$

$$x(x-12) = 0$$

$$x = 0 \quad \text{or} \quad x-12 = 0$$

$$x = 12$$

17. $\quad x^2 + 7x = 0$

$$x(x+7) = 0$$

$$x = 0 \quad \text{or} \quad x+7 = 0$$

$$x = -7$$

19. $\quad x^2 - 8x + 16 = 0$

$$(x-4)(x-4) = 0$$

$$x-4 = 0$$

$$x = 4$$

21. $\qquad x^2 + 12x = -20$

$$x^2 + 12x + 20 = 0$$

$$(x+10)(x+2) = 0$$

$$x+10 = 0 \quad \text{or} \quad x+2 = 0$$

$$x = -10 \qquad\qquad x = -2$$

23. $\quad x^2 + 12x + 22 = 2$

$$x^2 + 12x + 20 = 0$$

$$(x+2)(x+10) = 0$$

$$x+2 = 0 \quad \text{or} \quad x+10 = 0$$

$$x = -2 \qquad\qquad x = -10$$

25. $2x^2 - 5x - 24 = -3x$

$2x^2 - 2x - 24 = 0$

$2(x^2 - x - 12) = 0$

$2(x - 4)(x + 3) = 0$

$x - 4 = 0$ or $x + 3 = 0$

$x = 4$ $x = -3$

27. $23p - 24 = -p^2$

$p^2 + 23p - 24 = 0$

$(p + 24)(p - 1) = 0$

$p + 24 = 0$ or $p - 1 = 0$

$p = -24$ $p = 1$

29. $33w + 90 = -3w^2$

$3w^2 + 33w + 90 = 0$

$3(w^2 + 11w + 30) = 0$

$3(w + 5)(w + 6) = 0$

$w + 5 = 0$ or $w + 6 = 0$

$w = -5$ $w = -6$

31. $-2x - 15 = -x^2$

$x^2 - 2x - 15 = 0$

$(x - 5)(x + 3) = 0$

$x - 5 = 0$ or $x + 3 = 0$

$x = 5$ $x = -3$

33. $-x^2 + 29x + 30 = 0$

$x^2 - 29x - 30 = 0$

$(x - 30)(x + 1) = 0$

$x - 30 = 0$ or $x + 1 = 0$

$x = 30$ $x = -1$

35. $-15 = 4m^2 + 17m$

$4m^2 + 17m + 15 = 0$

$(4m + 5)(m + 3) = 0$

$4m + 5 = 0$ or $m + 3 = 0$

$4m = -5$ $m = -3$

$m = -\dfrac{5}{4}$

37. $9p^2 = -21p - 6$

$9p^2 + 21p + 6 = 0$

$3(3p^2 + 7p + 2) = 0$

$3(3p + 1)(p + 2) = 0$

$3p + 1 = 0$ or $p + 2 = 0$

$3p = -1$ $p = -2$

$p = -\dfrac{1}{3}$

39. $3r^2 + 13r = 10$

$3r^2 + 13r - 10 = 0$

$(3r - 2)(r + 5) = 0$

$3r - 2 = 0$ or $r + 5 = 0$

$3r = 2$ $r = -5$

$r = \dfrac{2}{3}$

41. $4x^2 + 4x - 48 = 0$

$4(x^2 + x - 12) = 0$

$4(x + 4)(x - 3) = 0$

$x + 4 = 0$ or $x - 3 = 0$

$x = -4$ $x = 3$

43. $8x^2 + 2x = 3$

$8x^2 + 2x - 3 = 0$

$(4x + 3)(2x - 1) = 0$

$4x + 3 = 0$ or $2x - 1 = 0$

$4x = -3$ $2x = 1$

$x = -\dfrac{3}{4}$ $x = \dfrac{1}{2}$

45. $c^2 = 64$

$c^2 - 64 = 0$

$c^2 - 8^2 = 0$

$(c + 8)(c - 8) = 0$

$c + 8 = 0$ or $c - 8 = 0$

$c = -8$ $c = 8$

47. $2x^2 = 50x$

$2x^2 - 50x = 0$

$2x(x - 25) = 0$

$2x = 0$ or $x - 25 = 0$

$x = 0$ $x = 25$

49.
$$x^2 = 100$$
$$x^2 - 100 = 0$$
$$x^2 - 10^2 = 0$$
$$(x+10)(x-10) = 0$$
$$x+10 = 0 \quad \text{or} \quad x-10 = 0$$
$$x = -10 \qquad x = 10$$

51.
$$(x-2)(x-1) = 12$$
$$x^2 - 3x + 2 = 12$$
$$x^2 - 3x - 10 = 0$$
$$(x+2)(x-5) = 0$$
$$x+2 = 0 \quad \text{or} \quad x-5 = 0$$
$$x = -2 \qquad x = 5$$

53.
$$(3x+2)(x+1) = 4$$
$$3x^2 + 5x + 2 = 4$$
$$3x^2 + 5x - 2 = 0$$
$$(3x-1)(x+2) = 0$$
$$3x-1 = 0 \qquad x+2 = 0$$
$$x = \frac{1}{3} \qquad x = -2$$

55.
$$2(a^2 + 9) = 15a$$
$$2a^2 + 18 = 15a$$
$$2a^2 - 15a + 18 = 0$$
$$(2a-3)(a-6) = 0$$
$$2a-3 = 0 \quad \text{or} \quad a-6 = 0$$
$$2a = 3 \qquad a = 6$$
$$a = \frac{3}{2}$$

57. The solutions are 6 and –4, so the factors are $x - 6$ and $x + 4$.
$$(x-6)(x+4) = x^2 - 2x - 24$$
The equation is $x^2 - 2x - 24 = 0$.

59. The solutions are 6 and 0, so the factors are $x - 0$ and $x - 6$.
$$(x-0)(x-6) = x(x-6)$$
$$= x^2 - 6x$$
The equation is $x^2 - 6x = 0$.

61. a. The solutions are
$$x = \frac{1}{2} \quad \text{or} \quad x = -\frac{1}{3}$$
$$2x = 1 \qquad 3x = -1$$
$$2x - 1 = 0 \qquad 3x + 1 = 0$$
Thus the factors are:
$(2x-1)$ and $(3x+1)$.

b. The equation is $(2x-1)(3x+1)$
$$= 6x^2 - x - 1 = 0.$$

63.
$$(2x-3)(x-4) = (x-5)(x+3) + 7$$
$$2x^2 - 11x + 12 = x^2 - 2x - 15 + 7$$
$$2x^2 - 11x + 12 = x^2 - 2x - 8$$
$$x^2 - 9x + 20 = 0$$
$$(x-5)(x-4) = 0$$
$$x-5 = 0 \quad \text{or} \quad x-4 = 0$$
$$x = 5 \qquad x = 4$$

65.
$$x(x-3)(x+2) = 0$$
$$x = 0 \quad \text{or} \quad x-3 = 0 \quad \text{or} \quad x+2 = 0$$
$$x = 3 \qquad x = -2$$

67. $\dfrac{3}{5} - \dfrac{2}{9} = \dfrac{27}{45} - \dfrac{10}{45} = \dfrac{27-10}{45} = \dfrac{17}{45}$

68. a. identity

b. contradiction

69. Let x be the number of people admitted in 60 minutes.
$$\frac{160 \text{ people}}{13 \text{ minutes}} = \frac{x}{60 \text{ minutes}}$$
$$13x = 160(60)$$
$$13x = 9600$$
$$x \approx 738$$
About 738 people were admitted in 60 minutes.

70. $\left(\dfrac{3p^5 q^7}{p^9 q^8}\right)^2 = \left(3 \cdot p^{5-9} \cdot q^{7-8}\right)^2$
$$= \left(3p^{-4} q^{-1}\right)^2$$
$$= \left(\frac{3}{p^4 q}\right)^2$$
$$= \frac{3^2}{p^{4\cdot2} q^{1\cdot2}}$$
$$= \frac{9}{p^8 q^2}$$

71. monomial

72. binomial

73. not a polynomial

74. trinomial

Exercise Set 5.7

1. A right triangle is a triangle with a 90° angle.

3. The Pythagorean Theorem is $a^2 + b^2 = c^2$.

5. $a^2 + b^2 = c^2$

$a^2 + 4^2 = 5^2$

$a^2 + 16 = 25$

$a^2 = 9$

$a = 3$

7. $a^2 + b^2 = c^2$

$12^2 + 5^2 = c^2$

$144 + 25 = c^2$

$169 = c^2$

$13 = c$

9. $a^2 + b^2 = c^2$

$24^2 + b^2 = 30^2$

$576 + b^2 = 900$

$b^2 = 324$

$b = 18$

11. $a^2 + b^2 = c^2$

$15^2 + 36^2 = c^2$

$225 + 1296 = c^2$

$1521 = c^2$

$39 = c$

13. Let x be the smaller of the two positive integers. Then $x + 4$ is the other integer.

$x(x+4) = 117$

$x^2 + 4x + 117 = 0$

$(x-9)(x+13) = 0$

$x - 9 = 0 \quad \text{or} \quad x + 13 = 0$

$x = 9 \qquad\qquad x = -13$

Since x must be positive, the two integers are 9 and $9 + 4 = 13$.

15. Let $x =$ first positive number. Then $2x + 2$ is the other number.

$x(2x+2) = 84$

$2x^2 + 2x = 84$

$2x^2 + 2x - 84 = 0$

$2(x^2 + x - 42) = 0$

$2(x+7)(x-6) = 0$

$x + 7 = 0 \quad \text{or} \quad x - 6 = 0$

$x = -7 \qquad\qquad x = 6$

The numbers have to be positive. Thus the numbers are 6 and $2(6) + 2 = 14$.

17. Let x be the first even integer. Then $x + 2$ is the next even integer.

$x(x+2) = 288$

$x^2 + 2x = 288$

$x^2 + 2x - 288 = 0$

$(x+18)(x-16) = 0$

$x + 18 = 0 \quad \text{or} \quad x - 16 = 0$

$x = -18 \qquad\qquad x = 16$

Since x must be positive, the numbers are 16 and 18.

19. Let $w =$ width. Then length $= 4w$.

$A = lw$

$36 = (4w)(w)$

$36 = 4w^2$

$0 = 4w^2 - 36$

$0 = 4(w^2 - 9)$

$0 = 4(w+3)(w-3)$

$w + 3 = 0 \quad \text{or} \quad w - 3 = 0$

$w = -3 \qquad\qquad w = 3$

Since dimensions must be positive, the width is 3 feet and the length is $4(3) = 12$ feet.

21. Let $l =$ length of the garden and $\dfrac{2}{3}l =$ width of the garden.

$lw = A$

$l\left(\dfrac{2}{3}l\right) = 150$

$2l^2 = 450$

$2l^2 - 450 = 0$

$2(l^2 - 225) = 0$

$2(l^2 - 15^2) = 0$

$2(l+15)(l-15) = 0$

$$l + 15 = 0 \quad \text{or} \quad l - 15 = 0$$
$$l = -15 \qquad\qquad l = 15$$

Since dimensions must be positive, the length is 15 feet and the width is $\frac{2}{3}(15) = 10$ feet.

23. Let a = length of a side of the original square. Then $a + 5$ is the length of the new side.

$$(\text{side}) \cdot (\text{side}) = \text{Area}$$
$$(a+5)(a+5) = 81$$
$$a^2 + 10a + 25 = 81$$
$$a^2 + 10a - 56 = 0$$
$$(a+14)(a-4) = 0$$
$$a + 14 = 0 \quad \text{or} \quad a - 4 = 0$$
$$a = -14 \quad \text{or} \quad a = 4$$

Since length must be positive, the original square had sides of length 4 meters.

25. $d = 16t^2$
$$256 = 16t^2$$
$$\frac{256}{16} = t^2$$
$$16 = t^2$$
$$0 = t^2 - 16$$
$$0 = (t+4)(t-4)$$
$$t + 4 = 0 \quad \text{or} \quad t - 4 = 0$$
$$t = -4 \qquad\qquad t = 4$$

Since time must be positive, it would take the egg 4 seconds to hit the ground.

27. $a^2 + b^2 = c^2$
$$7^2 + 24^2 = 25^2$$
$$49 + 576 = 625$$
$$625 = 625 \quad \text{True}$$

Since these values are true for the Pythagorean Theorem, a right triangle can exist.

29. $a^2 + b^2 = c^2$
$$9^2 + 40^2 = 41^2$$
$$81 + 1600 = 1681$$
$$1681 = 1681 \quad \text{True}$$

Since these values are true for the Pythagorean Theorem, a right triangle can exist.

31. $a^2 + b^2 = c^2$
$$30^2 + b^2 = 34^2$$
$$900 + b^2 = 1156$$
$$b^2 = 256$$
$$b = 16 \text{ feet}$$

33. $a^2 + b^2 = c^2$
$$9^2 + 40^2 = c^2$$
$$81 + 1600 = c^2$$
$$1681 = c^2$$
$$41 = c$$
$$c = 41 \text{ feet}$$

35. Let x be the length of one leg of the triangle. Then $x + 2$ is the length of the other leg.

$$a^2 + b^2 = c^2$$
$$x^2 + (x+2)^2 = 10^2$$
$$x^2 + x^2 + 4x + 4 = 100$$
$$2x^2 + 4x + 4 = 100$$
$$2x^2 + 4x - 96 = 0$$
$$2(x^2 + 2x - 48) = 0$$
$$2(x+8)(x-6) = 0$$
$$x + 8 = 0 \quad \text{or} \quad x - 6 = 0$$
$$x = -8 \qquad\qquad x = 6$$

Since length is positive, the lengths are 6 ft, 8ft and 10ft.

37. Let w = width of the frame, then $w + 3$ = the length of the frame. The diagonal is 15.

$$a^2 + b^2 = c^2$$
$$(w+3)^2 + w^2 = 15^2$$
$$w^2 + 6w + 9 + w^2 = 225$$
$$2w^2 + 6w + 9 = 225$$
$$2w^2 + 6w - 216 = 0$$
$$2(w^2 + 3w - 108) = 0$$
$$2(w+12)(w-9) = 0$$
$$w + 12 = 0 \quad \text{or} \quad w - 9 = 0$$
$$w = -12 \qquad\qquad w = 9$$

The width is 9 in. and the length is $9 + 3 = 12$ in.

39. Let w be the width of the rectangle. Then $3w + 3$ is the length and $3w + 4$ is the length of the diagonal.

$$a^2 + b^2 = c^2$$
$$w^2 + (3w + 3)^2 = (3w + 4)^2$$
$$w^2 + 9w^2 + 18w + 9 = 9w^2 + 24w + 16$$
$$10w^2 + 18w + 9 = 9w^2 + 24w + 16$$
$$w^2 - 6w - 7 = 0$$
$$(w - 7)(w + 1) = 0$$
$$w - 7 = 0 \quad \text{or} \quad w + 1 = 0$$
$$w = 7 \qquad\qquad w = -1$$

Since length is positive, the dimensions of the garden are 7 ft for the width and $3w + 3 = 3(7) + 3 = 24$ ft for the length.

41.
$$P = x^2 - 15x - 50$$
$$x^2 - 15x - 50 = 400$$
$$x^2 - 15 - 450 = 0$$
$$(x - 30)(x + 15) = 0$$
$$x - 30 = 0 \quad \text{or} \quad x + 15 = 0$$
$$x = 30 \qquad\qquad x = -15$$

Since x must be positive, she must sell 30 bookss for a profit of $400.

43. a.
$$n^2 + n = 20$$
$$n^2 + n - 20 = 0$$
$$(n - 4)(n + 5) = 0$$
$$n - 4 = 0 \quad \text{or} \quad n + 5 = 0$$
$$n = 4 \qquad\qquad n = -5$$

Since n must be positive, $n = 4$.

b.
$$n^2 + n = 90$$
$$n^2 + n - 90 = 0$$
$$(n - 9)(n + 10) = 0$$
$$n - 9 = 0 \quad \text{or} \quad n + 10 = 0$$
$$n = 9 \qquad\qquad n = -10$$

Since n must be positive, $n = 9$.

45. Before area can be determined, the length of the rectangle must be found first. Let x be the length of the rectangle.
$$a^2 + b^2 = c^2$$
$$x^2 + 18^2 = 30^2$$
$$x^2 + 324 = 900$$
$$x^2 = 576$$
$$x = 24$$

Area of a rectangle can be found by multiplying the length and width.

$$A = lw$$
$$= 24 \cdot 18$$
$$= 432$$

The area of the rectangle is 432 square feet.

47.
$$x^3 - 4x^2 - 32x = 0$$
$$x(x^2 - 4x - 32) = 0$$
$$x(x - 8)(x + 4) = 0$$
$$x = 0 \quad \text{or} \quad x - 8 = 0 \quad \text{or} \quad x + 4 = 0$$
$$\qquad\qquad x = 8 \qquad\qquad x = -4$$

49. Solutions are -2, 0, and 3, so the factors are $x + 2$, x, and $x - 3$.
$$x(x + 2)(x - 3) = x(x^2 - x - 6)$$
$$= x^3 - x^2 - 6x$$

The equation is $x^3 - x^2 - 6x = 0$.

51. $x + y = 9$ and $x^2 + y^2 = 45$
$$y = 9 - x$$
$$x^2 + (9 - x)^2 = 45$$
$$x^2 + 81 - 18x + x^2 = 45$$
$$2x^2 - 18x + 81 - 45 = 0$$
$$2(x^2 - 9x + 18) = 0$$
$$2(x - 3)(x - 6) = 0$$
$$x - 3 = 0 \quad \text{or} \quad x - 6 = 0$$
$$x = 3 \qquad\qquad x = 6$$

When $x = 3$, $y = 6$ and when $x = 6$, $y = 3$.
The numbers are 3 and 6.

53.
$$C = R$$
$$2x^2 - 20x + 600 = x^2 + 50x - 400$$
$$x^2 - 70x + 1000 = 0$$
$$(x - 50)(x - 20) = 0$$
$$x - 50 = 0 \quad \text{or} \quad x - 20 = 0$$
$$x = 50 \qquad\qquad x = 20$$

The manufacturer must produce 20 or 50 units to break even.

55. "Seven less than three a number" is $3x - 7$.

56. $(3x + 2) - (x^2 - 4x + 6) = 3x + 2 - x^2 + 4x - 6$
$$= -x^2 + 3x + 4x + 2 - 6$$
$$= -x^2 + 7x - 4$$

57. $\left(3x^2 + 2x - 4\right)\left(2x - 1\right)$

$$= 3x^2\left(2x - 1\right) + 2x\left(2x - 1\right) - 4\left(2x - 1\right)$$

$$= 6x^3 - 3x^2 + 4x^2 - 2x - 8x + 4$$

$$= 6x^3 + x^2 - 10x + 4$$

58.
$$
\begin{array}{r}
2x - 3 \\
3x - 5 \overline{\smash{\big)}\ 6x^2 - 19x + 15} \\
\underline{6x^2 - 10x} \\
-9x + 15 \\
\underline{-9x + 15} \\
0
\end{array}
$$

$$\frac{6x^2 - 19x + 15}{3x - 5} = 2x - 3$$

59. $\dfrac{6x^2 - 19x + 15}{3x - 5} = \dfrac{\left(3x - 5\right)\left(2x - 3\right)}{3x - 5}$

$$= 2x - 3$$

Review Exercises

1. The greatest common factor is y^3.

2. The greatest common factor is $3p$.

3. The greatest common factor is $6c^2$.

4. The greatest common factor is $5x^2y^2$.

5. The greatest common factor is 1.

6. The greatest common factor is s.

7. The greatest common factor is $x - 3$.

8. The greatest common factor is $x + 5$.

9. $7x - 35 = 7\left(x - 5\right)$

10. $35x - 5 = 5\left(7x - 1\right)$

11. $24y^2 - 4y = 4y\left(6y - 1\right)$

12. $55p^3 - 20p^2 = 5p^2\left(11p - 4\right)$

13. $60a^2b - 36ab^2 = 12ab\left(5a - 3b\right)$

14. $9xy - 36x^3y^2 = 9xy\left(1 - 4x^2y\right)$

15. $20x^3y^2 + 8x^9y^3 - 16x^5y^2$

$$= 4x^3y^2\left(5 + 2x^6y - 4x^2\right)$$

16. $24x^2 - 13y^2 + 6xy$ is prime.

17. $14a^2b - 7b - a^3$ is prime.

18. $x\left(5x + 3\right) - 2\left(5x + 3\right) = \left(5x + 3\right)\left(x - 2\right)$

19. $3x\left(x - 1\right) + 4\left(x - 1\right) = \left(x - 1\right)\left(3x + 4\right)$

20. $2x\left(4x - 3\right) + 4x - 3 = 2x\left(4x - 3\right) + 1\left(4x - 3\right)$

$$= \left(4x - 3\right)\left(2x + 1\right)$$

21. $x^2 + 6x + 2x + 12 = x\left(x + 6\right) + 2\left(x + 6\right)$

$$= \left(x + 6\right)\left(x + 2\right)$$

22. $x^2 - 5x + 4x - 20 = x\left(x - 5\right) + 4\left(x - 5\right)$

$$= \left(x - 5\right)\left(x + 4\right)$$

23. $y^2 - 6y - 6y + 36 = y\left(y - 6\right) - 6\left(y - 6\right)$

$$= \left(y - 6\right)\left(y - 6\right)$$

$$= \left(y - 6\right)^2$$

24. $3xy + 3x + 2y + 2 = 3x\left(y + 1\right) + 2\left(y + 1\right)$

$$= \left(y + 1\right)\left(3x + 2\right)$$

25. $4a^2 - 4ab - a + b = 4a\left(a - b\right) - 1\left(a - b\right)$

$$= \left(a - b\right)\left(4a - 1\right)$$

26. $2x^2 + 12x - x - 6 = 2x\left(x + 6\right) - 1\left(x + 6\right)$

$$= \left(x + 6\right)\left(2x - 1\right)$$

27. $x^2 + 3x - 2xy - 6y = x\left(x + 3\right) - 2y\left(x + 3\right)$

$$= \left(x + 3\right)\left(x - 2y\right)$$

28. $5x^2 - xy + 20xy - 4y^2$

$$= x\left(5x - y\right) + 4y\left(5x - y\right)$$

$$= \left(5x - y\right)\left(x + 4y\right)$$

29. $4x^2 + 12xy - 5xy - 15y^2$

$$= 4x\left(x + 3y\right) - 5y\left(x + 3y\right)$$

$$= \left(x + 3y\right)\left(4x - 5y\right)$$

30. $6a^2 - 10ab - 3ab + 5b^2$

$$= 2a\left(3a - 5b\right) - b\left(3a - 5b\right)$$

$$= \left(3a - 5b\right)\left(2a - b\right)$$

31. $pq - 3q + 4p - 12 = q\left(p - 3\right) + 4\left(p - 3\right)$

$$= \left(p - 3\right)\left(q + 4\right)$$

32. $3x^2 - 9xy + 2xy - 6y^2 = 3x\left(x - 3y\right) + 2y\left(x - 3y\right)$

$$= \left(x - 3y\right)\left(3x + 2y\right)$$

33. $7a^2 + 14ab - ab - 2b^2 = 7a(a+2b) - b(a+2b)$
$\qquad\qquad = (a+2b)(7a-b)$

34. $8x^2 - 4x + 6x - 3 = 4x(2x-1) + 3(2x-1)$
$\qquad\qquad = (2x-1)(4x+3)$

35. $x^2 - x - 6 = (x+2)(x-3)$

36. $x^2 + 4x - 15$ is prime.

37. $x^2 + 11x + 18 = (x+9)(x+2)$

38. $n^2 + 3n - 40 = (n+8)(n-5)$

39. $b^2 + b - 20 = (b-4)(b+5)$

40. $x^2 - 15x + 56 = (x-8)(x-7)$

41. $c^2 - 10c - 20$ is prime.

42. $y^2 - 10y - 22$ is prime.

43. $x^3 - 17x^2 + 72x = x(x^2 - 17x + 72)$
$\qquad\qquad = x(x-9)(x-8)$

44. $t^3 - 5t^2 - 36t = t(t^2 - 5t - 36)$
$\qquad\qquad = t(t-9)(t+4)$

45. $x^2 - 2xy - 15y^2 = (x-5y)(x+3y)$

46. $4x^3 + 32x^2y + 60xy^2 = 4x(x^2 + 8xy + 15y^2)$
$\qquad\qquad = 4x(x+3y)(x+5y)$

47. $2x^2 - x - 15 = (2x+5)(x-3)$

48. $6x^2 - 29x - 5 = (6x+1)(x-5)$

49. $4x^2 - 9x + 5 = (4x-5)(x-1)$

50. $5m^2 - 14m + 8 = (5m-4)(m-2)$

51. $16y^2 + 8y - 3 = (4y+3)(4y-1)$

52. $5x^2 - 32x + 12 = (5x-2)(x-6)$

53. $2t^2 + 14t + 9$ is prime.

54. $5x^2 + 37x - 24 = (5x-3)(x+8)$

55. $6s^2 + 13s + 5 = (2s+1)(3s+5)$

56. $6x^2 + 11x - 10 = (3x-2)(2x+5)$

57. $12x^2 + 2x - 4 = 2(6x^2 + x - 2)$
$\qquad\qquad = 2(3x+2)(2x-1)$

58. $25x^2 - 30x + 9 = (5x-3)(5x-3)$
$\qquad\qquad = (5x-3)^2$

59. $9x^3 - 12x^2 + 4x = x(9x^2 - 12x + 4)$
$\qquad\qquad = x(3x-2)(3x-2)$
$\qquad\qquad = x(3x-2)^2$

60. $18x^3 + 12x^2 - 16x = 2x(9x^2 + 6x - 8)$
$\qquad\qquad = 2x(3x+4)(3x-2)$

61. $4a^2 - 16ab + 15b^2 = (2a-3b)(2a-5b)$

62. $16a^2 - 22ab - 3b^2 = (8a+b)(2a-3b)$

63. $x^2 - 100 = x^2 - 10^2$
$\qquad\qquad = (x+10)(x-10)$

64. $x^2 - 36 = x^2 - 6^2$
$\qquad\qquad = (x+6)(x-6)$

65. $3x^2 - 48 = 3(x^2 - 16)$
$\qquad\qquad = 3(x^2 - 4^2)$
$\qquad\qquad = 3(x+4)(x-4)$

66. $81x^2 - 9y^2 = 9(9x^2 - y^2)$
$\qquad\qquad = 9\left[(3x)^2 - y^2\right]$
$\qquad\qquad = 9(3x+y)(3x-y)$

67. $81 - a^2 = 9^2 - a^2$
$\qquad\qquad = (9+a)(9-a)$

68. $64 - x^2 = 8^2 - x^2$
$\qquad\qquad = (8+x)(8-x)$

69. $16x^4 - 49y^2 = \left(4x^2\right)^2 - (7y)^2$
$\qquad\qquad = (4x^2 + 7y)(4x^2 - 7y)$

70. $64x^6 - 49y^6 = \left(8x^3\right)^2 - \left(7y^3\right)^2$
$\qquad\qquad = (8x^3 + 7y^3)(8x^3 - 7y^3)$

71. $a^3 + y^3 = (a+b)(a^2 - ab + b^2)$

72. $x^3 - y^3 = (x - y)(x^2 + xy + y^2)$

73. $x^3 - 1 = (x - 1)(x^2 + x + 1)$

74. $x^3 + 8 = x^3 + 2^3$
$$= (x + 2)(x^2 - 2x + 4)$$

75. $a^3 + 27 = a^3 + 3^3$
$$= (a + 3)(a^2 - 3a + 9)$$

76. $b^3 - 64 = b^3 - 4^3$
$$= (b - 4)(b^2 + 4b + 16)$$

77. $125a^3 + b^3 = (5a)^3 + b^3$
$$= (5a + b)(25a^2 - 5ab + b^2)$$

78. $27 - 8y^3 = 3^3 - (2y)^3$
$$= (3 - 2y)(9 + 6y + 4y^2)$$

79. $3x^3 - 192y^3 = 3(x^3 - 64y^3)$
$$= 3\left[x^3 - (4y)^3\right]$$
$$= 3(x - 4y)(x^2 + 4xy + 16y^2)$$

80. $27x^4 - 75y^2 = 3(9x^4 - 25y^2)$
$$= 3\left[(3x^2)^2 - (5y)^2\right]$$
$$= 3(3x^2 + 5y)(3x^2 - 5y)$$

81. $x^2 - 14x + 48 = (x - 6)(x - 8)$

82. $3x^2 - 18x + 27 = 3(x^2 - 6x + 9)$
$$= 3(x - 3)^2$$

83. $5q^2 - 5 = 5(q^2 - 1)$
$$= 5(q^2 - 1^2)$$
$$= 5(q + 1)(q - 1)$$

84. $8x^2 + 16x - 24 = 8(x^2 + 2x - 3)$
$$= 8(x + 3)(x - 1)$$

85. $4y^2 - 36 = 4(y^2 - 9)$
$$= 4(y^2 - 3^2)$$
$$= 4(y + 3)(y - 3)$$

86. $x^2 - 6x - 27 = (x - 9)(x + 3)$

87. $9x^2 - 6x + 1 = (3x - 1)(3x - 1)$
$$= (3x - 1)^2$$

88. $7x^2 + 25x - 12 = (7x - 3)(x + 4)$

89. $6b^3 - 6 = 6(b^3 - 1)$
$$= 6(b^3 - 1^3)$$
$$= 6(b - 1)(b^2 + b + 1)$$

90. $x^3y - 27y = y(x^3 - 27)$
$$= y(x^3 - 3^3)$$
$$= y(x - 3)(x^2 + 3x + 9)$$

91. $a^2b - 2ab - 15b = b(a^2 - 2a - 15)$
$$= b(a + 3)(a - 5)$$

92. $6x^3 + 30x^2 + 9x^2 + 45x$
$$= 3x(2x^2 + 10x + 3x + 15)$$
$$= 3x[2x(x + 5) + 3(x + 5)]$$
$$= 3x(2x + 3)(x + 5)$$

93. $x^2 - 4xy + 3y^2 = (x - 3y)(x - y)$

94. $3m^2 + 2mn - 8n^2 = (3m - 4n)(m + 2n)$

95. $4x^2 + 12xy + 9y^2 = (2x + 3y)(2x + 3y)$
$$= (2x + 3y)^2$$

96. $25a^2 - 49b^2 = (5a)^2 - (7b)^2$
$$= (5a + 7b)(5a - 7b)$$

97. $xy - 7x + 2y - 14 = x(y - 7) + 2(y - 7)$
$$= (x + 2)(y - 7)$$

98. $16y^5 - 25y^7 = y^5(16 - 25y^2)$
$$= y^5\left[4^2 - (5y)^2\right]$$
$$= y^5(4 + 5y)(4 - 5y)$$

99. $6x^2 + 5xy - 21y^2 = (2x - 3y)(3x + 7y)$

100. $4x^3 + 18x^2y + 20xy^2 = 2x(2x^2 + 9xy + 10y^2)$
$$= 2x(2x + 5y)(x + 2y)$$

101. $16x^4 - 8x^3 - 3x^2 = x^2(16x^2 - 8x - 3)$
$$= x^2(4x + 1)(4x - 3)$$

102. $d^4 - 16 = \left(d^2\right)^2 - 4^2$

$\qquad = \left(d^2 + 4\right)\left(d^2 - 4\right)$

$\qquad = \left(d^2 + 4\right)(d + 2)(d - 2)$

103. $x(x + 9) = 0$

$\qquad x = 0 \quad \text{or} \quad x + 9 = 0$

$\qquad\qquad\qquad\qquad x = -9$

104. $(a - 2)(a + 6) = 0$

$\qquad a - 2 = 0 \quad \text{or} \quad a + 6 = 0$

$\qquad\quad a = 2 \qquad\qquad a = -6$

105. $(x + 5)(4x - 3) = 0$

$\qquad x + 5 = 0 \quad \text{or} \quad 4x - 3 = 0$

$\qquad\quad x = -5 \qquad\qquad 4x = 3$

$\qquad\qquad\qquad\qquad\qquad x = \dfrac{3}{4}$

106. $x^2 + 7x = 0$

$\qquad x(x + 7) = 0$

$\qquad x = 0 \quad \text{or} \quad x + 7 = 0$

$\qquad\qquad\qquad\qquad x = -7$

107. $6x^2 + 30x = 0$

$\qquad 6x(x + 5) = 0$

$\qquad 6x = 0 \quad \text{or} \quad x + 5 = 0$

$\qquad\; x = 0 \qquad\qquad x = -5$

108. $6x^2 + 18x = 0$

$\qquad 6x(x + 3) = 0$

$\qquad 6x = 0 \quad \text{or} \quad x + 3 = 0$

$\qquad\; x = 0 \qquad\qquad x = -3$

109. $r^2 + 9r + 18 = 0$

$\qquad (r + 3)(r + 6) = 0$

$\qquad r + 3 = 0 \quad \text{or} \quad r + 6 = 0$

$\qquad\quad r = -3 \qquad\qquad r = -6$

110. $\qquad x^2 - 3x = -2$

$\qquad x^2 - 3x + 2 = 0$

$\qquad (x - 1)(x - 2) = 0$

$\qquad x - 1 = 0 \quad \text{or} \quad x - 2 = 0$

$\qquad\quad x = 1 \qquad\qquad x = 2$

111. $\qquad x^2 - 12 = -x$

$\qquad x^2 + x - 12 = 0$

$\qquad (x + 4)(x - 3) = 0$

$\qquad x + 4 = 0 \quad \text{or} \quad x - 3 = 0$

$\qquad\quad x = -4 \qquad\qquad x = 3$

112. $\qquad 15x + 12 = -3x^2$

$\qquad 3x^2 + 15x + 12 = 0$

$\qquad 3\left(x^2 + 5x + 4\right) = 0$

$\qquad 3(x + 1)(x + 4) = 0$

$\qquad x + 1 = 0 \quad \text{or} \quad x + 4 = 0$

$\qquad\quad x = -1 \qquad\qquad x = -4$

113. $\qquad x^2 - 6x + 8 = 0$

$\qquad (x - 4)(x - 2) = 0$

$\qquad x - 4 = 0 \quad \text{or} \quad x - 2 = 0$

$\qquad\quad x = 4 \qquad\qquad x = 2$

114. $\qquad 3p^2 + 6p = 45$

$\qquad 3p^2 + 6p - 45 = 0$

$\qquad 3\left(p^2 + 2p - 15\right) = 0$

$\qquad 3(x - 3)(x + 5) = 0$

$\qquad x - 3 = 0 \quad \text{or} \quad x + 5 = 0$

$\qquad\quad x = 3 \qquad\qquad x = -5$

115. $\qquad 8x^2 - 3 = -10x$

$\qquad 8x^2 + 10x - 3 = 0$

$\qquad (4x - 1)(2x + 3) = 0$

$\qquad 4x - 1 = 0 \quad \text{or} \quad 2x + 3 = 0$

$\qquad\quad 4x = 1 \qquad\qquad 2x = -3$

$\qquad\quad x = \dfrac{1}{4} \qquad\qquad x = -\dfrac{3}{2}$

116. $\qquad 3p^2 - 11p = 4$

$\qquad 3p^2 - 11p - 4 = 0$

$\qquad (3p + 1)(p - 4) = 0$

$\qquad 3p + 1 = 0 \quad \text{or} \quad p - 4 = 0$

$\qquad\quad 3p = -1 \qquad\qquad p = 4$

$\qquad\quad x = -\dfrac{1}{3}$

117.
$$4x^2 - 16 = 0$$
$$4(x^2 - 4) = 0$$
$$4(x^2 - 2^2) = 0$$
$$4(x+2)(x-2) = 0$$
$$x + 2 = 0 \quad \text{or} \quad x - 2 = 0$$
$$x = -2 \qquad\qquad x = 2$$

118.
$$49x^2 - 100 = 0$$
$$(7x)^2 - 10^2 = 0$$
$$(7x+10)(7x-10) = 0$$
$$7x + 10 = 0 \quad \text{or} \quad 7x - 10 = 0$$
$$7x = -10 \qquad\qquad 7x = 10$$
$$x = -\frac{10}{7} \qquad\qquad x = \frac{10}{7}$$

119.
$$8x^2 - 14x + 3 = 0$$
$$(2x-3)(4x-1) = 0$$
$$2x - 3 = 0 \quad \text{or} \quad 4x - 1 = 0$$
$$2x = 3 \qquad\qquad 4x = 1$$
$$x = \frac{3}{2} \qquad\qquad x = \frac{1}{4}$$

120.
$$-48x = -12x^2 - 45$$
$$12x^2 - 48x + 45 = 0$$
$$3(4x^2 - 16x + 15) = 0$$
$$3(2x-3)(2x-5) = 0$$
$$2x - 3 = 0 \quad \text{or} \quad 2x - 5 = 0$$
$$2x = 3 \qquad\qquad 2x = 5$$
$$x = \frac{3}{2} \qquad\qquad x = \frac{5}{2}$$

121. $a^2 + b^2 = c^2$

122. hypotenuse

123.
$$a^2 + b^2 = c^2$$
$$6^2 + 8^2 = c^2$$
$$36 + 64 = c^2$$
$$100 = c^2$$
$$10 \text{ ft} = c$$

124.
$$a^2 + b^2 = c^2$$
$$a^2 + 5^2 = 13^2$$
$$a^2 + 25 = 169$$
$$a^2 = 144$$
$$a = 12 \text{ m}$$

125. Let x be the smaller integer. The larger is $x + 2$.
$$x(x+2) = 99$$
$$x^2 + 2x = 99$$
$$x^2 + 2x - 99 = 0$$
$$(x+11)(x-9) = 0$$
$$x + 11 = 0 \quad \text{or} \quad x - 9 = 0$$
$$x = -11 \qquad\qquad x = 9$$
Since the integers must be positive, they are 9 and 11.

126. Let x be the smaller integer. Then the larger is $2x + 6$.
$$x(2x+6) = 56$$
$$2x^2 + 6x = 56$$
$$2x^2 + 6x - 56 = 0$$
$$2(x^2 + 3x - 28) = 0$$
$$(x+7)(x-4) = 0$$
$$x + 7 = 0 \quad \text{or} \quad x - 4 = 0$$
$$x = -7 \qquad\qquad x = 4$$
Since the integers must be positive, they are 4 and 14.

127. Let w be the width of the rectangle. Then the length is $w + 3$.
$$w(w+3) = 180$$
$$w^2 + 3w = 180$$
$$w^2 + 3w - 180 = 0$$
$$(w+15)(w-12) = 0$$
$$w + 15 = 0 \quad \text{or} \quad w - 12 = 0$$
$$w = -15 \qquad\qquad w = 12$$
Since the width must be positive, it is 12 feet, and the length is 15 feet.

128. Let x be the length of one leg of the triangle. Then $x + 7$ is the length of the other leg and $x + 9$ is the length of the hypotenuse.

$$a^2 + b^2 = c^2$$
$$x^2 + (x+7)^2 = (x+9)^2$$
$$x^2 + x^2 + 14x + 49 = x^2 + 18x + 81$$
$$2x^2 + 14x + 49 = x^2 + 18x + 81$$
$$x^2 - 4x - 32 = 0$$
$$(x-8)(x+4) = 0$$
$$x - 8 = 0 \quad \text{or} \quad x + 4 = 0$$
$$x = 8 \qquad x = -4$$

Since lengths must be positive, the lengths of the three sides are 8 ft, 15 ft, and 17 ft.

129. Let x be the length of a side of the original square. Then $x - 4$ is the length of a side of the smaller square.
$$(x-4)^2 = 25$$
$$x^2 - 8x + 16 = 25$$
$$x^2 - 8x + 16 - 25 = 0$$
$$x^2 - 8x - 9 = 0$$
$$(x-9)(x+1) = 0$$
$$x - 9 = 0 \quad \text{or} \quad x + 1 = 0$$
$$x = 9 \qquad x = -1$$

Since lengths must be positive, the length of a side of the original square is 9 inches.

130. Let w be the width of the table. Then the length is $w + 2$ and the diagonal is $w + 4$.
$$a^2 + b^2 = c^2$$
$$w^2 + (w+2)^2 = (w+4)^2$$
$$w^2 + w^2 + 4x + 4 = w^2 + 8x + 16$$
$$2w^2 + 4x + 4 = w^2 + 8x + 16$$
$$w^2 - 4w - 12 = 0$$
$$(w-6)(w+2) = 0$$
$$w - 6 = 0 \quad \text{or} \quad w + 2 = 0$$
$$w = 6 \qquad w = -2$$

Since lengths must be positive, the diagonal is $w + 4 = 6 + 4 = 10$ ft.

131.
$$d = 16t^2$$
$$16 = 16t^2$$
$$1 = t^2$$
$$1 = t$$

It will take 1 second for the pear to hit the ground.

132.
$$C = x^2 - 79x + 20$$
$$100 = x^2 - 79x + 20$$
$$0 = x^2 - 79x - 80$$
$$0 = (x-80)(x+1)$$
$$x - 80 = 0 \quad \text{or} \quad x + 1 = 0$$
$$x = 80 \qquad x = -1$$

Since only a positive number of dozens of brownies can be made, the association can make 80 dozen brownies.

Practice Test

1. The greatest common factor is $3y^3$.

2. The greatest common factor is $8p^2q^2$.

3. $5x^2y^3 - 15x^5y^2 = 5x^2y^2(y - 3x^3)$

4. $8a^3b - 12a^2b^2 + 28a^2b = 4a^2b(2a - 3b + 7)$

5. $4x^2 - 20x + x - 5 = 4x(x-5) + 1(x-5)$
$$= (4x+1)(x-5)$$

6. $a^2 - 4ab - 5ab + 20b^2 = a(a-4b) - 5b(a-4b)$
$$= (a-4b)(a-5b)$$

7. $r^2 + 5r - 24 = (r+8)(r-3)$

8. $25a^2 - 5ab - 6b^2 = (5a-3b)(5a+2b)$

9. $4x^2 - 16x - 48 = 4(x^2 - 4x - 12)$
$$= 4(x+2)(x-6)$$

10. $2y^3 - y^2 - 3y = y(2y^2 - y - 3)$
$$= y(2y-3)(y+1)$$

11. $12x^2 - xy - 6y^2 = (3x+2y)(4x-3y)$

12. $x^2 - 9y^2 = x^2 - (3y)^2$
$$= (x+3y)(x-3y)$$

13. $x^3 - 64 = x^3 - 4^3$
$$= (x-4)(x^2 + 4x + 16)$$

14. $(6x-5)(x+3) = 0$
$$6x - 5 = 0 \quad \text{or} \quad x + 3 = 0$$
$$6x = 5 \qquad x = -3$$
$$x = \frac{5}{6}$$

15. $x^2 - 6x = 0$

$x(x-6) = 0$

$x = 0$ or $x - 6 = 0$

$x = 6$

16. $x^2 = 64$

$x^2 - 64 = 0$

$x^2 - 8^2 = 0$

$(x+8)(x-8) = 0$

$x + 8 = 0$ or $x - 8 = 0$

$x = -8$ $x = 8$

17. $x^2 + 18x + 81 = 0$

$(x+9)^2 = 0$

$x + 9 = 0$

$x = -9$

18. $x^2 - 7x + 12 = 0$

$(x-3)(x-4) = 0$

$x - 3 = 0$ or $x - 4 = 0$

$x = 3$ $x = 4$

19. $x^2 + 6 = -5x$

$x^2 + 5x + 6 = 0$

$(x+2)(x+3) = 0$

$x - 2 = 0$ or $x + 3 = 0$

$x = -2$ $x = -3$

20. Use Pythagorean Theorem.

$a^2 + b^2 = c^2$

$a^2 + 10^2 = 26^2$

$a^2 + 100 = 676$

$a^2 = 576$

$a = 24$ in.

21. Let x be the length of one leg. Then $2x - 2$ is the length of the other leg and $2x + 2$ is the length of the hypotenuse.

$x^2 + (2x-2)^2 = (2x+2)^2$

$x^2 + 4x^2 - 8x + 4 = 4x^2 + 8x + 4$

$5x^2 - 8x + 4 = 4x^2 + 8x + 4$

$x^2 - 16x = 0$

$x(x-16) = 0$

$x = 0$ or $x - 16 = 0$

$x = 16$

Since length has to be positive, the hypotenuse is $2x + 2 = 2(16) + 2 = 32 + 2 = 34$ ft.

22. Let x be the smaller of the two integers. Then $2x + 1$ is the larger.

$x(2x+1) = 36$

$2x^2 + x - 36 = 0$

$(x-4)(2x+9) = 0$

$x - 4 = 0$ or $2x + 9 = 0$

$x = 4$ $2x = -9$

$x = -\dfrac{9}{2}$

Since x must be positive and an integer, the smaller integer is 4 and the larger is $2 \cdot 4 + 1 = 9$.

23. Let x be the smaller of the two consecutive even integers. Then $x + 2$ is the larger.

$x(x+2) = 168$

$x^2 + 2x - 168 = 0$

$(x+14)(x-12) = 0$

$x + 14 = 0$ or $x - 12 = 0$

$x = -14$ $x = 12$

Since x must be positive, then the smaller integer is 12 and the larger is 14.

24. Let w be the width of the rectangle. Then the length is $w + 2$.

$w(w+2) = 24$

$w^2 + 2w = 24$

$w^2 + 2w - 24 = 0$

$(w+6)(w-4) = 0$

$w + 6 = 0$ or $w - 4 = 0$

$w = -6$ $w = 4$

Since the width is positive, it is 4 meters, and the length is 6 meters.

25. $d = 16t^2$

$1600 = 16t^2$

$16t^2 - 1600 = 0$

$16(t^2 - 100) = 0$

$16(t^2 - 10^2) = 0$

$16(t+10)(t-10) = 0$

$t + 10 = 0$ or $t - 10 = 0$

$t = -10$ $t = 10$

Since time must be positive, then it would take the object 10 seconds to fall 1600 feet to the ground.

Cumulative Review Test

1. $4 - 5(2x + 4x^2 - 21)$

   $= 4 - 5[2(-4) + 4(-4)^2 - 21]$

   $= 4 - 5[-8 + 4(16) - 21]$

   $= 4 - 5(-8 + 64 - 21)$

   $= 4 - 5(35)$

   $= 4 - 175$

   $= -171$

2. $5x^2 - 3y + 7(2 + y^2 - 4x)$

   $= 5(3)^2 - 3(-2) + 7[2 + (-2)^2 - 4(3)]$

   $= 5(9) + 6 + 7(2 + 4 - 12)$

   $= 45 + 6 + 7(-6)$

   $= 51 - 42$

   $= 9$

3. Let $x =$ the cost of the room before tax.

   $x + (.15x) = 103.50$

   $1.15x = 103.50$

   $x = 90$

   The motel room costs $90 before taxes.

4. **a.** 7 is a natural number

   b. $-6, -0.2, \dfrac{3}{5}, 7, 0, -\dfrac{5}{9}$, and 1.34 are rational

   numbers.

   c. $\sqrt{7}$ and $-\sqrt{2}$ are irrational numbers.

   d. All of the numbers are real numbers.

5. $|-8|$ is greater than $-|8|$ since $-|8| = -(8) = -8$.

6. $4x - 2 = 4(x - 7) + 2x$

   $4x - 2 = 4x - 28 + 2x$

   $4x - 2 = 6x - 28$

   $26 = 2x$

   $13 = x$

7. $\dfrac{5}{12} = \dfrac{8}{x}$

   $5x = 8(12)$

   $5x = 96$

   $x = \dfrac{96}{5} = 19.2$

8. $3x - 5 \geq 10(6 - x)$

   $3x - 5 \geq 60 - 10x$

   $13x \geq 65$

   $x \geq 5$

9. $4x + 3y = 7$

   $3y = -4x + 7$

   $y = \dfrac{-4x + 7}{3}$

   $y = -\dfrac{4}{3}x + \dfrac{7}{3}$

10. Let x be the amount of 10% acid solution needed.

    $0.10x + 0.04(3) = 0.08(x + 3)$

    $0.10x + 0.12 = 0.08x + 0.24$

    $0.02x + 0.12 = 0.24$

    $0.02x = 0.12$

    $x = 6$

    Six liters of the 10% solution is needed.

11. Let x be the first of two consecutive odd integers. Then the other odd integer is $x + 2$.

    $x + x + 2 = 96$

    $2x + 2 = 96$

    $2x = 94$

    $x = 47$

    The two integers are 47 and 49.

12. Let $t =$ the number of hours that Brooke has been skiing. Then Bob has been skiing for $\left(t + \dfrac{1}{4}\right)$ hours.

	rate	time	distance
Brooke	8 kph	t	$8t$
Bob	4 kph	$t + \dfrac{1}{4}$	$4\left(t + \dfrac{1}{4}\right)$

    Brooke catches Bob when they have both gone the same distance.

$$8t = 4\left(t + \frac{1}{4}\right)$$
$$8t = 4t + 1$$
$$4t = 1$$
$$t = \frac{1}{4}$$

It will take Brooke $\frac{1}{4}$ hour to catch Bob.

20. $7y^3 - 63y = 7y(y^2 - 9)$
$$= 7y(y^2 - 3^2)$$
$$= 7y(y + 3)(y - 3)$$

13. $\left(\dfrac{4x^3}{9y^4}\right)^2 = \dfrac{4^2 x^{3\cdot2}}{9^2 y^{4\cdot2}} = \dfrac{16x^6}{81y^8}$

14. $(2x^{-3})^{-2}(4x^{-3}y^2)^3 = 2^{-2}x^{-3(-2)}4^3 x^{-3(3)}y^{2(3)}$
$$= 2^{-2}x^6 4^3 x^{-9}y^6$$
$$= 2^{-2} \cdot 4^3 x^{-3}y^6$$
$$= \frac{4^3 y^6}{2^2 x^3}$$
$$= \frac{64y^6}{4x^3}$$
$$= \frac{16y^6}{x^3}$$

15. $(x^3 - x^2 + 6x - 5) - (4x^3 - 3x^2 + 7)$
$$= x^3 - x^2 + 6x - 5 - 4x^3 + 3x^2 - 7$$
$$= x^3 - 4x^3 - x^2 + 3x^2 + 6x - 5 - 7$$
$$= -3x^3 + 2x^2 + 6x - 12$$

16. $(3x - 2)(x^2 + 5x - 6)$
$$= 3x(x^2) - 2(x^2) + 3x(5x) - 2(5x) + 3x(-6) - 2(-6)$$
$$= 3x^3 - 2x^2 + 15x^2 - 10x - 18x + 12$$
$$= 3x^3 + 13x^2 - 28x + 12$$

17.
$$\begin{array}{r}
x - 5 \\
x + 3 \overline{\smash{)}\, x^2 - 2x + 6} \\
\underline{x^2 + 3x} \\
-5x + 6 \\
\underline{-5x - 15} \\
21
\end{array}$$

$$\frac{x^2 - 2x + 6}{x + 3} = x - 5 + \frac{21}{x + 3}$$

18. $qr + 2q - 8r - 16 = q(r + 2) - 8(r + 2)$
$$= (r + 2)(q - 8)$$

19. $5x^2 - 7x - 6 = (5x + 3)(x - 2)$

Chapter 6

Exercise Set 6.1

1. Answers will vary.

3. The value of the variable does not make the denominator equal to 0.

5. There is no factor common to both the numerator and denominator of $\dfrac{4+3x}{9}$.

7. The denominator cannot be 0.

9. $x - 2 = 0$
$x \neq 2$

11. $\dfrac{x+8}{8-x} = \dfrac{x+8}{-(-8+x)} = -\dfrac{x+8}{x-8} \neq -1$

No

13. The expression is defined for all real numbers except $x = 0$.

15. $4n - 16 = 0$
$4n = 16$
$n = 4$

The expression is defined for all real numbers except $n = 4$.

17. $x^2 - 4 = 0$
$(x-2)(x+2) = 0$
$x - 2 = 0$ or $x + 2 = 0$
$x = 2$ $\qquad$ $x = -2$
The expression is defined for all real numbers except $x = 2$, $x = -2$.

19. $2x^2 - 9x + 9 = 0$
$(2x-3)(x-3) = 0$
$2x - 3 = 0$ or $x - 3 = 0$
$x = \dfrac{3}{2}$ $\qquad$ $x = 3$

The expression is defined for all real numbers except $x = \dfrac{3}{2}$, $x = 3$.

21. All real numbers because $x^2 + 36 \neq 0$.

23. $4p^2 - 25 = 0$
$(2p+5)(2p-5) = 0$
$2p + 5 = 0$ or $2p - 5 = 0$
$p = -\dfrac{5}{2}$ $\qquad$ $p = \dfrac{5}{2}$
The expression is defined for all real numbers except $p = \pm\dfrac{5}{2}$.

25. $\dfrac{8x^3y}{24x^2y^5} = \dfrac{8}{24} \cdot x^{3-2} \cdot y^{1-5}$
$= \dfrac{1}{3}xy^{-4}$
$= \dfrac{x}{3y^4}$

27. $\dfrac{\left(2a^4b^5\right)^3}{2a^{12}b^{20}} = \dfrac{2^3 \cdot a^{4(3)} \cdot b^{5(3)}}{2a^{12}b^{20}}$
$= \dfrac{8a^{12}b^{15}}{2a^{12}b^{20}}$
$= 4a^{12-12}b^{15-20}$
$= 4a^0b^{-5}$
$= \dfrac{4}{b^5}$

29. $\dfrac{2x}{x+xy} = \dfrac{2x}{x(1+y)}$
$= \dfrac{2}{1+y}$

31. $\dfrac{5x+15}{x+3} = \dfrac{5(x+3)}{x+3}$
$= 5$

33. $\dfrac{x^3 + 6x^2 + 7x}{2x} = \dfrac{x\left(x^2 + 6x + 7\right)}{2x}$
$= \dfrac{x^2 + 6x + 7}{2}$

35. $\dfrac{r^2 - r - 2}{r-2} = \dfrac{(r-2)(r+1)}{(r-2)}$
$= r + 1$

37. $\dfrac{x^2+2x}{x^2+4x+4}=\dfrac{x(x+2)}{(x+2)^2}$

$\qquad = \dfrac{x}{x+2}$

39. $\dfrac{z^2-10z+25}{z^2-25}=\dfrac{(z-5)^2}{(z-5)(z+5)}$

$\qquad = \dfrac{z-5}{z+5}$

41. $\dfrac{x^2-2x-3}{x^2-x-6}=\dfrac{(x+1)(x-3)}{(x+2)(x-3)}$

$\qquad = \dfrac{x+1}{x+2}$

43. $\dfrac{4x-3}{3-4x}=\dfrac{4x-3}{-(4x-3)}$

$\qquad = -1$

45. $\dfrac{x^2-2x-8}{4-x}=\dfrac{(x-4)(x+2)}{-(x-4)}$

$\qquad = -(x+2)$

47. $\dfrac{x^2+3x-18}{-2x^2+6x}=\dfrac{(x+6)(x-3)}{-2x(x-3)}$

$\qquad = -\dfrac{x+6}{2x}$

49. $\dfrac{2x^2+5x-3}{1-2x}=\dfrac{(2x-1)(x+3)}{-(2x-1)}$

$\qquad = -(x+3)$

51. $\dfrac{m-2}{4m^2-13m+10}=\dfrac{m-2}{(4m-5)(m-2)}=\dfrac{1}{4m-5}$

53. $\dfrac{x^2-25}{(x+5)^2}=\dfrac{(x-5)(x+5)}{(x+5)^2}$

$\qquad = \dfrac{x-5}{x+5}$

55. $\dfrac{6x^2-13x+6}{3x-2}=\dfrac{(3x-2)(2x-3)}{3x-2}$

$\qquad = 2x-3$

57. $\dfrac{x^2-3x+4x-12}{x+4}=\dfrac{x(x-3)+4(x-3)}{x+4}$

$\qquad = \dfrac{(x+4)(x-3)}{(x+4)}$

$\qquad = x-3$

59. $\dfrac{2x^2-8x+3x-12}{2x^2+8x+3x+12}=\dfrac{2x(x-4)+3(x-4)}{2x(x+4)+3(x+4)}$

$\qquad = \dfrac{(x-4)(2x+3)}{(x+4)(2x+3)}$

$\qquad = \dfrac{x-4}{x+4}$

61. $\dfrac{a^3-8}{a-2}=\dfrac{(a-2)(a^2+2a+4)}{(a-2)}$

$\qquad = a^2+2a+4$

63. $\dfrac{9s^2-16t^2}{3s-4t}=\dfrac{(3s+4t)(3s-4t)}{3s-4t}=3s+4t$

65. $\dfrac{6x+9y}{2x^2+xy-3y^2}=\dfrac{3(2x+3y)}{(2x+3y)(x-y)}=\dfrac{3}{x-y}$

67. $\dfrac{3\odot}{15}=\dfrac{3\odot}{3\cdot5}=\dfrac{\odot}{5}$

69. $\dfrac{7\triangle}{14\triangle+63}=\dfrac{7\triangle}{7(2\triangle+9)}=\dfrac{\triangle}{2\triangle+9}$

71. $\dfrac{3\triangle-4}{4-3\triangle}=\dfrac{-(2-4\triangle)}{(2-4\triangle)}=-1$

73. $x^2-x-6=(x-3)(x+2)$

Denominator $= x+2$

75. $(x+3)(x+5)=x^2+9x+20$

Numerator $= x^2+9x+20$

77. a.

$\dfrac{x-2}{x^2-2x+3x-6}=\dfrac{x-2}{x(x-2)+3(x-2)}$

$\qquad = \dfrac{(x-2)}{(x+3)(x-2)}$

$\qquad x\neq-3,\ x\neq2$

b. $\dfrac{(x-2)}{(x+3)(x-2)}=\dfrac{1}{x+3}$

79. a.

$\dfrac{x+5}{2x^3+7x^2-15x}=\dfrac{x+5}{x(2x^2+7x-15)}$

$\qquad = \dfrac{x+5}{x(2x-3)(x+5)}$

$\qquad x\neq0,\ x\neq\dfrac{3}{2},\ x\neq-5$

b. $\dfrac{(x+5)}{x(2x-3)(x+5)}=\dfrac{1}{x(2x-3)}$

81. $\dfrac{\left(\dfrac{1}{5}x^5 - \dfrac{2}{3}x^4\right)}{\left(\dfrac{1}{5}x^5 - \dfrac{2}{3}x^4\right)} = 1$

83. a. $\dfrac{x^2 - 25}{x^3 + 2x^2 - 15x} = \dfrac{(x+5)(x-5)}{x(x^2 + 2x - 15)}$

$\qquad = \dfrac{(x+5)(x-5)}{x(x+5)(x-3)}$

Undefined at $x = 0, x = 3,$ and $x = -5$.

b. $\dfrac{x^2 - 25}{x^3 + 2x^2 - 15x} = \dfrac{(x+5)(x-5)}{x(x^2 + 2x - 15)}$

$\qquad = \dfrac{(x+5)(x-5)}{x(x+5)(x-3)}$

$\qquad = \dfrac{x-5}{x(x-3)}$

c. $\dfrac{x^2 - 25}{x^3 + 2x^2 - 15x} = \dfrac{6^2 - 25}{6^3 + 2(6^2) - 15(6)}$

$\qquad = \dfrac{36 - 25}{216 + 72 - 90}$

$\qquad = \dfrac{11}{198}$

$\qquad = \dfrac{1}{18}$

d. $\dfrac{x-5}{x(x-3)} = \dfrac{6-5}{6(6-3)} = \dfrac{1}{18}$

e. $\dfrac{x^2 - 25}{x^3 + 2x^2 - 15x} = \dfrac{(-2)^2 - 25}{(-2)^3 + 2(-2)^2 - 15(-2)}$

$\qquad = \dfrac{4 - 25}{-8 + 8 + 30}$

$\qquad = \dfrac{-21}{30}$

$\qquad = -\dfrac{7}{10}$

$\dfrac{x-5}{x(x-3)} = \dfrac{(-2)-5}{(-2)((-2)-3)} = \dfrac{-7}{(-2)(-5)} = -\dfrac{7}{10}$

f. When a value that is defined is substituted in the original expression and in the simplified expression, the results are the same.

g. Since the expression is not defined for this value, −5 may not be substituted in the expression.

h. No, only for those values for which the expression is defined.

84. $z = \dfrac{x - y}{4}$

$\qquad 4z = x - y$

$\qquad 4z - x = -y$

$\qquad y = x - 4z$

85. Let x = measure of the smallest angle. Then the second angle = $x + 30$ and third angle = $3x + 10$.
angle 1 + angle 2 + angle 3 = 180°

$x + (x + 30) + (3x + 10) = 180$

$\qquad\qquad\qquad 5x + 40 = 180$

$\qquad\qquad\qquad\qquad 5x = 140$

$\qquad\qquad\qquad\qquad\quad x = 28$

$x + 30 = 28 + 30 = 58$

$3x + 10 = 3(28) + 10 = 84 + 10 = 94$

The three angles are 28°, 58°, and 94°.

86. $\left(\dfrac{5x^2 y^2}{9x^4 y^3}\right)^2 = \left(\dfrac{5}{9x^2 y}\right)^2$

$\qquad = \dfrac{25}{81x^4 y^2}$

87. $3x^2 - 4x - 8 - \left(-5x^2 + 6x + 11\right)$

$\qquad = 3x^2 - 4x - 8 + 5x^2 - 6x - 11$

$\qquad = 8x^2 - 10x - 19$

88. $3a^2 - 6a + 72 = 3(a^2 - 2a + 24)$

$\qquad\qquad\qquad\quad = 3(a - 6)(a + 4)$

89. $a^2 + b^2 = c^2$

$\qquad 5^2 + 12^2 = c^2$

$\qquad 25 + 144 = c^2$

$\qquad\qquad 169 = c^2$

$\qquad \sqrt{169} = \sqrt{c^2}$

$\qquad\qquad 13 = c$

The hypotenuse is 13 inches long.

Exercise Set 6.2

1. Answers will vary.

3. $\dfrac{x+3}{x-4} \cdot \dfrac{\boxed{}}{x+3} = x + 5$

Numerator must be $(x+5)(x-4) = x^2 + x - 20$

5. $\dfrac{x-5}{x+5} \cdot \dfrac{x+5}{\boxed{}} = \dfrac{1}{x+7}$

Denominator must be
$(x+7)(x-5) = x^2 + 2x - 35$

7. $\left(\dfrac{2}{5}\right)\left(\dfrac{15}{19}\right) = \dfrac{2}{\underset{1}{\cancel{5}}} \cdot \dfrac{\overset{3}{\cancel{15}}}{19} = \dfrac{2 \cdot 3}{1 \cdot 19} = \dfrac{6}{19}$

9. $\left(\dfrac{6}{8}\right)\left(-\dfrac{10}{14}\right) = \dfrac{6}{8} \cdot \dfrac{-10}{14} = \dfrac{3}{4} \cdot \dfrac{-5}{7} = \dfrac{3 \cdot (-5)}{4 \cdot 7} = -\dfrac{15}{28}$

11. $\left(-\dfrac{4}{11}\right)\left(-\dfrac{55}{64}\right) = \dfrac{-\overset{1}{\cancel{4}}}{\underset{1}{\cancel{11}}} \cdot \dfrac{-\overset{5}{\cancel{55}}}{\underset{16}{\cancel{64}}} = \dfrac{-1 \cdot (-5)}{1 \cdot 16} = \dfrac{5}{16}$

13. $\dfrac{3}{7} \div \dfrac{5}{7} = \dfrac{3}{\cancel{7}} \cdot \dfrac{\cancel{7}}{5} = \dfrac{3}{5}$

15. $-\dfrac{2}{9} \div \dfrac{32}{39} = \dfrac{-\overset{1}{\cancel{2}}}{\underset{3}{\cancel{9}}} \cdot \dfrac{\overset{13}{\cancel{39}}}{\underset{16}{\cancel{32}}} = \dfrac{-1 \cdot 13}{3 \cdot 16} = -\dfrac{13}{48}$

17. $\dfrac{6x}{4y} \cdot \dfrac{y^2}{12} = \dfrac{6x}{4y} \cdot \dfrac{y^2}{6 \cdot 2}$

$= \dfrac{xy}{8}$

19. $\dfrac{14x^2}{y^4} \cdot \dfrac{5x^2}{y^2} = \dfrac{70x^4}{y^6}$

21. $\dfrac{6x^5y^3}{5z^3} \cdot \dfrac{6x^4}{5yz^4} = \dfrac{36x^9y^2}{25z^7}$

23. $\dfrac{3x-2}{3x+2} \cdot \dfrac{x-1}{1-x} = \dfrac{3x-2}{3x+2} \cdot \dfrac{\cancel{(x-1)}}{-\cancel{(x-1)}}$

$= \dfrac{-3x+2}{3x+2}$

25. $\dfrac{x^2+7x+6}{x+6} \cdot \dfrac{1}{x+1} = \dfrac{\cancel{(x+6)}\,\cancel{(x+1)}}{\cancel{(x+6)}\,\cancel{(x+1)}}$

$= 1$

27. $\dfrac{a}{a^2-b^2} \cdot \dfrac{a+b}{a^2+ab} = \dfrac{\cancel{a}}{(a+b)(a-b)} \cdot \dfrac{\cancel{(a+b)}}{\cancel{a}\,\cancel{(a+b)}}$

$= \dfrac{1}{(a-b)(a+b)}$

$= \dfrac{1}{a^2-b^2}$

29. $\dfrac{6x^2-14x-12}{6x+4} \cdot \dfrac{2x+4}{2x^2-2x-12}$

$= \dfrac{2\left(3x^2-7x-6\right)}{2(3x+2)} \cdot \dfrac{2(x+2)}{2\left(x^2-x-6\right)}$

$= \dfrac{\cancel{2}\,(3x+2)\,(x-3)}{\cancel{2}\,(3x+2)} \cdot \dfrac{\cancel{2}\,(x+2)}{\cancel{2}\,(x-3)\,(x+2)}$

$= 1$

31. $\dfrac{3x^2-13x-10}{x^2-2x-15} \cdot \dfrac{x^2+x-2}{3x^2-x-2}$

$= \dfrac{(3x+2)\,\cancel{(x-5)}}{(x+3)\,\cancel{(x-5)}} \cdot \dfrac{(x+2)\,\cancel{(x-1)}}{(3x+2)\,\cancel{(x-1)}}$

$= \dfrac{x+2}{x+3}$

33. $\dfrac{x+9}{x-3} \cdot \dfrac{x^3-27}{x^2+3x+9}$

$= \dfrac{(x+9)}{\cancel{(x-3)}} \cdot \dfrac{\cancel{(x-3)}\left(x^2+3x+9\right)}{\left(x^2+3x+9\right)}$

$= x+9$

35. $\dfrac{12x^3}{y^2} \div \dfrac{3x}{y^3} = \dfrac{12x^3}{y^2} \cdot \dfrac{y^3}{3x}$

$= \dfrac{3 \cdot 4x^3}{y^2} \cdot \dfrac{y^3}{3x}$

$= 4x^2y$

37. $\dfrac{15xy^2}{4z} \div \dfrac{5x^2y^2}{12z^2} = \dfrac{3 \cdot 5xy^2}{4z} \cdot \dfrac{12z^2}{5x^2y^2}$

$= \dfrac{3 \cdot 5xy^2}{4z} \cdot \dfrac{3 \cdot 4z^2}{5x^2y^2}$

$= \dfrac{9z}{x}$

39. $\dfrac{11xy}{7ab^2} \div \dfrac{6xy}{7} = \dfrac{11xy}{7ab^2} \cdot \dfrac{7}{6xy}$

$= \dfrac{11}{6ab^2}$

41. $\dfrac{12r+6}{r} \div \dfrac{2r+1}{r^3} = \dfrac{6\cancel{(2r+1)}}{\cancel{r}} \cdot \dfrac{\cancel{r} \cdot r^2}{\cancel{(2r+1)}}$

$\qquad\qquad = 6r^2$

43. $\dfrac{x^2+11x+18}{x} \div \dfrac{x+2}{x} = \dfrac{(x+9)\cancel{(x+2)}}{\cancel{x}} \cdot \dfrac{\cancel{x}}{\cancel{(x+2)}}$

$\qquad\qquad\qquad = x+9$

45. $\dfrac{x^2-12x+32}{x^2-6x-16} \div \dfrac{x^2-x-12}{x^2-5x-24}$

$\quad = \dfrac{x^2-12x+32}{x^2-6x-16} \cdot \dfrac{x^2-5x-24}{x^2-x-12}$

$\quad = \dfrac{(x-8)\cancel{(x-4)}}{\cancel{(x-8)}(x+2)} \cdot \dfrac{\cancel{(x-8)}\cancel{(x+3)}}{\cancel{(x-4)}\cancel{(x+3)}}$

$\quad = \dfrac{x-8}{x+2}$

47. $\dfrac{2x^2+9x+4}{x^2+7x+12} \div \dfrac{2x^2-x-1}{(x+3)^2}$

$\quad = \dfrac{\cancel{(2x+1)}\cancel{(x+4)}}{\cancel{(x+3)}\cancel{(x+4)}} \cdot \dfrac{(x+3)(x+3)}{\cancel{(2x+1)}(x-1)}$

$\quad = \dfrac{x+3}{x-1}$

49. $\dfrac{x^2-y^2}{x^2-2xy+y^2} \div \dfrac{x+y}{y-x}$

$\quad = \dfrac{\cancel{(x-y)}\cancel{(x+y)}}{\cancel{(x-y)}\cancel{(x-y)}} \cdot \dfrac{-1\cancel{(x-y)}}{\cancel{(x+y)}}$

$\quad = -1$

51. $\dfrac{5x^2-4x-1}{5x^2+6x+1} \div \dfrac{x^2-5x+4}{x^2+2x+1}$

$\quad = \dfrac{\cancel{(5x+1)}\cancel{(x-1)}}{\cancel{(5x+1)}\cancel{(x+1)}} \cdot \dfrac{\cancel{(x+1)}(x+1)}{(x-4)\cancel{(x-1)}}$

$\quad = \dfrac{x+1}{x-4}$

53. $\dfrac{11z}{6y^2} \cdot \dfrac{24x^2y^4}{11z} = \dfrac{\cancel{11z}}{\cancel{6}\,\cancel{y^2}} \cdot \dfrac{\cancel{6} \cdot 4 \cdot x^2 \cdot y^2 \cdot \cancel{y^2}}{\cancel{11z}}$

$\qquad\qquad\qquad = 4x^2y^2$

55. $\dfrac{63a^2b^3}{20c^3} \cdot \dfrac{4c^4}{9a^3b^5} = \dfrac{7 \cdot \cancel{9} \cdot \cancel{4}\cancel{a^2}\, \cancel{b^3}\, \cancel{c^4}\, c}{5 \cdot \cancel{4} \cdot \cancel{9}\cancel{c^3} a \cancel{b^3}\, b^2\, \cancel{c}} = \dfrac{7c}{5ab^2}$

57. $\dfrac{-xy}{a} \div \dfrac{-2ax}{6y} = \dfrac{-xy}{a} \cdot \dfrac{6y}{-2ax}$

$\qquad\qquad = \dfrac{\cancel{-}\cancel{x}y}{a} \cdot \dfrac{\cancel{6} \cdot 3y}{\cancel{-2}a\cancel{x}}$

$\qquad\qquad = \dfrac{3y^2}{a^2}$

59. $\dfrac{64m^6}{21x^5y^7} \cdot \dfrac{14x^{12}y^5}{16m^5}$

$\quad = \dfrac{\cancel{16} \cdot 4 \,\cancel{m^5}\, m}{3 \cdot \cancel{7}\,\cancel{x^5}\,\cancel{y^5}\, y^2} \cdot \dfrac{2 \cdot \cancel{7}\,\cancel{x^5}\, x^7\, \cancel{y^5}}{\cancel{16}\,\cancel{m^5}}$

$\quad = \dfrac{8mx^7}{3y^2}$

61. $\dfrac{(x+3)^2}{5x^2} \cdot \dfrac{10x}{x^2-9}$

$\quad = \dfrac{(x+3)\cancel{(x+3)}}{\cancel{5}\,\cancel{x}x} \cdot \dfrac{\cancel{5} \cdot 2\cancel{x}}{\cancel{(x+3)}(x-3)}$

$\quad = \dfrac{2(x+3)}{x(x-3)}$

63. $\dfrac{1}{5x^2y^2} \div \dfrac{1}{35x^3y} = \dfrac{1}{\cancel{5}\,\cancel{x^2}\,\cancel{y}y} \cdot \dfrac{\cancel{5} \cdot 7\,\cancel{x^2}\, x\,\cancel{y}}{1}$

$\qquad\qquad\qquad = \dfrac{7x}{y}$

65. $\dfrac{(4m)^2}{8n^3} \div \dfrac{m^6n^8}{2} = \dfrac{16m^2}{8n^3} \cdot \dfrac{2}{m^6n^8}$

$\qquad\quad = \dfrac{\cancel{8} \cdot 2\,\cancel{m^2}}{\cancel{8}n^3} \cdot \dfrac{2}{m^4\,\cancel{m^2}\,n^8}$

$\qquad\quad = \dfrac{4}{m^4n^{11}}$

67. $\dfrac{r^2+5r+6}{r^2+9r+18} \cdot \dfrac{r^2+4r-12}{r^2-5r+6}$

$\quad = \dfrac{(r+2)\cancel{(r+3)}}{\cancel{(r+6)}\cancel{(r+3)}} \cdot \dfrac{\cancel{(r+6)}\cancel{(r-2)}}{(r-3)\cancel{(r-2)}}$

$\quad = \dfrac{r+2}{r-3}$

69. $\dfrac{x^2-12x+36}{x^2-8x+12} \div \dfrac{x^2-7x+12}{x^2-6x+8}$

$=\dfrac{x^2-12x+36}{x^2-8x+12}\cdot\dfrac{x^2-6x+8}{x^2-7x+12}$

$=\dfrac{\cancel{(x-6)}(x-6)}{\cancel{(x-6)}\cancel{(x-2)}}\cdot\dfrac{\cancel{(x-4)}\cancel{(x-2)}}{\cancel{(x-4)}(x-3)}$

$=\dfrac{x-6}{x-3}$

71. $\dfrac{2w^2+3w-35}{w^2-7w-8}\cdot\dfrac{w^2-5w-24}{w^2+8w+15}$

$=\dfrac{(2w-7)\cancel{(w+5)}}{\cancel{(w-8)}(w+1)}\cdot\dfrac{\cancel{(w-8)}\cancel{(w+3)}}{\cancel{(w+5)}\cancel{(w+3)}}$

$=\dfrac{2w-7}{w+1}$

73. $\dfrac{q^2-11q+30}{2q^2-7q-15}\div\dfrac{q^2-2q-24}{q^2-q-20}$

$=\dfrac{q^2-11q+30}{2q^2-7q-15}\cdot\dfrac{q^2-q-20}{q^2-2q-24}$

$=\dfrac{\cancel{(q-6)}(q-5)}{(2q+3)\cancel{(q-5)}}\cdot\dfrac{\cancel{(q-5)}\cancel{(q+4)}}{\cancel{(q-6)}\cancel{(q+4)}}$

$=\dfrac{q-5}{2q+3}$

75. $\dfrac{4n^2-9}{9n^2-1}\cdot\dfrac{3n^2-2n-1}{2n^2-5n+3}$

$=\dfrac{(2n+3)\cancel{(2n-3)}}{\cancel{(3n+1)}(3n-1)}\cdot\dfrac{\cancel{(3n+1)}\cancel{(n-1)}}{\cancel{(2n-3)}\cancel{(n-1)}}$

$=\dfrac{2n+3}{3n-1}$

77. $\dfrac{6\Delta^2}{13}\cdot\dfrac{13}{36\Delta^5}=\dfrac{\cancel{6\Delta^2}}{\cancel{13}}\cdot\dfrac{\cancel{13}}{6\cdot\cancel{6\Delta^2}\Delta^3}=\dfrac{1}{6\Delta^3}$

79. $\dfrac{\Delta-\text{☺}}{9\Delta-9\text{☺}}\div\dfrac{\Delta^2-\text{☺}^2}{\Delta^2+2\Delta\text{☺}+\text{☺}^2}$

$=\dfrac{\Delta-\text{☺}}{9\Delta-9\text{☺}}\cdot\dfrac{\Delta^2+2\Delta\text{☺}+\text{☺}^2}{\Delta^2-\text{☺}^2}$

$=\dfrac{\cancel{\Delta-\text{☺}}}{9(\Delta-\text{☺})}\cdot\dfrac{(\Delta+\text{☺})(\Delta+\text{☺})}{\cancel{(\Delta+\text{☺})}\cancel{(\Delta-\text{☺})}}$

$=\dfrac{\Delta+\text{☺}}{9(\Delta-\text{☺})}$

81. $(x+2)(x+3)=x^2+3x+2x+6$

$=x^2+5x+6$

Numerator is x^2+5x+6.

83. $(x-6)(x+2)=x^2+2x-6x-12$

$=x^2-4x-12$

Numerator is $x^2-4x-12$.

85. $(x^2-4)(x-1)\div(x+2)$†

$(x-2)(x+2)(x-1)\cdot\dfrac{1}{x+2}=x^2-x-2x+2$

$=x^2-3x+2$

Numerator is x^2-3x+2.

87. $\left(\dfrac{x+2}{x^2-4x-12}\cdot\dfrac{x^2-9x+18}{x-2}\right)\div\dfrac{x^2+5x+6}{x^2-4}=\dfrac{x+2}{x^2-4x-12}\cdot\dfrac{x^2-9x+18}{x-2}\cdot\dfrac{x^2-4}{x^2+5x+6}$

$=\dfrac{\cancel{(x+2)}}{\cancel{(x-6)}\cancel{(x+2)}}\cdot\dfrac{(x-3)\cancel{(x-6)}}{\cancel{(x-2)}}\cdot\dfrac{\cancel{(x+2)}\cancel{(x-2)}}{\cancel{(x+2)}(x+3)}$

$=\dfrac{x-3}{x+3}$

89. $\left(\dfrac{x^2-x-6}{2x^2-9x+9} \div \dfrac{x^2+x-12}{x^2+3x-4}\right) \cdot \dfrac{2x^2-5x+3}{x^2+x-2} = \dfrac{x^2-x-6}{2x^2-9x+9} \cdot \dfrac{x^2+3x-4}{x^2+x-12} \cdot \dfrac{2x^2-5x+3}{x^2+x-2}$

$$= \dfrac{\cancel{(x-3)}\,\cancel{(x+2)}}{\cancel{(2x-3)}\,(x-3)} \cdot \dfrac{\cancel{(x+4)}\,(x-1)}{\cancel{(x+4)}\,\cancel{(x-3)}} \cdot \dfrac{\cancel{(2x-3)}\,\cancel{(x-1)}}{\cancel{(x+2)}\,\cancel{(x-1)}}$$

$$= \dfrac{x-1}{x-3}$$

91. $\dfrac{(x-3)(x-2)}{(x+4)(x-5)} \cdot \dfrac{(x+4)(x-1)}{(x-3)(x-1)} = \dfrac{x-2}{x-5}$

The numerator is $(x-3)(x-2) = x^2-5x+6$.

The denominator is $(x+4)(x-5) = x^2-x-20$.

93. a. (2) and (3)

b. (1) $\left(\dfrac{x+2}{x-3}\right) \div \left(\dfrac{x^2-5x+6}{x-2} \cdot \dfrac{x+2}{x-3}\right)$

$$= \left(\dfrac{x+2}{x-3}\right) \div \left(\dfrac{\cancel{(x-3)}\,\cancel{(x-2)}}{\cancel{(x-2)}} \cdot \dfrac{(x+2)}{\cancel{(x-3)}}\right)$$

$$= \dfrac{x+2}{x-3} \div (x+2)$$

$$= \dfrac{\cancel{x+2}}{x-3} \cdot \dfrac{1}{\cancel{x+2}}$$

$$= \dfrac{1}{x-3}$$

(2) $\left(\dfrac{x+2}{x-3} \div \dfrac{x^2-5x+6}{x-2}\right) \cdot \left(\dfrac{x+2}{x-3}\right)$

$$= \left(\dfrac{x+2}{x-3} \cdot \dfrac{x-2}{x^2-5x+6}\right) \cdot \left(\dfrac{x+2}{x-3}\right)$$

$$= \left(\dfrac{x+2}{x-3} \cdot \dfrac{\cancel{x-2}}{(x-3)\,\cancel{(x-2)}}\right) \cdot \left(\dfrac{x+2}{x-3}\right)$$

$$= \dfrac{x+2}{(x-3)^2} \cdot \dfrac{x+2}{x-3}$$

$$= \dfrac{(x+2)^2}{(x-3)^3}$$

(3) $\left(\dfrac{x+2}{x-3}\right) \div \left(\dfrac{x^2-5x+6}{x-2}\right) \cdot \left(\dfrac{x+2}{x-3}\right)$

$$= \dfrac{x+2}{x-3} \cdot \dfrac{x-2}{x^2-5x+6}$$

$$= \dfrac{x+2}{x-3} \cdot \dfrac{\cancel{x-2}}{(x-3)\,\cancel{(x-2)}} \cdot \dfrac{x+2}{x-3}$$

$$= \dfrac{x+2}{x-3} \cdot \dfrac{1}{x-3} \cdot \dfrac{x+2}{x-3}$$

$$= \dfrac{(x+2)^2}{(x-3)^3}$$

94. Let x = the time it takes the tug boat to reach the barge.

Then $x + 2$ = the time it takes the tug boat to return to the dock.

	Rate	Time	Distance
Trip Out	15	x	$15(x)$
Return Trip	5	$x+2$	$5(x+2)$

Distance to barge = Distance back to dock

$15(x) = 5(x + 2)$

$15x = 5x + 10$

$10x = 10$

$x = 1$

It took 1 hour for the tug boat to reach the barge.

95. $(4x^3y^2z^4)(3xy^3z^7) = 4 \cdot 3 \cdot x^3 x y^2 y^3 z^4 z^7$

$$= 12x^4y^5z^{11}$$

96.

$$2x-1 \overline{)\, 4x^3 + 0x^2 - 5x + 0\,}$$

quotient: $2x^2 + x - 2$

$$\underline{4x^3 - 2x^2}$$
$$2x^2 - 5x$$
$$\underline{2x^2 - \; x}$$
$$-4x + 0$$
$$\underline{-4x + 2}$$
$$-2$$

$$\frac{4x^3 - 5x}{2x-1} = 2x^2 + x - 2 - \frac{2}{2x-1}$$

97. $6x^2 - 18x - 60 = 6\left(x^2 - 3x - 10\right)$
$$= 6(x-5)(x+2)$$

98. $3x^2 - 9x - 30 = 0$
$$3\left(x^2 - 3x - 10\right) = 0$$
$$3(x-5)(x+2) = 0$$
$$x - 5 = 0 \quad \text{or} \quad x + 2 = 0$$
$$x = 5 \qquad\qquad x = -2$$

Exercise Set 6.3

1. Answers will vary.

3. Answers will vary.

5. $\dfrac{9}{x+6} - \dfrac{2}{x}$

The only factor (other than 1) of the first denominator is $x + 6$. The only factor (other than 1) of the second denominator is x. The LCD is therefore $x(x+6)$.

7. $\dfrac{2}{x+3} + \dfrac{1}{x} + \dfrac{1}{4}$

The only factor (other than 1) of the first denominator is $x + 3$. The only factor (other than 1) of the second denominator is x. The only factor (other than 1) of the third denominator is 4. The LCD is therefore $4x(x+3)$.

9. a. The negative sign in $-(2x-9)$ was not distributed.

b. $\dfrac{4x-3}{5x+4} - \dfrac{2x-9}{5x+4} = \dfrac{4x-3-(2x-9)}{5x+4}$
$$= \dfrac{4x-3-2x+9}{5x+4}$$
$$\neq \dfrac{4x-3-2x-9}{5x+4}$$

11. a. The negative sign in $-\left(3x^2 - 4x + 5\right)$ was not distributed.

b. $\dfrac{8x-2}{x^2-4x+3} - \dfrac{3x^2-4x+5}{x^2-4x+3}$
$$= \dfrac{8x-2-\left(3x^2-4x+5\right)}{x^2-4x+3}$$
$$= \dfrac{8x-2-3x^2+4x-5}{x^2-4x+3}$$
$$\neq \dfrac{8x-2-3x^2-4x+5}{x^2-4x+3}$$

13. $\dfrac{4}{7} + \dfrac{2}{7} = \dfrac{4+2}{7} = \dfrac{6}{7}$

15. $\dfrac{5r+2}{4} - \dfrac{3}{4} = \dfrac{5r+2-3}{4} = \dfrac{5r-1}{4}$

17. $\dfrac{2}{x} + \dfrac{x+4}{x} = \dfrac{2+x+4}{x}$
$$= \dfrac{x+6}{x}$$

19. $\dfrac{6}{n+1} + \dfrac{n+2}{n+1} = \dfrac{6+n+2}{n+1}$
$$= \dfrac{n+8}{n+1}$$

21. $\dfrac{x}{x-3} + \dfrac{4x+9}{x-3} = \dfrac{x+4x+9}{x-3} = \dfrac{5x+9}{x-3}$

23. $\dfrac{4t+7}{5t^2} - \dfrac{3t+4}{5t^2} = \dfrac{4t+7-(3t+4)}{5t^2}$
$$= \dfrac{4t+7-3t-4}{5t^2}$$
$$= \dfrac{t+3}{5t^2}$$

25. $\dfrac{5x+4}{x^2-x-12} + \dfrac{-4x-1}{x^2-x-12} = \dfrac{5x+4-4x-1}{x^2-x-12}$
$$= \dfrac{x+3}{(x+3)(x-4)}$$
$$= \dfrac{1}{x-4}$$

27. $\dfrac{2m+5}{(m+4)(m-3)} - \dfrac{m+1}{(m+4)(m-3)}$

$= \dfrac{2m+5-(m+1)}{(m+4)(m-3)}$

$= \dfrac{2m+5-m-1}{(m+4)(m-3)}$

$= \dfrac{m+4}{(m+4)(m-3)}$

$= \dfrac{1}{m-3}$

29. $\dfrac{2p-6}{p-5} - \dfrac{p+6}{p-5} = \dfrac{2p-6-(p+6)}{p-5}$

$= \dfrac{2p-6-p-6}{p-5}$

$= \dfrac{p-12}{p-5}$

31. $\dfrac{x^2+4x+1}{x+2} - \dfrac{5x+7}{x+2}$

$= \dfrac{x^2+4x+1-(5x+7)}{x+2}$

$= \dfrac{x^2+4x+1-5x-7}{x+2}$

$= \dfrac{x^2-x-6}{x+2}$

$= \dfrac{(x-3)(x+2)}{x+2}$

$= x-3$

33. $\dfrac{3x+13}{2x+10} - \dfrac{2(x+4)}{2x+10} = \dfrac{3x+13-2(x+4)}{2x+10}$

$= \dfrac{3x+13-2x-8}{2x+10}$

$= \dfrac{x+5}{2(x+5)}$

$= \dfrac{1}{2}$

35. $\dfrac{b^2-2b-2}{b^2-b-6} + \dfrac{b-4}{b^2-b-6} = \dfrac{b^2-2b-2+b-4}{b^2-b-6}$

$= \dfrac{b^2-b-6}{b^2-b-6}$

$= 1$

37. $\dfrac{t-3}{t+3} - \dfrac{-3t-15}{t+3} = \dfrac{t-3-(-3t-15)}{t+3}$

$= \dfrac{t-3+3t+15}{t+3}$

$= \dfrac{4t+12}{t+3}$

$= \dfrac{4(t+3)}{t+3}$

$= 4$

39. $\dfrac{3x^2+15x}{x^3+2x^2-8x} + \dfrac{2x^2+5x}{x^3+2x^2-8x}$

$= \dfrac{3x^2+15x+2x^2+5x}{x^3+2x^2-8x}$

$= \dfrac{5x^2+20x}{x(x^2+2x-8)}$

$= \dfrac{5x(x+4)}{x(x-2)(x+4)}$

$= \dfrac{5}{x-2}$

41. $\dfrac{3x^2-9x}{4x^2-8x} + \dfrac{3x}{4x^2-8x} = \dfrac{3x^2-9x+3x}{4x^2-8x}$

$= \dfrac{3x^2-6x}{4x^2-8x}$

$= \dfrac{3x(x-2)}{4x(x-2)}$

$= \dfrac{3}{4}$

43. $\dfrac{3x^2-4x+6}{3x^2+7x+2} - \dfrac{10x+11}{3x^2+7x+2}$

$= \dfrac{3x^2-4x+6-(10x+11)}{3x^2+7x+2}$

$= \dfrac{3x^2-4x+6-10x-11}{3x^2+7x+2}$

$= \dfrac{3x^2-14x-5}{3x^2+7x+2}$

$= \dfrac{(3x+1)(x-5)}{(3x+1)(x+2)}$

$= \dfrac{x-5}{x+2}$

45. $\dfrac{x^2+3x-6}{x^2-5x+4}-\dfrac{-2x^2+4x-4}{x^2-5x+4}$

$=\dfrac{x^2+3x-6-(-2x^2+4x-4)}{x^2-5x+4}$

$=\dfrac{x^2+3x-6+2x^2-4x+4}{x^2-5x+4}$

$=\dfrac{3x^2-x-2}{x^2-5x+4}$

$=\dfrac{(3x+2)(x-1)}{(x-4)(x-1)}$

$=\dfrac{3x+2}{x-4}$

47. $\dfrac{5x^2+30x+8}{x^2-64}+\dfrac{x^2+19x}{x^2-64}$

$=\dfrac{5x^2+30x+8+x^2+19x}{x^2-64}$

$=\dfrac{6x^2+49x+8}{x^2-64}$

$=\dfrac{(6x+1)(x+8)}{(x-8)(x+8)}$

$=\dfrac{6x+1}{x-8}$

49. $\dfrac{x}{5}+\dfrac{x+4}{5}$

Least common denominator = 5

51. $\dfrac{3}{n}+\dfrac{1}{9n}$

Least common denominator = $9n$

53. $\dfrac{3}{5x}+\dfrac{7}{3}$

Least common denominator $=5x\cdot3=15x$

55. $\dfrac{6}{p}+\dfrac{9}{p^3}$

Least common denominator $= p^3$

57. $\dfrac{m+3}{3m-4}+m=\dfrac{m+3}{3m-4}+\dfrac{m}{1}$

Least common denominator $=3m-4$

59. $\dfrac{x}{6x}+\dfrac{4}{x^2}$

Least common denominator $=6x^2$

61. $\dfrac{x+1}{12x^2y}-\dfrac{7}{9x^3}=\dfrac{x+1}{3\cdot4x^2y}-\dfrac{7}{3^2x^3}$

Least common denominator
$=4\cdot3^2\cdot x^3\cdot y=36x^3y$

63. $\dfrac{4}{2r^4s^5}-\dfrac{5}{9r^3s^7}=\dfrac{4}{2r^4s^5}-\dfrac{5}{3\cdot3r^3s^7}$

Least common denominator
$=2\cdot3\cdot3r^4s^7=18r^4s^7$

65. $\dfrac{3}{m}-\dfrac{17m}{m+2}$

Least common denominator $=m(m+2)$

67. $\dfrac{5x-2}{x^2+x}-\dfrac{13}{x}=\dfrac{5x-2}{x(x+1)}-\dfrac{13}{x}$

Least common denominator $=x(x+1)$

69. $\dfrac{n}{4n-1}+\dfrac{n-8}{1-4n}=\dfrac{n}{4n-1}+\dfrac{(-1)(n-8)}{(-1)(1-4n)}$

$\qquad\qquad=\dfrac{n}{4n-1}+\dfrac{-n+8}{4n-1}$

Least common denominator $=4n-1$ or $1-4n$

71. $\dfrac{3}{4k-5r}-\dfrac{10}{-4k+5r}$

$=\dfrac{3}{4k-5r}-\dfrac{(-1)10}{(-1)(-4k+5r)}$

$=\dfrac{3}{4k-5r}-\dfrac{-10}{4k-5r}$

Least common denominator $=4k-5r$ or
$-4k+5r$

73. $\dfrac{4}{2q^2+2q}-\dfrac{5}{9q}=\dfrac{4}{2q(q+1)}-\dfrac{5}{3\cdot3q}$

Least common denominator $=2\cdot3\cdot3q(q+1)$

$\qquad\qquad\qquad\qquad\quad=18q(q+1)$

75. $\dfrac{21}{24x^2y}+\dfrac{x+4}{15xy^3}=\dfrac{21}{3\cdot8x^2y}+\dfrac{x+4}{3\cdot5xy^3}$

Least common denominator
$=8\cdot3\cdot5x^2y^3=120x^2y^3$

77. $\dfrac{11}{3x+12}+\dfrac{3x+1}{2x+4}=\dfrac{11}{3(x+4)}+\dfrac{3x+1}{2(x+2)}$

Least common denominator
$=3\cdot2(x+4)(x+2)=6(x+4)(x+2)$

79. $\dfrac{9x+4}{x+1} - \dfrac{2x-6}{x+8}$

Least common denominator $= (x+1)(x+8)$

81. $\dfrac{x-2}{x^2-5x-24} + \dfrac{3}{x^2+11x+24}$

$= \dfrac{x-2}{(x-8)(x+3)} + \dfrac{3}{(x+8)(x+3)}$

Least common denominator
$= (x-8)(x+3)(x+8)$

83. $\dfrac{5}{(a-4)^2} - \dfrac{a+2}{a^2-7a+12}$

$= \dfrac{5}{(a-4)^2} - \dfrac{a+2}{(a-4)(a-3)}$

Least common denominator
$= (a-4)^2(a-3)$

85. $\dfrac{9x}{x^2+6x+5} - \dfrac{5x^2}{x^2+4x+3}$

$= \dfrac{9x}{(x+5)(x+1)} - \dfrac{5x^2}{(x+3)(x+1)}$

Least common denominator
$= (x+5)(x+1)(x+3)$

87. $\dfrac{3x-5}{x^2-6x+9} + \dfrac{3}{x-3}$

$= \dfrac{3x+5}{(x-3)^2} + \dfrac{3}{x-3}$

Least common denominator $= (x-3)^2$

89. $\dfrac{8x^2}{x^2-7x+6} + x - 9$

$= \dfrac{8x^2}{(x-6)(x-1)} + \dfrac{x-9}{1}$

Least common denominator $= (x-6)(x-1)$

91. $\dfrac{t-1}{3t^2+10t-8} - \dfrac{11}{3t^2+11t-4}$

$= \dfrac{t-1}{(3t-2)(t+4)} - \dfrac{11}{(3t-1)(t+4)}$

Least common denominator
$= (3t-2)(t+4)(3t-1)$

93. $\dfrac{3x-1}{4x^2+4x+1} + \dfrac{x^2+x-9}{8x^2+10x+3}$

$= \dfrac{3x-1}{(2x+1)^2} + \dfrac{x^2+x-9}{(2x+1)(4x+3)}$

Least common denominator
$= (2x+1)^2(4x+3)$

95. $\dfrac{1}{7} + \dfrac{2}{5} = \dfrac{5}{5} \cdot \dfrac{1}{7} + \dfrac{2}{5} \cdot \dfrac{7}{7} = \dfrac{5}{35} + \dfrac{14}{35} = \dfrac{19}{35}$

97. $\dfrac{2}{9} + \dfrac{3}{4} = \dfrac{4}{4} \cdot \dfrac{2}{9} + \dfrac{3}{4} \cdot \dfrac{9}{9} = \dfrac{8}{36} + \dfrac{27}{36} = \dfrac{35}{36}$

99. $\dfrac{5}{9} - \dfrac{1}{2} = \dfrac{2}{2} \cdot \dfrac{5}{9} - \dfrac{1}{2} \cdot \dfrac{9}{9} = \dfrac{10}{18} - \dfrac{9}{18} = \dfrac{1}{18}$

101. $x^2 - 6x + 3 + \boxed{} = 2x^2 - 5x - 6$

$\boxed{} = 2x^2 - 5x - 6 - (x^2 - 6x + 3)$

$= 2x^2 - 5x - 6 - x^2 + 6x - 3$

$= x^2 + x - 9$

Sum of numerators must be $2x^2 - 5x - 6$

103. $-x^2 - 4x + 3 + \boxed{} = 5x - 7$

$\boxed{} = 5x - 7 - (-x^2 - 4x + 3)$

$= 5x - 7 + x^2 + 4x - 3$

$= x^2 + 9x - 10$

Sum of numerator must be $5x - 7$

105. $\dfrac{3}{☺} + \dfrac{4}{5☺}$

Least common denominator $= 5☺$

107. $\dfrac{8}{\Delta^2-9} - \dfrac{2}{\Delta+3} = \dfrac{8}{(\Delta+3)(\Delta-3)} - \dfrac{2}{\Delta+3}$

Least common denominator $= (\Delta+3)(\Delta-3)$

109. $\dfrac{4x-1}{x^2-25} - \dfrac{3x^2-8}{x^2-25} + \dfrac{8x-7}{x^2-25}$

$= \dfrac{4x-1-(3x^2-8)+(8x-7)}{x^2-25}$

$= \dfrac{4x-1-3x^2+8+8x-7}{x^2-25}$

$= \dfrac{-3x^2+12x}{x^2-25}$

111. $\dfrac{7}{6x^5y^9} - \dfrac{9}{2x^3y} + \dfrac{6}{5x^{12}y^2}$

$= \dfrac{7}{2 \cdot 3x^5y^9} - \dfrac{9}{2x^3y} + \dfrac{6}{5x^{12}y^2}$

Least common denominator
$= 2 \cdot 3 \cdot 5x^{12}y^9 = 30x^{12}y^9$

113. $\dfrac{3x}{x^2 - x - 12} + \dfrac{2}{x^2 - 6x + 8} + \dfrac{3}{x^2 + x - 6}$

$= \dfrac{3x}{(x-4)(x+3)} + \dfrac{2}{(x-4)(x-2)}$

$\quad + \dfrac{3}{(x+3)(x-2)}$

Least common denominator
$= (x-4)(x+3)(x-2)$

115. $4\dfrac{3}{5} - 2\dfrac{5}{9} = \dfrac{23}{5} - \dfrac{23}{9}$

$\qquad = \dfrac{207}{45} - \dfrac{115}{45}$

$\qquad = \dfrac{92}{45}$

$\qquad = 2\dfrac{2}{45}$

116. $6x + 4 = -(x+2) - 3x + 4$

$6x + 4 = -x - 2 - 3x + 4$

$6x + 4 = -4x + 2$

$6x + 4x = 2 - 4$

$10x = -2$

$x = \dfrac{-2}{10} = -\dfrac{1}{5}$

117. $\dfrac{6}{128} = \dfrac{x}{48}$

$128x = 6 \cdot 48$

$128x = 288$

$x = \dfrac{288}{128}$

$x = \dfrac{9}{4} = 2\dfrac{1}{4}$

You should use 2.25 ounces of concentrate.

118. Let h = the number of hours played.
The cost under Plan 1 is $C = 250 + 5h$ while the cost under Plan 2 is $C = 600$.

Set the two costs equal
$250 + 5h = 600$

$5h = 350$

$h = 70$

If Malcolm plays 70 hours in a year, the cost of the two plans is equal.

119. $\dfrac{8.4 \times 10^8}{2.1 \times 10^{-3}} = 4.0 \times 10^{8-(-3)} = 4.0 \times 10^{11}$

120.
$2x^2 - 3 = x$

$2x^2 - x - 3 = 0$

$(2x - 3)(x + 1) = 0$

$2x - 3 = 0 \quad$ or $\quad x + 1 = 0$

$2x = 3 \qquad\qquad x = -1$

$x = \dfrac{3}{2}$

Exercise Set 6.4

1. For each fraction, divide the LCD by the denominator.

3. a. Answers will vary.

b. $\dfrac{x}{x^2 - x - 6} + \dfrac{3}{x^2 - 4}$

$= \dfrac{x}{(x-3)(x+2)} + \dfrac{3}{(x-2)(x+2)}$

$= \dfrac{x(x-2)}{(x-3)(x+2)(x-2)} + \dfrac{3(x-3)}{(x-2)(x+2)(x-3)}$

$= \dfrac{x^2 - 2x + 3x - 9}{(x-3)(x+2)(x-2)}$

$= \dfrac{x^2 + x - 9}{(x-3)(x+2)(x-2)}$

5. a. $\dfrac{y}{4z} + \dfrac{5}{6z^2}$

$4z = 2 \cdot 2 \cdot z$

$6z^2 = 2 \cdot 3 \cdot z^2$

Least common denominator
$2 \cdot 2 \cdot 3 \cdot z^2 = 12z^2$

b. $\dfrac{y}{4z} + \dfrac{5}{6z^2} = \dfrac{y}{4z} \cdot \dfrac{3z}{3z} + \dfrac{5}{6z^2} \cdot \dfrac{2}{2}$

$= \dfrac{3yz}{12z^2} + \dfrac{10}{12z^2}$

$= \dfrac{3yz + 10}{12z^2}$

c. Yes. After factoring out the common factors, the reduced form would be the same.

7. $\dfrac{2}{x} + \dfrac{3}{y} = \dfrac{y}{y} \cdot \dfrac{2}{x} + \dfrac{3}{y} \cdot \dfrac{x}{x}$

$\qquad = \dfrac{2y}{xy} + \dfrac{3x}{xy}$

$\qquad = \dfrac{2y + 3x}{xy}$

9. $\dfrac{5}{x^2} + \dfrac{1}{2x} = \dfrac{2}{2} \cdot \dfrac{5}{x^2} + \dfrac{1}{2x} \cdot \dfrac{x}{x}$

$\qquad = \dfrac{10}{2x^2} + \dfrac{x}{2x^2}$

$\qquad = \dfrac{x + 10}{2x^2}$

11. $3 + \dfrac{8}{x} = \dfrac{x}{x} \cdot 3 + \dfrac{8}{x} = \dfrac{3x}{x} + \dfrac{8}{x} = \dfrac{3x + 8}{x}$

13. $\dfrac{2}{x^2} + \dfrac{3}{5x} = \dfrac{5}{5} \cdot \dfrac{2}{x^2} + \dfrac{3}{5x} \cdot \dfrac{x}{x}$

$\qquad = \dfrac{10}{5x^2} + \dfrac{3x}{5x^2}$

$\qquad = \dfrac{3x + 10}{5x^2}$

15. $\dfrac{9}{4x^2y} + \dfrac{3}{5xy^2} = \dfrac{5y}{5y} \cdot \dfrac{9}{4x^2y} + \dfrac{3}{5xy^2} \cdot \dfrac{4x}{4x}$

$\qquad = \dfrac{45y}{20x^2y^2} + \dfrac{12x}{20x^2y^2}$

$\qquad = \dfrac{45y + 12x}{20x^2y^2}$

17. $4y + \dfrac{x}{y} = \dfrac{y}{y} \cdot \dfrac{4y}{1} + \dfrac{x}{y} = \dfrac{4y^2}{y} + \dfrac{x}{y} = \dfrac{4y^2 + x}{y}$

19. $\dfrac{3a - 1}{2a} + \dfrac{2}{3a} = \dfrac{3}{3} \cdot \dfrac{3a - 1}{2a} + \dfrac{2}{3a} \cdot \dfrac{2}{2}$

$\qquad = \dfrac{3(3a - 1)}{3 \cdot 2a} + \dfrac{2 \cdot 2}{3a \cdot 2}$

$\qquad = \dfrac{9a - 3}{6a} + \dfrac{4}{6a}$

$\qquad = \dfrac{9a - 3 + 4}{6a}$

$\qquad = \dfrac{9a + 1}{6a}$

21. $\dfrac{6x}{y} + \dfrac{2y}{xy} = \dfrac{x}{x} \cdot \dfrac{6x}{y} + \dfrac{2y}{xy}$

$\qquad = \dfrac{6x^2}{xy} + \dfrac{2y}{xy}$

$\qquad = \dfrac{6x^2 + 2y}{xy}$

23. $\dfrac{9}{b} - \dfrac{4}{5a^2} = \dfrac{5a^2}{5a^2} \cdot \dfrac{9}{b} - \dfrac{4}{5a^2} \cdot \dfrac{b}{b}$

$\qquad = \dfrac{45a^2}{5a^2b} - \dfrac{4b}{5a^2b}$

$\qquad = \dfrac{45a^2 - 4b}{5a^2b}$

25. $\dfrac{4}{x} + \dfrac{9}{x - 3} = \dfrac{x - 3}{x - 3} \cdot \dfrac{4}{x} + \dfrac{9}{(x - 3)} \cdot \dfrac{x}{x}$

$\qquad = \dfrac{4(x - 3)}{x(x - 3)} + \dfrac{9x}{x(x - 3)}$

$\qquad = \dfrac{4x - 12}{x(x - 3)} + \dfrac{9x}{x(x - 3)}$

$\qquad = \dfrac{4x - 12 + 9x}{x(x - 3)}$

$\qquad = \dfrac{13x - 12}{x(x - 3)}$

27. $\dfrac{9}{p + 3} + \dfrac{2}{p} = \dfrac{p}{p} \cdot \dfrac{9}{p + 3} + \dfrac{2}{p} \cdot \dfrac{p + 3}{p + 3}$

$\qquad = \dfrac{9p}{p(p + 3)} + \dfrac{2(p + 3)}{p(p + 3)}$

$\qquad = \dfrac{9p}{p(p + 3)} + \dfrac{2p + 6}{p(p + 3)}$

$\qquad = \dfrac{9p + 2p + 6}{p(p + 3)}$

$\qquad = \dfrac{11p + 6}{p(p + 3)}$

29. $\dfrac{5}{d+1}-\dfrac{d}{3d+5}$

$=\dfrac{3d+5}{3d+5}\cdot\dfrac{5}{d+1}-\dfrac{d}{3d+5}\cdot\dfrac{d+1}{d+1}$

$=\dfrac{5(3d+5)}{(3d+5)(d+1)}-\dfrac{d(d+1)}{(3d+5)(d+1)}$

$=\dfrac{15d+25}{(3d+5)(d+1)}-\dfrac{d^2+d}{(3d+5)(d+1)}$

$=\dfrac{15d+25-d^2-d}{(3d+5)(d+1)}$

$=\dfrac{-d^2+14d+25}{(3d+5)(d+1)}$

31. $\dfrac{8}{p-3}+\dfrac{2}{3-p}=\dfrac{8}{p-3}+\dfrac{2}{3-p}\cdot\dfrac{-1}{-1}$

$=\dfrac{8}{p-3}+\dfrac{-2}{p-3}$

$=\dfrac{6}{p-3}$

33. $\dfrac{9}{x+7}-\dfrac{5}{-x-7}=\dfrac{9}{x+7}-\dfrac{5}{-x-7}\cdot\dfrac{-1}{-1}$

$=\dfrac{9}{x+7}-\dfrac{-5}{x+7}$

$=\dfrac{14}{x+7}$

35. $\dfrac{8}{a-2}+\dfrac{a}{2a-4}=\dfrac{2}{2}\cdot\dfrac{8}{a-2}+\dfrac{a}{2(a-2)}$

$=\dfrac{16}{2(a-2)}+\dfrac{a}{2(a-2)}$

$=\dfrac{a+16}{2(a-2)}$

37. $\dfrac{x+5}{x-5}-\dfrac{x-5}{x+5}=\dfrac{x+5}{x+5}\cdot\dfrac{x+5}{x-5}-\dfrac{x-5}{x+5}\cdot\dfrac{x-5}{x-5}$

$=\dfrac{(x+5)^2}{(x+5)(x-5)}-\dfrac{(x-5)^2}{(x+5)(x-5)}$

$=\dfrac{x^2+10x+25-(x^2-10x+25)}{(x-5)(x+5)}$

$=\dfrac{x^2+10x+25-x^2+10x-25}{(x-5)(x+5)}$

$=\dfrac{20x}{(x-5)(x+5)}$

39. $\dfrac{5}{6n+3}-\dfrac{2}{n}=\dfrac{n}{n}\cdot\dfrac{5}{3(2n+1)}-\dfrac{2}{n}\cdot\dfrac{3(2n+1)}{3(2n+1)}$

$=\dfrac{5n}{3n(2n+1)}-\dfrac{6(2n+1)}{3n(2n+1)}$

$=\dfrac{5n}{3n(2n+1)}-\dfrac{12n+6}{3n(2n+1)}$

$=\dfrac{5n-12n-6}{3n(2n+1)}$

$=\dfrac{-7n-6}{3n(2n+1)}$

41. $\dfrac{3}{2w+10}+\dfrac{6}{w+2}$

$=\dfrac{w+2}{w+2}\cdot\dfrac{3}{2(w+5)}+\dfrac{6}{w+2}\cdot\dfrac{2(w+5)}{2(w+5)}$

$=\dfrac{3(w+2)}{2(w+2)(w+5)}+\dfrac{12(w+5)}{2(w+2)(w+5)}$

$=\dfrac{3w+6+12w+60}{2(w+2)(w+5)}$

$=\dfrac{15w+66}{2(w+2)(w+5)}$

43. $\dfrac{z}{z^2-16}+\dfrac{4}{z+4}=\dfrac{z}{(z+4)(z-4)}+\dfrac{4}{(z+4)}\cdot\dfrac{z-4}{z-4}$

$=\dfrac{z+4z-16}{(z+4)(z-4)}$

$=\dfrac{5z-16}{(z+4)(z-4)}$

45. $\dfrac{x+2}{x^2-4}-\dfrac{2}{x+2}=\dfrac{x+2}{(x+2)(x-2)}-\dfrac{2}{x+2}\cdot\dfrac{x-2}{x-2}$

$=\dfrac{x+2}{(x+2)(x-2)}-\dfrac{2(x-2)}{(x+2)(x-2)}$

$=\dfrac{x+2-(2x-4)}{(x+2)(x-2)}$

$=\dfrac{x+2-2x+4}{(x+2)(x-2)}$

$=\dfrac{-x+6}{(x+2)(x-2)}$

47. $\dfrac{3r+4}{r^2-10r+24}-\dfrac{2}{r-6}$

$=\dfrac{3r+4}{(r-6)(r-4)}-\dfrac{2}{r-6}\cdot\dfrac{r-4}{r-4}$

$=\dfrac{3r+4}{(r-6)(r-4)}-\dfrac{2(r-4)}{(r-6)(r-4)}$

$=\dfrac{3r+4-(2r-4)}{(r-6)(r-4)}$

$=\dfrac{3r+4-2r+8}{(r-6)(r-4)}$

$=\dfrac{r+12}{(r-6)(r-4)}$

49. $\dfrac{x^2-3}{x^2+2x-8}-\dfrac{x-4}{x+4}$

$=\dfrac{x^2-3}{(x+4)(x-2)}-\dfrac{x-4}{x+4}\cdot\dfrac{x-2}{x-2}$

$=\dfrac{x^2-3}{(x+4)(x-2)}-\dfrac{(x-4)(x-2)}{(x+4)(x-2)}$

$=\dfrac{x^2-3-(x^2-6x+8)}{(x+4)(x-2)}$

$=\dfrac{x^2-3-x^2+6x-8}{(x+4)(x-2)}$

$=\dfrac{6x-11}{(x+4)(x-2)}$

51. $\dfrac{x-6}{x^2+10x+25}+\dfrac{x-3}{x+5}$

$=\dfrac{x-6}{(x+5)^2}+\dfrac{x-3}{x+5}\cdot\dfrac{x+5}{x+5}$

$=\dfrac{x-6}{(x+5)^2}+\dfrac{(x-3)(x+5)}{(x+5)^2}$

$=\dfrac{x-6+x^2+2x-15}{(x+5)^2}$

$=\dfrac{x^2+3x-21}{(x+5)^2}$

53. $\dfrac{5}{a^2-9a+8}-\dfrac{6}{a^2-6a-16}$

$=\dfrac{a+2}{a+2}\cdot\dfrac{5}{(a-8)(a-1)}-\dfrac{6}{(a-8)(a+2)}\cdot\dfrac{a-1}{a-1}$

$=\dfrac{5(a+2)}{(a-8)(a-1)(a+2)}-\dfrac{6(a-1)}{(a-8)(a-1)(a+2)}$

$=\dfrac{5a+10-(6a-6)}{(a-8)(a-1)(a+2)}$

$=\dfrac{5a+10-6a+6}{(a-8)(a-1)(a+2)}$

$=\dfrac{-a+16}{(a-8)(a-1)(a+2)}$

55. $\dfrac{2}{x^2+6x+9}+\dfrac{7}{x^2+x-6}$

$=\dfrac{x-2}{x-2}\cdot\dfrac{2}{(x+3)(x+3)}+\dfrac{7}{(x+3)(x-2)}\cdot\dfrac{x+3}{x+3}$

$=\dfrac{2(x-2)}{(x+3)(x+3)(x-2)}+\dfrac{7(x+3)}{(x+3)(x+3)(x-2)}$

$=\dfrac{2x-4+7x+21}{(x+3)(x+3)(x-2)}$

$=\dfrac{9x+17}{(x+3)^2(x-2)}$

57. $\dfrac{x}{2x^2+7x+3}-\dfrac{5}{3x^2+7x-6}$

$=\dfrac{3x-2}{3x-2}\cdot\dfrac{x}{(2x+1)(x+3)}-\dfrac{5}{(3x-2)(x+3)}\cdot\dfrac{2x+1}{2x+1}$

$=\dfrac{x(3x-2)}{(2x+1)(3x-2)(x+3)}-\dfrac{5(2x+1)}{(2x+1)(3x-2)(x+3)}$

$=\dfrac{3x^2-2x-(10x+5)}{(2x+1)(3x-2)(x+3)}$

$=\dfrac{3x^2-2x-10x-5}{(2x+1)(3x-2)(x+3)}$

$=\dfrac{3x^2-12x-5}{(2x+1)(3x-2)(x+3)}$

59. $\dfrac{x}{4x^2+11x+6}-\dfrac{2}{8x^2+2x-3}$

$=\dfrac{2x-1}{2x-1}\cdot\dfrac{x}{(4x+3)(x+2)}-\dfrac{2}{(4x+3)(2x-1)}\cdot\dfrac{x+2}{x+2}$

$=\dfrac{x(2x-1)}{(4x+3)(x+2)(2x-1)}-\dfrac{2(x+2)}{(4x+3)(x+2)(2x-1)}$

$=\dfrac{2x^2-x-(2x+4)}{(4x+3)(x+2)(2x-1)}$

$=\dfrac{2x^2-x-2x-4}{(4x+3)(x+2)(2x-1)}$

$=\dfrac{2x^2-3x-4}{(4x+3)(x+2)(2x-1)}$

61. $\dfrac{3w+12}{w^2+w-12}-\dfrac{2}{w-3}$

$=\dfrac{3(w+4)}{(w-3)(w+4)}-\dfrac{2}{w-3}$

$=\dfrac{3\cancel{(w+4)}}{(w-3)\cancel{(w+4)}}-\dfrac{2}{w-3}$

$=\dfrac{3}{w-3}-\dfrac{2}{w-3}$

$=\dfrac{1}{w-3}$

63. $\dfrac{4r}{2r^2-10r+12}+\dfrac{4}{r-2}$

$=\dfrac{4r}{2(r^2-5r+6)}+\dfrac{4}{r-2}$

$=\dfrac{\cancel{2}\cdot 2r}{\cancel{2}(r-3)(r-2)}+\dfrac{4}{r-2}\cdot\dfrac{r-3}{r-3}$

$=\dfrac{2r}{(r-3)(r-2)}+\dfrac{4r-12}{(r-3)(r-2)}$

$=\dfrac{6r-12}{(r-3)(r-2)}$

$=\dfrac{6\cancel{(r-2)}}{(r-3)\cancel{(r-2)}}$

$=\dfrac{6}{(r-3)}$

65. $\dfrac{4}{x^2-4x}-\dfrac{x}{4x-16}$

$=\dfrac{4}{x(x-4)}-\dfrac{x}{4(x-4)}$

$=\dfrac{4}{4}\cdot\dfrac{4}{x(x-4)}-\dfrac{x}{4(x-4)}\cdot\dfrac{x}{x}$

$=\dfrac{16}{4x(x-4)}-\dfrac{x^2}{4x(x-4)}$

$=\dfrac{16-x^2}{4x(x-4)}$

$=\dfrac{-1(x+4)\cancel{(x-4)}}{4x\cancel{(x-4)}}$

$=-\dfrac{x+4}{4x}$

67. $\dfrac{8}{x}+6$ is defined for all real numbers
except $x=0$

69. $\dfrac{3}{x-4}+\dfrac{7}{x+6}$
$x-4=0$ when $x=4$ and $x+6=0$ when $x=-6$
The expression is defined for all real
numbers except $x=4$ and $x=-6$.

71. $\dfrac{3}{\Delta-2}-\dfrac{4}{2-\Delta}=\dfrac{3}{\Delta-2}+\dfrac{4}{\Delta-2}$

$=\dfrac{3+4}{\Delta-2}$

$=\dfrac{7}{\Delta-2}$

73. $\dfrac{5}{a+b}+\dfrac{4}{a}$
$a+b=0$ when $a=-b$. The expression is defined
for all real numbers except $a=0$ and $a=-b$.

75. $\dfrac{x}{x^2-9}+\dfrac{2x}{x+3}+\dfrac{2x^2-5x}{9-x^2}$

$=\dfrac{x}{x^2-9}+\dfrac{2x}{x+3}+\dfrac{2x^2-5x}{-1\left(x^2-9\right)}$

$=\dfrac{x}{(x+3)(x-3)}+\dfrac{2x}{(x+3)}\cdot\dfrac{x-3}{x-3}-\dfrac{2x^2-5x}{(x+3)(x-3)}$

$=\dfrac{x+2x^2-6x-\left(2x^2-5x\right)}{(x+3)(x-3)}$

$=\dfrac{x+2x^2-6x-2x^2+5x}{(x+3)(x-3)}$

$=\dfrac{0}{(x+3)(x-3)}$

$=0$

77. $\dfrac{x+6}{4-x^2}-\dfrac{x+3}{x+2}+\dfrac{x-3}{2-x}$

$=\dfrac{x+6}{(2-x)(2+x)}-\dfrac{x+3}{x+2}+\dfrac{x-3}{2-x}$

$=\dfrac{x+6}{(2-x)(2+x)}-\dfrac{x+3}{x+2}\cdot\dfrac{2-x}{2-x}+\dfrac{x-3}{2-x}\cdot\dfrac{x+2}{x+2}$

$=\dfrac{x+6-(2x-x^2+6-3x)+(x^2-x-6)}{(2-x)(2+x)}$

$=\dfrac{x+6+x^2+x-6+x^2-x-6}{(2-x)(2+x)}$

$=\dfrac{2x^2+x-6}{(2-x)(2+x)}$

$=\dfrac{(2x-3)\,\cancel{(x+2)}}{(2-x)\,\cancel{(2+x)}}$

$=\dfrac{2x-3}{2-x}$

79. $\dfrac{2}{x^2-x-6}+\dfrac{3}{x^2-2x-3}+\dfrac{1}{x^2+3x+2}=\dfrac{2}{(x+2)(x-3)}+\dfrac{3}{(x-3)(x+1)}+\dfrac{1}{(x+2)(x+1)}$

$=\dfrac{2(x+1)}{(x+2)(x-3)(x+1)}+\dfrac{3(x+2)}{(x+2)(x-3)(x+1)}+\dfrac{x-3}{(x+2)(x-3)(x+1)}$

$=\dfrac{2x+2+3x+6+x-3}{(x+2)(x-3)(x+1)}$

$=\dfrac{6x+5}{(x+2)(x-3)(x+1)}$

81. a. $\dfrac{x+3y}{x^2+3xy+2y^2}+\dfrac{y-x}{2x^2+3xy+y^2}=\dfrac{x+3y}{(x+y)(x+2y)}+\dfrac{y-x}{(2x+y)(x+y)}$

The LCD is $(x+y)(x+2y)(2x+y)$.

b. $\dfrac{x+3y}{x^2+3xy+2y^2}+\dfrac{y-x}{2x^2+3xy+y^2}=\dfrac{x+3y}{(x+y)(x+2y)}+\dfrac{y-x}{(2x+y)(x+y)}$

$=\dfrac{2x+y}{2x+y}\cdot\dfrac{x+3y}{(x+y)(x+2y)}+\dfrac{y-x}{(2x+y)(x+y)}\cdot\dfrac{x+2y}{x+2y}$

$=\dfrac{(2x+y)(x+3y)}{(2x+y)(x+y)(x+2y)}+\dfrac{(y-x)(x+2y)}{(2x+y)(x+y)(x+2y)}$

c. $\dfrac{x+3y}{x^2+3xy+2y^2}+\dfrac{y-x}{2x^2+3xy+y^2}=\dfrac{x+3y}{(x+y)(x+2y)}+\dfrac{y-x}{(2x+y)(x+y)}$

$$=\dfrac{2x+y}{2x+y}\cdot\dfrac{x+3y}{(x+y)(x+2y)}+\dfrac{y-x}{(2x+y)(x+y)}\cdot\dfrac{x+2y}{x+2y}$$

$$=\dfrac{(2x+y)(x+3y)}{(2x+y)(x+y)(x+2y)}+\dfrac{(y-x)(x+2y)}{(2x+y)(x+y)(x+2y)}$$

$$=\dfrac{2x^2+7xy+3y^2+-xy+2y^2-x^2}{(2x+y)(x+y)(x+2y)}$$

$$=\dfrac{x^2+6xy+5y^2}{(2x+y)(x+y)(x+2y)}$$

$$=\dfrac{\cancel{(x+y)}(x+5y)}{(2x+y)\cancel{(x+y)}(x+2y)}$$

$$=\dfrac{x+5y}{(2x+y)(x+2y)}$$

d. $\dfrac{x+3y}{x^2+3xy+2y^2}=\dfrac{2+3(1)}{2^2+3(2)(1)+2(1)^2}=\dfrac{2+3}{4+6+2}=\dfrac{5}{12}$

e. $\dfrac{y-x}{2x^2+3xy+y^2}=\dfrac{1-2}{2(2)^2+3(2)(1)+1^2}=\dfrac{-1}{8+6+1}=-\dfrac{1}{15}$

f. $\dfrac{5}{12}+\left(-\dfrac{1}{15}\right)=\dfrac{5}{3\cdot4}-\dfrac{1}{3\cdot5}=\dfrac{5}{5}\cdot\dfrac{5}{3\cdot4}-\dfrac{1}{3\cdot5}\cdot\dfrac{4}{4}=\dfrac{25}{60}-\dfrac{4}{60}=\dfrac{21}{60}=\dfrac{7}{20}$

g. $\dfrac{(2x+y)(x+3y)}{(2x+y)(x+y)(x+2y)}+\dfrac{(y-x)(x+2y)}{(2x+y)(x+y)(x+2y)}$

$$=\dfrac{(2(2)+1)(2+3(1))}{(2(2)+1)(2+1)(2+2(1))}+\dfrac{(1-2)(2+2(1))}{(2(2)+1)(2+1)(2+2(1))}$$

$$=\dfrac{5\cdot5}{5\cdot3\cdot4}+\dfrac{-1\cdot4}{5\cdot3\cdot4}$$

$$=\dfrac{25}{60}+\dfrac{-4}{60}$$

$$=\dfrac{21}{60}=\dfrac{7}{20}$$

h. $\dfrac{x+5y}{(2x+y)(x+2y)}=\dfrac{2+5(1)}{(2(2)+1)(2+2(1))}=\dfrac{7}{5\cdot4}=\dfrac{7}{20}$

i. The simplified answer is equivalent to the unsimplified answer.

j. Yes.

82. Let $x=$ the number of hours it takes the train to travel 42 miles.

$$\frac{22 \text{ miles}}{0.8 \text{ hours}} = \frac{42 \text{ miles}}{x \text{ hours}}$$

$$22x = 0.8(42)$$

$$22x = 33.6$$

$$x \approx 1.53$$

It takes about 1.53 hours for the train to travel 42 miles.

83. $3(x-2)+2 < 4(x+1)$

$$3x-6+2 < 4x+4$$

$$3x-4 < 4x+4$$

$$-8 < x$$

$$x > -8$$

84.

$$\begin{array}{r} 4x-3 \\ 2x+3\overline{)\ 8x^2+6x-15} \\ \underline{8x^2+12x} \\ -6x-15 \\ \underline{-6x-\ 9} \\ -\ 6 \end{array}$$

$$(8x^2+6x-15) \div (2x+3) = 4x-3-\frac{6}{2x+3}$$

85. $\dfrac{x^2+xy-6y^2}{x^2-xy-2y^2} \cdot \dfrac{y^2-x^2}{x^2+2xy-3y^2}$

$$= \frac{(x+3y)(x-2y)}{(x+y)(x-2y)} \cdot \frac{-1(x-y)(x+y)}{(x+3y)(x-y)}$$

$$= -1$$

Mid-Chapter Test: Sections 6.1-6.4

1. $\dfrac{9}{3x-2}$

$3x-2=0$ when $x=\dfrac{2}{3}$

The expression is defined for all real numbers except $x=\dfrac{2}{3}$.

2. $\dfrac{2x+1}{x^2-5x-14}$

$$x^2-5x-14=0$$

$$(x-7)(x+2)=0$$

$$x-7=0 \quad \text{or} \quad x+2=0$$

$$x=7 \qquad\qquad x=-2$$

The expression is defined for all real numbers except $x=7$, $x=-2$.

3. $\dfrac{9x+18}{x+2} = \dfrac{9\cancel{(x+2)}}{\cancel{(x+2)}} = 9$

4. $\dfrac{2x^2+13x+15}{3x^2+14x-5} = \dfrac{(2x+3)\cancel{(x+5)}}{(3x-1)\cancel{(x+5)}} = \dfrac{2x+3}{3x-1}$

5. $\dfrac{25r^2-36t^2}{5r-6t} = \dfrac{(5r+6t)\cancel{(5r-6t)}}{\cancel{(5r-6t)}} = 5r+6t$

6. $\dfrac{15x^2}{2y} \cdot \dfrac{4y^4}{5x^5} = \dfrac{3 \cdot \cancel{5} \cdot \cancel{x}}{\cancel{2}\cancel{y}} \cdot \dfrac{2 \cdot \cancel{2} \cdot y^3 \cdot \cancel{y}}{\cancel{5} \cdot x^3 \cdot \cancel{x}} = \dfrac{6y^3}{x^3}$

7. $\dfrac{m-3}{m+4} \cdot \dfrac{m^2+8m+16}{3-m}$

$$= \frac{\cancel{m-3}}{\cancel{m+4}} \cdot \frac{\cancel{(m+4)}(m+4)}{-1\cancel{(m-3)}}$$

$$= -(m+4) \text{ or } -m-4$$

8. $\dfrac{x^3+27}{x^2-2x-15} \cdot \dfrac{x^2-7x+10}{x^2-3x+9}$

$$= \frac{\cancel{(x+3)}\cancel{(x^2-3x+9)}}{\cancel{(x-5)}\cancel{(x+3)}} \cdot \frac{\cancel{(x-5)}(x-2)}{\cancel{(x^2-3x+9)}}$$

$$= x-2$$

9. $\dfrac{5x-1}{x^2+11x+10} \div \dfrac{10x-2}{x^2+17x+70}$

$$= \frac{5x-1}{x^2+11x+10} \cdot \frac{x^2+17x+70}{10x-2}$$

$$= \frac{\cancel{5x-1}}{(x+10)(x+1)} \cdot \frac{(x+10)(x+7)}{2\cancel{(5x-1)}}$$

$$= \frac{x+7}{2(x+1)}$$

10.
$$\frac{5x^2+7x+2}{x^2+6x+5} \div \frac{7x^2-39x-18}{x^2-x-30}$$
$$= \frac{5x^2+7x+2}{x^2+6x+5} \cdot \frac{x^2-x-30}{7x^2-39x-18}$$
$$= \frac{(5x+2)\,\cancel{(x+1)}}{\cancel{(x+5)}\,\cancel{(x+1)}} \cdot \frac{\cancel{(x-6)}\,\cancel{(x+5)}}{(7x+3)\,\cancel{(x-6)}}$$
$$= \frac{5x+2}{7x+3}$$

11.
$$\frac{x^2}{x+6} - \frac{36}{x+6} = \frac{x^2-36}{x+6}$$
$$= \frac{\cancel{(x+6)}\,(x-6)}{\cancel{(x+6)}}$$
$$= x-6$$

12.
$$\frac{2x^2-2x}{2x+5} + \frac{x-15}{2x+5} = \frac{2x^2-2x+x-15}{2x+5}$$
$$= \frac{2x^2-x-15}{2x+5}$$
$$= \frac{\cancel{(2x+5)}\,(x-3)}{\cancel{(2x+5)}}$$
$$x-3$$

13.
$$\frac{3x^2-x}{4x^2-9x+2} - \frac{3x+4}{4x^2-9x+2} = \frac{3x^2-x-3x-4}{4x^2-9x+2}$$
$$= \frac{3x^2-4x-4}{4x^2-9x+2}$$
$$= \frac{(3x+2)\,\cancel{(x-2)}}{(4x-1)\,\cancel{(x-2)}}$$
$$= \frac{3x+2}{4x-1}$$

14.
$$\frac{2m}{6m^2+3m} + \frac{m+7}{2m+1} = \frac{2m}{3m(2m+1)} + \frac{m+7}{2m+1}$$
The LCD is $3m(2m+1)$.

15.
$$\frac{9x+8}{2x^2-5x-12} + \frac{2x+3}{x^2-9x+20}$$
$$= \frac{9x+8}{(2x+3)(x-4)} + \frac{2x+3}{(x-5)(x-4)}$$
The LCD is $(2x+3)(x-4)(x-5)$.

16.
$$\frac{x+1}{2x} + \frac{4x-3}{5x} = \frac{5}{5} \cdot \frac{x+1}{2x} + \frac{4x-3}{5x} \cdot \frac{2}{2}$$
$$= \frac{5x+5}{10x} + \frac{8x-6}{10x}$$
$$= \frac{5x+5+8x-6}{10x}$$
$$= \frac{13x-1}{10x}$$

17.
$$\frac{2a+5}{a+3} - \frac{3a+1}{a-4}$$
$$= \frac{a-4}{a-4} \cdot \frac{2a+5}{a+3} - \frac{3a+1}{a-4} \cdot \frac{a+3}{a+3}$$
$$= \frac{(a-4)(2a+5)}{(a-4)(a+3)} - \frac{(3a+1)(a+3)}{(a-4)(a+3)}$$
$$= \frac{2a^2-3a-20}{(a-4)(a+3)} - \frac{3a^2+10a+3}{(a-4)(a+3)}$$
$$= \frac{2a^2-3a-20-3a^2-10a-3}{(a-4)(a+3)}$$
$$= \frac{-a^2-13a-23}{(a-4)(a+3)}$$
$$= \frac{-1(a^2+13a+23)}{a^2-a-12}$$
$$= -\frac{a^2+13a+23}{a^2-a-12}$$

18.
$$\frac{x^2+5}{2x^2+13x+6} + \frac{3x-1}{2x+1}$$
$$= \frac{x^2+5}{(2x+1)(x+6)} + \frac{3x-1}{2x+1}$$
$$= \frac{x^2+5}{(2x+1)(x+6)} + \frac{3x-1}{2x+1} \cdot \frac{x+6}{x+6}$$
$$= \frac{x^2+5}{(2x+1)(x+6)} + \frac{3x^2+17x-6}{(2x+1)(x+6)}$$
$$= \frac{x^2+5+3x^2+17x-6}{(2x+1)(x+6)}$$
$$= \frac{4x^2+17x-1}{2x^2+13x+6}$$

19. $\dfrac{x}{x^2+3x+2} - \dfrac{4}{x^2-x-6}$

$= \dfrac{x}{(x+2)(x+1)} - \dfrac{4}{(x-3)(x+2)}$

$= \dfrac{x-3}{x-3} \cdot \dfrac{x}{(x+2)(x+1)} - \dfrac{4}{(x-3)(x+2)} \cdot \dfrac{x+1}{x+1}$

$= \dfrac{x^2-3x}{(x-3)(x+2)(x+1)} - \dfrac{4x+4}{(x-3)(x+2)(x+1)}$

$= \dfrac{x^2-3x-4x-4}{(x-3)(x+2)(x+1)}$

$= \dfrac{x^2-7x-4}{(x-3)(x+2)(x+1)}$

20. To add these fractions a common denominator of $x(x+1)$ is needed.

$\dfrac{7}{x+1} + \dfrac{8}{x} = \dfrac{x}{x} \cdot \dfrac{7}{x+1} + \dfrac{8}{x} \cdot \dfrac{x+1}{x+1}$

$\qquad = \dfrac{7x}{x(x+1)} + \dfrac{8x+8}{x(x+1)}$

$\qquad = \dfrac{7x+8x+8}{x(x+1)}$

$\qquad = \dfrac{15x+8}{x(x+1)}$

Exercise Set 6.5

1. A complex fraction is a fraction whose numerator or denominator (or both) contains a fraction.

3. a. $\dfrac{\dfrac{x+9}{4}}{\dfrac{7}{x^2+5x+6}}$

     Numerator: $\dfrac{x+9}{4}$

     Denominator: $\dfrac{7}{x^2+5x+6}$

b. $\dfrac{\dfrac{1}{2y}+x}{\dfrac{3}{y}+x^2}$

     Numerator, $\dfrac{1}{2y}+x$

     Denominator, $\dfrac{3}{y}+x^2$

5. $\dfrac{4+\dfrac{2}{3}}{5+\dfrac{1}{3}} = \dfrac{\left(4+\dfrac{2}{3}\right)3}{\left(5+\dfrac{1}{3}\right)3}$

$\qquad = \dfrac{12+2}{15+1}$

$\qquad = \dfrac{14}{16}$

$\qquad = \dfrac{7}{8}$

7. $\dfrac{2+\dfrac{3}{8}}{1+\dfrac{1}{3}} = \dfrac{\left(2+\dfrac{3}{8}\right)24}{\left(1+\dfrac{1}{3}\right)24}$

$\qquad = \dfrac{48+9}{24+8}$

$\qquad = \dfrac{57}{32}$

9. $\dfrac{\dfrac{2}{3}+\dfrac{1}{4}}{\dfrac{5}{6}-\dfrac{1}{3}} = \dfrac{\left(\dfrac{2}{3}+\dfrac{1}{4}\right)12}{\left(\dfrac{5}{6}-\dfrac{1}{3}\right)12}$

$\qquad = \dfrac{8+3}{10-4}$

$\qquad = \dfrac{11}{6}$

11. $\dfrac{\dfrac{xy^2}{7}}{\dfrac{3}{x^2}} = \dfrac{xy^2}{7} \cdot \dfrac{x^2}{3} = \dfrac{x^3y^2}{21}$

13. $\dfrac{\dfrac{6a^2b}{7}}{\dfrac{9ac^2}{b^2}} = \dfrac{6a^2b}{7} \cdot \dfrac{b^2}{9ac^2}$

$\qquad = \dfrac{6a^2b^3}{63ac^2}$

$\qquad = \dfrac{2ab^3}{21c^2}$

15. $\dfrac{a-\dfrac{a}{b}}{\dfrac{3+a}{b}} = \dfrac{\left(a-\dfrac{a}{b}\right)b}{\left(\dfrac{3+a}{b}\right)b} = \dfrac{ab-a}{3+a}$

17.
$$\frac{\dfrac{9}{x}+\dfrac{3}{x^2}}{3+\dfrac{1}{x}}=\frac{\left(\dfrac{9}{x}+\dfrac{3}{x^2}\right)x^2}{\left(3+\dfrac{1}{x}\right)x^2}$$

$$=\frac{9x+3}{3x^2+x}$$

$$=\frac{3(3x+1)}{x(3x+1)}$$

$$=\frac{3}{x}$$

19.
$$\frac{5-\dfrac{1}{x}}{4-\dfrac{1}{x}}=\frac{\left(5-\dfrac{1}{x}\right)x}{\left(4-\dfrac{1}{x}\right)x}=\frac{5x-1}{4x-1}$$

21.
$$\frac{\dfrac{m}{n}-\dfrac{n}{m}}{\dfrac{m+n}{n}}=\frac{\left(\dfrac{m}{n}-\dfrac{n}{m}\right)mn}{\left(\dfrac{m+n}{n}\right)mn}$$

$$=\frac{m^2-n^2}{m(m+n)}$$

$$=\frac{(m+n)(m-n)}{m(m+n)}$$

$$=\frac{m-n}{m}$$

23.
$$\frac{\dfrac{a^2}{b}-b}{\dfrac{b^2}{a}-a}=\frac{\left(\dfrac{a^2}{b}-b\right)ab}{\left(\dfrac{b^2}{a}-a\right)ab}$$

$$=\frac{(a^2-b^2)a}{(b^2-a^2)b}$$

$$=\frac{a(a^2-b^2)}{-b(a^2-b^2)}$$

$$=-\frac{a}{b}$$

25.
$$\frac{2-\dfrac{a}{b}}{\dfrac{a}{b}-2}=\frac{\left(2-\dfrac{a}{b}\right)b}{\left(\dfrac{a}{b}-2\right)b}$$

$$=\frac{2b-a}{a-2b}$$

$$=\frac{-1(-2b+a)}{a-2b}$$

$$=\frac{-1\cancel{(a-2b)}}{\cancel{(a-2b)}}$$

$$=-1$$

27.
$$\frac{\dfrac{4}{x^2}+\dfrac{4}{x}}{\dfrac{4}{x}+\dfrac{4}{x^2}}=\frac{\dfrac{4}{x^2}+\dfrac{4}{x}}{\dfrac{4}{x^2}+\dfrac{4}{x}}=1$$

29.
$$\frac{\dfrac{1}{a}-\dfrac{1}{b}}{\dfrac{1}{ab}}=\frac{\left(\dfrac{1}{a}-\dfrac{1}{b}\right)ab}{\left(\dfrac{1}{ab}\right)ab}=\frac{b-a}{1}=b-a$$

31.
$$\frac{\dfrac{a}{b}+\dfrac{1}{a}}{\dfrac{b}{a}+\dfrac{1}{a}}=\frac{\left(\dfrac{a}{b}+\dfrac{1}{a}\right)ab}{\left(\dfrac{b}{a}+\dfrac{1}{a}\right)ab}=\frac{a^2+b}{b^2+b}=\frac{a^2+b}{b(b+1)}$$

33.
$$\frac{x}{\dfrac{1}{x}-\dfrac{1}{y}}=\frac{(x)xy}{\left(\dfrac{1}{x}-\dfrac{1}{y}\right)xy}=\frac{x^2y}{y-x}$$

35.
$$\frac{\dfrac{5}{a}+\dfrac{5}{a^2}}{\dfrac{5}{b}+\dfrac{5}{b^2}}=\frac{\left(\dfrac{5}{a}+\dfrac{5}{a^2}\right)a^2b^2}{\left(\dfrac{5}{b}+\dfrac{5}{b^2}\right)a^2b^2}$$

$$=\frac{5ab^2+5b^2}{5a^2b+5a^2}$$

$$=\frac{5b^2(a+1)}{5a^2(b+1)}$$

$$=\frac{ab^2+b^2}{a^2(b+1)}$$

37. a. Answers will vary.

b. $\dfrac{5+\dfrac{3}{5}}{\dfrac{1}{8}-4}=\dfrac{\dfrac{25}{5}+\dfrac{3}{5}}{\dfrac{1}{8}-\dfrac{32}{8}}$

$=\dfrac{\dfrac{28}{5}}{-\dfrac{31}{8}}$

$=\dfrac{28}{5}\cdot\left(-\dfrac{8}{31}\right)$

$=-\dfrac{224}{155}$

c. $\dfrac{5+\dfrac{3}{5}}{\dfrac{1}{8}-4}=\dfrac{\left(5+\dfrac{3}{5}\right)40}{\left(\dfrac{1}{8}-4\right)40}=\dfrac{200+24}{5-160}=-\dfrac{224}{155}$

39. a. Answers will vary.

b. $\dfrac{\dfrac{x-y}{x+y}+\dfrac{6}{x+y}}{2-\dfrac{7}{x+y}}=\dfrac{\dfrac{x-y+6}{x+y}}{\dfrac{2(x+y)}{x+y}-\dfrac{7}{x+y}}$

$=\dfrac{\dfrac{x-y+6}{x+y}}{\dfrac{2x+2y-7}{x+y}}$

$=\dfrac{x-y+6}{\cancel{x+y}}\cdot\dfrac{\cancel{x+y}}{2x+2y-7}$

$=\dfrac{x-y+6}{2x+2y-7}$

c. $\dfrac{\dfrac{x-y}{x+y}+\dfrac{6}{x+y}}{2-\dfrac{7}{x+y}}=\dfrac{\dfrac{x-y+6}{x+y}}{2-\dfrac{7}{x+y}}$

$=\dfrac{\left(\dfrac{x-y+6}{x+y}\right)(x+y)}{\left(2-\dfrac{7}{x+y}\right)(x+y)}$

$=\dfrac{x-y+6}{2(x+y)-7}$

$=\dfrac{x-y+6}{2x+2y-7}$

41. a. $\dfrac{\dfrac{5}{12x}}{\dfrac{8}{x^2}-\dfrac{4}{3x}}$

b. $\dfrac{\dfrac{5}{12x}}{\dfrac{8}{x^2}-\dfrac{4}{3x}}=\dfrac{\dfrac{5}{12x}}{\dfrac{24-4x}{3x^2}}$

$=\dfrac{5}{12x}\cdot\dfrac{3x^2}{(24-4x)}$

$=\dfrac{5x}{4(24-4x)}$

$=\dfrac{5x}{96-16x}$

43. $\dfrac{x^{-1}+y^{-1}}{3}=\dfrac{\dfrac{1}{x}+\dfrac{1}{y}}{3}$

$=\dfrac{\left(\dfrac{1}{x}+\dfrac{1}{y}\right)xy}{3xy}$

$=\dfrac{y+x}{3xy}$

45. $\dfrac{x^{-1}+y^{-1}}{x^{-1}y^{-1}}=\dfrac{\dfrac{1}{x}+\dfrac{1}{y}}{\dfrac{1}{xy}}$

$=\dfrac{\left(\dfrac{1}{x}+\dfrac{1}{y}\right)xy}{\left(\dfrac{1}{xy}\right)xy}$

$=\dfrac{y+x}{1}$

$=x+y$

47. a. $E=\dfrac{\dfrac{1}{2}\left(\dfrac{2}{3}\right)}{\dfrac{2}{3}+\dfrac{1}{2}}=\dfrac{\dfrac{2}{6}}{\dfrac{4+3}{6}}=\dfrac{2}{\cancel{6}}\cdot\dfrac{\cancel{6}}{7}=\dfrac{2}{7}$

b. $E=\dfrac{\dfrac{1}{2}\left(\dfrac{4}{5}\right)}{\dfrac{4}{5}+\dfrac{1}{2}}=\dfrac{\dfrac{4}{10}}{\dfrac{8+5}{10}}=\dfrac{4}{\cancel{10}}\cdot\dfrac{\cancel{10}}{13}=\dfrac{4}{13}$

49. $\dfrac{\dfrac{a}{b}+b-\dfrac{1}{a}}{\dfrac{a}{b^2}-\dfrac{b}{a}+\dfrac{3}{a^2}} = \dfrac{\dfrac{a^2+b^2a-b}{ba}}{\dfrac{a^3-ab^3+3b^2}{a^2b^2}}$

$= \dfrac{a^2+b^2a-b}{\cancel{a}\,\cancel{b}} \cdot \dfrac{\cancel{a}^a\,\cancel{b}^b}{a^3-ab^3+3b^2}$

$= \dfrac{(a^2+b^2a-b)ab}{a^3-ab^3+3b^2}$

$= \dfrac{a^3b+a^2b^3-ab^2}{a^3-ab^3+3b^2}$

51. $2x-8(5-x)=9x-3(x+2)$

$2x-40+8x=9x-3x-6$

$10x-40=6x-6$

$4x=34$

$x=\dfrac{34}{4}=\dfrac{17}{2}$

52. A polynomial is a sum of terms of the form ax^n where a is a real number and n is a whole number.

53. $x^2-13x+40=(x-8)(x-5)$

54. $\dfrac{x}{3x^2+17x-6}-\dfrac{2}{x^2+3x-18}$

$= \dfrac{x}{(3x-1)(x+6)}-\dfrac{2}{(x+6)(x-3)}$

$= \dfrac{x}{(3x-1)(x+6)}\cdot\dfrac{x-3}{x-3}-\dfrac{2}{(x+6)(x-3)}\cdot\dfrac{3x-1}{3x-1}$

$= \dfrac{x^2-3x-(6x-2)}{(3x-1)(x+6)(x-3)}$

$= \dfrac{x^2-3x-6x+2}{(3x-1)(x+6)(x-3)}$

$= \dfrac{x^2-9x+2}{(3x-1)(x+6)(x-3)}$

Exercise Set 6.6

1. a. Answers will vary.

b. $\dfrac{1}{x-1}-\dfrac{1}{x+1}=\dfrac{3x}{x^2-1}$

$\dfrac{1}{x-1}-\dfrac{1}{x+1}=\dfrac{3x}{(x-1)(x+1)}$

Multiply both sides of the equation by the least common denominator, $(x-1)(x+1)$.

$$(x-1)(x+1)\left(\dfrac{1}{x-1}-\dfrac{1}{x+1}\right)=\left(\dfrac{3x}{(x-1)(x+1)}\right)(x-1)(x+1)$$

$$(x-1)(x+1)\left(\dfrac{1}{x-1}\right)-(x-1)(x+1)\left(\dfrac{1}{x+1}\right)=3x$$

$$x+1-(x-1)=3x$$

$$x+1-x+1=3x$$

$$2=3x$$

$$\dfrac{2}{3}=x$$

3. a. The problem on the left is an expression to be simplified while the problem on the right is an equation to be solved.

b. Left: Write the fractions with the LCD, $12(x-1)$, then combine numerators.
Right: Multiply both sides of the equation by the LCD, $12(x-1)$, then solve.

c. Left: $\dfrac{x}{3} - \dfrac{x}{4} + \dfrac{1}{x-1} = \dfrac{x \cdot 4(x-1)}{3 \cdot 4(x-1)} - \dfrac{x \cdot 3(x-1)}{4 \cdot 3(x-1)} + \dfrac{1 \cdot 3 \cdot 4}{(x-1)3 \cdot 4}$

$$= \dfrac{4x(x-1) - 3x(x-1) + 12}{3 \cdot 4(x-1)}$$

$$= \dfrac{4x^2 - 4x - 3x^2 + 3x + 12}{12(x-1)}$$

$$= \dfrac{x^2 - x + 12}{12(x-1)}$$

Right:

$$\dfrac{x}{3} - \dfrac{x}{4} = \dfrac{1}{x-1}$$

$$12(x-1)\left(\dfrac{x}{3} - \dfrac{x}{4}\right) = \left(\dfrac{1}{x-1}\right)12(x-1)$$

$$12(x-1)\left(\dfrac{x}{3}\right) - 12(x-1)\left(\dfrac{x}{4}\right) = 12$$

$$4x(x-1) - 3x(x-1) = 12$$

$$4x^2 - 4x - 3x^2 + 3x = 12$$

$$x^2 - x - 12 = 0$$

$$(x-4)(x+3) = 0$$

$$x - 4 = 0 \quad \text{or} \quad x + 3 = 0$$

$$x = 4 \qquad\qquad x = -3$$

5. You must check for extraneous when there is a variable in the denominator.

7. 2 cannot be a solution because it makes the denominator zero in the first term.

9. No, because there are no variables in the denominator.

11. Yes, because there is a variable in the denominator.

13.
$$\dfrac{x}{3} - \dfrac{x}{4} = 1$$

$$12\left(\dfrac{x}{3} - \dfrac{x}{4}\right) = 12(1)$$

$$4x - 3x = 12$$

$$x = 12$$

15.
$$\dfrac{r}{6} = \dfrac{r}{4} + \dfrac{1}{3}$$

$$12\left(\dfrac{r}{6}\right) = 12\left(\dfrac{r}{4} + \dfrac{1}{3}\right)$$

$$2r = 3r + 4$$

$$-r = 4$$

$$r = -4$$

17.
$$\dfrac{z}{2} + 6 = \dfrac{z}{5}$$

$$10\left(\dfrac{z}{2} + 6\right) = 10\left(\dfrac{z}{5}\right)$$

$$5z + 60 = 2z$$

$$3z = -60$$

$$z = -20$$

19. $\dfrac{z}{6}+\dfrac{2}{3}=\dfrac{z}{5}-\dfrac{1}{3}$

$30\left(\dfrac{z}{6}+\dfrac{2}{3}\right)=30\left(\dfrac{z}{5}-\dfrac{1}{3}\right)$

$5z+20=6z-10$

$-z=-30$

$z=30$

21. $d+7=\dfrac{3}{2}d+5$

$2(d+7)=2\left(\dfrac{3}{2}d+5\right)$

$2d+14=3d+10$

$-d=-4$

$d=4$

23. $3k+\dfrac{1}{6}=4k-4$

$6\left(3k+\dfrac{1}{6}\right)=6(4k-4)$

$18k+1=24k-24$

$-6k=-25$

$k=\dfrac{25}{6}$

25. $\dfrac{(n+6)}{3}=\dfrac{5(n-8)}{10}$

$10(n+6)=3\cdot5(n-8)$

$10n+60=15n-120$

$180=5n$

$36=n$

27. $\dfrac{x-5}{15}=\dfrac{3}{5}-\dfrac{x-4}{10}$

$30\left(\dfrac{x-5}{15}\right)=30\left(\dfrac{3}{5}-\dfrac{x-4}{10}\right)$

$2(x-5)=6(3)-3(x-4)$

$2x-10=18-3x+12$

$2x-10=30-3x$

$5x=40$

$x=8$

29. $\dfrac{-p+1}{4}+\dfrac{13}{20}=\dfrac{p}{5}-\dfrac{p-1}{2}$

$20\left(\dfrac{-p+1}{4}+\dfrac{13}{20}\right)=20\left(\dfrac{p}{5}-\dfrac{p-1}{2}\right)$

$5(-p+1)+13=4p-10(p-1)$

$-5p+5+13=4p-10p+10$

$-5p+18=-6p+10$

$p=-8$

31. $\dfrac{d-3}{4}+\dfrac{1}{15}=\dfrac{2d+1}{3}-\dfrac{34}{15}$

$60\left(\dfrac{d-3}{4}+\dfrac{1}{15}\right)=60\left(\dfrac{2d+1}{3}-\dfrac{34}{15}\right)$

$15(d-3)+4=20(2d+1)-4(34)$

$15d-45+4=40d+20-136$

$15d-41=40d-116$

$-25d=-75$

$d=3$

33. $2+\dfrac{3}{x}=\dfrac{11}{4}$

$4x\left(2+\dfrac{3}{x}\right)=4x\left(\dfrac{11}{4}\right)$

$8x+12=44$

$8x=32$

$x=4$

Check: $2+\dfrac{3}{4}=\dfrac{11}{4}$

$\dfrac{8}{4}+\dfrac{3}{4}=\dfrac{11}{4}$

$\dfrac{11}{4}=\dfrac{11}{4}$ True

35. $7-\dfrac{5}{x}=\dfrac{9}{2}$

$2x\left(7-\dfrac{5}{x}\right)=2x\left(\dfrac{9}{2}\right)$

$14x-10=9x$

$5x=10$

$x=2$

Check: $7-\dfrac{5}{2}=\dfrac{9}{2}$

$\dfrac{14}{2}-\dfrac{5}{2}=\dfrac{9}{2}$

$\dfrac{9}{2}=\dfrac{9}{2}$ True

37.
$$\frac{4}{n} - \frac{3}{2n} = \frac{1}{2}$$
$$2n\left(\frac{4}{n} - \frac{3}{2n}\right) = 2n\left(\frac{1}{2}\right)$$
$$8 - 3 = n$$
$$5 = n$$

Check: $\dfrac{4}{5} - \dfrac{3}{10} = \dfrac{1}{2}$

$$\frac{8}{10} - \frac{3}{10} = \frac{1}{2}$$
$$\frac{5}{10} = \frac{1}{2}$$
$$\frac{1}{2} = \frac{1}{2} \quad \text{True}$$

39.
$$\frac{x-1}{x-5} = \frac{4}{x-5}$$
$$(x-5)\left(\frac{x-1}{x-5}\right) = \left(\frac{4}{x-5}\right)(x-5)$$
$$x - 1 = 4$$
$$x = 5$$

Check: $\dfrac{x-1}{x-5} = \dfrac{4}{x-5}$

$$\frac{5-1}{5-5} = \frac{4}{5-5}$$
$$\frac{4}{0} = \frac{4}{0}$$

Since $\dfrac{4}{0}$ is not a real number, 5 is an extraneous solution. This equation has no solution.

41.
$$\frac{5}{a+3} = \frac{4}{a+1}$$
$$5(a+1) = 4(a+3)$$
$$5a + 5 = 4a + 12$$
$$a = 7$$

Check: $\dfrac{5}{a+3} = \dfrac{4}{a+1}$

$$\frac{5}{7+3} = \frac{4}{7+1}$$
$$\frac{5}{10} = \frac{4}{8}$$
$$\frac{1}{2} = \frac{1}{2} \quad \text{True}$$

43.
$$\frac{y+3}{y-3} = \frac{6}{4}$$
$$4(y+3) = 6(y-3)$$
$$4y + 12 = 6y - 18$$
$$30 = 2y$$
$$15 = y$$

Check: $\dfrac{y+3}{y-3} = \dfrac{6}{4}$

$$\frac{15+3}{15-3} = \frac{6}{4}$$
$$\frac{18}{12} = \frac{6}{4}$$
$$\frac{3}{2} = \frac{3}{2} \quad \text{True}$$

45.
$$\frac{2x-3}{x-4} = \frac{5}{x-4}$$
$$(x-4)\left(\frac{2x-3}{x-4}\right) = \left(\frac{5}{x-4}\right)(x-4)$$
$$2x - 3 = 5$$
$$2x = 8$$
$$x = 4$$

Check: $\dfrac{2x-3}{x-4} = \dfrac{5}{x-4}$

$$\frac{2(4)-3}{4-4} = \frac{5}{4-4}$$
$$\frac{5}{0} = \frac{5}{0}$$

Since $\dfrac{5}{0}$ is not a real number, 4 is an extraneous solution. This equation has no solution.

47.
$$\frac{x^2}{x-3} = \frac{9}{x-3}$$
$$(x-3)\left(\frac{x^2}{x-3}\right) = (x-3)\left(\frac{9}{x-3}\right)$$
$$x^2 = 9$$
$$x^2 - 9 = 0$$
$$(x+3)(x-3) = 0$$
$$x + 3 = 0 \quad \text{or} \quad x - 3 = 0$$
$$x = -3 \qquad\qquad x = 3$$

$$x = -3 \qquad\qquad x = 3$$

Check: $\dfrac{(-3)^2}{-3-3} = \dfrac{9}{-3-3} \qquad \dfrac{(3)^2}{3-3} = \dfrac{9}{3-3}$

$$\dfrac{9}{-6} = \dfrac{9}{-6}\ \text{True} \qquad \dfrac{9}{0} = \dfrac{9}{0}$$

Since $\dfrac{9}{0}$ is not a real number, 3 is an extraneous solution. The solution is $x = -3$.

49. $\qquad \dfrac{n-3}{n+2} = \dfrac{n+4}{n+10}$

$$(n-3)(n+10) = (n+2)(n+4)$$

$$n^2 + 7n - 30 = n^2 + 6n + 8$$

$$n = 38$$

Check: $\dfrac{38-3}{38+2} = \dfrac{38+4}{38+10}$

$$\dfrac{35}{40} = \dfrac{42}{48}$$

$$\dfrac{7}{8} = \dfrac{7}{8}\quad \text{True}$$

51. $\qquad \dfrac{1}{r} = \dfrac{3r}{8r+3}$

$$1(8r+3) = 3r^2$$

$$0 = 3r^2 - 8r - 3$$

$$0 = (3r+1)(r-3)$$

$$3r+1 = 0 \quad \text{or} \quad r-3 = 0$$

$$3r = -1 \qquad\qquad r = 3$$

$$r = -\dfrac{1}{3}$$

Check: $\dfrac{1}{\frac{-1}{3}} = \dfrac{3\left(-\frac{1}{3}\right)}{8\left(\frac{-1}{3}\right)+3} \qquad \dfrac{1}{3} = \dfrac{3(3)}{8(3)+3}$

$$\dfrac{1}{\frac{-1}{3}} = \dfrac{-1}{\frac{-8}{3}+\frac{9}{3}} \qquad\qquad \dfrac{1}{3} = \dfrac{9}{27}$$

$$-3 = \dfrac{-1}{\frac{1}{3}} \qquad\qquad\qquad \dfrac{1}{3} = \dfrac{1}{3}\quad \text{True}$$

$$-3 = -3\ \text{True}$$

53. $\qquad \dfrac{k}{k+2} = \dfrac{3}{k-2}$

$$k(k-2) = 3(k+2)$$

$$k^2 - 2k = 3k + 6$$

$$k^2 - 5k - 6 = 0$$

$$(k-6)(k+1) = 0$$

$$k-6 = 0 \quad \text{or} \quad k+1 = 0$$

$$k = 6 \qquad\qquad k = -1$$

Check: $\dfrac{6}{6+2} = \dfrac{3}{6-2} \qquad\quad \dfrac{-1}{-1+2} = \dfrac{3}{-1-2}$

$$\dfrac{6}{8} = \dfrac{3}{4} \qquad\qquad\qquad \dfrac{-1}{1} = \dfrac{3}{-3}$$

$$\dfrac{3}{4} = \dfrac{3}{4}\quad \text{True} \qquad\qquad -1 = -1\ \text{True}$$

55. $\qquad \dfrac{4}{r} + r = \dfrac{20}{r}$

$$r\left(\dfrac{4}{r} + r\right) = r\left(\dfrac{20}{r}\right)$$

$$4 + r^2 = 20$$

$$r^2 - 16 = 0$$

$$(r+4)(r-4) = 0$$

$$r+4 = 0 \quad \text{or} \quad r-4 = 0$$

$$r = -4 \qquad\qquad r = 4$$

Check: $\dfrac{4}{4} + 4 = \dfrac{20}{4} \qquad\quad \dfrac{4}{-4} - 4 = \dfrac{20}{-4}$

$$\dfrac{4}{4} + \dfrac{16}{4} = \dfrac{20}{4} \qquad\quad \dfrac{4}{-4} - \dfrac{16}{4} = \dfrac{20}{-4}$$

$$\dfrac{20}{4} = \dfrac{20}{4}\ \text{True} \qquad -\dfrac{20}{4} = -\dfrac{20}{4}\ \text{True}$$

57. $\qquad x + \dfrac{20}{x} = -9$

$$x\left(x + \dfrac{20}{x}\right) = -9x$$

$$x^2 + 20 = -9x$$

$$x^2 + 9x + 20 = 0$$

$$(x+4)(x+5) = 0$$

$$x+4 = 0 \quad \text{or} \quad x+5 = 0$$

$$x = -4 \qquad\qquad x = -5$$

Check $x = -4$: $x + \dfrac{20}{x} = -9$

$$-4 + \dfrac{20}{-4} = -9$$

$$-4 + (-5) = -9 \quad \text{True}$$

Check $x = -5$: $x + \dfrac{20}{x} = -9$

$$-5 + \dfrac{20}{-5} = -9$$

$$5 + (-4) = -9 \quad \text{True}$$

59.
$$\frac{3y-2}{y+1} = 4 - \frac{y+2}{y-1}$$

$$(y+1)(y-1)\left(\frac{3y-2}{y+1}\right) = \left(4 - \frac{y+2}{y-1}\right)(y+1)(y-1)$$

$$(y-1)(3y-2) = 4(y+1)(y-1) - \left(\frac{y+2}{y-1}\right)(y+1)(y-1)$$

$$3y^2 - 5y + 2 = 4\left(y^2 - 1\right) - (y+2)(y+1)$$

$$3y^2 - 5y + 2 = 4y^2 - 4 - (y^2 + 3y + 2)$$

$$3y^2 - 5y + 2 = 3y^2 - 3y - 6$$

$$-5y + 2 = -3y - 6$$

$$8 = 2y$$

$$4 = y$$

Check: $\dfrac{3y-2}{y+1} = 4 - \dfrac{y+2}{y-1}$

$$\frac{3(4)-2}{4+1} = 4 - \frac{4+2}{4-1}$$

$$\frac{12-2}{5} = 4 - \frac{6}{3}$$

$$\frac{10}{5} = 4 - 2$$

$$2 = 2 \quad \text{True}$$

61.
$$\frac{1}{x+3} + \frac{1}{x-3} = \frac{-5}{x^2 - 9}$$

$$\frac{1}{x+3} + \frac{1}{x-3} = \frac{-5}{(x-3)(x+3)}$$

$$(x-3)(x+3)\left[\frac{1}{x+3} + \frac{1}{x-3}\right] = \left[\frac{-5}{(x-3)(x+3)}\right](x-3)(x+3)$$

$$(x-3)(x+3)\left(\frac{1}{x+3}\right) + (x-3)(x+3)\left(\frac{1}{x-3}\right) = -5$$

$$x - 3 + x + 3 = -5$$

$$2x = -5$$

$$x = -\frac{5}{2}$$

Check: $\dfrac{1}{x+3} + \dfrac{1}{x-3} = \dfrac{-5}{x^2-9}$

$\dfrac{1}{-\dfrac{5}{2}+3} + \dfrac{1}{-\dfrac{5}{2}-3} = \dfrac{-5}{\left(-\dfrac{5}{2}\right)^2 - 9}$

$\dfrac{1}{\dfrac{1}{2}} - \dfrac{1}{\left(-\dfrac{11}{2}\right)} = \dfrac{-5}{\dfrac{25}{4} - 9}$

$2 - \dfrac{2}{11} = \dfrac{-5}{-\dfrac{11}{4}}$

$\dfrac{20}{11} = \dfrac{20}{11}$ True

63.

$\dfrac{x}{x-3} + \dfrac{3}{2} = \dfrac{3}{x-3}$

$2(x-3)\left(\dfrac{x}{x-3} + \dfrac{3}{2}\right) = 2(x-3)\left(\dfrac{3}{x-3}\right)$

$2x + 3(x-3) = 2(3)$

$2x + 3x - 9 = 6$

$5x = 15$

$x = 3$

Check: $\dfrac{x}{x-3} + \dfrac{3}{2} = \dfrac{3}{x-3}$

$\dfrac{3}{3-3} + \dfrac{3}{2} = \dfrac{3}{3-3}$

$\dfrac{3}{0} + \dfrac{3}{2} = \dfrac{3}{0}$

Since $\dfrac{3}{0}$ is not a real number, 3 is an extraneous solution. This equation has no solution.

65.

$\dfrac{3}{x-5} - \dfrac{4}{x+5} = \dfrac{11}{x^2-25}$

$\dfrac{3}{x-5} - \dfrac{4}{x+5} = \dfrac{11}{(x-5)(x+5)}$

$(x-5)(x+5)\left[\dfrac{3}{x-5} - \dfrac{4}{x+5}\right] = \left[\dfrac{11}{(x-5)(x+5)}\right](x-5)(x+5)$

$(x-5)(x+5)\left(\dfrac{3}{x-5}\right) - (x-5)(x+5)\left(\dfrac{4}{x+5}\right) = 11$

$3(x+5) - 4(x-5) = 11$

$3x + 15 - 4x + 20 = 11$

$-x + 35 = 11$

$24 = x$

Check: $\dfrac{3}{x-5} - \dfrac{4}{x+5} = \dfrac{11}{x^2-25}$

$\dfrac{3}{24-5} - \dfrac{4}{24+5} = \dfrac{11}{24^2-25}$

$\dfrac{3}{19} - \dfrac{4}{29} = \dfrac{11}{576-25}$

$\dfrac{87}{551} - \dfrac{76}{551} = \dfrac{11}{551}$

$\dfrac{11}{551} = \dfrac{11}{551}$ True

67.

$$\dfrac{3x}{x^2-9} + \dfrac{1}{x-3} = \dfrac{3}{x+3}$$

$$\dfrac{3x}{(x-3)(x+3)} + \dfrac{1}{x-3} = \dfrac{3}{x+3}$$

$$(x-3)(x+3)\left[\dfrac{3x}{(x-3)(x+3)} + \dfrac{1}{x-3}\right] = \left[\dfrac{3}{x+3}\right](x-3)(x+3)$$

$$(x-3)(x+3)\left(\dfrac{3x}{(x-3)(x+3)}\right) + (x-3)(x+3)\left(\dfrac{1}{x-3}\right) = 3(x-3)$$

$$3x + x + 3 = 3x - 9$$

$$4x + 3 = 3x - 9$$

$$x + 3 = -9$$

$$x = -12$$

Check: $\dfrac{3x}{x^2-9} + \dfrac{1}{x-3} = \dfrac{3}{x+3}$

$\dfrac{3(-12)}{(-12)^2-9} + \dfrac{1}{-12-3} = \dfrac{3}{-12+3}$

$\dfrac{-36}{144-9} + \dfrac{1}{-15} = \dfrac{3}{-9}$

$-\dfrac{36}{135} - \dfrac{1}{15} = -\dfrac{1}{3}$

$-\dfrac{4}{15} - \dfrac{1}{15} = -\dfrac{1}{3}$

$-\dfrac{5}{15} = -\dfrac{1}{3}$

$-\dfrac{1}{3} = -\dfrac{1}{3}$ True

69.

$$\frac{1}{y-1} + \frac{1}{2} = \frac{2}{y^2-1}$$

$$\frac{1}{y-1} + \frac{1}{2} = \frac{2}{(y+1)(y-1)}$$

$$2(y+1)(y-1)\left[\frac{1}{y-1} + \frac{1}{2}\right] = 2(y+1)(y-1)\left[\frac{2}{(y+1)(y-1)}\right]$$

$$2(y+1)(y-1)\left(\frac{1}{y-1}\right) + 2(y+1)(y-1)\left(\frac{1}{2}\right) = 2(2)$$

$$2(y+1) + (y+1)(y-1) = 4$$

$$2y+2+y^2-1 = 4$$

$$y^2+2y-3 = 0$$

$$(y+3)(y-1) = 0$$

$$y+3 = 0 \quad \text{or} \quad y-1 = 0$$

$$y = -3 \qquad\qquad y = 1$$

Check: $y = -3$

$$\frac{1}{y-1} + \frac{1}{2} = \frac{2}{y^2-1}$$

$$\frac{1}{-3-1} + \frac{1}{2} = \frac{2}{(-3)^2-1}$$

$$\frac{1}{-4} + \frac{1}{2} = \frac{2}{8}$$

$$\frac{1}{4} = \frac{1}{4} \qquad \text{True}$$

Check: $y = 1$

$$\frac{1}{y-1} + \frac{1}{2} = \frac{2}{y^2-1}$$

$$\frac{1}{1-1} + \frac{1}{2} = \frac{2}{1^2-1}$$

$$\frac{1}{0} + \frac{1}{2} = \frac{2}{0}$$

The solution to the equation is -3. Since $\frac{1}{0}$ and $\frac{2}{0}$ are not real numbers, 1 is an extraneous solution.

71.

$$\frac{3t}{6t+6} + \frac{t}{2t+2} = \frac{2t-3}{t+1}$$

$$\frac{3t}{6(t+1)} + \frac{t}{2(t+1)} = \frac{2t-3}{t+1}$$

$$6(t+1)\left[\frac{3t}{6(t+1)} + \frac{t}{2(t+1)}\right] = 6(t+1)\left(\frac{2t-3}{t+1}\right)$$

$$3t+3t = 6(2t-3)$$

$$6t = 12t-18$$

$$-6t = -18$$

$$t = 3$$

Check:

$$\frac{3(3)}{6(3)+6} + \frac{3}{2(3)+2} = \frac{2(3)-3}{3+1}$$

$$\frac{9}{18+6} + \frac{3}{6+2} = \frac{6-3}{4}$$

$$\frac{9}{24} + \frac{3}{8} = \frac{3}{4}$$

$$\frac{3}{8} + \frac{3}{8} = \frac{3}{4}$$

$$\frac{6}{8} = \frac{3}{4}$$

$$\frac{3}{4} = \frac{3}{4} \quad \text{True}$$

73. The solution is 5. Since $3 = x-2$, $x = 5$.

75. The solution is 0.
Since $x + x = 0$, $x = 0$.

77. x can be any real number.
$x - 2 + x - 2 = 2x - 4$.

79. $\dfrac{1}{p} + \dfrac{1}{q} = \dfrac{1}{f}$

$\dfrac{1}{30} + \dfrac{1}{q} = \dfrac{1}{10}$

$\dfrac{1}{q} = \dfrac{1}{10} - \dfrac{1}{30}$

$\dfrac{1}{q} = \dfrac{2}{30}$

$2q = 30$

$q = 15$

The image will appear 15 cm from the mirror.

81.
$$\dfrac{x-4}{x^2 - 2x} = \dfrac{-4}{x^2 - 4}$$

$$\dfrac{x-4}{x(x-2)} = \dfrac{-4}{(x+2)(x-2)}$$

$$x(x+2)(x-2)\left(\dfrac{x-4}{x(x-2)}\right) = x(x+2)(x-2)\left(\dfrac{-4}{(x+2)(x-2)}\right)$$

$$(x+2)(x-4) = -4x$$

$$x^2 - 2x - 8 = -4x$$

$$x^2 + 2x - 8 = 0$$

$$(x+4)(x-2) = 0$$

$$x+4 = 0 \ \text{ or } \ x-2 = 0$$

$$x = -4 \qquad x = 2$$

Since $\dfrac{-2}{0}$ and $\dfrac{-4}{0}$ are not a real numbers, 2 is an extraneous solution.

The solution to the equation is –4.

83. No, it is impossible for both sides of the equation to be equal.

85. Let x be the number of minutes of internet access over 5 hours.
Plan 1: $7.95 + 0.15x$
Plan 2: 19.95
$7.95 + 0.15x = 19.95$

$\qquad 0.15x = 12$

$\qquad\quad x = 80$

80 minutes $= \dfrac{80}{60}$ hours $= 1\dfrac{1}{3}$ hours

Jake would have to use the internet more than

$5 + 1\dfrac{1}{3} = 6\dfrac{1}{3}$ hours.

86. $\dfrac{600 \text{ gallons}}{4 \text{ gallons/minute}} = 150 \text{ minutes}$

87. Let x = measure of larger angle
$\dfrac{1}{2}x - 30$ = measure of smaller angle

$x + \left(\dfrac{1}{2}x - 30\right) = 180$

$\qquad \dfrac{3}{2}x - 30 = 180$

$\qquad\quad \dfrac{3}{2}x = 210$

$\dfrac{2}{3} \cdot \dfrac{3}{2}x = \dfrac{2}{3} \cdot 210$

$\qquad\quad x = 140$

The angles measure 40° and 140°.

88. $(3.4 \times 10^{-5})(2 \times 10^{13})$

$= (3.4 \cdot 2) \times (10^{-5} \cdot 10^{13})$

$= 6.8 \times 10^{-5+13}$

$= 6.8 \times 10^{8}$

Exercise Set 6.7

1. Some examples are:

$A = \dfrac{1}{2}bh$, $A = \dfrac{1}{2}h(b_1 + b_2)$, $V = \dfrac{1}{3}\pi r^2 h$, and

$V = \dfrac{4}{3}\pi r^3$

3. It represents 1 complete task.

5. Let w = width, then

$\dfrac{2}{3}w + 5 =$ length

area = width · length

$$99 = w\left(\dfrac{2}{3}w + 5\right)$$

$$99 = \dfrac{2w^2}{3} + 5w$$

$$3(99) = 3\left(\dfrac{2w^2}{3} + 5w\right)$$

$$297 = 2w^2 + 15w$$

$2w^2 + 15w - 297 = 0$

$2w^2 + 15w - 297 = 0$

$(2w + 33)(w - 9) = 0$

$2w + 33 = 0$ or $w - 9 = 0$

$$w = -\dfrac{33}{2} \qquad\qquad w = 9$$

Since the width cannot be negative, $w = 9$

$l = \dfrac{2}{3}w + 5$

$l = \dfrac{2}{3}(9) + 5$

$l = 6 + 5 = 11$

The length is 11 inches and the width is 9 inches.

7. Let x = height, then $x + 5$ = base

area $= \dfrac{1}{2} \cdot$ height · base

$$42 = \dfrac{1}{2}x(x + 5)$$

$$2(42) = 2\left[\dfrac{1}{2}x(x + 5)\right]$$

$$84 = x(x + 5)$$

$$84 = x^2 + 5x$$

$$0 = x^2 + 5x - 84$$

$$0 = (x - 7)(x + 12)$$

$x - 7 = 0$ or $x + 12 = 0$

$\quad x = 7 \qquad\qquad x = -12$

Since the height cannot be negative, $x = 7$.

base $= x + 5 = 7 + 15 = 12$

The base is 12 cm and the height is 7 cm.

9. Let b = the base of the triangle, then $\left(\dfrac{1}{2}b - 1\right)$ is

the height.

$$A = \dfrac{1}{2}bh$$

$$12 = \dfrac{1}{2}b\left(\dfrac{1}{2}b - 1\right)$$

$$12 = \dfrac{1}{4}b^2 - \dfrac{1}{2}b$$

$$4(12) = 4\left(\dfrac{1}{4}b^2 - \dfrac{1}{2}b\right)$$

$$48 = b^2 - 2b$$

$$0 = b^2 - 2b - 48$$

$$0 = (b - 8)(b + 6)$$

$b - 8 = 0$ or $b + 6 = 0$

$\quad b = 8 \quad$ or $\qquad b = -6$

Since a length cannot be negative, the base is 8 feet.

11. Let one number be x, then the other number is $9x$.

$$\frac{1}{x} - \frac{1}{9x} = 1$$

$$9x\left(\frac{1}{x} - \frac{1}{9x}\right) = 9x(1)$$

$$9 - 1 = 9x$$

$$8 = 9x$$

$$\frac{8}{9} = x$$

The numbers are $\frac{8}{9}$ and $9\left(\frac{8}{9}\right) = 8$.

13. Let x = amount by which the numerator was increased.

$$\frac{3+x}{4} = \frac{5}{2}$$

$$4\left(\frac{3+x}{4}\right) = \left(\frac{5}{2}\right)4$$

$$3 + x = 10$$

$$x = 7$$

The numerator was increased by 7.

15. Let r = speed of Creole Queen paddle boat.

$$t = \frac{d}{r}$$

Time upstream = time downstream

$$\frac{6}{r-3} = \frac{12}{r+3}$$

$$6(r+3) = 12(r-3)$$

$$6r + 18 = 12r - 36$$

$$54 = 6r$$

$$9 = r$$

The boat's speed in still water is 9 mph.

17. Let d = distance and $t = \frac{d}{r}$.

Time going + Time returning = $\frac{5}{2}$.

$$\frac{d}{12} + \frac{d}{12} = \frac{5}{2}$$

$$\frac{2d}{12} = \frac{5}{2}$$

$$4d = 60$$

$$d = 15$$

The trolley traveled 15 miles in one direction.

19. Let r be the speed of the propeller plane, then $4r$ is the speed of the jet.

$$\frac{d}{r} = t$$

time by jet + time by propeller plane = 6 hr

$$\frac{1600}{4r} + \frac{500}{r} = 6$$

$$\frac{400}{r} + \frac{300}{r} = 6$$

$$\frac{900}{r} = 6$$

$$r = \frac{900}{6} = 150$$

The speed of the propeller plane is 150 mph and the speed of the jet is 600 mph.

21. Let d = distance from the dock to the no wake zone, then $36.6 - d$ = distance from the no wake zone to Paradise Island.

$$t = \frac{d}{r}$$

time traveled to no wake zone + time traveled from no wake zone = total time

$$\frac{d}{4} + \frac{36.6 - d}{28} = 1.7$$

$$28\left(\frac{d}{4} + \frac{36.6 - d}{28}\right) = 1.7(28)$$

$$7d + 36.6 - d = 47.6$$

$$6d = 11$$

$$d = \frac{11}{6} \approx 1.83$$

$$36.6 - d = 36.6 - 1.83 \approx 34.77$$

The dock is about 1.83 miles from the no wake zone and about 34.77 miles from the no wake zone to the island..

23. Let d = the distance flown with the wind, then $2900 - d$ = the time flown against the wind.

$$\text{time with wind} = \frac{d}{600}$$

$$\text{time against wind} = \frac{2900 - d}{550}$$

$$\frac{d}{600} + \frac{2900 - d}{550} = 5$$

$$3300\left(\frac{d}{600} + \frac{2900 - d}{550}\right) = 5(3300)$$

$$5.5d + 17,400 - 6d = 16,500$$

$$-0.5d = -900$$

$$d = 1800$$

$$\text{time with wind} = \frac{1800}{600} = 3$$

time against wind $= \dfrac{2900-800}{550} = 2$

It flew 3 hours at 600 mph and 2 hours at 550 mph.

25. time at 30 ft/s $= \dfrac{d}{30}$

time at 25 ft/s $= \dfrac{d}{25}$

$$\dfrac{d}{25} = \dfrac{d}{30} + 8$$

$$150\left(\dfrac{d}{25}\right) = \left(\dfrac{d}{30} + 8\right)150$$

$$6d = 5d + 1200$$

$$d = 1200$$

The boat traveled 1200 feet in one direction.

27. Felicia's rate $= \dfrac{1}{6}$

Reynaldo's rate $= \dfrac{1}{8}$

$$\dfrac{t}{6} + \dfrac{t}{8} = 1$$

$$48\left(\dfrac{t}{6} + \dfrac{t}{8}\right) = 48(1)$$

$$8t + 6t = 48$$

$$14t = 48$$

$$t = 3\dfrac{3}{7}$$

It will take them $3\dfrac{3}{7}$ hours.

29. Gary's rate $= \dfrac{1}{6}$

Alex's rate $= \dfrac{1}{12}$

$$\dfrac{t}{6} + \dfrac{t}{12} = 1$$

$$12\left(\dfrac{t}{6} + \dfrac{t}{12}\right) = 12(1)$$

$$2t + t = 12$$

$$3t = 12$$

$$t = 4$$

It will take them 4 hours.

31. Eric's rate $= \dfrac{1}{60}$

Jessup's rate $= \dfrac{1}{40}$

$$\dfrac{t}{60} + \dfrac{t}{40} = 1$$

$$120\left(\dfrac{t}{60} + \dfrac{t}{40}\right) = 120(1)$$

$$2t + 3t = 120$$

$$5t = 120$$

$$t = 24$$

It will take them 24 minutes.

33. input rate $= \dfrac{1}{40}$

output rate $= \dfrac{1}{60}$

$$\dfrac{t}{40} - \dfrac{t}{60} = 1$$

$$120\left(\dfrac{t}{40} - \dfrac{t}{60}\right) = 120(1)$$

$$3t - 2t = 120$$

$$t = 120$$

It will take 120 minutes or 2 hours for the tub to fill.

35. Rate for first $= \dfrac{1}{40}$

Rate for second $= \dfrac{1}{t}$

In 24 minutes, the first computer completes

$\dfrac{24}{40} = \dfrac{3}{5}$ of the checks and the second computer

completes $\dfrac{24}{t}$.

$$\dfrac{3}{5} + \dfrac{24}{t} = 1$$

$$5t\left(\dfrac{3}{5} + \dfrac{24}{t}\right) = 5t(1)$$

$$3t + 120 = 5t$$

$$120 = 2t$$

$$60 = t$$

It would take the second computer 60 minutes or 1 hour.

37. Rate for first backhoe $= \dfrac{1}{12}$

Rate for second backhoe $= \dfrac{1}{15}$

Work done by first $= \dfrac{1}{12} \cdot 5 = \dfrac{5}{12}$

Work done by second $= \dfrac{1}{15} \cdot t = \dfrac{t}{15}$

$$\frac{5}{12} + \frac{t}{15} = 1$$

$$60\left(\frac{5}{12} + \frac{t}{15}\right) = 1 \cdot 60$$

$$25 + 4t = 60$$

$$4t = 35$$

$$t = \frac{35}{4} = 8\frac{3}{4}$$

It takes the smaller backhoe $8\frac{3}{4}$ days to finish the trench.

39. Ken's rate $= \frac{1}{4}$

Bettina's rate $= \frac{1}{6}$

$$\frac{t+3}{6} + \frac{t}{4} = 1$$

$$12\left(\frac{t+3}{6} + \frac{t}{4}\right) = 12 \cdot 1$$

$$2(t+3) + 3t = 12$$

$$2t + 6 + 3t = 12$$

$$5t = 6$$

$$t = \frac{6}{5}$$

It will take them $\frac{6}{5}$ hour or 1 hr, 12 min longer.

41. Rate of first skimmer $= \frac{1}{60}$

Rate of second skimmer $= \frac{1}{50}$

Rate of transfer $= \frac{1}{30}$

$$\frac{t}{60} + \frac{t}{50} - \frac{t}{30} = 1$$

$$300\left(\frac{t}{60} + \frac{t}{50} - \frac{t}{30}\right) = 300$$

$$5t + 6t - 10t = 300$$

$$t = 300$$

It will take 300 hours to fill the tank.

43. Let x be the number.

$$\frac{3}{x} + 2x = 7$$

$$x\left(\frac{3}{x} + 2x\right) = 7x$$

$$3 + 2x^2 = 7x$$

$$2x^2 - 7x + 3 = 0$$

$$(2x - 1)(x - 3) = 0$$

$$2x - 1 = 0 \quad \text{or} \quad x - 3 = 0$$

$$x = \frac{1}{2} \qquad\qquad x = 3$$

The numbers are 3 or $\frac{1}{2}$.

45. Ed's rate $= \frac{1}{8}$

Samantha's rate $= \frac{1}{4}$

$$\frac{p}{4} - 1 = \frac{p}{8}$$

$$8\left(\frac{p}{4} - 1\right) = 8\left(\frac{p}{8}\right)$$

$$2p - 8 = p$$

$$p = 8$$

Each must pick 8 pints.

47. $\frac{1}{2}(x+3) - (2x+5) = \frac{1}{2}x + \frac{3}{2} - 2x - 5$

$$= \frac{x}{2} - \frac{4x}{2} + \frac{3}{2} - \frac{10}{2}$$

$$= -\frac{3x}{2} - \frac{7}{2}$$

48. $y^2 + 6y - y - 6 = y(y+6) - 1(y+6)$

$$= (y+6)(y-1)$$

49. $\dfrac{x^2 - 14x + 48}{x^2 - 5x - 24} \div \dfrac{2x^2 - 13x + 6}{2x^2 + 5x - 3} = \dfrac{x^2 - 14x + 48}{x^2 - 5x - 24} \cdot \dfrac{2x^2 + 5x - 3}{2x^2 - 13x + 6}$

$$= \frac{(x-6)(x-8)}{(x+3)(x-8)} \cdot \frac{(2x-1)(x+3)}{(2x-1)(x-6)}$$

$$= 1$$

50. $\dfrac{x}{6x^2-x-15}-\dfrac{5}{9x^2-12x-5}=\dfrac{x}{(2x+3)(3x-5)}-\dfrac{5}{(3x+1)(3x-5)}$

$$=\dfrac{x(3x+1)}{(2x+3)(3x-5)(3x+1)}-\dfrac{5(2x+3)}{(2x+3)(3x-5)(3x+1)}$$

$$=\dfrac{3x^2+x-(10x+15)}{(2x+3)(3x-5)(3x+1)}$$

$$=\dfrac{3x^2+x-10x-15}{(2x+3)(3x-5)(3x+1)}$$

$$=\dfrac{3x^2-9x-15}{(2x+3)(3x-5)(3x+1)}$$

Exercise Set 6.8

1. 30

3. $y=kx$

5. direct; The radius of the hose varies directly as the water coming out of the hose.

7. inverse; The speed of the turtle varies inversely as the length of time it takes the turtle to cross the road.

9. inverse; The temperature of the water varies inversely as the time it tales for an ice cube placed in the water to melt.

11. direct: The length of a roll of scotch tape varies directly with the number of two inch strips that can be obtained from the roll.

13. direct: The cubic inch displacement varies directly as the horsepower of the engine.

15. a. $x=kz$

　　b. $x=4(11)=44$

17. a. $x=\dfrac{k}{y}$

　　b. $x=\dfrac{5}{25}=\dfrac{1}{5}$

19. a. $C=kZ^2$

　　b. $C=3(5)^2=3(25)=75$

21. a. $y=\dfrac{k}{x^2}$

　　b. $y=\dfrac{250}{10^2}=\dfrac{250}{100}=2.5$

23. a. $x=ky$

　　b. k must be determined first; $x=ky$

$$9=k(18)$$

$$\dfrac{1}{2}=k$$

Now substitute 40 for y and $\dfrac{1}{2}$ for k.

$$x=ky=\dfrac{1}{2}(40)=20$$

25. a. $C=\dfrac{k}{J}$

　　b. k must be determined first; $C=\dfrac{k}{J}$

$$7=\dfrac{k}{1}$$

$$7=k$$

Now substitute 2 for J and 7 for k.

$$C=\dfrac{k}{J}=\dfrac{7}{2}=3.5$$

27. a. $y=kR^2$

　　b. k must be determined first; $y=kR^2$

$$4=k(4)^2$$

$$4=16k$$

$$\dfrac{1}{4}=k$$

Now substitute 12 for R and $\dfrac{1}{4}$ for k.

$$y=kR^2=\dfrac{1}{4}(12)^2=\dfrac{1}{4}(144)=36$$

29. a. $L=\dfrac{k}{P^2}$

b. k must be determined first; $L = \dfrac{k}{P^2}$

$$320 = \dfrac{k}{20^2}$$

$$320 = \dfrac{k}{400}$$

$$128,000 = k$$

Now substitute 40 for P and 128,000 for k.

$$L = \dfrac{k}{P^2} = \dfrac{128,000}{40^2} = \dfrac{128,000}{1600} = 80$$

31. $a = kb = k(2b) = 2kb$ If b is doubled, then a is also doubled.

33. $y = \dfrac{k}{x} = \dfrac{k}{2x} = \dfrac{1}{2} \cdot \dfrac{k}{x}$ If x is doubled, then y is halved.

35. a. $d = ks$

    b. Substitute 2 for k and 55 for s.
$d = ks = 2(55) = 110$
The distance traveled was 110 miles.

37. a. $t = \dfrac{k}{s}$

    b. $t = \dfrac{k}{s} = \dfrac{150}{50} = 3$
It will take 3 hours to reach the destination.

39. a. $I = kn$

    b. k must be determined first; $I = kn$

$$33 = k(22)$$

$$\dfrac{33}{22} = k$$

$$\dfrac{3}{2} = k$$

Now substitute 38 for n and $\dfrac{3}{2}$ for k.

$$I = kn = \dfrac{3}{2}(38) = 57$$

The income will be $57.

41. a. $t = \dfrac{k}{n}$

b. k must be determined first; $t = \dfrac{k}{n}$

$$7 = \dfrac{k}{3}$$

$$21 = k$$

Now substitute 5 for n and 21 for k.

$$t = \dfrac{k}{n} = \dfrac{21}{5} \approx 4.2$$

It will take them about 4.2 hours to nail the shingles.

43. a. $r = kn$

    b. k must be determined first; $r = kn$

$$18000 = k(800)$$

$$22.5 = k$$

Now substitute 22,500 for r and 22.5 for k.

$$r = kn$$

$$22,500 = 22.5n$$

$$1000 = n$$

The number of people that attended the game was 1,000.

45. a. $A = kE$

    b. k must be determined first; $A = kE$

$$1630 = k(500)$$

$$3.26 = k$$

Now substitute 2500 for A and 3.26 for k.

$$A = kE$$

$$2500 = 3.26E$$

$$766.9 \approx E$$

The CO_2 saved annually would be 766.9 tons.

47. a. $A = kr^2$

    b. k must be determined first; $A = kr^2$

$$78.5 = k(5)^2$$

$$78.5 = k(25)$$

$$3.14 = k$$

Now substitute 12 for r and 3.14 for k.

$$A = kr^2$$

$$= 3.14(12)^2$$

$$= 3.14(144)$$

$$\approx 452.16$$

The area of the circle is about 452.16 square inches.

49 a. $r = \dfrac{k}{c^2}$

    b. k must be determined first;

$$r = \frac{k}{c^2}$$

$$100 = \frac{k}{0.4^2}$$

$$100 = \frac{k}{.16}$$

$$16 = k$$

Now substitute 0.6 for c and 16 for k.

$$r = \frac{k}{c^2} = \frac{16}{0.6^2} = \frac{16}{.36} \approx 44.44$$

The resistance is about 44.44 ohms.

51. a. $I = kr$

    b. k must be determined first; $I = kr$

$$40 = k(0.04)$$

$$1000 = k$$

Now substitute 0.05 for r and 1000 for k.
$I = kr = 1000(0.05) = 50$
The amount of interest earned was $50.

53. a. $V = \dfrac{k}{P}$

    b. k must be determined first; $V = \dfrac{k}{P}$

$$800 = \frac{k}{200}$$

$$160,000 = k$$

Now substitute 25 for P and 160,000 for k.

$$V = \frac{k}{P}$$

$$= \frac{160,000}{25}$$

$$= 6400$$

The volume is 6400 cubic centimeters.

55. a. $x = kyz$

    b. k must be determined first; $x = kyz$

$$72 = k(18)(2)$$

$$72 = k(36)$$

$$2 = k$$

Now substitute 36 for y, 3 for z and 2 for k.
$x = kyz = 2(36)(3) = 216$
Thus, $x = 216$.

57.

$$4x + 9 \overline{\smash{\big)}\, 8x^2 + 6x - 21}$$

$$\underline{8x^2 + 18x}$$

$$-12x - 21$$

$$\underline{-12x - 27}$$

$$6$$

$$\frac{8x^2 + 6x - 25}{4x + 9} = 2x - 3 + \frac{6}{4x + 9}$$

58. $y(z - 2) + 8(z - 2) = (z - 2)(y + 8)$

59.
$$3x^2 - 24 = -6x$$
$$3x^2 + 6x - 24 = 0$$
$$3(x^2 + 2x - 8) = 0$$
$$3(x + 4)(x - 2) = 0$$
$$x + 4 = 0 \quad \text{or} \quad x - 2 = 0$$
$$x = -4 \qquad\qquad x = 2$$

60.
$$\frac{x + 8}{x - 3} \cdot \frac{x^3 - 27}{x^2 + 3x + 9}$$

$$= \frac{x + 8}{\cancel{x - 3}} \cdot \frac{\cancel{(x - 3)}(x^2 + 3x + 9)}{x^2 + 3x + 9}$$

$$= x + 8$$

Review Exercises

1. $\dfrac{5}{2x - 18}$
$$2x - 18 = 0$$
$$2(x - 9) = 0$$
$$x - 9 = 0$$
$$x = 9$$
The expression is defined for all real numbers except $x = 9$.

2. $\dfrac{2x + 1}{x^2 - 8x + 15}$
$$x^2 - 8x + 15 = 0$$
$$(x - 3)(x - 5) = 0$$
$$x - 3 = 0 \quad \text{or} \quad x - 5 = 0$$
$$x = 3 \qquad\qquad x = 5$$
The expression is defined for all real numbers except $x = 3$, $x = 5$.

3. $\dfrac{7x-1}{5x^2+4x-1}$

$5x^2+4x-1=0$

$(5x-1)(x+1)=0$

$5x-1=0 \quad \text{or} \quad x+1=0$

$x=\dfrac{1}{5} \qquad\qquad x=-1$

The expression is defined for all real numbers

except $x=\dfrac{1}{5},\ x=-1$.

4. $\dfrac{y}{xy-3y}=\dfrac{y}{y(x-3)}=\dfrac{1}{x-3}$

5. $\dfrac{x^3+5x^2+12x}{x}=\dfrac{x(x^2+5x+12)}{x}$

$\qquad = x^2+5x+12$

6. $\dfrac{9x^2+3xy}{3x}=\dfrac{\cancel{3x}(3x+y)}{\cancel{3x}}=3x+y$

7. $\dfrac{x^2+2x-8}{x-2}=\dfrac{(x-2)(x+4)}{\cancel{x-2}}=x+4$

8. $\dfrac{a^2-81}{a-9}=\dfrac{(a-9)(a+9)}{\cancel{a-9}}=a+9$

9. $\dfrac{-2x^2+7x+4}{x-4}=\dfrac{-1(2x^2+7x+4)}{(x-4)}$

$\qquad = \dfrac{-1(2x+1)\cancel{(x-4)}}{\cancel{(x-4)}}$

$\qquad = -(2x+1)$

10. $\dfrac{b^2-2b+10}{b^2-3b-10}=\dfrac{\cancel{(b-5)}(b-2)}{\cancel{(b-5)}(b+2)}=\dfrac{b-2}{b+2}$

11. $\dfrac{4x^2-11x-3}{4x^2-7x-2}=\dfrac{\cancel{(4x+1)}(x-3)}{\cancel{(4x+1)}(x-2)}$

$\qquad = \dfrac{x-3}{x-2}$

12. $\dfrac{2x^2-21x+40}{4x^2-4x-15}=\dfrac{(x-8)\cancel{(2x-5)}}{(2x+3)\cancel{(2x-5)}}$

$\qquad = \dfrac{x-8}{2x+3}$

13. $\dfrac{5a^2}{6b}\cdot\dfrac{2}{4a^2b}=\dfrac{5\cdot2}{6\cdot4}\cdot\dfrac{a^2}{a^2}\cdot\dfrac{1}{b\cdot b}$

$\qquad = \dfrac{10}{24b^2}$

$\qquad = \dfrac{5}{12b^2}$

14. $\dfrac{30x^2y^3}{3z}\cdot\dfrac{6z^3}{5xy^3}=\dfrac{15\cdot2\cdot6}{15}\left(\dfrac{x^2}{x}\right)\left(\dfrac{y^3}{y^3}\right)\left(\dfrac{z^3}{z}\right)$

$\qquad = 12xz^2$

15. $\dfrac{20a^3b^4}{7c^3}\cdot\dfrac{14c^7}{5a^5b}=\dfrac{20}{5}\cdot\dfrac{14}{7}\cdot\dfrac{a^3}{a^5}\cdot\dfrac{b^4}{b}\cdot\dfrac{c^7}{c^3}$

$\qquad = 8\dfrac{1}{a^2}b^3c^4$

$\qquad = \dfrac{8b^3c^4}{a^2}$

16. $\dfrac{1}{x-4}\cdot\dfrac{4-x}{9}=\dfrac{1}{\cancel{x-4}}\cdot\dfrac{-1\cancel{(x-4)}}{9}$

$\qquad = -\dfrac{1}{9}$

17. $\dfrac{-m+4}{15m}\cdot\dfrac{10m}{m-4}=\dfrac{-1\cancel{(m-4)}}{3\cdot\cancel{5m}}\cdot\dfrac{2\cdot\cancel{5m}}{\cancel{m-4}}$

$\qquad = \dfrac{-2}{3}$

18. $\dfrac{a-2}{a+3}\cdot\dfrac{a^2+4a+3}{a^2-a-2}=\dfrac{\cancel{(a-2)}\cancel{(a+3)}\cancel{(a+1)}}{\cancel{(a+3)}\cancel{(a-2)}\cancel{(a+1)}}$

$\qquad = 1$

19. $\dfrac{9x^6}{y^2}\div\dfrac{x^4}{4y}=\dfrac{9x^6}{y^2}\cdot\dfrac{4y}{x^4}=\dfrac{36x^6y}{x^4y^2}=\dfrac{36x^2}{y}$

20. $\dfrac{5xy^2}{z}\div\dfrac{x^4y^2}{4z^2}=\dfrac{5xy^2}{z}\cdot\dfrac{4z^2}{x^4y^2}=\dfrac{20z}{x^3}$

21. $\dfrac{6a+6b}{a^2}\div\dfrac{a^2-b^2}{a^2}=\dfrac{6\cancel{(a+b)}}{\cancel{a^2}}\cdot\dfrac{\cancel{a^2}}{\cancel{(a+b)}(a-b)}$

$\qquad = \dfrac{6}{a-b}$

22. $\dfrac{1}{a^2+8a+15}\div\dfrac{8}{a+5}=\dfrac{1}{\cancel{(a+5)}(a+3)}\cdot\dfrac{\cancel{a+5}}{8}$

$\qquad = \dfrac{1}{8(a+3)}$

23. $(t+8) \div \dfrac{t^2+5t-24}{t-3} = \dfrac{\cancel{(t+8)}}{1} \cdot \dfrac{\cancel{t-3}}{\cancel{(t-3)}\cancel{(t+8)}}$

$$= 1$$

24. $\dfrac{x^2+xy-2y^2}{2y} \div \dfrac{x+2y}{12y^2} = \dfrac{(x-y)\cancel{(x+2y)}}{2y} \cdot \dfrac{12y^2}{\cancel{x+2y}}$

$$= 6y(x-y)$$

25. $\dfrac{n}{n+5} - \dfrac{2}{n+5} = \dfrac{n-2}{n+5}$

26. $\dfrac{4x}{x+7} + \dfrac{28}{x+7} = \dfrac{4x+28}{x+7} = \dfrac{4\cancel{(x+7)}}{\cancel{x+7}} = 4$

27. $\dfrac{5x-4}{x+8} + \dfrac{44}{x+8} = \dfrac{5x-4+44}{x+8}$

$$= \dfrac{5x+40}{x+8}$$

$$= \dfrac{5\cancel{(x+8)}}{\cancel{x+8}}$$

$$= 5$$

28. $\dfrac{7x-3}{x^2+7x-30} - \dfrac{3x+9}{x^2+7x-30} = \dfrac{7x-3-(3x+9)}{x^2+7x-30}$

$$= \dfrac{7x-3-3x-9}{x^2+7x-30}$$

$$= \dfrac{4x-12}{x^2+7x-30}$$

$$= \dfrac{4\cancel{(x-3)}}{(x+10)\cancel{(x-3)}}$$

$$= \dfrac{4}{x+10}$$

29. $\dfrac{5h^2+12h-1}{h+5} - \dfrac{h^2-5h+14}{h+5}$

$$= \dfrac{5h^2+12h-1-\left(h^2-5h+14\right)}{h+5}$$

$$= \dfrac{5h^2+12h-1-h^2+5h-14}{h+5}$$

$$= \dfrac{4h^2+17h-15}{h+5}$$

$$\dfrac{(4h-3)\cancel{(h+5)}}{\cancel{h+5}}$$

$$= 4h-3$$

30. $\dfrac{6x^2-4x}{2x-3} - \dfrac{-3x+12}{2x-3}$

$$= \dfrac{6x^2+4x-(-3x+12)}{2x-3}$$

$$= \dfrac{6x^2-4x+3x-12}{2x-3}$$

$$= \dfrac{6x^2-x-12}{2x-3}$$

$$= \dfrac{(3x+4)\cancel{(2x-3)}}{\cancel{2x-3}}$$

$$= 3x+4$$

31. $\dfrac{a}{8} + \dfrac{4a}{3}$

Least common denominator $= 2(2)(2)(3) = 24$

32. $\dfrac{10}{x+3} + \dfrac{2x}{x+3}$

Least common denominator $= x + 3$

33. $\dfrac{10}{4xy^3} - \dfrac{11}{10x^2y}$

Least common denominator $= 20x^2y^3$

34. $\dfrac{6}{x-3} - \dfrac{2}{x}$

Least common denominator $= x(x-3)$

35. $\dfrac{8}{n+5} + \dfrac{2n-3}{n-4}$

Least common denominator $= (n+5)(n-4)$

36. $\dfrac{5x-12}{x^2+2x} - \dfrac{4}{x+2} = \dfrac{5x-12}{x(x+2)} - \dfrac{4}{x+2}$

Least common denominator $= x(x+2)$

37. $\dfrac{2r+1}{r-s} - \dfrac{6}{r^2-s^2} = \dfrac{2r+1}{r-s} - \dfrac{6}{(r+s)(r-s)}$

Least common denominator $= (r+s)(r-s)$

38. $\dfrac{3x^2}{x-9} + 10x^3 = \dfrac{4x^2}{x-9} + \dfrac{10x^3}{1}$

Least common denominator $= x - 9$

39. $\dfrac{19x-5}{x^2+2x-35} + \dfrac{-10x+1}{x^2+9x+14}$

$$= \dfrac{19x-5}{(x+7)(x-5)} + \dfrac{-10x+1}{(x+7)(x+2)}$$

Least common denominator

$$= (x+7)(x-5)(x+2)$$

40.
$$\frac{5}{3y^2} + \frac{y}{2y} = \frac{5}{3y^2} + \frac{1}{2}$$
$$= \frac{5}{3y^2} \cdot \frac{2}{2} + \frac{1}{2} \cdot \frac{3y^2}{3y^2}$$
$$= \frac{10}{6y^2} + \frac{3y^2}{6y^2}$$
$$= \frac{10 + 3y^2}{6y^2}$$
$$= \frac{3y^2 + 10}{6y^2}$$

41.
$$\frac{3x}{xy} + \frac{1}{4x} = \frac{3x}{xy} \cdot \frac{4}{4} + \frac{1}{4x} \cdot \frac{y}{y}$$
$$= \frac{12x}{4xy} + \frac{y}{4xy}$$
$$= \frac{12x + y}{4xy}$$

42.
$$\frac{5x}{3xy} - \frac{6}{x^2} = \frac{5x}{3xy} \cdot \frac{x}{x} - \frac{6}{x^2} \cdot \frac{3y}{3y}$$
$$= \frac{5x^2}{3x^2y} - \frac{18y}{3x^2y}$$
$$= \frac{5x^2 - 18y}{3x^2y}$$

43.
$$7 - \frac{2}{x+2} = 7\left(\frac{x+2}{x+2}\right) - \frac{2}{x+2}$$
$$= \frac{7x + 14 - 2}{x+2}$$
$$= \frac{7x + 12}{x+2}$$

44.
$$\frac{x-y}{y} - \frac{x+y}{x} = \frac{x-y}{y} \cdot \frac{x}{x} - \frac{x+y}{x} \cdot \frac{y}{y}$$
$$= \frac{x(x-y)}{xy} - \frac{y(x+y)}{xy}$$
$$= \frac{x^2 - xy - xy - y^2}{xy}$$
$$= \frac{x^2 - 2xy - y^2}{xy}$$

45.
$$\frac{7}{x+4} + \frac{2}{x} = \frac{7}{x+4} \cdot \frac{x}{x} + \frac{2}{x} \cdot \frac{x+4}{x+4}$$
$$= \frac{7x}{x(x+4)} + \frac{2(x+4)}{x(x+4)}$$
$$= \frac{7x + 2x + 8}{x(x+4)}$$
$$= \frac{9x + 8}{x(x+4)}$$

46.
$$\frac{2}{3x} - \frac{3}{3x-6} = \frac{2}{3x} - \frac{3}{3(x-2)}$$
$$= \frac{2}{3x} \cdot \frac{x-2}{x-2} - \frac{3}{3(x-2)} \cdot \frac{x}{x}$$
$$= \frac{2(x-2)}{3x(x-2)} - \frac{3x}{3x(x-2)}$$
$$= \frac{2x - 4 - 3x}{3x(x-2)}$$
$$= \frac{-x - 4}{3x(x-2)}$$

47.
$$\frac{1}{z+5} + \frac{9}{(z+5)^2} = \frac{1}{z+5} \cdot \frac{z+5}{z+5} + \frac{9}{(z+5)^2}$$
$$= \frac{1(z+5)}{(z+5)^2} + \frac{9}{(z+5)^2}$$
$$= \frac{z+5+9}{(z+5)^2}$$
$$= \frac{z+14}{(z+5)^2}$$

48.
$$\frac{x+2}{x^2 - x - 6} + \frac{x-3}{x^2 - 8x + 15}$$
$$= \frac{x+2}{(x-3)(x+2)} + \frac{x-3}{(x-3)(x-5)}$$
$$= \frac{1}{x-3} + \frac{1}{x-5}$$
$$= \frac{1}{x-3} \cdot \frac{x-5}{x-5} + \frac{1}{x-5} \cdot \frac{x-3}{x-3}$$
$$= \frac{x-5}{(x-3)(x-5)} + \frac{x-3}{(x-5)(x-3)}$$
$$= \frac{x-5+x-3}{(x-5)(x-3)}$$
$$= \frac{2x-8}{(x-5)(x-3)}$$

49.
$$\frac{x+4}{x+6} - \frac{x-5}{x+2} = \frac{(x+4)(x+2)}{(x+6)(x+2)} - \frac{(x-5)(x+6)}{(x+2)(x+6)}$$
$$= \frac{x^2+6x+8-(x^2+x-30)}{(x+6)(x+2)}$$
$$= \frac{x^2+6x+8-x^2+x+30}{(x+6)(x+2)}$$
$$= \frac{5x+38}{(x+6)(x+2)}$$

50.
$$2 + \frac{x}{x-4} = \frac{2(x-4)}{x-4} + \frac{x}{x-4}$$
$$= \frac{2x-8+x}{x-4}$$
$$= \frac{3x-8}{x-4}$$

51.
$$\frac{a+2}{b} \div \frac{a-2}{5b^2} = \frac{a+2}{b} \cdot \frac{5b^2}{a-2}$$
$$= \frac{5b(a+2)}{a-2}$$
$$= \frac{5ab+10b}{a-2}$$

52.
$$\frac{x+5}{x^2-9} + \frac{2}{x+3} = \frac{x+5}{(x-3)(x+3)} + \frac{2}{x+3}$$
$$= \frac{x+5}{(x-3)(x+3)} + \frac{2(x-3)}{(x-3)(x+3)}$$
$$= \frac{x+5+2x-6}{(x-3)(x+3)}$$
$$= \frac{3x-1}{(x-3)(x+3)}$$

53.
$$\frac{6p+12q}{p^2q} \cdot \frac{p^4}{p+2q} = \frac{6\cancel{(p+2q)}p^4}{\cancel{(p+2q)}p^2q} = \frac{6p^2}{q}$$

54.
$$\frac{8}{(x+2)(x-3)} - \frac{6}{(x-2)(x+2)}$$
$$= \frac{8(x-2)}{(x+2)(x-3)(x-2)} - \frac{6(x-3)}{(x+2)(x-3)(x-2)}$$
$$= \frac{8(x-2)-6(x-3)}{(x+2)(x-3)(x-2)}$$
$$= \frac{8x-16-6x+18}{(x+2)(x-3)(x-2)}$$
$$= \frac{2x+2}{(x+2)(x-3)(x-2)}$$

55.
$$\frac{x+7}{x^2+9x+14} - \frac{x-10}{x^2-49}$$
$$= \frac{x+7}{(x+7)(x+2)} - \frac{x-10}{(x+7)(x-7)}$$
$$= \frac{x+7}{(x+7)(x+2)} \cdot \frac{(x-7)}{(x-7)} - \frac{x-10}{(x+7)(x-7)} \cdot \frac{(x+2)}{(x+2)}$$
$$= \frac{x^2-49-(x^2-8x-20)}{(x+7)(x-7)(x+2)}$$
$$= \frac{8x-29}{(x+7)(x-7)(x+2)}$$

56.
$$\frac{x-y}{x+y} \cdot \frac{xy+x^2}{x^2-y^2} = \frac{\cancel{x-y}}{x+y} \cdot \frac{x\cancel{(y+x)}}{\cancel{(x+y)}\cancel{(x-y)}}$$
$$= \frac{x}{x+y}$$

57.
$$\frac{3x^2-27y^2}{30} \div \frac{(x-3y)^2}{6}$$
$$= \frac{3(x^2-9y^2)}{30} \cdot \frac{6}{(x-3y)^2}$$
$$= \frac{3\cancel{(x-3y)}(x+3y)}{\cancel{6}\cdot 5} \cdot \frac{\cancel{6}}{\cancel{(x-3y)}(x-3y)}$$
$$= \frac{3(x+3y)}{5(x-3y)}$$

58.
$$\frac{a^2-11a+30}{a-6} \cdot \frac{a^2-8a+15}{a^2-10a+25}$$
$$= \frac{\cancel{(a-6)}(a-5)}{\cancel{a-6}} \cdot \frac{\cancel{(a-5)}(a-3)}{\cancel{(a-5)^2}}$$
$$= a-3$$

59.
$$\frac{a}{a^2-1} - \frac{3}{3a^2-2a-5}$$
$$= \frac{a}{(a-1)(a+1)} - \frac{3}{(3a-5)(a+1)}$$
$$= \frac{a(3a-5)}{(a-1)(a+1)(3a-5)} - \frac{3(a-1)}{(a-1)(a+1)(3a-5)}$$
$$= \frac{a(3a-5)-3(a-1)}{(a-1)(a+1)(3a-5)}$$
$$= \frac{3a^2-5a-3a+3}{(a-1)(a+1)(3a-5)}$$
$$= \frac{3a^2-8a+3}{(a-1)(a+1)(3a-5)}$$

60. $\dfrac{2x^2+6x-20}{x^2-2x} \div \dfrac{x^2+7x+10}{2x^2-8}$

$= \dfrac{2(x^2+3x-10)}{x(x-2)} \cdot \dfrac{2(x^2-4)}{(x+5)(x+2)}$

$= \dfrac{2(x+5)(x-2)}{x(x-2)} \cdot \dfrac{2(x+2)(x-2)}{(x+5)(x+2)}$

$= \dfrac{4(x-2)}{x}$

$= \dfrac{4x-8}{x}$

61. $\dfrac{5+\dfrac{2}{3}}{\dfrac{3}{4}} = \dfrac{12\left(5+\dfrac{2}{3}\right)}{12\left(\dfrac{3}{4}\right)} = \dfrac{60+8}{9} = \dfrac{68}{9}$

62. $\dfrac{1+\dfrac{5}{8}}{3-\dfrac{9}{16}} = \dfrac{16\left(1+\dfrac{5}{8}\right)}{16\left(3-\dfrac{9}{16}\right)}$

$= \dfrac{16+10}{48-9}$

$= \dfrac{26}{39}$

$= \dfrac{2}{3}$

63. $\dfrac{\dfrac{12ab}{9c}}{\dfrac{4a}{c^2}} = \dfrac{12ab}{9c} \cdot \dfrac{c^2}{4a} = \dfrac{bc}{3}$

64. $\dfrac{\dfrac{18x^4y^2}{9xy^5}}{\dfrac{9xy^5}{4z^2}} = \dfrac{18x^4y^2 \cdot 4z^2}{\dfrac{9xy^5}{4z^2} \cdot 4z^2} = \dfrac{72x^4y^2z^2}{9xy^5} = \dfrac{8x^3z^2}{y^3}$

65. $\dfrac{a-\dfrac{a}{b}}{\dfrac{1+a}{b}} = \dfrac{\left(a-\dfrac{a}{b}\right)b}{\left(\dfrac{1+a}{b}\right)b} = \dfrac{ab-a}{1+a}$

66. $\dfrac{r^2+\dfrac{7}{s}}{s^2} = \dfrac{\left(r^2+\dfrac{7}{s}\right)s}{\left(s^2\right)s} = \dfrac{r^2s+7}{s^3}$

67. $\dfrac{\dfrac{3}{x}+\dfrac{2}{x^2}}{5-\dfrac{1}{x}} = \dfrac{\left(\dfrac{3}{x}+\dfrac{2}{x^2}\right)x^2}{\left(5-\dfrac{1}{x}\right)x^2} = \dfrac{3x+2}{5x^2-x} = \dfrac{3x+2}{x(5x-1)}$

68. $\dfrac{\dfrac{x}{x+y}}{\dfrac{x^2}{4x+4y}} = \dfrac{x}{x+y} \cdot \dfrac{4x+4y}{x^2}$

$= \dfrac{1}{\cancel{x+y}} \cdot \dfrac{4\cancel{(x+y)}}{x}$

$= \dfrac{4}{x}$

69. $\dfrac{\dfrac{9}{x}}{\dfrac{9}{x^2}} = \dfrac{9}{x} \cdot \dfrac{x^2}{9} = x$

70. $\dfrac{\dfrac{1}{a}+2}{\dfrac{1}{a}+\dfrac{3}{a}} = \dfrac{\dfrac{1}{a}+2}{\dfrac{4}{a}} = \dfrac{\left(\dfrac{1}{a}+2\right)a}{\left(\dfrac{4}{a}\right)a} = \dfrac{1+2a}{4}$

71. $\dfrac{\dfrac{1}{x^2}-\dfrac{1}{x}}{\dfrac{1}{x^2}+\dfrac{1}{x}} = \dfrac{x^2\left(\dfrac{1}{x^2}-\dfrac{1}{x}\right)}{x^2\left(\dfrac{1}{x^2}+\dfrac{1}{x}\right)}$

$= \dfrac{1-x}{1+x}$

$= \dfrac{-x+1}{x+1}$

72. $\dfrac{\dfrac{8x}{y}-x}{\dfrac{y}{x}-1} = \dfrac{\left(\dfrac{8x}{y}-x\right)xy}{\left(\dfrac{y}{x}-1\right)xy}$

$= \dfrac{8x^2-x^2y}{y^2-xy}$

$= \dfrac{8x^2-x^2y}{y(y-x)}$

73. $\dfrac{5}{9} = \dfrac{10}{x+3}$

$5(x+3) = 10(9)$

$5x+15 = 90$

$5x = 75$

$x = 15$

74. $\dfrac{x}{4} = \dfrac{x-3}{2}$

$2x = 4(x-3)$

$2x = 4x-12$

$12 = 2x$

$6 = x$

75.
$$\frac{12}{n} + 2 = \frac{n}{4}$$

$$4n\left(\frac{12}{n} + 2\right) = 4n\left(\frac{n}{4}\right)$$

$$48 + 8n = n^2$$

$$0 = n^2 - 8n - 48$$

$$0 = (n - 12)(n + 4)$$

$$n - 12 = 0 \quad \text{or} \quad n + 4 = 0$$

$$n = 12 \qquad\qquad n = -4$$

Since –4 is an extraneous root, $n = 12$ is the solution.

76.
$$\frac{10}{m} + \frac{3}{2} = \frac{m}{10}$$

$$10m\left(\frac{10}{m} + \frac{3}{2}\right) = 10m\left(\frac{m}{10}\right)$$

$$100 + 15m = m^2$$

$$0 = m^2 - 15m - 100$$

$$0 = (m - 20)(m + 5)$$

$$m - 20 = 0 \quad \text{or} \quad m + 5 = 0$$

$$m = 20 \qquad\qquad m = -5$$

Since –5 is an extraneous root, $m = 20$ is the solution.

77.
$$\frac{-4}{d} = \frac{3}{2} + \frac{4 - d}{d}$$

$$2d\left(\frac{-4}{d}\right) = 2d\left(\frac{3}{2} + \frac{4 - d}{d}\right)$$

$$-8 = 3d + 8 - 2d$$

$$-8 = d + 8$$

$$-16 = d$$

78.
$$\frac{1}{x - 7} + \frac{1}{x + 7} = \frac{1}{x^2 - 49}$$

$$\frac{1}{x - 7} + \frac{1}{x + 7} = \frac{1}{(x - 7)(x + 7)}$$

$$(x - 7)(x + 7)\left[\frac{1}{x - 7} + \frac{1}{x + 7}\right] = \left[\frac{1}{(x - 7)(x + 7)}\right](x - 7)(x + 7)$$

$$x + 7 + x - 7 = 1$$

$$2x = 1$$

$$x = \frac{1}{2}$$

79.
$$\frac{x - 3}{x - 2} + \frac{x + 1}{x + 3} = \frac{2x^2 + x + 1}{x^2 + x - 6}$$

$$\frac{x - 3}{x - 2} + \frac{x + 1}{x + 3} = \frac{2x^2 + x + 1}{(x - 2)(x + 3)}$$

$$(x - 2)(x + 3)\left(\frac{x - 3}{x - 2} + \frac{x + 1}{x + 3}\right) = (x - 2)(x + 3)\left[\frac{2x^2 + x + 1}{(x - 2)(x + 3)}\right]$$

$$(x + 3)(x - 3) + (x - 2)(x + 1) = 2x^2 + x + 1$$

$$x^2 - 9 + x^2 - x - 2 = 2x^2 + x + 1$$

$$2x^2 - x - 11 = 2x^2 + x + 1$$

$$-12 = 2x$$

$$-6 = x$$

80.
$$\frac{a}{a^2-64}+\frac{4}{a+8}=\frac{3}{a-8}$$

$$\frac{a}{(a+8)(a-8)}+\frac{4}{a+8}=\frac{3}{a-8}$$

$$(a+8)(a-8)\left[\frac{a}{(a+8)(a-8)}+\frac{4}{a+8}\right]=(a+8)(a-8)\left(\frac{3}{a-8}\right)$$

$$a+4(a-8)=3(a+8)$$
$$a+4a-32=3a+24$$
$$5a-32=3a+24$$
$$2a=56$$
$$a=28$$

81.
$$\frac{d}{d-4}-4=\frac{4}{d-4}$$

$$(d-4)\left(\frac{d}{d-4}-4\right)=(d-4)\left(\frac{4}{d-4}\right)$$

$$d-4(d-4)=4$$
$$d-4d+16=4$$
$$-3d+16=4$$
$$-3d=-12$$
$$d=4$$

Since $\frac{4}{0}$ is not a real number, there is no solution.

82. John and Amy rate $=\frac{1}{6}$

Paul and Cindy rate $=\frac{1}{4}$

$$\frac{t}{6}+\frac{t}{4}=1$$

$$24\left(\frac{t}{6}+\frac{t}{4}\right)=24(1)$$

$$4t+6t=24$$
$$10t=24$$
$$t=\frac{24}{10}=2.4$$

It will take the 4 people 2.4 hours.

83. $\frac{3}{4}$-inch hose's rate $=\frac{1}{7}$

$\frac{5}{16}$-inch hose's rate $=\frac{1}{12}$

$$\frac{t}{7}-\frac{t}{12}=1$$

$$\frac{12t-7t}{84}=1$$

$$5t=84$$

$$t=\frac{84}{5}=16\frac{4}{5}$$

It will take $16\frac{4}{5}$ hours to fill the pool.

84. Let x be one number then, $6x$ is the other number.

$$\frac{1}{x}+\frac{1}{6x}=7$$

$$6x\left(\frac{1}{x}+\frac{1}{6x}\right)=6x(7)$$

$$6+1=42x$$

$$7=42x$$

$$\frac{7}{42}=x$$

$$\frac{1}{6}=x$$

$$6x=6\left(\frac{1}{6}\right)=1$$

The numbers are $\frac{1}{6}$ and 1.

85. Let $x=$ Robert's speed, then
$3.5+x=$ Tran's speed

$$t=\frac{d}{r}$$

Robert's time = Tran's time

$$\frac{3}{x} = \frac{8}{3.5 + x}$$

$$3(3.5 + x) = 8x$$

$$10.5 + 3x = 8x$$

$$10.5 = 5x$$

$$2.1 = x$$

$$x + 3.5 = 2.1 + 3.5 = 5.6$$

Robert's speed is 2.1 mph and Tran's speed is 5.6 mph.

86.

$$d = kw$$

$$182 = k \cdot 132$$

$$182 = 132k$$

$$1.379 \approx k$$

Now we have to substitute 198 for w and 1.379 for k to find the recommended dosage for Bill.

$$d = kw$$

$$d = 1.379 \cdot 198$$

$$d \approx 273$$

Thus, 273 mg is needed for Bill.

87.

$$t = \frac{k}{s}$$

$$1.4 = \frac{k}{6}$$

$$8.4 = k$$

Now we have to substitute 5 for s and 8.4 for k to find Leif's time.

$$t = \frac{k}{s}$$

$$t = \frac{8.4}{5}$$

$$t = 1.68$$

Thus, it will take Leif 1.68 hours.

Practice Test

1. $\dfrac{-8 + x}{x - 8} = \dfrac{x - 8}{x - 8} = 1$

2. $\dfrac{x^3 - 1}{x^2 - 1} = \dfrac{(x - 1)(x^2 + x + 1)}{(x - 1)(x + 1)} = \dfrac{x^2 + x + 1}{x + 1}$

3. $\dfrac{20x^2 y^3}{4z^2} \cdot \dfrac{8xz^3}{5xy^4} = \dfrac{4 \cdot 5x^2 y^3}{4z^2} \cdot \dfrac{2 \cdot 4xz^3}{5xy^4}$

$$= \dfrac{8x^3 y^3 z^3}{xy^4 z^2} = \dfrac{8x^2 z}{y}$$

4. $\dfrac{a^2 - 9a + 14}{a - 2} \cdot \dfrac{a^2 - 4a - 21}{(a - 7)^2}$

$$= \dfrac{(a - 7)(a - 2)}{a - 2} \cdot \dfrac{(a - 7)(a + 3)}{(a - 7)^2}$$

$$= a + 3$$

5. $\dfrac{x^2 - x - 6}{x^2 - 9} \cdot \dfrac{x^2 - 6x + 9}{x^2 + 4x + 4}$

$$= \dfrac{(x - 3)(x + 2)}{(x - 3)(x + 3)} \cdot \dfrac{(x - 3)(x - 3)}{(x + 2)(x + 2)}$$

$$= \dfrac{(x - 3)^2}{(x + 3)(x + 2)}$$

$$= \dfrac{x^2 - 6x + 9}{(x + 3)(x + 2)}$$

6. $\dfrac{x^2 - 1}{x + 2} \cdot \dfrac{x + 2}{1 - x^2}$

$$= \dfrac{(x - 1)(x + 1)}{x + 2} \cdot \dfrac{x + 2}{-1(x - 1)(x + 1)}$$

$$= -1$$

7. $\dfrac{x^2 - 4y^2}{5x + 20y} \div \dfrac{x + 2y}{x + 4y} = \dfrac{(x - 2y)(x + 2y)}{5(x + 4y)} \cdot \dfrac{x + 4y}{x + 2y}$

$$= \dfrac{x - 2y}{5}$$

8. $\dfrac{15}{y^2 + 2y - 15} \div \dfrac{5}{y - 3} = \dfrac{\overset{3}{15}}{(y - 3)(y + 5)} \cdot \dfrac{y - 3}{\underset{1}{5}}$

$$= \dfrac{3}{y + 5}$$

9. $\dfrac{m^2 + 3m - 18}{m - 3} \div \dfrac{m^2 - 8m + 15}{3 - m}$

$$= \dfrac{(m + 6)(m - 3)}{m - 3} \cdot \dfrac{-1(m - 3)}{(m - 5)(m - 3)}$$

$$= \dfrac{-(m + 6)}{m - 5}$$

$$= -\dfrac{m + 6}{m - 5}$$

10.
$$\frac{4x+3}{8y}+\frac{2x-5}{8y}=\frac{4x+3+2x-5}{8y}$$
$$=\frac{6x-2}{8y}$$
$$=\frac{2(3x-1)}{8y}$$
$$=\frac{3x-1}{4y}$$

11.
$$\frac{7x^2-4}{x+3}-\frac{6x+9}{x+3}=\frac{7x^2-4-(6x+9)}{x+3}$$
$$=\frac{7x^2-4-6x-9}{x+3}$$
$$=\frac{7x^2-6x-13}{x+3}$$

12.
$$\frac{2}{xy}-\frac{8}{xy^3}=\frac{2}{xy}\cdot\frac{y^2}{y^2}-\frac{8}{xy^3}$$
$$=\frac{2y^2}{xy^3}-\frac{8}{xy^3}$$
$$=\frac{2y^2-8}{xy^3}$$

13.
$$3-\frac{5z}{z-5}=3\left(\frac{z-5}{z-5}\right)-\frac{5z}{z-5}$$
$$=\frac{3z-15}{z-5}-\frac{5z}{z-5}$$
$$=\frac{3z-15-5z}{z-5}$$
$$=\frac{-2z-15}{z-5}$$
$$=-\frac{2z+15}{z-5}$$

14.
$$\frac{x-5}{x^2-16}-\frac{x-2}{x^2+2x-8}$$
$$=\frac{x-5}{(x-4)(x+4)}-\frac{x-2}{(x-2)(x+4)}$$
$$=\frac{x-5}{(x-4)(x+4)}-\frac{1}{x+4}$$
$$=\frac{x-5}{(x-4)(x+4)}-\frac{1}{x+4}\cdot\frac{x-4}{x-4}$$
$$=\frac{x-5-(x-4)}{(x-4)(x+4)}$$
$$=\frac{x-5-x+4}{(x-4)(x+4)}$$
$$=\frac{-1}{(x-4)(x+4)}$$

15.
$$\frac{2+\frac{1}{2}}{3-\frac{1}{5}}=\frac{10\left(2+\frac{1}{2}\right)}{10\left(3-\frac{1}{5}\right)}=\frac{20+5}{30-2}=\frac{25}{28}$$

16.
$$\frac{x+\frac{x}{y}}{\frac{7}{x}}=\left(x+\frac{x}{y}\right)\frac{x}{7}$$
$$=\left(\frac{xy+x}{y}\right)\left(\frac{x}{7}\right)$$
$$=\frac{yx^2+x^2}{7y}$$

17.
$$\frac{4+\frac{3}{x}}{\frac{9}{x}-5}=\frac{x\left(4+\frac{3}{x}\right)}{x\left(\frac{9}{x}-5\right)}=\frac{4x+3}{9-5x}$$

18.
$$2+\frac{8}{x}=6$$
$$x\left(2+\frac{8}{x}\right)=6x$$
$$2x+8=6x$$
$$8=4x$$
$$2=x$$

19.
$$\frac{2x}{3} - \frac{x}{4} = x + 1$$
$$12\left(\frac{2x}{3} - \frac{x}{4}\right) = 12(x+1)$$
$$8x - 3x = 12x + 12$$
$$5x = 12x + 12$$
$$-7x = 12$$
$$x = -\frac{12}{7}$$

20.
$$\frac{x}{x-8} + \frac{6}{x-2} = \frac{x^2}{x^2 - 10x + 16}$$
$$\frac{x}{x-8} + \frac{6}{x-2} = \frac{x^2}{(x-8)(x-2)}$$
$$(x-8)(x-2)\left(\frac{x}{x-8} + \frac{6}{x-2}\right) = (x-8)(x-2)\left[\frac{x^2}{(x-8)(x-2)}\right]$$
$$x(x-2) + 6(x-8) = x^2$$
$$x^2 - 2x + 6x - 48 = x^2$$
$$4x - 48 = 0$$
$$4x = 48$$
$$x = 12$$

21.
$$\frac{t}{10} + \frac{t}{15} = 1$$
$$30\left(\frac{t}{10} + \frac{t}{15}\right) = 30(1)$$
$$3t + 2t = 30$$
$$5t = 30$$
$$t = 6$$
It will take them 6 hours to level one acre together.

22. Let x be the number.
$$x + \frac{1}{x} = 2$$
$$x\left(x + \frac{1}{x}\right) = x(2)$$
$$x^2 + 1 = 2x$$
$$x^2 - 2x + 1 = 0$$
$$(x-1)(x-1) = 0$$
$$x - 1 = 0$$
$$x = 1$$
The number is 1

23. Let x = base, then $2x - 2$ = height.
$$\text{area} = \frac{1}{2} \cdot \text{base} \cdot \text{height}$$
$$30 = \frac{1}{2}x(2x - 2)$$
$$2(30) = 2\left[\frac{1}{2}x(2x - 2)\right]$$
$$60 = x(2x - 2)$$
$$60 = 2x^2 - 2x$$
$$0 = 2x^2 - 2x - 60$$
$$0 = 2(x^2 - x - 30)$$
$$0 = 2(x-6)(x+5)$$
$$x - 6 = 0 \quad \text{or} \quad x + 5 = 0$$
$$x = 6 \quad\quad\quad x = -5$$
Since the base cannot be negative, the base is 6 inches and the height is 2(6) – 2 = 10 inches.

24. Let d = the distance she rollerblades, then $12 - d$ is the distance she bicycles.

$$t = \frac{d}{r}$$

$$\frac{d}{4} + \frac{12 - d}{10} = 1.5$$

$$20\left(\frac{d}{4} + \frac{12 - d}{10}\right) = 20(1.5)$$

$$5d + 2(12 - d) = 30$$

$$5d + 24 - 2d = 30$$

$$3d = 6$$

$$d = 2$$

She rollerblades for 2 miles.

25. $w = \dfrac{k}{f}$

$$4.3 = \frac{k}{263}$$

$$1130.9 = k$$

Now substitute 1000 for f and 1130.9 for k.

$$w = \frac{k}{f}$$

$$w = \frac{1130.9}{1000}$$

$$w \approx 1.1309$$

The wavelength would be about 1.13 feet.

Cumulative Review Test

1. $3x^2 - 5xy^2 - 7 = 3(-4)^2 - 5(-4)(-2)^2 - 7$
$$= 3(16) - 5(-4)(4) - 7$$
$$= 48 + 80 - 7$$
$$= 121$$

2. $5z + 4 = -3(z - 7)$
$$5z + 4 = -3z + 21$$
$$5z + 3z = 21 - 4$$
$$8z = 17$$
$$z = \frac{17}{8}$$

3. $\left(\dfrac{10x^6 y^3}{2x^5 y^5}\right)^3 = \left(\dfrac{5x}{y^2}\right)^3 = \dfrac{125x^3}{y^6}$

4. $c + (c + 0.012c)$

5. $(6x^2 - 3x - 5) - (-2x^2 - 8x - 19)$
$$= 6x^2 - 3x - 5 + 2x^2 + 8x + 19$$
$$= 6x^2 + 2x^2 - 3x + 8x - 5 + 19$$
$$= 8x^2 + 5x + 14$$

6. $(3n^2 - 4n + 3)(2n - 5)$
$$= 3n^2(2n - 5) - 4n(2n - 5) + 3(2n - 5)$$
$$= 6n^3 - 15n^2 - 8n^2 + 20n + 6n - 15$$
$$= 6n^3 - 23n^2 + 26n - 15$$

7. $8a^2 - 8a - 5a + 5 = 8a(a - 1) - 5(a - 1)$
$$= (a - 1)(8a - 5)$$

8. $13x^2 + 26x - 39 = 13(x^2 + 2x - 3)$
$$= 13(x + 3)(x - 1)$$

9. $[6 - [3(8 \div 4)]^2 + 9 \cdot 4]^2$
$$= [6 - [3(2)]^2 + 9 \cdot 4]^2$$
$$= [6 - (6)^2 + 9 \cdot 4]^2$$
$$= [6 - 36 + 9 \cdot 4]^2$$
$$= [6 - 36 + 36]^2$$
$$= [6]^2$$
$$= 36$$

10. $2(x + 4) \le -(x + 3) - 1$
$$2x + 8 \le -x - 3 - 1$$
$$2x + 8 \le -x - 4$$
$$3x \le -12$$
$$x \le -4$$

11. $\dfrac{4x - 38}{8} = \dfrac{4x}{8} - \dfrac{38}{8} = \dfrac{1}{2}x - \dfrac{19}{4}$

12. $2x^2 = 11x - 12$
$$2x^2 - 11x + 12 = 0$$
$$(x - 4)(2x - 3) = 0$$
$$x - 4 = 0 \quad \text{or} \quad 2x - 3 = 0$$
$$x = 4 \qquad\qquad x = \frac{3}{2}$$

13. $\dfrac{x^2 + x - 12}{x^2 - x - 6} \cdot \dfrac{x^2 - 2x - 8}{2x^2 - 7x - 4}$

$= \dfrac{(x+4)\cancel{(x-3)}}{\cancel{(x-3)}\cancel{(x+2)}} \cdot \dfrac{\cancel{(x-4)}\cancel{(x+2)}}{(2x+1)\cancel{(x-4)}}$

$= \dfrac{x+4}{2x+1}$

14. $\dfrac{r}{r+2} - \dfrac{3}{r-5} = \dfrac{r}{r+2} \cdot \dfrac{r-5}{r-5} - \dfrac{3}{r-5} \cdot \dfrac{r+2}{r+2}$

$= \dfrac{r(r-5)}{(r+2)(r-5)} - \dfrac{3(r+2)}{(r+2)(r-5)}$

$= \dfrac{r^2 - 5r - (3r+6)}{(r+2)(r-5)}$

$= \dfrac{r^2 - 5r - 3r - 6}{(r+2)(r-5)}$

$= \dfrac{r^2 - 8r - 6}{(r+2)(r-5)}$

15. $\dfrac{4}{x^2 - 3x - 10} + \dfrac{6}{x^2 + 5x + 6}$

$= \dfrac{4}{(x-5)(x+2)} + \dfrac{6}{(x+2)(x+3)}$

$= \dfrac{4(x+3)}{(x-5)(x+2)(x+3)} + \dfrac{6(x-5)}{(x-5)(x+2)(x+3)}$

$= \dfrac{4(x+3) + 6(x-5)}{(x-5)(x+2)(x+3)}$

$= \dfrac{4x + 12 + 6x - 30}{(x-5)(x+2)(x+3)}$

$= \dfrac{10x - 18}{(x-5)(x+2)(x+3)}$

16. $\dfrac{x}{9} - \dfrac{x}{6} = \dfrac{1}{12}$

$36\left(\dfrac{x}{9} - \dfrac{x}{6}\right) = 36\left(\dfrac{1}{12}\right)$

$4x - 6x = 3$

$-2x = 3$

$x = -\dfrac{3}{2}$

17. $\dfrac{7}{x+3} + \dfrac{5}{x+2} = \dfrac{5}{x^2 + 5x + 6}$

$\dfrac{7}{x+3} + \dfrac{5}{x+2} = \dfrac{5}{(x+3)(x+2)}$

$(x+3)(x+2)\left(\dfrac{7}{x+3} + \dfrac{5}{x+2}\right) = (x+3)(x+2)\left[\dfrac{5}{(x+3)(x+2)}\right]$

$7(x+2) + 5(x+3) = 5$

$7x + 14 + 5x + 15 = 5$

$12x + 29 = 5$

$12x = -24$

$x = -2$

Check:

$\dfrac{7}{x+3} + \dfrac{5}{x+2} = \dfrac{5}{x^2 + 5x + 6}$

$\dfrac{7}{-2+3} + \dfrac{5}{-2+2} = \dfrac{5}{(-2)^2 + 5(-2) + 6}$

$\dfrac{7}{1} + \dfrac{5}{0} = \dfrac{5}{0}$

Since $\dfrac{5}{0}$ is not a real number, there is no solution.

18. Let x = the total medical bills. The cost under plan 1 is $0.10x$, while the cost under plan 2 is $100 + 0.05x$.

$$0.10x = 150 + 0.05x$$
$$0.05x = 150$$
$$x = 3000$$

The cost under both plans is the same for $3000 in total medical bills.

19. Let x = pounds of sunflower seed and
      y = pounds of premixed assorted seed mix

$$x + y = 50$$
$$0.50x + 0.20y = 16.00$$

Solve the first equation for y.

$$y = 50 - x$$

Substitute $50 - x$ for y in the second equation.

$$0.50x + 0.20(50 - x) = 16$$
$$0.50x + 10 - 0.20x = 16$$
$$0.30x = 6$$
$$x = 20$$
$$y = 50 - x = 50 - 20 = 30$$

He will have to use 20 pounds of sunflower seed and 30 pounds of premixed assorted seed mix.

20. Let d = distance on first leg, then the distance on the second leg is $12.75 - d$.

$$t = \frac{d}{r}$$

Time for first leg + time for second leg = total time

$$\frac{d}{6.5} + \frac{12.75 - d}{9.5} = 1.5$$
$$(9.5)(6.5)\left[\frac{d}{6.5} + \frac{12.75 - d}{9.5}\right] = (9.5)(6.5)(1.5)$$
$$9.5d + 6.5(12.75 - d) = 92.625$$
$$9.5d + 82.875 - 6.5d = 92.625$$
$$3d = 9.75$$
$$d = 3.25$$
$$12.75 - d = 12.75 - 3.25 = 9.5$$

The distance traveled during the first leg of the race was 3.25 miles and the distance traveled in the second leg of the race was 9.5 miles.

Chapter 7

Exercise Set 7.1

1. The *x*-coordinate is always listed first.

3. a. The horizontal axis is the *x*-axis.

  b. The vertical axis is the *y*-axis.

5. Axis is singular, while axes is plural.

7. The graph of a linear equation is an illustration of the set of points whose coordinates satisfy the equation.

9. a. Two points are needed to graph a linear equation.

  b. It is a good idea to use three or more points when graphing a linear equation to catch errors.

11. $ax + by = c$

13.

15. II

17. IV

19. I

21. III

23. III

25. II

27. $A(3, 1)$; $B(-3, 0)$; $C(1, -3)$; $D(-2, -3)$; $E(0, 3)$; $F\left(\dfrac{3}{2}, -1\right)$

29.

31.

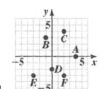

33.

The points are collinear.

35.

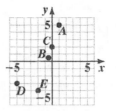

The points are not collinear since $(-5, -3)$ is not on the line.

37. a.

$\begin{aligned} y &= x + 2 \\ 4 &= 2 + 2 \\ 4 &= 4 \quad \text{True} \end{aligned}$ $\qquad$ $\begin{aligned} y &= x + 2 \\ 0 &= -2 + 2 \\ 0 &= 0 \quad \text{True} \end{aligned}$

$\begin{aligned} y &= x + 2 \\ 5 &= -1 + 2 \\ 5 &= 1 \quad \text{False} \end{aligned}$ $\qquad$ $\begin{aligned} y &= x + 2 \\ 2 &= 0 + 2 \\ 2 &= 2 \quad \text{True} \end{aligned}$

Point c) does not satisfy the equation.

  b.

39. a.

$\begin{aligned} 3x - 2y &= 6 \\ 3(4) - 2(0) &= 6 \\ 12 &= 6 \quad \text{False} \end{aligned}$ $\qquad$ $\begin{aligned} 3x - 2y &= 6 \\ 3(2) - 2(0) &= 6 \\ 6 &= 6 \quad \text{True} \end{aligned}$

$\begin{aligned} 3x - 2y &= 6 \\ 3\left(\tfrac{2}{3}\right) - 2(-2) &= 6 \\ 2 + 4 &= 6 \\ 6 &= 6 \quad \text{True} \end{aligned}$ $\qquad$ $\begin{aligned} 3x - 2y &= 6 \\ 3\left(\tfrac{4}{3}\right) - 2(-1) &= 6 \\ 4 + 2 &= 6 \\ 6 &= 6 \quad \text{True} \end{aligned}$

Point a) does not satisfy the equation.

  b.

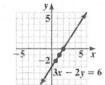

41. a.

$$\frac{1}{2}x + 4y = 4$$

$$\frac{1}{2}(-2) + 4(3) = 4$$

$$-1 + 12 = 4$$

$$11 = 4 \quad \text{False}$$

$$\frac{1}{2}x + 4y = 4$$

$$\frac{1}{2}(2) + 4\left(\frac{3}{4}\right) = 4$$

$$1 + 3 = 4$$

$$4 = 4 \quad \text{True}$$

$$\frac{1}{2}x + 4y = 4$$

$$\frac{1}{2}(0) + 4(1) = 4$$

$$0 + 4 = 4$$

$$4 = 4 \quad \text{True}$$

$$\frac{1}{2}x + 4y = 4$$

$$\frac{1}{2}(-4) + 4\left(\frac{3}{2}\right) = 4$$

$$-2 + 6 = 4$$

$$4 = 4 \quad \text{True}$$

Point a) does not satisfy the equation.

b.

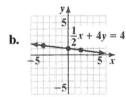

43. $y = 3x - 4$

$y = 3(2) - 4$

$y = 6 - 4$

$y = 2$

45. $y = 3x - 4$

$y = 3(0) - 4$

$y = 0 - 4$

$y = -4$

47. $2x + 3y = 12$

$2x + 3(2) = 12$

$2x + 6 = 12$

$2x = 6$

$x = 3$

49. $2x + 3y = 12$

$2x + 3\left(\frac{11}{3}\right) = 12$

$2x + 11 = 12$

$2x = 1$

$x = \frac{1}{2}$

51. The value of y is 0 when a straight line crosses the x-axis, because any point on the x-axis is neither above or below the origin.

53. a. Latitude: 16°N   Longitude: 56°W

   b. Latitude: 29°N   Longitude: 90.5°W

   c. Latitude: 26°N   Longitude: 80.5°W

   d. Answers will vary.

55.

57.

$$\frac{1}{2}(x - 3) = \frac{1}{3}x + 2$$

$$\frac{1}{2}x - \frac{3}{2} = \frac{1}{3}x + 2$$

$$6\left(\frac{1}{2}x - \frac{3}{2}\right) = 6\left(\frac{1}{3}x + 2\right)$$

$$3x - 9 = 2x + 12$$

$$x = 21$$

58.

$$2x - 5y = 8$$

$$2x - 2x - 5y = 8 - 2x$$

$$-5y = 8 - 2x$$

$$\frac{-5y}{-5} = \frac{8 - 2x}{-5}$$

$$y = \frac{8 - 2x}{-5}$$

$$y = \frac{2x - 8}{5}$$

$$y = \frac{2}{5}x - \frac{8}{5}$$

59. $(2x^3)^4 = 2^4(x^3)^4 = 16x^{3 \cdot 4} = 16x^{12}$

60. $x^2 - 6x - 27 = (x + 3)(x - 9)$

61. $y(y - 7) = 0$

$y = 0 \quad \text{or} \quad y - 7 = 0$

$\qquad\qquad\qquad y = 7$

The solutions are 0 and 7.

62.

$$\frac{6}{x^2} + \frac{5}{3x} = \frac{6}{x^2} \cdot \frac{3}{3} + \frac{5}{3x} \cdot \frac{x}{x}$$

$$= \frac{18}{3x^2} + \frac{5x}{3x^2}$$

$$= \frac{18 + 5x}{3x^2}$$

$$= \frac{5x + 18}{3x^2}$$

Exercise Set 7.2

1. To find the x-intercept, substitute 0 for y and find the corresponding value of x. To find the y-intercept, substitute 0 for x and find the corresponding value of y.

3. The graph of $y = b$ is a horizontal line.

5. You may not be able to read exact answers from a graph.

7. Yes. The equation goes through the origin because the point (0, 0) satisfies the equation.

9. $3x + y = 9$
$3(3) + y = 9$
$9 + y = 9$
$y = 0$

11. $3x + y = 9$
$3x + (-6) = 9$
$3x - 6 = 9$
$3x = 15$
$x = 5$

Let $x = 2$, $y = 4(2) - 2 = 6$, $(2, 6)$

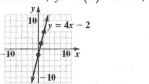

13. $3x + y = 9$
$3x + 0 = 9$
$3x = 9$
$x = 3$

15. $3x - 2y = 8$
$3(4) - 2y = 8$
$12 - 2y = 8$
$-2y = -4$
$y = 2$

29. Let $x = 0$, then, $0 + 2y = 6$ $(0, 3)$
$2y = 6$
$y = 3$
Let $x = 2$, $2 + 2y = 6$, $(2, 2)$
$2y = 4$
$y = 2$
Let $x = 4$, $4 + 2y = 6$, $(4, 1)$
$2y = 2$
$y = 1$

17. $3x - 2y = 8$
$3x - 2(0) = 8$
$3x = 8$
$x = \dfrac{8}{3}$

19. $3x - 2y = 8$
$3(-2) - 2y = 8$
$-6 - 2y = 8$
$-2y = 14$
$y = -7$

21. $x = -3$ is a vertical line with x-intercept at $(-3, 0)$

23. An equation of the form $y = 4$ is a horizontal line with y-intercept at $(0, 4)$.

31. $3x - 2y = 4$
$-2y = -3x + 4$
$y = \dfrac{3}{2}x - 2$
Let $x = 0$, $y = \dfrac{3}{2}(0) - 2 = -2$, $(0, -2)$
Let $x = 2$, $y = \dfrac{3}{2}(2) - 2 = 1$, $(2, 1)$
Let $x = 4$, $y = \dfrac{3}{2}(4) - 2 = 4$, $(4, 4)$

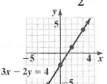

25. Let $x = 0$, $y = 3(0) - 1 = -1$, $(0, -1)$
Let $x = 1$, $y = 3(1) - 1 = 2$, $(1, 2)$
Let $x = 2$, $y = 3(2) - 1 = 5$, $(2, 5)$

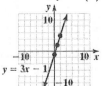

27. Let $x = 0$, $y = 4(0) - 2 = -2$, $(0, -2)$
Let $x = 1$, $y = 4(1) - 2 = 2$, $(1, 2)$

33. $4x + 3y = -9$
$3y = -4x - 9$
$y = -\dfrac{4}{3}x - 3$
Let $x = -3$, $y = -\dfrac{4}{3}(-3) - 3 = 1$, $(-3, 1)$
Let $x = 0$, $y = -\dfrac{4}{3}(0) - 3 = -3$, $(0, -3)$
Let $x = 3$, $y = -\dfrac{4}{3}(3) - 3 = -7$, $(3, -7)$

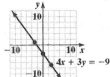

35. $6x + 5y = 30$

$$5y = -6x + 30$$

$$y = -\frac{6}{5}x + 6$$

Let $x = 0$, $y = -\frac{6}{5}(0) + 6 = 6$, $(0, 6)$

Let $x = 5$, $y = -\frac{6}{5}(5) + 6 = 0$, $(5, 0)$

Let $x = 10$, $y = -\frac{6}{5}(10) + 6 = -6$, $(10, -6)$

37. $-4x + 5y = 0$

$$5y = 4x$$

$$y = \frac{4}{5}x$$

Let $x = -5$, $y = \frac{4}{5}(-5) = -4$, $(-5, -4)$

Let $x = 0$, $y = \frac{4}{5}(0) = 0$, $(0, 0)$

Let $x = 5$, $y = \frac{4}{5}(5) = 4$, $(5, 4)$

39. Let $x = 0$, $y = -20(0) + 60 = 60$, $(0, 60)$

Let $x = 2$, $y = -20(2) + 60 = 20$, $(2, 20)$

Let $x = 4$, $y = -20(4) + 60 = -20$, $(4, -20)$

41. Let $x = -3$, $y = \frac{4}{3}(-3) = -4$, $(-3, -4)$

Let $x = 0$, $y = \frac{4}{3}(0) = 0$, $(0, 0)$

Let $x = 3$, $y = \frac{4}{3}(3) = 4$, $(3, 4)$

43. Let $x = 0$, $y = \frac{1}{2}(0) + 4 = 4$, $(0, 4)$

Let $x = 2$, $y = \frac{1}{2}(2) + 4 = 5$, $(2, 5)$

Let $x = 4$, $y = \frac{1}{2}(4) + 4 = 6$, $(4, 6)$

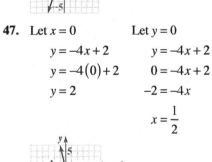

45. Let $x = 0$ Let $y = 0$

$\quad y = 3x + 3$ $y = 3x + 3$

$\quad y = 3(0) + 3$ $0 = 3x + 3$

$\quad y = 3$ $-3x = 3$

                       $x = -1$

47. Let $x = 0$ Let $y = 0$

$\quad y = -4x + 2$ $y = -4x + 2$

$\quad y = -4(0) + 2$ $0 = -4x + 2$

$\quad y = 2$ $-2 = -4x$

                       $x = \frac{1}{2}$

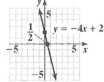

49. Let $x = 0$ Let $y = 0$

$$y = 4x + 16 \qquad y = 4x + 16$$
$$y = 4(0) + 16 \qquad 0 = 4x + 16$$
$$y = 16 \qquad -4x = 16$$
$$x = -4$$

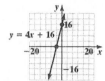

51. $4y + 6x = 24$

$$4y = -6x + 24$$
$$y = -\frac{3}{2}x + 6$$

Let $x = 0$ Let $y = 0$

$$y = -\frac{3}{2}(0) + 6 \qquad 0 = -\frac{3}{2}x + 6$$
$$y = 6 \qquad \frac{3}{2}x = 6$$
$$x = 4$$

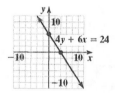

53. Let $x = 0$ Let $y = 0$

$$\frac{1}{2}x + 2y = 4 \qquad \frac{1}{2}x + 2y = 4$$
$$\frac{1}{2}(0) + 2y = 4 \qquad \frac{1}{2}x + 0 = 4$$
$$2y = 4 \qquad \frac{1}{2}x = 4$$
$$y = 2 \qquad x = 8$$

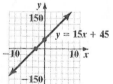

55. Let $x = 0$ Let $y = 0$

$$12x - 24y = 48 \qquad 12x - 24y = 48$$
$$12(0) - 24y = 48 \qquad 12x - 12(0) = 48$$
$$-24y = 48 \qquad 12x = 48$$
$$y = -2 \qquad x = 4$$

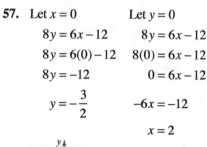

57. Let $x = 0$ Let $y = 0$

$$8y = 6x - 12 \qquad 8y = 6x - 12$$
$$8y = 6(0) - 12 \qquad 8(0) = 6x - 12$$
$$8y = -12 \qquad 0 = 6x - 12$$
$$y = -\frac{3}{2} \qquad -6x = -12$$
$$x = 2$$

59. Let $x = 0$ Let $y = 0$

$$y = 15x + 45 \qquad y = 15x + 45$$
$$y = 15(0) + 45 \qquad 0 = 15x + 45$$
$$y = 45 \qquad -15x = 45$$
$$x = -3$$

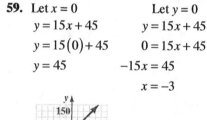

61. Let $x = 0$ Let $y = 0$

$$\frac{1}{3}x + \frac{1}{4}y = 12 \qquad \frac{1}{3}x + \frac{1}{4}y = 12$$
$$\frac{1}{3}(0) + \frac{1}{4}y = 12 \qquad \frac{1}{3}x + \frac{1}{4}(0) = 12$$
$$\frac{1}{4}y = 12 \qquad \frac{1}{3}x = 12$$
$$y = 48 \qquad x = 36$$

63. Let $x = 0$ Let $y = 0$

$$\frac{1}{2}x = \frac{2}{5}y - 80 \qquad \frac{1}{2}x = \frac{2}{5}y - 80$$

$$\frac{1}{2}(0) = \frac{2}{5}y - 80 \qquad \frac{1}{2}x = \frac{2}{5}(0) - 80$$

$$0 = \frac{2}{5}y - 80 \qquad \frac{1}{2}x = -80$$

$$-\frac{2}{5}y = -80 \qquad\qquad x = -160$$

$$y = 200$$

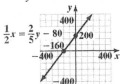

65. $x = -2$

67. $y = 6$

69.
$$ax + 3y = 10$$
$$a(2) + 3(0) = 10$$
$$2a + 0 = 10$$
$$2a = 10$$
$$a = 5$$

71.
$$3x + by = 14$$
$$3(0) + b(7) = 14$$
$$0 + 7b = 14$$
$$7b = 14$$
$$b = 2$$

73. Yes. For each 15 minutes of time, the number of calories burned increases by 200 calories.

75. a. $C = 0.10n + 15$

b.
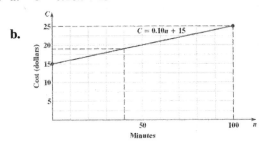

c. $19

d. 100 minutes

77. a. $C = m + 40$

b.
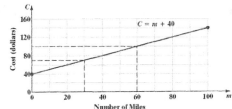

c. $100

d. 30 miles

79. a.
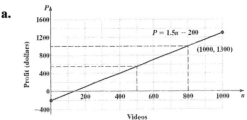

b. $550

c. 800 tapes

81. Since each shaded area multiplied by the corresponding intercept must equal 6, the coefficients are 3 and 2 respectively.

83. Since the first shaded area multiplied by the x-intercept must equal -12, the coefficient of x is 6. Since the opposite of the second shaded area multiplied by the y-intercept must equal -12, the coefficient of y is 4.

85. a.

b. $(2, 3)$

c.
$$y = 2x - 1 \qquad\qquad y = -x + 5$$
$$3 = 2(2) - 1 \qquad\quad 3 = -2 + 5$$
$$3 = 3 \qquad\qquad\qquad 3 = 3$$

d. no

87. a.
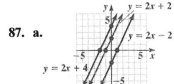

b. They appear to be parallel.

c. The constant is the y-intercept.

88.
$$2\left[6-(4-5)\right]\div 2-8^2 = 2\left[6-(-1)\right]\div 2-64$$
$$= 2\left[7\right]\div 2-64$$
$$= 14\div 2-64$$
$$= 7-64$$
$$= -57$$

89.
$$\frac{8 \text{ ounces}}{3 \text{ gallons}} = \frac{x \text{ ounces}}{2.5 \text{ gallons}}$$
$$\frac{8}{3} = \frac{x}{2.5}$$
$$20 = 3x$$
$$6.67 \approx x$$

You should use 6.67 ounces of cleaner.

90. Let x = smaller integer. Then $3x+1$ = larger integer.
$$x+(3x+1) = 37$$
$$4x+1 = 37$$
$$4x = 36$$
$$x = 9$$
The smaller integer is 9.
The larger is $3(9)+1 = 27+1 = 28$.

91.
$$\frac{3xy^3}{z} \div \frac{x^2 y^2}{5z^3} = \frac{3xy^3}{z} \cdot \frac{5z^3}{x^2 y^2} = \frac{15yz^2}{x}$$

92.
$$\frac{3}{x-2}+\frac{4}{x-3}+2 = \frac{3(x-3)}{(x-2)(x-3)}+\frac{4(x-2)}{(x-2)(x-3)}+\frac{2(x-2)(x-3)}{(x-2)(x-3)}$$
$$= \frac{3x-9}{(x-2)(x-3)}+\frac{4x-8}{(x-2)(x-3)}+\frac{2x^2-10x+12}{(x-2)(x-3)}$$
$$= \frac{3x-9+4x-8+2x^2-10x+12}{(x-2)(x-3)}$$
$$= \frac{2x^2-3x-5}{(x-2)(x-3)}$$

93.
$$\frac{3}{x-2}+\frac{4}{x-3} = 3$$
$$(x-2)(x-3)\cdot\frac{3}{x-2}+(x-2)(x-3)\cdot\frac{4}{x-3} = 3(x-2)(x-3)$$
$$3(x-3)+4(x-2) = 3(x-2)(x-3)$$
$$3x-9+4x-8 = 3x^2-15x+18$$
$$7x-17 = 3x^2-15x+18$$
$$0 = 3x^2-22x+35$$
$$0 = (3x-7)(x-5)$$
$$3x-7=0 \quad \text{or} \quad x-5=0$$
$$3x=7 \qquad\qquad x=5$$
$$x=\frac{7}{3}$$

Exercise Set 7.3

1. The slope of a line is the ratio of the vertical change to the horizontal change between any two points on the line.

3. A line with a positive slope rises from left to right.

5. Lines that rise from the left to right have a positive slope. Lines that fall from left to right have a negative slope.

7. No, since we cannot divide by 0, the slope is undefined.

9. Their slopes are the same.

10. Their slopes are negative reciprocals.

11. $m = \dfrac{5-1}{6-4}$

$\quad = \dfrac{4}{2}$

$\quad = 2$

13. $m = \dfrac{-2-0}{4-8}$

$\quad = \dfrac{-2}{-4}$

$\quad = \dfrac{1}{2}$

15. $m = \dfrac{\frac{1}{2}-\frac{1}{2}}{-3-9}$

$\quad = \dfrac{0}{-12}$

$\quad = 0$

17. $m = \dfrac{-3-(-6)}{8-5}$

$\quad = \dfrac{3}{3}$

$\quad = 1$

19. $m = \dfrac{2-4}{6-6}$

$\quad = \dfrac{-2}{0}$

$\quad$ is undefined

21. $m = \dfrac{3-0}{-2-6}$

$\quad = \dfrac{3}{-8}$

$\quad = -\dfrac{3}{8}$

23. $m = \dfrac{2-\frac{5}{2}}{-\frac{3}{4}-0}$

$\quad = \dfrac{-\frac{1}{2}}{-\frac{3}{4}}$

$\quad = \dfrac{-1}{2}\cdot\dfrac{4}{-3}$

$\quad = \dfrac{-4}{-6}$

$\quad = \dfrac{2}{3}$

25. $m = \dfrac{6}{3} = 2$

27. $m = \dfrac{6}{-3} = -2$

29. $m = \dfrac{4}{-7} = -\dfrac{4}{7}$

31. $m = \dfrac{7}{4}$

33. $m = \dfrac{0}{3} = 0$

35. $m = \dfrac{-2}{3} = -\dfrac{2}{3}$

37. Vertical line, slope is undefined.

39.

41.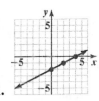

43.

45.

47.

49. The lines are parallel because the slopes are the same.

51. The lines are perpendicular because the slopes are negative reciprocals.

53. The lines are perpendicular because the slopes are negative reciprocals.

55. The lines are neither parallel nor perpendicular.

57. The lines are neither parallel nor perpendicular.

59. The lines are parallel because the slopes are the same.

61. The lines are parallel because the slopes are the same.

63. The lines are perpendicular because if the slope is 0, the line is horizontal and if the slope is undefined the line is vertical.

65. Its slope would be 3.

67. Its slope would be $\dfrac{1}{4}$.

69. The first graph appears to pass through the points $(-1, 0)$ and $(0, 6)$. Its slope is $m = \dfrac{6-0}{0-(-1)} = \dfrac{6}{1} = 6$. The second graph appears to pass through the points $(-4, 0)$ and $(0, 6)$. Its slope is $m = \dfrac{6-0}{0-(-4)} = \dfrac{6}{4} = \dfrac{6}{4} = \dfrac{3}{2}$.

The first graph has the greater slope.

71. a. $m = \dfrac{45-22}{1957-1961} = \dfrac{23}{-4} = -\dfrac{23}{4}$

b. $m = \dfrac{51-7}{1989-1985} = \dfrac{44}{4} = 11$

73. $m = \dfrac{-2-6}{4-2} = \dfrac{-8}{2} = -4$

A line parallel to the given line would have a slope of –4.

75. $m = \dfrac{1-(-7)}{2-1} = \dfrac{1+7}{1} = 8$

A line perpendicular to the given line would

have slope of $-\dfrac{1}{8}$.

77. $m = \dfrac{-\dfrac{7}{2}-\left(-\dfrac{3}{8}\right)}{-\dfrac{4}{9}-\dfrac{1}{2}}$

$= \dfrac{-\dfrac{28}{8}+\dfrac{3}{8}}{-\dfrac{8}{18}-\dfrac{9}{18}}$

$= \dfrac{-\dfrac{25}{8}}{-\dfrac{17}{18}}$

$= \left(-\dfrac{25}{{}_{4}\cancel{8}}\right)\left(-\dfrac{\cancel{18}^{9}}{17}\right)$

$= \dfrac{(-25)(-9)}{(4)(17)}$

$= \dfrac{225}{68}$

79. a.

b. AC; $m = \dfrac{4-1}{5-0} = \dfrac{3}{5}$

CB; $m = \dfrac{4-2}{5-6} = \dfrac{2}{-1} = -2$

DB; $m = \dfrac{2-(-1)}{6-1} = \dfrac{3}{5}$

AD; $m = \dfrac{-1-1}{1-0} = \dfrac{-2}{1} = -2$

c. Yes; opposite sides are parallel.

81. a. AB; $m = \dfrac{12-4}{2-0} = \dfrac{8}{2} = 4$

BC; $m = \dfrac{8-12}{4-2} = \dfrac{-4}{2} = -2$

CD; $m = \dfrac{16-8}{6-4} = \dfrac{8}{2} = 4$

b. $\dfrac{4+(-2)+4}{3} = \dfrac{6}{3} = 2$

c. $m = \dfrac{16-4}{6-0} = \dfrac{12}{6} = 2$

d. yes

e. Answers will vary.

83. $4x^2 + 9x + \dfrac{x}{3} = 4(0)^2 + 9(0) + \dfrac{0}{3}$

$\qquad\qquad = 0 + 0 + 0$

$\qquad\qquad = 0$

84. a. $\qquad -x = -\dfrac{5}{2}$

$(-1)(-x) = (-1)\left(-\dfrac{5}{2}\right)$

$\qquad\quad x = \dfrac{5}{2}$

b. $8x = 0$

$\dfrac{8x}{8} = \dfrac{0}{8}$

$x = 0$

85. $(4x+7)-(2x-9) = 4x+7-2x+9$

$\qquad\qquad\qquad\qquad = 4x-2x+7+9$

$\qquad\qquad\qquad\qquad = 2x+16$

86. $\qquad\qquad \dfrac{2x}{x-3} = 2 + \dfrac{3}{x}$

$x(x-3)\left(\dfrac{2x}{x-3}\right) = x(x-3)\left[2+\dfrac{3}{x}\right]$

$x \cdot 2x = x(x-3)\cdot 2 + (x-3)3$

$2x^2 = 2x^2 - 6x + 3x - 9$

$9 = -3x$

$-3 = x$

87. $5x - 3y = 30$

$x = 0$	$y = 0$
$5(0) - 3y = 30$	$5x - 3(0) = 30$
$-3y = 30$	$5x = 30$
$y = -10$	$x = 6$
$(0, -10)$	$(6, 0)$

Mid-Chapter Test: 7.1-7.3

1. IV

2.

3. a. $\frac{1}{3}x + y = -2$

$$\frac{1}{3}(3) + (-3) = -2$$

$$1 - 3 = -2$$

$$-2 = -2 \text{ True}$$

b. $\frac{1}{3}x + y = -2$

$$\frac{1}{3}(0) + (2) = -2$$

$$0 + 2 = -2$$

$$2 = -2 \text{ False}$$

c. $\frac{1}{3}x + y = -2$

$$\frac{1}{3}(-6) + (0) = -2$$

$$-2 + 0 = -2$$

$$-2 = -2 \text{ True}$$

4. $y = 5x + 1$

$y = 5(-1) + 1$

$y = -5 + 1$

$y = -4$

5. $3x - 4y = 1$

$3x - 4(2) = 1$

$3x - 8 = 1$

$3x = 9$

$x = 3$

6. A graph of an equation in two variables is an illustration of a set of points whose coordinates satisfy the equation.

7.

8.

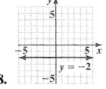

9. Let $x = -1$; $y = 3(-1) + 1 = -2$; $(-1, -2)$

Let $x = 0$; $y = 3(0) + 1 = 1$; $(0, 1)$

Let $x = 1$; $y = 3(1) + 1 = 4$; $(1, 4)$

10. Let $x = 2$; $y = -\frac{1}{2}(2) + 4 = 3$; $(2, 3)$

Let $x = 4$; $y = -\frac{1}{2}(4) + 4 = 2$; $(4, 2)$

Let $x = 6$; $y = -\frac{1}{2}(6) + 4 = 1$; $(6, 1)$

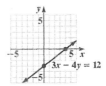

11.

Let $x = 0$	Let $y = 0$
$3(0) - 4y = 12$	$3x - 4(0) = 12$
$-4y = 12$	$3x = 12$
$y = -3$	$x = 4$

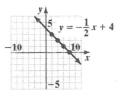

12.

Let $x = 0$	Let $y = 0$
$\frac{1}{2}(0) + \frac{1}{5}y = 10$	$\frac{1}{2}x + \frac{1}{5}(0) = 10$
$\frac{1}{5}y = 10$	$\frac{1}{2}x = 10$
$y = 50$	$x = 20$

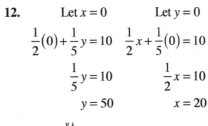

13. $m = \dfrac{3 - 5}{6 - (-1)} = -\dfrac{2}{7}$

14. $m = \dfrac{2 - 2}{7 - 4} = \dfrac{0}{-3} = 0$

15. $m = \dfrac{5-0}{-3-(-3)} = \dfrac{5}{0}$

is undefined

19. $-2x + y = -3$

$y = 2x - 3$

$m = 2$; y-intercept: $(0, -3)$

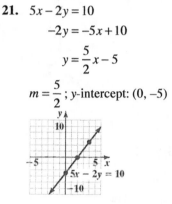

16.   **17.**

18. The lines are neither parallel nor perpendicular.

19. The lines are perpendicular because the slopes are negative reciprocals.

20. Use the points $(0, 0)$ and $(10, 100)$.

The slope is $m = \dfrac{100-0}{10-0} = \dfrac{100}{10} = 10$.

Exercise Set 7.4

1. $y = mx + b$

3. $y = 3x - 5$

5. Compare their slopes: If slopes are the same and their y-intercepts are different, the lines are parallel.

7. $y - y_1 = m(x - x_1)$

9. $m = 2$; y-intercept: $(0, -6)$

11. $m = \dfrac{4}{3}$; y-intercept: $(0, -7)$

13. $m = 1$; y-intercept: $(0, -3)$

15. $m = 3$; y-intercept: $(0, 2)$

17. $m = 2$; y-intercept: $(0, 0)$

21. $5x - 2y = 10$

$-2y = -5x + 10$

$y = \dfrac{5}{2}x - 5$

$m = \dfrac{5}{2}$; y-intercept: $(0, -5)$

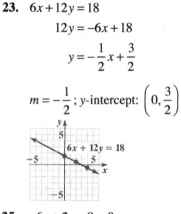

23. $6x + 12y = 18$

$12y = -6x + 18$

$y = -\dfrac{1}{2}x + \dfrac{3}{2}$

$m = -\dfrac{1}{2}$; y-intercept: $\left(0, \dfrac{3}{2}\right)$

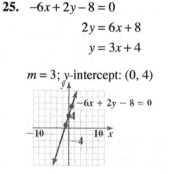

25. $-6x + 2y - 8 = 0$

$2y = 6x + 8$

$y = 3x + 4$

$m = 3$; y-intercept: $(0, 4)$

27. $3x = 2y - 4$

$-2y = -3x - 4$

$y = \dfrac{3}{2}x + 2$

$m = \dfrac{3}{2}$; y-intercept: (0, 2)

29. $m = \dfrac{4}{4} = 1$, $b = -2$

$y = x - 2$

31. $m = \dfrac{-2}{6} = -\dfrac{1}{3}$, $b = 2$

$y = -\dfrac{1}{3}x + 2$

33. $m = \dfrac{-3}{1} = -3$, $b = -5$

$y = -3x - 5$

35. $m = \dfrac{10}{30} = \dfrac{1}{3}$, $b = 5$

$y = \dfrac{1}{3}x + 5$

37. Since the slopes of the lines are the same and y-intercepts are different, the lines are parallel.

39. $4x + 2y = 7 \qquad\qquad 4x = 8y + 12$

$2y = -4x + 7 \quad -8y = -4x + 12$

$y = -2x + \dfrac{7}{2} \qquad y = \dfrac{1}{2}x - \dfrac{3}{2}$

Since the slopes of the lines are opposite reciprocals, the lines are perpendicular.

41. $3x + 5y = 9 \qquad\qquad 6x = -10y + 9$

$5y = -3x + 9 \qquad 10y = -6x + 9$

$y = -\dfrac{3}{5}x + \dfrac{9}{5} \qquad y = \dfrac{-6}{10}x + \dfrac{9}{10}$

$\qquad\qquad\qquad\qquad y = -\dfrac{3}{5}x + \dfrac{9}{10}$

Since the slopes of the lines are the same and y-intercepts are different, the lines are parallel.

43. $y = \dfrac{1}{2}x - 2 \quad 2y = 6x + 9$

$\qquad\qquad\qquad y = 3x + \dfrac{9}{2}$

Since the slopes of the lines are not equal and are not opposite reciprocals, the lines are neither parallel nor perpendicular.

45. $5y = 2x + 9 \qquad -10x = 4y + 11$

$y = \dfrac{2}{5}x + \dfrac{9}{5} \qquad -4y = 10x + 11$

$\qquad\qquad\qquad\qquad y = -\dfrac{5}{2} - \dfrac{11}{4}$

Since the slopes of the lines are opposite reciprocals, the lines are perpendicular.

47. $3x + 7y = 21 \qquad\qquad 7x + 3y = 21$

$7y = -3x + 21 \qquad 3y = -7x + 21$

$y = -\dfrac{3}{7}x + 3 \qquad y = -\dfrac{7}{3}x + 7$

Since the slopes of the lines are not equal and are not opposite reciprocals, the lines are neither parallel nor perpendicular.

49. $y - 2 = 3(x - 0)$

$y = 3x + 2$

51. $y - 5 = -3\left[x - (-4)\right]$

$y - 5 = -3(x + 4)$

$y - 5 = -3x - 12$

$y = -3x - 7$

53. $y - (-3) = \dfrac{1}{2}\left[x - (-1)\right]$

$y + 3 = \dfrac{1}{2}(x + 1)$

$y + 3 = \dfrac{1}{2}x + \dfrac{1}{2}$

$y = \dfrac{1}{2}x - \dfrac{5}{2}$

55. $y - 6 = \dfrac{2}{3}(x - 0)$

$y - 6 = \dfrac{2}{3}x$

$y = \dfrac{2}{3}x + 6$

57. $m = \dfrac{4-(-2)}{-2-(-4)} = \dfrac{6}{2} = 3$

$y-(-2) = 3\left[x-(-4)\right]$

$y+2 = 3(x+4)$

$y+2 = 3x+12$

$y = 3x+10$

59. $m = \dfrac{-12-9}{8-(-6)} = \dfrac{-21}{14} = -\dfrac{3}{2}$

$y-9 = -\dfrac{3}{2}\left(x-(-6)\right)$

$y-9 = -\dfrac{3}{2}(x+6)$

$y-9 = -\dfrac{3}{2}x-9$

$y = -\dfrac{3}{2}x$

61. $m = \dfrac{-2-3}{0-10} = \dfrac{-5}{-10} = \dfrac{1}{2}$

$y-3 = \dfrac{1}{2}(x-10)$

$y-3 = \dfrac{1}{2}x-5$

$y = \dfrac{1}{2}x-2$

63. $y-(-4.5) = 7.4(x-0)$

$y+4.5 = 7.4x$

$y = 7.4x-4.5$

65. a. $y = 5x+60$

    b. $y = 5(30)+60 = 150+60 = \$210$

67. a. Use the slope-intercept form.

    b. Use the point-slope form.

    c. Use the point-slope form but first find the slope.

69. a. No. The equations will look different because different points are used.

    b. $y-(-4) = 2\left[x-(-5)\right]$

        $y+4 = 2(x+5)$

    c. $y-12 = 2(x-3)$

d. $y+4 = 2(x+5)$

    $y+4 = 2x+10$

       $y = 2x+6$

e. $y-12 = 2(x-3)$

    $y-12 = 2x-6$

       $y = 2x+6$

f. Yes

71. a. Use the points $(0,0)$ and $(200, 293)$ and substitute into the slope formula.

$$m = \dfrac{293-0}{200-0} = \dfrac{293}{200} \approx 1.465$$

    b. Using the point-slope formula, the equation of the line is:

$$y-y_1 = m(x-x_1)$$

$$f-0 = 1.465(m-0)$$

$$f = 1.465m$$

    c. $f = 1.465m$

$$f = 1.465(142.7)$$

$$f \approx 209.06$$

The speed was 209.06 feet per second.

    d. It is about 150 feet per second.

    e. It is about 55 miles per hour.

73. First, find the slope of the line $2x+y = 6$.

$2x+y = 6$

    $y = -2x+6$

$m = -2$

Use $m = -2$ and $b = 5$ in the slope-intercept equation.

$y = -2x+5$

74. Line with points $(2, 0)$ and $(0,3)$:

$$m = \dfrac{3-0}{0-2} = \dfrac{3}{-2} = -\dfrac{3}{2}$$

Line with points $(60, 30)$ and $(20, 90)$:

$$m = \dfrac{90-30}{20-60} = \dfrac{60}{-40} = -\dfrac{3}{2}$$

$$y-30 = -\dfrac{3}{2}(x-60)$$

$$y-30 = -\dfrac{3}{2}x+90$$

$$y = -\dfrac{3}{2}x+120$$

Yes

Since slopes are the same and the
y-intercepts are different, they are parallel.

75. $3x - 4y = 6$

$$4y = 3x - 6$$

$$y = \frac{3}{4}x - \frac{3}{2}$$

$$m = \frac{3}{4}$$

$$y - (-1) = \frac{3}{4}\left[x - (-8)\right]$$

$$y + 1 = \frac{3}{4}(x + 8)$$

$$y + 1 = \frac{3}{4}x + 6$$

$$y = \frac{3}{4}x + 5$$

76. $y = x - 3$

77. a. $-3x + 2y = 4$

$$2y = 3x + 4$$

$$y = \frac{3}{2}x + 2$$

Let $x = -2$; $y = \frac{3}{2}(-2) + 2 = -1$

Let $x = 0$; $y = \frac{3}{2}(0) + 2 = 2$

Let $x = 2$; $y = \frac{3}{2}(2) + 2 = 5$

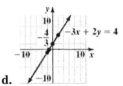

d.

78. $\left|-4\right| < \left|-9\right|$ because $4 < 9$.

79. $i = prt$

$$\frac{i}{pt} = \frac{prt}{pt}$$

$$\frac{i}{pt} = r$$

80. $2(x - 3) \geq 5x + 6$

$$2x - 6 \geq 5x + 6$$

$$-6 \geq 3x + 6$$

$$-12 \geq 3x$$

$$-4 \geq x$$

$$x \leq -4$$

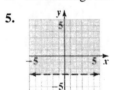

81. $x^2 - 4xy + 3xy - 12y^2 = x(x - 4y) + 3y(x - 4y)$

$$= (x - 4y)(x + 3y)$$

82. $\dfrac{x}{3} - \dfrac{3x + 2}{6} = \dfrac{1}{2}$

$$6\left(\frac{x}{3} - \frac{3x + 2}{6}\right) = 6\left(\frac{1}{2}\right)$$

$$6\left(\frac{x}{3}\right) - 6\left(\frac{3x + 2}{6}\right) = 3$$

$$2x - (3x + 2) = 3$$

$$2x - 3x - 2 = 3$$

$$-x = 5$$

$$x = -5$$

Exercise Set 7.5

1. Points on the line satisfy the = part of the inequality.

3. The shadings are on opposite sides of the line.

5. 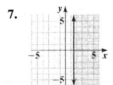

Check $(0, 0)$: $0 > -3$ Tru

7.

Check $(0, 0)$: $x \geq \dfrac{3}{2}$

$$0 \geq \frac{3}{2}$$ False

9.

Check $(1, 0)$: $y \leq 3x$

$$0 \leq 3(1)$$

$$0 \leq 3$$ True

11.

Check (0, 0): $y < x - 4$
$$0 < 0 - 4$$
$$0 < -4 \qquad \text{False}$$

13.

Check (0, 0): $y < -3x + 4$
$$0 < -3(0) + 4$$
$$0 < 4 \qquad \text{True}$$

15.

Check (0, 0): $y \geq \dfrac{1}{2}x - 4$
$$0 \geq \dfrac{1}{2}(0) - 4$$
$$0 \geq -4 \qquad \text{True}$$

17.

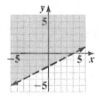

Check (0, 0): $y > \dfrac{1}{2}x - 2$
$$0 > \dfrac{1}{2}(0) - 2$$
$$0 > -2 \qquad \text{True}$$

19.

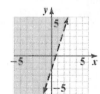

Check (0, 0): $3x - 2 < y$
$$3(0) - 2 < 0$$
$$-2 < 0 \text{ True}$$

21.

Check (0, 0): $2x + y \leq 3$
$$2(0) + 0 \leq 3$$
$$0 \leq 3 \text{ True}$$

23.

Check (0, 0): $3y > 2x - 3$
$$3(0) > 2(0) - 3$$
$$0 > -3 \text{ True}$$

25. a. $2(4) + 4(2) < 16$
$$8 + 8 < 16$$
$$16 < 16$$
No

b. $2(4) + 4(2) > 16$
$$16 > 16$$
No

c. $2(4) + 4(2) \geq 16$
$$16 \geq 16$$
Yes

d. $2(4) + 4(2) \leq 16$
$$16 \leq 16$$
Yes

27. No, the ordered pair could be a solution to $ax + by = c$.

29. No. If an ordered pair satisfies $ax + by > c$, it means the ordered pair lies on one side of the line $ax + by = c$. The ordered pair cannot lie on the other side of the line or on the line itself.

31. a. less than or equal to

b. greater than or equal to

c. less than or equal to

d. greater than or equal to

33. a. $2x - y > 4$

$$-y > -2x + 4$$

$$y < 2x - 4$$

b. $-2x + y < -4$

$$y < 2x - 4$$

c. $y < 2x - 4$

d. $-2y + 4x < -8$

$$-2y < -4x - 8$$

$$y > 2x + 4$$

After solving each inequality for y, compare the inequalities. Only (a), (b), and (c) will have the same graphs.

34. a. 2

b. $2, 0$

c. $2, -5, 0, \dfrac{2}{5}, -6.3, -\dfrac{23}{34}$

d. $\sqrt{7}, \sqrt{3}$

e. $2, -5, 0, \sqrt{7}, \dfrac{2}{5}, -6.3, \sqrt{3}, -\dfrac{23}{34}$

35. $3(x - 2) + 4x = 5x - 2$

$$3x - 6 + 4x = 5x - 2$$

$$7x - 6 = 5x - 2$$

$$2x = 4$$

$$x = 2$$

36. $\dfrac{10x^2 - 15x + 25}{5x} = \dfrac{10x^2}{5x} - \dfrac{15x}{5x} + \dfrac{25}{5x}$

$$= 2x - 3 + \dfrac{5}{x}$$

37. $\dfrac{3x}{3x^2 + 6xy} = \dfrac{3x}{3x(x + 2y)} = \dfrac{1}{x + 2y}$

Exercise Set 7.6

1. A relation is any set of ordered pairs.

3. A function is a set of ordered pairs in which each first component corresponds to exactly one second component.

5. a. The domain is the set of first components in the set of ordered pairs.

b. The range is the set of second components in the set of ordered pairs.

7. No, each x must have a unique y for it to be a function.

9. Function
Domain $\{1, 2, 3, 4, 5\}$
Range $\{1, 2, 3, 4, 5\}$

11. Relation
Domain $\{1, 2, 3, 5, 7\}$
Range $\{-2, 0, 2, 4, 5\}$

13. Function
Domain $\{0, 1, 3, 4, 5\}$
Range $\{-4, -1, 0, 1, 2\}$

15. Relation
Domain $\{0, 1, 3\}$
Range $\{-3, 0, 2, 5\}$

17. Function
Domain $\{0, 1, 2, 3, 4\}$
Range $\{3\}$

19. a. $\{(1, 4), (2, 5), (3, 5), (4, 7)\}$

b. The relation is a function; every element of the domain corresponds to exactly one element of the range.

21. a. $\{(-5, 4), (0, 7), (6, 9), (6, 3)\}$
The relation is not a function; 6, a first component, is paired with more than 1 value.

23. Function   **25.** Not a function

27. Function   **29.** Function

31. Since a vertical line drawn at $x = -1$ will intersect the graph at more than one point, the relation is not a function.

33. Function

35. a. $f(3) = 4(3) + 2 = 14$

b. $f(-1) = 4(-1) + 2 = -2$

37. a. $f(6) = 6^2 - 5 = 31$

b. $f(-3) = (-3)^2 - 5 = 4$

39. a. $f(0) = 3(0)^2 - 0 + 4 = 4$

b. $f(1) = 3(1)^2 - 1 + 4 = 6$

41. a. $f(2) = \dfrac{2 + 4}{2} = \dfrac{6}{2} = 3$

b. $f(12) = \dfrac{12 + 4}{2} = \dfrac{16}{2} = 8$

43. Let $x = 0$, $y = f(0) = 0 + 3 = 3$, $(0, 3)$

Let $x = 1$, $y = f(1) = 1 + 3 = 4$, $(1, 4)$

Let $x = 2$, $y = f(2) = 2 + 3 = 5$, $(2, 5)$

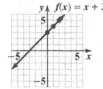

45. Let $x = -2$, $y = f(-2) = 2(-2) - 1 = -5$, $(-2, -5)$

Let $x = 0$, $y = f(0) = 2 \cdot 0 - 1 = -1$, $(0, -1)$

Let $x = 2$, $y = f(2) = 2 \cdot 2 - 1 = 3$, $(2, 3)$

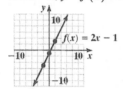

47. Let $x = 0$, $y = f(0) = -2 \cdot 0 + 4 = 4$, $(0, 4)$

Let $x = 1$, $y = f(1) = -2 \cdot 1 + 4 = 2$, $(1, 2)$

Let $x = 2$, $y = f(2) = -2 \cdot 2 + 4 = 0$, $(2, 0)$

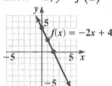

49. Let $x = 0$, $y = f(0) = -\dfrac{1}{2}(0) + 2 = 2$, $(0, 2)$

Let $x = 2$, $y = f(2) = -\dfrac{1}{2}(2) + 2 = 1$, $(2, 1)$

Let $x = 4$, $y = f(4) = -\dfrac{1}{2}(4) + 2 = 0$, $(4, 0)$

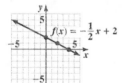

51. $c = 0.35n$

53. No, each x cannot have a unique y.

55. Yes, each year has only one value for the number registered.

57. a.

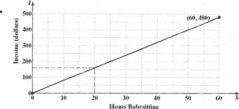

b. $160

59. a.

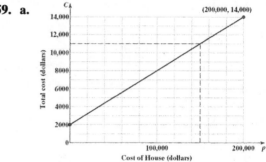

b. $11,000

61. a.

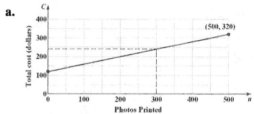

b. $240

63. a.

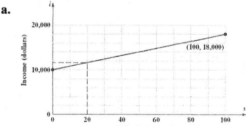

b. $11,600

65. Yes.

67. No. At $x = 1$, there are two y values: $y = 1$ and $y = 2$.

69. a. $f\left(\dfrac{1}{2}\right) = \dfrac{1}{2}\left(\dfrac{1}{2}\right)^2 - 3\left(\dfrac{1}{2}\right) + 5$

$\qquad\qquad = \dfrac{1}{8} - \dfrac{3}{2} + 5$

$\qquad\qquad = \dfrac{1}{8} - \dfrac{12}{8} + \dfrac{40}{8}$

$\qquad\qquad = \dfrac{29}{8}$

b. $f\left(\dfrac{2}{3}\right) = \dfrac{1}{2}\left(\dfrac{2}{3}\right)^2 - 3\left(\dfrac{2}{3}\right) + 5$

$\qquad\qquad = \dfrac{4}{18} - 2 + 5$

$\qquad\qquad = \dfrac{2}{9} + 3$

$\qquad\qquad = \dfrac{2}{9} + \dfrac{27}{9}$

$\qquad\qquad = \dfrac{29}{9}$

c. $f(0.4) = \dfrac{1}{2}(0.4)^2 - 3(0.4) + 5$

$\qquad\qquad = 0.08 - 1.2 + 5$

$\qquad\qquad = 3.88$

71. Answers will vary.

73. $\dfrac{4}{9} - \dfrac{3}{7} = \dfrac{28}{63} - \dfrac{27}{63} = \dfrac{1}{63}$

74. $2x - 3(x + 2) = 8$

$\qquad 2x - 3x - 6 = 8$

$\qquad\quad -x - 6 = 8$

$\qquad\qquad -x = 14$

$\qquad\qquad\ x = -14$

75. Let x = the number of additional miles.
Then

Cost $= \$2.00 + \$1.50x$

$20.00 = 2.00 + 1.50x$

$\quad 20 = 2 + 1.5x$

$\quad 18 = 1.5x$

$\quad 12 = x$

Andrew can travel 12 additional miles for a total
of 13 miles.

76. $25x^2 - 49y^2 = (5x)^2 - (7y)^2$

$\qquad\qquad\qquad\ = (5x + 7y)(5x - 7y)$

77. $\dfrac{\dfrac{28x}{y^2}}{\dfrac{7}{xy}} = \dfrac{28x}{y^2} \div \dfrac{7}{xy} = \dfrac{28x}{y^2} \cdot \dfrac{xy}{7} = \dfrac{4x^2}{y}$

78. A graph is an illustration of a set of points
whose coordinates satisfy an equation.

Review Exercises

1.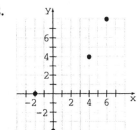

2.

The points are not collinear.

3. a. $\qquad 2x + 3y = 9$

$\qquad 2(5) + 3\left(-\dfrac{1}{3}\right) = 9$

$\qquad\qquad\quad 10 - 1 = 9$

$\qquad\qquad\qquad\quad 9 = 9$ True

b. $\qquad 2x + 3y = 9$

$\qquad 2(3) + 3(1) = 9$

$\qquad\qquad\quad 9 = 9$ True

c. $\qquad 2x + 3y = 9$

$\qquad 2(-2) + 3(4) = 9$

$\qquad\qquad\quad 8 = 9$ False

d. $\qquad 2x + 3y = 9$

$\qquad 2(2) + 3\left(\dfrac{5}{3}\right) = 9$

$\qquad\qquad\quad 9 = 9$ True

4. a. $3x - 2y = 8$ **b.** $3x - 2y = 8$
$$3(2) - 2y = 8 \qquad 3(0) - 2y = 8$$
$$-2y = 2 \qquad\qquad -2y = 8$$
$$y = -1 \qquad\qquad\quad y = -4$$

c. $3x - 2y = 8$ **d.** $3x - 2y = 8$
$$3x - 2(5) = 8 \qquad 3x - 2(0) = 8$$
$$3x - 10 = 8 \qquad\qquad 3x = 8$$
$$3x = 18 \qquad\qquad\qquad x = \frac{8}{3}$$
$$x = 6$$

5. $y = 4$ is a horizontal line with
y-intercept = $(0, 4)$.

6. $x = 2$ is a vertical line with x-intercept = $(2, 0)$.

7. Let $x = -1$, $y = 3(-1) = -3$, $(-1, -3)$
Let $x = 0$, $y = 3 \cdot 0 = 0$, $(0, 0)$
Let $x = 1$, $y = 3 \cdot 1 = 3$, $(1, 3)$

8. Let $x = 0$, $y = 2 \cdot 0 - 1 = -1$, $(0, -1)$
Let $x = 1$, $y = 2 \cdot 1 - 1 = 1$, $(1, 1)$
Let $x = 2$, $y = 2 \cdot 2 - 1 = 3$, $(2, 3)$

9. Let $x = 0$, $y = -2 \cdot 0 + 5 = 5$, $(0, 5)$
Let $x = 1$, $y = -2 \cdot 1 + 5 = 3$, $(1, 3)$
Let $x = 2$, $y = -2 \cdot 2 + 5 = 1$, $(2, 1)$

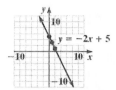

10. $2y + x = 8$
$$2y = -x + 8$$
$$y = -\frac{1}{2}x + 4$$

Let $x = 0$, $y = -\frac{1}{2}(0) + 4 = 4$, $(0, 4)$

Let $x = 2$, $y = -\frac{1}{2}(2) + 4 = 3$, $(2, 3)$

Let $x = 4$, $y = -\frac{1}{2}(4) + 4 = 2$, $(4, 2)$

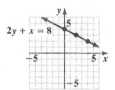

11. Let $x = 0$ Let $y = 0$
$$-2x + 3y = 6 \qquad -2x + 3y = 6$$
$$-2 \cdot 0 + 3y = 6 \qquad -2x + 3 \cdot 0 = 6$$
$$3y = 6 \qquad\qquad\quad -2x = 6$$
$$y = 2 \qquad\qquad\qquad x = -3$$

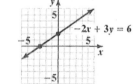

12. Let $x = 0$ Let $y = 0$
$$5x + 2y = -10 \qquad 5x + 2y = -10$$
$$5 \cdot 0 + 2y = -10 \qquad 5x + 2 \cdot 0 = -10$$
$$2y = -10 \qquad\qquad 5x = -10$$
$$y = -5 \qquad\qquad\quad x = -2$$

13. Let $x = 0$ Let $y = 0$

$5x + 10y = 20$ $5x + 10y = 20$

$5 \cdot 0 + 10y = 20$ $5x + 10 \cdot 0 = 20$

$10y = 20$ $5x = 20$

$y = 2$ $x = 4$

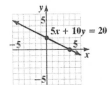

14. Let $x = 0$ Let $y = 0$

$\dfrac{2}{3}x = \dfrac{1}{4}y + 20$ $\dfrac{2}{3}x = \dfrac{1}{4}y + 20$

$\dfrac{2}{3} \cdot 0 = \dfrac{1}{4}y + 20$ $\dfrac{2}{3}x = \dfrac{1}{4} \cdot 0 + 20$

$0 = \dfrac{1}{4}y + 20$ $\dfrac{2}{3}x = 20$

$-\dfrac{1}{4}y = 20$ $x = 30$

$y = -80$

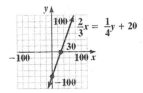

15. $m = \dfrac{5 - (-4)}{1 - 6}$

$= \dfrac{9}{-5}$

$= -\dfrac{9}{5}$

16. $m = \dfrac{-7 - (-6)}{8 - (-4)}$

$= \dfrac{-1}{12}$

$= -\dfrac{1}{12}$

17. $m = \dfrac{1 - (-3)}{-4 - (-2)}$

$= \dfrac{4}{-2}$

$= -2$

18. The slope of a horizontal line is 0.

19. The slope of a vertical line is undefined.

20. The slope of a straight line is the ratio of the vertical change to the horizontal change between any two points on the line.

21. $m = \dfrac{-6}{3} = -2$ **22.** $m = \dfrac{2}{8} = \dfrac{1}{4}$

23. Neither. For the lines to be parallel the slopes have to be the same. For the lines to be perpendicular the slopes have to be opposite reciprocals.

24. Perpendicular, because the slopes are opposite reciprocals.

25. a. $m = \dfrac{415 - 201}{1996 - 1995} = \dfrac{214}{1} = 214$

     b. $m = \dfrac{415 - 268}{1996 - 1999} = \dfrac{147}{-3} = -49$

26. $6x + 7y = 21$

$7y = -6x + 14$

$y = -\dfrac{6}{7}x + \dfrac{21}{7}$

$y = -\dfrac{6}{7}x + 3$

$m = -\dfrac{6}{7}, b = 3$

The slope is $-\dfrac{6}{7}$; the y-intercept is $(0, 3)$.

27. $2x + 7 = 0$

$2x = -7$

$x = -\dfrac{7}{2}$

This is a vertical line, so the slope is undefined and there is no y-intercept.

28. $4y + 12 = 0$

$4y = -12$

$y = -3$

This is a horizontal line, so the slope is 0 and the y-intercept is $(0, -3)$.

29. $m = \dfrac{3}{1} = 3, b = -3$

$y = 3x - 3$

30. $m = \dfrac{-2}{4} = -\dfrac{1}{2}, b = 2$

$y = -\dfrac{1}{2}x + 2$

31. $y = 2x - 7$ $6y = 12x + 18$

                $y = 2x + 3$

Since the slopes are the same and the y-intercepts are different, the lines are parallel.

32. $2x - 3y = 15$ $3x + 2y = 12$

$-3y = -2x + 15$ $2y = -3x + 12$

$y = \dfrac{2}{3}x - 5$ $y = -\dfrac{3}{2}x + 6$

Since the slopes are opposite reciprocals, the lines are perpendicular.

33. $y - 7 = 3(x - 2)$

$y - 7 = 3x - 6$

$y = 3x + 1$

34. $y - 2 = -\dfrac{2}{3}(x - 3)$

$y - 2 = -\dfrac{2}{3}x + 2$

$y = -\dfrac{2}{3}x + 4$

35. $y - 2 = 0(x - 6)$

$y - 2 = 0$

$y = 2$

36. Lines with undefined slopes are vertical and have the form $x = c$ where c is the value of x for any point on the line.

$x = 4$

37. $m = \dfrac{-3 - 4}{0 - (-2)} = \dfrac{-7}{2} = -\dfrac{7}{2}$

$y - (-3) = -\dfrac{7}{2}[x - 0]$

$y + 3 = -\dfrac{7}{2}x$

$y = -\dfrac{7}{2}x - 3$

38. $m = \dfrac{3 - (-2)}{-5 - (-5)} = \dfrac{5}{0}$ is undefined

Lines with undefined slopes are vertical and have the form $x = c$ where c is the value of x for any point on the line.

$x = -5$

39.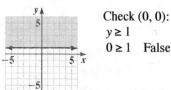

Check $(0, 0)$:

$y \ge 1$

$0 \ge 1$ False

40.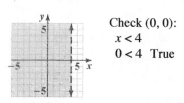

Check $(0, 0)$:

$x < 4$

$0 < 4$ True

41.

Check $(1, -1)$:

$y < 3x$

$-1 < 3 \cdot 1$

$-1 < 3$ True

42.

Check $(0, 0)$:

$y > 2x + 1$

$0 > 2(0) + 1$

$0 > 1$ False

43.

Check $(0, 0)$:

$-6x + y \ge 5$

$-6(0) + 0 \ge 5$

$0 \ge 5$ False

44.

Check $(0, 0)$:

$3y + 6 \le x$

$3(0) + 6 \le 0$

$6 \le 0$ False

45. Function
Domain $\{1, 2, 3, 4, 6\}$
Range $\{-3, -1, 2, 4, 5\}$

46. Not a function
Domain $\{3, 4, 6, 7\}$
Range $\{0, 1, 2, 5\}$

47. Not a function
Domain $\{3, 4, 5, 6\}$
Range $\{-3, 1, 2\}$

48. Function
Domain $\{-2, 3, 4, 5, 9\}$
Range $\{-2\}$

49. a. $\{(1, 3), (4, 5), (7, 2), (9, 2)\}$

b. The relation is a function; every element of the domain corresponds to exactly one element of the range.

50. a. {(4, 1), (6, 3), (6, 5), (8, 7)}

    b. The relation is not a function; 6 is paired with more than 1 value.

51. a. Domain: {Mary, Pete, George, Carlos}
Range: {Apple, Orange, Grape}

    b. Not a function.

52. a. Domain: {Sarah, Jacob, Kristen, Erin}
Range: {Seat 1, Seat 2, Seat 3, Seat 4}

    b. Not a function.

53. a. Domain: {Blue, Green , Yellow}
Range: {Paul, Maria, Lalo, Duc}

    b. Function

54. a. Domain: {1, 2, 3, 4}
Range: {A, B, C}

    b. Function

55. Function   **56.** Function

57. Since a vertical line at $x = 0$ will intersect the graph more than once, the graph is not a function.

58. Function

59. a. $f(1) = 6 \cdot 1 - 1 = 6 - 1 = 5$

    b. $f(-5) = 6 \cdot (-5) - 1 = -30 - 1 = -31$

60. a. $f(-4) = -4(-4) - 7 = 16 - 7 = 9$

    b. $f(8) = -4 \cdot 8 - 7 = -32 - 7 = -39$

61. a. $f(3) = \frac{1}{3}(3) - 5 = 1 - 5 = -4$

    b. $f(-9) = \frac{1}{3}(-9) - 5 = -3 - 5 = -8$

62. a. $f(3) = 2 \cdot 3^2 - 4 \cdot 3 + 6 = 12$

    b. $f(-5) = 2(-5)^2 - 4(-5) + 6 = 76$

63. Yes, it is a function since each year has only one value of net income.

64. Yes, it is a function since it passes the vertical line test.

65. Let $x = 0$, $y = f(0) = 3 \cdot 0 - 5 = -5$, $(0, -5)$
Let $x = 1$, $y = f(1) = 3 \cdot 1 - 5 = -2$, $(1, -2)$
Let $x = 2$, $y = f(2) = 3 \cdot 2 - 5 = 1$, $(2, 1)$

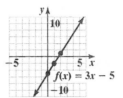

66. Let $x = 0$, $y = f(0) = -2 \cdot 0 + 3 = 3$, $(0, 3)$
Let $x = 1$, $y = f(1) = -2 \cdot 1 + 3 = 1$, $(1, 1)$
Let $x = 2$, $y = f(2) = -2 \cdot 2 + 3 = -1$, $(2, -1)$

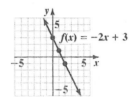

67.a.

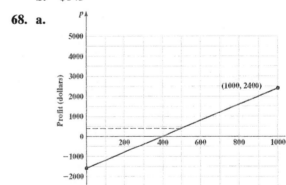

    b. $145

68. a.

    b. $400

Practice Test

1. A graph is an illustration of the set of points that satisfy an equation.

2. a. IV   **b.** II

3. a. $ax + by = c$

b.　$y = mx + b$

c.　$y - y_1 = m(x - x_1)$

4. a.　$3y = 5x - 9$

$$3(2) = 5(4) - 9$$
$$6 = 20 - 9$$
$$6 = 11 \qquad \text{False}$$

b.　$3y = 5x - 9$

$$3(0) = 5\left(\frac{9}{5}\right) - 9$$
$$0 = 9 - 9$$
$$0 = 0 \qquad \text{True}$$

c.　$3y = 5x - 9$

$$3(-10) = 5(-1) - 9$$
$$-30 = -5 - 9$$
$$-30 = -14 \qquad \text{False}$$

d.　$3y = 5x - 9$

$$3(-3) = 5(0) - 9$$
$$-9 = -9 \qquad \text{True}$$

$\left(\dfrac{9}{5}, 0\right)$ and $(0, -3)$ satisfy the equation.

5.　$m = \dfrac{-3 - 5}{4 - (-2)} = \dfrac{-8}{6} = -\dfrac{4}{3}$

6.　$4x - 9y = 15$

$$-9y = -4x + 15$$
$$y = \frac{4}{9}x - \frac{5}{3}$$
$$m = \frac{4}{9}, \; b = -\frac{5}{3}$$

The slope is $\dfrac{4}{9}$; the y-intercept is $\left(0, -\dfrac{5}{3}\right)$.

7.　$m = \dfrac{-1}{1} = -1$, $b = -1$

$$y = -x - 1$$

8.　$x = -4$ is a vertical line with x-intercept $= (-4, 0)$.

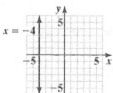

9.　$y = 2$ is a horizontal line with y-intercept $= (0, 2)$.

10.　Let $x = 0$, $y = 3 \cdot 0 - 2 = -2$, $(0, -2)$

Let $x = 1$, $y = 3 \cdot 1 - 2 = 1$, $(1, 1)$

Let $x = 2$, $y = 3 \cdot 2 - 2 = 4$, $(2, 4)$

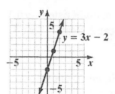

11. a.　$3x - 6y = 12$

$$-6y = -3x + 12$$
$$y = \frac{1}{2}x - 2$$

b.　Let $x = 0$, $y = \dfrac{1}{2}(0) - 2 = -2$, $(0, -2)$

Let $x = 2$, $y = \dfrac{1}{2}(2) - 2 = -1$, $(2, -1)$

Let $x = 4$, $y = \dfrac{1}{2}(4) - 2 = 0$, $(4, 0)$

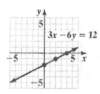

12.　$3x + 5y = 15$

Let $x = 0$ 　　　　 Let $y = 0$

$3(0) + 5y = 15$ 　　 $3x + 5(0) = 15$

$5y = 15$ 　　　　　 $3x = 15$

$y = 3$ 　　　　　　 $x = 5$

13.　$y - (-5) = 4(x - 2)$

$$y + 5 = 4x - 8$$
$$y = 4x - 13$$

14. $m = \dfrac{2-(-1)}{-4-3} = \dfrac{3}{-7} = -\dfrac{3}{7}$

$y-(-1) = -\dfrac{3}{7}(x-3)$

$y+1 = -\dfrac{3}{7}x + \dfrac{9}{7}$

$y = -\dfrac{3}{7}x + \dfrac{2}{7}$

15. $2y = 3x - 6 \quad y - \dfrac{3}{2}x = -5$

$y = \dfrac{3}{2}x - 3 \qquad y = \dfrac{3}{2}x - 5$

The lines are parallel since they have the same slope but different y-intercepts.

16. slope $= 3$, y-intercept is $(0, -4)$.

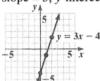

17. $4x - 2y = 6$

$-2y = -4x + 6$

$y = 2x - 3$

Slope $= 2$, y intercept is $(0, -3)$.

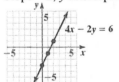

18. A function is a set of ordered pairs in which each first component corresponds to exactly one second component.

19. a. The relation is not a function; 1, a first component, is paired with more than 1 value.

    b. Domain $\{1, 3, 5, 6\}$
        Range $\{-4, 0, 2, 3, 5\}$

20. a. The graph is a function because it passes the vertical line test.

    b. The graph is not a function because a vertical line can be drawn that intersects the graph at more than one point.

21. a. $f(2) = 2(2)^2 + 3(2) + 1$

        $= 8 + 6 + 1$

        $= 15$

b. $f(-3) = 2(-3)^2 + 3(-3) + 1$

     $= 18 - 9 + 1$

     $= 10$

22. Let $x = 0$, $y = f(0) = 2 \cdot 0 - 4 = -4$, $(0, -4)$
    Let $x = 1$, $y = f(1) = 2 \cdot 1 - 4 = -2$, $(1, -2)$
    Let $x = 2$, $y = f(2) = 2 \cdot 2 - 4 = 0$, $(2, 0)$

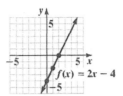

23.

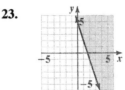

Check $(0, 0)$: $y \geq -3x + 5$

               $0 \geq -3(0) + 5$

                  $0 \geq 5$ False

24.

Check $(0, 0)$: $y < 4x - 2$

               $0 < 4(0) - 2$

                $0 < -2$ False

25. a.

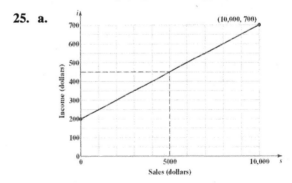

    b. $\$450$

Cumulative Review Test

1. a. $\{1, 2, 3, \ldots\}$

    b. $\{0, 1, 2, 3, \ldots\}$

2. a. Distributive Property

  b. Commutative Property of Addition

3. $2x + 5 = 3(x - 5)$

  $2x + 5 = 3x - 15$

  $-x + 5 = -15$

  $-x = -20$

  $x = 20$

4. $3(x - 1) - (x + 4) = 2x - 7$

  $3x - 3 - x - 4 = 2x - 7$

  $2x - 7 = 2x - 7$

  $0 = 0$

  All real numbers are solutions.

5. $2x - 14 > 5x + 1$

  $-3x > 15$

  $x < -5$

6. $\dfrac{3 \text{ cans}}{\$1.50} = \dfrac{8 \text{ cans}}{x \text{ dollars}}$

  $\dfrac{3}{1.50} = \dfrac{8}{x}$

  $3x = 12$

  $x = \dfrac{12}{3} = 4$

  8 cans sell for $4.00.

7. Let x = width of rectangle.
  Then $2x + 3$ = length of rectangle.
  $P = 2l + 2w$

  $36 = 2(2x + 3) + 2x$

  $36 = 4x + 6 + 2x$

  $36 = 6x + 6$

  $30 = 6x$

  $5 = x$

  The width is 5 feet and the length is
  $2(5) + 3 = 13$ feet.

8. Let x = number of hours until the runners are 28 miles apart.

Runner	Rate	Time	Distance
First	6 mph	x	$6x$
Second	8 mph	x	$8x$

(Distance run by first runner) + (Distance run by second runner) = 28 miles

$6x + 8x = 28$

$14x = 28$

$x = 2$

It will take 2 hours.

9. $\dfrac{x^{-4}}{x^{11}} = x^{-4-11} = x^{-15} = \dfrac{1}{x^{15}}$

10. $652.3 = 6.523 \times 10^2$

11. $2x^2 - 12x + 10 = 2(x^2 - 6x + 5)$

  $\qquad\qquad\qquad = 2(x - 5)(x - 1)$

12. $4a^2 + 4a - 35 = (2a - 5)(2a + 7)$

13. $\qquad\quad 3x^2 = 21x$

  $3x^2 - 21x = 0$

  $3x(x - 7) = 0$

  $3x = 0 \quad$ or $\quad x - 7 = 0$

  $x = 0 \quad$ or $\qquad x = 7$

14. $\dfrac{2r - 7}{14 - 4r} = \dfrac{2r - 7}{-2(2r - 7)} = -\dfrac{1}{2}$

15. $\dfrac{\cancel{x - 2}}{3x + 7} \cdot \dfrac{8x}{\cancel{x - 2}} = \dfrac{8x}{3x + 7}$

16. $\qquad\qquad \dfrac{y^2}{y - 6} = \dfrac{36}{y - 6}$

  $(y - 6)\left(\dfrac{y^2}{y - 6}\right) = \left(\dfrac{36}{y - 6}\right)(y - 6)$

  $\qquad\qquad\quad y^2 = 36$

  $\qquad\qquad y^2 - 36 = 0$

  $\qquad (y + 6)(y - 6) = 0$

  $y + 6 = 0 \quad$ or $\quad y - 6 = 0$

  $\quad y = -6 \qquad\qquad y = 6$

  $y = 6$ is an extraneous solution since $\dfrac{y}{y - 6}$ and

  $\dfrac{36}{y - 6}$ are undefined when $y = 6$. The only

  solution is $y = -6$.

17. $6x - 3y = -12$

Let $x = 0$ Let $y = 0$

$6(0) - 3y = -12$ $6x - 3(0) = -12$

$\qquad -3y = -12 \qquad\qquad 6x = -12$

$\qquad\qquad y = 4 \qquad\qquad\qquad x = -2$

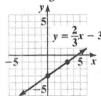

18. Slope $= \dfrac{2}{3}$, y intercept is $(0, -3)$

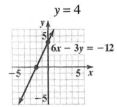

19. $y - 2 = 3(x - 5)$

20. a. The relation is not a function; it does not pass the vertical line test.

    b. The relation is a function; each first component corresponds to exactly one second component.

Chapter 8

Exercise Set 8.1

1. The solution to a system of equations represents the ordered pairs that satisfy all the equations in the system.

3. Write the equations in slope-intercept form and compare their slopes and y-intercepts.

5. The point of intersection can only be estimated.

7. a.

$$y = 3x - 6 \qquad\qquad y = -3x$$
$$0 = 3(2) - 6 \qquad\quad 0 = -3(2)$$
$$0 = 6 - 6 \qquad\qquad 0 = -6 \;\; \text{False}$$
$$0 = 0 \;\; \text{True}$$

Since $(2, 0)$ does not satisfy both equations, it is not a solution to the system of equations.

b.

$$y = 3x - 6$$
$$0 = 3(0) - 6$$
$$0 = -6 \;\; \text{False}$$

Since $(0, 0)$ does not satisfy the first equation, it is not a solution to the system of equations.

c.

$$y = 3x - 6 \qquad\qquad y = -3x$$
$$-3 = 3(1) - 6 \qquad\quad -3 = -3(1)$$
$$-3 = 3 - 6 \qquad\qquad -3 = -3 \;\; \text{True}$$
$$-3 = -3 \;\; \text{True}$$

Since $(1, -3)$ satisfies both equations, it is a solution to the system of equations.

9. a.

$$y = 2x - 3 \qquad\qquad y = x + 5$$
$$13 = 2(8) - 3 \qquad\quad 13 = 8 + 5$$
$$13 = 13 \;\; \text{True} \qquad 13 = 13 \;\; \text{True}$$

Since $(8, 13)$ satisfies both equations, it is a solution to the system.

b.

$$y = 2x - 3 \qquad\qquad y = x + 5$$
$$5 = 2(4) - 3 \qquad\quad 5 = 4 + 5$$
$$5 = 5 \;\; \text{True} \qquad\;\; 5 = 9 \;\; \text{False}$$

Since $(4, 5)$ does not satisfy both equations, it is not a solution to the system.

c.

$$y = 2x - 3 \qquad\qquad y = x + 5$$
$$7 = 2(5) - 3 \qquad\quad 7 = 5 + 5$$
$$7 = 7 \;\; \text{True} \qquad\;\; 7 = 10 \;\; \text{False}$$

Since $(5, 7)$ does not satisfy both equations, it is not a solution to the system

11. a.

$$4x + y = 15 \qquad\qquad 5x + y = 10$$
$$4(3) + 3 = 15 \qquad\quad 5(3) + 3 = 10$$
$$15 = 15 \;\; \text{True} \qquad 18 = 10 \;\; \text{False}$$

Since $(3, 3)$ does not satisfy both equations, it is not a solution to the system.

b.

$$4x + y = 15$$
$$4(2) + (0) = 15$$
$$8 = 15 \;\; \text{False}$$

Since $(2, 0)$ does not satisfy the first equation, it is not a solution to the system.

c.

$$4x + y = 15 \qquad\qquad 5x + y = 10$$
$$4(-1) + 19 = 15 \qquad 5(-1) + 19 = 10$$
$$15 = 15 \qquad\qquad\quad 14 = 10$$
$$\text{True} \qquad\qquad\qquad \text{False}$$

Since $(-1, 19)$ does not satisfy both equations, it is not a solution to the system.

13. Solve the first equation for y.
$$4x - 6y = 12$$
$$-6y = -4x + 12$$
$$y = \frac{2}{3}x - 2$$

Notice that it is the same as the second equation. If the ordered pair satisfies the first equation, then it also satisfies the second equation.

a.

$$4x - 6y = 12$$
$$4(3) - 6(0) = 12$$
$$12 = 12 \;\; \text{True}$$

Since $(3, 0)$ satisfies both equations, it is a solution to the system.

b. $4x - 6y = 12$

$4(9) - 6(4) = 12$

$12 = 12$ True

Since (9, 4) satisfies both equations, it is a solution to the system.

c. $4x - 6y = 12$

$4(6) - 6(1) = 12$

$18 = 12$ False

Since (6, 1) does not satisfy the first equation, it is not a solution to the system.

15. a. $3x - 4y = 8$

$3(0) - 4(-2) = 8$

$8 = 8$ True

$2y = \dfrac{2}{3}x - 4$

$2(-2) = \dfrac{2}{3}(0) - 4$

$-4 = -4$ True

Since (0, –2) satisfies both equations, it is a solution to the system.

b. $3x - 4y = 8$

$3(1) - 4(-6) = 8$

$27 = 8$ False

Since (1, –6) does not satisfy the first equation, it is not a solution to the system.

c. $3x - 4y = 8$

$3\left(-\dfrac{1}{3}\right) - 4\left(-\dfrac{9}{4}\right) = 8$

$8 = 8$ True

$2y = \dfrac{2}{3}x - 4$

$2\left(-\dfrac{9}{4}\right) = \dfrac{2}{3}\left(-\dfrac{1}{3}\right) - 4$

$-\dfrac{9}{2} = -\dfrac{38}{9}$ False

Since $\left(-\dfrac{1}{3}, -\dfrac{9}{4}\right)$ does not satisfy both equations, it is not a solution to the system.

17. consistent—one solution

19. dependent—infinite number of solutions

21. consistent—one solution

23. inconsistent—no solution

25. Write each equation in slope-intercept form.

$y = 2x - 1 \qquad 3y = 5x - 6$

$\qquad\qquad\qquad y = \dfrac{5}{3}x - 2$

Since the slopes of the lines are not the same, the lines intersect to produce one solution. This is a consistent system.

27. Write each equation in slope-intercept form.

$2y = 3x + 3$

$y = \dfrac{3}{2}x + \dfrac{3}{2} \qquad y = \dfrac{3}{2}x - 2$

Since the lines have the same slope, $\dfrac{3}{2}$, and different y-intercepts, the lines are parallel. There is no solution. This is an inconsistent system.

29. Write each equation in slope-intercept form.

$3x = 3y + 5$

$2x = y - 6 \qquad\quad 3y = 3x - 5$

$y = 2x + 6$

$\qquad\qquad\qquad y = x - \dfrac{5}{3}$

Since the slopes of the lines are not the same, the lines intersect to produce one solution. This is a consistent system.

31. Write each equation in slope-intercept form.

$3x + 5y = -7 \qquad\quad -3x - 5y = -10$

$5y = -3x - 7 \qquad\quad -5y = 3x - 10$

$y = -\dfrac{3}{5}x - \dfrac{7}{5} \qquad y = -\dfrac{3}{5}x + 2$

Since the lines have the same slope and different y-intercepts, the lines are parallel. There is no solution. This is an inconsistent system.

33. Write each equation in slope-intercept form.

$x = 3y + 5 \qquad\qquad 2x - 6y = 10$

$x - 5 = 3y \qquad\qquad -6y = -2x + 10$

$\dfrac{1}{3}x - \dfrac{5}{3} = y \qquad\quad y = \dfrac{1}{3}x - \dfrac{5}{3}$

Since both equations are identical, the line is the same for both of them. There are an infinite number of solutions. This is a dependent system.

35. Write each equation in slope-intercept form.

$3x - 2y = \dfrac{5}{2}$

$y = \dfrac{3}{2}x + \dfrac{1}{2} \qquad -2y = -3x - \dfrac{5}{2}$

$\qquad\qquad\qquad y = \dfrac{3}{2}x + \dfrac{5}{4}$

Since the lines have the same slope and different

y-intercepts, the lines are parallel. There is no solution. This is an inconsistent system.

37. Graph the equations $y = x + 3$ and $y = -x + 3$.

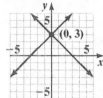

The lines intersect and the point of intersection is (0, 3). This is a consistent system.

39. Graph the equations $y = 3x - 6$ and $y = -x + 6$.

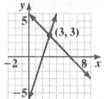

The lines intersect and the point of intersection is (3, 3). This is a consistent system.

41. Graph the equations $4x = 8$ or $x = 2$ and $y = -3$.

The lines intersect and the point of intersection is (2, –3). This is a consistent system.

43. Graph the equations $x + y = 5$ or $y = -x + 5$ and $-x + y = 1$ or $y = x + 1$.

The lines intersect and the point of intersection is (2, 3). This is a consistent system.

45. Graph the equations $y = -\dfrac{1}{2}x + 4$ and

$x + 2y = 6$ or $y = -\dfrac{1}{2}x + 3$.

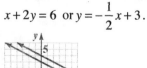

The lines are parallel. The system is inconsistent and there is no solution.

47. Graph the equations $x + 2y = 8$ or $y = -\dfrac{1}{2}x + 4$

and $5x + 2y = 0$ or $y = -\dfrac{5}{2}x$.

The lines intersect and the point of intersection is (–2, 5). This is a consistent system.

49. Graph the equations $2x + 3y = 6$ or

$y = -\dfrac{2}{3}x + 2$ and $4x = -6y + 12$

or $y = -\dfrac{2}{3}x + 2$.

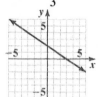

The lines are identical. There are an infinite number of solutions. This is a dependent system.

51. Graph the equations $y = 3$ and $y = 2x - 3$.

The lines intersect and the point of intersection is (3, 3). This is a consistent system.

53. Graph the equations $x - 2y = 4$ or $y = \dfrac{1}{2}x - 2$

and $2x - 4y = 8$ or $y = \dfrac{1}{2}x - 2$.

The lines are identical. There are an infinite number of solutions. This is a dependent system.

55. Graph the equations $2x + y = -2$ or $y = -2x - 2$ and $6x + 3y = 6$ or $y = -2x + 2$.

The lines are parallel. The system is inconsistent and there is no solution.

57. Graph the equations $4x - 3y = 6$ or $y = \frac{4}{3}x - 2$

and $2x + 4y = 14$ or $y = -\frac{1}{2}x + \frac{7}{2}$.

The lines intersect and the point of intersection is $(3, 2)$. This is a consistent system.

59. Graph the equations $2x - 3y = 0$ or $y = \frac{2}{3}x$ and

$x + 2y = 0$ or $y = -\frac{1}{2}x$.

The lines intersect and the point of intersection is $(0, 0)$. This is a consistent system.

61. Write each equation in slope-intercept form.

$\begin{aligned} 6x - 4y &= 12 \\ -4y &= -6x + 12 \\ y &= \frac{3}{2}x - 3 \end{aligned}$ $\begin{aligned} 12y &= 18x - 24 \\ y &= \frac{3}{2}x - 2 \end{aligned}$

The lines are parallel because they have the same slope, $\frac{3}{2}$, and different y-intercepts.

63. The system has an infinite number of solutions. If the two lines have two points in common then they must be the same line.

65. The system has no solutions. Distinct parallel lines do not intersect.

67. $x = 5$, $y = 3$ has one solution, $(5, 3)$.

69. (repair) $c = 600 + 650n$
     (replacement) $c = 1800 + 450n$

Graph the equations and determine the intersection.

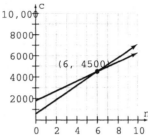

The solution is $(6, 4500)$. Therefore, the total cost of repair equals the total cost of replacement at 6 years.

71. $c = 25h$

$c = 21h + 28$
Graph the equations and determine the intersection.

The solution $(6, 150)$. Therefore, the boats must be rented for 6 hours for the cost to be the same.

73. 0

75. 2

77. 3

79. $\begin{aligned} 7x - (x - 6) + 4(3 - x) &= 7x - x + 6 + 12 - 4x \\ &= 7x - x - 4x + 6 + 12 \\ &= 2x + 18 \end{aligned}$

80. $\begin{aligned} 2(x + 3) - x &= 5x + 2 \\ 2x + 6 - x &= 5x + 2 \\ x + 6 &= 5x + 2 \\ -4x &= -4 \\ x &= 1 \end{aligned}$

81. $\dfrac{x^2 - 9x + 14}{2 - x} = \dfrac{(x - 7)(x - 2)}{-(x - 2)} = -(x - 7)$

82. $\dfrac{2}{b} + b = \dfrac{19}{3}$

$3b\left(\dfrac{2}{b} + b\right) = 3b\left(\dfrac{19}{3}\right)$

$6 + 3b^2 = 19b$

$3b^2 - 19b + 6 = 0$

$(3b - 1)(b - 6) = 0$

$3b - 1 = 0$ or $b - 6 = 0$

$b = \dfrac{1}{3}$ $b = 6$

83. a. For the x-intercept, set $y = 0$.

$$2x + 3y = 12$$
$$2x + 3(0) = 12$$
$$2x = 12$$
$$x = 6$$

The x-intercept is $(6, 0)$.

For the y-intercept, set $x = 0$.

$$2x + 3y = 12$$
$$2(0) + 3y = 12$$
$$3y = 12$$
$$y = 4$$

The y-intercept is $(0, 4)$.

b.

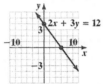

Exercise Set 8.2

1. The x in the first equation, since both 6 and 12 are divisible by 3.

3. You will obtain a false statement, such as $3 = 0$.

5. $x + 2y = 6$

$2x - 3y = 5$

Solve the first equation for x, $x = 6 - 2y$.

Substitute $6 - 2y$ for x in the second equation.

$$2(6 - 2y) - 3y = 5$$
$$12 - 4y - 3y = 5$$
$$-7y = -7$$
$$y = 1$$

Substitute 1 for y in the equation $x = 6 - 2y$.

$$x = 6 - 2(1)$$
$$x = 4$$

The solution is $(4, 1)$.

7. $x + y = -2$

$x - y = 0$

Solve the first equation for y, $y = -2 - x$.

Substitute $-2 - x$ for y in the second equation.

$$x - (-2 - x) = 0$$
$$x + 2 + x = 0$$
$$2x = -2$$
$$x = -1$$

Substitute -1 for x in the equation $y = -2 - x$.

$$y = -2 - (-1)$$
$$y = -2 + 1$$
$$y = -1$$

The solution is $(-1, -1)$.

9. $3x + y = 3$

$3x + y + 5 = 0$

Solve the first equation for y, $y = -3x + 3$.

Substitute $-3x + 3$ for y in the second equation.

$$3x + y + 5 = 0$$
$$3x - 3x + 3 + 5 = 0$$
$$8 = 0 \text{ False}$$

There is no solution.

11. $x = 3$

$x + y + 5 = 0$

Substitute 3 for x in the second equation.

$$x + y + 5 = 0$$
$$3 + y + 5 = 0$$
$$y = -8$$

The solution is $(3, -8)$.

13. $x = y + 1$

$4x + 2y = -14$

Substitute $y + 1$ for x in the second equation.

$$4x + 2y = -14$$
$$4(y + 1) + 2y = -14$$
$$4y + 4 + 2y = -14$$
$$6y + 4 = -14$$
$$6y = -18$$
$$y = \frac{-18}{6} = -3$$

Now, substitute -3 for y in the first equation.

$$x = y + 1$$
$$x = -3 + 1$$
$$x = -2$$

The solution is $(-2, -3)$.

15. $2x + y = 11$

$y = 3x - 4$

Substitute $3x - 4$ for y in the first equation.

$$2x + y = 11$$
$$2x + 3x - 4 = 11$$
$$5x - 4 = 11$$
$$5x = 15$$
$$x = 3$$

Now substitute 3 for x in the second equation.

$y = 3x - 4$

$y = 3(3) - 4$

$y = 9 - 4$

$y = 5$

The solution is (3, 5).

17. $y = \dfrac{1}{3}x - 2$

$x - 3y = 6$

Substitute $\dfrac{1}{3}x - 2$ for y in the second equation.

$x - 3y = 6$

$x - 3\left(\dfrac{1}{3}x - 2\right) = 6$

$x - x + 6 = 6$

$6 = 6$

Since this is a true statement, there are an infinite number of solutions. This is a dependent system.

19. $2x + 5y = 9$

$6x - 2y = 10$

First solve the second equation for y.

$\dfrac{1}{2}(6x - 2y) = \dfrac{1}{2}(10)$

$3x - y = 5$

$y = 3x - 5$

Now substitute $3x - 5$ for y in the first equation.

$2x + 5y = 9$

$2x + 5(3x - 5) = 9$

$2x + 15x - 25 = 9$

$17x = 34$

$x = 2$

Finally substitute 2 for x in the equation $y = 3x - 5$.

$y = 3(2) - 5$

$y = 6 - 5$

$y = 1$

The solution is (2, 1).

21. $y = 2x - 13$

$-4x - 7 = 9y$

Substitute $2x - 13$ for y in the second equation.

$-4x - 7 = 9y$

$-4x - 7 = 9(2x - 13)$

$-4x - 7 = 18x - 117$

$-22x - 7 = -117$

$-22x = -110$

$x = \dfrac{-110}{-22} = 5$

Now substitute 5 for x in the first equation.

$y = 2x - 13$

$y = 2(5) - 13$

$y = 10 - 13$

$y = -3$

The solution is (5, -3).

23. $4x - 5y = -4$

$3x = 2y - 3$

First solve the second equation for x.

$\dfrac{1}{3}(3x) = \dfrac{1}{3}(2y - 3)$

$x = \dfrac{2}{3}y - 1$

Now substitute $\dfrac{2}{3}y - 1$ for x in the first equation.

$4x - 5y = -4$

$4\left(\dfrac{2}{3}y - 1\right) - 5y = -4$

$\dfrac{8}{3}y - 4 - 5y = -4$

$\dfrac{8}{3}y - \dfrac{15}{3}y = 0$

$-\dfrac{7}{3}y = 0$

$y = 0$

Finally substitute 0 for y in the equation $x = \dfrac{2}{3}y - 1$.

$x = \dfrac{2}{3}(0) - 1$

$x = -1$

The solution is (-1, 0).

25. $4x + 5y = -6$

$2x - \dfrac{10}{3}y = -4$

First solve the second equation for x,

$$2x - \frac{10}{3}y = -4$$

$$3\left(2x - \frac{10}{3}y\right) = 3(-4)$$

$$6x - 10y = -12$$

$$6x = 10y - 12$$

$$x = \frac{5}{3}y - 2$$

Now substitute $\frac{5}{3}y - 2$ for x in the first

equation.

$$4x + 5y = -6$$

$$4\left(\frac{5}{3}y - 2\right) + 5y = -6$$

$$\frac{20}{3}y - 8 + 5y = -6$$

$$\frac{20}{3}y + \frac{15}{3}y = 8 - 6$$

$$\frac{35}{3}y = 2$$

$$y = \frac{6}{35}$$

Finally, substitute $\frac{9}{37}$ for y in the

equation $x = \frac{5}{3}y - 2$.

$$x = \frac{5}{3}\left(\frac{6}{35}\right) - 2$$

$$x = \frac{2}{7} - \frac{14}{7}$$

$$x = -\frac{12}{7}$$

The solution is $\left(-\frac{12}{7}, \frac{6}{35}\right)$.

27. $\quad 3x - 4y = 15$

$-6x + 8y = -14$

First solve the second equation for y,

$-6x + 8y = -14$

$$8y = 6x - 14$$

$$y = \frac{3}{4}x - \frac{7}{4}$$

Now substitute $\frac{3}{4}x - \frac{7}{4}$ for y in the first

equation.

$$3x - 4\left(\frac{3}{4}x - \frac{7}{4}\right) = 15$$

$$3x - 3x + 7 = 15$$

$$7 = 15 \quad \text{False}$$

Since this is a false statement, there is no
solution to this system.

29. $\quad 4x - y = 1$

$$10x + \frac{1}{2}y = 1$$

Solve the first equation for y.

$y = 4x - 1$

Now substitute $4x - 1$ for y in the second
equation.

$$10x + \frac{1}{2}(4x - 1) = 1$$

$$10x + 2x - \frac{1}{2} = 1$$

$$12x - \frac{1}{2} = 1$$

$$12x = \frac{3}{2}$$

$$\frac{1}{12}(12x) = \frac{1}{12}\left(\frac{3}{2}\right)$$

$$x = \frac{1}{8}$$

Now substitute $\frac{1}{8}$ for x in the first equation;

$$y = 4x - 1$$

$$y = 4\left(\frac{1}{8}\right) - 1$$

$$y = \frac{1}{2} - 1$$

$$y = -\frac{1}{2}$$

The solution to the system is $\left(\frac{1}{8}, -\frac{1}{2}\right)$.

31. Let x = the smaller number,
then y = the larger number.

$x + y = 80$

$x + 8 = y$

Substitute $x + 8$ for y in the first equation.

$$x + y = 80$$

$$x + (x + 8) = 80$$

$$2x + 8 = 80$$

$$2x = 72$$

$$x = 36$$

Now substitute 36 for x in the second equation:

$x + 8 = y$

$36 + 8 = y$

$44 = y$

The two integers are 36 and 44.

33. Let l = the length of the rectangle, then w = the width.

$2l + 2w = 50$

$l = 9 + w$

Substitute $9 + w$ for l in the first equation and solve for w.

$2l + 2w = 50$

$2(9 + w) + 2w = 50$

$18 + 2w + 2w = 50$

$4w = 32$

$w = 8$

Now substitute 8 for w in the second equation to find l.

$l = 9 + w$

$l = 9 + 8$

$l = 17$

The length of the rectangle is 17 feet and the width is 8 feet.

35. Let f = the number of attendees who paid the full fee and d = the number of attendees who received the discount.

$f + d = 2500$

$d = f - 622$

Substitute $f - 622$ for d in the first equation.

$f + d = 2500$

$f + (f - 622) = 2500$

$2f - 622 = 2500$

$2f = 3122$

$f = 1561$

Now substitute 1561 for f in the second equation and solve for d.

$d = f - 622$

$d = 1561 - 622$

$d = 939$

The number of attendees who paid the full amount was 1561 and then 939 got the discount fee.

37. Let c = the client's portion of the award and a = the attorneys portion.

$c + a = 40,000$

$c = 3a$

Now solve the first equation for a and substitute it for a in the second equation.

$c + a = 40000$

$a = 40000 - c$

$c = 3a$

$c = 3(40000 - c)$

$c = 120,000 - 3c$

$4c = 120,000$

$c = 30,000$

The client received \$30,000.

39. $c = 1280 + 794n$

$c = 874n$

a. Substitute $874n$ for c in the first equation.

$874n = 1280 + 794n$

$80n = 1280$

$n = 16$

The mortgage plans will have the same total cost at 16 months.

b. $12 \text{ years} \cdot \left(\dfrac{12 \text{ months}}{1 \text{ year}} \right) = 144 \text{ months}$

$c = 1280 + 794(144) = 115,616$

$c = 874(144) = 125,856$

Yes, since \$115,616 is less than \$125,856, she should refinance.

41. a. Substitute $65 + 72t$ for m in the first equation and solve for t.

$65 + 72t = 80 + 60t$

$12t = 15$

$t = \dfrac{15}{12} = 1.25$

It will take Roberta 1.25 hours to catch up to Jean.

Now substitute 1.25 for t
in one of the original equtions.

b. $m = 80 + 60(1.25)$

$m = 80 + 75$

$m = 155$

They will be at mile marker 155 when they meet.

43. a. $T = 180 - 10t$

b. $T = 20 + 6t$

c. $T = 180 - 10t$

$T = 20 + 6t$

Substitute $20 + 6t$ for T in the first equation.
$20 + 6t = 180 - 10t$

$16t = 160$

$t = 10$

It will take 10 minutes for the ball and oil to reach the same temperature.

d. Substitute 10 for t in one of the original equations.

$T = 180 - 10t$

$T = 180 - 10(10)$

$T = 180 - 100$

$T = 80$

The temperature will be 80°F.

45. $\dfrac{27.6}{1.2} = 23$

The willow tree is about 23 years old.

46. $(6x + 7)(3x - 2) = 18x^2 - 12x + 21x - 14$

$\qquad\qquad\qquad\quad = 18x^2 + 9x - 14$

47. $4x - 8y = 16$

Let $x = 0$ and solve for y.
$4(0) - 8y = 16$

$y = -2$

Let $y = 0$ and solve for x.
$4x - 8(0) = 16$

$x = 4$

The intercepts are $(0, -2)$ and $(4, 0)$.

48. $3x - 5y = 25$

Write in slope-intercept form.

$-5y = -3x + 25$

$y = \dfrac{3}{5}x - 5$

The slope is $\dfrac{3}{5}$ and the y intercept is $(0, -5)$.

49. Find the slope of the line using points $(-2, 0)$ and $(0, 4)$.

$m = \dfrac{4 - 0}{0 - (-2)} = \dfrac{4}{2} = 2$

The y-intercept is 4, therefore $b = 4$.
$y = mx + b$
$y = 2x + 4$ is the equation of the line

Exercise Set 8.3

1. Multiply the top equation by 2.
Now the top equation contains a $-2x$ and the bottom equation contains a $2x$. When the equations are added together, the variable x will be eliminated.

3. You will obtain a false statement, such as $0 = 6$

5. $x + y = 6$

$\underline{x - y = 4}$

Add: $2x \quad = 10$

$x = 5$

Substitute 5 for x in the first equation.
$x + y = 6$
$5 + y = 6$

$y = 1$

The solution is $(5, 1)$.

7. Add: $x + y = 9$

$\underline{-x + y = 1}$

$2y = 10$

$y = 5$

Substitute 5 for y in the first equation.
$x + y = 9$
$x + 5 = 9$

$x = 4$

The solution is $(4, 5)$.

9. Add: $x + 2y = 21$

$\underline{2x - 2y = -6}$

$3x \qquad = 15$

$x = 5$

Substitute 5 for x in the first equation.

$$x + 2y = 21$$
$$5 + 2y = 21$$
$$2y = 16$$
$$y = 8$$
The solution is (5, 8).

11. $\quad 4x + y = 6 \quad (eq. 1)$

$\quad -8x - 2y = 20 \quad (eq. 2)$

Multiply the first equation by 2, then add to the second equation.
$$2[4x + y = 6]$$
gives
$$8x + 2y = 12$$
$$\underline{-8x - 2y = 20}$$
$$0 = 32 \quad \text{False}$$
There is no solution.

13. $\quad -5x + y = 14 \quad (eq. 1)$

$\quad -3x + y = -2 \quad (eq. 2)$

To eliminate y, multiply the first equation by -1 and then add.
$$-1[-5x + y = 14]$$
gives
$$5x - y = -14$$
$$\underline{-3x + y = -2}$$
$$2x \quad\quad = -16$$
$$x = -8$$
Substitute -8 for x in the first equation.
$$-5x + y = 14$$
$$-5(-8) + y = 14$$
$$40 + y = 14$$
$$y = -26$$
The solution is $(-8, -26)$.

15. $\quad 2x + \quad y = -6$

$\quad 2x - 2y = \quad 3$

To eliminate y, multiply the first equation by 2 and then add.
$$2[2x + y = -6]$$
gives
$$4x + 2y = -12$$
$$\underline{2x - 2y = \quad 3}$$
$$6x \quad\quad = -9$$
$$x = -\frac{3}{2}$$
Substitute $-\frac{3}{2}$ for x in the first equation.

$$2x + y = -6$$
$$2\left(-\frac{3}{2}\right) + y = -6$$
$$-3 + y = -6$$
$$y = -3$$
The solution is $\left(-\frac{3}{2}, -3\right)$.

17. $\quad 2y = 6x + 16 \quad (eq. 1)$

$\quad y = -3x - 4 \quad (eq. 2)$

Rewrite the equations to align the variables on the left hand side of the equal sign.
$$-6x + 2y = 16$$
$$3x + y = -4$$
To eliminate x, multiply the second equation by 2, then add.
$$2[3x + y = -4]$$
gives
$$-6x + 2y = 16$$
$$\underline{6x + 2y = -8}$$
$$4y = 8$$
$$y = 2$$
Substitute 2 for y in the second equation.
$$3x + y = -4$$
$$3x + 2 = -4$$
$$3x = -6$$
$$x = -2$$
The solution is $(-2, 2)$.

19. $\quad 5x + 3y = 12 \quad (eq. 1)$

$\quad 3x - 6y = 15 \quad (eq. 2)$

To eliminate y, multiply the first equation by 2 and then add.
$$2[5x + 3y = 12]$$
gives
$$10x + 6y = 24$$
$$\underline{3x - 6y = 15}$$
$$13x \quad\quad = 39$$
$$x = 3$$
Substitute 3 for x in the first equation.
$$5x + 3y = 12$$
$$5(3) + 3y = 12$$
$$15 + 3y = 12$$
$$3y = -3$$
$$y = -1$$
The solution is $(3, -1)$.

21. $-2y = -4x + 12$

$y = 2x - 6$

Align x- and y-terms on the left side.

$4x - 2y = 12$ $(eq. 1)$

$-2x + y = -6$ $(eq. 2)$

To eliminate x, multiply the second equation by 2 and then add.

$2[-2x + y = -6]$

gives

$4x - 2y = 12$

$\underline{-4x + 2y = -12}$

$ 0 = 0$

Since this is a true statement, there are an infinite number of solutions. This is a dependent system.

23. $5x - 4y = -3$

$7y = 2x + 12$

Align x- and y-terms on the left side.

$5x - 4y = -3$ $(eq. 1)$

$-2x + 7y = 12$ $(eq. 2)$

To eliminate x, multiply the first equation by 2 and the second equation by 5 and then add.

$2[5x - 4y = -3]$

$5[-2x + 7y = 12]$

gives

$10x - 8y = -6$

$\underline{-10x + 35y = 60}$

$ 27y = 54$

$ y = 2$

Substitute 2 for y in the first equation.

$5x - 4y = -3$

$5x - 4(2) = -3$

$5x - 8 = -3$

$5x = 5$

$x = 1$

The solution is (1, 2).

25. $5x - 4y = 1$ $(eq. 1)$

$-10x + 8y = -3$ $(eq. 2)$

Multiply the first equation by 2, then add.

$2[5x - 4y = 1]$

gives

$10x - 8y = 1$

$\underline{-10x + 8y = -3}$

$ 0 = -2$ False

There is no solution.

27. $5x - 6y = 0$ $(eq. 1)$

$3x + 4y = 0$ $(eq. 2)$

To eliminate y, multiply the first equation by 3 and the second equation by -5 and then add.

$3[5x - 6y = 0]$

$-5[3x + 4y = 0]$

gives

$15x - 18y = 0$

$\underline{-15x - 20y = 0}$

$ -38y = 0$

$ y = 0$

Substitute 0 for y in the second equation.

$3x + 4y = 0$

$3x + 4(0) = 0$

$3x = 0$

$x = 0$

The solution is (0, 0).

29. $-5x + 4y = -20$ $(eq. 1)$

$3x - 2y = 15$ $(eq. 2)$

To eliminate y, multiply the second equation by 2, then add.

$2[3x - 2y = 15]$

gives

$-5x + 4y = -20$

$\underline{6x - 4y = 30}$

$x = 10$

Substitute 10 for x in the first equation.

$-5x + 4y = -20$

$-5(10) + 4y = -20$

$-50 + 4y = -20$

$4y = 30$

$y = \dfrac{15}{2}$

The solution is $\left(10, \dfrac{15}{2}\right)$.

31. $6x = 4y + 12$

$3y - 5x = -6$

Align the x- and y-terms on the left side.

$6x - 4y = 12$

$5x - 3y = 6$

To eliminate x, multiply the first equation by 5 and the second equation by -6 and then add.

$5(6x - 4y = 12)$

$-6(5x - 3y = 6)$

gives

$$30x - 20y = 60$$
$$-30x + 18y = -36$$
$$\overline{ -2y = 24}$$
$$y = -12$$

Substitute -12 for y in the first equation.

$$6x - 4y = 12$$
$$6x - 4(-12) = 12$$
$$6x + 48 = 12$$
$$6x = -36$$
$$x = -6$$

The solution is $(-6, -12)$.

33. $4x + 5y = 0$

$3x = 6y + 4$

Align the x- and y-terms on the left side.

$4x + 5y = 0$

$3x - 6y = 4$

To eliminate y, multiply the first equation by 6 and the second equation by 5 and then add.

$6[4x + 5y = 0]$

$5[3x - 6y = 4]$

gives

$$24x + 30y = 0$$
$$15x - 30y = 20$$
$$\overline{39x = 20}$$
$$x = \frac{20}{39}$$

Substitute $\frac{20}{39}$ for x in the first equation.

$$4x + 5y = 0$$
$$4\left(\frac{20}{39}\right) + 5y = 0$$
$$5y = -\frac{80}{39}$$
$$y = -\frac{16}{39}$$

The solution is $\left(\frac{20}{39}, -\frac{16}{39}\right)$.

35. $x - \dfrac{1}{2}y = 4$

$3x + y = 6$

To eliminate y, multiply the first equation by 2 and then add.

$2\left[x - \dfrac{1}{2}y = 4\right]$

gives

$$2x - y = 8$$
$$3x + y = 6$$
$$\overline{5x = 14}$$
$$x = \frac{14}{5}$$

Substitute $\dfrac{14}{5}$ for x in the second equation.

$$3x + y = 6$$
$$3\left(\frac{14}{5}\right) + y = 6$$
$$\frac{42}{5} + y = 6$$
$$y = 6 - \frac{42}{5}$$
$$y = \frac{30}{5} - \frac{42}{5}$$
$$y = -\frac{12}{5}$$

The solution is $\left(\dfrac{14}{5}, -\dfrac{12}{5}\right)$.

37. $3x - y = 4$

$2x - \dfrac{2}{3}y = 8$

To eliminate y, multiply the first equation by $-\dfrac{2}{3}$ and then add.

$-\dfrac{2}{3}[3x - y = 4]$

gives

$$-2x + \frac{2}{3}y = \frac{8}{3}$$
$$2x - \frac{2}{3}y = 8$$
$$\overline{0 = \frac{32}{3}} \quad \text{False}$$

There is no solution.

39.   Add: $x + y = 20$

$$\underline{x - y = 8}$$
$$2x = 28$$
$$x = 14$$

Substitute 14 for x in the first equation to find the second number.

$$x + y = 20$$
$$14 + y = 20$$
$$y = 6$$

The numbers are 14 and 6.

41. $x + 2y = 14$

$x - y = 2$

To eliminate y, multiply the second equation by 2 and then add.

$$2[x - y = 2]$$

gives

$$x + 2y = 14$$
$$\underline{2x - 2y = 4}$$
$$3x = 18$$
$$x = 6$$

Substitute 6 for x in the second equation to find the other number.

$$x - y = 2$$
$$6 - y = 2$$
$$y = 4$$

The numbers are 6 and 4.

43. Let x be the length of the rectangle and y be the width.

$$2x + 2y = 18$$
$$\underline{x = 2y}$$

Align the x and y variables on the left hand side of the equal sign.

$$2x + 2y = 18$$
$$\underline{x - 2y = 0}$$

Now add the equations to eliminate the y.

$$3x = 18$$
$$x = 6$$

Substitute 6 for x in the second equation and solve for y.

$$x = 2y$$
$$6 = 2y$$
$$3 = y$$

The width is 3 inches and the length is 6 inches.

45. Let l = the length and w = the width of the photograph.

$$2l + 2w = 36$$
$$\underline{l - w = 2}$$

Multiply the second equation by 2

$$2[l - w = 2]$$

gives

$$2l + 2w = 36$$
$$\underline{2l - 2w = 4}$$
$$4l = 40$$
$$l = 10$$
$$10 - w = 2$$
$$w = 8$$

The length is 10 inches and the width is 8 inches.

47. Answers will vary.

49. a.

$$4x + 2y = 1000$$
$$2x + 4y = 800$$

To eliminate x, multiply the first equation by -2.

$$-2[4x + 2y = 1000]$$

gives

$$-8x - 4y = -2000$$
$$\underline{2x + 4y = 800}$$
$$-6x = -1200$$
$$x = 200$$

Substitute 200 for x in the first equation.

$$4x + 2y = 1000$$
$$4(200) + 2y = 1000$$
$$800 + 2y = 1000$$
$$2y = 200$$
$$y = 100$$

The solution is (200, 100).

b. They will have the same solution. Dividing an equation by a nonzero number does not change the solutions.

$$2x + y = 500$$
$$2x + 4y = 800$$

To eliminate x, multiply the first equation by -1 and then add.

$$-1[2x + y = 500]$$

gives

$$-2x - y = -500$$
$$\underline{2x + 4y = 800}$$
$$3y = 300$$
$$y = 100$$

Substitute 100 for y in the first equation.

$$2x + y = 500$$
$$2x + 100 = 500$$
$$2x = 400$$
$$x = 200$$

The solution is (200, 100).

51.　$\dfrac{x+2}{2} - \dfrac{y+4}{3} = 4$

$\dfrac{x+y}{2} = \dfrac{1}{2} + \dfrac{x-y}{3}$

Start by writing each equation in standard form after clearing fractions.
For the first equation:

$$6\left[\dfrac{x+2}{2} - \dfrac{y+4}{3} = 4\right]$$

$3(x+2) - 2(y+4) = 24$

$3x + 6 - 2y - 8 = 24$

$3x - 2y - 2 = 24$

$3x - 2y = 26$

For the second equation:

$$6\left[\dfrac{x+y}{2} = \dfrac{1}{2} + \dfrac{x-y}{3}\right]$$

$3(x+y) = 3 + 2(x-y)$

$3x + 3y = 3 + 2x - 2y$

$x + 5y = 3$

The new system is:

$3x - 2y = 26$

$x + 5y = 3$

To eliminate x, multiply the second equation by -3 and then add.

$-3[x + 5y = 3]$

gives

$3x - 2y = 26$

$\underline{-3x - 15y = -9}$

$-17y = 17$

$y = -1$

Now, substitute -1 for y in the equation $x + 5y = 3$.

$x + 5(-1) = 3$

$x - 5 = 3$

$x = 8$

The solution is $(8, -1)$.

53.　$x + 2y - z = 2$

$2x - y + z = 3$

$3x + y + z = 8$

Add the second and third equations to eliminate y.

$2x - y + z = 3$

$\underline{3x + y + z = 8}$

$5x + 2z = 11$

Multiply the second equation by 2 and then add the first equation to eliminate y.

$2[2x - y + z = 3]$

gives

$4x - 2y + 2z = 6$

$\underline{x + 2y - z = 2}$

$5x + z = 8$

Now we have two equations with two unknowns.

$5x + 2z = 11$

$5x + z = 8$

To eliminate z, multiply the second equation by -2 and then add.

$-2[5x + z = 8]$

gives

$5x + 2z = 11$

$\underline{-10x - 2z = -16}$

$-5x = -5$

$x = 1$

Substitute 1 for x in the second equation and solve for z

$5x + z = 8$

$5(1) + z = 8$

$5 + z = 8$

$z = 3$

Now go back to one of the original equations and substitute 1 for x and 3 for z and then find y.
The third equation is used below.

$3x + y + z = 8$

$3(1) + y + 3 = 8$

$3 + y + 3 = 8$

$y + 6 = 8$

$y = 2$

The solution to the system is $(1, 2, 3)$.

55.　$5^3 = 5 \cdot 5 \cdot 5 = 125$

56.　$2(2x - 5) = 2x + 4$

$4x - 10 = 2x + 4$

$4x - 2x = 10 + 4$

$2x = 14$

$x = 7$

57.　$\left(4x^2y - 3xy + y\right) - \left(2x^2y + 6xy - 7y\right)$

$= 4x^2y - 3xy + y - 2x^2y - 6xy + 7y$

$= 4x^2y - 2x^2y - 3xy - 6xy + y + 7y$

$= 2x^2y - 9xy + 8y$

58. $\left(9a^4b^2c\right)\left(4a^2b^7c^4\right)$

$= 9 \cdot 4 \cdot a^4 \cdot a^2 \cdot b^2 \cdot b^7 \cdot c \cdot c^4$

$= 36a^{4+2}b^{2+7}c^{1+4}$

$= 36a^6b^9c^5$

59. $xy + xc - ay - ac$

$= x(y+c) - a(y+c)$

$= (y+c)(x-a)$

60. $f(x) = 2x^2 - 13$

$f(3) = 2(3)^2 - 13$

$\quad\quad = 2(9) - 13$

$\quad\quad = 18 - 13$

$\quad\quad = 5$

$f(3) = 5$

Mid-Chapter Test: Sections 8.1-8.3

1. **a.** $(-1, 1)$

$4(-1) + 3(1) = -1$

$-4 + 3 = -1$

$-1 = -1$

$-1 - 2(1) = 8$

$-1 - 2 = 8$

$-3 = 8$ False

$(-1, 1)$ is not a solution.

b. $(2, -3)$

$4(2) + 3(-3) = -1$

$8 - 9 = -1$

$-1 = -1$

$2 - 2(-3) = 8$

$2 + 6 = 8$

$8 = 8$ True

$(2, -3)$ is a solution.

2. **a.** $\left(\frac{1}{2}, 5\right)$

$6\left(\frac{1}{2}\right) - 5 = -2$

$3 - 5 = -2$

$-2 = -2$

$7\left(\frac{1}{2}\right) + \frac{1}{2}(5) = 6$

$\frac{7}{2} + \frac{5}{2} = 6$

$6 = 6$ True

$\left(\frac{1}{2}, 5\right)$ is a solution.

b. $\left(\frac{1}{3}, 4\right)$

$6\left(\frac{1}{3}\right) - 4 = -2$

$2 - 4 = -2$

$-2 = -2$

$7\left(\frac{1}{3}\right) + \frac{1}{2}(4) = 6$

$\frac{7}{3} + 2 = 6$

$\frac{13}{3} = 6$ False

$\left(\frac{1}{3}, 4\right)$ is not a solution.

3. Solve each equation for y.

$\quad 2x + y = 8 \quad\quad\quad\quad 3x - 4y = 1$

$\quad\quad y = -2x + 8 \quad\quad\quad -4y = -3x + 1$

$\quad\quad\quad\quad\quad\quad\quad\quad\quad\quad y = \frac{3}{4}x - \frac{1}{4}$

Since the equations have different slopes the system will have one solution.

4. Solve each equation for y.

$\quad \frac{1}{2}x - 3y = 5 \quad\quad\quad\quad -2x + 12y = -20$

$\quad\quad -3y = -\frac{1}{2}x + 5 \quad\quad\quad 12y = 2x - 20$

$\quad\quad\quad\quad y = \frac{1}{6}x - \frac{5}{3} \quad\quad\quad\quad y = \frac{1}{6}x - \frac{5}{3}$

Since both equations are the same, the system has infinite solutions.

5. Solve each equation for y.

$$y = \frac{3}{2}x + \frac{5}{2} \qquad 3x - 2y = 7$$
$$-2y = -3x + 7$$
$$y = \frac{3}{2}x - \frac{7}{2}$$

Since the two equations have the same slope but different y-intercepts, the lines are parallel which means there is no solution.

6. $y = 2x + 1$ has slope of 2 and y-intercept of 1.

$y = -x + 4$ has slope of -1 and y-intercept of 4.

The solution is $(1, 3)$.

7. $x = 5$ is a vertical line passing through 5 on the x–axis. $y = -3$ is a horizontal line passing through -3 on the y-axis.

The solution is $(5, -3)$

8. $3x + y = -2$

$2x - 3y = -16$

Solve the first equation for y, $y = -3x - 2$.

Substitute $-3x - 2$ for y in the second equation.
$$2x - 3(-3x - 2) = -16$$
$$2x + 9x + 6 = -16$$
$$11x + 6 = -16$$
$$11x = -22$$
$$x = -2$$

To find y, substitute -2 for x in the equation $y = -3x - 2$.
$$y = -3(-2) - 2$$
$$y = 6 - 2$$
$$y = 4$$

The solution is $(-2, 4)$.

9. $x - 3y = 2$

$4x + 9y = 1$

Solve the first equation for x, $x = 3y + 2$.

Substitute $-3x - 2$ for x in the second equation.
$$4(3y + 2) + 9y = 1$$
$$12y + 8 + 9y = 1$$
$$21y + 8 = 1$$
$$21y = -7$$
$$y = -\frac{1}{3}$$

To find x, substitute $-\frac{1}{3}$ for y in the equation
$$x = 3\left(-\frac{1}{3}\right) + 2.$$
$$x = -1 + 2$$
$$x = 1$$

The solution is $\left(1, -\frac{1}{3}\right)$.

10. $3x - y = 5$

$x - \frac{1}{3}y = 2$

Solve the second equation for x, $x = \frac{1}{3}y + 2$.

Substitute $\frac{1}{3}y + 2$ for x in the first equation.
$$3\left(\frac{1}{3}y + 2\right) - y = 5$$
$$y + 2 - y = 5$$
$$2 = 5 \quad \text{False}$$

Since this is a false statement the system has no solution.

11. Let l be the length of the rectangle and w be its width.

$$2l + 2w = 44$$
$$l = w + 8$$

Substitute $w + 8$ for l in the first equation and solve for w.
$$2(w + 8) + 2w = 44$$
$$2w + 16 + 2w = 44$$
$$4w + 16 = 44$$
$$4w = 28$$
$$w = 7$$

Now substitute 7 for w in the equation $l = w + 8$.

$l = 7 + 8 = 15$.

The length of the rectangle is 15 feet and the width is 7 feet.

12. $x + 3y = 1$

$\underline{2x - 3y = 11}$

$3x \qquad = 12$

$x = 4$

Substitute 4 for x in the first equation and then find y.

$4 + 3y = 1$

$3y = -3$

$y = -1$

The solution is $(4, -1)$.

13. $4x + 3y = 4 \quad (eq. 1)$

$-8x + 5y = 14 \quad (eq. 2)$

Multiply equation 1 by 2 giving $2[4x + 3y = 4]$. Now add the two equations to eliminate x and solve for y.

$8x + 6y = 8$

$\underline{-8x + 5y = 14}$

$11y = 22$

$y = 2$

Substitute 2 for y in equation 1 and solve for x.

$4x + 3(2) = 4$

$4x + 6 = 4$

$4x = -2$

$x = -\dfrac{1}{2}$

The solution is $\left(-\dfrac{1}{2}, 2\right)$.

14. $5x - 2y = 1 \quad (eq. 1)$

$-10x + 4y = -2 \quad (eq. 2)$

Multiply equation 1 by 2 giving $2[5x - 2y = 1]$. Now add the two equations.

$10x - 4y = 2$

$\underline{-10x + 4y = -2}$

$0 = 0$

The system has an infinite number of solutions.

15. A system's solution has to have two values, one for x and one for y.

$3x - 5y = -16 \quad (eq. 1)$

$2x + 3y = 21 \quad (eq. 2)$

Multiply equation 1 by 3 and equation 2 by 5, then add to eliminate y and solve for x.

$3(3x - 5y = -16)$

$\underline{5(2x + 3y = 21)}$

$9x - 15y = -48$

$\underline{10x + 15y = 105}$

$19x = 57$

$x = 3$

Substitute 3 for x in equation 2 and solve for y.

$2(3) + 3y = 21$

$6 + 3y = 21$

$3y = 15$

$y = 5$

The solution is $(3, 5)$.

Exercise Set 8.4

1. Let x and y be the integers, with x the larger integer.

$x + y = 43$

$x = y + 9$

Substitute $y + 9$ for x in the first equation.

$(y + 9) + y = 43$

$2y + 9 = 43$

$2y = 34$

$y = \dfrac{34}{2} = 17$

$x = y + 9$

$x = 17 + 9$

$x = 26$

The integers are 17 and 26.

3. $A + B = 90$

$B = A + 18$

Substitute $A + 18$ for B in the first equation.

$A + (A + 18) = 90$

$2A + 18 = 90$

$2A = 72$

$A = \dfrac{72}{2} = 36$

$B = A + 18$

$B = 36 + 18$

$B = 54$

The angles are $A = 36°$ and $B = 54°$.

5. $A + B = 180$

$A = B + 44$

Substitute $B + 44$ for A in the first equation.

$(B+44)+B=180$

$2B+44=180$

$2B=136$

$B=68$

$A=B+48$

$A=68+44$

$A=112$

The angles are $A=112°$ and $B=68°$.

7. Let w = the width of the flag

l = the length of the flag

The formula for the perimeter of the flag is $P=2w+2l$.

$2w+2l=2260$

$l=w+350$

Substitute $w+350$ for l in the first equation.

$2w+2l=2260$

$2w+2(w+350)=2260$

$2w+2w+700=2260$

$4w=1560$

$w=390$

$l=w+350$

$l=390+350$

$l=740$

The width of the flag is 390 feet and the length is 740 feet.

9. Let p = the population

y = the number of years that have passed

For Birch Mountain, $p=40,000+800y$, while for Hidden Valley, $p=67,000-550y$. Set the two populations equal.

$40,000+800y=67,000-550y$

$1350y=27,000$

$y=20$

The populations of both areas will be the same after 20 years.

11. Let k = the speed of the kayak

c = the speed of the current

$k+c=4.7$

$\underline{k-c=3.4}$

$2k=8.1$

$k=4.05$

$k+c=4.7$

$4.05+c=4.7$

$c=0.65$

The speed of the kayak in still water is

4.05 miles per hour and the speed of the current is 0.65 miles per hour.

13. Let c = number of acres of corn

w = number of acres of wheat

$c+w=100$

$450c+430w=49,000$

Solve the first equation for w.

$w=100-c$

Substitute $100-c$ for w in the second equation.

$500c+475(100-c)=49,0000$

$500c+47,500-475c=49,000$

$25c+47,500=49,000$

$25c=1500$

$c=\dfrac{1500}{25}=60$

$w=100-c$

$w=100-60$

$w=40$

She planted 60 acres of corn and 40 acres of wheat.

15. Let a = the number of adult tickets purchased

c = the number of children's tickets purchased

$a+c=27$

$40a+30c=930$

Solve the first equation for c.

$c=27-a$

Substitute it in for c in the second equation.

$40a+30(27-a)=930$

$40a+810-30a=930$

$10a+810=930$

$10a=120$

$a=12$

Substitute 12 for a in the first equation to find c.

$a+c=27$

$12+c=27$

$c=15$

There were 12 adult tickets and 15 children's tickets purchased.

17. **a.** Let n = the number of copies

c = the monthly cost

With the Kate Spence Company, $c=18+0.02n$, while with Office Copier Depot, $c=25+0.015n$. Set the monthly costs equal

$18+0.02n=25+0.015n$

$0.005n=7$

$n=1400$

When 1400 copies are made, the monthly costs of both plans are the same.

b. With Kate Spence Company:
$$c = 18 + 0.02(2500)$$
$$c = 18 + 50$$
$$c = 68$$
With Office Copier Depot:
$$c = 25 + 0.015(2500)$$
$$c = 25 + 37.5$$
$$c = 62.5$$
When 2500 copies are made, it is less expensive to get the service contract from Office Copier Depot.

19. Let x = the amount giving 5% interest
y = the amount giving 4% interest
$$x + y = 8000$$
$$0.05x + 0.04y = 375$$
Eliminate the decimal numbers.
$$x + y = 8000$$
$$5x + 4y = 37,500$$
Multiply the first equation by –4.
$$-4[x + y = 8000]$$
$$5x + 4y = 37,500$$
gives
$$-4x - 4y = -32,000$$
$$\underline{5x + 4y = 37,500}$$
$$x = 5500$$
$$x + y = 8000$$
$$5500 + y = 8000$$
$$y = 2500$$
They invested $5500 at 5%, and $2500 at 4%.

21. a. Let y = the number of yards of carpet
c = the total cost of the carpet
At Carpet U.S.A., $c = 200 + 20y$, while at Tom Taylor's National Carpet Stores, $c = 260 + 16y$. Set the two costs equal.
$$200 + 20y = 260 + 16y$$
$$4y = 60$$
$$y = 15$$
The total cost of the carpet is the same at both stores when 15 square yards are purchased.

b. Carpet U.S.A.:
$$c = 200 + 20(25)$$
$$= 200 + 500$$
$$= 700$$
Tom Taylor's:
$$c = 260 + 16(25)$$
$$= 260 + 400$$
$$= 660$$
The total cost of 25 square yards of carpet is less at Tom Taylor's National Carpet Stores.

23. Let d = Dave's speed
a = Alice's speed
The distance that Dave has traveled after 7 hours is $7d$ and the distance that Alice has traveled is $7a$. These distances add up to 903 miles.
$$7d + 7a = 903$$
$$a = d + 15$$
Substitute $d + 15$ for a in the first equation.
$$7d + 7(d + 15) = 903$$
$$7d + 7d + 105 = 903$$
$$14d = 798$$
$$d = 57$$
$$a = d + 15$$
$$a = 57 + 15$$
$$a = 72$$
Dave's speed is 57 miles per hour and Alice's speed is 72 miles per hour.

25. Let e = the speed of Elizabeth's boat
m = the speed of Melissa's boat
If d is the distance that both boats travel, then $d = 3e$ and $d = 3.4m$.
$$e = m + 4$$
$$3e = 3.4m$$
Multiply the first equation by –3.
$$-3[e = m + 4]$$
$$3e = 3.4m$$
gives
$$-3e = -3m - 12$$
$$\underline{3e = 3.4m}$$
$$0 = 0.4m - 12$$
$$12 = 0.4m$$
$$30 = m$$
$$e = m + 4$$
$$e = 30 + 4$$
$$e = 34$$
The speed of Elizabeth's boat is 34 miles per

hour and the speed of Melissa's boat is 30 miles per hour.

27. Let a = time that Amanda jogs

d = time that Dolores jogs

The distance that Amanda jogs is $5a$ and the distance that Dolores jogs is $8d$.

$5a = 8d$

$a = d + 1.2$

Substitute $d + 1.2$ for a in the first equation.

$5(d + 1.2) = 8d$

$5d + 5 = 8d$

$6 = 3d$

$2 = d$

Dolores will catch up to Amanda when Dolores has been jogging for 2 hours.

29. Let t = the amount of time it took Randy to catch up to Terri

r = the distance that Terri and Randy traveled

Traveler	Rate	Time	Distance
Terri	5	$0.75 + t$	r
Randy	10.5	t	r

$5(0.75 + t) = r$

$10.5t = r$

Substitute 10.5 for r in the first equation.

$5(0.75 + t) = 10.5t$

$3.75 + 5t = 10.5t$

$3.75 = 5.5t$

$.68 \approx t$

They met after about 0.68 hours.

31. Let x = amount of 15% solution

y = amount of 40% solution

Solution	Number of Liters	Concentration	Acid Content
15% solution	x	0.15	$0.15x$
40% solution	y	0.40	$0.40y$
Mixture	20	0.30	0.30(20)

$x + y = 20$

$0.15x + 0.40y = 6$

Solve the first equation for x.

$x = 20 - y$

Substitute $20 - y$ for x in the second equation.

$0.15(20 - y) + 0.40y = 6$

$3 - 0.15y + 0.40y = 6$

$0.25y = 3$

$y = 12$

$x = 20 - y$

$x = 20 - 12$

$x = 8$

She must use 8 liters of the 15% solution and 12 liters of the 40% solution.

33. Let x = the number of $3 tiles
$\quad\quad y$ = the number of $5 tiles
$\quad\quad x + y = 380$

$3x + 5y = 1500$

Solve the first equation for x.
$x = 380 - y$

Substitute $380 - y$ for x in the second equation.

$3(380 - y) + 5y = 1500$

$1140 - 3y + 5y = 1500$

$\quad\quad\quad\quad\quad 2y = 360$

$\quad\quad\quad\quad\quad\ y = 180$

She can purchase at most 180 of the $5 tiles.

35. Let x = the amount of 5% butterfat milk
$\quad\quad y$ = the amount of skim milk

Milk	Number of Gallons	Percentage butterfat	Butterfat Content
5% butterfat	x	0.05	0.05x
skim	y	0	0
Mixture	200	0.035	0.035(200)

$x + y = 200$

$0.05x = 7$

From the second equation, $x = 140$.

$\quad\quad x + y = 200$

$140 + y = 100$

$\quad\quad\quad\ y = 60$

Wayne must use 140 gallons of 5% butterfat milk and 60 gallons of skim milk.

37. Let x = the amount of apple juice
$\quad\quad y$ = the amount of apple drink

Liquid	Number of ounces	Cost per ounce	Total cost
Apple juice	x	12	12x
Apple drink	y	6	6y
Mixture	8	10	10(8)

$\quad\quad x + y = 8$

$12x + 6y = 80$

Solve the first equation for y.
$y = 8 - x$

Substitute $8 - x$ for y in the second equation.

$12x + 6(8 - x) = 80$

$12x + 48 - 6x = 80$

$6x = 32$

$x = \dfrac{32}{6} = 5\dfrac{1}{3}$

$y = 8 - x$

$y = 8 - 5\dfrac{1}{3}$

$y = \dfrac{24}{3} - \dfrac{16}{3}$

$y = \dfrac{8}{3} = 2\dfrac{2}{3}$

The cans should contain $5\dfrac{1}{3}$ ounces apple juice

and $2\dfrac{2}{3}$ ounces apple drink.

39. $p = -1.4t + 72$

$p = 1.4t + 28$

Set the equations equal to each other and solve
for t.

$-1.4t + 72 = 1.4t + 28$

$-2.8t = -44$

$t \approx 15.71$

$1995 + 15 = 2010$

In 2010 the percent living in rural areas will be
the same as that in urban cities.

41. Let t = the amount of time they jog
d = the distance to the school
The distance that Sean jogs is $9t$, while the
distance that Meghan jogs is $5t$.

$9t = d$

$5t = d - 0.5$

Substitute $9t$ for d in the second equation.

$5t = 9t - 0.5$

$0.5 = 4t$

$0.125 = t$

$d = 9t$

$d = 9(0.125)$

$d = 1.125$

The school is 1.125 miles from their house.

43. Let x = number of minutes
a = pressure in tank one and
b = pressure in tank two

$a = 200 - 2x$

$b = 20 + 2x$

Let $a = b$

$200 - 2x = 20 + 2x$

$180 = 4x$

$45 = x$

It will take 45 minutes for the pressure in the
tanks to be equal.

45. a. $x + 4 = 4 + x$ illustrates the commutative
property of addition.

b. $(3x)y = 3(xy)$ illustrates the associative
property of multiplication.

c. $4(x + 2) = 4x + 8$ illustrates the distributive
property.

46. Let l = the length of the rectangle
w = the width of the rectangle

$l = 2w + 2$

The formula for the perimeter of a rectangle
is $P = 2l + 2w$.

$22 = 2l + 2w$

$22 = 2(2w + 2) + 2w$

$22 = 4w + 4 + 2w$

$18 = 6w$

$3 = w$

$l = 2w + 2$

$l = 2(3) + 2$

$l = 8$

The length of the rectangle is 8 feet and the
width is 3 feet.

47. $x + \dfrac{2}{x} = \dfrac{6}{x}$

$x\left(x + \dfrac{2}{x}\right) = x\left(\dfrac{6}{x}\right)$

$x^2 + \dfrac{2x}{x} = \dfrac{6x}{x}$

$x^2 + 2 = 6$

$x^2 = 4$

$x = \pm 2$

48. A graph is an illustration of the set of points that
satisfy an equation.

Exercise Set 8.5

1. Yes, the solution to a system of linear
inequalities contains all of the ordered pairs
which satisfy both inequalities.

3. Yes, when the lines are parallel. One possible
system is $x + y > 2$, $x + y < 1$.

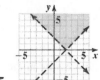

5.

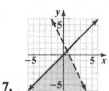

7.

9.

11.

13.

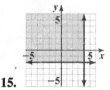

15.

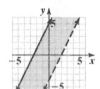

17.

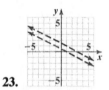

19.

21.

23.

25. No, the system can have no solutions or infinitely many solutions. If the lines involved are parallel, the system will have no solutions or infinitely many solutions. If the lines intersect, they will divide the plane into 4 regions, each containing infinitely many points. One of these regions will be the solution to the system.

27. $x + 2y \le 6$

29. $6(x - 2) < 4x - 3 + 2x$

$6x - 12 < 6x - 3$

$-12 < -3$

Since this is a true statement, the solution is all real numbers.

30. $3x - 5y = 6$

$3x = 5y + 6$

$3x - 6 = 5y$

$\dfrac{3x - 6}{5} = y$

$\dfrac{3}{5}x - \dfrac{6}{5} = y$

31. $4x^2 - 11x - 3 = 0$

$(4x + 1)(x - 3) = 0$

$4x + 1 = 0 \qquad x - 3 = 0$

$4x = -1 \qquad x - 3 = 0$

$x = -\dfrac{1}{4} \qquad x = 3$

32. $\dfrac{x^{-6}y^2}{x^3 y^{-5}} = x^{-6-3}y^{2-(-5)}$

$= x^{-9}y^7$

$= \dfrac{y^7}{x^9}$

Review Exercises

1. a. $\quad y = 4x - 2 \qquad\qquad 2x + 3y = 8$

$\qquad 6 = 4(2) - 2 \qquad 2(2) + 3(6) = 8$

$\qquad 6 = 6 \ \text{True} \qquad\qquad 22 = 8 \ \text{False}$

Since (2, 6) does not satisfy both equations, it is not a solution to the system.

b. $\quad y = 4x - 2$

$\qquad 0 = 4(4) - 2$

$\qquad 0 = 14 \ \text{False}$

Since (4, 0) does not satisfy the first equation, it is not a solution to the system.

c. $\quad y = 4x - 2 \qquad\qquad 2x + 3y = 8$

$\qquad 2 = 4(1) - 2 \qquad 2(1) + 3(2) = 8$

$\qquad 2 = 2 \ \text{True} \qquad\qquad 8 = 8 \ \text{True}$

Since (1, 2) satisfies both equations, it is a solution to the system.

2. a.　$y = -x + 4$

$$\frac{3}{2} = -\frac{5}{2} + 4$$

$$\frac{3}{2} = \frac{3}{2} \text{ True}$$

$$3x + 5y = 15$$

$$3\left(\frac{5}{2}\right) + 5\left(\frac{3}{2}\right) = 15$$

$$15 = 15 \text{ True}$$

Since $\left(\frac{5}{2}, \frac{3}{2}\right)$ satisfies both equations, it is

a solution to the system.

b.　$y = -x + 4$

$$5 = -(-1) + 4$$

$$5 = 5 \text{ True}$$

$$3x + 5y = 15$$

$$3(-1) + 5(5) = 15$$

$$22 = 15 \text{ False}$$

Since $(-1, 5)$ does not satisfy both equations, it is not a solution to the system.

c.　$y = -x + 4$

$$\frac{3}{5} = -\frac{1}{2} + 4$$

$$\frac{3}{5} = \frac{7}{2} \text{ False}$$

Since $\left(\frac{1}{2}, \frac{3}{5}\right)$ does not satisfy the first

equation, it is not a solution to the system.

3. consistent, one solution

4. inconsistent, no solutions

5. dependent, infinite number of solutions

6. consistent, one solution

7. Write each equation in slope-intercept form.

$$x + 2y = 10 \qquad\qquad 4x = -8y + 16$$

$$2y = -x + 10 \qquad\qquad 8y = -4x + 16$$

$$y = -\frac{1}{2}x + 5 \qquad\qquad y = -\frac{1}{2}x + 2$$

Since the slope of each line is $-\frac{1}{2}$ but the

y-intercepts are different, the two lines are parallel. There is no solution. This is an inconsistent system.

8. Write each equation in slope-intercept form.
$y = -2x + 5$ is already in this form.

$$2x + 5y = 10$$

$$5y = -2x + 10$$

$$y = -\frac{2}{5}x + 2$$

Since the slopes of the lines are different, the lines intersect to produce one solution. This is a consistent system.

9. Write each equation in slope-intercept form.

$y = \frac{1}{3}x + \frac{2}{3}$ is already in this form.

$$6y - 2x = 4$$

$$6y = 2x + 4$$

$$y = \frac{1}{3}x + \frac{2}{3}$$

Since both equations are identical, the line is the same for both of them. There are an infinite number of solutions. This is a dependent system.

10. Write each equation in slope-intercept form.

$$6x = 4y - 20 \qquad\qquad 4x = 6y + 20$$

$$6x + 20 = 4y \qquad\qquad 4x - 20 = 6y$$

$$\frac{3}{2}x + 5 = y \qquad\qquad \frac{2}{3}x - \frac{10}{5} = y$$

Since the slopes of the lines are different, the lines intersect to produce one solution. This is a consistent system.

11. Graph $y = x - 4$ and $y = 2x - 7$.

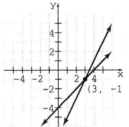

The lines intersect and the point of intersection is $(3, -1)$. This is a consistent system.

12. Graph $x = -2$ and $y = 5$.

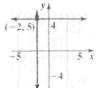

The lines intersect and the point of intersection is $(-2, 5)$. This is a consistent system.

13. Graph the equations $x + 2y = 8$ and $2x - y = -4$.

The lines intersect and the point of intersection is $(0, 4)$. This is a consistent system.

14. Graph $x + 4y = 8$ and $y = 2$.

The lines intersect and the point of intersection is $(0, 2)$. This is a consistent system.

15. Graph $y = 3$ and $y = -2x + 5$.

The lines intersect and the point of intersection is $(1, 3)$. This is a consistent system.

16. Graph the equations $y = x - 3$ and $3x - 3y = 9$.

Both equations produce the same line. This is a dependent system. There are an infinite number of solutions.

17. Graph $3x + y = 0$ and $3x - 3y = 12$.

The lines intersect and the point of intersection is $(1, -3)$. This is a consistent system.

18. Graph $x + 5y = 10$ and $\dfrac{1}{5}x + y = -1$.

The lines are parallel and do not intersect. The system is inconsistent and there is no solution.

19.
$$y = 4x - 18$$
$$2x - 5y = 0$$

Substitute $4x - 18$ for y in the second equation.
$$2x - 5y = 0$$
$$2x - 5(4x - 18) = 0$$
$$2x - 20x + 90 = 0$$
$$-18x + 90 = 0$$
$$-18x = -90$$
$$x = 5$$

Now, substitute 5 for x in the first equation.
$$y = 4x - 18$$
$$y = 4(5) - 18$$
$$y = 20 - 18$$
$$y = 2$$

The solution is $(5, 2)$.

20.
$$x = 3y - 9$$
$$x + 2y = 1$$

Substitute $3y - 9$ for x in the second equation.
$$x + 2y = 1$$
$$3y - 9 + 2y = 1$$
$$5y - 9 = 1$$
$$5y = 10$$
$$y = 2$$

Now substitute 2 for y in the first equation.
$$x = 3y - 9$$
$$x = 3(2) - 9$$
$$x = 6 - 9$$
$$x = -3$$

The solution is $(-3, 2)$.

21.
$$2x - y = 7$$
$$x + 2y = 6$$

Solve the second equation for x, $x = 6 - 2y$.
Substitute $6 - 2y$ for x in the first equation.

$$2x - y = 7$$
$$2(6 - 2y) - y = 7$$
$$12 - 4y - y = 7$$
$$-5y = -5$$
$$y = 1$$

Substitute 1 for y in the equation $x = 6 - 2y$.

$$x = 6 - 2(1)$$
$$x = 6 - 2$$
$$x = 4$$

The solution is (4, 1).

22.
$$x = -3y$$
$$x + 4y = 5$$

Substitute $-3y$ for x in the second equation.

$$x + 4y = 5$$
$$-3y + 4y = 5$$
$$y = 5$$

Substitute 5 for y in the first equation.

$$x = -3y$$
$$x = -3(5)$$
$$x = -15$$

The solution is (−15, 5).

23. $4x - 2y = 7$
$$y = 2x + 3$$

Substitute $2x + 3$ for y in the first equation.
$$4x - 2y = 7$$
$$4x - 2(2x + 3) = 7$$
$$4x - 4x - 6 = 7$$
$$-6 = 7 \text{ False}$$

There is no solution.

24. $2x - 4y = 7$
$$-4x + 8y = -14$$

Solve the first equation for x.
$$2x - 4y = 7$$
$$2x = 4y + 7$$
$$x = 2y + \frac{7}{2}$$

Substitute $2y + \dfrac{7}{2}$ for x in the second equation.

$$-4x + 8y = -14$$
$$-4\left(2y + \frac{7}{2}\right) + 8y = -14$$
$$-8y - 14 + 8y = -14$$
$$-14 = -14 \text{ True}$$

There are an infinite number of solutions.

25. $2x - 3y = 8$
$$6x - 5y = 20$$

Solve the first equation for x.
$$2x - 3y = 8$$
$$2x = 3y + 8$$
$$x = \frac{3}{2}y + 4$$

Substitute $\dfrac{3}{2}y + 4$ for x in the second equation.

$$6x - 5y = 20$$
$$6\left(\frac{3}{2}y + 4\right) - 5y = 20$$
$$9y + 24 - 5y = 20$$
$$4y + 24 = 20$$
$$4y = -4$$
$$y = -1$$

Substitute −1 for y in the equation $x = \dfrac{3}{2}y + 4$.

$$x = \frac{3}{2}(-1) + 4$$
$$x = -\frac{3}{2} + \frac{8}{2}$$
$$x = \frac{5}{2}$$

The solution is $\left(\dfrac{5}{2}, -1\right)$.

26. $3x - y = -5$
$$x + 2y = 8$$

Solve the second equation for x, $x = 8 - 2y$.

Substitute $8 - 2y$ for x in the first equation.

$$3x - y = -5$$
$$3(8 - 2y) - y = -5$$
$$24 - 6y - y = -5$$
$$-7y = -29$$
$$y = \frac{29}{7}$$

Substitute $\dfrac{29}{7}$ for y in the equation $x = 8 - 2y$.

$$x = 8 - 2\left(\frac{29}{7}\right)$$

$$x = \frac{56}{7} - \frac{58}{7}$$

$$x = -\frac{2}{7}$$

The solution is $\left(-\frac{2}{7}, \frac{29}{7}\right)$.

27. $x - y = -4$
     $\underline{-x + 6y = -6}$
         $5y = -10$
          $y = -2$

Substitute -2 for y in the first equation.
     $x - y = -4$
   $x - (-2) = -4$
     $x + 2 = -4$
         $x = -6$
The solution is $(-6, -2)$.

28. $x + 2y = -3$
     $\underline{5x - 2y = 9}$
     $6x = 6$
          $x = 1$

Substitute 1 for x in the first equation.
$x + 2y = -3$
$1 + 2y = -3$
     $2y = -4$
      $y = -2$
The solution is $(1, -2)$.

29. $x + y = 12$
       $2x + y = 5$

To eliminate y, multiply the first equation by -1 and then add.
$-1[x + y = 12]$
gives
     $-x - y = -12$
     $\underline{2x + y = 5}$
      $x = -7$

Substitute -7 for x in the first equation.
     $x + y = 12$
   $-7 + y = 12$
        $y = 19$
The solution is $(-7, 19)$.

30. $4x - 3y = 8$
       $2x + 5y = 8$

To eliminate x, multiply the second equation by -2 and then add.
$-2[2x + 5y = 8]$
gives
     $4x - 3y = 8$
     $\underline{-4x - 10y = -16}$
       $-13y = -8$
          $y = \frac{8}{13}$

Substitute $\frac{8}{13}$ for y in the first equation.
     $4x - 3y = 8$
   $4x - 3\left(\frac{8}{13}\right) = 8$
   $4x - \frac{24}{13} = 8$
        $4x = \frac{104}{13} + \frac{24}{13}$
        $4x = \frac{128}{13}$
         $x = \frac{32}{13}$

The solution is $\left(\frac{32}{13}, \frac{8}{13}\right)$.

31. $-2x + 3y = 15$
        $7x + 3y = 6$

To eliminate y, multiply the second equation by -1 and then add.
$-1[7x + 3y = 6]$
gives
     $-2x + 3y = 15$
     $\underline{-7x - 3y = -6}$
     $-9x = 9$
          $x = -1$

Substitute -1 for x in the second equation.
     $7x + 3y = 6$
   $7(-1) + 3y = 6$
     $-7 + 3y = 6$
          $3y = 13$
           $y = \frac{13}{3}$

The solution is $\left(-1, \frac{13}{3}\right)$.

32. $2x + y = 3$

$-4x - 2y = 5$

Multiply the first equation by 2, and then add.

$2[2x + y = 3]$

gives

$4x + 2y = 6$

$\underline{-4x - 2y = 3}$

$0 = 9$ False

There is no solution.

33. $3x = -4y + 15$

$8y = -6x + 30$

Align the x and y terms.

$3x + 4y = 15$

$6x + 8y = 30$

To eliminate x, multiply the first equation by -2, and then add.

$-2[3x + 4y = 15]$

gives

$-6x - 8y = -30$

$\underline{6x + 8y = 30}$

$0 = 0$ True

There are an infinite number of solutions.

34. $2x - 5y = 12$

$3x - 4y = -6$

To eliminate x, multiply the first equation by -3 and the second equation by 2 and then add.

$-3[2x - 5y = 12]$

$2[3x - 4y = -6]$

gives

$-6x + 15y = -36$

$\underline{6x - 8y = -12}$

$7y = -48$

$y = -\dfrac{48}{7}$

Now, substitute $-\dfrac{48}{7}$ for y in the first equation.

$2x - 5y = 12$

$2x - 5\left(-\dfrac{48}{7}\right) = 12$

$2x + \dfrac{240}{7} = 12$

$2x = \dfrac{84}{7} - \dfrac{240}{7}$

$2x = -\dfrac{156}{7}$

$x = -\dfrac{78}{7}$

The solution is $\left(-\dfrac{78}{7}, -\dfrac{48}{7}\right)$.

35. Let x be the larger number and y be the smaller number.

$x + y = 22$

$x = 2y - 8$

Substitute $2y - 8$ for x in the first equation.

$x + y = 22$

$2y - 8 + y = 22$

$3y = 30$

$y = 10$

Substitute 10 for y in the second equation.

$x = 2y - 8$

$x = 2(10) - 8$

$x = 12$

The numbers are 10 and 12.

36. Let x be the speed of the plane in still air and y be the speed of the wind.

$x + y = 580$

$\underline{x - y = 520}$

Add: $2x = 1100$

$x = 550$

Substitute 550 for x in the first equation.

$x + y = 580$

$550 + y = 580$

$y = 30$

The speed of the plane is 550 miles per hour and the speed of the wind is 30 miles per hour.

37. Let x be the number of miles traveled and c be the cost.

$c = 35 + 0.5x$

$c = 40 + 0.4x$

Substitute $35 + 0.5x$ for c in the second equation.

$$35 + 0.5x = 40 + 0.4x$$
$$0.1x = 5$$
$$x = 50$$

The cost is the same for 50 miles of travel.

38. Let x be the amount invested at 4% and y be the amount invested at 6%.

$$x + y = 16,000$$

$$0.04x + 0.06y = 760$$

Solve the first equation for x, $x = 16,000 - y$.

Substitute $16,000 - y$ for x in the second equation.

$$0.04(16,000 - y) + 0.06y = 760$$
$$640 - 0.04y + 0.06y = 760$$
$$0.02y = 120$$
$$y = 6000$$

Substitute 6000 for y in the equation $x = 16,000 - y$.

$$x = 16,000 - 6000$$

$$x = 10,000$$

She invested \$10,000 at 4% and \$6000 at 6%.

39. Let l be Liz's speed and m be Mary's speed. The distance that Liz traveled is $5l$ and the distance that Mary traveled is $5m$.

$$m = l + 6$$

$$5l + 5m = 600$$

Substitute $l + 6$ for m in the second equation.

$$5l + 5(l + 6) = 600$$
$$5l + 5l + 30 = 600$$
$$10l = 570$$
$$l = 57$$

Substitute 57 for l in the first equation.

$$m = 57 + 6$$

$$m = 63$$

Liz's speed was 57 miles per hour and Mary's speed was 63 miles per hour.

40. Let g be the pounds of Green Turf's grass seed and a be the pounds of Agway's grass seed.

$$0.6g + 0.45a = 25.50$$

$$g + a = 50$$

Solve the second equation for a, $a = 50 - g$.

Substitute $50 - g$ for a in the first equation.

$$0.6g + 0.45(50 - g) = 25.50$$
$$0.6g + 22.5 - 0.45g = 25.50$$
$$0.15g = 3$$
$$g = 20$$

Substitute 20 for g in the equation $a = 50 - g$.

$$a = 50 - 20$$
$$a = 30$$

There were 20 pounds of Green Turf's grass seed and 30 pounds of Agway's grass seed.

41. Let x be the amount of 25% acid solution and y be the amount of 55% acid solution.

$$x + y = 10$$

$$0.25x + 0.55y = 0.4(10)$$

To clear decimals, multiply the second equation by 100.

$$x + y = 10$$

$$25x + 55y = 400$$

Solve the first equation for y, $y = -x + 10$.

Substitute $-x + 10$ for y in the second equation.

$$25x + 55y = 400$$
$$25x + 55(-x + 10) = 400$$
$$25x - 55x + 550 = 400$$
$$-30x = -150$$
$$x = 5$$

Finally, substitute 5 for x in the equation $y = -x + 10$.

$$y = -x + 10$$
$$y = -5 + 10$$
$$y = 5$$

The chemist should combine 5 liters of each solution to produce the desired result.

42. $2x - 6y > 6$

$x > -2$

43. $x < 2$

$y \geq -3$

44. $2x + y > 2$

$2x - y \leq 4$

45. $2x - 3y \leq 6$

$2x + 8y > 8$

Practice Test

1. a. $x + 2y = -6$
$$-6 + 2(0) = -6$$
$$-6 = -6 \quad \text{True}$$

$$3x + 2y = -12$$
$$3(-6) + 2(0) = -12$$
$$-18 = -12 \quad \text{False}$$

Since $(-6, 0)$ does not satisfy both equations, it is not a solution to the system.

b. $x + 2y = -6$
$$-3 + 2\left(-\frac{3}{2}\right) = -6$$
$$-6 = -6 \quad \text{True}$$

$$3x + 2y = -12$$
$$3(-3) + 2\left(-\frac{3}{2}\right) = -12$$
$$-12 = -12 \quad \text{True}$$

$\left(-3, -\frac{3}{2}\right)$ is a solution to the system.

c. $x + 2y = -6$
$$2 + 2(-4) = -6$$
$$-6 = -6 \quad \text{True}$$

$$3x + 2y = -12$$
$$3(2) + 2(-4) = -12$$
$$-2 = -12 \quad \text{False}$$
Since $(2, -4)$ does not satisfy both equations, it is not a solution to the system.

2. The system is consistent; it has exactly one solution.

3. The system is inconsistent, it has no solution.

4. The system is dependent; it has an infinite number of solutions.

5. $-3y = 6x - 10 \qquad\qquad 2x + y = 5$
$$y = -2x + \frac{10}{3} \qquad\qquad y = -2x + 5$$

The lines have the same slope, but different y-intercepts, so they are parallel. Thus, the system of equations is inconsistent and has no solution.

6. $5x + 2y = 12 \qquad\qquad 5x - 2y = 16$
$$2y = -5x + 12 \qquad\qquad -2y = -5x + 16$$
$$y = -\frac{5}{2}x + 6 \qquad\qquad y = \frac{5}{2}x - 8$$

The slopes of the lines are different. Thus, the system of equations is consistent and has one solution.

7. $4x = 6y - 12 \qquad\qquad 2x - 3y = -6$
$$6y = 4x + 12 \qquad\qquad -3y = -2x - 6$$
$$y = \frac{2}{3}x + 2 \qquad\qquad y = \frac{2}{3}x + 2$$

The lines are the same. Thus, the system of equations is consistent and dependent, and it has infinite number of solutions.

8. a. You will obtain a false statement, such as $6 = 0$.

b. You will obtain a true statement, such as $0 = 0$.

9. $y = 2x - 4 \qquad y = -2x + 8$

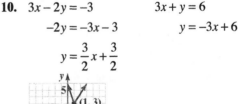

It appears that $(3, 2)$ is the solution to the system.
$$y = 2x - 4 \qquad\qquad y = -2x + 8$$
$$2 = 2(3) - 4 \qquad\qquad 2 = -2(3) + 8$$
$$4 = 4 \quad \text{True} \qquad\qquad 2 = 2 \quad \text{True}$$
$(3, 2)$ is the solution to the system.

10. $3x - 2y = -3 \qquad\qquad 3x + y = 6$
$$-2y = -3x - 3 \qquad\qquad y = -3x + 6$$
$$y = \frac{3}{2}x + \frac{3}{2}$$

It appears that $(1, 3)$ is the solution to the system.
$$3x - 2y = -3 \qquad\qquad 3x + y = 6$$
$$3(1) - 2(3) = -3 \qquad\qquad 3(1) + 3 = 6$$
$$-3 = -3 \quad \text{True} \qquad\qquad 6 = 6 \quad \text{True}$$
$(1, 3)$ is the solution to the system.

11. $y = 2x + 4$ $4x - 2y = 6$

$-2y = -4x + 6$

$y = 2x - 3$

The lines are parallel, so the system has no solution.

12. $y = 5x - 9$

$y = 3x + 3$

Both equations are solved for *y*. Substitute $5x - 7$ for *y* in the second equation.

$5x - 9 = 3x + 3$

$2x = 12$

$x = 6$

Substitute 6 for *x* in the first equation.

$y = 5x - 9$

$y = 5(6) - 9$

$y = 21$

The solution to the system is (6, 21).

13. $3x + y = 8$

$x - y = 6$

Solve the first equation for *y*,

$y = 8 - 3x$.

Substitute $8 - 3x$ for *y* in the second equation.

$x - (8 - 3x) = 6$

$x - 8 + 3x = 6$

$4x = 14$

$x = \dfrac{14}{4} = \dfrac{7}{2}$

Substitute $\dfrac{7}{2}$ for *x* in the equation $y = 8 - 3x$.

$y = 8 - 3x$

$y = 8 - 3\left(\dfrac{7}{2}\right)$

$y = \dfrac{16}{2} - \dfrac{21}{2}$

$y = -\dfrac{5}{2}$

The solution to the system is $\left(\dfrac{7}{2}, -\dfrac{5}{2}\right)$.

14. $3x - 2y = 2$

$-5x + 4y = 0$

Solve the second equation for *y*.

$-5x + 4y = 0$

$4y = 5x$

$y = \dfrac{5x}{4}$

Substitute $\dfrac{5x}{4}$ for *y* in the first equation.

$3x - 2\left(\dfrac{5x}{4}\right) = 2$

$3x - \dfrac{5x}{2} = 2$

$\dfrac{6x}{2} - \dfrac{5x}{2} = 2$

$\dfrac{x}{2} = 2$

$x = 4$

Substitute 4 for *x* in the equation $y = \dfrac{5x}{4}$.

$y = \dfrac{5x}{4}$

$y = \dfrac{5(4)}{4}$

$y = 5$

The solution to the system is (4, 5).

15. $4x + y = -6$

$x + 3y = 4$

To eliminate *x*, multiply the second equation by –4.

$-4[x + 3y = 4]$

gives

$\begin{aligned} 4x + y &= -6 \\ -4x - 12y &= -16 \\ \hline -11y &= -22 \\ y &= 2 \end{aligned}$

Substitute 2 for *y* in the first equation.

$4x + y = -6$

$4x + 2 = -6$

$4x = -8$

$x = -2$

The solution to the system is (–2, 2).

16. $4x - y = 8$

$10x + 3y = -13$

To eliminate *x*, multiply the first equation by 3.

$3[4x - y = 8]$
gives
$12x - 3y = 24$
$\underline{10x + 3y = -13}$
$\qquad 22x = 11$

$$x = \frac{1}{2}$$

Substitute $\frac{1}{2}$ for x in the first equation and solve for y.

$$4\left(\frac{1}{2}\right) - y = 8$$
$$2 - y = 8$$
$$-y = 6$$
$$y = -6$$

The solution to the system is $\left(\frac{1}{2}, -6\right)$.

17. $5x - 10y = 20$
$\qquad 2x = 4y + 8$

Align the x- and y-terms on the left side of each equation.

$5x - 10y = 20 \quad (eq. 1)$
$\;2x - 4y = 8 \quad (eq. 2)$

Multiply the first equation by -2 and the second equation by 5.

$-2[5x - 10y = 20]$
$5[2x - 4y = 8\;]$

gives

$-10x + 20y = -40$
$\underline{\;10x - 20y = 40\;}$
$\qquad\quad 0 = 0$

This is a true statement for all values of x and y. Thus, the system is dependent and has an infinite number of solutions.

18. $y = 5x - 13$
$\quad\; y = -2x + 8$

Substitute $5x - 13$ for y in the second equation.
$5x - 13 = -2x + 8$
$7x - 13 = 8$
$\quad\; 7x = 21$
$\qquad x = 3$
Substitute 3 for x in the first equation.

$y = 5x - 13$
$y = 5(3) - 13$
$y = 2$
The solution to the system is $(3, 2)$.

19. $\quad 3x - 4y = 1 \quad (eq. 1)$
$\quad -2x + 5y = -10 \;\; (eq. 2)$

To eliminate x, multiply the first equation by 2 and the second equation by 3.

$\quad 2[3x - 4y = 1]$
$\quad 3[-2x + 5y = -10]$
gives
$\quad 6x - 8y = 2$
$\quad \underline{-6x + 15y = -30}$
$\qquad\quad 7y = -28$
$\qquad\quad\; y = -4$

To find x, substitute -4 for y in equation 2.

$\quad -2x + 5y = -10$
$\quad -2x + 5(-4) = -10$
$\quad -2x - 20 = -10$
$\qquad -2x = 10$
$\qquad\quad x = -5$

The solution to the system is $(-5, -4)$.

20. $3x + 5y = 20$
$\quad 6x + 3y = -12$

To eliminate x, multiply the first equation by -2.
$-2[3x + 5y = 20]$
gives
$-6x - 10y = -40$
$\underline{\;6x + 3y = -12\;}$
$\qquad -7y = -52$

$$y = \frac{52}{7}$$

To eliminate y, multiply the first equation by -3 and the second equation by 5.
$-3[3x + 5y = 20]$
$\;5[6x + 3y = -12]$

gives
$-9x - 15y = -60$
$\underline{\;30x + 15y = -60\;}$
$21x \qquad\;\; = -120$

$$x = -\frac{120}{21} = -\frac{40}{7}$$

The solution to the system is $\left(-\dfrac{40}{7}, \dfrac{52}{7}\right)$.

21. Let m = the number of miles driven
    c = the total cost per day
With Charley's Rent A Truck,
$c = 47 + 0.08m$, while with Hugh's Rent a

Truck, $c = 40 + 0.15m$. Set the two costs equal.
$$47 + 0.08m = 40 + 0.15m$$
$$7 = 0.07m$$
$$100 = m$$

The cars cost an equal amount when they are driven 100 miles per day.

22. Let l = amount of lemon candies
    b = amount of butterscotch candies

Candy	Number of pounds	Cost per pound	Total cost
lemon	l	6	$6l$
butterscotch	b	4.5	$4.5b$
Mixture	20	5	$5(20)$

$$l + b = 20$$
$$6l + 4.5b = 100$$
Solve the first equation for b.
$$l + b = 20$$
$$b = 20 - l$$
Substitute $20 - l$ for b in the second equation.
$$6l + 4.5(20 - l) = 100$$
$$6l + 90 - 4.5l = 100$$
$$1.5l = 10$$
$$l = \frac{10}{1.5} = 6\frac{2}{3}$$
$$b = 20 - l$$
$$b = 20 - 6\frac{2}{3}$$
$$b = 13\frac{1}{3}$$
The mixture must contain $6\dfrac{2}{3}$ pounds of lemon candies and $13\dfrac{1}{3}$ pounds of butterscotch candies.

23. Let h = the speed of Dante Hull's boat
    r = the speed of Deja Rocket's boat
In 2.5 hours, Dante's boat travels $2.5h$ miles, while in 3 hours, Deja's boat travels $3r$ miles. The distance that the two boats travel are the same.
$$2.5h = 3r$$
$$h = r + 4$$
Substitute $r + 4$ for h in the first equation.

$$2.5(r + 4) = 3r$$
$$2.5r + 10 = 3r$$
$$10 = 0.5r$$
$$20 = r$$
Substitute 20 for r in the second equation.
$$h = r + 4$$
$$h = 20 + 4$$
$$h = 24$$

The speed of Dante Hull's boat is 24 miles per hour and the speed of Deja Rocket's boat is 20 miles per hour.

24. $x + 3y \geq 6$

$y < 3$

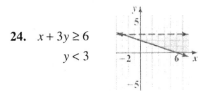

25. $2x + 4y < 8$

$x - 3y \geq 6$

Cumulative Review Test

1. a. Air Force and Army

  b. Air Force, Army and Navy

2. a. 7

  b. $-5, -0.6, \dfrac{3}{5}, 7, 0, -\dfrac{5}{9}, 1.34$

  c. $\sqrt{10}, -\sqrt{2}$

  d. $-5, -0.6, \dfrac{3}{5}, \sqrt{10}, -\sqrt{2}, 7, 0, -\dfrac{5}{9}, 1.34$

3. $-115 + 63 + (-192) = -52 + (-192) = -244$

4. $10 - (3a - 2) + 4(a + 3) = 10 - 3a + 2 + 4a + 12$
$$= (-3a + 4a) + (10 + 2 + 12)$$
$$= a + 24$$

5. $2(x - 4) + 2 = 3x - 4$
$$2x - 8 + 2 = 3x - 4$$
$$2x - 6 = 3x - 4$$
$$-2 = x$$

6. $3x - 2 \leq x + 8$
$$2x \leq 10$$
$$x \leq 5$$

7. $39 - y$

8. Let s = Maria's weekly sales
w = Maria's weekly salary
Under plan A, $w = 0.12s$, while under plan B, $w = 348 + 0.06s$. Set the two salaries equal.

$0.12s = 348 + 0.06s$

$0.06s = 348$

$s = \dfrac{348}{0.06} = 5800$

Maria's weekly sales must be \$5800 for both plans to pay the same amount.

9. Let x = the measure of the smallest angle
Then the other angles measure $x + 30$ and $8x$.
The sum of the measures of the angles in any triangle is 180°.
$$x + (x + 30) + 8x = 180$$
$$10x + 30 = 180$$
$$10x = 150$$
$$x = 15$$
$$x + 30 = 15 + 30 = 45$$
$$8x = 8(15) = 120$$
The angles of the triangle measure 15°, 45°, and 120°.

10. $(4x^3 y^2)^3 (x^2 y) = (4^3 x^9 y^6)(x^2 y)$
$$= 64x^{9+2} y^{6+1}$$
$$= 64x^{11} y^7$$

11. $(x - 2y)^2 = (x - 2y)(x - 2y)$
$$= x^2 - 2xy - 2xy + 4y^2$$
$$= x^2 - 4xy + 4y^2$$

12. $2n^2 - 5n - 12 = (2n + 3)(n - 4)$

13. $x^2 - 3x - 54 = 0$
$$(x + 6)(x - 9) = 0$$
$$x + 6 = 0 \qquad x - 9 = 0$$
$$x = -6 \qquad x = 9$$

14. $\dfrac{x^2 - 4x - 12}{7x} \cdot \dfrac{x^2 - x}{x^2 - 7x + 6}$

$= \dfrac{(x - 6)(x + 2)}{7x} \cdot \dfrac{x(x - 1)}{(x - 1)(x - 6)}$

$= \dfrac{(x - 6)(x + 2) \cdot x(x - 1)}{7x \cdot (x - 1)(x - 6)}$

$= \dfrac{x + 2}{7}$

15. $\dfrac{2x+3}{5} = \dfrac{x-2}{2}$

$2(2x+3) = 5(x-2)$

$4x+6 = 5x-10$

$-x = -16$

$x = 16$

16.

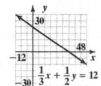

17.

18. $3x - y = 6$

$-y = -3x + 6$

$y = 3x - 6$

$\dfrac{3}{2}x - 3 = \dfrac{1}{2}y$

$\dfrac{1}{2}y = \dfrac{3}{2}x - 3$

$y = 3x - 6$

The lines are the same, so the system has an infinite number of solutions.

19. Graph $2x + y = 5$ and $x - 2y = 0$.

The solution is $(2, 1)$.

20. $3x + 5y = 6$

$-6x + 7y = -29$

To eliminate x, multiply the first equation by 2.

$2[3x + 5y = 6]$

gives

$6x + 10y = 12$

$\underline{-6x + 7y = -29}$

$17y = -17$

$y = -1$

To find x, substitute -1 for y in the first equation.

$6x + 10y = 12$

$6x + 10(-1) = 12$

$6x - 10 = 12$

$6x = 22$

$x = \dfrac{22}{6} = \dfrac{11}{3}$

The solution to the system is $\left(\dfrac{11}{3}, -1\right)$.

Chapter 9

Exercise Set 9.1

1. The principal square root of a positive real number x is a positive number whose square equals x.

3. Answers will vary.

5. Answers will vary.

7. Yes, since $5^2 = 25$.

9. No, because the square root of a negative number is not a real number.

11. Yes, since $\sqrt{\dfrac{16}{25}} = \dfrac{4}{5}$ which is a rational number.

13. $\sqrt{0} = 0$ since $(0)^2 = 0$

15. $\sqrt{36} = 6$ since $(6)^2 = 36$

17. $\sqrt{49} = 7$ since $(7)^2 = 49$
    Take the opposite of both sides to get
    $-\sqrt{49} = -7$

19. $\sqrt{400} = 20$ since $20^2 = 400$

21. $\sqrt{16} = 4$ since $(4)^2 = 16$
    Take the opposite of both sides to get
    $-\sqrt{16} = -4$

23. $\sqrt{144} = 12$ since $(12)^2 = 144$

25. $\sqrt{225} = 15$ since $(15)^2 = 225$

27. $\sqrt{1} = 1$ since $(1)^2 = 1$
    Take the opposite of both sides to get $-\sqrt{1} = -1$

29. $\sqrt{144} = 12$ since $(12)^2 = 144$
    Take the opposite of both sides to get
    $-\sqrt{144} = -12$

31. $\sqrt{121} = 11$ since $(11)^2 = 121$
    Take the opposite of both sides to get
    $-\sqrt{121} = -11$

33. $\sqrt{\dfrac{1}{4}} = \dfrac{1}{2}$ since $\left(\dfrac{1}{2}\right)^2 = \dfrac{1}{4}$

35. $\sqrt{\dfrac{25}{4}} = \dfrac{5}{2}$ since $\left(\dfrac{5}{2}\right)^2 = \dfrac{25}{4}$

37. $\sqrt{\dfrac{25}{30}} = \dfrac{5}{6}$ since $\left(\dfrac{5}{6}\right)^2 = \dfrac{25}{36}$
    Take the opposite of both sides to get
    $-\sqrt{\dfrac{25}{30}} = -\dfrac{5}{6}$

39. $\sqrt{\dfrac{81}{100}} = \dfrac{9}{10}$ since $\left(\dfrac{9}{10}\right)^2 = \dfrac{81}{100}$

41. $\sqrt{12} \approx 3.4641016$

43. $\sqrt{15} \approx 3.8729833$

45. $\sqrt{80} \approx 8.9442719$

47. $\sqrt{324} = 18$

49. $\sqrt{97} \approx 9.8488578$

51. $\sqrt{30} \approx 5.4772256$

53. False; since 28 is not a perfect square, $\sqrt{28}$ is an irrational number.

55. True; since 25 is a perfect square, $\sqrt{25}$ is a rational number

57. False; since 9 is a perfect square, $\sqrt{9}$ is a rational number

59. True; $\sqrt{\dfrac{9}{16}} = \dfrac{3}{4}$ which is a rational number

61. True; since 125 is not a perfect square, $\sqrt{125}$ is an irrational number

63. True; $\sqrt{(12)^2} = \sqrt{144} = 12$ which is an integer

65. $\sqrt{7} = 7^{1/2}$

67. $\sqrt{29} = (29)^{1/2}$

69. $\sqrt{8x} = (8x)^{1/2}$

71. $\sqrt{12x^2} = \left(12x^2\right)^{1/2}$

73. $\sqrt{17ab^2} = (17ab^2)^{1/2}$

75. $\sqrt{38n^3} = (38n^3)^{1/2}$

77. Rational:

$$5,\ 9.83, \frac{3}{7}, \frac{3}{5}, 0.333\ldots, \sqrt{\frac{4}{49}}, -\sqrt{9}$$

Irrational: $\sqrt{\dfrac{5}{16}}$

Imaginary: $\sqrt{-4}, -\sqrt{-16}$

79. 6 and 7 since $6^2 = 36, 7^2 = 49$, and $36 < 47 < 49$

81. a. Square 4.6 and compare it with 20.

     b. $(4.6)^2 = 21.16 > 20$, so 4.6 is greater.

83. $-\sqrt{9}, -\sqrt{7}, -\dfrac{1}{2}, 2.5,\ \sqrt{16}, 4.01,\ 5, 12$

85. $\quad \sqrt{4} = 2$

$\qquad 6^{1/2} \approx 2.45$

$\qquad -\sqrt{9} = -3$

$\qquad -(25)^{1/2} = -5$

$\qquad (30)^{1/2} \approx 5.48$

$\qquad (-4)^{1/2}$, imaginary number

87. $\sqrt{0} = 0$ which is neither a positive nor negative number.

0 is a perfect square since $0^2 = 0$

a. Yes

b. No

c. No

d. Yes

e. No

89. a. Yes, $\sqrt{3^2} = \sqrt{9} = 3$.

     b. Yes, $\sqrt{8^2} = \sqrt{64} = 8$.

     c. $\sqrt{a^2} = a, a \geq 0$

91. $(x^3)^{1/2} = x^{3 \cdot (1/2)} = x^{3/2}$

93. $x^{1/2} x^{5/2} = x^{(1/2)+(5/2)} = x^{6/2} = x^3$

95. Let j = the number of jumps the mother did, then $2j$ = the number of jumps Allison did.

$$j + 2j = 78$$
$$3j = 78$$
$$j = 26$$

Thus Allison made $2j = 2(26) = 52$ jumps.

96.

$$\frac{2x}{x^2 - 4} + \frac{1}{x - 2} = \frac{2}{x + 2}$$

$$\frac{2x}{(x-2)(x+2)} + \frac{1}{x-2} = \frac{2}{x+2}$$

$$(x-2)(x+2)\left[\frac{2x}{(x-2)(x+2)} + \frac{1}{(x-2)}\right] = \frac{2}{x+2} \cdot (x-2)(x+2)$$

$$2x + (x+2) = 2(x-2)$$
$$2x + x + 2 = 2x - 4$$
$$3x + 2 = 2x - 4$$
$$3x = 2x - 6$$
$$x = -6$$

97.

$$\frac{4x}{x^2 + 6x + 9} - \frac{2x}{x + 3} = \frac{x+1}{x+3}$$

$$\frac{4x}{(x+3)^2} - \frac{2x}{x+3} = \frac{x+1}{x+3}$$

$$(x+3)^2\left[\frac{4x}{(x+3)^2}-\frac{2x}{x+3}\right]=\frac{x+1}{x+3}\cdot(x+3)^2$$

$$4x-2x(x+3)=(x+1)(x+3)$$

$$4x-2x^2-6x=x^2+4x+3$$

$$0=3x^2+6x+3$$

$$0=3(x^2+2x+1)$$

$$0=3(x+1)^2$$

$$0=x+1$$

$$x=-1$$

98. $m=\dfrac{7-2}{6-(-5)}=\dfrac{5}{11}$

99. $f(x)=x^2-4x-15$

$$f(-3)=(-3)^2-4(-3)-15$$

$$=9+12-15$$

$$=6$$

Exercise Set 9.2

1. Answers will vary.

3. The product rule cannot be used when radicands are negative.

5. a. Answers will vary.

   b. $\sqrt{x^{13}}=\sqrt{x^{12}\cdot x}=\sqrt{x^{12}}\sqrt{x}=x^6\sqrt{x}$

7. a. There can be no perfect square factors or any exponents greater than 1 in the radicand.

   b. $\sqrt{75x^5}=\sqrt{25x^4}\cdot\sqrt{3x}=5x^2\sqrt{3x}$

9. Yes; since $\sqrt{75}=\sqrt{25\cdot3}=\sqrt{25}\sqrt{3}=5\sqrt{3}$

11. No; $\sqrt{32}=\sqrt{16\cdot2}=\sqrt{16}\sqrt{2}=4\sqrt{2}$

13. $\sqrt{18}=\sqrt{9\cdot2}=\sqrt{9}\cdot\sqrt{2}=3\sqrt{2}$

15. $\sqrt{8}=\sqrt{4\cdot2}$

$$=\sqrt{4}\cdot\sqrt{2}$$

$$=2\sqrt{2}$$

17. $\sqrt{28}=\sqrt{4\cdot7}$

$$=\sqrt{4}\cdot\sqrt{7}$$

$$=2\sqrt{7}$$

19. $\sqrt{20}=\sqrt{4\cdot5}$

$$=\sqrt{4}\cdot\sqrt{5}$$

$$=2\sqrt{5}$$

21. $\sqrt{160}=\sqrt{16\cdot10}$

$$=\sqrt{16}\cdot\sqrt{10}$$

$$=4\sqrt{10}$$

23. $\sqrt{80}=\sqrt{16\cdot5}$

$$=\sqrt{16}\cdot\sqrt{5}$$

$$=4\sqrt{5}$$

25. $\sqrt{72}=\sqrt{36\cdot2}$

$$=\sqrt{36}\cdot\sqrt{2}$$

$$=6\sqrt{2}$$

27. $\sqrt{120}=\sqrt{4\cdot30}$

$$=\sqrt{4}\cdot\sqrt{30}$$

$$=2\sqrt{30}$$

29. $\sqrt{243}=\sqrt{81\cdot3}$

$$=\sqrt{81}\cdot\sqrt{3}$$

$$=9\sqrt{3}$$

31. $\sqrt{150}=\sqrt{25\cdot6}$

$$=\sqrt{25}\cdot\sqrt{6}$$

$$=5\sqrt{6}$$

33. $\sqrt{x^6}=x^3$ since $(x^3)^2=x^6$

35. $\sqrt{x^2y^8}=\sqrt{x^2}\sqrt{y^8}=xy^4$

37. $\sqrt{a^{12}b^9}=\sqrt{a^{12}b^8}\sqrt{b}=a^6b^4\sqrt{b}$

39. $\sqrt{a^2b^4c} = \sqrt{a^2b^4} \cdot \sqrt{c} = ab^2\sqrt{c}$

41. $\sqrt{3n^3} = \sqrt{n^2}\sqrt{3n} = n\sqrt{3n}$

43. $\sqrt{108a^3b^2} = \sqrt{36a^2b^2}\sqrt{3a} = 6ab\sqrt{3a}$

45. $\sqrt{300a^5b^{11}} = \sqrt{100a^4b^{10}}\sqrt{3ab} = 10a^2b^5\sqrt{3ab}$

47. $\sqrt{243x^3y^4} = \sqrt{81x^2y^4}\sqrt{3x} = 9xy^2\sqrt{3x}$

49. $\sqrt{108a^2b^9c} = \sqrt{36a^2b^8}\sqrt{3bc} = 6ab^4\sqrt{3bc}$

51. $\sqrt{180r^3s^{10}t^5} = \sqrt{36r^2s^{10}t^4} \cdot \sqrt{5rt} = 6rs^5t^2\sqrt{5rt}$

53. $\sqrt{7} \cdot \sqrt{7} = \sqrt{7 \cdot 7} = \sqrt{49} = 7$

55. $\sqrt{24} \cdot \sqrt{3} = \sqrt{72} = \sqrt{36} \cdot \sqrt{2} = 6\sqrt{2}$

57. $\sqrt{48} \cdot \sqrt{15} = \sqrt{720}$
$$= \sqrt{144} \cdot \sqrt{5}$$
$$= 12\sqrt{5}$$

59. $\sqrt{2x}\sqrt{7x} = \sqrt{14x^2} = \sqrt{14}\sqrt{x^2} = x\sqrt{14}$

61. $\sqrt{4a^2}\sqrt{12ab^2} = \sqrt{48a^3b^2}$
$$= \sqrt{16a^2b^2}\sqrt{3a}$$
$$= 4ab\sqrt{3a}$$

63. $\sqrt{3xy^3}\sqrt{24x^2y} = \sqrt{72x^3y^4}$
$$= \sqrt{36x^2y^4}\sqrt{2x}$$
$$= 6xy^2\sqrt{2x}$$

65. $\sqrt{3r^4s^7}\sqrt{21r^6s^5} = \sqrt{63r^{10}s^{12}}$
$$= \sqrt{9r^{10}s^{12}}\sqrt{7}$$
$$= 3r^5s^6\sqrt{7}$$

67. $\sqrt{15xy^6}\sqrt{6xyz} = \sqrt{90x^2y^7z}$
$$= \sqrt{9x^2y^6}\sqrt{10yz}$$
$$= 3xy^3\sqrt{10yz}$$

69. $\sqrt{6a^2b^4}\sqrt{9a^4b^6} = \sqrt{54a^6b^{10}}$
$$= \sqrt{9a^6b^{10}}\sqrt{6}$$
$$= 3a^3b^5\sqrt{6}$$

71. $\left(\sqrt{2x}\right)^2 = (2x)^{(1/2)\cdot 2}$
$$= (2x)^1$$
$$= 2x$$

73. $\left(\sqrt{13x^4y^6}\right)^2 = (13x^4y^6)^{(1/2)\cdot 2}$
$$= (13x^4y^6)^1$$
$$= 13x^4y^6$$

75. $\left(\sqrt{5a}\right)^2\left(\sqrt{7a}\right)^2 = (5a)^{(1/2)\cdot 2}(7a)^{(1/2)\cdot 2}$
$$= (5a)^1(7a)^1$$
$$= 5a \cdot 7a$$
$$= 35a^2$$

77. Coefficient is 5 because
$\sqrt{25} = 5$.
Exponent on x is 8 because $\sqrt{x^8} = x^4$.

79. Exponent on x is 12 because $\sqrt{x^{12}} = x^6$;
exponent on y is 5 because
$\sqrt{y^5} = \sqrt{y^4}\sqrt{y} = y^2\sqrt{y}$.

81. Coefficient is 8 because
$\sqrt{2} \cdot \sqrt{8} = \sqrt{16} = 4$.
Exponent on x is 12 because
$\sqrt{x^{12}} \cdot \sqrt{x^3} = \sqrt{x^{15}} = x^7\sqrt{x}$.
Exponent on y is 7 because
$\sqrt{y^5} \cdot \sqrt{y^7} = \sqrt{y^{12}} = y^6$.

83. a. $\left(\sqrt{7x^4}\right)^2 = \left(7x^4\right)^{(1/2)\cdot 2} = \left(7x^4\right)^1 = 7x^4$

   b. $\sqrt{\left(7x^4\right)^2} = \left(7x^4\right)^{2\cdot(1/2)} = \left(7x^4\right)^1 = 7x^4$

   c. Yes

85. $\sqrt{x^{2/6}} = \left(x^{2/6}\right)^{1/2} = x^{(2/6)(1/2)} = x^{1/6}$

87. $\sqrt{4x^{4/5}} = \sqrt{4}\sqrt{x^{4/5}}$
$$= 2\left(x^{4/5}\right)^{1/2}$$
$$= 2x^{(4/5)(1/2)}$$
$$= 2x^{2/5}$$

89. It is rational since $\sqrt{6.25} = 2.5$ and 2.5 is a terminating decimal number.

91. a. $\sqrt{16} = 4$
      The side has length 4 feet.

   b. No, it is increased $\sqrt{2}$ or ≈ 1.414 times.

   c. 4 times

93. a. Yes; a rational number is one that can be written in the form $\dfrac{a}{b}$ where a and b are integers and $b \neq 0$.

Let x and y be 2 rational numbers

$x = \dfrac{a}{b}$, a, b, integers $b \neq 0$

$y = \dfrac{c}{d}$, c, d integers $d \neq 0$

$xy = \dfrac{a}{b} \cdot \dfrac{c}{d} = \dfrac{ac}{bd}$, ac and bd are integers and $bd \neq 0$, hence xy is rational.

b. No, for example $\sqrt{2} \cdot \sqrt{2} = 2$

95. $\sqrt{x^{8b}} = \left(x^{8b}\right)^{1/2} = x^{4b}$

97. $\sqrt{x^{10b}y^{6c}} = \left(x^{10b}y^{6c}\right)^{1/2} = x^{5b}y^{3c}$

98. Substitute 15 for b and 18 for d.

$A = \dfrac{1}{2}h(b+d)$

$= \dfrac{1}{2}(9)(15+18)$

$= \dfrac{1}{2}(9)(33)$

$= (4.5)(33)$

$= 148.5$

The area of the trapezoid is 148.5 square inches.

99. Substitute 2 for r and 6 for h.

$V = \dfrac{1}{3}\pi r^2 h$

$= \dfrac{1}{3}\pi (2)^2 (6)$

$= \dfrac{1}{3}\pi (4)(6)$

$= 8\pi$

≈ 25.13

The volume of the cone is about 25.13 cubic feet.

100. $\dfrac{3x^2 - 16x - 12}{3x^2 - 10x - 8} \div \dfrac{x^2 - 7x + 6}{3x^2 - 11x - 4}$

$= \dfrac{3x^2 - 16x - 12}{3x^2 - 10x - 8} \cdot \dfrac{3x^2 - 11x - 4}{x^2 - 7x + 6}$

$= \dfrac{(3x+2)(x-6)}{(3x+2)(x-4)} \cdot \dfrac{(3x+1)(x-4)}{(x-6)(x-1)}$

$= \dfrac{3x+1}{x-1}$

101. $3x + 6y = 9$

$6y = -3x + 9$

$\dfrac{6y}{6} = \dfrac{-3x+9}{6}$

$y = -\dfrac{1}{2}x + \dfrac{3}{2}$

$m = -\dfrac{1}{2}, \left(0, \dfrac{3}{2}\right)$

102. Graph the line $6x - 5y = 30$.

Since the inequality symbol is $\geq$, draw a solid line.

Check $(0, 0)$: $\quad 6x - 5y \geq 30$

$6(0) - 5(0) \geq 30$

$0 - 0 \geq 30$

$0 \geq 30 \quad$ False

Since $(0, 0)$ does not satisfy the inequality, shade the region that does not include $(0, 0)$.

103. $2x + 3y = -8$

$6x - y = 6$

Multiply the second equation by 3, then add..

$3[6x - y = 6]$

gives

$2x + 3y = -8$

$\underline{18x + 3y = 18}$

$20x = 10$

$x = \dfrac{1}{2}$

Substitute $\dfrac{1}{2}$ for x in the second equation.

$$6x - y = 6$$

$$6\left(\frac{1}{2}\right) - y = 6$$

$$3 - y = 6$$

$$-y = 3$$

$$y = -3$$

The solution is $\left(\dfrac{1}{2}, -3\right)$.

Exercise Set 9.3

1. Like square roots are square roots having the same radicand. One example is $\sqrt{3}, 5\sqrt{3}$.

3. Only like square roots can be added or subtracted.

5. $7\sqrt{5} - 4\sqrt{5} = (7 - 4)\sqrt{5} = 3\sqrt{5}$

7. $9\sqrt{5} - 11\sqrt{5} = (9 - 11)\sqrt{5} = -2\sqrt{5}$

9. $\sqrt{7} + 4\sqrt{7} - 3\sqrt{7} + 8 = (1 + 4 - 3)\sqrt{7} + 8$
$$= 2\sqrt{7} + 8$$

11. $6\sqrt{x} + \sqrt{x} = (6 + 1)\sqrt{x} = 7\sqrt{x}$

13. $-\sqrt{y} + 3\sqrt{y} - 6\sqrt{y} = (-1 + 3 - 6)\sqrt{y} = -4\sqrt{y}$

15. $-6\sqrt{t} + 2\sqrt{t} - 11 = (-6 + 2)\sqrt{t} - 11 = -4\sqrt{t} - 11$

17. $\sqrt{x} + \sqrt{y} + x + 7\sqrt{y} = \sqrt{x} + (1 + 7)\sqrt{y} + x$
$$= \sqrt{x} + 8\sqrt{y} + x$$

19. $11 + 4\sqrt{m} - 6\sqrt{m} + 5m - 2$
$$= 5m + (4 - 6)\sqrt{m} + (11 - 2)$$
$$= 5m - 2\sqrt{m} + 9$$

21. $-3\sqrt{7} + \sqrt{7} - 2\sqrt{x} - 7\sqrt{x}$
$$= (-3 + 1)\sqrt{7} + (-2 - 7)\sqrt{x}$$
$$= -2\sqrt{7} - 9\sqrt{x}$$

23. $\sqrt{40} + \sqrt{18} = \sqrt{4 \cdot 10} + \sqrt{9 \cdot 2}$
$$= \sqrt{4}\sqrt{10} + \sqrt{9}\sqrt{2}$$
$$= 2\sqrt{10} + 3\sqrt{2}$$

25. $\sqrt{300} - \sqrt{12} = \sqrt{100 \cdot 3} - \sqrt{4 \cdot 3}$
$$= \sqrt{100}\sqrt{3} - \sqrt{4}\sqrt{3}$$
$$= 10\sqrt{3} - 2\sqrt{3}$$
$$= 8\sqrt{3}$$

27. $\sqrt{75} + \sqrt{108} = \sqrt{25 \cdot 3} + \sqrt{36 \cdot 3}$
$$= \sqrt{25}\sqrt{3} + \sqrt{36}\sqrt{3}$$
$$= 5\sqrt{3} + 6\sqrt{3}$$
$$= 11\sqrt{3}$$

29. $4\sqrt{50} - \sqrt{72} + \sqrt{8}$
$$= 4\sqrt{25 \cdot 2} - \sqrt{36 \cdot 2} + \sqrt{4 \cdot 2}$$
$$= 4\sqrt{25}\sqrt{2} - \sqrt{36}\sqrt{2} + \sqrt{4}\sqrt{2}$$
$$= 4 \cdot 5\sqrt{2} - 6\sqrt{2} + 2\sqrt{2}$$
$$= 20\sqrt{2} - 6\sqrt{2} + 2\sqrt{2}$$
$$= 16\sqrt{2}$$

31. $-3\sqrt{125} + 8\sqrt{75} = -3\sqrt{25 \cdot 5} + 8\sqrt{25 \cdot 3}$
$$= -3\sqrt{25}\sqrt{5} + 8\sqrt{25}\sqrt{3}$$
$$= -3 \cdot 5\sqrt{5} + 8 \cdot 5\sqrt{3}$$
$$= -15\sqrt{5} + 40\sqrt{3}$$

33. $2\sqrt{360} + 4\sqrt{160} = 2\sqrt{36 \cdot 10} + 4\sqrt{16 \cdot 10}$
$$= 2\sqrt{36}\sqrt{10} + 4\sqrt{16}\sqrt{10}$$
$$= 2 \cdot 6\sqrt{10} + 4 \cdot 4\sqrt{10}$$
$$= 12\sqrt{10} + 16\sqrt{10}$$
$$= (12 + 16)\sqrt{10}$$
$$= 28\sqrt{10}$$

35. $7\sqrt{16} - \sqrt{48} = 7 \cdot 4 - \sqrt{16 \cdot 3}$
$$= 28 - \sqrt{16}\sqrt{3}$$
$$= 28 - 4\sqrt{3}$$

37. $\sqrt{3}\left(2 + \sqrt{3}\right) = \sqrt{3} \cdot 2 + \sqrt{3} \cdot \sqrt{3}$
$$= 2\sqrt{3} + \sqrt{9}$$
$$= 2\sqrt{3} + 3$$

39. $3\left(\sqrt{x} - \sqrt{2}\right) = 3 \cdot \sqrt{x} - 3 \cdot \sqrt{2}$
$$= 3\sqrt{x} - 3\sqrt{2}$$

41. $y\left(\sqrt{y} + y\right) = y \cdot \sqrt{y} + y \cdot y$
$$= y\sqrt{y} + y^2$$

43. $\sqrt{5}\left(\sqrt{8}-3\right)=\sqrt{5}\cdot\sqrt{8}-\sqrt{5}\cdot 3$

$\qquad = \sqrt{40}-3\sqrt{5}$

$\qquad = \sqrt{4\cdot 10}-3\sqrt{5}$

$\qquad = \sqrt{4}\cdot\sqrt{10}-3\sqrt{5}$

$\qquad = 2\sqrt{10}-3\sqrt{5}$

45. $\sqrt{x}\left(\sqrt{x}+\sqrt{3}\right)=\sqrt{x}\cdot\sqrt{x}+\sqrt{x}\cdot\sqrt{3}$

$\qquad = \sqrt{x^2}+\sqrt{x\cdot 3}$

$\qquad = x+\sqrt{3x}$

47. $\sqrt{a}\left(9-\sqrt{2a}\right)=\sqrt{a}\cdot 9-\sqrt{a}\cdot\sqrt{2a}$

$\qquad = 9\sqrt{a}-\sqrt{2a^2}$

$\qquad = 9\sqrt{a}-a\sqrt{2}$

49. $x\left(x+8\sqrt{y}\right)=x\cdot x+x\cdot 8\sqrt{y}$

$\qquad = x^2+8x\sqrt{y}$

51. $3x\left(4x-3\sqrt{x}\right)=3x\cdot 4x+3x\cdot-3\sqrt{x}$

$\qquad = (3\cdot 4)x^2+(3\cdot-3)x\sqrt{x}$

$\qquad = 12x^2-9x\sqrt{x}$

53. $\left(6+\sqrt{3}\right)\left(1-\sqrt{2}\right)$

$\qquad = 6(1)+6\left(-\sqrt{2}\right)+\sqrt{3}(1)+\sqrt{3}\left(-\sqrt{2}\right)$

$\qquad = 6-6\sqrt{2}+\sqrt{3}-\sqrt{3\cdot 2}$

$\qquad = 6-6\sqrt{2}+\sqrt{3}-\sqrt{6}$

55. $\left(\sqrt{5}-4\right)\left(\sqrt{6}+3\right)$

$\qquad = \sqrt{5}\left(\sqrt{6}\right)+\sqrt{5}(3)+(-4)\left(\sqrt{6}\right)+(-4)(3)$

$\qquad = \sqrt{5\cdot 6}+3\sqrt{5}-4\sqrt{6}-12$

$\qquad = \sqrt{30}+3\sqrt{5}-4\sqrt{6}-12$

57. $\left(6-2\sqrt{7}\right)\left(8-2\sqrt{7}\right)$

$\qquad = 6(8)+6\left(-2\sqrt{7}\right)+\left(-2\sqrt{7}\right)(8)+\left(-2\sqrt{7}\right)\left(-2\sqrt{7}\right)$

$\qquad = 48-12\sqrt{7}-16\sqrt{7}+4\sqrt{49}$

$\qquad = 48-12\sqrt{7}-16\sqrt{7}+4(7)$

$\qquad = 48-12\sqrt{7}-16\sqrt{7}+28$

$\qquad = (48+28)+(-12-16)\sqrt{7}$

$\qquad = 76-28\sqrt{7}$

59. $\left(4-\sqrt{x}\right)\left(4-\sqrt{x}\right)$

$\qquad = 4(4)+4\left(-\sqrt{x}\right)+\left(-\sqrt{x}\right)(4)+\left(-\sqrt{x}\right)\left(-\sqrt{x}\right)$

$\qquad = 16-4\sqrt{x}-4\sqrt{x}+\sqrt{x^2}$

$\qquad = 16-4\sqrt{x}-4\sqrt{x}+x$

$\qquad = 16+(-4-4)\sqrt{x}+x$

$\qquad = 16-8\sqrt{x}+x$

61. $\left(\sqrt{3z}-4\right)\left(\sqrt{5z}+1\right)$

$\qquad = \left(\sqrt{3z}\right)\left(\sqrt{5z}\right)+\left(\sqrt{3z}\right)(1)+(-4)\left(\sqrt{5z}\right)+(-4)(1)$

$\qquad = \sqrt{3\cdot 5z^2}+\sqrt{3z}-4\sqrt{5z}-4$

$\qquad = \sqrt{15z^2}+\sqrt{3z}-4\sqrt{5z}-4$

$\qquad = z\sqrt{15}+\sqrt{3z}-4\sqrt{5z}-4$

63. $\left(r+6\sqrt{s}\right)\left(2r-3\sqrt{s}\right)$

$\qquad = r(2r)+r\left(-3\sqrt{s}\right)+\left(6\sqrt{s}\right)(2r)+\left(6\sqrt{s}\right)\left(-3\sqrt{s}\right)$

$\qquad = 2r^2-3r\sqrt{s}+12r\sqrt{s}-18\sqrt{s^2}$

$\qquad = 2r^2-3r\sqrt{s}+12r\sqrt{s}-18s$

$\qquad = 2r^2+(-3r+12r)\sqrt{s}-18s$

$\qquad = 2r^2+9r\sqrt{s}-18s$

65. $\left(x-\sqrt{2y}\right)\left(2x-2\sqrt{2y}\right)$

$\qquad = x(2x)+x\left(-2\sqrt{2y}\right)+\left(-\sqrt{2y}\right)(2x)$

$\qquad\quad +\left(-\sqrt{2y}\right)\left(-2\sqrt{2y}\right)$

$\qquad = 2x^2-2x\sqrt{2y}-2x\sqrt{2y}+2\sqrt{2y\cdot 2y}$

$\qquad = 2x^2-2x\sqrt{2y}-2x\sqrt{2y}+2\sqrt{4y^2}$

$\qquad = 2x^2-2x\sqrt{2y}-2x\sqrt{2y}+2(2y)$

$\qquad = 2x^2-2x\sqrt{2y}-2x\sqrt{2y}+4y$

$\qquad = 2x^2+(-2x-2x)\sqrt{2y}+4y$

$\qquad = 2x^2-4x\sqrt{2y}+4y$

67. $\left(4p - 2\sqrt{3q}\right)\left(p + 2\sqrt{3q}\right)$

$= 4p(p) + 4p\left(2\sqrt{3q}\right) + \left(-2\sqrt{3q}\right)(p)$

$\quad + \left(-2\sqrt{3q}\right)\left(2\sqrt{3q}\right)$

$= 4p^2 + 8p\sqrt{3q} - 2p\sqrt{3q} - 4\sqrt{3q \cdot 3q}$

$= 4p^2 + 8p\sqrt{3q} - 2p\sqrt{3q} - 4\sqrt{9q^2}$

$= 4p^2 + 8p\sqrt{3q} - 2p\sqrt{3q} - 4(3q)$

$= 4p^2 + (8p - 2p)\sqrt{3q} - 12q$

$= 4p^2 + 6p\sqrt{3q} - 12q$

69. $(1 + \sqrt{3})(1 - \sqrt{3})$

$= 1(1) + 1(-\sqrt{3}) + 1(\sqrt{3}) + \sqrt{3}(-\sqrt{3})$

$= 1 - \sqrt{3} + \sqrt{3} - \sqrt{9}$

$= 1 - 3$

$= -2$

71. $(5 - \sqrt{2})(5 + \sqrt{2})$

$= 5(5) + 5(\sqrt{2}) + 5(-\sqrt{2}) + \sqrt{2}(-\sqrt{2})$

$= 25 + 5\sqrt{2} - 5\sqrt{2} - 2$

$= 25 - 2$

$= 23$

73. $(\sqrt{x} + 2)(\sqrt{x} - 2)$

$= \sqrt{x}(\sqrt{x}) + \sqrt{x}(-2) + 2\sqrt{x} + 2(-2)$

$= x - 2\sqrt{x} + 2\sqrt{x} - 4$

$= x - 4$

75. $(\sqrt{7} + m)(\sqrt{7} - m)$

$= \sqrt{7}(\sqrt{7}) + \sqrt{7}(-m) + \sqrt{7}(m) + m(-m)$

$= 7 - \sqrt{7}m + \sqrt{7}m - m^2$

$= 7 - m^2$

77. $(\sqrt{5x} + \sqrt{y})(\sqrt{5x} - \sqrt{y})$

$= \sqrt{5x}(\sqrt{5x}) + \sqrt{5x}(-\sqrt{y}) + \sqrt{y}(\sqrt{5x}) + \sqrt{y}(-\sqrt{y})$

$= 5x - \sqrt{5x}\sqrt{y} + \sqrt{5x}\sqrt{y} - y$

$= 5x - y$

79. $(6\sqrt{x} + 3\sqrt{y})(6\sqrt{x} - 3\sqrt{y})$

$= (6\sqrt{x})(6\sqrt{x}) + (6\sqrt{x})(-3\sqrt{y}) + (3\sqrt{y})(6\sqrt{x})$

$\quad + (3\sqrt{y})(-3\sqrt{y})$

$= 36x - 18\sqrt{xy} + 18\sqrt{xy} - 9y$

$= 36x - 9y$

81. a. No

   b. $2 \cdot \sqrt{5} = 2\sqrt{5}$ is twice as large as $\sqrt{5}$.

83. $x + 3$

85. Yes

87. The missing expression is 343 since

$\sqrt{343} - \sqrt{63} = \sqrt{49 \cdot 7} - \sqrt{9 \cdot 7}$

$\qquad\qquad\qquad = 7\sqrt{7} - 3\sqrt{7}$

$\qquad\qquad\qquad = 4\sqrt{7}$

89. Perimeter:

$(\sqrt{2} + \sqrt{3}) + (\sqrt{2} + \sqrt{3}) + (\sqrt{2} + \sqrt{3}) + (\sqrt{2} + \sqrt{3})$

$= 4(\sqrt{2} + \sqrt{3})$ units

Area:

$(\sqrt{2} + \sqrt{3})(\sqrt{2} + \sqrt{3})$

$= (\sqrt{2})^2 + 2\sqrt{2}\sqrt{3} + (\sqrt{3})^2$

$= 2 + 2\sqrt{2}\sqrt{3} + 3$

$= 5 + 2\sqrt{6}$ square units

91. Perimeter:

$\sqrt{7} + \sqrt{15} + \sqrt{22}$ units

Area:

$= \dfrac{1}{2}bh$

$= \dfrac{1}{2}\left(\sqrt{7}\right)\left(\sqrt{15}\right)$

$= \dfrac{1}{2}\left(\sqrt{7 \cdot 15}\right)$

$= \dfrac{1}{2}\sqrt{105}$ square units

93. $\sqrt{(3^2) - 4 \cdot 1 \cdot 2} = \sqrt{9 - 8} = \sqrt{1} = 1$

95. $\sqrt{(-14)^2 - 4 \cdot 1 \cdot (-5)} = \sqrt{196 + 20}$

$\qquad\qquad\qquad\qquad = \sqrt{216}$

$\qquad\qquad\qquad\qquad = \sqrt{36 \cdot 6}$

$\qquad\qquad\qquad\qquad = 6\sqrt{6}$

97. $\sqrt{(4)^2 - 4 \cdot (-2)(7)} = \sqrt{16 + 56}$
$$= \sqrt{72}$$
$$= \sqrt{36 \cdot 2}$$
$$= 6\sqrt{2}$$

99. The missing expression is 48 since
$$-5\sqrt{48} + \sqrt{3} + 3\sqrt{27}$$
$$= -5\sqrt{16 \cdot 3} + \sqrt{3} + 3\sqrt{9 \cdot 3}$$
$$= -5 \cdot 4\sqrt{3} + \sqrt{3} + 3 \cdot 3\sqrt{3}$$
$$= -20\sqrt{3} + \sqrt{3} + 9\sqrt{3}$$
$$= (-20 + 1 + 9)\sqrt{3}$$
$$= -10\sqrt{3}$$

101. Let x = the amount of time he spent riding the sled downhill.

	Rate	Time	Distance
Riding	10	x	$10x$
Walking	2	$x + 0.2$	$2(x + 0.2)$

$10x = 2x + 0.4$
$8x = 0.4$
$x = 0.05$ hours or $(0.05 \times 60) = 3$ minutes
Jason's sleigh ride took 3 minutes.

102. $3x^2 - 12x - 96 = 3(x^2 - 4x - 32)$
$$= 3(x + 4)(x - 8)$$

103. $\dfrac{x^2 - 1}{x^3 - 1} = \dfrac{(x+1)\cancel{(x-1)}}{\cancel{(x-1)}(x^2 + x + 1)} = \dfrac{x + 1}{x^2 + x + 1}$

104. $x - \dfrac{24}{x} = 2$
$$x\left(x - \dfrac{24}{x}\right) = x \cdot 2$$
$$x^2 - 24 = 2x$$
$$x^2 - 2x - 24 = 0$$
$$(x - 6)(x + 4) = 0$$
$$x - 6 = 0 \quad \text{or} \quad x + 4 = 0$$
$$x = 6 \qquad\qquad x = -4$$

105.

The solution is (2, 2).

Exercise Set 9.4

1. Cannot be simplified: the radicand does not have a factor that is a perfect square, the radicand does not contain a fraction, and the denominator does not contain a square root.

3. The numerator and denominator have a common factor.
$$\frac{x^2\sqrt{3}}{x} = x\sqrt{3}$$

5. Cannot be simplified: the radicand does not have a factor that is a perfect square, the radicand does not contain a fraction, and the denominator does not contain a square root.

7. 1. No perfect square factors in any radicand.
2. No radicand contains a fraction.
3. No square roots in any denominator.

9. a. The radicand contains a perfect square factor.
$$\sqrt{27} = \sqrt{9 \cdot 3} = \sqrt{9} \cdot \sqrt{3} = 3\sqrt{3}$$

b. The radicand contains a fraction.
$$\sqrt{\frac{1}{3}} = \frac{\sqrt{1}}{\sqrt{3}} = \frac{1}{\sqrt{3}} = \frac{1}{\sqrt{3}} \cdot \frac{\sqrt{3}}{\sqrt{3}} = \frac{\sqrt{3}}{3}$$

c. The denominator contains a square root.
$$\frac{8}{\sqrt{5}} = \frac{8}{\sqrt{5}} \cdot \frac{\sqrt{5}}{\sqrt{5}} = \frac{8\sqrt{5}}{5}$$

11. $\sqrt{\dfrac{27}{3}} = \sqrt{9} = 3$

13. $\sqrt{\dfrac{63}{7}} = \sqrt{9} = 3$

15. $\dfrac{\sqrt{18}}{\sqrt{2}} = \sqrt{\dfrac{18}{2}} = \sqrt{9} = 3$

17. $\sqrt{\dfrac{3}{12}} = \dfrac{\sqrt{1}}{\sqrt{4}} = \dfrac{1}{2}$

19. $\sqrt{\dfrac{81}{100}} = \dfrac{\sqrt{81}}{\sqrt{100}} = \dfrac{9}{10}$

21. $\dfrac{\sqrt{20}}{\sqrt{2000}} = \sqrt{\dfrac{20}{2000}} = \sqrt{\dfrac{1}{100}} = \dfrac{\sqrt{1}}{\sqrt{100}} = \dfrac{1}{10}$

23. $\sqrt{\dfrac{48x^3}{2x}} = \sqrt{24x^2} = \sqrt{4x^2} \cdot \sqrt{6} = 2x\sqrt{6}$

25. $\sqrt{\dfrac{45x^2}{16x^2y^4}} = \sqrt{\dfrac{45}{16y^4}} = \dfrac{\sqrt{45}}{\sqrt{16y^4}} = \dfrac{\sqrt{9 \cdot 5}}{4y^2} = \dfrac{3\sqrt{5}}{4y^2}$

27. $\sqrt{\dfrac{16x^5y^3}{81x^7y}} = \sqrt{\dfrac{16y^2}{81x^2}} = \dfrac{\sqrt{16y^2}}{\sqrt{81x^2}} = \dfrac{4y}{9x}$

29. $\sqrt{\dfrac{14ab}{14a^5b^3}} = \sqrt{\dfrac{1}{a^4b^2}} = \dfrac{\sqrt{1}}{\sqrt{a^4b^2}} = \dfrac{1}{a^2b}$

31. $\dfrac{\sqrt{32n^5}}{\sqrt{8n}} = \sqrt{\dfrac{32n^5}{8n}} = \sqrt{4n^4} = 2n^2$

33. $\dfrac{\sqrt{81w^5z}}{\sqrt{144wz^3}} = \sqrt{\dfrac{81w^5z}{144wz^3}}$

$= \sqrt{\dfrac{81w^4}{144z^2}}$

$= \dfrac{\sqrt{81w^4}}{\sqrt{144z^2}}$

$= \dfrac{9w^2}{12z} = \dfrac{3w^2}{4z}$

35. $\dfrac{\sqrt{50ab^6}}{\sqrt{10ab^4c^2}} = \sqrt{\dfrac{50ab^6}{10ab^4c^2}} = \sqrt{\dfrac{5b^2}{c^2}} = \dfrac{\sqrt{5b^2}}{\sqrt{c^2}} = \dfrac{b\sqrt{5}}{c}$

37. $\dfrac{\sqrt{125a^6b^8}}{\sqrt{5a^2b^2}} = \sqrt{\dfrac{125a^6b^8}{5a^2b^2}} = \sqrt{25a^4b^6} = 5a^2b^3$

39. $\dfrac{1}{\sqrt{7}} = \dfrac{1}{\sqrt{7}} \cdot \dfrac{\sqrt{7}}{\sqrt{7}} = \dfrac{\sqrt{7}}{\sqrt{49}} = \dfrac{\sqrt{7}}{7}$

41. $\dfrac{4}{\sqrt{2}} = \dfrac{4}{\sqrt{2}} \cdot \dfrac{\sqrt{2}}{\sqrt{2}} = \dfrac{4\sqrt{2}}{\sqrt{4}} = \dfrac{4\sqrt{2}}{2} = 2\sqrt{2}$

43. $\dfrac{6}{\sqrt{12}} = \dfrac{6}{\sqrt{4 \cdot 3}}$

$= \dfrac{6}{2\sqrt{3}}$

$= \dfrac{3}{\sqrt{3}}$

$= \dfrac{3}{\sqrt{3}} \cdot \dfrac{\sqrt{3}}{\sqrt{3}}$

$= \dfrac{3\sqrt{3}}{\sqrt{9}}$

$= \dfrac{3\sqrt{3}}{3}$

$= \sqrt{3}$

45. $\sqrt{\dfrac{2}{5}} = \dfrac{\sqrt{2}}{\sqrt{5}} = \dfrac{\sqrt{2}}{\sqrt{5}} \cdot \dfrac{\sqrt{5}}{\sqrt{5}} = \dfrac{\sqrt{10}}{\sqrt{25}} = \dfrac{\sqrt{10}}{5}$

47. $\sqrt{\dfrac{2}{7}} = \dfrac{\sqrt{2}}{\sqrt{7}} = \dfrac{\sqrt{2}}{\sqrt{7}} \cdot \dfrac{\sqrt{7}}{\sqrt{7}} = \dfrac{\sqrt{14}}{\sqrt{49}} = \dfrac{\sqrt{14}}{7}$

49. $\sqrt{\dfrac{6}{18}} = \sqrt{\dfrac{1}{3}} = \dfrac{\sqrt{1}}{\sqrt{3}} = \dfrac{1}{\sqrt{3}} = \dfrac{1}{\sqrt{3}} \cdot \dfrac{\sqrt{3}}{\sqrt{3}} = \dfrac{\sqrt{3}}{\sqrt{9}} = \dfrac{\sqrt{3}}{3}$

51. $\sqrt{\dfrac{5}{8}} = \dfrac{\sqrt{5}}{\sqrt{8}} = \dfrac{\sqrt{5}}{\sqrt{4}\sqrt{2}}$

$= \dfrac{\sqrt{5}}{2\sqrt{2}}$

$= \dfrac{\sqrt{5}}{2\sqrt{2}} \cdot \dfrac{\sqrt{2}}{\sqrt{2}}$

$= \dfrac{\sqrt{10}}{2 \cdot 2}$

$= \dfrac{\sqrt{10}}{4}$

53. $\sqrt{\dfrac{6}{x}} = \dfrac{\sqrt{6}}{\sqrt{x}} = \dfrac{\sqrt{6}}{\sqrt{x}} \cdot \dfrac{\sqrt{x}}{\sqrt{x}} = \dfrac{\sqrt{6x}}{\sqrt{x^2}} = \dfrac{\sqrt{6x}}{x}$

55. $\sqrt{\dfrac{a}{b}} = \dfrac{\sqrt{a}}{\sqrt{b}} = \dfrac{\sqrt{a}}{\sqrt{b}} \cdot \dfrac{\sqrt{b}}{\sqrt{b}} = \dfrac{\sqrt{ab}}{b}$

57. $\sqrt{\dfrac{m}{n}} = \dfrac{\sqrt{m}}{\sqrt{n}} = \dfrac{\sqrt{m}}{\sqrt{n}} \cdot \dfrac{\sqrt{n}}{\sqrt{n}} = \dfrac{\sqrt{mn}}{n}$

59. $\sqrt{\dfrac{3x}{11}} = \dfrac{\sqrt{3x}}{\sqrt{11}} = \dfrac{\sqrt{3x}}{\sqrt{11}} \cdot \dfrac{\sqrt{11}}{\sqrt{11}} = \dfrac{\sqrt{33x}}{11}$

61. $\sqrt{\dfrac{x^2}{7}} = \dfrac{\sqrt{x^2}}{\sqrt{7}} = \dfrac{x}{\sqrt{7}} = \dfrac{x}{\sqrt{7}} \cdot \dfrac{\sqrt{7}}{\sqrt{7}} = \dfrac{x\sqrt{7}}{7}$

63. $\sqrt{\dfrac{a^2}{18}} = \dfrac{\sqrt{a^2}}{\sqrt{18}}$

$= \dfrac{a}{\sqrt{9} \cdot \sqrt{2}}$

$= \dfrac{a}{3\sqrt{2}}$

$= \dfrac{a}{3\sqrt{2}} \cdot \dfrac{\sqrt{2}}{\sqrt{2}}$

$= \dfrac{a\sqrt{2}}{3 \cdot 2}$

$= \dfrac{a\sqrt{2}}{6}$

65. $\sqrt{\dfrac{t^5}{6}} = \dfrac{\sqrt{t^5}}{\sqrt{6}} = \dfrac{\sqrt{t^4}\sqrt{t}}{\sqrt{6}} = \dfrac{t^2\sqrt{t}}{\sqrt{6}} \cdot \dfrac{\sqrt{6}}{\sqrt{6}} = \dfrac{t^2\sqrt{6t}}{6}$

67. $\sqrt{\dfrac{a^8}{14b}} = \dfrac{\sqrt{a^8}}{\sqrt{14b}}$

$= \dfrac{a^4}{\sqrt{14b}}$

$= \dfrac{a^4}{\sqrt{14b}} \cdot \dfrac{\sqrt{14b}}{\sqrt{14b}}$

$= \dfrac{a^4\sqrt{14b}}{\sqrt{196b^2}}$

$= \dfrac{a^4\sqrt{14b}}{14b}$

69. $\sqrt{\dfrac{6c^2d^4}{30c^2d^7}} = \sqrt{\dfrac{1}{5d^3}}$

$= \dfrac{\sqrt{1}}{\sqrt{5d^2 \cdot d}}$

$= \dfrac{1}{d\sqrt{5d}}$

$= \dfrac{1}{d\sqrt{5d}} \cdot \dfrac{\sqrt{5d}}{\sqrt{5d}}$

$= \dfrac{\sqrt{5d}}{d\sqrt{25d^2}}$

$= \dfrac{\sqrt{5d}}{d \cdot 5d}$

$= \dfrac{\sqrt{5d}}{5d^2}$

71. $\sqrt{\dfrac{50yz}{24x^4y^5z^9}} = \sqrt{\dfrac{25}{12x^4y^4z^8}}$

$= \dfrac{\sqrt{25}}{\sqrt{12x^4y^4z^8}}$

$= \dfrac{5}{x^2y^2z^4\sqrt{12}}$

$= \dfrac{5}{x^2y^2z^4\sqrt{12}} \cdot \dfrac{\sqrt{3}}{\sqrt{3}}$

$= \dfrac{5\sqrt{3}}{6x^2y^2z^4}$

73. $\dfrac{\sqrt{90x^4y}}{\sqrt{2x^5y^5}} = \sqrt{\dfrac{90x^4y}{2x^5y^5}}$

$= \sqrt{\dfrac{45}{xy^4}}$

$= \dfrac{\sqrt{45}}{\sqrt{xy^4}}$

$= \dfrac{\sqrt{9}\sqrt{5}}{\sqrt{y^4}\sqrt{x}}$

$= \dfrac{3\sqrt{5}}{y^2\sqrt{x}}$

$= \dfrac{3\sqrt{5}}{y^2\sqrt{x}} \cdot \dfrac{\sqrt{x}}{\sqrt{x}}$

$= \dfrac{3\sqrt{5x}}{xy^2}$

75. $\left(6+\sqrt{3}\right)\left(6-\sqrt{3}\right)$

$= 6(6) + 6\left(-\sqrt{3}\right) + \sqrt{3}(6) + \sqrt{3}\left(-\sqrt{3}\right)$

$= 36 - 6\sqrt{3} + 6\sqrt{3} - 3$

$= 33$

77. $\left(\sqrt{3}-\sqrt{11}\right)\left(\sqrt{3}+\sqrt{11}\right)$

$= \sqrt{3}\left(\sqrt{3}\right) + \sqrt{3}\left(\sqrt{11}\right) + \left(-\sqrt{11}\right)\left(\sqrt{3}\right)$

$\quad + \left(-\sqrt{11}\right)\left(\sqrt{11}\right)$

$= 3 + \sqrt{33} - \sqrt{33} - 11$

$= -8$

79. $(\sqrt{x} - y)(\sqrt{x} + y)$

$= \sqrt{x}\sqrt{x} + y\sqrt{x} - y\sqrt{x} - y(y)$

$= x + y\sqrt{x} - y\sqrt{x} - y^2$

$= x - y^2$

81. $(\sqrt{a} + \sqrt{b})(\sqrt{a} - \sqrt{b})$

$= \sqrt{a}\sqrt{a} + \sqrt{a}(-\sqrt{b}) + \sqrt{b}\sqrt{a} + \sqrt{b}(-\sqrt{b})$

$= a - \sqrt{a}\sqrt{b} + \sqrt{a}\sqrt{b} - b$

$= a - b$

83. $\dfrac{3}{\sqrt{5} + 2} = \dfrac{3}{\sqrt{5} + 2} \cdot \dfrac{\sqrt{5} - 2}{\sqrt{5} - 2}$

$= \dfrac{3(\sqrt{5} - 2)}{5 - 4}$

$= \dfrac{3\sqrt{5} - 6}{1}$

$= 3\sqrt{5} - 6$

85. $\dfrac{4}{\sqrt{6} - 1} = \dfrac{4}{\sqrt{6} - 1} \cdot \dfrac{\sqrt{6} + 1}{\sqrt{6} + 1}$

$= \dfrac{4(\sqrt{6} + 1)}{6 - 1}$

$= \dfrac{4\sqrt{6} + 4}{5}$

87. $\dfrac{12}{\sqrt{3} + \sqrt{5}} = \dfrac{12}{\sqrt{3} + \sqrt{5}} \cdot \dfrac{\sqrt{3} - \sqrt{5}}{\sqrt{3} - \sqrt{5}}$

$= \dfrac{12(\sqrt{3} - \sqrt{5})}{3 - 5}$

$= \dfrac{12(\sqrt{3} - \sqrt{5})}{-2}$

$= -6(\sqrt{3} - \sqrt{5})$

$= -6\sqrt{3} + 6\sqrt{5}$

89. $\dfrac{8}{\sqrt{5} - \sqrt{8}} = \dfrac{8}{\sqrt{5} - \sqrt{8}} \cdot \dfrac{\sqrt{5} + \sqrt{8}}{\sqrt{5} + \sqrt{8}}$

$= \dfrac{8(\sqrt{5} + \sqrt{8})}{5 - 8}$

$= \dfrac{8\sqrt{5} + 8\sqrt{8}}{-3}$

$= \dfrac{8\sqrt{5} + 8\sqrt{4}\sqrt{2}}{-3}$

$= \dfrac{8\sqrt{5} + 8 \cdot 2\sqrt{2}}{-3}$

$= \dfrac{8\sqrt{5} + 16\sqrt{2}}{-3}$

$= \dfrac{-8\sqrt{5} - 16\sqrt{2}}{3}$

91. $\dfrac{4}{\sqrt{y} + 3} = \dfrac{4}{\sqrt{y} + 3} \cdot \dfrac{\sqrt{y} - 3}{\sqrt{y} - 3}$

$= \dfrac{4(\sqrt{y} - 3)}{y - 9}$

$= \dfrac{4\sqrt{y} - 12}{y - 9}$

93. $\dfrac{7}{4 - \sqrt{y}} = \dfrac{7}{4 - \sqrt{y}} \cdot \dfrac{4 + \sqrt{y}}{4 + \sqrt{y}}$

$= \dfrac{7(4 + \sqrt{y})}{16 - y}$

$= \dfrac{28 + 7\sqrt{y}}{16 - y}$

95. $\dfrac{16}{\sqrt{y} + x} = \dfrac{16}{\sqrt{y} + x} \cdot \dfrac{\sqrt{y} - x}{\sqrt{y} - x}$

$= \dfrac{16(\sqrt{y} - x)}{y - x^2}$

$= \dfrac{16\sqrt{y} - 16x}{y - x^2}$

97. $\dfrac{x}{\sqrt{x} + \sqrt{y}} = \dfrac{9}{\sqrt{x} + \sqrt{y}} \cdot \dfrac{\sqrt{x} - \sqrt{y}}{\sqrt{x} - \sqrt{y}}$

$= \dfrac{9(\sqrt{x} - \sqrt{y})}{x - y}$

$= \dfrac{9\sqrt{x} - 9\sqrt{y}}{x - y}$

99.
$$\frac{\sqrt{3}}{\sqrt{3}-\sqrt{n}} = \frac{\sqrt{3}}{\sqrt{3}-\sqrt{n}} \cdot \frac{\sqrt{3}+\sqrt{n}}{\sqrt{3}+\sqrt{n}}$$
$$= \frac{\sqrt{3}(\sqrt{3}+\sqrt{n})}{3-n}$$
$$= \frac{3+\sqrt{3n}}{3-n}$$

101.
$$\frac{2\sqrt{x}}{6-\sqrt{x}} = \frac{2\sqrt{x}}{6-\sqrt{x}} \cdot \frac{6+\sqrt{x}}{6+\sqrt{x}}$$
$$= \frac{2\sqrt{x}\left(6+\sqrt{x}\right)}{36-x}$$
$$= \frac{12\sqrt{x}+2x}{36-x}$$

103. Yes, $\dfrac{a}{b} \div \dfrac{c}{d} = \dfrac{a}{b} \cdot \dfrac{d}{c} = \dfrac{ad}{bc}$, which is a rational

number since b, c, and d cannot be zero $\left(\dfrac{a}{b}, \dfrac{c}{d}\right.$

both rational and $\left.\dfrac{c}{d} \neq 0\right)$.

105. $\sqrt{5}+\sqrt{10} \approx 2.236 + 3.162 \approx 5.398 \approx 5.40$

107. $\dfrac{\sqrt{5}}{\sqrt{10}} \approx \dfrac{2.236}{3.162} \approx 0.71$

109. $\sqrt{7}+\sqrt{21} \approx 2.646 + 4.583 \approx 7.229 \approx 7.23$

111. $\dfrac{\sqrt{7}}{\sqrt{21}} \approx \dfrac{2.646}{4.583} \approx 0.58$

113.
$$lw = A$$
$$\left(4+\sqrt{3}\right)w = 24$$
$$w = \frac{24}{4+\sqrt{3}}$$
$$= \frac{24}{4+\sqrt{3}} \cdot \frac{4-\sqrt{3}}{4-\sqrt{3}}$$
$$= \frac{24\left(4-\sqrt{3}\right)}{16-3}$$
$$= \frac{24\left(4-\sqrt{3}\right)}{13}$$

115. The missing expression is 2 since
$$\frac{1}{\sqrt{2}} = \frac{1}{\sqrt{2}} \cdot \frac{\sqrt{2}}{\sqrt{2}} = \frac{\sqrt{2}}{2}.$$

117. The missing expression is $64x^{10}$ since
$$\sqrt{\frac{64x^{10}}{4x^2}} = \sqrt{16x^8} = 4x^4.$$

119.
$$\frac{\sqrt{x}}{1-\sqrt{3}} = \frac{\sqrt{x}}{1-\sqrt{3}} \cdot \frac{1+\sqrt{3}}{1+\sqrt{3}}$$
$$= \frac{\sqrt{x}(1+\sqrt{3})}{1-3}$$
$$= \frac{\sqrt{x}+\sqrt{3x}}{-2}$$
$$= \frac{-\sqrt{x}-\sqrt{3x}}{2}$$

121. a.
$$\frac{\sqrt{x}}{x+\sqrt{x}} = \frac{\sqrt{x}}{x+\sqrt{x}} \cdot \frac{x-\sqrt{x}}{x-\sqrt{x}}$$
$$= \frac{x\sqrt{x}-\sqrt{x^2}}{x^2-x}$$
$$= \frac{x\sqrt{x}-x}{x^2-x}$$
$$= \frac{x\left(\sqrt{x}-1\right)}{x\left(x-1\right)}$$
$$= \frac{\sqrt{x}-1}{x-1}$$

b.
$$\frac{\sqrt{x}}{x+\sqrt{x}} = \frac{\sqrt{4}}{4+\sqrt{4}} = \frac{2}{4+2} = \frac{2}{6} = \frac{1}{3}$$
$$\frac{\sqrt{x}-1}{x-1} = \frac{\sqrt{4}-1}{4-1} = \frac{2-1}{3} = \frac{1}{3}$$

c. $\dfrac{\sqrt{x}}{x+\sqrt{x}} = \dfrac{\sqrt{6}}{6+\sqrt{6}} \cdot \dfrac{6-\sqrt{6}}{6-\sqrt{6}}$
$$= \frac{6\sqrt{6}-6}{36-6}$$
$$= \frac{6\sqrt{6}-6}{30}$$
$$= \frac{6\left(\sqrt{6}-1\right)}{30}$$
$$= \frac{\sqrt{6}-1}{5}$$
$$\frac{\sqrt{x}-1}{x-1} = \frac{\sqrt{6}-1}{6-1} = \frac{\sqrt{6}-1}{5}$$

d. $\dfrac{\sqrt{x}}{x+\sqrt{x}} = \dfrac{\sqrt{9}}{9+\sqrt{9}} = \dfrac{3}{9+3} = \dfrac{3}{12} = \dfrac{1}{4}$

$\dfrac{\sqrt{x}-1}{x-1} = \dfrac{\sqrt{9}-1}{9-1} = \dfrac{3-1}{8} = \dfrac{2}{8} = \dfrac{1}{4}$

e. They are equal.

122.

$$x+4\overline{\smash{\big)}\,3x^2+4x-26} \quad \dfrac{3x-8}{}$$

$$\underline{3x^2+12x}$$

$$-8x-26$$

$$\underline{-8x-32}$$

$$6$$

$$\dfrac{3x^2+4x-25}{x+4} = 3x-8+\dfrac{6}{x+4}$$

123. $2x^2 - x - 36 = 0$

$(2x-9)(x+4)=0$

$2x-9=0$ or $x+4=0$

$x = \dfrac{9}{2} \qquad x = -4$

124. $\dfrac{1}{x^2-4} - \dfrac{3}{x-2}$

$= \dfrac{1}{(x-2)(x+2)} - \dfrac{3}{x-2}$

$= \dfrac{1}{(x-2)(x+2)} - \dfrac{3}{x-2}\cdot\dfrac{x+2}{x+2}$

$= \dfrac{1}{(x-2)(x+2)} - \dfrac{3x+6}{(x-2)(x+2)}$

$= \dfrac{1-(3x+6)}{(x-2)(x+2)}$

$= \dfrac{-3x-5}{(x-2)(x+2)}$

125. Mark's rate: $\dfrac{1}{20}$, Terry's rate: $\dfrac{1}{t}$

$\dfrac{12}{20} + \dfrac{12}{t} = 1$

$20t\left(\dfrac{12}{20} + \dfrac{12}{t}\right) = 20t$

$12t + 240 = 20t$

$240 = 8t$

$30 = t$

It would take Mrs. DeGroat 30 minutes to stack the wood by herself.

Mid-Chapter Test: 9.1-9.4

1. $\sqrt{81} = 9$ because $(9)^2 = 81$.

2. $\sqrt{121} = 11$ because $(11)^2 = 121$.
Now take the opposite $-\sqrt{121} = -11$.

3. $\sqrt{\dfrac{169}{49}} = \dfrac{\sqrt{169}}{\sqrt{49}} = \dfrac{13}{7}$ because $\left(\dfrac{13}{7}\right)^2 = \dfrac{169}{49}$.

4. a. irrational   **b.** rational
  b. imaginary   **d.** rational

5. $\sqrt{53xy^2} = \left(53xy^2\right)^{1/2}$

6. $\sqrt{40} = \sqrt{4}\cdot\sqrt{10} = 2\sqrt{10}$

7. $\sqrt{63} = \sqrt{9}\cdot\sqrt{7} = 3\sqrt{7}$

8. $\sqrt{a^2b^5c^8} = \sqrt{a^2b^4c^8}\cdot\sqrt{b} = ab^2c^4\sqrt{b}$

9. $\sqrt{128x^9y^{14}} = \sqrt{64x^8y^{14}}\cdot\sqrt{2x} = 8x^4y^7\sqrt{2x}$

10. $\sqrt{6x^2y^3}\sqrt{9x^3y^6} = \sqrt{54x^5y^9}$

$= \sqrt{9x^4y^8}\cdot\sqrt{6xy}$

$= 3x^2y^4\sqrt{6xy}$

11. $3\sqrt{x} + 2\sqrt{5} + 9\sqrt{x} + 4\sqrt{5} + 17$

$= 3\sqrt{x} + 9\sqrt{x} + 2\sqrt{5} + 4\sqrt{5} + 17$

$= 12\sqrt{x} + 6\sqrt{5} + 17$

12. $4\sqrt{75} - 2\sqrt{108} = 4\sqrt{25}\sqrt{3} - 2\sqrt{36}\sqrt{3}$

$= 4\cdot 5\sqrt{3} - 2\cdot 6\sqrt{3}$

$= 20\sqrt{3} - 12\sqrt{3}$

$= 8\sqrt{3}$

13. $\left(5-\sqrt{2}\right)\left(7+\sqrt{3}\right)$

$= 5(7) + 5\left(\sqrt{3}\right) + \left(-\sqrt{2}\right)(7) + \left(-\sqrt{2}\right)\left(\sqrt{3}\right)$

$= 35 + 5\sqrt{3} - 7\sqrt{2} - \sqrt{6}$

14. $\left(\sqrt{x}-4z\right)\left(\sqrt{x}+5z\right)$

$= \sqrt{x}\left(\sqrt{x}\right) + \sqrt{x}(5z) + (-4z)\left(\sqrt{x}\right) + (-4z)(5z)$

$= x + 5z\sqrt{x} - 4z\sqrt{x} - 20z^2$

$= x + z\sqrt{x} - 20z^2$

15. $\left(\sqrt{3a}+\sqrt{2b}\right)\left(\sqrt{3a}-\sqrt{2b}\right)$

$= \left(\sqrt{3a}\right)^2 - \left(\sqrt{2b}\right)^2$

$= 3a - 2b$

16. Radicals with like radicands can only be added.

$\sqrt{8} + \sqrt{32} = \sqrt{4 \cdot 2} + \sqrt{16 \cdot 2}$

$\qquad\qquad = 2\sqrt{2} + 4\sqrt{2}$

$\qquad\qquad = 6\sqrt{2}$

17. $\dfrac{\sqrt{17}}{\sqrt{68}} = \sqrt{\dfrac{17}{68}} = \sqrt{\dfrac{1}{4}} = \dfrac{1}{2}$

18. $\dfrac{\sqrt{45x^5 y^6}}{\sqrt{5xy^8}} = \sqrt{\dfrac{45x^5 y^6}{5xy^8}} = \sqrt{\dfrac{9x^4}{y^2}} = \dfrac{3x^2}{y}$

19. $\dfrac{7}{\sqrt{6}-2} = \dfrac{7}{\sqrt{6}-2} \cdot \dfrac{\sqrt{6}+2}{\sqrt{6}+2}$

$\qquad = \dfrac{7\sqrt{6}+14}{6-4}$

$\qquad = \dfrac{7\sqrt{6}+14}{2}$

20. $\dfrac{3\sqrt{x}}{\sqrt{x}+5} = \dfrac{3\sqrt{x}}{\sqrt{x}+5} \cdot \dfrac{\sqrt{x}-5}{\sqrt{x}-5} = \dfrac{3x-15\sqrt{x}}{x-25}$

Exercise Set 9.5

1. A radical equation is an equation that contains a variable in a radicand.

3. It is necessary to check solutions because they may be extraneous.

5. Yes

7. No; $-\sqrt{64} = -8$

9. Yes

11. No; $\sqrt{-9}$ is not a real number.

13. $\sqrt{x} = 5$

$\left(\sqrt{x}\right)^2 = (5)^2$

$x = 25$

Check: $\sqrt{x} = 5$

$\sqrt{25} = 5$

$5 = 5$ True

15. $\sqrt{m} = 11$

$\left(\sqrt{m}\right)^2 = 11^2$

$m = 121$

Check: $\sqrt{m} = 11$

$\sqrt{121} = 11$

$11 = 11$ True

17. $\sqrt{x+5} = 3$

$\left(\sqrt{x+5}\right)^2 = 3^2$

$x + 5 = 9$

$x + 5 - 5 = 9 - 5$

$x = 4$

Check: $\sqrt{x+5} = 3$

$\sqrt{4+5} = 3$

$\sqrt{9} = 3$

$3 = 3$ True

19. $\sqrt{x} + 5 = -7$

$\sqrt{x} = -7 - 5$

$\sqrt{x} = -12$

No solution.

21. $\sqrt{z} - 3 = 6$

$\sqrt{z} = 6 + 3$

$\sqrt{z} = 9$

$\left(\sqrt{z}\right)^2 = 9^2$

$z = 81$

Check: $\sqrt{z} - 3 = 6$

$\sqrt{81} - 3 = 6$

$9 - 3 = 6$

$6 = 6$ True

23. $11 = 6 + \sqrt{x}$

$\sqrt{x} = 11 - 6$

$\sqrt{x} = 5$

$\left(\sqrt{x}\right)^2 = 5^2$

$x = 25$

Check: $11 = 6 + \sqrt{x}$

$11 = 6 + \sqrt{25}$

$11 = 6 + 5$

$11 = 11$ True

25. $8 + \sqrt{n} = 4$

$\qquad \sqrt{n} = 4 - 8$

$\qquad \sqrt{n} = -4$

No solution.

27. $\sqrt{2x - 5} = x - 4$

$\qquad (\sqrt{2x - 5})^2 = (x - 4)^2$

$\qquad 2x - 5 = x^2 - 8x + 16$

$\qquad 0 = x^2 - 10x + 21$

$\qquad 0 = (x - 3)(x - 7)$

$x - 3 = 0$ or $x - 7 = 0$

$\qquad x = 3 \qquad\qquad x = 7$

Check:

$x = 3 \qquad\qquad\qquad x = 7$

$\sqrt{2x - 5} = x - 4 \qquad \sqrt{2x - 5} = x - 4$

$\sqrt{2(3) - 5} = 3 - 4 \qquad \sqrt{2(7) - 5} = 7 - 4$

$\qquad \sqrt{1} = -1 \qquad\qquad \sqrt{9} = 3$

$\qquad 1 = -1$ False $\qquad\quad 3 = 3$ True

The solution is 7; 3 is not a solution.

29. $\sqrt{2r - 3} = \sqrt{r + 3}$

$\qquad (\sqrt{2r - 3})^2 = (\sqrt{r + 3})^2$

$\qquad 2r - 3 = r + 3$

$\qquad 2r - r = 3 + 3$

$\qquad r = 6$

Check: $\sqrt{2r - 3} = \sqrt{r + 3}$

$\qquad \sqrt{2(6) - 3} = \sqrt{6 + 3}$

$\qquad \sqrt{12 - 3} = \sqrt{9}$

$\qquad \sqrt{9} = \sqrt{9}$ True

31. $\sqrt{4x + 4} = \sqrt{6x - 2}$

$\qquad (\sqrt{4x + 4})^2 = (\sqrt{6x - 2})^2$

$\qquad 4x + 4 = 6x - 2$

$\qquad 4 + 2 = 6x - 4x$

$\qquad 6 = 2x$

$\qquad x = 3$

Check: $\sqrt{4x + 4} = \sqrt{6x - 2}$

$\qquad \sqrt{4(3) + 4} = \sqrt{6(3) - 2}$

$\qquad \sqrt{16} = \sqrt{16}$ True

33. $\sqrt{x^2 + 5} = x + 1$

$\qquad (\sqrt{x^2 + 5})^2 = (x + 1)^2$

$\qquad x^2 + 5 = x^2 + 2x + 1$

$\qquad 4 = 2x$

$\qquad 2 = x$

Check: $\sqrt{x^2 + 5} = x + 1$

$\qquad \sqrt{2^2 + 5} = 2 + 1$

$\qquad \sqrt{9} = 3$

$\qquad 3 = 3$ True

35. $\sqrt{3x - 5} = \sqrt{x + 9}$

$\qquad (\sqrt{3x - 5})^2 = (\sqrt{x + 9})^2$

$\qquad 3x - 5 = x + 9$

$\qquad 2x - 5 = 9$

$\qquad 2x = 14$

$\qquad x = 7$

Check: $\sqrt{3x - 5} = \sqrt{x + 9}$

$\qquad \sqrt{3(7) - 5} = \sqrt{7 + 9}$

$\qquad \sqrt{16} = \sqrt{16}$ True

37. $3\sqrt{x} = \sqrt{x + 8}$

$\qquad (3\sqrt{x})^2 = (\sqrt{x + 8})^2$

$\qquad 9x = x + 8$

$\qquad 8x = 8$

$\qquad x = 1$

Check: $3\sqrt{x} = \sqrt{x + 8}$

$\qquad 3\sqrt{1} = \sqrt{1 + 8}$

$\qquad 3(1) = \sqrt{9}$

$\qquad 3 = 3$ True

39. $4\sqrt{x} = x + 3$

$\qquad (4\sqrt{x})^2 = (x + 3)^2$

$\qquad 16x = x^2 + 6x + 9$

$\qquad 0 = x^2 - 10x + 9$

$\qquad 0 = (x - 9)(x - 1)$

$x - 9 = 0$ or $x - 1 = 0$

$\qquad x = 9$ or $\qquad x = 1$

Check: $x = 9$ $x = 1$

$4\sqrt{x} = x + 3$ $4\sqrt{x} = x + 3$

$4\sqrt{9} = 9 + 3$ $4\sqrt{1} = 1 + 3$

$4 \cdot 3 = 12$ $4 \cdot 1 = 4$

$12 = 12$ True $4 = 4$ True

41. $\sqrt{3f - 4} = 2\sqrt{3f - 2}$

$(\sqrt{3f - 4})^2 = (2\sqrt{3f - 2})^2$

$3f - 4 = 4(3f - 2)$

$3f - 4 = 12f - 8$

$-4 + 8 = 12f - 3f$

$4 = 9f$

$\dfrac{4}{9} = f$

Check: $\sqrt{3f - 4} = 2\sqrt{3f - 2}$

$\sqrt{3\left(\dfrac{4}{9}\right) - 4} = 2\sqrt{3\left(\dfrac{4}{9}\right) - 2}$

$\sqrt{\dfrac{4}{3} - \dfrac{12}{3}} = 2\sqrt{\dfrac{4}{3} - \dfrac{6}{3}}$

$\sqrt{-\dfrac{8}{3}} = 2\sqrt{-\dfrac{2}{3}}$ False

$\dfrac{4}{9}$ is an extraneous root. There is no solution.

43. $\sqrt{x^2 - 25} = x + 5$

$\left(\sqrt{x^2 - 25}\right)^2 = (x + 5)^2$

$x^2 - 25 = x^2 + 10x + 25$

$0 = x^2 + 10x + 25 - x^2 + 25$

$0 = 10x + 50$

$-50 = 10x$

$-5 = x$

Check: $\sqrt{x^2 - 25} = x + 5$

$\sqrt{(-5)^2 - 25} = -5 + 5$

$\sqrt{25 - 25} = 0$

$0 = 0$ True

45. $3 + \sqrt{3x - 5} = x$

$\sqrt{3x - 5} = x - 3$

$(\sqrt{3x - 5})^2 = (x - 3)^2$

$3x - 5 = x^2 - 6x + 9$

$0 = x^2 - 6x + 9 - 3x + 5$

$0 = x^2 - 9x + 14$

$(x - 7)(x - 2) = 0$

$x - 7 = 0$ or $x - 2 = 0$

$x = 7$ or $x = 2$

Check: $x = 7$

$3 + \sqrt{3x - 5} = x$

$3 + \sqrt{3 \cdot 7 - 5} = 7$

$3 + \sqrt{16} = 7$

$3 + 4 = 7$

$7 = 7$ True

Check: $x = 2$

$3 + \sqrt{3x - 5} = x$

$3 + \sqrt{3 \cdot 2 - 5} = 2$

$3 + \sqrt{1} = 2$

$4 = 2$ False

The solution is 7; 2 is an extraneous root.

47. $\sqrt{8 - 7x} = x - 3$

$(\sqrt{8 - 7x})^2 = (x - 3)^2$

$8 - 7x = x^2 - 6x + 9$

$0 = x^2 + x + 1$

$x^2 + x + 1$ cannot be factored. There is no solution.

49. $2\sqrt{3b-5} - \sqrt{2b+10} = 0$

$$2\sqrt{3b-5} = \sqrt{2b+10}$$

$$\left(2\sqrt{3b-5}\right)^2 = \left(\sqrt{2b+10}\right)^2$$

$$4(3b-5) = 2b+10$$

$$12b - 20 = 2b + 10$$

$$10b - 20 = 10$$

$$10b = 30$$

$$b = 3$$

Check: $2\sqrt{3b-5} - \sqrt{2b+10} = 0$

$$2\sqrt{3(3)-5} - \sqrt{2(3)+10} = 0$$

$$2\sqrt{9-5} - \sqrt{6+10} = 0$$

$$2\sqrt{4} - \sqrt{16} = 0$$

$$2(2) - 4 = 0$$

$$0 = 0 \quad \text{True}$$

51. $4\sqrt{2w+3} = 4w$

$$\frac{1}{4}\left(4\sqrt{2w+3}\right) = \frac{1}{4}(4w)$$

$$\sqrt{2w+3} = w$$

$$\left(\sqrt{2w+3}\right)^2 = w^2$$

$$2w + 3 = w^2$$

$$0 = w^2 - 2w - 3$$

$$0 = (w-3)(w+1)$$

$w - 3 = 0$ or $w + 1 = 0$

$w = 3$ or $w = -1$

Check: $w = 3$

$$4\sqrt{2w+3} = 4w$$

$$4\sqrt{2(3)+3} = 4(3)$$

$$4\sqrt{6+3} = 12$$

$$4\sqrt{9} = 12$$

$$4(3) = 12$$

$$12 = 12 \quad \text{True}$$

Check: $w = -1$

$$4\sqrt{2w+3} = 4w$$

$$4\sqrt{2(-1)+3} = 4(-1)$$

$$4\sqrt{-2+3} = -4$$

$$4\sqrt{1} = -4$$

$$4 = -4 \quad \text{False}$$

The solution is 3; -1 is an extraneous solution.

53. $lw = A$

$$\sqrt{w+9}(6) = 24$$

$$\frac{1}{6}\left(6\sqrt{w+9}\right) = \frac{1}{6}(24)$$

$$\sqrt{w+9} = 4$$

$$\left(\sqrt{w+9}\right)^2 = 4^2$$

$$w + 9 = 16$$

$$w = 7$$

55. $lw = A$

$$6.2\sqrt{3n+3} = 37.2$$

$$\frac{6.2\sqrt{3n+3}}{6.2} = \frac{37.2}{6.2}$$

$$\sqrt{3n+3} = 6$$

$$\left(\sqrt{3n+3}\right)^2 = 6^2$$

$$3n + 3 = 36$$

$$3n = 33$$

$$n = 11$$

57. $(x+4)^{1/2} = 7$

$$\sqrt{x+4} = 7$$

$$(\sqrt{x+4})^2 = 7^2$$

$$x + 4 = 49$$

$$x = 45$$

Check: $\sqrt{45+4} = 7$

$$\sqrt{49} = 7$$

$$7 = 7 \quad \text{True}$$

59. $(x-2)^{1/2} = (2x-9)^{1/2}$

$$\sqrt{x-2} = \sqrt{2x-9}$$
$$(\sqrt{x-2})^2 = (\sqrt{2x-9})^2$$
$$x-2 = 2x-9$$
$$7 = x$$

Check: $\sqrt{7-2} = \sqrt{2\cdot 7-9}$
$$\sqrt{5} = \sqrt{14-9}$$
$$\sqrt{5} = \sqrt{5} \text{ True}$$

61. a. $(\sqrt{x}-3)(\sqrt{x}+3) = 40$

$$(\sqrt{x})(\sqrt{x}) + 3\sqrt{x} - 3\sqrt{x} - 3(3) = 40$$
$$x - 9 = 40$$

b. $x = 40 + 9$
$$x = 49$$

Check: $(\sqrt{49}-3)(\sqrt{49}+3) = 40$
$$(7-3)(7+3) = 40$$
$$4\cdot 10 = 40$$
$$40 = 40 \text{ True}$$

63. a. $(7-\sqrt{x})(5+\sqrt{x}) = 35$

$$7\cdot 5 + 7\sqrt{x} - 5\sqrt{x} + (-\sqrt{x})(\sqrt{x}) = 35$$
$$35 + 7\sqrt{x} - 5\sqrt{x} - x = 35$$
$$35 + 2\sqrt{x} - x = 35$$

b. $35 + 2\sqrt{x} - x = 35$

$$2\sqrt{x} - x = 0$$
$$2\sqrt{x} = x$$
$$(2\sqrt{x})^2 = x^2$$
$$4x = x^2$$
$$0 = x^2 - 4x$$
$$0 = x(x-4)$$
$$x = 0 \quad \text{or} \quad x = 4$$

Check $x = 0$:
$$(7-\sqrt{x})(5+\sqrt{x}) = 35$$
$$(7-\sqrt{0})(5+\sqrt{0}) = 35$$
$$(7)(5) = 35$$
$$35 = 35 \text{ True}$$

Check $x = 4$:
$$(7-\sqrt{x})(5+\sqrt{x}) = 35$$
$$(7-\sqrt{4})(5+\sqrt{4}) = 35$$
$$(7-2)(5+2) = 35$$
$$(5)(7) = 35$$
$$35 = 35 \text{ True}$$

65. $n + \sqrt{n} = 2$

$$\sqrt{n} = 2 - n$$
$$(\sqrt{n})^2 = (2-n)^2$$
$$n^2 = 4 - 4n + n^2$$
$$4n = 4$$
$$n = 1$$

Check: $1 + \sqrt{1} = 2$
$$2 = 2 \text{ True}$$

67. $\sqrt{x} + 1 = \sqrt{x+11}$

$$(\sqrt{x}+1)^2 = (\sqrt{x+11})^2$$
$$x + 2\sqrt{x} + 1 = x + 11$$
$$2\sqrt{x} = 10$$
$$\sqrt{x} = 5$$
$$(\sqrt{x})^2 = 5^2$$
$$x = 25$$

Check: $\sqrt{x} + 1 = \sqrt{x+11}$
$$\sqrt{25} + 1 = \sqrt{25+11}$$
$$5 + 1 = \sqrt{36}$$
$$6 = 6 \text{ True}$$

69. $\sqrt{x+7} = 3 + \sqrt{x-8}$

$$(\sqrt{x+7})^2 = (3+\sqrt{x-8})^2$$
$$x + 7 = 9 + 6\sqrt{x-8} + x - 8$$
$$x + 7 = x + 6\sqrt{x-8} + 1$$
$$6 = 6\sqrt{x-8}$$
$$1 = \sqrt{x-8}$$
$$1^2 = (\sqrt{x-8})^2$$
$$1 = x - 8$$
$$9 = x$$

Check: $\sqrt{x+7} = 3 + \sqrt{x-8}$

$\sqrt{9+7} = 3 + \sqrt{9-8}$

$\sqrt{16} = 3 + \sqrt{1}$

$4 = 3 + 1$

$4 = 4$ True

71. a. Answers will vary.

b.

x	y
2	0
3	1
6	2
11	3

c.

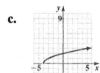

d. no

e. Yes, it passes the vertical line test.

f. Yes, (2, 0) is the x-intercept. There is no y-intercept.

72. a. Answers will vary.

b.

x	y
−4	0
−3	1
0	2
5	3

c.

d. no

e. Yes, it passes the vertical line test.

f. Yes, (−4, 0) is the x-intercept. The y-intercept is (0, 2).

73.

The solution is (2, 0).

74. Substitute $2x - 4$ for y in the first equation.

$3x - 2y = 6$

$3x - 2(2x - 4) = 6$

$3x - 4x + 8 = 6$

$-x + 8 = 6$

$-x = -2$

$x = 2$

Substitute 2 for x in the second equation.

$y = 2x - 4$

$y = 2(2) - 4 = 4 - 4 = 0$

The solution is (2, 0).

75. Align the x- and y-terms on the left side of the equation.

$3x - 2y = 6$

$-2x + y = -4$

Multiply the second equation by 2.

$2[-2x + y = -4]$

gives

$3x - 2y = 6$

$\underline{-4x + 2y = -8}$

$-x \quad\quad = -2$

$x = 2$

Substitute 2 for x in the second equation.

$y = 2x - 4$

$y = 2(2) - 4 = 4 - 4 = 0$

The solution is (2, 0).

76. Let b = the speed of the ferry in still water, c = speed of the current.

Speed of ferry with current = 18 mph.

Speed of ferry against current = 14 mph.

$b + c = 18$

$\underline{b - c = 14}$

$2b = 32$

$b = 16$

Substitute 16 for b in the first equation.

$b + c = 18$

$16 + c = 18$

$c = 2$

Speed of ferry in still water = 16 mph, speed of the current = 2 mph.

Exercise Set 9.6

1. A right triangle is a triangle that contains a 90° angle.

3. No; only with right triangles.

5. They represent the two points in the coordinate plane that you are trying to find the distance between.

7. $\sqrt{(0-0)^2 + [-11-(-4)]^2} = \sqrt{0+(-7)^2}$
$$= \sqrt{49}$$
$$= 7$$

9. $a^2 + b^2 = c^2$
$$x^2 + 4^2 = 7^2$$
$$x^2 + 16 = 49$$
$$x^2 = 33$$
$$x = \sqrt{33} \approx 5.74$$

11. $a^2 + b^2 = c^2$
$$(11)^2 + 7^2 = x^2$$
$$121 + 49 = x^2$$
$$170 = x^2$$
$$x = \sqrt{170} \approx 13.04$$

13. $a^2 + b^2 = c^2$
$$12^2 + (\sqrt{7})^2 = y^2$$
$$144 + 7 = y^2$$
$$151 = y^2$$
$$y = \sqrt{151} \approx 12.29$$

15. $a^2 + b^2 = c^2$
$$8^2 + (\sqrt{3})^2 = x^2$$
$$64 + 3 = x^2$$
$$67 = x^2$$
$$x = \sqrt{67} \approx 8.19$$

17. $a^2 + b^2 = c^2$
$$(\sqrt{6})^2 + 14^2 = x^2$$
$$6 + 196 = x^2$$
$$202 = x^2$$
$$x = \sqrt{202} \approx 14.21$$

19. $a^2 + b^2 = c^2$
$$4^2 + x^2 = 14^2$$
$$16 + x^2 = 196$$
$$x^2 = 180$$
$$x = \sqrt{180} \approx 13.42$$

21. $d = \sqrt{(3-8)^2 + (10-7)^2}$
$$= \sqrt{25+9}$$
$$= \sqrt{34}$$
$$\approx 5.83$$

23. $d = \sqrt{[4-(-8)]^2 + (11-4)^2}$
$$= \sqrt{(12)^2 + 7^2}$$
$$= \sqrt{193}$$
$$\approx 13.89$$

25. $a^2 + b^2 = c^2$
$$(120)^2 + (53.3)^2 = x^2$$
$$14,400 + 2840.89 = x^2$$
$$x^2 = 17,240.89$$
$$x = \sqrt{17,240.89}$$

The diagonal is $\sqrt{17,240.89} \approx 131.30$ yards.

27. $a^2 + b^2 = c^2$
$$2^2 + x^2 = 8^2$$
$$4 + x^2 = 64$$
$$x^2 = 60$$
$$x = \sqrt{60}$$

The top of the ladder will be $\sqrt{60} \approx 7.75$ meters high.

29. $A = s^2$
$$256 = s^2$$
$$\sqrt{256} = \sqrt{s^2}$$
$$16 = s$$

The sides are 16 feet long.

31. $A = \pi r^2$
$$1965 = (3.14)r^2$$
$$\frac{1965}{3.14} = r^2$$
$$625.80 \approx r^2$$
$$\sqrt{625.80} \approx \sqrt{r^2}$$
$$25.02 \approx r$$

The radius is about 25.02 ft.

33. $v = \pi r^2 h$

$402 = 3.14 r^2 \cdot 2$

$r^2 = \dfrac{402}{6.28}$

$r^2 \approx 64.01$

$r \approx \sqrt{64.01}$

The radius is about $\sqrt{64.01} \approx 8.00$ inches.

35. $a^2 + b^2 = c^2$

$(12)^2 + 5^2 = x^2$

$144 + 25 = x^2$

$169 = x^2$

$x = \sqrt{169} = 13$

The length of the diagonal is 13 inches.

37. $d = \sqrt{a^2 + b^2 + c^2}$

$= \sqrt{(24)^2 + (16)^2 + (10)^2}$

$= \sqrt{932}$

≈ 30.53 in.

39. $T = 2\pi \sqrt{\dfrac{L}{32}}$

43 in. $= \dfrac{43}{12}$ ft

$T = 2 \cdot 3.14 \sqrt{\dfrac{\left(\frac{43}{12}\right)}{32}}$

$\approx 6.28 \sqrt{0.11}$

≈ 2.08 sec

41. $T = 2\pi \sqrt{\dfrac{L}{32}}$

$= 2 \cdot 3.14 \sqrt{\dfrac{61.6}{32}}$

$= 6.28 \sqrt{1.925}$

≈ 8.71 sec

43. $N = 0.2(\sqrt{R})^3$

$N = 0.2(\sqrt{149.4})^3 \approx 365$ Earth days

45. $s = 5.5\sqrt{cl}$

$= 5.5\sqrt{0.72(50)}$

$= 5.5\sqrt{36}$

$= 5.5(6)$

$= 33$ mph

47. $s = 5.5\sqrt{cl}$

$= 5.5\sqrt{0.75(120)}$

$= 5.5\sqrt{90}$

$\approx 5.5(9.49)$

≈ 52.2 mph

49. $v = \sqrt{2gR}$

$v = \sqrt{2 \cdot 9.75(6,370,000)} \approx 11,145.18$ m/sec

51. $v = \sqrt{2gh}$

$= \sqrt{2(32)(1431)}$

$= \sqrt{91584}$

≈ 302.63

The velocity of the glasses is 302.63 feet per second.

53. $\text{BSA} = \sqrt{\dfrac{H \cdot W}{3600}} = \sqrt{\dfrac{120 \cdot 165}{3600}} = \sqrt{5.5} \approx 2.35 m^2$

55. Let the width be w, then the length is $w + 3$.

$w^2 + (w + 3)^2 = (15)^2$

$w^2 + w^2 + 6w + 9 = 225$

$2w^2 + 6w - 216 = 0$

$w^2 + 3w - 108 = 0$

$(w - 9)(w + 12) = 0$

$w = 9$ or $w = -12$

Since the width must be positive, $w = 9$.

Therefore the width is 9 inches and the length is $9 + 3 = 12$ inches.

57.
$$T = 2\pi\sqrt{\frac{L}{32}}$$
$$2 = 2\pi\sqrt{\frac{L}{32}}$$
$$\frac{2}{2\pi} = \frac{\sqrt{L}}{\sqrt{32}}$$
$$\frac{\sqrt{32}}{\pi} = \sqrt{L}$$
$$\left(\frac{\sqrt{32}}{\pi}\right)^2 = (\sqrt{L})^2$$
$$\frac{32}{\pi^2} = L$$
$$\frac{32}{(3.14)^2} = L$$
$$3.25 \approx L$$

The length is approximately 3.25 feet.

58. $2(x+3) < 4x - 6$
$$2x + 6 < 4x - 6$$
$$6 + 6 < 4x - 2x$$
$$12 < 2x$$
$$6 < x$$
$$x > 6$$

59. $(8x^{-4}y^3)^{-1} = (8y^3)^{-1}(x^{-4})^{-1}$
$$= (8y^3)^{-1}x^4$$
$$= \frac{x^4}{8y^3}$$

60. $3x + 4y = 12$
$$\frac{1}{2}x - 2y = 8$$

Multiply the second equation by 2.
$$2\left[\frac{1}{2}x - 2y = 8\right]$$

gives
$$3x + 4y = 12$$
$$\underline{+ \quad x - 4y = 16}$$
$$4x \qquad = 28$$
$$x = 7$$

Substitute 7 for x in the first equation.

$$3x + 4y = 12$$
$$3(7) + 4y = 12$$
$$21 + 4y = 12$$
$$4y = -9$$
$$y = -\frac{9}{4}$$

The solution is $\left(7, -\frac{9}{4}\right)$.

61. $5 + \dfrac{6}{x} = \dfrac{2}{3x}$
$$\frac{5x + 6}{x} = \frac{2}{3x}$$
$$3x(5x + 6) = 2x$$
$$15x^2 + 18x = 2x$$
$$15x^2 + 16x = 0$$
$$x(15x + 16) = 0$$
$$x = 0 \text{ or } 15x + 16 = 0$$
$$x = -\frac{16}{15}$$

The solution is $x = -\dfrac{16}{15}$ since x cannot be 0.

Exercise Set 9.7

1. a.   The square root of 8

    b.   The cube root of 8

    c.   The fourth root of 8

3. Write the radicand as a product of a perfect cube and another number.

5. a.   Answers will vary.

    b. $\sqrt[3]{y^7} = y^{7/3}$

7. Yes, because any real positive number raised to an odd power will be positive.

9. $\sqrt[3]{8} = 2$ since $2^3 = 8$

11. $\sqrt[3]{-27} = -3$ since $(-3)^3 = -27$

13. $\sqrt[3]{216} = 6$ since $6^3 = 216$

15. $\sqrt[3]{1} = 1$ since $1^3 = 1$

17. $\sqrt[4]{81} = 3$ since $3^4 = 81$

19. $\sqrt[4]{16} = 2$ since $2^4 = 16$

21. $\sqrt[3]{40} = \sqrt[3]{8 \cdot 5} = \sqrt[3]{8}\sqrt[3]{5} = 2\sqrt[3]{5}$

23. $\sqrt[3]{16} = \sqrt[3]{8 \cdot 2} = \sqrt[3]{8}\sqrt[3]{2} = 2\sqrt[3]{2}$

25. $\sqrt[3]{108} = \sqrt[3]{27 \cdot 4} = \sqrt[3]{27}\sqrt[3]{4} = 3\sqrt[3]{4}$

27. $\sqrt[4]{32} = \sqrt[4]{16 \cdot 2} = \sqrt[4]{16}\sqrt[4]{2} = 2\sqrt[4]{2}$

29. $\sqrt[4]{1250} = \sqrt[4]{625 \cdot 2} = \sqrt[4]{625}\sqrt[4]{2} = 5\sqrt[4]{2}$

31. $\sqrt[3]{x^7} = x^{7/3}$

33. $\sqrt[5]{a^2} = a^{2/5}$

35. $\sqrt[4]{y^{15}} = y^{15/4}$

37. $\sqrt[3]{y^8} = y^{8/3}$

39. $\sqrt[3]{x^3} = x^{3/3} = x$

41. $\sqrt[3]{y^{12}} = y^{12/3} = y^4$

43. $\sqrt[4]{x^4} = x^{4/4} = x$

45. $\sqrt[4]{a^{20}} = a^{20/4} = a^5$

47. $\sqrt[3]{x^{15}} = x^{15/3} = x^5$

49. $\sqrt[4]{m^2} = m^{2/4} = m^{1/2} = \sqrt{m}$

51. $\sqrt[10]{c^5} = c^{5/10} = c^{1/2} = \sqrt{c}$

53. $\sqrt[9]{x^3} = x^{3/9} = x^{1/3} = \sqrt[3]{x}$

55. $\sqrt[8]{w^4} = w^{4/8} = w^{1/2} = \sqrt{w}$

57. $= x^{2/3} = \sqrt[3]{x^2}$

59. $\sqrt[8]{z^6} = z^{6/8} = z^{3/4} = \sqrt[4]{z^3}$

61. $8^{4/3} = \left(\sqrt[3]{8}\right)^4 = 2^4 = 16$

63. $27^{4/3} = (\sqrt[3]{27})^4 = 3^4 = 81$

65. $1^{2/3} = (\sqrt[3]{1})^2 = 1^2 = 1$

67. $9^{3/2} = (\sqrt[2]{9})^3 = 3^3 = 27$

69. $27^{5/3} = (\sqrt[3]{27})^5 = 3^5 = 243$

71. $256^{3/4} = (\sqrt[4]{256})^3 = 4^3 = 64$

73. $8^{-1/3} = \dfrac{1}{8^{1/3}} = \dfrac{1}{\sqrt[3]{8}} = \dfrac{1}{2}$

75. $27^{-4/3} = \dfrac{1}{27^{4/3}} = \dfrac{1}{(\sqrt[3]{27})^4} = \dfrac{1}{3^4} = \dfrac{1}{81}$

77. $\sqrt[4]{4^2} = 4^{2/4} = 4^{1/2} = \sqrt{4} = 2$

79. $\sqrt[6]{9^3} = 9^{3/6} = 9^{1/2} = \sqrt{9} = 3$

81. $\sqrt[8]{64^4} = 64^{4/8} = 64^{1/2} = \sqrt{64} = 8$

83. $\sqrt[4]{7^8} = 7^{8/4} = 7^2 = 49$

85. $\sqrt[4]{3^{12}} = 3^{12/4} = 3^3 = 27$

87. $\sqrt[5]{6^{10}} = 6^{10/5} = 6^2 = 36$

89. $\sqrt[4]{x} \cdot \sqrt[4]{x^3} = x^{1/4} \cdot x^{3/4} = x^{(1/4)+(3/4)} = x^{4/4} = x$

91. $\sqrt[4]{t} \cdot \sqrt[4]{t^3} = t^{1/4} \cdot t^{3/4} = t^{(1/4)+(3/4)} = t^{4/4} = t$

93. $(\sqrt[3]{r^4})^6 = (r^{4/3})^6 = r^{(4/3) \cdot 6} = r^{24/3} = r^8$

95. $\left(\sqrt[4]{a^2}\right)^4 = (a^{2/4})^4 = (a^{1/2})^4 = a^{(1/2) \cdot 4} = a^2$

97. For $x = 27$, $(\sqrt[3]{x})^2 = (\sqrt[3]{27})^2 = 3^2 = 9$

For $x = 27$, $\left(\sqrt[3]{x^2}\right) = \left(\sqrt[3]{27^2}\right) = \sqrt[3]{729} = 9$

99. $\sqrt[3]{4^2}$ because $\sqrt[3]{4} \cdot \sqrt[3]{4^2} = \sqrt[3]{4^3} = 4$

101. $\sqrt[3]{6^2}$ because $\sqrt[3]{6} \cdot \sqrt[3]{6^2} = \sqrt[3]{6^3} = 6$

103. $\sqrt[4]{7^3}$ because $\sqrt[4]{7} \cdot \sqrt[4]{7^3} = \sqrt[4]{7^4} = 7$

105. The missing number is 3 since
$\sqrt[3]{6^2} \cdot \sqrt[3]{6} = \sqrt[3]{6^3} = 6$.

107. The missing number is 1 since
$\sqrt[3]{5^1} \cdot \sqrt[3]{5^2} = \sqrt[3]{5^3}$.

109. $\sqrt[3]{xy} \cdot \sqrt[3]{x^2 y^2} = \sqrt[3]{x^3 y^3} = xy$

111. $\sqrt[4]{32} - \sqrt[4]{2} = \sqrt[4]{16 \cdot 2} - \sqrt[4]{2}$
$= \sqrt[4]{16} \cdot \sqrt[4]{2} - \sqrt[4]{2}$
$= \sqrt[4]{2}(\sqrt[4]{16} - 1)$
$= \sqrt[4]{2}(2 - 1)$
$= \sqrt[4]{2}$

113. a. When multiplying $\sqrt[3]{2} \cdot \sqrt[3]{2^2}$, the radicand becomes a perfect cube.
$\sqrt[3]{2} \cdot \sqrt[3]{2^2} = \sqrt[3]{2^3} = \sqrt[3]{8} = 2$

b. $\dfrac{1}{\sqrt[3]{2}} \cdot \dfrac{\sqrt[3]{2^2}}{\sqrt[3]{2^2}} = \dfrac{\sqrt[3]{2^2}}{\sqrt[3]{2^8}} = \dfrac{\sqrt[3]{2^2}}{\sqrt[3]{8}} = \dfrac{\sqrt[3]{4}}{2}$

114. $-x^2 + 4xy - 8 = (-2)^2 + 4(2)(-4) - 8$

$\qquad\qquad\qquad\quad = -4 - 32 - 8$

$\qquad\qquad\qquad\quad = -44$

115. $3x^2 - 28x + 32 = 3x^2 - 24x - 4x + 32$

$\qquad\qquad\qquad\quad = 3x(x - 8) - 4(x - 8)$

$\qquad\qquad\qquad\quad = (3x - 4)(x - 8)$

116. Put $2x - 3y = 4$ in slope–intercept form.

$2x - 3y = 4$

$\qquad -3y = -2x + 4$

$\qquad\quad y = \dfrac{-2}{-3}x + \dfrac{4}{-3}$

$\qquad\quad y = \dfrac{2}{3}x - \dfrac{4}{3}$

Thus, the slope is $\dfrac{2}{3}$ and the y-intercept is $-\dfrac{4}{3}$.

117. $\sqrt{\dfrac{36x^3 y^7}{2x^4}} = \sqrt{\dfrac{18y^7}{x}}$

$\qquad\qquad\qquad = \dfrac{\sqrt{18y^7}}{\sqrt{x}}$

$\qquad\qquad\qquad = \dfrac{\sqrt{9y^6}\sqrt{2y}}{\sqrt{x}}$

$\qquad\qquad\qquad = \dfrac{3y^3\sqrt{2y}}{\sqrt{x}}$

$\qquad\qquad\qquad = \dfrac{3y^3\sqrt{2y}}{\sqrt{x}} \cdot \dfrac{\sqrt{x}}{\sqrt{x}}$

$\qquad\qquad\qquad = \dfrac{3y^3\sqrt{2xy}}{x}$

Review Exercises

1. $\sqrt{81} = 9$ since $9^2 = 81$

2. $\sqrt{121} = 11$ since $11^2 = 121$

3. $-\sqrt{49} = -7$ since $\sqrt{49} = 7 \,(7^2 = 49)$

4. $\sqrt{15} = 15^{1/2}$

5. $\sqrt{41x} = (41x)^{1/2}$

6. $\sqrt{23x^2 y} = (23x^2 y)^{1/2}$

7. $\sqrt{24} = \sqrt{4 \cdot 6} = \sqrt{4}\sqrt{6} = 2\sqrt{6}$

8. $\sqrt{5} = \sqrt{4 \cdot 13} = \sqrt{4}\sqrt{13} = 2\sqrt{13}$

9. $\sqrt{48x^7 y^5} = \sqrt{16x^6 y^4}\sqrt{3xy} = 4x^3 y^2 \sqrt{3xy}$

10. $\sqrt{125x^4 y^8} = \sqrt{25x^4 y^8}\sqrt{5} = 5x^2 y^4 \sqrt{5}$

11. $\sqrt{60ab^5 c^4} = \sqrt{4b^4 c^4}\sqrt{15ab} = 2b^2 c^2 \sqrt{15ab}$

12. $\sqrt{72a^2 b^2 c^7} = \sqrt{36a^2 b^2 c^6}\sqrt{2c} = 6abc^3 \sqrt{2c}$

13. $\sqrt{144}\sqrt{10} = 12\sqrt{10}$

14. $\sqrt{3y}\sqrt{3y} = \sqrt{9y^2} = 3y$

15. $\sqrt{32x}\sqrt{2xy} = \sqrt{64x^2 y} = \sqrt{64x^2}\sqrt{y} = 8x\sqrt{y}$

16. $\sqrt{25x^2 y}\sqrt{2y} = \sqrt{50x^2 y^2}$

$\qquad\qquad\qquad\quad = \sqrt{25x^2 y^2}\sqrt{2}$

$\qquad\qquad\qquad\quad = 5xy\sqrt{2}$

17. $\sqrt{12a^3 b^4}\sqrt{3b^4} = \sqrt{36a^3 b^8}$

$\qquad\qquad\qquad\quad = \sqrt{36a^2 b^8}\sqrt{a}$

$\qquad\qquad\qquad\quad = 6ab^4 \sqrt{a}$

18. $\sqrt{2ab^3}\sqrt{50ab^4} = \sqrt{100a^2 b^7}$

$\qquad\qquad\qquad\quad = \sqrt{100a^2 b^6}\sqrt{b}$

$\qquad\qquad\qquad\quad = 10ab^3 \sqrt{b}$

19. $9\sqrt{3} - 4\sqrt{3} = (9 - 4)\sqrt{3} = 5\sqrt{3}$

20. $4\sqrt{5} - 6\sqrt{5} - 3\sqrt{5} = (4 - 6 - 3)\sqrt{5} = -5\sqrt{5}$

21. $11\sqrt{x} - 5\sqrt{x} = (11 - 5)\sqrt{x} = 6\sqrt{x}$

22. $\sqrt{k} + 3\sqrt{k} - 8\sqrt{k} = (1 + 3 - 8)\sqrt{k} = -4\sqrt{k}$

23. $2\sqrt{18} - \sqrt{27} = 2\sqrt{9 \cdot 2} - \sqrt{9 \cdot 3}$

$\qquad\qquad\qquad = 2\sqrt{9}\sqrt{2} - \sqrt{9}\sqrt{3}$

$\qquad\qquad\qquad = 2 \cdot 3\sqrt{2} - 3\sqrt{3}$

$\qquad\qquad\qquad = 6\sqrt{2} - 3\sqrt{3}$

24. $7\sqrt{40} - 3\sqrt{10} = 7\sqrt{4}\sqrt{10} - 3\sqrt{10}$

$\qquad\qquad\qquad = 7 \cdot 2\sqrt{10} - 3\sqrt{10}$

$\qquad\qquad\qquad = 14\sqrt{10} - 3\sqrt{10}$

$\qquad\qquad\qquad = (14 - 3)\sqrt{10}$

$\qquad\qquad\qquad = 11\sqrt{10}$

25. $2\sqrt{98} - 4\sqrt{72} = 2\sqrt{49}\sqrt{2} - 4\sqrt{36}\sqrt{2}$

$\qquad = 2\cdot 7\sqrt{2} - 4\cdot 6\sqrt{2}$

$\qquad = 14\sqrt{2} - 24\sqrt{2}$

$\qquad = (14-24)\sqrt{2}$

$\qquad = -10\sqrt{2}$

26. $7\sqrt{50} + 2\sqrt{18} - 4\sqrt{32}$

$\qquad = 7\sqrt{25}\sqrt{2} + 2\sqrt{9}\sqrt{2} - 4\sqrt{16}\sqrt{2}$

$\qquad = 7\cdot 5\sqrt{2} + 2\cdot 3\sqrt{2} - 4\cdot 4\sqrt{2}$

$\qquad = (35 + 6 - 16)\sqrt{2}$

$\qquad = 25\sqrt{2}$

27. $\sqrt{6}\left(2 + \sqrt{6}\right) = \sqrt{6}(2) + \sqrt{6}\left(\sqrt{6}\right)$

$\qquad = 2\sqrt{6} + \sqrt{36}$

$\qquad = 2\sqrt{6} + 6$

28. $\sqrt{2}\left(\sqrt{2} + 3\right) = \sqrt{2}\left(\sqrt{2}\right) + \sqrt{2}(3)$

$\qquad = \sqrt{4} + 3\sqrt{2}$

$\qquad = 2 + 3\sqrt{2}$

29. $\sqrt{y}\left(x - 8\sqrt{y}\right) = \sqrt{y}(x) + \sqrt{y}\left(-8\sqrt{y}\right)$

$\qquad = x\sqrt{y} - 8\sqrt{y^2}$

$\qquad = x\sqrt{y} - 8y$

30. $4a\left(3a + \sqrt{2a}\right) = 4a(3a) + 4a\left(\sqrt{2a}\right)$

$\qquad = 12a^2 + 4a\sqrt{2a}$

31. $\left(\sqrt{7} - 2\right)\left(\sqrt{7} + 2\right)$

$\qquad = \sqrt{7}\left(\sqrt{7}\right) + 2\sqrt{7} - 2\sqrt{7} - 2(2)$

$\qquad = \sqrt{49} - 4$

$\qquad = 7 - 4$

$\qquad = 3$

32. $\left(9 - \sqrt{5}\right)\left(9 + \sqrt{5}\right)$

$\qquad = 9(9) + 9\sqrt{5} - 9\sqrt{5} - \sqrt{5}\left(\sqrt{5}\right)$

$\qquad = 81 - \sqrt{25}$

$\qquad = 81 - 5$

$\qquad = 76$

33. $\left(x - 5\sqrt{y}\right)\left(x + 5\sqrt{y}\right)$

$\qquad = x(x) + x\left(5\sqrt{y}\right) - 5\sqrt{y}(x) - 5\sqrt{y}\left(5\sqrt{y}\right)$

$\qquad = x^2 - 25\sqrt{y^2}$

$\qquad = x^2 - 25y$

34. $\left(\sqrt{c} - 3\sqrt{d}\right)\left(\sqrt{c} + 3\sqrt{d}\right)$

$\qquad = \sqrt{c}\left(\sqrt{c}\right) + \sqrt{c}\left(3\sqrt{d}\right) - 3\sqrt{d}\left(\sqrt{c}\right) - 3\sqrt{d}\left(3\sqrt{d}\right)$

$\qquad = \sqrt{c^2} - 9\sqrt{d^2}$

$\qquad = c - 9d$

35. $\left(m + 2\sqrt{r}\right)\left(m - 5\sqrt{r}\right)$

$\qquad = m(m) + m\left(-5\sqrt{r}\right) + 2\sqrt{r}(m) + 2\sqrt{r}\left(-5\sqrt{r}\right)$

$\qquad = m^2 - 5m\sqrt{r} + 2m\sqrt{r} - 10\sqrt{r^2}$

$\qquad = m^2 + (-5 + 2)m\sqrt{r} - 10r$

$\qquad = m^2 - 3m\sqrt{r} - 10r$

36. $\left(\sqrt{t} + 2s\right)\left(3\sqrt{t} - s\right)$

$\qquad = \sqrt{t}\left(3\sqrt{t}\right) + \sqrt{t}(-s) + 2s\left(3\sqrt{t}\right) + 2s(-s)$

$\qquad = 3\sqrt{t^2} - s\sqrt{t} + 6s\sqrt{t} - 2s^2$

$\qquad = 3t + (-1 + 6)s\sqrt{t} - 2s^2$

$\qquad = 3t + 5s\sqrt{t} - 2s^2$

37. $\left(\sqrt{5m} + 6\sqrt{n}\right)\left(3\sqrt{5m} - \sqrt{n}\right)$

$\qquad = \sqrt{5m}\left(3\sqrt{5m}\right) + \sqrt{5m}\left(-\sqrt{n}\right) + 6\sqrt{n}\left(3\sqrt{5m}\right)$

$\qquad\quad + 6\sqrt{n}\left(-\sqrt{n}\right)$

$\qquad = 3\sqrt{25m^2} - \sqrt{5mn} + 18\sqrt{5mn} - 6\sqrt{n^2}$

$\qquad = 3(5m) + (-1 + 18)\sqrt{5mn} - 6n$

$\qquad = 15m + 17\sqrt{5mn} - 6n$

38. $\left(\sqrt{7} - 3\sqrt{p}\right)\left(2\sqrt{7} - 3\sqrt{p}\right)$

$\qquad = \sqrt{7}\left(2\sqrt{7}\right) + \sqrt{7}\left(-3\sqrt{p}\right) - 3\sqrt{p}\left(2\sqrt{7}\right)$

$\qquad\quad - 3\sqrt{p}\left(-3\sqrt{p}\right)$

$\qquad = 2\sqrt{49} - 3\sqrt{7p} - 6\sqrt{7p} + 9\sqrt{p^2}$

$\qquad = 2(7) + (-3 - 6)\sqrt{7p} + 9p$

$\qquad = 14 - 9\sqrt{7p} + 9p$

39. $\dfrac{\sqrt{48}}{\sqrt{3}} = \sqrt{\dfrac{48}{3}} = \sqrt{16} = 4$

40. $\sqrt{\dfrac{5}{245}} = \sqrt{\dfrac{1}{49}} = \dfrac{\sqrt{1}}{\sqrt{49}} = \dfrac{1}{7}$

41. $\sqrt{\dfrac{6}{24}} = \sqrt{\dfrac{1}{4}} = \dfrac{\sqrt{1}}{\sqrt{4}} = \dfrac{1}{2}$

42. $\dfrac{2}{\sqrt{3}} = \dfrac{2}{\sqrt{3}} \cdot \dfrac{\sqrt{3}}{\sqrt{3}} = \dfrac{2\sqrt{3}}{3}$

43. $\sqrt{\dfrac{n}{7}} = \dfrac{\sqrt{n}}{\sqrt{7}} = \dfrac{\sqrt{n}}{\sqrt{7}} \cdot \dfrac{\sqrt{7}}{\sqrt{7}} = \dfrac{\sqrt{7n}}{7}$

44. $\sqrt{\dfrac{10a}{24}} = \sqrt{\dfrac{5a}{12}}$

$\qquad = \dfrac{\sqrt{5a}}{\sqrt{12}}$

$\qquad = \dfrac{\sqrt{5a}}{\sqrt{4}\sqrt{3}}$

$\qquad = \dfrac{\sqrt{5a}}{2\sqrt{3}}$

$\qquad = \dfrac{\sqrt{5a}}{2\sqrt{3}} \cdot \dfrac{\sqrt{3}}{\sqrt{3}}$

$\qquad = \dfrac{\sqrt{15a}}{6}$

45. $\sqrt{\dfrac{x^2}{5}} = \dfrac{\sqrt{x^2}}{\sqrt{5}} = \dfrac{x}{\sqrt{5}} = \dfrac{x}{\sqrt{5}} \cdot \dfrac{\sqrt{5}}{\sqrt{5}} = \dfrac{x\sqrt{5}}{5}$

46. $\sqrt{\dfrac{z^6}{8}} = \dfrac{\sqrt{z^6}}{\sqrt{8}}$

$\qquad = \dfrac{z^3}{\sqrt{4}\sqrt{2}}$

$\qquad = \dfrac{z^3}{2\sqrt{2}}$

$\qquad = \dfrac{z^3}{2\sqrt{2}} \cdot \dfrac{\sqrt{2}}{\sqrt{2}}$

$\qquad = \dfrac{z^3\sqrt{2}}{4}$

47. $\sqrt{\dfrac{28x^3y^7}{4x^3y^3}} = \sqrt{7y^4} = \sqrt{7}\sqrt{y^4} = y^2\sqrt{7}$

48. $\sqrt{\dfrac{20x^4y}{10x^2y^4}} = \sqrt{\dfrac{2x^2}{y^3}}$

$\qquad = \dfrac{\sqrt{2x^2}}{\sqrt{y^3}}$

$\qquad = \dfrac{\sqrt{2}\sqrt{x^2}}{\sqrt{y^2}\sqrt{y}}$

$\qquad = \dfrac{x\sqrt{2}}{y\sqrt{y}}$

$\qquad = \dfrac{x\sqrt{2}}{y\sqrt{y}} \cdot \dfrac{\sqrt{y}}{\sqrt{y}}$

$\qquad = \dfrac{x\sqrt{2y}}{y^2}$

49. $\dfrac{\sqrt{60}}{\sqrt{27a^3b^2}} = \sqrt{\dfrac{60}{27a^3b^2}}$

$\qquad = \sqrt{\dfrac{20}{9a^3b^2}}$

$\qquad = \dfrac{\sqrt{20}}{\sqrt{9a^3b^2}}$

$\qquad = \dfrac{\sqrt{4}\sqrt{5}}{\sqrt{9a^2b^2}\sqrt{a}}$

$\qquad = \dfrac{2\sqrt{5}}{3ab\sqrt{a}}$

$\qquad = \dfrac{2\sqrt{5}}{3ab\sqrt{a}} \cdot \dfrac{\sqrt{a}}{\sqrt{a}}$

$\qquad = \dfrac{2\sqrt{5a}}{3a^2b}$

50. $\dfrac{\sqrt{2a^4bc^4}}{\sqrt{7a^5bc^2}} = \sqrt{\dfrac{2a^4bc^4}{7a^5bc^2}}$

$\qquad = \sqrt{\dfrac{2c^2}{7a}}$

$\qquad = \dfrac{\sqrt{2c^2}}{\sqrt{7a}}$

$\qquad = \dfrac{c\sqrt{2}}{\sqrt{7a}}$

$\qquad = \dfrac{c\sqrt{2}}{\sqrt{7a}} \cdot \dfrac{\sqrt{7a}}{\sqrt{7a}}$

$\qquad = \dfrac{c\sqrt{14a}}{7a}$

51. $\dfrac{2}{1-\sqrt{6}} = \dfrac{2}{1-\sqrt{6}} \cdot \dfrac{1+\sqrt{6}}{1+\sqrt{6}}$

$\qquad = \dfrac{2(1+\sqrt{6})}{1-6}$

$\qquad = \dfrac{2(1+\sqrt{6})}{-5}$

$\qquad = \dfrac{2+2\sqrt{6}}{-5}$

$\qquad = \dfrac{(-1)(2+2\sqrt{6})}{(-1)(-5)}$

$\qquad = \dfrac{-2-2\sqrt{6}}{5}$

52. $\dfrac{4}{3-\sqrt{6}} = \dfrac{4}{3-\sqrt{6}} \cdot \dfrac{3+\sqrt{6}}{3+\sqrt{6}}$

$\qquad = \dfrac{4(3+\sqrt{6})}{9-6}$

$\qquad = \dfrac{12+4\sqrt{6}}{3}$

53. $\dfrac{\sqrt{3}}{2+\sqrt{y}} = \dfrac{\sqrt{3}}{2+\sqrt{y}} \cdot \dfrac{2-\sqrt{y}}{2-\sqrt{y}}$

$\qquad = \dfrac{\sqrt{3}(2-\sqrt{y})}{4-y}$

$\qquad = \dfrac{2\sqrt{3}-\sqrt{3y}}{4-y}$

54. $\dfrac{3}{\sqrt{x}-5} = \dfrac{3}{\sqrt{x}-5} \cdot \dfrac{\sqrt{x}+5}{\sqrt{x}+5}$

$\qquad = \dfrac{3(\sqrt{x}+5)}{x-25}$

$\qquad = \dfrac{3\sqrt{x}+15}{x-25}$

55. $\dfrac{\sqrt{10}}{\sqrt{x}+\sqrt{3}} = \dfrac{\sqrt{10}}{\sqrt{x}+\sqrt{3}} \cdot \dfrac{\sqrt{x}-\sqrt{3}}{\sqrt{x}-\sqrt{3}}$

$\qquad = \dfrac{\sqrt{10}(\sqrt{x}-\sqrt{3})}{x-3}$

$\qquad = \dfrac{\sqrt{10x}-\sqrt{30}}{x-3}$

56. $\dfrac{\sqrt{7}}{\sqrt{5}-x} = \dfrac{\sqrt{7}}{\sqrt{5}-x} \cdot \dfrac{\sqrt{5}+x}{\sqrt{5}+x}$

$\qquad = \dfrac{\sqrt{7}(\sqrt{5}+x)}{5-x^2}$

$\qquad = \dfrac{\sqrt{35}+x\sqrt{7}}{5-x^2}$

57. $\quad \sqrt{x} = 7$

$\quad (\sqrt{x})^2 = 7^2$

$\qquad x = 49$

Check: $\quad \sqrt{x} = 7$

$\qquad\qquad \sqrt{49} = 7$

$\qquad\qquad\quad 7 = 7$ True

58. $\sqrt{g} = -2$

No solution

59. $\quad \sqrt{h-6} = 3$

$\quad (\sqrt{h-6})^2 = 3^2$

$\qquad h-6 = 9$

$\qquad\quad h = 15$

Check: $\sqrt{15-6} = 3$

$\qquad\qquad \sqrt{9} = 3$

$\qquad\qquad\quad 3 = 3$ True

60. $\quad \sqrt{3x+4} = 5$

$\quad (\sqrt{3x+4})^2 = 5^2$

$\qquad 3x+4 = 25$

$\qquad\quad 3x = 21$

$\qquad\qquad x = 7$

Check: $\quad \sqrt{3x+4} = 5$

$\qquad\qquad \sqrt{3(7)+4} = 5$

$\qquad\qquad\quad \sqrt{25} = 5$

$\qquad\qquad\qquad 5 = 5$ True

61. $\quad \sqrt{5x+7} = \sqrt{4x+9}$

$\quad (\sqrt{5x+7})^2 = (\sqrt{4x+9})^2$

$\qquad 5x+7 = 4x+9$

$\qquad 5x-4x = 9-7$

$\qquad\qquad x = 2$

Check: $\quad \sqrt{5x+7} = \sqrt{4x+9}$

$\qquad\qquad \sqrt{5(2)+7} = \sqrt{4(2)+9}$

$\qquad\qquad\quad \sqrt{17} = \sqrt{17}$ True

62.

$$4\sqrt{x} - x = 4$$
$$4\sqrt{x} = x + 4$$
$$(4\sqrt{x})^2 = (x+4)^2$$
$$16x = x^2 + 8x + 16$$
$$0 = x^2 - 8x + 16$$
$$0 = (x-4)^2$$
$$x - 4 = 0$$
$$x = 4$$

Check: $4\sqrt{x} - x = 4$
$$4\sqrt{4} - 4 = 4$$
$$4 \cdot 2 - 4 = 4$$
$$4 = 4 \text{ True}$$

63.

$$\sqrt{x^2 + 7} = x + 1$$
$$\left(\sqrt{x^2 + 7}\right)^2 = (x+1)^2$$
$$x^2 + 7 = x^2 + 2x + 1$$
$$0 = 2x + 1 - 7$$
$$0 = 2x - 6$$
$$6 = 2x$$
$$3 = x$$

Check: $\sqrt{x^2 + 7} = x + 1$
$$\sqrt{3^2 + 7} = 3 + 1$$
$$\sqrt{16} = 4$$
$$4 = 4 \text{ True}$$

64.

$$\sqrt{4x + 8} - \sqrt{7x - 13} = 0$$
$$\sqrt{4x + 8} = \sqrt{7x - 13}$$
$$(\sqrt{4x + 8})^2 = (\sqrt{7x - 13})^2$$
$$4x + 8 = 7x - 13$$
$$8 + 13 = 7x - 4x$$
$$21 = 3x$$
$$7 = x$$

Check: $\sqrt{4x + 8} - \sqrt{7x - 13} = 0$
$$\sqrt{4(7) + 8} - \sqrt{7(7) - 13} = 0$$
$$\sqrt{36} - \sqrt{36} = 0$$
$$0 = 0 \text{ True}$$

65.

$$\sqrt{4p + 1} = 2p - 1$$
$$\left(\sqrt{4p + 1}\right)^2 = (2p - 1)^2$$
$$4p + 1 = 4p^2 - 4p + 1$$
$$0 = 4p^2 - 8p$$
$$0 = 4p(p - 2)$$
$$4p = 0 \quad \text{or} \quad p - 2 = 0$$
$$p = 0 \quad \text{or} \quad p = 2$$

Check: $p = 0$ $p = 2$
$$\sqrt{4(0) + 1} = 2(0) - 1 \qquad \sqrt{4(2) + 1} = 2(2) - 1$$
$$\sqrt{5} = -1 \quad \text{False} \qquad \sqrt{9} = 4 - 1$$
$$3 = 3 \quad \text{True}$$

Thus, $p = 2$ is a solution and $p = 0$ is an extraneous solution.

66.

$$a^2 + b^2 = c^2$$
$$10^2 + 24^2 = x^2$$
$$100 + 576 = x^2$$
$$x^2 = 676$$
$$x = \sqrt{676} = 26$$

67.

$$a^2 + b^2 = c^2$$
$$10^2 + x^2 = 15^2$$
$$100 + x^2 = 225$$
$$x^2 = 225 - 100$$
$$x^2 = 125$$
$$x = \sqrt{125} \approx 11.18$$

68.

$$a^2 + b^2 = c^2$$
$$x^2 + (\sqrt{3})^2 = (\sqrt{15})^2$$
$$x^2 + 3 = 15$$
$$x^2 = 12$$
$$x = \sqrt{12} \approx 3.46$$

69.

$$a^2 + b^2 = c^2$$
$$6^2 + 5^2 = x^2$$
$$36 + 25 = x^2$$
$$61 = x^2$$
$$x = \sqrt{61} \approx 7.81$$

70. $a^2 + b^2 = c^2$

$h^2 + 4^2 = 12^2$

$h^2 + 16 = 144$

$h^2 = 128$

$h = \sqrt{128} \approx 11.31$

The height of the ladder on the house is $\sqrt{128} \approx 11.31$ feet.

71. $a^2 + b^2 = c^2$

$15^2 + 10^2 = d^2$

$225 + 100 = d^2$

$325 = d^2$

$d = \sqrt{325} \approx 18.03$

The length of the diagonal is $\sqrt{325} \approx 18.03$ inches.

72. $d = \sqrt{(x_2 - x_1)^2 + (y_2 - y_1)^2}$

$= \sqrt{(1-4)^2 + [7-(-3)]^2}$

$= \sqrt{(-3)^2 + (10)^2}$

$= \sqrt{9 + 100}$

$= \sqrt{109}$

≈ 10.44

73. $d = \sqrt{(x_2 - x_1)^2 + (y_2 - y_1)^2}$

$= \sqrt{(-6-6)^2 + (8-5)^2}$

$= \sqrt{(-12)^2 + (3)^2}$

$= \sqrt{144 + 9}$

$= \sqrt{153}$

≈ 12.37

74. $A = \dfrac{s^2 \sqrt{3}}{4}$

$A = \dfrac{36^2 \sqrt{3}}{4}$

$= \dfrac{1296\sqrt{3}}{4}$

$= 324\sqrt{3}$

$\approx 324(1.732)$

≈ 561.18 square inches

75. $d = \sqrt{(3/2)h}$

$= \sqrt{(3/2)40}$

$= \sqrt{60}$

≈ 7.75

He can see about 7.75 miles.

76. $s = \sqrt{(3V)/h}$

$= \sqrt{3(48,686,866.67)/350}$

$= \sqrt{417,315.99}$

≈ 646

The sides are about 646 feet long.

77. $\sqrt[3]{8} = 2$ since $2^3 = 8$

78. $\sqrt[3]{-64} = -4$ since $(-4)^3 = -64$

79. $\sqrt[4]{16} = 2$ since $2^4 = 16$

80. $\sqrt[4]{81} = 3$ since $3^4 = 81$

81. $\sqrt[3]{16} = \sqrt[3]{8 \cdot 2} = \sqrt[3]{8}\sqrt[3]{2} = 2\sqrt[3]{2}$

82. $\sqrt[3]{-16} = \sqrt[3]{-8 \cdot 2} = \sqrt[3]{-8}\sqrt[3]{2} = -2\sqrt[3]{2}$

83. $\sqrt[3]{48} = \sqrt[3]{8 \cdot 6} = \sqrt[3]{8}\sqrt[3]{6} = 2\sqrt[3]{6}$

84. $\sqrt[4]{32} = \sqrt[4]{16 \cdot 2} = \sqrt[4]{16}\sqrt[4]{2} = 2\sqrt[4]{2}$

85. $\sqrt[3]{54} = \sqrt[3]{27 \cdot 2} = \sqrt[3]{27}\sqrt[3]{2} = 3\sqrt[3]{2}$

86. $\sqrt[4]{80} = \sqrt[4]{16 \cdot 5} = \sqrt[4]{16}\sqrt[4]{5} = 2\sqrt[4]{5}$

87. $\sqrt[3]{x^{21}} = x^{21/3} = x^7$

88. $\sqrt[4]{s^{48}} = s^{48/4} = s^{12}$

89. $27^{2/3} = \left(\sqrt[3]{27}\right)^2 = 3^2 = 9$

90. $36^{1/2} = \sqrt{36} = 6$

91. $27^{-2/3} = (\sqrt[3]{27})^{-2} = 3^{-2} = \dfrac{1}{3^2} = \dfrac{1}{9}$

92. $64^{4/3} = (\sqrt[3]{64})^4 = 4^4 = 256$

93. $125^{-4/3} = (\sqrt[3]{125})^{-4} = 5^{-4} = \dfrac{1}{5^4} = \dfrac{1}{625}$

94. $9^{5/2} = (\sqrt{9})^5 = 3^5 = 243$

95. $\sqrt{x^5} = x^{5/2}$

96. $\sqrt{a^7} = a^{7/2}$

97. $\sqrt[3]{z^{11}} = x^{11/3}$

98. $\sqrt[3]{x^{10}} = x^{10/3}$

99. $\sqrt[4]{y^{13}} = y^{13/4}$

100. $\sqrt[4]{m^6} = m^{6/4} = m^{3/2}$

101. $\sqrt[3]{x}\sqrt[3]{x^2} = x^{1/3}x^{2/3} = x^{(1/3)+(2/3)} = x^{3/3} = x$

102. $\sqrt[3]{x} \cdot \sqrt[3]{x} = x^{1/3} \cdot x^{1/3} = x^{(1/3)+(1/3)} = x^{2/3} = \sqrt[3]{x^2}$

103. $\sqrt[3]{a^4} \cdot \sqrt[3]{a^8} = a^{4/3} \cdot a^{8/3} = a^{(4/3)+(8/3)} = a^{12/3} = a^4$

104. $\sqrt[4]{x^2} \cdot \sqrt[4]{x^6} = x^{2/4} \cdot x^{6/4} = x^{(2/4)+(6/4)} = x^{8/4} = x^2$

105. $\left(\sqrt[3]{q^3}\right)^3 = (q^{3/3})^3 = q^{(3/3)\cdot3} = q^3$

106. $\left(\sqrt[4]{b^2}\right)^4 = (b^{2/4})^4 = b^{(2/4)\cdot4} = b^2$

107. $\left(\sqrt[4]{x^8}\right)^3 = (4^{8/4})^3 = (x^2)^3 = x^{2(3)} = x^6$

108. $\left(\sqrt[4]{x^5}\right)^8 = (x^{5/4})^8 = x^{(5/4)8} = x^{10}$

Practice Test

1. $\sqrt{5x} = (5x)^{1/2}$

2. $x^{3/4} = \sqrt[4]{x^3}$

3. $\sqrt{169} = 13$ because $13^2 = 169$

4. $\sqrt{90} = \sqrt{9(10)} = \sqrt{9}\sqrt{10} = 3\sqrt{10}$

5. $\sqrt{12x^2} = \sqrt{4x^2}\sqrt{3} = 2x\sqrt{3}$

6. $\sqrt{75x^7y^3} = \sqrt{25x^6y^2}\sqrt{3xy} = 5x^3y\sqrt{3xy}$

7. $\sqrt{4x^2y} \cdot \sqrt{20xy} = \sqrt{80x^3y^2}$
$$= \sqrt{16x^2y^2}\sqrt{5x}$$
$$= 4xy\sqrt{5x}$$

8. $\sqrt{10xy^2} \cdot \sqrt{5x^3y^3} = \sqrt{50x^4y^5}$
$$= \sqrt{25x^4y^4}\sqrt{2y}$$
$$= 5x^2y^2\sqrt{2y}$$

9. $\sqrt{\dfrac{5}{125}} = \sqrt{\dfrac{1}{25}} = \dfrac{\sqrt{1}}{\sqrt{25}} = \dfrac{1}{5}$

10. $\dfrac{\sqrt{3c^4d}}{\sqrt{3d^3}} = \sqrt{\dfrac{3c^4d}{3d^3}} = \sqrt{\dfrac{c^4}{d^2}} = \dfrac{\sqrt{c^4}}{\sqrt{d^2}} = \dfrac{c^2}{d}$

11. $\dfrac{1}{\sqrt{5}} = \dfrac{1}{\sqrt{5}} \cdot \dfrac{\sqrt{5}}{\sqrt{5}} = \dfrac{\sqrt{5}}{5}$

12. $\sqrt{\dfrac{9r}{5}} = \dfrac{\sqrt{9r}}{\sqrt{5}}$
$$= \dfrac{\sqrt{9}\sqrt{r}}{\sqrt{5}}$$
$$= \dfrac{3\sqrt{r}}{\sqrt{5}}$$
$$= \dfrac{3\sqrt{r}}{\sqrt{5}} \cdot \dfrac{\sqrt{5}}{\sqrt{5}}$$
$$= \dfrac{3\sqrt{5r}}{5}$$

13. $\sqrt{\dfrac{40x^2y^5}{3x^3y^7}} = \sqrt{\dfrac{40}{3xy^2}}$
$$= \dfrac{\sqrt{40}}{\sqrt{3xy^2}}$$
$$= \dfrac{\sqrt{4}\sqrt{10}}{\sqrt{y^2}\sqrt{3x}}$$
$$= \dfrac{2\sqrt{10}}{y\sqrt{3x}}$$
$$= \dfrac{2\sqrt{10}}{y\sqrt{3x}} \cdot \dfrac{\sqrt{3x}}{\sqrt{3x}}$$
$$= \dfrac{2\sqrt{30x}}{3xy}$$

14. $\dfrac{6}{2-\sqrt{7}} = \dfrac{6}{2-\sqrt{7}} \cdot \dfrac{2+\sqrt{7}}{2+\sqrt{7}}$
$$= \dfrac{6(2+\sqrt{7})}{4-7}$$
$$= \dfrac{6(2+\sqrt{7})}{-3}$$
$$= -2(2+\sqrt{7})$$
$$= -4 - 2\sqrt{7}$$

15. $\dfrac{7}{\sqrt{x}-3} = \dfrac{7}{\sqrt{x}-3} \cdot \dfrac{\sqrt{x}+3}{\sqrt{x}+3}$

$= \dfrac{7(\sqrt{x}+3)}{x-9}$

$= \dfrac{7\sqrt{x}+21}{x-9}$

16. $\sqrt{48} + 5\sqrt{12} + 2\sqrt{3} = \sqrt{16 \cdot 3} + 5\sqrt{4 \cdot 3} + 2\sqrt{3}$

$= 4\sqrt{3} + 5 \cdot 2\sqrt{3} + 2\sqrt{3}$

$= 4\sqrt{3} + 10\sqrt{3} + 2\sqrt{3}$

$= (4 + 10 + 2)\sqrt{3}$

$= 16\sqrt{3}$

17. $9\sqrt{y} - 3\sqrt{y} - \sqrt{y} = (9 - 3 - 1)\sqrt{y} = 5\sqrt{y}$

18. $\sqrt{x-10} = 4$

$(\sqrt{x-10})^2 = 4^2$

$x - 10 = 16$

$x = 26$

Check: $\sqrt{26-10} = 4$

$\sqrt{16} = 4$

$4 = 4$ True

19. $2\sqrt{x-4} + 4 = x$

$2\sqrt{x-4} = x - 4$

$(2\sqrt{x-4})^2 = (x-4)^2$

$4(x-4) = x^2 - 8x + 16$

$4x - 16 = x^2 - 8x + 16$

$0 = x^2 - 12x + 32$

$0 = (x-4)(x-8)$

$x - 4 = 0$ or $x - 8 = 0$

$x = 4$ or $x = 8$

Check: $x = 4$

$2\sqrt{x-4} + 4 = x$

$2\sqrt{4-4} + 4 = 4$

$2\sqrt{0} + 4 = 4$

$4 = 4$ True

Check: $x = 8$

$2\sqrt{x-4} + 4 = x$

$2\sqrt{8-4} + 4 = 8$

$2\sqrt{4} + 4 = 8$

$2 \cdot 2 + 4 = 8$

$8 = 8$ True

The solutions are 4 and 8.

20. $a^2 + b^2 = c^2$

$9^2 + 5^2 = x^2$

$81 + 25 = x^2$

$106 = x^2$

$x = \sqrt{106} \approx 10.30$

21. $\sqrt{(-4-3)^2 + (-1-2)^2} = \sqrt{(-7)^2 + (-3)^2}$

$= \sqrt{49 + 9}$

$= \sqrt{58}$

≈ 7.62

22. $27^{-4/3} = \dfrac{1}{27^{4/3}} = \dfrac{1}{(\sqrt[3]{27})^4} = \dfrac{1}{3^4} = \dfrac{1}{81}$

23. $\sqrt[4]{x^5} \cdot \sqrt[4]{x^7} = x^{5/4} x^{7/4}$

$= x^{(5/4)+(7/4)}$

$= x^{12/4}$

$= x^3$

24. $s^2 = A$

$s^2 = 169$

$s = \sqrt{169} = 13$

The side is 11 meters.

25. $v = \sqrt{2gh} = \sqrt{2(32)10} = \sqrt{640} \approx 25.30$ ft/sec

Cumulative Review Test

1. **a.** $-5, 735$, and 4 are integers.

     b. 4 and 735 are whole numbers.

     c. $-5, 735, 0.5, 4$, and $\dfrac{1}{2}$ are rational numbers.

     d. $\sqrt{12}$ is an irrational number.

     e. All of the numbers are real numbers.

2. $7a^2 - 4b^2 + 3ab$

$= 7(-3)^2 - 4(2)^2 + 3(-3)(2)$

$= 7(9) - 4(4) - 18$

$= 63 - 16 - 18$

$= 29$

3. $-7(3 - x) = 4(x + 2) - 3x$

$-21 + 7x = 4x + 8 - 3x$

$-21 + 7x = x + 8$

$7x - x = 8 + 21$

$6x = 29$

$x = \dfrac{29}{6}$

4. $3(x + 2) > 5 - 4(2x - 7)$

$3x + 6 > 5 - 8x + 28$

$3x + 8x > 5 + 28 - 6$

$11x > 27$

$x > \dfrac{27}{11}$

$\dfrac{27}{11}$

5. $4x^3 + x^2 + 8x + 2 = x^2(4x + 1) + 2(4x + 1)$

$\qquad\qquad\qquad\quad = (4x + 1)(x^2 + 2)$

6. $2x^2 - 19x + 24 = (2x - 3)(x - 8)$

7. $r^2 - 9r = 0$

$r(r - 9) = 0$

$r = 0 \quad \text{or} \quad r - 9 = 0$

$r = 0 \quad \text{or} \qquad r = 9$

8. $\dfrac{4a^3 b^{-5}}{20a^8 b} = \dfrac{1}{5a^5 b^6}$

9. To find x-intercept, substitute 0 for y and solve for x.

$4x - 6y = 24$

$4x - 6(0) = 24$

$4x = 24$

$x = 6$

$(6, 0)$

To find y-intercept, substitute 0 for x and solve for y.

$4x - 6y = 24$

$4(0) - 6y = 24$

$-6y = 24$

$y = -4$

$(0, -4)$

10. The y-intercept is $(0, -2)$ and the slope is

$m = \dfrac{1 - (-2)}{1 - 0} = \dfrac{1 + 2}{1} = 3.$

$y = 3x - 2$

11. Use the slope-intercept form with $m = \dfrac{2}{5}$ and

$(x_1, y_1) = (-5, 2).$

$y - y_1 = m(x - x_1)$

$y - 2 = \dfrac{2}{5}\left[x - (-5)\right]$

$y - 2 = \dfrac{2}{5}(x + 5)$

$y - 2 = \dfrac{2}{5}x + 2$

$y = \dfrac{2}{5}x + 4$

12. $-2x + 3y = 6$

$4x - 2y = -4$

Solve the second equation for y.

$y = 2x + 2$

Substitute $2x + 2$ for y in the first equation.

$-2x + 3(2x + 2) = 6$

$-2x + 6x + 6 = 6$

$4x + 6 = 6$

$4x + 6 - 6 = 6 - 6$

$4x = 0$

$x = 0$

Substitute 0 for x in the equation $y = 2x + 2$.

$y = -2(0) + 2 = 0 + 2 = 2$

The solution is $(0, 2)$.

13. $\dfrac{y + 9}{8} + \dfrac{2y - 14}{8} = \dfrac{y + 9 + 2y - 14}{8} = \dfrac{3y - 5}{8}$

14.
$$\frac{3}{5}+\frac{1}{z}=2$$
$$5z\left(\frac{3}{5}\right)+5z\left(\frac{1}{z}\right)=5z(2)$$
$$3z+5=10z$$
$$5=7z$$
$$\frac{5}{7}=z$$

15. $7\sqrt{11}-4\sqrt{11}=(7-4)\sqrt{11}=3\sqrt{11}$

16.
$$\sqrt{\frac{3z}{28y^5}}=\frac{\sqrt{3z}}{\sqrt{28y^5}}\cdot\frac{\sqrt{28y}}{\sqrt{28y}}$$
$$=\frac{\sqrt{84yz}}{\sqrt{28^2y^6}}$$
$$=\frac{\sqrt{4}\sqrt{21yz}}{28y^3}$$
$$=\frac{2\sqrt{21yz}}{28y^3}$$
$$=\frac{\sqrt{21yz}}{14y^3}$$

17.
$$\sqrt{x+10}=6$$
$$(\sqrt{x+10})^2=6^2$$
$$x+10=36$$
$$x=36-10$$
$$x=26$$
Check: $\sqrt{26+10}=6$
$$\sqrt{36}=6$$
$$6=6 \text{ True}$$

18.
$$\frac{3}{11}=\frac{x}{10}$$
$$11x=3(10)$$
$$11x=30$$
$$x=\frac{30}{11}=2\frac{8}{11}$$
She must use $2\frac{8}{11}$ cups of flour.

19. Let r = the Hyatt's regular room rate.
Regular room rate – 40% discount = Final cost

$$r-0.40r=75$$
$$0.6r=75$$
$$r=\frac{75}{0.6}=125$$
The regular room rate is \$125.

20. Let x = the distance. Since $d=rt$, $t=\frac{d}{r}$.
$$\frac{x}{100}+\frac{x}{125}=2$$
$$500\left(\frac{x}{100}+\frac{x}{125}\right)=500(2)$$
$$5x+4x=1000$$
$$9x=1000$$
$$x=\frac{1000}{9}\approx111.1$$

The distance is about 111.1 miles.

Chapter 10

Exercise Set 10.1

1. If $x^2 = a$, then $x = \sqrt{a}$ or $x = -\sqrt{a}$.

3. In any golden rectangle, the length is about 1.62 times its width.

5. a. $x^2 = 9$ has 2 solutions

   b. $x^2 = 0$ has 1 solution

   c. $(x - 2)^2 = 2$ has 2 solutions

   d. $(x - 3)^2 = -4$ has no real solutions

7. $x^2 - 64 = 0$
$$x^2 = 64$$
$$x = \pm\sqrt{64}$$
$$x = 8, -8$$

9. $x^2 = 81$
$$x = \pm\sqrt{81}$$
$$x = 9, -9$$

11. $y^2 = 169$
$$y = \pm\sqrt{169}$$
$$y = 13, -13$$

13. $x^2 + 3 = 103$
$$x^2 = 100$$
$$x = \pm\sqrt{100}$$
$$x = 10, -10$$

15. $x^2 + 10 = 30$
$$x^2 = 20$$
$$x = \pm\sqrt{20}$$
$$x = 2\sqrt{5}, -2\sqrt{5}$$

17. $3x^2 = 12$
$$x^2 = 4$$
$$x = \pm\sqrt{4}$$
$$x = 2, -2$$

19. $3w^2 = 51$
$$w^2 = 17$$
$$w = \pm\sqrt{17}$$
$$w = \sqrt{17}, -\sqrt{17}$$

21. $3z^2 + 4 = 31$
$$3z^2 = 27$$
$$z^2 = 9$$
$$z = \pm\sqrt{9}$$
$$z = 3, -3$$

23. $9w^2 + 5 = 20$
$$9w^2 = 15$$
$$w^2 = \frac{15}{9}$$
$$w = \pm\sqrt{\frac{15}{9}}$$
$$w = \pm\frac{\sqrt{15}}{3}$$
$$w = \frac{\sqrt{15}}{3}, -\frac{\sqrt{15}}{3}$$

25. $16x^2 - 7 = 66$
$$16x^2 = 73$$
$$x^2 = \frac{73}{16}$$
$$x = \pm\sqrt{\frac{73}{16}}$$
$$x = \pm\frac{\sqrt{73}}{\sqrt{16}}$$
$$x = \pm\frac{\sqrt{73}}{4}$$
$$x = \frac{\sqrt{73}}{4}, -\frac{\sqrt{73}}{4}$$

27. $(x - 4)^2 = 1$
$$x - 4 = \pm\sqrt{1}$$
$$x = 4 \pm 1$$
$$x = 4 + 1 \text{ or } x = 4 - 1$$
$$x = 5 \quad \text{ or } x = 3$$
The solutions are 5 and 3.

29. $(a + 3)^2 = 36$
$$a + 3 = \pm\sqrt{36}$$
$$a + 3 = \pm 6$$
$$a = -3 \pm 6$$
$$a = -3 + 6 \text{ or } a = -3 - 6$$
$$a = 3 \quad \text{ or } a = -9$$
The solutions are 3 and –9.

31. $(x + 2)^2 = 64$
$$x + 2 = \pm\sqrt{64}$$
$$x + 2 = \pm 8$$
$$x = -2 \pm 8$$
$$x = -2 + 8 \text{ or } x = -2 - 8$$
$$x = 6 \quad \text{ or } x = -10$$
The solutions are 6 and –10.

33. $(r+6)^2 = 32$

$$r+6 = \pm\sqrt{32}$$
$$r+6 = \pm\sqrt{16}\sqrt{2}$$
$$r+6 = \pm 4\sqrt{2}$$
$$r = -6 \pm 4\sqrt{2}$$

The solutions are $-6+4\sqrt{2}$ and $-6-4\sqrt{2}$.

35. $(d+1)^2 = 20$

$$d+1 = \pm\sqrt{20}$$
$$d+1 = \pm\sqrt{4}\sqrt{5}$$
$$d+1 = \pm 2\sqrt{5}$$
$$d = -1 \pm 2\sqrt{5}$$

The solutions are $-1+2\sqrt{5}$ and $-1-2\sqrt{5}$.

37. $(n-8)^2 = 49$

$$n-8 = \pm\sqrt{49}$$
$$n-8 = \pm 7$$
$$n = 8 \pm 7$$
$$n = 8+7 \quad \text{or} \quad n = 8-7$$
$$n = 15 \quad \text{or} \quad n = 1$$

The solutions are 15 and 1.

39. $(x+9)^2 = 100$

$$x+9 = \pm\sqrt{100}$$
$$x+9 = \pm 10$$
$$x = -9 \pm 10$$
$$x = -9+10 \quad \text{or} \quad x = -9-10$$
$$x = 1 \quad \text{or} \quad x = -19$$

The solutions are 1 and –19.

41. $(2x+3)^2 = 18$

$$2x+3 = \pm\sqrt{18}$$
$$2x+3 = \pm\sqrt{9}\sqrt{2}$$
$$2x+3 = \pm 3\sqrt{2}$$
$$2x = -3 \pm 3\sqrt{2}$$
$$x = \frac{-3 \pm 3\sqrt{2}}{2}$$

The solutions are $\dfrac{-3+3\sqrt{2}}{2}$ and $\dfrac{-3-3\sqrt{2}}{2}$.

43. $(4x+1)^2 - 3 = 17$

$$(4x+1)^2 = 20$$
$$4x+1 = \pm\sqrt{20}$$
$$4x+1 = \pm\sqrt{4}\sqrt{5}$$
$$4x+1 = \pm 2\sqrt{5}$$
$$4x = -1 \pm 2\sqrt{5}$$
$$x = \frac{-1 \pm 2\sqrt{5}}{4}$$

The solutions are $\dfrac{-1+2\sqrt{5}}{4}$ and $\dfrac{-1-2\sqrt{5}}{4}$.

45. $(2p-7)^2 + 6 = 24$

$$(2p-7)^2 = 18$$
$$2p-7 = \pm\sqrt{18}$$
$$2p-7 = \pm\sqrt{9}\sqrt{2}$$
$$2p-7 = \pm 3\sqrt{2}$$
$$2p = 7 \pm 3\sqrt{2}$$
$$p = \frac{7 \pm 3\sqrt{2}}{2}$$

The solutions are $\dfrac{7+3\sqrt{2}}{2}$ and $\dfrac{7-3\sqrt{2}}{2}$.

47. $x = \pm 7$

$$x^2 = (\pm 7)^2$$
$$x^2 = 49$$

Other answers are possible.

49. $x^2 - 19 = 17$; need an equation equivalent to $x^2 = 36$.

51. a. $-3x^2 + 9x - 6 = 0$

Multiply both sides by –1
$$-1(-3x^2 + 9x - 6) = (-1)(0)$$
$$3x^2 - 9x + 6 = 0$$

b. $-3x^2 + 9x - 6 = 0$

Multiply both sides by $-\dfrac{1}{3}$

$$-\frac{1}{3}(3x^2 + 9x - 6) = \left(-\frac{1}{3}\right)(0)$$
$$x^2 - 3x + 2 = 0$$

53. Let $x =$ the smaller positive number, then $4.25x =$ the larger number.
(smaller number)(larger number) = 68

$$x(4.25x) = 68$$
$$4.25x^2 = 68$$
$$x^2 = 16$$
$$x = \sqrt{16}$$
$$x = 4$$
$$4.25x = 4.25(4) = 17$$

The numbers are 4 and 17.

55. Let x = width of newspaper,
then $1.21x$ = length of newspaper.
Area = length · width

$$631.92 = 1.21x(x)$$
$$631.92 = 1.21x^2$$
$$522.25 = x^2$$
$$\sqrt{522.25} = x$$
$$x \approx 22.85$$

$1.21x \approx 1.21\sqrt{522.25} \approx 27.65$
The width is about 22.85 inches and
the length is about 27.65 inches.

57. Let x = width of rectangle,
then $1.62x$ = length of rectangle.
Area = length · width

$$2000 = (1.62x)x$$
$$2000 = 1.62x^2$$
$$\frac{2000}{1.62} = x^2$$
$$x = \pm\sqrt{\frac{2000}{1.62}} \approx \pm 35.14$$

Since the width is positive $x \approx 35.14$ feet. The
length is $1.62 \cdot 35.14 \approx 56.93$ feet.

59. a. Left x^2, right $(x+3)^2$

b. $x^2 = 36$
$$x = \pm\sqrt{36}.$$
$$x = \pm 6$$
Since the length cannot be negative, the
length of each side of the square is
= 6 inches.

c. $x^2 = 50$
$$x = \pm\sqrt{50}$$
$$x = \pm\sqrt{25}\sqrt{2}$$
$$x = \pm 5\sqrt{2}$$
Since the length cannot be negative, the

length of each side of the square is
$5\sqrt{2} \approx 7.07$ inches.

d. $(x+3)^2 = 81$
$$x + 3 = \pm\sqrt{81}$$
$$x + 3 = \pm 9$$
Since the length cannot be negative, the
length of each side of the square is
= 9 inches.

e. $(x+3)^2 = 92$
$$x + 3 = \pm\sqrt{92}$$
Since the length cannot be negative, the
length of each side of the square is
$\sqrt{92} \approx 9.59$ inches.

61. $A = s^2$
$$\sqrt{A} = \sqrt{s^2}$$
$$\sqrt{A} = s$$
$$s = \sqrt{A}$$

63. $A = \pi r^2$
$$\frac{A}{\pi} = r^2$$
$$\sqrt{\frac{A}{\pi}} = \sqrt{r^2}$$
$$\sqrt{\frac{A}{\pi}} = r$$
$$r = \sqrt{\frac{A}{\pi}}$$

65. $I = \dfrac{k}{d^2}$
$$d^2 I = k$$
$$d^2 = \frac{k}{I}$$
$$\sqrt{d^2} = \sqrt{\frac{k}{I}}$$
$$d = \sqrt{\frac{k}{I}}$$

67. $6x^2 - 15x - 36 = 3(2x^2 - 5x - 12)$
$$= 3(2x^2 - 8x + 3x - 12)$$
$$= 3[2x(x-4) + 3(x-4)]$$
$$= 3(2x+3)(x-4)$$

68. $\dfrac{5 - \dfrac{1}{y}}{6 - \dfrac{1}{y}} = \dfrac{\left(5 - \dfrac{1}{y}\right)y}{\left(6 - \dfrac{1}{y}\right)y} = \dfrac{5y - 1}{6y - 1}$

69. $m = \dfrac{y_2 - y_1}{x_2 - x_1} = \dfrac{3-(-1)}{1-0} = \dfrac{3+1}{1} = 4$

The *y*-intercept is (0, −1). Thus, the equation of the line is $y = 4x - 1$.

70. $\dfrac{\sqrt{135a^4 b}}{\sqrt{3a^5 b^7}} = \sqrt{\dfrac{135a^4 b}{3a^5 b^7}}$

$= \sqrt{\dfrac{45}{ab^4}6}$

$= \dfrac{\sqrt{45}}{\sqrt{ab^4}6}$

$= \dfrac{\sqrt{9}\sqrt{5}}{\sqrt{b^6}\sqrt{a}}$

$= \dfrac{3\sqrt{5}}{b^3\sqrt{a}}$

$= \dfrac{3\sqrt{5}}{b3\sqrt{a}} \cdot \dfrac{\sqrt{a}}{\sqrt{a}}$

$= \dfrac{3\sqrt{5a}}{ab^3}$

Exercise Set 10.2

1. a. A perfect square trinomial is a trinomial that can be expressed as the square of a binomial.

b. $x^2 + 8x + 16$; the constant is the square of half the coefficient of the *x*-term.

3. The constant is the square of half the coefficient of the *x*-term.

5. $\left(\dfrac{-14}{2}\right)^2 = (-7)^2 = 49$

7. $\quad x^2 + 7x + 10 = 0$

$x^2 + 7x = -10$

$x^2 + 7x + \dfrac{49}{4} = -10 + \dfrac{49}{4}$

$\left(x + \dfrac{7}{2}\right)^2 = -\dfrac{40}{4} + \dfrac{49}{4}$

$\left(x + \dfrac{7}{2}\right)^2 = \dfrac{9}{4}$

$x + \dfrac{7}{2} = \pm\sqrt{\dfrac{9}{4}}$

$x + \dfrac{7}{2} = \pm\dfrac{3}{2}$

$x = -\dfrac{7}{2} \pm \dfrac{3}{2}$

$x = -\dfrac{7}{2} + \dfrac{3}{2} \text{ or } x = -\dfrac{7}{2} - \dfrac{3}{2}$

$x = -2 \qquad \text{ or } x = -5$

The solutions are −2 and −5.

9. $\quad x^2 - 8x + 7 = 0$

$x^2 - 8x = -7$

$x^2 - 8x + 16 = -7 + 16$

$(x - 4)^2 = 9$

$x - 4 = \pm\sqrt{9}$

$x - 4 = \pm 3$

$x = 4 \pm 3$

$x = 4 + 3 \text{ or } x = 4 - 3$

$x = 7 \qquad \text{ or } x = 1$

The solutions are 7 and 1.

11.
$$x^2 + 13x + 12 = 0$$
$$x^2 + 13x = -12$$
$$x^2 + 13x + \frac{169}{4} = -12 + \frac{169}{4}$$
$$\left(x + \frac{13}{2}\right)^2 = -\frac{48}{4} + \frac{169}{4}$$
$$\left(x + \frac{13}{2}\right)^2 = \frac{121}{4}$$
$$x + \frac{13}{2} = \pm\sqrt{\frac{121}{4}}$$
$$x + \frac{13}{2} = \pm\frac{11}{2}$$
$$x = -\frac{13}{2} \pm \frac{11}{2}$$
$$x = -\frac{13}{2} + \frac{11}{2} \text{ or } x = -\frac{13}{2} - \frac{11}{2}$$
$$x = -1 \qquad \text{ or } \quad x = -12$$
The solutions are -1 and -12.

13.
$$z^2 - 6z + 8 = 0$$
$$x^2 - 6z = -8$$
$$z^2 - 6z + 9 = -8 + 9$$
$$(z - 3)^2 = 1$$
$$z - 3 = \pm\sqrt{1}$$
$$z - 3 = \pm 1$$
$$z = 3 \pm 1$$
$$z = 3 + 1 \text{ or } z = 3 - 1$$
$$z = 4 \quad \text{ or } \quad z = 2$$
The solutions are 4 and 2.

15.
$$n^2 = -6n - 9$$
$$n^2 + 6n = -9$$
$$n^2 + 6n + 9 = -9 + 9$$
$$(n + 3)^2 = 0$$
$$n + 3 = \pm\sqrt{0}$$
$$n + 3 = \pm 0$$
$$n = -3 \pm 0$$
$$n = -3$$
The solution is -3.

17.
$$x^2 = 2x + 15$$
$$x^2 - 2x = 15$$
$$x^2 - 2x + 1 = 15 + 1$$
$$(x - 1)^2 = 16$$
$$x - 1 = \pm\sqrt{16}$$
$$x - 1 = \pm 4$$
$$x = 1 \pm 4$$
$$x = 1 + 4 \text{ or } x = 1 - 4$$
$$x = 5 \qquad \text{ or } x = -3$$
The solutions are 5 and -3.

19.
$$x^2 + 10x + 24 = 0$$
$$x^2 + 10x = -24$$
$$x^2 + 10x + 25 = -24 + 25$$
$$(x + 5)^2 = 1$$
$$x + 5 = \pm\sqrt{1}$$
$$x + 5 = \pm 1$$
$$x = -5 \pm 1$$
$$x = -5 + 1 \text{ or } x = -5 - 1$$
$$x = -4 \quad \text{ or } x = -6$$
The solutions are -4 and -6.

21.
$$x^2 = 10x - 16$$
$$x^2 - 10x = -16$$
$$x^2 - 10 + 25 = -16 + 25$$
$$(x - 5)^2 = 9$$
$$(x - 5)^2 = \pm\sqrt{9}$$
$$x - 5 = \pm 3$$
$$x = 5 \pm 3$$
$$x = 5 + 3 \text{ or } x = 5 - 3$$
$$x = 8 \qquad \text{ or } \quad x = 2$$

The solutions are 8 and 2.

23.
$$-60 = -p^2 + 4p$$
$$p^2 - 4p = 60$$
$$p^2 - 4p + 4 = 60 + 4$$
$$(p-2)^2 = 64$$
$$p - 2 = \pm\sqrt{64}$$
$$p - 2 = \pm 8$$
$$p = 2 \pm 8$$
$$p = 2 + 8 \text{ or } p = 2 - 8$$
$$p = 10 \quad \text{ or } \quad p = -6$$
The solutions are 10 and –6.

25.
$$z^2 - 4z = -2$$
$$z^2 - 4z + 4 = -2 + 4$$
$$(z-2)^2 = 2$$
$$z - 2 = \pm\sqrt{2}$$
$$z = 2 \pm \sqrt{2}$$
The solutions are $2 + \sqrt{2}$ and $2 - \sqrt{2}$.

27.
$$w^2 + 6w = -3$$
$$w^2 + 6w = -3$$
$$w^2 + 6w + 9 = -3 + 9$$
$$(w + 3)^2 = 6$$
$$w + 3 = \pm\sqrt{6}$$
$$w = -3 \pm \sqrt{6}$$
The solutions are $-3 + \sqrt{6}$ and $-3 - \sqrt{6}$.

29.
$$m^2 + 7m + 2 = 0$$
$$m^2 + 7m = -2$$
$$m^2 + 7m + \frac{49}{4} = -2 + \frac{49}{4}$$
$$\left(m + \frac{7}{2}\right)^2 = \frac{41}{4}$$
$$m + \frac{7}{2} = \pm\sqrt{\frac{41}{4}}$$
$$m + \frac{7}{2} = \pm\frac{\sqrt{41}}{2}$$
$$m = -\frac{7}{2} \pm \frac{\sqrt{41}}{2}$$
$$m = \frac{-7 \pm \sqrt{41}}{2}$$

The solutions are $\dfrac{-7 + \sqrt{41}}{2}$ and $\dfrac{-7 - \sqrt{41}}{2}$.

31.
$$3x^2 + 6x - 9 = 0$$
$$\frac{1}{3}(3x^2 + 6x - 9) = \frac{1}{2}(0)$$
$$x^2 + 2x - 3 = 0$$
$$x^2 + 2x = 3$$
$$x^2 + 2x + 1 = 3 + 1$$
$$(x + 1)^2 = 4$$
$$x + 1 = \pm\sqrt{4}$$
$$x + 1 = \pm 2$$
$$x = -1 \pm 2$$
$$x = -1 + 2 \text{ or } x = -1 - 2$$
$$x = 1 \quad \text{ or } x = -3$$
The solutions are 1 and –3.

33.
$$2x^2 + 18x + 4 = 0$$
$$\frac{1}{2}(2x^2 + 18x + 4) = \frac{1}{2}(0)$$
$$x^2 + 9x + 2 = 0$$
$$x^2 + 9x = -2$$
$$x^2 + 9x + \frac{81}{4} = -2 + \frac{81}{4}$$
$$\left(x + \frac{9}{2}\right)^2 = \frac{73}{4}$$
$$x + \frac{9}{2} = \pm\sqrt{\frac{73}{4}}$$
$$x + \frac{9}{2} = \pm\frac{\sqrt{73}}{2}$$
$$x = -\frac{9}{2} \pm \frac{\sqrt{73}}{2}$$
$$x = \frac{-9 \pm \sqrt{73}}{2}$$

The solutions are $\dfrac{-9 + \sqrt{73}}{2}$ and $\dfrac{-9 - \sqrt{73}}{2}$.

35.
$$3h^2 - 15h = 18$$
$$\frac{1}{3}(3h^2 - 15h) = \frac{1}{3}(18)$$
$$h^2 - 5h = 6$$
$$h^2 - 5h + \frac{25}{4} = 6 + \frac{25}{4}$$
$$\left(h - \frac{5}{2}\right)^2 = \frac{24}{4} + \frac{25}{4}$$
$$\left(h - \frac{5}{2}\right)^2 = \frac{49}{4}$$
$$h - \frac{5}{2} = \pm\sqrt{\frac{49}{4}}$$
$$h - \frac{5}{2} = \pm\frac{7}{2}$$
$$h = \frac{5}{2} \pm \frac{7}{2}$$
$$x = \frac{5}{2} + \frac{7}{2} \text{ or } x = \frac{5}{2} - \frac{7}{2}$$
$$x = 6 \qquad \text{or } x = -1$$

The solutions are 6 and −1.

37.
$$3x^2 - 11x - 4 = 0$$
$$\frac{1}{3}(3x^2 - 11x - 4) = \frac{1}{3}(0)$$
$$x^2 - \frac{11}{3}x - \frac{4}{3} = 0$$
$$x^2 - \frac{11}{3}x = \frac{4}{3}$$
$$x^2 - \frac{11}{3}x + \frac{121}{36} = \frac{4}{3} + \frac{121}{36}$$
$$\left(x - \frac{11}{6}\right)^2 = \frac{48}{36} + \frac{121}{36}$$
$$\left(x - \frac{11}{6}\right)^2 = \frac{169}{36}$$
$$x - \frac{11}{6} = \pm\sqrt{\frac{169}{36}}$$
$$x - \frac{11}{6} = \pm\frac{13}{6}$$
$$x = \frac{11}{6} \pm \frac{13}{6}$$
$$x = \frac{11}{6} + \frac{13}{6} \text{ or } x = \frac{11}{6} - \frac{13}{6}$$
$$x = 4 \qquad \text{or } x = -\frac{1}{3}$$

The solutions are 4 and $-\frac{1}{3}$.

39.
$$9t^2 + 6t = 6$$
$$\frac{1}{9}(9t^2 + 6t) = \frac{1}{9}(6)$$
$$t^2 + \frac{6}{9}t = \frac{6}{9}$$
$$t^2 + \frac{6}{9}x + \frac{1}{9} = \frac{6}{9} + \frac{1}{9}$$
$$(t + \frac{1}{3})^2 = \frac{7}{9}$$
$$t + \frac{1}{3} = \pm\sqrt{\frac{7}{9}}$$
$$t = -\frac{1}{3} \pm \frac{\sqrt{7}}{3}$$

The solutions are
$$t = \frac{-1 + \sqrt{7}}{3} \text{ and } t = \frac{-1 - \sqrt{7}}{3}.$$

41.
$$x^2 - 8x = 0$$
$$x^2 - 8x + 16 = 0 + 16$$
$$(x - 4)^2 = 16$$
$$x - 4 = \pm\sqrt{16}$$
$$x - 4 = \pm 4$$
$$x = 4 \pm 4$$
$$x = 4 + 4 \text{ or } x = 4 + 4$$
$$x = 8 \qquad \text{or } x = 0$$

The solutions are 8 and 0.

43.
$$2x^2 = 18x$$
$$2x^2 - 18x = 0$$
$$\frac{1}{2}(2x^2 - 18x) = \frac{1}{2}(0)$$
$$x^2 - 9x = 0$$
$$x^2 - 9x + \frac{81}{4} = 0 + \frac{81}{4}$$
$$\left(x - \frac{9}{2}\right)^2 = \frac{81}{4}$$
$$x - \frac{9}{2} = \pm\sqrt{\frac{81}{4}}$$
$$x - \frac{9}{2} = \pm\frac{9}{2}$$
$$x = \frac{9}{2} \pm \frac{9}{2}$$

$$x = \frac{9}{2} + \frac{9}{2} \text{ or } x = \frac{9}{2} - \frac{9}{2}$$

$$x = 9 \qquad \text{ or } \quad x = 0$$

The solutions are 9 and 0.

45. a. $x^2 + 10x + 25$

   b.   The constant is the square of half the coefficient of the x-term.

$$\left(\frac{10}{2}\right)^2 = 5^2 = 25$$

47. Let x be the number.

$$x^2 + 3x = 4$$

$$x^2 + 3x + \frac{9}{4} = 4 + \frac{9}{4}$$

$$\left(x + \frac{3}{2}\right)^2 = \frac{16}{4} + \frac{9}{4}$$

$$\left(x + \frac{3}{2}\right)^2 = \frac{25}{4}$$

$$x + \frac{3}{2} = \pm\sqrt{\frac{25}{4}}$$

$$x + \frac{3}{2} = \pm\frac{5}{2}$$

$$x = -\frac{3}{2} \pm \frac{5}{2}$$

$$x = -\frac{3}{2} + \frac{5}{2} \text{ or } x = -\frac{3}{2} - \frac{5}{2}$$

$$x = 1 \qquad \text{ or } x = -4$$

The numbers are 1 and –4.

49. Let x be the number.

$$(x + 3)^2 = 9$$

$$x + 3 = \pm\sqrt{9}$$

$$x + 3 = \pm 3$$

$$x = -3 \pm 3$$

$$x = -3 + 3 \text{ or } x = -3 - 3$$

$$x = 0 \qquad \text{ or } x = -6$$

The numbers are 0 and –6.

51. Let x and y be the numbers.

$$xy = 21$$

$$y = x + 4$$

Substitute $x + 4$ for y in the first equation.

$$xy = 21$$

$$x(x + 4) = 21$$

$$x^2 + 4x = 21$$

$$x^2 + 4x + 4 = 21 + 4$$

$$(x + 2)^2 = 25$$

$$x + 2 = \pm\sqrt{25}$$

$$x + 2 = \pm 5$$

$$x = -2 \pm 5$$

$$x = -2 + 5 \text{ or } x = -2 - 5$$

$$x = 3 \qquad \text{ or } x = -7$$

Since the numbers must be positive, $x = 3$; $y = 3 + 4 = 7$. The numbers are 3 and 7.

53. Use Pythagorean Theorem

$$a^2 + b^2 = c^2$$

$$a^2 + (a + 18)^2 = 30^2$$

$$a^2 + a^2 + 36a + 324 = 900$$

$$2a^2 + 36a = 576$$

$$\frac{1}{2}\left(2a^2 + 36a\right) = \frac{1}{2}(576)$$

$$a^2 + 18a = 288$$

$$a^2 + 18a + 81 = 288 + 81$$

$$(a + 9)^2 = 369$$

$$a + 9 = \pm\sqrt{369}$$

$$a = -9 \pm \sqrt{369}$$

Since a must be positive,
$a = -9 + \sqrt{369} \approx 10.21$.
The vertical distance is $a + 18 = 10.21 + 18 = 28.21$ feet.

55. Substitute 240 for s.

$$240 = -16t^2 + 128t$$

$$-\frac{1}{16}(240) = -\frac{1}{16}\left(-16t^2 + 128t\right)$$

$$-15 = t^2 - 8t$$

$$-15 + 16 = t^2 - 8t + 16$$

$$1 = (t - 4)^2$$

$$\pm\sqrt{1} = t - 4$$

$$4 \pm 1 = t$$

$t = 4 + 1 = 5$ and $t = 4 - 1 = 3$
It takes 3 and 5 seconds for the object to reach a height of 240 feet.

57. $+18x$ or $-18x$

The coefficient of the x-term is plus or minus twice the square root of the constant.
$$b = \pm 2\sqrt{c} = \pm 2\sqrt{81} = \pm 2(9) = \pm 18.$$

59. a.
$$x^2 - 14x - 1 = 0$$
$$x^2 - 14x = 1$$
$$x^2 - 14x + 49 = 1 + 49$$
$$(x - 7)^2 = 50$$
$$x - 7 = \pm\sqrt{50}$$
$$x - 7 = \pm 5\sqrt{2}$$
$$x = 7 \pm 5\sqrt{2}$$

b. Check $x = 7 + 5\sqrt{2}$:
$$x^2 - 14x - 1 = 0$$
$$\left(7 + 5\sqrt{2}\right)^2 - 14\left(7 + 5\sqrt{2}\right) - 1 = 0$$
$$49 + 70\sqrt{2} + 50 - 98 - 70\sqrt{2} - 1 = 0$$
$$0 = 0$$

Check $x = 7 - 5\sqrt{2}$:
$$x^2 - 14x - 1 = 0$$
$$\left(7 - 5\sqrt{2}\right)^2 - 14\left(7 - 5\sqrt{2}\right) - 1 = 0$$
$$49 - 70\sqrt{2} + 50 - 98 + 70\sqrt{2} - 1 = 0$$
$$0 = 0$$

61.
$$x^2 + \frac{3}{5}x - \frac{1}{2} = 0$$
$$x^2 + \frac{3}{5}x = \frac{1}{2}$$
$$x^2 + \frac{3}{5}x + \frac{9}{100} = \frac{1}{2} + \frac{9}{100}$$
$$\left(x + \frac{3}{10}\right)^2 = \frac{59}{100}$$
$$x + \frac{3}{10} = \pm\sqrt{\frac{59}{100}}$$
$$x + \frac{3}{10} = \pm\frac{\sqrt{59}}{10}$$
$$x = \frac{-3 \pm \sqrt{59}}{10}$$

The solutions are: $\dfrac{-3 + \sqrt{59}}{10}$ and $\dfrac{-3 - \sqrt{59}}{10}$.

63.
$$3x^2 + \frac{1}{2}x = 4$$
$$x^2 + \frac{1}{6}x = \frac{4}{3}$$
$$x + \frac{1}{6}x + \frac{1}{144} = \frac{4}{3} + \frac{1}{144}$$
$$\left(x + \frac{1}{12}\right)^2 = \frac{194}{144}$$
$$x + \frac{1}{12} = \pm\sqrt{\frac{193}{144}}$$
$$x + \frac{1}{12} = \pm\frac{\sqrt{193}}{12}$$
$$x = -\frac{1}{12} \pm \frac{\sqrt{193}}{12}$$
$$x = \frac{-1 \pm \sqrt{193}}{12}$$

The solutions are:
$$\frac{-1 + \sqrt{193}}{12} \text{ and } \frac{-1 - \sqrt{193}}{12}.$$

65.
$$-5.26x^2 + 7.89x + 15.78 = 0$$
$$x^2 - 1.5x - 3 = 0$$
$$x^2 - 1.5x = 3$$
$$x^2 - 1.5x + 0.5625 = 3 + 0.5625$$
$$(x - 0.75)^2 = 3.5625$$
$$x - 0.75 = \pm\sqrt{3.5625}$$
$$x = 0.75 \pm \sqrt{3.5625}$$

The solutions are:
$$0.75 + \sqrt{3.5625} \text{ and } 0.75 - \sqrt{3.5625}$$

66.
$$\frac{x^2}{x^2 - x - 6} - \frac{x - 2}{x - 3}$$
$$= \frac{x^2}{(x - 3)(x + 2)} - \frac{x - 2}{x - 3}$$
$$= \frac{x^2}{(x - 3)(x + 2)} - \frac{(x - 2)}{(x - 3)} \cdot \frac{(x + 2)}{(x + 2)}$$
$$= \frac{x^2}{(x - 3)(x + 2)} - \frac{x^2 - 4}{(x - 3)(x + 2)}$$
$$= \frac{x^2 - (x^2 - 4)}{(x - 3)(x + 2)}$$
$$= \frac{4}{(x - 3)(x + 2)}$$

67. If the slopes are the same and the y-intercepts are different, the equations represent parallel lines.

68. $2x + 3y = 6$

$-x + 4y = 19$

Multiply the second equation by 2.

$2[-x + 4y = 19]$

gives

$2x + 3y = 6$

$\underline{-2x + 8y = 38}$

$\quad 11y = 44$

$\quad\quad y = 4$

Substitute 4 for y in the first equation.

$2x + 3y = 6$

$2x + 3(4) = 6$

$2x + 12 = 6$

$2x = -6$

$x = -3$

The solution is $(-3, 4)$.

69. $\sqrt{2x + 3} = 2x - 3$

$(\sqrt{2x + 3})^2 = (2x - 3)^2$

$2x + 3 = 4x^2 - 12x + 9$

$0 = 4x^2 - 14x + 6$

$0 = 2(2x - 1)(x - 3)$

$2x - 1 = 0$ or $x - 3 = 0$

$x = \dfrac{1}{2}\quad$ or $x = 3$

Check:

$$x = \frac{1}{2}$$

$$\sqrt{2x + 3} = 2x - 3$$

$$\sqrt{2\left(\frac{1}{2}\right) + 3} = 2\left(\frac{1}{2}\right) - 3$$

$$\sqrt{4} = -2$$

$$2 = -2 \text{ False}$$

Check:$\quad x = 3$

$$\sqrt{2x + 3} = 2x - 3$$

$$\sqrt{2(3) + 3} = 2(3) - 3$$

$$\sqrt{9} = 3$$

$$3 = 3 \text{ True}$$

$\dfrac{1}{2}$ is an extraneous root. The solution is 3.

Exercise Set 10.3

1. a. $b^2 - 4ac$

b. If the discriminant is:
greater than 0 there are two solutions;
equal to 0 there is one solution;
less than 0 there is no real solution.

3. $x = \dfrac{-b \pm \sqrt{b^2 - 4ac}}{2a}$

5. The first step to take when solving a quadratic equation is to write the equation in standard form.

7. The values used for b and c are incorrect because the equation was not first put in standard form.

9. $b^2 - 4ac = (5)^2 - 4(1)(-9) = 25 + 36 = 61$
Since the discriminant is positive, this equation has two distinct real number solutions.

11. $b^2 - 4ac = (1)^2 - 4(2)(1) = 1 - 8 = -7$
Since the discriminant is negative, this equation has no real number solution.

13. $b^2 - 4ac = (3)^2 - 4(6)(-5) = 9 + 120 = 129$
Since the discriminant is positive, this equation has two distinct real number solutions.

15. $\quad 2m^2 - 16m = -32$
$2m^2 - 16m + 32 = 0$
$b^2 - 4ac = (-16)^2 - 4(2)(32) = 256 - 256 = 0$
Since the discriminant is zero, this equation has one real number solution.

17. $b^2 - 4ac = (-7)^2 - 4(2)(10) = 49 - 80 = -31$
Since the discriminant is negative, this equation has no real number solution.

19. $4x = 8 + x^2$
$0 = x^2 - 4x + 8$
$b^2 - 4ac = (-4)^2 - 4(1)(8) = 16 - 32 = -16$
Since the discriminant is negative, this equation has no real number solution.

21. $b^2 - 4ac = (7)^2 - 4(1)(-2) = 49 + 8 = 57$
Since the discriminant is positive, this equation has two distinct real number solutions.

23. $b^2 - 4ac = (0)^2 - 4(2.1)(-0.5) = 0 + 4.2 = 4.2$
Since the discriminant is positive, this equation has two distinct real number solutions.

25.
$$9 = -t^2 + 6t$$
$$t^2 - 6t + 9 = 0$$
$$b^2 - 4ac = (-6)^2 - 4(1)(9) = 36 - 36 = 0$$

Since the discriminant is zero, this equation has one real number solution.

27. $a = 1, b = -10, c = 24$
$$x = \frac{-b \pm \sqrt{b^2 - 4ac}}{2a}$$
$$= \frac{-(-10) \pm \sqrt{(-10)^2 - 4(1)(24)}}{2(1)}$$
$$= \frac{10 \pm \sqrt{100 - 96}}{2}$$
$$= \frac{10 \pm \sqrt{4}}{2}$$
$$= \frac{10 \pm 2}{2}$$
$$x = \frac{10 + 2}{2} \text{ or } x = \frac{10 - 2}{2}$$
$$x = 6 \qquad \text{or} \quad x = 4$$

29. $a = 1, b = 9, c = 18$
$$x = \frac{-b \pm \sqrt{b^2 - 4ac}}{2a}$$
$$= \frac{-9 \pm \sqrt{(9)^2 - 4(1)(18)}}{2(1)}$$
$$= \frac{-9 \pm \sqrt{81 - 72}}{2}$$
$$= \frac{-9 \pm \sqrt{9}}{2}$$
$$= \frac{-9 \pm 3}{2}$$
$$x = \frac{-9 + 3}{2} \text{ or } x = \frac{-9 - 3}{2}$$
$$x = -3 \qquad \text{or } x = -6$$

31. Write in standard form
$$m^2 - 8m + 15 = 0$$

$a = 1, b = -8, c = 15$
$$x = \frac{-b \pm \sqrt{b^2 - 4ac}}{2a}$$
$$= \frac{-(-8) \pm \sqrt{(-8)^2 - 4(1)(15)}}{2(1)}$$
$$= \frac{8 \pm \sqrt{64 - 60}}{2}$$
$$= \frac{8 \pm \sqrt{4}}{2}$$
$$= \frac{8 \pm 2}{2}$$
$$x = \frac{8 + 2}{2} \text{ or } x = \frac{8 - 2}{2}$$
$$x = 5 \qquad \text{or } x = 3$$

33. $a = 1, b = 0, c = -49$
$$x = \frac{-b \pm \sqrt{b^2 - 4ac}}{2a}$$
$$= \frac{-0 \pm \sqrt{(0)^2 - 4(1)(-49)}}{2(1)}$$
$$= \frac{\pm\sqrt{196}}{2}$$
$$= \frac{\pm 14}{2}$$
$$= \pm 7$$
$$x = 7 \text{ or } x = -7$$

35. $a = 1, b = -6, c = 0$
$$x = \frac{-b \pm \sqrt{b^2 - 4ac}}{2a}$$
$$= \frac{-(-6) \pm \sqrt{(-6)^2 - 4(1)(0)}}{2(1)}$$
$$= \frac{6 \pm \sqrt{36}}{2}$$
$$= \frac{6 \pm 6}{2}$$
$$x = \frac{6 + 6}{2} \text{ or } x = \frac{6 - 6}{2}$$
$$x = 6 \qquad \text{or } x = 0$$

37. Write in standard form
$$z^2 + 11z + 30 = 0$$

$a = 1, b = 11, c = 30$

$$x = \frac{-b \pm \sqrt{b^2 - 4ac}}{2a}$$

$$= \frac{-(11) \pm \sqrt{(11)^2 - 4(1)(30)}}{2(1)}$$

$$= \frac{-11 \pm \sqrt{121 - 120}}{2}$$

$$= \frac{-11 \pm \sqrt{1}}{2}$$

$$= \frac{-11 \pm 1}{2}$$

$$x = \frac{-11 + 1}{2} \quad \text{or} \quad x = \frac{-11 - 1}{2}$$

$$x = -5 \quad \text{or} \quad x = -6$$

39. $a = 1, b = -7, c = -8$

$$x = \frac{-b \pm \sqrt{b^2 - 4ac}}{2a}$$

$$= \frac{-(-7) \pm \sqrt{(-7)^2 - 4(1)(-8)}}{2(1)}$$

$$= \frac{7 \pm \sqrt{49 + 32}}{2}$$

$$= \frac{7 \pm \sqrt{81}}{2}$$

$$= \frac{7 \pm 9}{2}$$

$$x = \frac{7 + 9}{2} \quad \text{or} \quad x = \frac{7 - 9}{2}$$

$$x = 8 \quad \text{or} \quad x = -1$$

41. $a = 2, b = -7, c = 4$

$$y = \frac{-b \pm \sqrt{b^2 - 4ac}}{2a}$$

$$= \frac{-(-7) \pm \sqrt{(-7)^2 - 4(2)(4)}}{2(2)}$$

$$= \frac{7 \pm \sqrt{49 - 32}}{4}$$

$$= \frac{7 \pm \sqrt{17}}{4}$$

$$y = \frac{7 + \sqrt{17}}{4} \quad \text{or} \quad y = \frac{7 - \sqrt{17}}{4}$$

43. Write in standard form

$6x^2 + x - 1 = 0$

$a = 6, b = 1, c = -1$

$$x = \frac{-b \pm \sqrt{b^2 - 4ac}}{2a}$$

$$= \frac{-1 \pm \sqrt{(1)^2 - 4(6)(-1)}}{2(6)}$$

$$= \frac{-1 \pm \sqrt{1 + 24}}{12}$$

$$= \frac{-1 \pm \sqrt{25}}{12}$$

$$= \frac{-1 \pm 5}{12}$$

$$x = \frac{-1 + 5}{12} \quad \text{or} \quad x = \frac{-1 - 5}{12}$$

$$x = \frac{1}{3} \quad \text{or} \quad x = -\frac{1}{2}$$

45. Write in standard form

$2x^2 - 5x - 7 = 0$

$a = 2, b = -5, c = -7$

$$x = \frac{-b \pm \sqrt{b^2 - 4ac}}{2a}$$

$$= \frac{-(-5) \pm \sqrt{(-5)^2 - 4(2)(-7)}}{2(2)}$$

$$= \frac{5 \pm \sqrt{25 + 56}}{4}$$

$$= \frac{5 \pm \sqrt{81}}{4}$$

$$= \frac{5 \pm 9}{4}$$

$$x = \frac{5 + 9}{4} \quad \text{or} \quad x = \frac{5 - 9}{4}$$

$$x = \frac{7}{2} \quad \text{or} \quad x = -1$$

47. $a = 2, b = -4, c = 5$

$$s = \frac{-b \pm \sqrt{b^2 - 4ac}}{2a}$$

$$= \frac{-(-4) \pm \sqrt{(-4)^2 - 4(2)(5)}}{2(2)}$$

$$= \frac{4 \pm \sqrt{16 - 40}}{4}$$

$$= \frac{4 \pm \sqrt{-24}}{4}$$

Since $\sqrt{-24}$ is not a real number, this equation has no real number solution.

49. $a = 1, b = -7, c = 3$

$$x = \frac{-b \pm \sqrt{b^2 - 4ac}}{2a}$$

$$= \frac{(-7) \pm \sqrt{(-7)^2 - 4(1)(3)}}{2(1)}$$

$$= \frac{7 \pm \sqrt{49 - 12}}{2}$$

$$= \frac{7 \pm \sqrt{37}}{2}$$

$$x = \frac{7 + \sqrt{37}}{2} \text{ or } x = \frac{7 - \sqrt{37}}{2}$$

51. Write in standard form

$2x^2 - 7x - 9 = 0$

$a = 2, b = -7, c = -9$

$$x = \frac{-b \pm \sqrt{b^2 - 4ac}}{2a}$$

$$= \frac{-(-7) \pm \sqrt{(-7)^2 - 4(2)(-9)}}{2(2)}$$

$$= \frac{7 \pm \sqrt{49 + 72}}{4}$$

$$= \frac{7 \pm \sqrt{121}}{4}$$

$$= \frac{7 \pm 11}{4}$$

$$x = \frac{7 + 11}{4} \text{ or } x = \frac{7 - 11}{4}$$

$$x = \frac{9}{2} \qquad \text{or } x = -1$$

53. $a = -1, b = 2, c = 15$

$$x = \frac{-b \pm \sqrt{b^2 - 4ac}}{2a}$$

$$= \frac{-2 \pm \sqrt{2^2 - 4(-1)(15)}}{2(-1)}$$

$$= \frac{-2 \pm \sqrt{4 + 60}}{-2}$$

$$= \frac{-2 \pm \sqrt{64}}{-2}$$

$$= \frac{-2 \pm 8}{-2}$$

$$x = \frac{-2 + 8}{-2} \text{ or } x = \frac{-2 - 8}{-2}$$

$$x = -3 \qquad \text{or } x = 5$$

55. Factor out a 2.

$2\left(t^2 - 3t - 28\right) = 0$

Multiply both sides by $\frac{1}{2}$ and use

$t^2 - 3t - 28 = 0$

$a = 1, b = -3, c = -28$

$$t = \frac{-b \pm \sqrt{b^2 - 4ac}}{2a}$$

$$= \frac{-(-3) \pm \sqrt{(-3)^2 - 4(1)(-28)}}{2(1)}$$

$$= \frac{3 \pm \sqrt{9 + 112}}{2}$$

$$= \frac{3 \pm \sqrt{121}}{2}$$

$$= \frac{3 \pm 11}{2}$$

$$t = \frac{3 + 11}{2} \text{ or } t = \frac{3 - 11}{2}$$

$$t = 7 \qquad \text{or } t = -4$$

57. Write in standard form

$6y^2 + 5y + 9 = 0$

$a = 6, b = 5, c = 9$

$$x = \frac{-b \pm \sqrt{b^2 - 4ac}}{2a}$$

$$= \frac{-5 \pm \sqrt{(5)^2 - 4(6)(9)}}{2(6)}$$

$$= \frac{-5 \pm \sqrt{25 - 216}}{12}$$

$$= \frac{-5 \pm \sqrt{-191}}{12}$$

Since $\sqrt{-191}$ is not a real number, this equation has no real number solution.

59. Let $x =$ the smaller integer,
then $x + 1 =$ the larger integer.

$$x(x + 1) = 56$$

$$x^2 + x = 56$$

$$x^2 + x - 56 = 0$$

$a = 1, b = 1, c = -56$

$$x = \frac{-b \pm \sqrt{b^2 - 4ac}}{2a}$$

$$= \frac{-1 \pm \sqrt{(1)^2 - 4(1)(-56)}}{2(1)}$$

$$= \frac{-1 \pm \sqrt{1 + 224}}{2}$$

$$= \frac{-1 \pm \sqrt{225}}{2}$$

$$= \frac{-1 \pm 15}{2}$$

$$x = \frac{-1 + 15}{2} \text{ or } x = \frac{-1 - 15}{2}$$

$$x = 7 \qquad \text{or } x = -8$$

Since the numbers are positive, $x = 7$. The numbers are 7 and $7 + 1 = 8$.

61. Let w = width of rectangle,
then $2w - 3$ = length of rectangle.
Area=length $\cdot$ width

$$20 = (2w - 3)w$$

$$20 = 2w^2 - 3w$$

$$0 = 2w^2 - 3w - 20$$

$a = 2, b = -3, c = -20$

$$x = \frac{-b \pm \sqrt{b^2 - 4ac}}{2a}$$

$$= \frac{-(-3) \pm \sqrt{(-3)^2 - 4(2)(-20)}}{2(2)}$$

$$= \frac{3 \pm \sqrt{9 + 160}}{4}$$

$$= \frac{3 \pm \sqrt{169}}{4}$$

$$= \frac{3 \pm 13}{4}$$

$$x = \frac{3 + 13}{4} \text{ or } x = \frac{3 - 13}{4}$$

$$x = 4 \qquad \text{or } x = -\frac{5}{2}$$

Since the width is positive, $w = 4$. The width is 4 feet and the length is $2(4) - 3 = 5$ feet.

63. Let x = the width of the tile border.
Area of the pool = $(25)(35) = 875$ square feet
Area of the pool plus border = $(2x + 25)(2x + 35)$

$$= 4x^2 + 120x + 875$$

Area of the border = $4x^2 + 120x + 875 - 875$

$$= 4x^2 + 120x$$

$$4x^2 + 120x = 256$$

$$4x^2 + 120x - 256 = 0$$

$$x^2 + 30x - 64 = 0$$

$a = 1, b = 30, c = -64$

$$x = \frac{-b \pm \sqrt{b^2 - 4ac}}{2a}$$

$$= \frac{-30 \pm \sqrt{(30)^2 - 4(1)(-64)}}{2(1)}$$

$$= \frac{-30 \pm \sqrt{900 + 256}}{2}$$

$$= \frac{-30 \pm \sqrt{1156}}{2}$$

$$= \frac{-30 \pm 34}{2}$$

$$x = \frac{-30 + 34}{2} \text{ or } x = \frac{-30 - 34}{2}$$

$$x = 2 \qquad \text{or } x = -32$$

Since the width must be positive, the border can be 2 feet wide.

65. Substitute 14 for d.

$$d = \frac{n^2 - 3n}{2}$$

$$14 = \frac{n^2 - 3n}{2}$$

$$28 = n^2 - 3n$$

$$0 = n^2 - 3n - 28$$

$a = 1, b = -3, c = -28$

$$n = \frac{-b \pm \sqrt{b^2 - 4ac}}{2a}$$

$$= \frac{-(-3) \pm \sqrt{(-3)^2 - 4(1)(-28)}}{2(1)}$$

$$= \frac{3 \pm \sqrt{9 + 112}}{2}$$

$$= \frac{3 \pm \sqrt{121}}{2}$$

$$= \frac{3 \pm 11}{2}$$

$$n = \frac{3 + 11}{2} \text{ or } n = \frac{3 - 11}{2}$$

$$n = 7 \qquad \text{or } n = -4$$

Since the number of sides must be positive, the polygon has 7 sides.

67. Substitute 120 for c.

$$c = x^2 - 16x + 40$$

$$120 = x^2 - 16x + 40$$

$$0 = x^2 - 16x - 80$$

$$a = 1,\ b = -16,\ c = -80$$

$$x = \frac{-b \pm \sqrt{b^2 - 4ac}}{2a}$$

$$= \frac{-(-16) \pm \sqrt{(-16)^2 - 4(1)(-80)}}{2(1)}$$

$$= \frac{16 \pm \sqrt{256 + 320}}{2}$$

$$= \frac{16 \pm \sqrt{576}}{2}$$

$$= \frac{16 \pm 24}{2}$$

$$x = \frac{16 + 24}{2} \quad \text{or} \quad x = \frac{16 - 24}{2}$$

$$x = 20 \qquad \text{or} \quad x = -4$$

x must be positive. Therefore, 20 flags were manufactured.

69. Substitute 80 for s.

$$s = -16t^2 + 90t$$

$$80 = -16t^2 + 90t$$

$$16t^2 - 90t + 80 = 0$$

$$8t^2 - 45t + 40 = 0$$

$$a = 8,\ b = -45,\ c = 40$$

$$t = \frac{-b \pm \sqrt{b^2 - 4ac}}{2a}$$

$$= \frac{-(-45) \pm \sqrt{(-45)^2 - 4(8)(40)}}{2(8)}$$

$$= \frac{45 \pm \sqrt{2025 - 1280}}{16}$$

$$= \frac{45 \pm \sqrt{745}}{16}$$

$$\approx \frac{45 \pm 27.29}{16}$$

$$t \approx \frac{45 + 27.29}{16} \quad \text{or} \quad t \approx \frac{45 - 27.29}{16}$$

$$t \approx 4.52 \qquad \text{or} \quad t \approx 1.11$$

t must be positive. Therefore, it will take 1.11 and 4.52 seconds.

71. $x^2 + 8x + c = 0$

$a = 1,\ b = 8$

The discriminant is

$$b^2 - 4ac = 8^2 - 4(1)c = 64 - 4c = 4(16 - c)$$

a. The equation has two real number solutions when $b^2 - 4ac > 0$.

$$4(16 - c) > 0$$

$$16 - c > 0$$

$$16 > c$$

$$c < 16$$

b. The equation has one real number solution when $b^2 - 4ac = 0$.

$$4(16 - c) = 0$$

$$16 - c = 0$$

$$16 = c$$

$$c = 16$$

c. The equation has no real number solution when $b^2 - 4ac < 0$.

$$4(16 - c) < 0$$

$$16 - c < 0$$

$$16 < c$$

$$c > 16$$

73. $-3x^2 + 6x + c = 0$

$a = -3,\ b = 6$

The discriminant is

$$b^2 - 4ac = 6^2 - 4(-3)c = 36 + 12c = 12(3 + c).$$

a. The equation has two real number solutions when $b^2 - 4ac > 0$.

$$12(3 + c) > 0$$

$$3 + c > 0$$

$$c > -3$$

b. The equation has one real number solution when $b^2 - 4ac = 0$.

$$12(3 + c) = 0$$

$$3 + c = 0$$

$$c = -3$$

c. The equation has no real number solution when $b^2 - 4ac < 0$.

$$12(3 + c) < 0$$

$$3 + c < 0$$

$$c < -3$$

75. a. Each member copies graph.

b. A, $(-2, 0)$; B, $(0, -8)$

c. C, $(1. -9)$; D, $(2, -8)$

d. E, (4, 0)

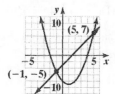

e.

f. (−1, −5), (5, 7)

g.
$$x^2 - 2x - 8 = 2x - 3$$
$$x^2 - 4x - 5 = 0$$
$$a = 1, b = -4, c = -5$$
$$x = \frac{-b \pm \sqrt{b^2 - 4ac}}{2a}$$
$$= \frac{-(-4) \pm \sqrt{(-4)^2 - 4(1)(-5)}}{2(1)}$$
$$= \frac{4 \pm \sqrt{16 + 20}}{2}$$
$$= \frac{4 \pm \sqrt{36}}{2}$$
$$= \frac{4 \pm 6}{2}$$
$$x = \frac{4 + 6}{2} \quad \text{or} \quad x = \frac{4 - 6}{2}$$
$$x = 5 \quad \text{or} \quad x = -1$$

h.
$$x = 5$$

$y = x^2 - 2x - 8$	$y = 2x - 3$
$y = 5^2 - 2(5) - 8$	$y = 2(5) - 3$
$y = 7$	$y = 7$

$$(5, 7)$$

$$x = -1$$

$y = x^2 - 2x - 8$	$y = 2x - 3$
$y = (-1)^2 - 2(-1) - 8$	$y = 2(-1) - 3$
$y = -5$	$y = -5$

$$(-1, -5)$$

76. a.
$$x^2 - 14x + 40 = 0$$
$$(x - 10)(x - 4) = 0$$
$$x - 10 = 0 \quad \text{or} \quad x - 4 = 0$$
$$x = 10 \quad \text{or} \quad x = 4$$

b.
$$x^2 - 14x + 40 = 0$$
$$x^2 - 14x = -40$$
$$x^2 - 14x + 49 = -40 + 49$$
$$(x - 7)^2 = 9$$
$$x - 7 = \pm\sqrt{9}$$
$$x = 7 \pm 3$$
$$x = 7 + 3 \quad \text{or} \quad x = 7 - 3$$
$$x = 10 \quad \text{or} \quad x = 4$$

c. $a = 1, b = -14, c = 40$
$$x = \frac{-b \pm \sqrt{b^2 - 4ac}}{2a}$$
$$= \frac{-(-14) \pm \sqrt{(-14)^2 - 4(1)(40)}}{2(1)}$$
$$= \frac{14 \pm \sqrt{196 - 160}}{2}$$
$$= \frac{14 \pm \sqrt{36}}{2}$$
$$= \frac{14 \pm 6}{2}$$
$$x = \frac{14 + 6}{2} \quad \text{or} \quad x = \frac{14 - 6}{2}$$
$$x = 10 \quad \text{or} \quad x = 4$$

77. a.
$$6x^2 + 11x - 35 = 0$$
$$6x^2 + 21x - 10x - 35 = 0$$
$$3x(2x + 7) - 5(2x + 7) = 0$$
$$(3x - 5)(2x + 7) = 0$$
$$3x - 5 = 0 \quad \text{or} \quad 2x + 7 = 0$$
$$x = \frac{5}{3} \quad \text{or} \quad x = -\frac{7}{2}$$

b.
$$6x^2 + 11x - 35 = 0$$
$$x^2 + \frac{11}{6}x - \frac{35}{6} = 0$$
$$x^2 + \frac{11}{6}x = \frac{35}{6}$$
$$x^2 + \frac{11}{6}x + \frac{121}{144} = \frac{35}{6} + \frac{121}{144}$$
$$\left(x + \frac{11}{12}\right)^2 = \frac{961}{144}$$
$$x + \frac{11}{12} = \pm\sqrt{\frac{961}{144}}$$
$$x + \frac{11}{12} = \pm\frac{31}{12}$$
$$x = -\frac{11}{12} \pm \frac{31}{12}$$

$$x = -\frac{11}{12} + \frac{31}{12} \text{ or } x = -\frac{11}{12} - \frac{31}{12}$$
$$x = \frac{20}{12} = \frac{5}{3} \quad \text{ or } x = -\frac{42}{12} = -\frac{7}{2}$$

c. $a = 6, b = 11, c = -35$
$$x = \frac{-b \pm \sqrt{b^2 - 4ac}}{2a}$$
$$= \frac{-11 \pm \sqrt{11^2 - 4(6)(-35)}}{2(6)}$$
$$= \frac{-11 \pm \sqrt{121 + 840}}{12}$$
$$= \frac{-11 \pm \sqrt{961}}{12}$$
$$= \frac{-11 \pm 31}{12}$$
$$x = \frac{-11 + 31}{12} \text{ or } x = \frac{-11 - 31}{12}$$
$$x = \frac{20}{12} = \frac{5}{3} \quad \text{ or } x = \frac{-42}{12} = -\frac{7}{2}$$

78. a. $2x^2 + 3x - 4 = 0$
Since there are no integers whose product is
−8 and whose sum is 3, this equation cannot
be solved by factoring.

b.
$$2x^2 + 3x - 4 = 0$$
$$x^2 + \frac{3}{2}x - 2 = 0$$
$$x^2 + \frac{3}{2}x = 2$$
$$x^2 + \frac{3}{2}x + \frac{9}{16} = 2 + \frac{9}{16}$$
$$\left(x + \frac{3}{4}\right)^2 = \frac{41}{16}$$
$$x + \frac{3}{4} = \pm\sqrt{\frac{41}{16}}$$
$$x + \frac{3}{4} = \pm\frac{\sqrt{41}}{4}$$
$$x = -\frac{3}{4} \pm \frac{\sqrt{41}}{4}$$
$$x = \frac{-3 \pm \sqrt{41}}{4}$$

$$x = \frac{-3 + \sqrt{41}}{4} \text{ or } x = \frac{-3 - \sqrt{41}}{4}$$

c. $a = 2, b = 3, c = -4$
$$x = \frac{-b \pm \sqrt{b^2 - 4ac}}{2(a)}$$
$$= \frac{-3 \pm \sqrt{3^2 - 4(2)(-4)}}{2(2)}$$
$$= \frac{-3 \pm \sqrt{9 + 32}}{4}$$
$$= \frac{-3 \pm \sqrt{41}}{4}$$
$$x = \frac{-3 + \sqrt{41}}{4} \text{ or } x = \frac{-3 - \sqrt{41}}{4}$$

79. a.
$$3x^2 = 48$$
$$3x^2 - 48 = 0$$
$$3(x^2 - 16) = 0$$
$$3(x - 4)(x + 4) = 0$$
$$x - 4 = 0 \text{ or } x + 4 = 0$$
$$x = 4 \text{ or } \qquad x = -4$$

b.
$$3x^2 = 48$$
$$x^2 = 16$$
$$x = \pm\sqrt{16}$$
$$x = \pm 4$$
$$x = 4 \text{ or } x = -4$$

c. $3x^2 - 48 = 0$

$a = 3,\ b = 0,\ c = -48$

$$x = \frac{-b \pm \sqrt{b^2 - 4ac}}{2(a)}$$

$$= \frac{-0 \pm \sqrt{0^2 - 4(3)(-48)}}{2(3)}$$

$$= \frac{\pm\sqrt{576}}{6}$$

$$= \frac{\pm 24}{6}$$

$$= \pm 4$$

$x = 4$ or $x = -4$

80. $\dfrac{x}{2x^2 + 7x - 4} - \dfrac{2}{x^2 - x - 20}$

$$= \frac{x}{(2x-1)(x+4)} - \frac{2}{(x-5)(x+4)}$$

LCD is $(2x-1)(x+4)(x-5)$

$$= \frac{x-5}{x-5} \cdot \frac{x}{(2x-1)(x+4)} - \frac{2x-1}{2x-1} \cdot \frac{2}{(x-5)(x+4)}$$

$$= \frac{x^2 - 5x}{(2x-1)(x+4)(x-5)} - \frac{4x-2}{(2x-1)(x+4)(x-5)}$$

$$= \frac{x^2 - 5x - 4x + 2}{(2x-1)(x+4)(x-5)}$$

$$= \frac{x^2 - 9x + 2}{(2x-1)(x+4)(x-5)}$$

Mid-Chapter Test: 10.1-10.3

1. $x^2 = 64$ **2.** $a^2 = 19$

$x = \pm\sqrt{64}$ $a = \pm\sqrt{19}$

$x = \pm 8$

3. $16m^2 + 10 = 25$

$16m^2 = 15$

$$m^2 = \frac{15}{16}$$

$$m = \pm\sqrt{\frac{15}{16}}$$

$$m = \pm\frac{\sqrt{15}}{\sqrt{16}}$$

$$m = \pm\frac{\sqrt{15}}{4}$$

4. $(y-3)^2 = 4$

$y - 3 = \pm\sqrt{4}$

$y - 3 = \pm 2$

$y = 3 \pm 2$

$y = 3 + 2$ or $y = 3 - 2$

$y = 5$ or $y = 1$

5. $(z+6)^2 = 81$

$z + 6 = \pm\sqrt{81}$

$z + 6 = \pm 9$

$z = -6 \pm 9$

$z = -6 + 9$ or $z = -6 - 9$

$z = 3$ or $z = -15$

6. $(b-7)^2 = 24$

$b - 7 = \pm\sqrt{24}$

$b - 7 = \pm\sqrt{4}\sqrt{6}$

$b - 7 = \pm 2\sqrt{6}$

$b = 7 \pm 2\sqrt{6}$

7. Let $n =$ the smaller number and $2.5n =$ the larger number.

$n \cdot 2.5n = 40$

$2.5n^2 = 40$

$n^2 = 16$

$n = \pm\sqrt{16}$

$n = \pm 4$

Since n has to be positive, the smaller number is 4 and the larger is $4(2.5) = 10$.

8. Let n be the number and n^2 be the squared number.

$2n + n^2 = 8$

$n^2 + 2n - 8 = 0$

$(n+4)(n-2) = 0$

$n + 4 = 0$ or $n - 2 = 0$

$n = -4$ or $n = 2$

The numbers are 2 and –4.

9. $x^2 + 2x - 15 = 0$

$$x^2 + 2x = 15$$
$$x^2 + 2x + 1 = 15 + 1$$
$$x^2 + 2x + 1 = 16$$
$$(x+1)^2 = 16$$
$$x + 1 = \pm\sqrt{16}$$
$$x + 1 = \pm 4$$
$$x = -1 \pm 4$$
$$x = -1 + 4 \quad \text{or} \quad x = -1 - 4$$
$$x = 3 \quad\quad \text{or} \quad x = -5$$

The solutions are 3 and –5.

10. $x^2 - 11x + 18 = 0$

$$x^2 - 11x = -18$$
$$x^2 - 11x + \frac{121}{4} = -18 + \frac{121}{4}$$
$$x^2 - 11x + \frac{121}{4} = -\frac{72}{4} + \frac{121}{4}$$
$$x^2 - 11x + \frac{121}{4} = \frac{49}{4}$$
$$\left(x - \frac{11}{2}\right)^2 = \pm\sqrt{\frac{49}{4}}$$
$$\left(x - \frac{11}{2}\right)^2 = \pm\frac{7}{2}$$
$$x = \frac{11}{2} \pm \frac{7}{2}$$
$$x = \frac{11}{2} + \frac{7}{2} \quad \text{or} \quad x = \frac{11}{2} - \frac{7}{2}$$
$$x = 9 \quad\quad \text{or} \quad x = 2$$

The solutions are 9 and 2.

11. $p^2 - 7p = 0$

$$p^2 - 7p + \frac{49}{4} = 0 + \frac{49}{4}$$
$$p^2 - 7p + \frac{49}{4} = \frac{49}{4}$$
$$\left(p - \frac{7}{2}\right)^2 = \pm\sqrt{\frac{49}{4}}$$
$$\left(p - \frac{7}{2}\right)^2 = \pm\frac{7}{2}$$
$$p = \frac{7}{2} \pm \frac{7}{2}$$
$$p = \frac{7}{2} + \frac{7}{2} \quad \text{or} \quad p = \frac{7}{2} - \frac{7}{2}$$
$$p = 7 \quad\quad \text{or} \quad p = 0$$

The solutions are 7 and 0.

12. $h^2 + 2h - 6 = 0$

$$h^2 + 2h = 6$$
$$h^2 + 2h + 1 = 6 + 1$$
$$h^2 + 2h + 1 = 7$$
$$(h+1)^2 = 7$$
$$h + 1 = \pm\sqrt{7}$$
$$h = -1 \pm \sqrt{7}$$

The solutions are $-1 + \sqrt{7}$ and $-1 - \sqrt{7}$.

13. $x^2 - 9x + 1 = 0$

$$x^2 - 9x = -1$$
$$x^2 - 9x + \frac{81}{4} = -1 + \frac{81}{4}$$
$$x^2 - 9x + \frac{81}{4} = -\frac{4}{4} + \frac{81}{4}$$
$$x^2 - 9x + \frac{81}{4} = \frac{77}{4}$$
$$\left(x - \frac{9}{2}\right)^2 = \pm\sqrt{\frac{77}{4}}$$
$$\left(x - \frac{9}{2}\right)^2 = \pm\frac{\sqrt{77}}{2}$$
$$x = \frac{9}{2} \pm \frac{\sqrt{77}}{2}$$
$$x = \frac{9 \pm \sqrt{77}}{2}$$

The solutions are $\dfrac{9 + \sqrt{77}}{2}$ and $\dfrac{9 - \sqrt{77}}{2}$.

14. $x^2 - 5x - 24 = 0$

$a = 1, b = -5, c = -24$

$x = \dfrac{-b \pm \sqrt{b^2 - 4ac}}{2a}$

$x = \dfrac{-(-5) \pm \sqrt{(-5)^2 - 4(1)(-24)}}{2(1)}$

$x = \dfrac{5 \pm \sqrt{25 + 96}}{2}$

$x = \dfrac{5 \pm \sqrt{121}}{2}$

$x = \dfrac{5 \pm 11}{2}$

$x = \dfrac{5 + 11}{2}$ or $x = \dfrac{5 - 11}{2}$

$x = 8$ or $x = -3$

15. $x^2 + 11x + 30 = 0$

$a = 1, b = 11, c = 30$

$x = \dfrac{-b \pm \sqrt{b^2 - 4ac}}{2a}$

$x = \dfrac{-11 \pm \sqrt{11^2 - 4(1)(30)}}{2(1)}$

$x = \dfrac{-11 \pm \sqrt{121 - 120}}{2}$

$x = \dfrac{-11 \pm \sqrt{1}}{2}$

$x = \dfrac{-11 \pm 1}{2}$

$x = \dfrac{-11 + 1}{2}$ or $x = \dfrac{-11 - 1}{2}$

$x = -5$ or $x = -6$

16. $m^2 - 5m - 3 = 0$

$a = 1, b = -5, c = -3$

$m = \dfrac{-b \pm \sqrt{b^2 - 4ac}}{2a}$

$m = \dfrac{-(-5) \pm \sqrt{(-5)^2 - 4(1)(-3)}}{2(1)}$

$m = \dfrac{5 \pm \sqrt{25 + 12}}{2}$

$m = \dfrac{5 \pm \sqrt{37}}{2}$

The solutions are $\dfrac{5 + \sqrt{37}}{2}$ and $\dfrac{5 - \sqrt{37}}{2}$.

17. a. $b^2 - 4ac > 0$

   b. $b^2 - 4ac = 0$

   c. $b^2 - 4ac < 0$

18. $3x^2 - x - 2 = 0$

$a = 3, b = -1, c = -2$

$b^2 - 4ac = (-1)^2 - 4(3)(-2) = 1 + 24 = 25$

Since the discriminant, $25 > 0$, there are two distinct solutions.

19. $\dfrac{1}{2}x^2 + 4x + 11 = 0$

$a = \dfrac{1}{2}, b = 4, c = +11$

$b^2 - 4ac = 4^2 - 4\left(\dfrac{1}{2}\right)(11) = 16 - 22 = -6$

Since the discriminant, $-6 < 0$, there are no real number solutions.

20. Let w be the width of the screen, then $w + 3$ is the length of the screen.

$$lw = A$$
$$(w + 3)w = 88$$
$$w^2 + 3w = 88$$
$$w^2 + 3w - 88 = 0$$
$$(w + 11)(w - 8) = 0$$
$$w + 11 = 0 \quad \text{or} \quad w - 8 = 0$$
$$w = -11 \quad \text{or} \quad w = 8$$

Since the width has to be positive, the width is 8 inches and the length is 8 + 3 = 11 inches.

Exercise Set 10.4

1. The graph of a quadratic equation of the form $y = ax^2 + bx + c, a \neq 0$ is called a parabola.

3. Answers will vary.

5. a. Where the graph crosses the x-axis.

   b. The x-intercepts are found by setting $y = 0$ and solving for x.

7. a. $x = -\dfrac{b}{2a}$

b. This line is called the axis of symmetry.

9. $a = 1$, $b = 2$, $c = -7$

$$x = -\frac{b}{2a} = -\frac{2}{2(1)} = -1$$

The axis of symmetry is $x = -1$.
Find the y-coordinate of the vertex:

$$y = x^2 + 2x - 7$$

$$y = (-1)^2 + 2(-1) - 7$$

$$= 1 - 2 - 7$$

$$= -8$$

The vertex is $(-1, -8)$
Since $a > 0$, the parabola opens upward.

11. $a = 4$, $b = 8$, $c = 3$

$$x = -\frac{b}{2a} = -\frac{8}{2(4)} = -1$$

The axis of symmetry is $x = -1$.
Find the y-coordinate of the vertex:

$$y = 4x^2 + 8x + 3$$

$$y = 4(-1)^2 + 8(-1) + 3$$

$$= 4 - 8 + 3$$

$$= -1$$

The vertex is $(-1, -1)$.
Since $a > 0$, the parabola opens upward.

13. $a = -3$, $b = 2$, $c = 1$

$$x = -\frac{b}{2a} = -\frac{2}{2(-3)} = \frac{2}{6} = \frac{1}{3}$$

The axis of symmetry is $x = \frac{1}{3}$
Find the y-coordinate of the vertex:

$$y = -3x^2 + 2x + 1$$

$$y = -3\left(\frac{1}{3}\right)^2 + 2\left(\frac{1}{3}\right) + 1$$

$$= -\frac{1}{3} + \frac{2}{3} + \frac{3}{3}$$

$$= \frac{4}{3}$$

The vertex is $\left(\frac{1}{3}, \frac{4}{3}\right)$.

Since $a < 0$, the parabola opens downward.

15. $a = -1$, $b = 3$, $c = -4$

$$x = -\frac{b}{2a} = -\frac{3}{2(-1)} = \frac{3}{2}$$

The axis of symmetry is $x = \frac{3}{2}$
Find the y-coordinate of the vertex:

$$y = -x^2 + 3x - 4$$

$$y = -\left(\frac{3}{2}\right)^2 + 3\left(\frac{3}{2}\right) - 4$$

$$= -\frac{9}{4} + \frac{9}{2} - 4$$

$$= -\frac{7}{4}$$

The vertex is $\left(\frac{3}{2}, -\frac{7}{4}\right)$

Since $a < 0$, the parabola opens downward.

17. $a = 2$, $b = 3$, $c = 4$

$$x = -\frac{b}{2a} = -\frac{3}{2(2)} = -\frac{3}{4}$$

The axis of symmetry is $x = -\frac{3}{4}$.
Find the y-coordinate of the vertex:

$$y = 2x^2 + 3x + 4$$

$$y = 2\left(-\frac{3}{4}\right)^2 + 3\left(-\frac{3}{4}\right) + 4$$

$$= \frac{9}{8} - \frac{9}{4} + 4$$

$$= \frac{9}{8} - \frac{18}{8} + \frac{32}{8}$$

$$= \frac{23}{8}$$

The vertex is $\left(-\frac{3}{4}, \frac{23}{8}\right)$.

Since $a > 0$, the parabola opens upward.

19. $a = -1$, $b = 1$, $c = 8$

$$x = -\frac{b}{2a} = -\frac{1}{2(-1)} = \frac{1}{2}$$

The axis of symmetry is $x = \frac{1}{2}$.
Find the y-coordinate of the vertex:

$$y = -x^2 + x + 8$$

$$y = -\left(\frac{1}{2}\right)^2 + \frac{1}{2} + 8$$

$$= -\frac{1}{4} + \frac{1}{2} + 8$$

$$= \frac{33}{4}$$

The vertex is $\left(\frac{1}{2}, \frac{33}{4}\right)$.

Since $a < 0$, the parabola opens downward.

21. $a = 1, b = 0, c = 3$

Since $a > 0$, the parabola opens upward.

Axis of symmetry is $x = -\dfrac{b}{2a} = -\dfrac{0}{2(1)} = 0$

y-coordinate of the vertex:

$y = x^2 + 3$

$y = 0^2 + 3 = 3$

The vertex is $(0, 3)$.

$$y = x^2 + 3$$

Let $x = -1$ $y = (-1)^2 + 3 = 4$

Let $x = 1$ $y = 1^2 + 3 = 4$

x	y
-1	4
1	4

$0 = x^2 + 3$

$x = \dfrac{-0 \pm \sqrt{0^2 - 4(1)(3)}}{2(1)}$

$= \dfrac{\pm\sqrt{-12}}{2}$

No real number solution

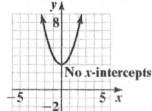

No *x*-intercepts

23. $a = -1, b = 0, c = 5$

Since $a < 0$, the parabola opens downward.

Axis of symmetry is $x = -\dfrac{b}{2a} = -\dfrac{0}{2(-1)} = 0$

y-coordinate of the vertex:

$y = -x^2 + 5$

$y = -0^2 + 5 = 5$

The vertex is $(0, 5)$.

$$y = -x^2 + 5$$

Let $x = -1$ $y = -(-1)^2 + 5 = 4$

Let $x = 1$ $y = -(1)^2 + 5 = 4$

x	y
-1	4
1	4

$0 = -x^2 + 5$

$x^2 = 5$

$x = \pm\sqrt{5}$

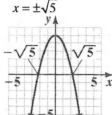

25. $a = 1, b = 4, c = 3$

Since $a > 0$, the parabola opens upward.

Axis of symmetry is $x = -\dfrac{b}{2a} = -\dfrac{4}{2(1)} = -2$

y-coordinate of the vertex:

$y = x^2 + 4x + 3$

$y = (-2)^2 + 4(-2) + 3 = 1$

The vertex is $(-2, -1)$.

$$y = x^2 + 4x + 3$$

Let $x = -1$ $y = (-1)^2 + 4(-1) + 3 = 0$

Let $x = 0$ $y = 0^2 + 4(0) + 3 = 3$

x	y
-1	0
0	3

$0 = x^2 + 4x + 3$

$0 = (x + 3)(x + 1)$

$x = -3$ or $x = -1$

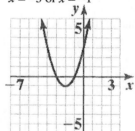

27. $a = 1, b = 4, c = 4$

Since $a > 0$, the parabola opens upward.

Axis of symmetry is $x = -\dfrac{b}{2a} = -\dfrac{4}{2(1)} = -2$

y-coordinate of the vertex:

$y = x^2 + 4x + 4$

$y = (-2)^2 + 4(-2) + 4 = 0$

The vertex is $(-2, 0)$

$$y = x^2 + 4x + 4$$

Let $x = -3$ $y = (-3)^2 + 4(-3) + 4 = 1$

Let $x = -1$ $y = (-1)^2 + 4(-1) + 4 = 1$

x	y
-3	1
-1	1

$$0 = x^2 + 4x + 4$$
$$0 = (x+2)^2$$
$$x = -2$$

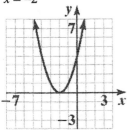

29. $a = -1$, $b = -5$, $c = -4$

Since $a < 0$, the parabola opens downward.

Axis of symmetry is $x = -\dfrac{b}{2a} = -\dfrac{-5}{2(-1)} = -\dfrac{5}{2}$

y-coordinate of the vertex:
$$y = -x^2 - 5x - 4$$
$$y = -\left(-\frac{5}{2}\right)^2 - 5\left(-\frac{5}{2}\right) - 4$$
$$= -\frac{25}{4} + \frac{25}{2} - 4$$
$$= \frac{9}{4}$$

The vertex is $\left(-\dfrac{5}{2}, \dfrac{9}{4}\right)$.

$$y = -x^2 - 5x - 4$$

Let $x = -1$ $y = -(-1)^2 - 5(-1) - 4 = 0$

Let $x = -4$ $y = -(-4)^2 - 5(-4) - 4 = 0$

x	y
-4	0
-1	0

$$0 = -x^2 - 5x - 4$$
$$0 = x^2 + 5x + 4$$
$$0 = (x+4)(x+1)$$
$$x = -4 \text{ or } x = -1$$

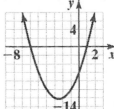

31. $a = 1$, $b = 5$, $c = -6$

Since $a > 0$, the parabola opens upward.

Axis of symmetry is $x = -\dfrac{b}{2a} = -\dfrac{5}{2(1)} = -\dfrac{5}{2}$

y-coordinate of the vertex:
$$y = x^2 + 5x - 6$$
$$y = \left(-\frac{5}{2}\right)^2 + 5\left(-\frac{5}{2}\right) - 6 = -\frac{49}{4}$$

The vertex is $\left(-\dfrac{5}{2}, -\dfrac{49}{4}\right)$.

$$y = x^2 + 5x - 6$$

Let $x = -6$ $y = (-6)^2 + 5(-6) - 6 = 0$

Let $x = 1$ $y = 1^2 + 5(1) - 6 = 0$

x	y
-6	0
1	0

$$0 = x^2 + 5x - 6$$
$$0 = (x+6)(x-1)$$
$$x = -6 \text{ or } x = 1$$

33. $a = 1$, $b = 5$, $c = -14$

Since $a > 0$, the parabola opens upward.

Axis of symmetry is $x = -\dfrac{b}{2a} = -\dfrac{5}{2(1)} = -\dfrac{5}{2}$

y-coordinate of the vertex:
$$y = x^2 + 5x - 14$$
$$y = \left(-\frac{5}{2}\right)^2 + 5\left(-\frac{5}{2}\right) - 14 = -\frac{81}{4}$$

The vertex is $\left(-\dfrac{5}{2}, -\dfrac{81}{4}\right)$

$$y = x^2 + 5x - 14$$

Let $x = -7$ $\quad y = (-7)^2 + 5(-7) - 14 = 0$

Let $x = 2$ $\quad y = 2^2 + 5(2) - 14 = 0$

x	y
-7	0
2	0

$$0 = x^2 + 5x - 14$$

$$0 = (x + 7)(x - 2)$$

$$x = -7 \text{ or } x = 2$$

35. $a = 1,\ b = -6,\ c = 9$

Since $a > 0$, the parabola opens upward.

Axis of symmetry: $x = -\dfrac{b}{2a} = -\dfrac{-6}{2(1)} = 3$

y-coordinate of the vertex:

$$y = x^2 - 6x + 9$$

$$y = 3^2 - 6(3) + 9 = 0$$

The vertex is at $(3, 0)$

$$y = x^2 - 6x + 9$$

Let $x = 4$ $\quad y = 4^2 - 6(4) + 9 = 1$

Let $x = 5$ $\quad y = 5^2 - 6(5) + 9 = 4$

Let $x = 6$ $\quad y = 6^2 - 6(6) + 9 = 9$

x	y
4	1
5	4
6	9

$$0 = x^2 - 6x + 9$$

$$0 = (x - 3)^2$$

$$x = 3$$

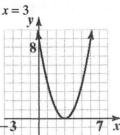

37. $a = 1,\ b = -6,\ c = 0$

Since $a > 0$, the parabola opens upward.

axis of symmetry is $x = -\dfrac{b}{2a} = -\dfrac{-6}{2(1)} = 3$

y-coordinate of the vertex:

$$y = x^2 - 6x$$

$$y = 3^2 - 6(3) = -9$$

The vertex is $(3, -9)$.

$$y = x^2 - 6x$$

Let $x = 0$ $\quad y = 0^2 - 6(0) = 0$

Let $x = 6$ $\quad y = 6^2 - 6(6) = 0$

x	y
0	0
6	0

$$0 = x^2 - 6x$$

$$0 = x(x - 6)$$

$$x = 0 \text{ or } x = 6$$

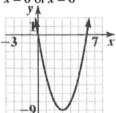

39. $a = 1,\ b = -2,\ c = 1$

Since $a > 0$, the parabola opens upward.

Axis of symmetry is $x = -\dfrac{b}{2a} = -\dfrac{-2}{2(1)} = 1$

y-coordinate of the vertex:

$$y = x^2 - 2x + 1$$

$$y = 1^2 - 2(1) + 1 = 0$$

The vertex is $(1, 0)$.

$$y = x^2 - 2x + 1$$

Let $x = -1$ $\quad y = (-1)^2 - 2(-1) + 1 = 4$

Let $x = 3$ $\quad y = 3^2 - 2(3) + 1 = 4$

x	y
-1	4
3	4

$0 = x^2 - 2x + 1$

$0 = (x-1)^2$

$x = 1$

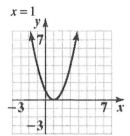

41. $a = -1, b = 7, c = -10$

Since $a < 0$, the parabola opens downward.

Axis of symmetry: $x = -\dfrac{b}{2a} = -\dfrac{7}{2(-1)} = \dfrac{7}{2}$

y-coordinate of the vertex:

$y = -x^2 + 7x - 10$

$y = -\left(\dfrac{7}{2}\right)^2 + 7\left(\dfrac{7}{2}\right) - 10 = \dfrac{9}{4}$

The vertex is at $\left(\dfrac{7}{2}, \dfrac{9}{4}\right)$.

$$y = -x^2 + 7x - 10$$

Let $x = 1$ $y = -1^2 + 7(1) - 10 = -4$

Let $x = 6$ $y = -6^2 + 7(6) - 10 = -4$

Let $x = 3$ $y = -3^2 + 7(3) - 10 = 2$

x	y
1	-4
6	-4
3	2

$0 = -x^2 + 7x - 10$

$0 = x^2 - 7x + 10$

$0 = (x-5)(x-2)$

$x = 5$ or $x = 2$

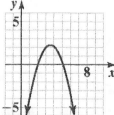

43. $a = 4, b = 12, c = 9$

Since $a > 0$, the parabola opens upward.

Axis of symmetry is $x = -\dfrac{b}{2a} = -\dfrac{12}{2(4)} = -\dfrac{3}{2}$

y-coordinate of the vertex:

$y = 4x^2 + 12x + 9$

$y = 4\left(-\dfrac{3}{2}\right)^2 + 12\left(-\dfrac{3}{2}\right) + 9 = 0$

The vertex is $\left(-\dfrac{3}{2}, 0\right)$.

$$y = 4x^2 + 12x + 9$$

Let $x = -1$ $y = 4(-1)^2 + 12(-1) + 9 = 1$

Let $x = 0$ $y = 4(0)^2 + 12(0) + 9 = 9$

x	y
-1	1
0	9

$0 = 4x^2 + 12x + 9$

$0 = (2x+3)^2$

$x = -\dfrac{3}{2}$

45. $a = -2, b = 3, c = -2$

Since $a < 0$, the parabola opens downward.

Axis of symmetry: $x = -\dfrac{b}{2a} = -\dfrac{3}{2(-2)} = \dfrac{3}{4}$

y-coordinate of the vertex:

$y = -2x^2 + 3x - 2$

$y = -2\left(\dfrac{3}{4}\right)^2 + 3\left(\dfrac{3}{4}\right) - 2 = -\dfrac{7}{8}$

The vertex is $\left(\dfrac{3}{4}, -\dfrac{7}{8}\right)$.

$$y = -2x^2 + 3x - 2$$

Let $x = -1$ $y = -2(-1)^2 + 3(-1) - 2 = -7$

Let $x = 0$ $y = -2(0)^2 + 3(0) - 2 = -2$

Let $x = 1$ $y = -2(1)^2 + 3(1) - 2 = -1$

Let $x = 2$ $y = -2(2)^2 + 3(2) - 2 = -4$

x	y
−1	−7
0	−2
1	−1
2	−4

$$0 = -2x^2 + 3x - 2$$

$$x = \frac{-3 \pm \sqrt{3^2 - 4(-2)(-2)}}{2(-2)}$$

$$= \frac{-3 \pm \sqrt{-7}}{-4}$$

No real number solution

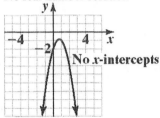

No *x*-intercepts

47. $a = 2$, $b = -1$, $c = -15$

Since $a > 0$, the parabola opens upward.

Axis of symmetry is $x = -\dfrac{b}{2a} = -\dfrac{-1}{2(2)} = \dfrac{1}{4}$

y-coordinate of the vertex:

$$y = 2x^2 - x - 15$$

$$y = 2\left(\frac{1}{4}\right)^2 - \frac{1}{4} - 15 = -\frac{121}{8}$$

The vertex is $\left(\dfrac{1}{4}, -\dfrac{121}{8}\right)$

$$y = 2x^2 - x - 15$$

Let $x = -2$ $y = 2(-2)^2 - (-2) - 15 = -5$

Let $x = 2$ $y = 2(2)^2 - 2 - 15 = -9$

x	y
−2	−5
2	−9

$$0 = 2x^2 - x - 15$$

$$0 = (2x + 5)(x - 3)$$

$$x = -\frac{5}{2} \text{ or } x = 3$$

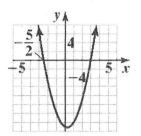

49. $b^2 - 4ac = (-2)^2 - 4(4)(-7)$

$$= 4 + 112$$

$$= 116$$

Since the discriminant is positive, there will be two *x*-intercepts.

51. $b^2 - 4ac = (-6)^2 - 4(4)(-5) = 36 + 80 = 116$

Since the discriminant is positive, there will be two *x*-intercepts.

53. $b^2 - 4ac = (-22)^2 - 4(1)(121) = 484 - 484 = 0$

Since the discriminant is zero, there will be one *x*-intercept.

55. $b^2 - 4ac = 2^2 - 4(1.6)(-1.5)$

$$= 4 + 9.6$$

$$= 13.6$$

Since the discriminant is positive, there will be two *x*-intercepts.

57. None; the vertex is below the *x*-axis and the parabola opens downward.

59. One; the vertex of the parabola is on the *x*-axis.

61. Yes; if *y* is set to 0, both equations have the same solutions, 5 and −3.

63. a. The maximum height is about 255 feet.

    b. It will take 4 seconds.

    c. It will strike the ground in 8 seconds.

    d. At 2 seconds it is about 190 feet high and about 240 feet high at 5 seconds.

65. a.

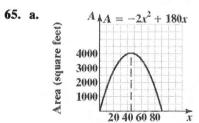

    b. The maximum area is when $x = 45$ feet.

c. Substitute 45 for x.

$A = -2x^2 + 180x$

$\quad = -2(45)^2 + 180(45)$

$\quad = -4050 + 8100$

$\quad = 4050$

The maximum are is 4050 square feet.

67. a. $a = -1, b = 6, c = 0$

Since $a < 0$, the parabola opens downward.

Axis of symmetry is $x = -\dfrac{b}{2a} = -\dfrac{6}{2(-1)} = 3$

y-coordinate of the vertex:

$y = -x^2 + 6x$

$y = -(3)^2 + 6(3) = 9$

The vertex is $(3, 9)$.

$$y = -x^2 + 6x$$

Let $x = 0$　　$y = -(0)^2 + 6(0) = 0$

Let $x = 6$　　$y = -(6)^2 + 6(6) = 6$

x	y
0	0
6	0

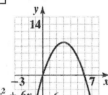

$y = -x^2 + 6x$

b. For $y = x^2 - 2x$

$a = 1, b = -2, c = 0$

Since $a > 0$, the parabola opens upward.

Axis of symmetry is $x = -\dfrac{b}{2a} = -\dfrac{-2}{2(1)} = 1$

y-coordinate of the vertex:

$y = x^2 - 2x$

$y = (1)^2 - 2(1) = -1$

The vertex is $(1, -1)$.

$$y = x^2 - 2x$$

Let $x = 2$　　$y = 2^2 - 2(2) = 0$

Let $x = -1$　　$y = (-1)^2 - 2(-1) = 3$

x	y
2	0
-1	3

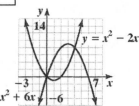

$y = x^2 - 2x$

$y = -x^2 + 6x$

c. $(0, 0), (4, 8)$

69. $\dfrac{5}{x+3} - \dfrac{x-2}{x-4} = \dfrac{5}{x+3} \cdot \dfrac{x-4}{x-4} - \dfrac{x-2}{x-4} \cdot \dfrac{x+3}{x+3}$

$\qquad = \dfrac{5x-20}{(x+3)(x-4)} - \dfrac{x^2+x-6}{(x+3)(x-4)}$

$\qquad = \dfrac{5x-20-x^2-x+6}{(x+3)(x-4)}$

$\qquad = \dfrac{-x^2+4x-14}{(x+3)(x-4)}$

70. $\dfrac{1}{3}(x+6) = 3 - \dfrac{1}{4}(x-5)$

$12\left[\dfrac{1}{3}(x+6)\right] = 12\left[3 - \dfrac{1}{4}(x-5)\right]$

$4(x+6) = 36 - 3(x-5)$

$4x + 24 = 36 - 3x + 15$

$7x = 27$

$x = \dfrac{27}{7}$

71. $2x + 3y = -3$

$3x + 5y = -7$

Multiply the first equation by -3.

Multiply the second equation by 2.

$-6x - 9y = 9$

$\underline{6x + 10y = -14}$

$\qquad y = -5$

Substitute -5 for y in the first equation and solve for x.

$2x + 3(-5) = -3$

$2x - 15 = -3$

$2x = 12$

$x = 6$

The solution is $(6, -5)$.

72. $\sqrt{x+9} - x = -3$

$$\sqrt{x+9} = x - 3$$

$$\left(\sqrt{x+9}\right)^2 = \left(x-3\right)^2$$

$$x + 9 = x^2 - 6x + 9$$

$$0 = x^2 - 7x$$

$$0 = x(x-7)$$

$$x = 0 \quad \text{or} \quad x - 7 = 0$$

$$x = 7$$

Check $x = 0$ $\quad \sqrt{x+9} - x = -3$

$$\sqrt{0+9} - 0 = -3$$

$$3 - 0 = -3 \quad \text{False}$$

Check $x = 7$ $\quad \sqrt{x+9} - x = -3$

$$\sqrt{7+9} - 7 = -3$$

$$-3 = -3 \quad \text{True}$$

The solution is 7.

Exercise Set 10.5

1. Yes, every real number is a complex number because it can be written in the form $a + bi$ where $b = 0$.

3. $i = \sqrt{-1}$

5. The general form of a complex number is $a + bi$.

7. $\sqrt{-16} = \sqrt{16}\sqrt{-1} = 4i$

9. $\sqrt{-100} = \sqrt{100}\sqrt{-1} = 10i$

11. $\sqrt{-15} = i\sqrt{15}$

13. $\sqrt{-13} = i\sqrt{13}$

15. $\sqrt{-32} = \sqrt{16}\sqrt{2}\sqrt{-1} = 4\sqrt{2}i = 4i\sqrt{2}$

17. $\sqrt{-45} = \sqrt{9}\sqrt{5}\sqrt{-1} = 3\sqrt{5}i = 3i\sqrt{5}$

19. $8 + \sqrt{-4} = 8 + i\sqrt{4} = 8 + 2i$

21. $10 + \sqrt{-25} = 10 + i\sqrt{25} = 10 + 5i$

23. $-3 - \sqrt{-9} = -3 - i\sqrt{9} = -3 - 3i$

25. $-7 - \sqrt{-15} = -7 - i\sqrt{15}$

27. $5.2 + \sqrt{-48} = 5.2 + i\sqrt{48}$

$$= 5.2 + i\sqrt{16}\sqrt{3}$$

$$= 5.2 + 4i\sqrt{3}$$

29. $\dfrac{1}{4} + \sqrt{-75} = \dfrac{1}{2} + i\sqrt{75}$

$$= \dfrac{1}{4} + i\sqrt{25}\sqrt{3}$$

$$= \dfrac{1}{4} + 5i\sqrt{3}$$

31. $(2 + 3i) + 8 = 2 + 8 + 3i = 10 + 3i$

33. $(4 - 2i) - 9i = 4 - 2i - 9i = 4 - (2+9)i = 4 - 11i$

35. $(5 + 3i) + (6 + 2i) = 5 + 6 + 3i + 2i$

$$= 11 + (3+2)i$$

$$= 11 + 5i$$

37. $(4 - 3i) - (6 + 4i) = 4 - 3i - 6 - 4i$

$$= 4 - 6 - 3i - 4i$$

$$= -2 - (3+4)i$$

$$= -2 - 7i$$

39. $(13 - 6i) - (13 - 6i) = 13 - 6i - 13 + 6i$

$$= 13 - 13 - 6i + 6i$$

$$= 0$$

41. $(35 - 3i) - (26 + i) = 35 - 3i - 26 - i$

$$= 35 - 26 - 3i - i$$

$$= 9 - (3+1)i$$

$$= 9 - 4i$$

43. $x^2 = -16$

$$x = \pm\sqrt{-16}$$

$$x = \pm\sqrt{16}\sqrt{-1}$$

$$x = \pm 4i$$

The solutions are $4i$ and $-4i$.

45. $3x^2 = -30$

$$x^2 = -10$$

$$x = \pm\sqrt{-10}$$

$$x = \pm\sqrt{-1}\sqrt{10}$$

$$x = \pm i\sqrt{10}$$

The solutions are $i\sqrt{10}$ and $-i\sqrt{10}$.

47. $x^2 - 4x + 5 = 0$

$a = 1,\ b = -4,\ c = 5$

$x = \dfrac{-b \pm \sqrt{b^2 - 4ac}}{4ac}$

$x = \dfrac{-(-4) \pm \sqrt{(-4)^2 - 4(1)(5)}}{2(1)}$

$x = \dfrac{4 \pm \sqrt{16 - 20}}{2}$

$x = \dfrac{4 \pm \sqrt{-4}}{2}$

$x = \dfrac{4 \pm \sqrt{4}\sqrt{-1}}{2}$

$x = \dfrac{4 \pm 2i}{2} = 2 \pm i$

The solutions are $2 + i$ and $2 - i$.

49. $2r^2 + 3r + 5 = 0$

$a = 2,\ b = 3,\ c = 5$

$r = \dfrac{-b \pm \sqrt{b^2 - 4ac}}{2a}$

$r = \dfrac{-3 \pm \sqrt{3^2 - 4(2)(5)}}{2(2)}$

$r = \dfrac{-3 \pm \sqrt{9 - 40}}{4}$

$r = \dfrac{-3 \pm \sqrt{-31}}{4}$

$r = \dfrac{-3 \pm \sqrt{-1}\sqrt{31}}{4}$

$r = \dfrac{-3 \pm i\sqrt{31}}{4}$

The solutions are $\dfrac{-3 + i\sqrt{31}}{4}$ and $\dfrac{-3 - i\sqrt{31}}{4}$.

51. $2p^2 + 4p + 7 = 0$

$a = 2,\ b = 4,\ c = 7$

$p = \dfrac{-b \pm \sqrt{b^2 - 4ac}}{2a}$

$p = \dfrac{-4 \pm \sqrt{4^2 - 4(2)(7)}}{2(2)}$

$p = \dfrac{-4 \pm \sqrt{16 - 56}}{4}$

$p = \dfrac{-4 \pm \sqrt{-40}}{4}$

$p = \dfrac{-4 \pm \sqrt{-1}\sqrt{4}\sqrt{10}}{4}$

$p = \dfrac{-4 \pm 2i\sqrt{10}}{4} = \dfrac{-2 \pm i\sqrt{10}}{2}$

The solutions are $\dfrac{-2 + i\sqrt{10}}{2}$ and $\dfrac{-2 - i\sqrt{10}}{2}$.

53. $-4w^2 + 7w - 6 = 0$

$a = -4,\ b = 7,\ c = -6$

$w = \dfrac{-b \pm \sqrt{b^2 - 4ac}}{2a}$

$w = \dfrac{-7 \pm \sqrt{7^2 - 4(-4)(-6)}}{2(-4)}$

$w = \dfrac{-7 \pm \sqrt{49 - 96}}{-8}$

$w = \dfrac{-7 \pm \sqrt{-47}}{-8}$

$w = \dfrac{-7 \pm \sqrt{-1}\sqrt{47}}{-8}$

$w = \dfrac{-7 \pm i\sqrt{47}}{-8}$

The solutions are $\dfrac{7 - i\sqrt{47}}{8}$ and $\dfrac{7 + i\sqrt{47}}{8}$.

55. The equation will have imaginary solutions when $c < 0$.

57. It will have non-real solutions when $b^2 - 4ac < 0$.

59. Substitute 6 for x.

$$-\left\{\left[3(x-4)^2-5\right]-2x\right\}$$
$$=-\left\{\left[3(6-4)^2-5\right]-2(6)\right\}$$
$$=-\left\{\left[3(4)-5\right]-12\right\}$$
$$=-\left\{\left[12-5\right]-12\right\}$$
$$=-\left\{7-12\right\}$$
$$=-(-5)$$
$$=5$$

60.
$$\frac{1}{2}x+\frac{3}{5}x=\frac{1}{2}(x-2)$$
$$\frac{1}{2}x+\frac{3}{5}x=\frac{1}{2}x-1$$
$$10\left(\frac{1}{2}x+\frac{3}{5}x\right)=10\left(\frac{1}{2}x-1\right)$$
$$5x+6x=5x-10$$
$$11x=5x+10$$
$$6x=-10$$
$$x=-\frac{10}{6}=-\frac{5}{3}$$

61.
$$\frac{w-2}{w-5}=\frac{3}{w-6}+\frac{3}{4}$$
$$4(w-5)(w-6)\left(\frac{w-2}{w-5}\right)=4(w-5)(w-6)\left(\frac{3}{w-6}+\frac{3}{4}\right)$$
$$4(w-6)(w-2)=12(w-5)+3(w-5)(w-6)$$
$$4\left(w^2-8w+12\right)=12w-60+3\left(w^2-11w+30\right)$$
$$4w^2-32w+48=12w-60+3w^2-33w+90$$
$$4w^2-32w+48=3w^2-21w+30$$
$$w^2-11w+18=0$$
$$(w-2)(w-9)=0$$
$$w-2=0 \quad \text{or} \quad w-9=0$$
$$w=2 \quad \text{or} \qquad w=9$$

62. $2\sqrt{r-4}+5=11$
$$2\sqrt{r-4}=6$$
$$\sqrt{r-4}=3$$
$$\left(\sqrt{r-4}\right)^2=3^2$$
$$r-4=9$$
$$r=13$$

Review Exercises

1. $x^2=25$
$$x=\pm\sqrt{25}$$
$$x=\pm5$$
The solutions are 5 and –5.

2. $x^2=121$
$$x=\pm\sqrt{121}$$
$$x=\pm11$$
The solutions are 11 and –11.

3. $x^2+4=9$
$$x^2=5$$
$$x=\pm\sqrt{5}$$
The solutions are $\sqrt{5}$ and $-\sqrt{5}$.

4. $2x^2=12$
$$\frac{1}{2}(2x^2)=\frac{1}{2}(12)$$
$$x^2=6$$
$$x=\pm\sqrt{6}$$
The solutions are $\sqrt{6}$ and $-\sqrt{6}$.

5. $2x^2-3=11$
$$2x^2=14$$
$$x^2=7$$
$$x=\pm\sqrt{7}$$
The solutions are $\sqrt{7}$ and $-\sqrt{7}$.

6. $x^2-2=18$
$$x^2=20$$
$$x=\pm\sqrt{20}$$
$$x=\pm2\sqrt{5}$$
The solutions are $2\sqrt{5}$ and $-2\sqrt{5}$.

7. $4x^2-31=1$
$$4x^2=32$$
$$x^2=8$$
$$x=\pm\sqrt{8}$$
$$x=\pm2\sqrt{2}$$
The solutions are $2\sqrt{2}$ and $-2\sqrt{2}$.

8. $(r-3)^2 = 24$

$\qquad r-3 = \pm\sqrt{24}$

$\qquad r-3 = \pm 2\sqrt{6}$

$\qquad\quad x = 3 \pm 2\sqrt{6}$

The solutions are $3+2\sqrt{6}$ and $3-2\sqrt{6}$.

9. $(4t-9)^2 = 50$

$\qquad 4t-9 = \pm\sqrt{50}$

$\qquad 4t-9 = \pm 5\sqrt{2}$

$\qquad\quad 4t = 9 \pm 5\sqrt{2}$

$\qquad\quad t = \dfrac{9 \pm 5\sqrt{2}}{4}$

The solutions are $\dfrac{9+5\sqrt{2}}{4}$ and $\dfrac{9-5\sqrt{2}}{4}$.

10. $(3x+4)^2 = 30$

$\qquad 3x+4 = \pm\sqrt{30}$

$\qquad 3x = -4 \pm \sqrt{30}$

$\qquad x = \dfrac{-4 \pm \sqrt{30}}{3}$

The solutions are $\dfrac{-4+\sqrt{30}}{3}$ and $\dfrac{-4-\sqrt{30}}{3}$.

11. $\qquad x^2 - 7x + 10 = 0$

$\qquad\quad x^2 - 7x = -10$

$\qquad x^2 - 7x + \dfrac{49}{4} = -10 + \dfrac{49}{4}$

$\qquad\quad \left(x - \dfrac{7}{2}\right)^2 = \dfrac{9}{4}$

$\qquad\quad x - \dfrac{7}{2} = \pm\sqrt{\dfrac{9}{4}}$

$\qquad\quad x - \dfrac{7}{2} = \pm\dfrac{3}{2}$

$\qquad\quad x = \dfrac{7}{2} \pm \dfrac{3}{2}$

$x = \dfrac{7}{2} + \dfrac{3}{2}$ or $x = \dfrac{7}{2} - \dfrac{3}{2}$

$x = 5 \qquad$ or $x = 2$

The solutions are 5 and 2.

12. $\qquad x^2 - 11x + 28 = 0$

$\qquad\quad x^2 - 11x = -28$

$\qquad x^2 - 11x + \dfrac{121}{4} = -28 + \dfrac{121}{4}$

$\qquad\quad \left(x - \dfrac{11}{2}\right)^2 = \dfrac{9}{4}$

$\qquad\quad x - \dfrac{11}{2} = \pm\sqrt{\dfrac{9}{4}}$

$\qquad\quad x - \dfrac{11}{2} = \pm\dfrac{3}{2}$

$\qquad\quad x = \dfrac{11}{2} \pm \dfrac{3}{2}$

$x = \dfrac{11}{2} + \dfrac{3}{2}$ or $x = \dfrac{11}{2} - \dfrac{3}{2}$

$x = 7 \qquad$ or $x = 4$

The solutions are 7 and 4.

13. $\qquad x^2 + 18x + 17 = 0$

$\qquad\quad x^2 + 18x = -17$

$\qquad x^2 + 18x + 81 = -17 + 81$

$\qquad\quad (x+9)^2 = 64$

$\qquad\quad x + 9 = \pm\sqrt{64}$

$\qquad\quad x + 9 = \pm 8$

$\qquad\quad x = -9 \pm 8$

$x = -9 + 8$ or $x = -9 - 8$

$x = -1 \quad$ or $x = -17$

The solutions are −1 and −17.

14. $\qquad x^2 + 19x + 90 = 0$

$\qquad\quad x^2 + 19x = -90$

$\qquad x^2 + 19x + \dfrac{361}{4} = \dfrac{-360}{4} + \dfrac{361}{4}$

$\qquad\quad \left(x + \dfrac{19}{2}\right)^2 = \dfrac{1}{4}$

$\qquad\quad x + \dfrac{19}{2} = \pm\sqrt{\dfrac{1}{4}}$

$\qquad\quad x + \dfrac{19}{2} = \pm\dfrac{1}{2}$

$\qquad\quad x = -\dfrac{19}{2} \pm \dfrac{1}{2}$

$x = -\dfrac{19}{2} + \dfrac{1}{2}$ or $x = -\dfrac{19}{2} - \dfrac{1}{2}$

$x = -9 \qquad$ or $x = -10$

The solutions are –9 and –10.

15.
$$t^2 - 3t - 54 = 0$$
$$t^2 - 3t = 54$$
$$t^2 - 3t + \frac{9}{4} = 54 + \frac{9}{4}$$
$$\left(t - \frac{3}{2}\right)^2 = \frac{225}{4}$$
$$t - \frac{3}{2} = \pm\sqrt{\frac{225}{4}}$$
$$t - \frac{3}{2} = \pm\frac{15}{2}$$
$$t = \frac{3}{2} \pm \frac{15}{2}$$

$$t^2 - 3x - 54 = 0$$
$$t^2 - 3x = 54$$
$$t = \frac{3}{2} + \frac{15}{2} \text{ or } t = \frac{3}{2} - \frac{15}{2}$$
$$t = 9 \qquad \text{or } t = -6$$

The solutions are 9 and –6.

16.
$$x^2 = -5x + 6$$
$$x^2 + 5x = 6$$
$$x^2 + 5x + \frac{25}{4} = 6 + \frac{25}{4}$$
$$\left(x + \frac{5}{2}\right)^2 = \frac{49}{4}$$
$$x + \frac{5}{2} = \pm\sqrt{\frac{49}{4}}$$
$$x + \frac{5}{2} = \pm\frac{7}{2}$$
$$x- = -\frac{5}{2} \pm \frac{7}{2}$$
$$x = -\frac{5}{2} + \frac{7}{2} \text{ or } x = -\frac{5}{2} - \frac{7}{2}$$
$$x = 1 \qquad \text{or } x = -6$$

The solutions are 1 and –6.

17.
$$2x^2 - 8x = 64$$
$$\frac{1}{2}(2x^2 - 8x) = \frac{1}{2}(64)$$
$$x^2 - 4x = 32$$
$$x^2 - 4x + 4 = 32 + 4$$
$$(x - 2)^2 = 36$$
$$x - 2 = \pm\sqrt{36}$$
$$x - 2 = \pm 6$$
$$x = 2 \pm 6$$
$$x = 2 + 6 \text{ or } x = 2 - 6$$
$$x = 8 \qquad \text{or } x = -4$$

The solutions are 8 and –4.

18.
$$30 = 2n^2 - 4n$$
$$2n^2 - 4n = 30$$
$$\frac{1}{2}(2n^2 - 4n) = \frac{1}{2}(30)$$
$$n^2 - 2n = 15$$
$$n^2 - 2n + 1 = 15 + 1$$
$$(n - 1)^2 = 16$$
$$n - 1 = \pm\sqrt{16}$$
$$n - 1 = \pm 4$$
$$n = 1 \pm 4$$
$$n = 1 + 4 \text{ or } n = 1 - 4$$
$$n = 5 \qquad \text{or } n = -3$$

The solutions are 5 and –3.

19.
$$x^2 + 2x - 12 = 0$$
$$x^2 + 2x = 12$$
$$x^2 + 2x + 1 = 12 + 1$$
$$(x + 1)^2 = 13$$
$$x + 1 = \pm\sqrt{13}$$
$$x = -1 \pm \sqrt{13}$$
$$x = -1 + \sqrt{13} \text{ or } x = -1 - \sqrt{13}$$

The solutions are
$$-1 + \sqrt{13} \text{ and } -1 - \sqrt{13}.$$

20.

$$y^2 - 5y - 2 = 0$$
$$y^2 - 5y = 2$$
$$y^2 - 5y + \frac{25}{4} = 2 + \frac{25}{4}$$
$$\left(y - \frac{5}{2}\right)^2 = \frac{33}{4}$$
$$y - \frac{5}{2} = \pm\sqrt{\frac{33}{4}}$$
$$y - \frac{5}{2} = \pm\frac{\sqrt{33}}{2}$$
$$y = \frac{5}{2} \pm \frac{\sqrt{33}}{2}$$
$$y = \frac{5 \pm \sqrt{33}}{2}$$
$$y = \frac{5 + \sqrt{33}}{2} \text{ or } y = \frac{5 - \sqrt{33}}{2}$$

The solutions are $\dfrac{5+\sqrt{33}}{2}$ and $\dfrac{5-\sqrt{33}}{2}$.

21.

$$3p^2 = -2p + 8$$
$$3p^2 + 2p - 8 = 0$$
$$\frac{1}{3}(3p^2 + 2p - 8) = \frac{1}{3}(0)$$
$$p^2 + \frac{2}{3}p - \frac{8}{3} = 0$$
$$p^2 + \frac{2}{3}p = \frac{8}{3}$$
$$p^2 + \frac{2}{3}p + \frac{1}{9} = \frac{8}{3} + \frac{1}{9}$$
$$\left(p + \frac{1}{3}\right)^2 = \frac{25}{9}$$
$$p + \frac{1}{3} = \pm\sqrt{\frac{25}{9}}$$
$$p + \frac{1}{3} = \pm\frac{5}{3}$$
$$p = -\frac{1}{3} \pm \frac{5}{3}$$
$$p = -\frac{1}{3} + \frac{5}{3} \text{ or } p = -\frac{1}{3} - \frac{5}{3}$$
$$p = \frac{4}{3} \qquad \text{or } p = -2$$

The solutions are $\dfrac{4}{3}$ and -2.

22.

$$12x^2 - 11x + 2 = 0$$
$$\frac{1}{12}(12x^2 - 11x + 2) = \frac{1}{12}(0)$$
$$x^2 - \frac{11}{12}x + \frac{2}{12} = 0$$
$$x^2 - \frac{11}{12}x = -\frac{2}{12}$$
$$x^2 - \frac{11}{12}x + \frac{121}{576} = -\frac{2}{12} + \frac{121}{576}$$
$$\left(x - \frac{11}{24}\right)^2 = \frac{25}{576}$$
$$x - \frac{11}{24} = \pm\sqrt{\frac{25}{576}}$$
$$x - \frac{11}{24} = \pm\frac{5}{24}$$
$$x = \frac{11}{24} \pm \frac{5}{24}$$
$$x = \frac{11}{24} + \frac{5}{24} \text{ or } x = \frac{11}{24} - \frac{5}{24}$$
$$x = \frac{2}{3} \qquad \text{or } x = \frac{1}{4}$$

The solutions are $\dfrac{2}{3}$ and $\dfrac{1}{4}$.

23. $b^2 - 4ac = 4^2 - 4(-4)(-9) = 16 - 144 = -128$
Since the discriminant is negative, there is no real number solution.

24. Write in standard form.
$$-3x^2 + 4x - 10 = 0$$
$$b^2 - 4ac = (4)^2 - 4(-3)(-10) = 16 - 120 = -104$$
Since the discriminant is negative, there is no real number solution.

25. $b^2 - 4ac = (-12)^2 - 4(1)(36) = 144 - 144 = 0$
Since the discriminant is zero, there is one real number solution.

26. $b^2 - 4ac = (5)^2 - 4(1)(-8) = 25 + 32 = 57$
Since the discriminant is positive, there are two real number solutions.

27. Write in standard form.
$$4z^2 - 3z - 2 = 0$$
$$b^2 - 4ac = (-3)^2 - 4(4)(-2) = 9 + 32 = 41$$
Since the discriminant is positive, there are two real number solutions.

28. $b^2 - 4ac = (-2)^2 - 4(3)(4) = 4 - 48 = -44$

Since the discriminant is negative, there is no real number solution.

29. $b^2 - 4ac = (-4)^2 - 4(-3)(1) = 16 + 12 = 28$

Since the discriminant is positive, there are two real number solutions.

30. $b^2 - 4ac = (-9)^2 - 4(1)(7) = 81 - 28 = 53$

Since the discriminant is positive, there are two real number solutions.

31. $a = 1, b = -10, c = 16$

$$x = \frac{-b \pm \sqrt{b^2 - 4ac}}{2a}$$

$$= \frac{-(-10) \pm \sqrt{(-10)^2 - 4(1)(16)}}{2(1)}$$

$$= \frac{10 \pm \sqrt{100 - 64}}{2}$$

$$= \frac{10 \pm \sqrt{36}}{2}$$

$$= \frac{10 \pm 6}{2}$$

$$x = \frac{10 + 6}{2} \text{ or } x = \frac{10 - 6}{2}$$

$$x = 8 \qquad \text{or } x = 2$$

The solutions are 8 and 2.

32. Write in standard form.

$x^2 + 11x + 18 = 0$

$a = 1, b = 11, c = 18$

$$x = \frac{-b \pm \sqrt{b^2 - 4ac}}{2a}$$

$$= \frac{-11 \pm \sqrt{11^2 - 4(1)(18)}}{2(1)}$$

$$= \frac{-11 \pm \sqrt{121 - 72}}{2}$$

$$= \frac{-11 \pm \sqrt{49}}{2}$$

$$= \frac{-11 \pm 7}{2}$$

$$x = \frac{-11 + 7}{2} \text{ or } x = \frac{-11 - 7}{2}$$

$$x = -2 \qquad \text{or } x = -9$$

The solutions are -2 and 9.

33. $a = 1, b = -7, c = -44$

$$x = \frac{-b \pm \sqrt{b^2 - 4ac}}{2a}$$

$$= \frac{-(-7) \pm \sqrt{(-7)^2 - 4(1)(-44)}}{2(1)}$$

$$= \frac{7 \pm \sqrt{49 + 176}}{2}$$

$$= \frac{7 \pm \sqrt{225}}{2}$$

$$= \frac{7 \pm 15}{2}$$

$$x = \frac{7 + 15}{2} \text{ or } x = \frac{7 - 15}{2}$$

$$x = 11 \qquad \text{or } x = -4$$

The solutions are 11 and -4.

34. Write in standard form.

$5x^2 - 9x + 4 = 0$

$a = 5, b = -9, c = 4$

$$x = \frac{-b \pm \sqrt{b^2 - 4ac}}{2a}$$

$$= \frac{-(-9) \pm \sqrt{(-9)^2 - 4(5)(4)}}{2(5)}$$

$$= \frac{9 \pm \sqrt{81 - 80}}{10}$$

$$= \frac{9 \pm \sqrt{1}}{10}$$

$$= \frac{9 \pm 1}{10}$$

$$x = \frac{9 + 1}{10} \text{ or } x = \frac{9 - 1}{10}$$

$$x = 1 \qquad \text{or } x = \frac{4}{5}$$

The solutions are 1 and $\frac{4}{5}$.

35. Write in standard form.

$r^2 + 4r - 21 = 0$

$a = 1, b = 4, c = -21$

$r = \dfrac{-b \pm \sqrt{b^2 - 4ac}}{2a}$

$= \dfrac{-4 \pm \sqrt{4^2 - 4(1)(-21)}}{2(1)}$

$= \dfrac{-4 \pm \sqrt{16 + 84}}{2}$

$= \dfrac{-4 \pm \sqrt{100}}{2}$

$= \dfrac{-4 \pm 10}{2}$

$r = \dfrac{-4 + 10}{2}$ or $r = \dfrac{-4 - 10}{2}$

$r = 3$ or $r = -7$

The solutions are 3 and –7.

36. $a = 1, b = -1, c = 1$

$x = \dfrac{-b \pm \sqrt{b^2 - 4ac}}{2a}$

$= \dfrac{-(-1) \pm \sqrt{(-1)^2 - 4(1)(1)}}{2(1)}$

$= \dfrac{1 \pm \sqrt{1 - 4}}{2}$

$= \dfrac{1 \pm \sqrt{-3}}{2}$

Since $\sqrt{-3}$ is not a real number, there is no real number solution.

37. $a = 6, b = 1, c = -15$

$x = \dfrac{-b \pm \sqrt{b^2 - 4ac}}{2a}$

$= \dfrac{-1 \pm \sqrt{1^2 - 4(6)(-15)}}{2(6)}$

$= \dfrac{-1 \pm \sqrt{1 + 360}}{12}$

$= \dfrac{-1 \pm \sqrt{361}}{12}$

$= \dfrac{-1 \pm 19}{12}$

$x = \dfrac{-1 + 19}{12}$ or $x = \dfrac{-1 - 19}{12}$

$x = \dfrac{3}{2}$ or $x = -\dfrac{5}{3}$

The solutions are $\dfrac{3}{2}$ and $-\dfrac{5}{3}$.

38. $a = -2, b = 3, c = 6$

$x = \dfrac{-b \pm \sqrt{b^2 - 4ac}}{2a}$

$= \dfrac{-3 \pm \sqrt{3^2 - 4(-2)(6)}}{2(-2)}$

$= \dfrac{-3 \pm \sqrt{9 + 48}}{-4}$

$= \dfrac{-3 \pm \sqrt{57}}{-4}$

$= \dfrac{3 \pm \sqrt{57}}{4}$

$x = \dfrac{3 + \sqrt{57}}{4}$ or $x = \dfrac{3 - \sqrt{57}}{4}$

The solutions are $\dfrac{3 + \sqrt{57}}{4}$ and $\dfrac{3 - \sqrt{57}}{4}$.

39. $a = -2, b = -4, c = 3$

$x = \dfrac{-b \pm \sqrt{b^2 - 4ac}}{2a}$

$= \dfrac{-(-4) \pm \sqrt{(-4)^2 - 4(-2)(3)}}{2(-2)}$

$= \dfrac{4 \pm \sqrt{16 + 24}}{-4}$

$= \dfrac{4 \pm \sqrt{40}}{-4}$

$= \dfrac{4 \pm 2\sqrt{10}}{4}$

$= \dfrac{2(2 \pm \sqrt{10})}{-4}$

$= \dfrac{-2 \pm \sqrt{10}}{2}$

$x = \dfrac{-2 + \sqrt{10}}{2}$ or $x = \dfrac{-2 - \sqrt{10}}{2}$

The solutions are $\dfrac{-2 + \sqrt{10}}{2}$ and $\dfrac{-2 - \sqrt{10}}{2}$.

40. $a = 1, b = -6, c = 3$

$$y = \frac{-b \pm \sqrt{b^2 - 4ac}}{2a}$$

$$= \frac{-(-6) \pm \sqrt{(-6)^2 - 4(1)(3)}}{2(1)}$$

$$= \frac{6 \pm \sqrt{36 - 12}}{2}$$

$$= \frac{6 \pm \sqrt{24}}{2}$$

$$= \frac{6 \pm 2\sqrt{6}}{2}$$

$$= \frac{2(3 \pm \sqrt{6})}{2}$$

$$= 3 \pm \sqrt{6}$$

$y = 3 + \sqrt{6}$ or $y = 3 - \sqrt{6}$

The solutions are $3 + \sqrt{6}$ and $3 - \sqrt{6}$.

41. $a = 3, b = -4, c = 5$

$$x = \frac{-b \pm \sqrt{b^2 - 4ac}}{2a}$$

$$= \frac{-(-4) \pm \sqrt{(-4)^2 - 4(3)(5)}}{2(3)}$$

$$= \frac{4 \pm \sqrt{16 - 60}}{6}$$

$$= \frac{4 \pm \sqrt{-44}}{6}$$

Since $\sqrt{-44}$ is not a real number, there is no real number solution.

42. $a = 3, b = -6, c = -8$

$$x = \frac{-b \pm \sqrt{b^2 - 4ac}}{2a}$$

$$= \frac{-(-6) \pm \sqrt{(-6)^2 - 4(3)(-8)}}{2(3)}$$

$$= \frac{6 \pm \sqrt{36 + 96}}{6}$$

$$= \frac{6 \pm \sqrt{132}}{6}$$

$$= \frac{6 \pm 2\sqrt{33}}{6}$$

$$= \frac{2(3 \pm \sqrt{33})}{6}$$

$$= \frac{3 \pm \sqrt{33}}{3}$$

$x = \frac{3 + \sqrt{33}}{3}$ or $x = \frac{3 - \sqrt{33}}{3}$

The solutions are $\frac{3 + \sqrt{33}}{3}$ and $\frac{3 - \sqrt{33}}{3}$.

43. $a = 7, b = -4, c = 0$

$$x = \frac{-b \pm \sqrt{b^2 - 4ac}}{2a}$$

$$= \frac{-(-4) \pm \sqrt{(-4)^2 - 4(7)(0)}}{2(7)}$$

$$= \frac{4 \pm \sqrt{16}}{14}$$

$$= \frac{4 \pm 4}{14}$$

$x = \frac{4 + 4}{14}$ or $x = \frac{4 - 4}{14}$

$x = \frac{4}{7}$ or $x = 0$

The solutions are $\frac{4}{7}$ and 0.

44. Write in standard form.

$4z^2 - 10z = 0$

$a = 4, b = -10, c = 0$

$$z = \frac{-b \pm \sqrt{b^2 - 4ac}}{2a}$$

$$= \frac{-(-10) \pm \sqrt{(-10)^2 - 4(4)(0)}}{2(4)}$$

$$= \frac{10 \pm \sqrt{100}}{8}$$

$$= \frac{10 \pm 10}{8}$$

$z = \frac{10 + 10}{8}$ or $z = \frac{10 - 10}{8}$

$z = \frac{5}{2}$ or $z = 0$

The solutions are $\frac{5}{2}$ and 0.

45. $x^2 - 10x + 24 = 0$

$(x - 6)(x - 4) = 0$

$x - 6 = 0$ or $x - 4 = 0$

$\qquad x = 6$ or $x = 4$

46. $x^2 - 16x + 55 = 0$

$(x - 5)(x - 11) = 0$

$x - 5 = 0$ or $x - 11 = 0$

$\qquad x = 5$ or $x = 11$

47. $r^2 - 3r - 70 = 0$

$(r - 10)(r + 7) = 0$

$r - 10 = 0$ or $r + 7 = 0$

$\qquad r = 10$ or $r = -7$

48. $\qquad x^2 + 6x = 27$

$x^2 + 6x - 27 = 0$

$(x - 3)(x + 9) = 0$

$x - 3 = 0$ or $x + 9 = 0$

$\qquad x = 3$ or $x = -9$

49. $x^2 - 4x - 60 = 0$

$(x + 6)(x - 10) = 0$

$x + 6 = 0$ or $x - 10 = 0$

$\qquad x = -6$ or $x = 10$

50. $x^2 - 13x - 22 = 0$

$(x - 11)(x - 2) = 0$

$x - 11 = 0$ or $x - 2 = 0$

$\qquad x = 11$ or $x = 2$

51. $y^2 + 9y - 36 = 0$

$(y + 12)(y - 3) = 0$

$y + 12 = 0$ or $y - 3 = 0$

$\qquad y = -12$ or $y = 3$

52. $\qquad t^2 = 8t$

$t^2 - 8t = 0$

$t(t - 8) = 0$

$t = 0$ or $t - 8 = 0$

$t = 0$ or $t = 8$

53. $x^2 = 64$

$x = \pm\sqrt{64}$

$x = \pm 8$

$x = 8$ or $x = -8$

54. $x^2 = 169$

$x = \pm\sqrt{169}$

$x = \pm 13$

$x = 13$ or $x = -13$

55. $\qquad\qquad 2x^2 = 9x - 10$

$2x^2 - 9x + 10 = 0$

$(2x - 5)(x - 2) = 0$

$2x - 5 = 0$ or $x - 2 = 0$

$\qquad x = \dfrac{5}{2}$ or $x = 2$

56. $\qquad\qquad 6x^2 + 5x = 6$

$6x^2 + 5x - 6 = 0$

$(2x + 3)(3x - 2) = 0$

$2x + 3 = 0$ or $3x - 2 = 0$

$\qquad x = -\dfrac{3}{2}$ or $\qquad x = \dfrac{2}{3}$

57. $a = 4, b = -11, c = 0$

$x = \dfrac{-b \pm \sqrt{b^2 - 4ac}}{2a}$

$\quad = \dfrac{-(-11) \pm \sqrt{(-11)^2 - 4(4)(0)}}{2(4)}$

$\quad = \dfrac{11 \pm \sqrt{121}}{8}$

$\quad = \dfrac{11 \pm 11}{8}$

$x = \dfrac{11 + 11}{8}$ or $x = \dfrac{11 - 11}{8}$

$x = \dfrac{11}{4}$ or $x = 0$

58. $3x^2 + 10x = 0$

$x(3x + 10) = 0$

$x = 0$ or $3x + 10 = 0$

$x = 0$ or $x = -\dfrac{10}{3}$

59. $\qquad -3x^2 - 5x + 8 = 0$

$-1(-3x^2 - 5x + 8) = (-1)(0)$

$3x^2 + 5x - 8 = 0$

$(3x + 8)(x - 1) = 0$

$3x + 8 = 0$ or $x - 1 = 0$

$\qquad x = -\dfrac{8}{3}$ or $x = 1$

60. $3x^2 - 11x + 10 = 0$

$(3x - 5)(x - 2) = 0$

$3x - 5 = 0 \quad$ or $\quad x - 2 = 0$

$x = \dfrac{5}{3} \quad$ or $\qquad x = 2$

61. $a = -2, b = 6, c = 9$

$x = \dfrac{-b \pm \sqrt{b^2 - 4ac}}{2a}$

$= \dfrac{-6 \pm \sqrt{6^2 - 4(-2)(9)}}{2(-2)}$

$= \dfrac{-6 \pm \sqrt{36 + 72}}{-4}$

$= \dfrac{-6 \pm \sqrt{108}}{-4}$

$= \dfrac{-6 \pm 6\sqrt{3}}{-4}$

$= \dfrac{-2(3 \pm 3\sqrt{2})}{-2(2)}$

$= \dfrac{3 \pm 3\sqrt{2}}{2}$

$x = \dfrac{3 + 3\sqrt{3}}{2} \quad$ or $\quad x = \dfrac{3 - 3\sqrt{3}}{2}$

62. Write in standard form.

$x^2 + 3x - 6 = 0$

$a = 1, b = 3, c = -6$

$x = \dfrac{-b \pm \sqrt{b^2 - 4ac}}{2a}$

$= \dfrac{-3 \pm \sqrt{3^2 - 4(1)(-6)}}{2(1)}$

$= \dfrac{-3 \pm \sqrt{9 + 24}}{2}$

$= \dfrac{-3 \pm \sqrt{33}}{2}$

$x = \dfrac{-3 + \sqrt{33}}{2} \quad$ or $\quad x = \dfrac{-3 - \sqrt{33}}{2}$

63. $a = 1, b = -4, c = -5$

$x = -\dfrac{b}{2a} = -\dfrac{-4}{2(1)} = 2$

The axis of symmetry is $x = 2$.

y-coordinate of the vertex:

$y = x^2 - 4x - 5$

$y = (2)^2 - 4(2) - 5$

$\quad = 4 - 8 - 5$

$\quad = -9$

The vertex is $(2, -9)$

Since $a > 0$, the parabola opens upward.

64. $a = 1, b = -12, c = 17$

$x = -\dfrac{b}{2a} = -\dfrac{-12}{2(1)} = 6$

The axis of symmetry is $x = 6$

y-coordinate of the vertex:

$y = x^2 - 12x + 17$

$y = 6^2 - 12(6) + 17$

$\quad = 36 - 72 + 17$

$\quad = -19$

The vertex is $(6, -19)$

Since $a > 0$, the parabola opens upward.

65. $a = 1, b = -3, c = 7$

$x = -\dfrac{b}{2a} = -\dfrac{-3}{2(1)} = \dfrac{3}{2}$

The axis of symmetry is $x = \dfrac{3}{2}$.

y-coordinate of the vertex:

$y = x^2 - 3x + 7$

$y = \left(\dfrac{3}{2}\right)^2 - 3\left(\dfrac{3}{2}\right) + 7$

$\quad = \dfrac{9}{4} - \dfrac{9}{2} + 7$

$\quad = \dfrac{19}{4}$

The vertex is $\left(\dfrac{3}{2}, \dfrac{19}{4}\right)$.

Since $a > 0$, the parabola opens upward.

66. $a = -1, b = -2, c = 13$

$x = -\dfrac{b}{2a} = -\dfrac{-2}{2(-1)} = -1$

The axis of symmetry is $x = -1$.

y-coordinate of the vertex:

$y = -x^2 - 2x + 13$

$y = -(-1)^2 - 2(-1) + 13$

$\quad = -1 + 2 + 13$

$\quad = 14$

The vertex is $(-1, 14)$.

Since $a < 0$, the parabola opens downward.

67. $a = 3, b = 7, c = 3$

$$x = -\frac{b}{2a} = -\frac{7}{2(3)} = -\frac{7}{6}$$

The axis of symmetry is $x = -\frac{7}{6}$.

y-coordinate of the vertex:

$$y = 3x^2 + 7x + 3$$

$$y = 3\left(-\frac{7}{6}\right)^2 + 7\left(-\frac{7}{6}\right) + 3$$

$$= \frac{49}{12} - \frac{49}{6} + 3$$

$$= -\frac{13}{12}$$

The vertex is $\left(-\frac{7}{6}, -\frac{13}{12}\right)$.

Since $a > 0$, the parabola opens upward.

68. $a = -1, b = -5, c = 0$

$$x = -\frac{b}{2a} = -\frac{-5}{2(-1)} = \frac{-5}{2}$$

The axis of symmetry is $x = -\frac{5}{2}$.

y-coordinate of the vertex:

$$y = -x^2 - 5x$$

$$y = -\left(-\frac{5}{2}\right)^2 - 5\left(-\frac{5}{2}\right)$$

$$= -\frac{25}{4} + \frac{25}{2}$$

$$= \frac{25}{4}$$

The vertex is $\left(-\frac{5}{2}, \frac{25}{4}\right)$.

Since $a < 0$, the parabola opens downward.

69. $a = -1, b = 0, c = -10$

$$x = -\frac{b}{2a} = -\frac{0}{2(-1)} = 0$$

The axis of symmetry is $x = 0$.

y-coordinate of the vertex:

$$y = -x^2 - 10$$

$$y = -0^2 - 8 = -10$$

The vertex is $(0, -10)$.

Since $a < 0$, the parabola opens downward.

70. $a = -2, b = -1, c = 15$

$$x = -\frac{b}{2a} = -\frac{-1}{2(-2)} = -\frac{1}{4}$$

The axis of symmetry is $x = -\frac{1}{4}$.

y-coordinate of the vertex:

$$y = -2x^2 - x + 15$$

$$y = -2\left(-\frac{1}{4}\right)^2 - \left(-\frac{1}{4}\right) + 15$$

$$= -\frac{1}{8} + \frac{1}{4} + 15$$

$$= \frac{121}{8}$$

The vertex is $\left(-\frac{1}{4}, \frac{121}{8}\right)$.

Since $a < 0$, the parabola opens downward.

71. $a = -4, b = 8, c = 9$

$$x = -\frac{b}{2a} = -\frac{8}{2(-4)} = 1$$

The axis of symmetry is $x = 1$.

y-coordinate of the vertex:

$$y = -4x^2 + 8x + 9$$

$$y = -4(1)^2 + 8(1) + 9$$

$$= -4 + 8 + 9$$

$$= 13$$

The vertex is $(1, 13)$.

Since $a < 0$, the parabola opens downward.

72. $a = 3, b = 5, c = -6$

$$x = -\frac{b}{2a} = -\frac{5}{2(3)} = -\frac{5}{6}$$

The axis of symmetry is $x = -\frac{5}{6}$.

y-coordinate of the vertex:

$$y = 3x^2 + 5x - 6$$

$$y = 3\left(-\frac{5}{6}\right)^2 + 5\left(-\frac{5}{6}\right) - 6$$

$$= \frac{25}{12} - \frac{25}{6} - 6$$

$$= -\frac{97}{12}$$

The vertex is $\left(-\frac{5}{6}, -\frac{97}{12}\right)$.

Since $a > 0$, the parabola opens upward.

73. $a = 1, b = -2, c = 0$

Since $a > 0$, the parabola opens upward.

The axis of symmetry is

$$y = -\frac{b}{2a} = -\frac{-2}{2(1)} = 1$$

y-coordinate of the vertex:

$y = x^2 - 2x$

$y = (1)^2 - 2(1) = -1$

The vertex is $(1, -1)$.

$$y = x^2 - 2x$$

Let $x = 2$ $y = 2^2 - 2(2) = 0$

Let $x = 0$ $y = 0^2 - 2(0) = 0$

x	y
2	0
0	0

$0 = x^2 - 2x$

$0 = x(x - 2)$

$x = 0$ or $x = 2$

74. $a = -1$, $b = -6$, $c = 0$

Since $a < 0$, the parabola opens downward.
The axis of symmetry is

$x = -\dfrac{b}{2a} = -\dfrac{-6}{2(-1)} = -3$

y-coordinate of the vertex:

$y = -x^2 - 6x$

$y = -(-3)^2 - 6(-3) = -9 + 18 = 9$

The vertex is $(-3, 9)$.

$$y = -x^2 - 6x$$

Let $x = 0$ $y = -0^2 - 6(0) = 0$

Let $x = -6$ $y = -(-6)^2 - 6(-6) = -36 + 36 = 0$

x	y
0	0
-6	0

$0 = -x^2 - 6x$

$0 = -x(x + 6)$

$x = 0$ or $x = -6$

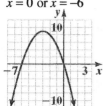

75. $a = -1$, $b = 0$, $c = 9$

Since $a < 0$, the parabola opens downward.
The axis of symmetry is

$x = -\dfrac{b}{2a} = -\dfrac{0}{2(-1)} = 0$

y-coordinate of the vertex:

$y = -x^2 + 9$

$y = -(0)^2 + 9$

$\quad = 9$

The vertex is $(0, 9)$

$$y = -x^2 + 9$$

Let $x = -3$ $y = -(-3)^2 + 9 = 0$

Let $x = 3$ $y = -(3)^2 + 9 = 0$

x	y
-3	0
3	0

$0 = -x^2 + 9$

$0 = -1(x^2 - 9)$

$0 = -1(x + 3)(x - 3)$

$x = -3$ or $x = 3$

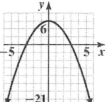

76. $a = -3$, $b = 0$, $c = 6$

Since $a < 0$, the parabola opens downward.
The axis of symmetry is

$x = -\dfrac{b}{2a} = -\dfrac{0}{2(-3)} = 0$

y-coordinate of the vertex:

$y = -3x^2 + 6$

$y = -3(0)^2 + 6 = 6$

The vertex is $(0, 6)$.

$$y = -3x^2 + 6$$

Let $x = -1$ $y = -3(-1)^2 + 6 = 3$

Let $x = 1$ $y = -3(1)^2 + 6 = 3$

x	y
-1	3
1	3

$$0 = -3x^2 + 6$$
$$3x^2 = 6$$
$$x^2 = 2$$
$$x = \pm\sqrt{2}$$

77. $a = 1, b = -1, c = 1$

Since $a > 0$, the parabola opens upward.
The axis of symmetry is

$$x = -\frac{b}{2a} = -\frac{-1}{2(1)} = \frac{1}{2}$$

y-coordinate of the vertex:

$$y = x^2 - x + 1$$

$$y = \left(\frac{1}{2}\right)^2 - \frac{1}{2} + 1 = \frac{3}{4}$$

The vertex is $\left(\frac{1}{2}, \frac{3}{4}\right)$.

$$y = x^2 - x + 1$$

Let $x = 0$ $y = 0^2 - 0 + 1 = 1$
Let $x = 2$ $y = 2^2 - (2) + 1 = 3$

x	y
0	1
2	3

$$0 = x^2 - x + 1$$

$$x = \frac{-(-1) \pm \sqrt{(-1)^2 - 4(1)(1)}}{2(1)}$$

$$= \frac{1 \pm \sqrt{-3}}{2}$$

No real number solution

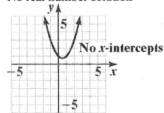

78. $a = 1, b = 5, c = 4$

Since $a > 0$, the parabola opens upward.
The axis of symmetry is

$$x = -\frac{b}{2a} = -\frac{5}{2(1)} = -\frac{5}{2}$$

y-coordinate of the vertex:

$$y = x^2 + 5x + 4$$

$$y = \left(-\frac{5}{2}\right)^2 + 5\left(-\frac{5}{2}\right) + 4$$

$$= \frac{25}{4} - \frac{25}{2} + 4$$

$$= -\frac{9}{4}$$

The vertex is $\left(-\frac{5}{2}, -\frac{9}{4}\right)$.

$$y = x^2 + 5x + 4$$

Let $x = -2$ $y = (-2)^2 + 5(-2) + 4 = -2$
Let $x = -1$ $y = (-1)^2 + 5(-1) + 4 = 0$
Let $x = 0$ $y = (0)^2 + 5(0) + 4 = 4$

x	y
−2	−2
−1	0
0	4

$$0 = x^2 + 5x + 4$$
$$0 = (x + 1)(x + 4)$$
$$x + 1 = 0 \text{ or } x + 4 = 0$$
$$x = -1 \quad \text{ or } x = -4$$

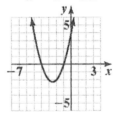

79. $a = -1, b = 2, c = -3$

Since $a < 0$, the parabola opens downward.

The axis of symmetry is $x = -\dfrac{b}{2a} = -\dfrac{2}{2(-1)} = 1$

y-coordinate of the vertex:

$$y = -x^2 + 2x - 3$$
$$y = -(1)^2 + 2(1) - 3$$
$$= -1 + 2 - 3$$
$$= -2$$

The vertex is $(1, -2)$.

$$y = -x^2 + 2x - 3$$

Let $x = 0$ $y = -0^2 + 0 - 3 = -3$
Let $x = 2$ $y = -(2)^2 + 2(2) - 3 = -3$

x	y
0	−3
2	−3

$$0 = -x^2 + 2x - 3$$

$$x = \frac{-2 \pm \sqrt{1^2 - 4(-1)(-3)}}{2(-1)}$$

$$= \frac{-2 \pm \sqrt{-11}}{-2}$$

No real number solution

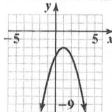

No *x*-intercepts

80. $a = -1$, $b = 5$, $c = -6$

Since $a < 0$, the parabola opens downward.
The axis of symmetry is

$$x = -\frac{b}{2a} = -\frac{5}{2(-1)} = \frac{5}{2}$$

y-coordinate of the vertex:

$$y = -x^2 + 5x - 6$$

$$y = -\left(\frac{5}{2}\right)^2 + 5\left(\frac{5}{2}\right) - 6$$

$$= -\frac{25}{4} + \frac{25}{2} - 6$$

$$= \frac{1}{4}$$

The vertex is $\left(\frac{5}{2}, \frac{1}{4}\right)$

$$y = -x^2 + 5x - 6$$

Let $x = 0$ $\quad y = -0^2 + 5(0) - 6 = -6$

Let $x = 3$ $\quad y = -(3)^2 + 5(3) - 6 = 0$

x	y
0	−6
3	0

$$0 = -x^2 + 5x - 6$$

$$x^2 - 5x + 6 = 0$$

$$(x - 2)(x - 3) = 0$$

$x = 2$ or $x = 3$

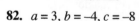

81. $a = 1$, $b = 4$, $c = 3$

Since $a > 0$, the parabola opens upward.

The axis of symmetry is $x = -\frac{b}{2a} = -\frac{4}{2(1)} = -2$

y-coordinate of the vertex:

$$y = x^2 + 4x + 3$$

$$y = (-2)^2 + 4(-2) + 3$$

$$= 4 - 8 + 3$$

$$= -1$$

The vertex is $(-2, -1)$.

$$y = x^2 + 4x + 3$$

Let $x = -1$ $\quad y = (-1)^2 + 4(-1) + 3 = 0$

Let $x = 0$ $\quad y = (0)^2 + 4(0) + 3 = 3$

x	y
−1	0
0	3

$$0 = x^2 + 4x + 3$$

$$0 = (x + 1)(x + 3)$$

$x + 1 = 0$ or $x + 3 = 0$

$x = -1$ or $\quad x = -3$

82. $a = 3$, $b = -4$, $c = -8$

Since $a > 0$, the parabola opens upward.
The axis of symmetry is

$$x = -\frac{b}{2a} = -\frac{-4}{2(3)} = \frac{2}{3}$$

y-coordinate of the vertex:

$$y = 3x^2 - 4x - 8$$

$$y = 3\left(\frac{2}{3}\right)^2 - 4\left(\frac{2}{3}\right) - 8$$

$$= \frac{4}{3} - \frac{8}{3} - 8$$

$$= -\frac{28}{3}$$

The vertex is $\left(\frac{2}{3}, -\frac{28}{3}\right)$.

$$y = 3x^2 - 4x - 8$$

Let $x = 0$ $y = 3(0)^2 - 4(0) - 8 = -8$

Let $x = 2$ $y = 3(2)^2 - 4(2) - 8 = -4$

x	y
0	-8
2	-4

$$0 = 3x^2 - 4x - 8$$

$$x = \frac{-(-4) \pm \sqrt{(-4)^2 - 4(3)(-8)}}{2(3)}$$

$$= \frac{4 \pm \sqrt{112}}{6}$$

$$= \frac{2(2 \pm 2\sqrt{7})}{2(3)}$$

$$= \frac{2 \pm 2\sqrt{7}}{3}$$

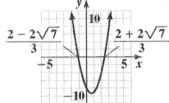

83. $a = -2, b = 7, c = -3$

Since $a < 0$, the parabola opens downward.

The axis of symmetry is

$$x = -\frac{b}{2a} = -\frac{7}{2(-2)} = \frac{7}{4}$$

y-coordinate of the vertex:

$$y = -2x^2 + 7x - 3$$

$$y = -2\left(\frac{7}{4}\right)^2 + 7\left(\frac{7}{4}\right) - 3 = -\frac{49}{8} + \frac{49}{4} - 3 = \frac{25}{8}$$

The vertex is $\left(\frac{7}{4}, \frac{25}{8}\right)$.

$$y = -2x^2 + 7x - 3$$

Let $x = 0$ $y = -2(0)^2 + 7(0) - 3 = -3$

Let $x = 3$ $y = -2(3)^2 + 7(3) - 3 = 0$

x	y
0	-3
3	0

$$0 = -2x^2 + 7x - 3$$

$$0 = -(2x - 1)(x - 3)$$

$$x = \frac{1}{2} \text{ or } x = 3$$

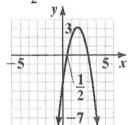

84. $a = 1, b = -5, c = 4$

Since $a > 0$, the parabola opens upward.

The axis of symmetry is $x = -\frac{b}{2a} = -\frac{-5}{2(1)} = \frac{5}{2}$

y-coordinate of the vertex:

$$y = x^2 - 5x + 4$$

$$y = \left(\frac{5}{2}\right)^2 - 5\left(\frac{5}{2}\right) + 4 = \frac{25}{4} - \frac{25}{2} + 4 = -\frac{9}{4}$$

The vertex is $\left(\frac{5}{2}, -\frac{9}{4}\right)$.

$$y = x^2 - 5x + 4$$

Let $x = 4$ $y = 4^2 - 5(4) + 4 = 0$

Let $x = 1$ $y = 1^2 - 5(1) + 4 = 0$

x	y
4	0
1	0

$$0 = x^2 - 5x + 4$$

$$0 = (x - 1)(x - 4)$$

$$x = 1 \text{ or } x = 4$$

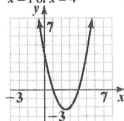

85. Let x = the smaller integer,
then $x + 2$ = the larger integer.
$$x(x+2) = 35$$
$$x^2 + 2x = 35$$
$$x^2 + 2x + 1 = 35 + 1$$
$$(x+1)^2 = 36$$
$$x + 1 = \pm\sqrt{36}$$
$$x + 1 = \pm 6$$
$$x = -1 \pm 6$$
$$x = -1 + 6 \text{ or } x = -1 - 6$$
$$x = 5 \qquad \text{or } x = -7$$
Since the numbers are positive,
$x = 5$ and $x + 2 = 5 + 2 = 7$.

86. Let x = the smaller integer,
then $x + 4$ = the larger integer.
$$x(x+4) = 96$$
$$x^2 + 4x = 96$$
$$x^2 + 4x + 4 = 96 + 4$$
$$(x+2)^2 = 100$$
$$x + 2 = \pm\sqrt{100}$$
$$x + 2 = \pm 10$$
$$x = -2 \pm 10$$
$$x = -2 + 10 \text{ or } x = -2 - 10$$
$$x = 8 \qquad \text{or } x = -12$$
Since the numbers are positive,
$x = 8$ and $x + 4 = 8 + 4 = 12$.

87. Let w = width of table,
then $2w + 6$ = length of table.
$$\text{Area=length} \cdot \text{width}$$
$$920 = w(2w+6)$$
$$2w^2 + 6w = 920$$
$$\frac{1}{2}(2w^2 + 6w) = \frac{1}{2}(920)$$
$$w^2 + 3w = 460$$
$$w^2 + 3w + \frac{9}{4} = 460 + \frac{9}{4}$$
$$\left(w + \frac{3}{2}\right)^2 = \frac{1849}{4}$$
$$w + \frac{3}{2} = \pm\sqrt{\frac{1849}{4}}$$
$$w + \frac{3}{2} = \pm\frac{43}{2}$$
$$w = -\frac{3}{2} \pm \frac{43}{2}$$

$$w = -\frac{3}{2} + \frac{43}{2} \text{ or } w = -\frac{3}{2} - \frac{43}{2}$$
$$w = 20 \qquad \text{or } w = -23$$
Since w is positive, the width is 20 inches and
the length is $2(20) + 6 = 46$ inches.

88. Let w = width of the desktop,
then $w + 16$ = length of the desktop.
$$\text{Area} = \text{length} \cdot \text{width}$$
$$960 = w(w+16)$$
$$960 = w^2 + 16w$$
$$960 + 64 = w^2 + 16w + 64$$
$$1024 = (w+8)^2$$
$$\pm\sqrt{1024} = w + 8$$
$$\pm 32 = w + 8$$
$$-8 \pm 32 = w$$
$$-8 + 32 = w \text{ or } -8 - 32 = w$$
$$24 = w \text{ or } \qquad -40 = w$$
Since w is positive, the width is 24 inches and
the length is $24 + 16 = 40$ inches.

89. $\sqrt{-9} = \sqrt{9}\sqrt{-1} = 3i$

90. $\sqrt{-26} = \sqrt{-1}\sqrt{26} = i\sqrt{26}$

91. $8 - \sqrt{-25} = 8 - \sqrt{25}\sqrt{-1} = 8 - 5i$

92. $6 - \sqrt{-60} = 6 - \sqrt{4}\sqrt{-1}\sqrt{15} = 6 - 2i\sqrt{15}$

93. $(4 - 6i) + (7 - 3i) = 4 + 7 - 6i - 3i$
$$= 11 - (6+3)i$$
$$= 11 - 9i$$

94. $(9 + 5i) - (6 - 3i) = 9 + 5i - 6 + 3i$
$$= 9 - 6 + 5i + 3i$$
$$= 3 + (5+3)i$$
$$= 3 + 8i$$

95. $3x^2 = -48$
$$x^2 = -16$$
$$x = \pm\sqrt{-16}$$
$$x = \pm 4i$$
The solutions are $4i$ and $-4i$.

96. $5a^2 = -30$

$a^2 = -6$

$a = \pm\sqrt{-6}$

$a = \pm i\sqrt{6}$

The solutions are $i\sqrt{6}$ and $-i\sqrt{6}$.

97. $2r^2 - 5r + 6 = 0$

$a = 2,\ b = -5,\ c = 6$

$r = \dfrac{-b \pm \sqrt{b^2 - 4ac}}{2a}$

$= \dfrac{-(-5) \pm \sqrt{(-5)^2 - 4(2)(6)}}{2(2)}$

$= \dfrac{5 \pm \sqrt{25 - 48}}{4}$

$= \dfrac{5 \pm \sqrt{-23}}{4}$

$= \dfrac{5 \pm i\sqrt{23}}{4}$

The solutions are $\dfrac{5 + i\sqrt{23}}{4}$ and $\dfrac{5 - i\sqrt{23}}{4}$.

98. $4w^2 - 8w + 9 = 0$

$a = 4,\ b = -8,\ c = 9$

$w = \dfrac{-b \pm \sqrt{b^2 - 4ac}}{2a}$

$= \dfrac{-(-8) \pm \sqrt{(-8)^2 - 4(4)(9)}}{2(4)}$

$= \dfrac{8 \pm \sqrt{64 - 144}}{8}$

$= \dfrac{8 \pm \sqrt{-80}}{8}$

$= \dfrac{8 \pm 4i\sqrt{5}}{8}$

$= \dfrac{4\left(2 \pm i\sqrt{5}\right)}{4(2)}$

$= \dfrac{2 \pm i\sqrt{5}}{2}$

The solutions are $\dfrac{2 + i\sqrt{5}}{2}$ and $\dfrac{2 - i\sqrt{5}}{2}$.

Practice Test

1. $x^2 - 2 = 30$

$x^2 = 32$

$x = \pm\sqrt{32}$

$x = \pm 4\sqrt{2}$

The solutions are $4\sqrt{2}$ and $-4\sqrt{2}$.

2. $(2p - 3)^2 = 13$

$2p - 3 = \pm\sqrt{13}$

$2p = 3 \pm \sqrt{13}$

$p = \dfrac{3 \pm \sqrt{13}}{2}$

The solutions are $\dfrac{3 + \sqrt{13}}{2}$ and $\dfrac{3 - \sqrt{13}}{2}$.

3. $x^2 - 5x = 50$

$x^2 - 5x + \dfrac{25}{4} = 50 + \dfrac{25}{4}$

$\left(x - \dfrac{5}{2}\right)^2 = \dfrac{225}{4}$

$x - \dfrac{5}{2} = \pm\sqrt{\dfrac{225}{4}}$

$x - \dfrac{5}{2} = \pm\dfrac{15}{2}$

$x = \dfrac{5}{2} \pm \dfrac{15}{2}$

$x = \dfrac{5}{2} + \dfrac{15}{2}$ or $x = \dfrac{5}{2} - \dfrac{15}{2}$

$x = 10$ or $x = -5$

The solutions are 10 and –5.

4. $r^2 + 8r = 33$

$r^2 + 8r + 16 = 33 + 16$

$(r + 4)^2 = 49$

$r + 4 = \pm\sqrt{49}$

$r + 4 = \pm 7$

$r = -4 \pm 7$

$r = -4 + 7$ or $r = -4 - 7$

$r = 3$ or $r = -11$

The solutions are 3 and –11.

5. Write in standard form.

$k^2 - 13k + 42 = 0$

$a = 1,\ b = -13,\ c = 42$

$$k = \frac{-b \pm \sqrt{b^2 - 4ac}}{2a}$$

$$= \frac{-(-13) \pm \sqrt{(-13)^2 - 4(1)(42)}}{2(1)}$$

$$= \frac{13 \pm \sqrt{169 - 168}}{2}$$

$$= \frac{13 \pm \sqrt{1}}{2}$$

$$= \frac{13 \pm 1}{2}$$

$$k = \frac{13 + 1}{2} \text{ or } k = \frac{13 - 1}{2}$$

$$k = 7 \qquad \text{or } k = 6$$

The solutions are 7 and 6.

6. $\qquad 2x^2 + 5 = -8x$

$$2x^2 + 8x + 5 = 0$$
$$a = 2,\, b = 8,\, c = 5$$

$$x = \frac{-b \pm \sqrt{b^2 - 4ac}}{2a}$$

$$= \frac{-8 \pm \sqrt{8^2 - 4(2)(5)}}{2(2)}$$

$$= \frac{-8 \pm \sqrt{64 - 40}}{4}$$

$$= \frac{-8 \pm \sqrt{24}}{4}$$

$$= \frac{-8 \pm 2\sqrt{6}}{4}$$

$$= \frac{-4 \pm \sqrt{6}}{2}$$

$$x = \frac{-4 + \sqrt{6}}{2} \text{ or } x = \frac{-4 - \sqrt{6}}{2}$$

The solutions are $\dfrac{-4 + \sqrt{6}}{2}$ and $\dfrac{-4 - \sqrt{6}}{2}$.

7. $16x^2 = 25$

$$x^2 = \frac{25}{16}$$

$$x = \pm\sqrt{\frac{25}{16}}$$

$$x = \pm\frac{5}{4}$$

The solutions are $\dfrac{5}{4}$ and $-\dfrac{5}{4}$.

8. $x = \dfrac{-b \pm \sqrt{b^2 - 4ac}}{2a}$

9. Answers will vary. One example is $x^2 + 6x + 9$.

10. $b^2 - 4ac = (-4)^2 - 4(-2)(7) = 16 + 56 = 72$
Since the discriminant is positive, the equation has two distinct real solutions.

11. $b^2 - 4ac = (10)^2 - 4(1)(25) = 100 - 100 = 0$
Since the discriminant is zero, the equation has one real solution.

12. $a = -1,\, b = -8,\, c = 11$
Axis of symmetry: $x = -\dfrac{b}{2a} = -\dfrac{-8}{2(-1)} = -4$
The axis of symmetry is $x = -4$.

13. $a = 4,\, b = -16,\, c = 9$
Axis of symmetry: $x = -\dfrac{b}{2a} = -\dfrac{-16}{2(4)} = 2$
The axis of symmetry is $x = 2$.

14. $a = -1,\, b = -10,\, c = 3$
Since $a < 0$, the graph opens downward.

15. $a = 5,\, b = -2,\, c = 9$
Since $a > 0$, the graph opens upward.

16. The vertex of the graph of a parabola is the lowest point on a parabola that opens upward or the highest point on a parabola that opens downward.

17. $a = -1,\, b = -4,\, c = -12$
Axis of symmetry: $x = -\dfrac{b}{2a} = -\dfrac{-4}{2(-1)} = -2$
The axis of symmetry is $x = -2$.
y-coordinate of vertex:
$$y = -x^2 - 4x - 12$$
$$y = -(-2)^2 - 4(-2) - 12$$
$$= -4 + 8 - 12$$
$$= -8$$
The vertex is $(-2, -8)$.

18. $a = 3,\, b = -8,\, c = 9$
Axis of symmetry: $x = -\dfrac{b}{2a} = -\dfrac{-8}{2(3)} = \dfrac{4}{3}$
The axis of symmetry is $x = \dfrac{4}{3}$.
y-coordinate of vertex:

$y = 3x^2 - 8x + 9$

$y = 3\left(\dfrac{4}{3}\right)^2 - 8\left(\dfrac{4}{3}\right) + 9$

$= \dfrac{16}{3} - \dfrac{32}{3} + 9$

$= \dfrac{11}{3}$

The vertex is $\left(\dfrac{4}{3}, \dfrac{11}{3}\right)$.

19. $a = 1,\, b = 2,\, c = -8$

Since $a > 0$, the parabola opens upward.

Axis of symmetry: $x = -\dfrac{b}{2a} = -\dfrac{2}{2(1)} = -1$

y-coordinate of vertex:

$y = x^2 + 2x - 8$

$y = (-1)^2 + 2(-1) - 8 = 1 - 2 - 8 = -9$

The vertex is $(-1, -9)$

$$y = x^2 + 2x - 8$$

Let $x = 0$ $y = 0^2 + 2(0) - 8 = -8$

Let $x = 1$ $y = 1^2 + 2(1) - 8 = -5$

Let $x = 2$ $y = 2^2 + 2(2) - 8 = 0$

Let $x = 3$ $y = 3^2 + 2(3) - 8 = 7$

x	y
0	-8
1	-5
2	0
3	7

$0 = x^2 + 2x - 8$

$0 = (x + 4)(x - 2)$

$x = -4$ or $x = 2$

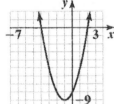

20. $a = 2,\, b = -6,\, c = 0$

Since $a > 0$, the parabola opens upward.

Axis of symmetry: $x = -\dfrac{b}{2a} = -\dfrac{-6}{2(2)} = \dfrac{3}{2}$

y-coordinate of vertex:

$y = 2x^2 - 6x$

$y = 2\left(\dfrac{3}{2}\right)^2 - 6\left(\dfrac{3}{2}\right) = \dfrac{9}{2} - \dfrac{18}{2} = -\dfrac{9}{2}$

The vertex is $\left(\dfrac{3}{2}, -\dfrac{9}{2}\right)$.

$$y = 2x^2 - 6x$$

Let $x = 1$ $y = 2(1)^2 - 6(1) = -4$

Let $x = 2$ $y = 2(2)^2 - 6(2) = -4$

x	y
1	-4
2	-4

$0 = 2x^2 - 6x$

$0 = 2x(x - 3)$

$x = 0$ or $x = 3$

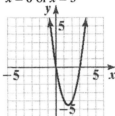

21. $a = -1,\, b = 6,\, c = -9$

Since $a < 0$, the parabola opens downward.

Axis of symmetry: $x = -\dfrac{b}{2a} = -\dfrac{6}{2(-1)} = 3$

y-coordinate of vertex:

$y = -x^2 + 6x - 9$

$y = -3^2 + 6(3) - 9 = -9 + 18 - 9 = 0$

The vertex is $(3, 0)$.

$$y = -x^2 + 6x - 9$$

Let $x = 0$ $y = -0^2 + 6(0) - 9 = -9$

Let $x = 1$ $y = -1^2 + 6(1) - 9 = -4$

Let $x = 2$ $y = -2^2 + 6(2) - 9 = -1$

x	y
0	-9
1	-4
2	-1

$$0 = -x^2 + 6x - 9$$
$$0 = -(x - 3)^2$$
$$x = 3$$

22. Let w = width of the mural,
then $3w + 2$ = length of the mural.
$$\text{Area} = \text{length} \cdot \text{width}$$
$$33 = (3w + 2)w$$
$$3w^2 + 2w = 33$$
$$3w^2 + 2w - 33 = 0$$
$$(3w + 11)(w - 3) = 0$$
$$3w + 11 = 0 \quad \text{or} \quad w - 3 = 0$$
$$w = -\frac{11}{3} \quad \text{or} \quad w = 3$$
Since w is positive, the width is 3 feet and the length is $3(3) + 2 = 11$ feet.

23. Let x = the larger integer,
then $x - 2$ = the smaller integer.
$$x(x - 2) = 35$$
$$x^2 - 2x = 35$$
$$x^2 - 2x + 1 = 35 + 1$$
$$(x - 1)^2 = 36$$
$$x - 1 = \pm\sqrt{36}$$
$$x - 1 = \pm 6$$
$$x = 1 \pm 6$$
$$x = 1 + 6 \quad \text{or} \quad x = 1 - 6$$
$$x = 7 \quad \text{or} \quad x = -5$$
Since the integer is positive, it is 7.

24. Let x = Shawn's age,
then $x - 6$ = Aaron's age.
$$x(x - 6) = 55$$
$$x^2 - 6x = 55$$
$$x^2 - 6x + 9 = 55 + 9$$
$$(x - 3)^2 = 64$$
$$x - 3 = \pm\sqrt{64}$$
$$x - 3 = \pm 8$$
$$x = 3 \pm 8$$

$$x = 3 + 8 \quad \text{or} \quad x = 3 - 8$$
$$x = 11 \quad \text{or} \quad x = -5$$
Since the age must be positive, Shawn is 11 years old.

25. $a = 3, b = -2, c = 6$
$$p = \frac{-b \pm \sqrt{b^2 - 4ac}}{2a}$$
$$= \frac{-(-2) \pm \sqrt{(-2)^2 - 4(3)(6)}}{2(3)}$$
$$= \frac{2 \pm \sqrt{4 - 72}}{6}$$
$$= \frac{2 \pm \sqrt{-68}}{6}$$
$$= \frac{2 \pm 2i\sqrt{17}}{6}$$
$$= \frac{2(1 + i\sqrt{17})}{2(3)}$$
$$= \frac{1 + i\sqrt{17}}{3}$$
The solutions are $\dfrac{1 + i\sqrt{17}}{3}$ and $\dfrac{1 - i\sqrt{17}}{3}$.

Cumulative Review Test

1. $-5x^2y + 3y^2 + xy$
$$= -5(4)^2(-3) + 3(-3)^2 + 4(-3)$$
$$= 240 + 27 - 12$$
$$= 255$$

2. $\dfrac{1}{2}z - \dfrac{2}{7}z = \dfrac{1}{5}(3z - 1)$
$$70\left[\frac{1}{2}z - \frac{2}{7}z\right] = 70\left[\frac{1}{5}(3z - 1)\right]$$
$$35z - 20z = 14(3z - 1)$$
$$15z = 42z - 14$$
$$-27z = -14$$
$$z = \frac{14}{27}$$

3. $\dfrac{x}{8} = \dfrac{2}{3}$

$3x = (8)(2)$

$3x = 16$

$x = \dfrac{16}{3}$ or $5\dfrac{1}{3}$

The length of side x is $5\dfrac{1}{3}$ inches.

4. $2(x-3) \le 6x - 5$

$2x - 6 \le 6x - 5$

$2x - 1 \le 6x$

$-1 \le 4x$

$-\dfrac{1}{4} \le x$

$x \ge -\dfrac{1}{4}$

$\xleftarrow{\quad\bullet\qquad\qquad}\rightarrow$
$-\frac{1}{4}$

5. $\qquad A = \dfrac{m+n+P}{6}$

$\qquad 6A = m + n + P$

$6A - m - n = P$

$\qquad P = 6A - m - n$

6. $(2a^4 b^5)^3 (3a^2 b^5)^2$

$= 2^3 a^{4(3)} b^{5(3)} \cdot 3^2 a^{2(2)} b^{5(2)}$

$= 8a^{12} b^{15} \cdot 9a^4 b^{10}$

$= 72 a^{12+4} b^{15+10}$

$= 72 a^{16} b^{25}$

7. $\quad x+2 \overline{)\,x^2 + 6x - 1\,}$ with quotient $x + 4$

$\quad\underline{x^2 + 2x}$

$\qquad\quad 4x - 1$

$\qquad\quad \underline{4x + 8}$

$\qquad\qquad -9$

$\dfrac{x^2 + 6x + 5}{x+2} = x + 4 - \dfrac{9}{x+2}$

8. $2x^2 - 3xy - 4xy + 6y^2$

$= x(2x - 3y) - 2y(2x - 3y)$

$= (x - 2y)(2x - 3y)$

9. $6x^2 - 27x + 54$

$= 3(2x^2 - 9x + 18)$

$= 3(2x + 3)(x - 6)$

10. $\dfrac{4}{a^2 - 16} + \dfrac{5}{(a-4)^2}$

$= \dfrac{4}{(a-4)(a+4)} + \dfrac{5}{(a-4)^2}$

$= \dfrac{4}{(a-4)(a+4)} \cdot \dfrac{a-4}{a-4} + \dfrac{5}{(a-4)^2} \cdot \dfrac{a+4}{a+4}$

$= \dfrac{4a - 16}{(a+4)(a-4)^2} + \dfrac{5a + 20}{(a+4)(a-4)^2}$

$= \dfrac{9a + 4}{(a+4)(a-4)^2}$

11. $\qquad x + \dfrac{24}{x} = 11$

$\qquad x\left[x + \dfrac{24}{x}\right] = 11 \cdot x$

$\qquad x^2 + 24 = 11x$

$x^2 - 11x + 24 = 0$

$(x-3)(x-8) = 0$

$x - 3 = 0 \quad\text{or}\quad x - 8 = 0$

$\quad x = 3 \quad\text{or}\qquad x = 8$

The solutions are 3 and 8.

12. Write in standard form.
$\quad y = 4x - 8$

                            Ordered Pair

Let $x = 0$, then $y = -8$ $(0, -8)$

Let $x = 2$, then $y = 0$ $(2, 0)$

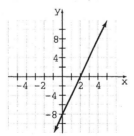

13. $5x - 3y = 12$

$4x - 2y = 6$

Multiply the first equation by 4 and the second equation by -5.

$\quad 4[5x - 3y = 12]$

$-5[4x - 2y = 6]$

gives

$$20x - 12y = 48$$
$$\underline{-20x + 10y = -30}$$
$$-2y = 18$$
$$y = -9$$

Substitute -9 for y in the first equation.
$$5x - 3y = 12$$
$$5x - 3(-9) = 12$$
$$5x + 27 = 12$$
$$5x = -15$$
$$x = -3$$

The solution is $(-3, -9)$

14.
$$\sqrt{\frac{2x^2 y^3}{12x}} = \sqrt{\frac{xy^3}{6}}$$
$$= \frac{\sqrt{xy^3}}{\sqrt{6}}$$
$$= \frac{\sqrt{y^2}\sqrt{xy}}{\sqrt{6}}$$
$$= \frac{y\sqrt{xy}}{\sqrt{6}}$$
$$= \frac{y\sqrt{xy}}{\sqrt{6}} \cdot \frac{\sqrt{6}}{\sqrt{6}}$$
$$= \frac{y\sqrt{6xy}}{6}$$

15. $2\sqrt{28} - 3\sqrt{7} + \sqrt{63} = 2\sqrt{4}\sqrt{7} - 3\sqrt{7} + \sqrt{9}\sqrt{7}$
$$= 2 \cdot 2\sqrt{7} - 3\sqrt{7} + 3\sqrt{7}$$
$$= 4\sqrt{7} - 3\sqrt{7} + 3\sqrt{7}$$
$$= 4\sqrt{7}$$

16.
$$x - 1 = \sqrt{x^2 - 7}$$
$$(x-1)^2 = \left(\sqrt{x^2 - 7}\right)^2$$
$$x^2 - 2x + 1 = x^2 - 7$$
$$-2x + 1 = -7$$
$$-2x = -8$$
$$x = 4$$

Check: $x - 1 = \sqrt{x^2 - 7}$
$$4 - 1 = \sqrt{4^2 - 7}$$
$$3 = \sqrt{16 - 7}$$
$$3 = \sqrt{9}$$
$$3 = 3 \text{ True}$$

17. $2x^2 + 3x - 8 = 0$
$$a = 2, b = 3, c = -8$$
$$x = \frac{-b \pm \sqrt{b^2 - 4ac}}{2a}$$
$$= \frac{-3 \pm \sqrt{(3)^2 - 4(2)(-8)}}{2(2)}$$
$$= \frac{-3 \pm \sqrt{9 + 64}}{4}$$
$$= \frac{-3 \pm \sqrt{73}}{4}$$
$$x = \frac{-3 + \sqrt{73}}{4} \quad \text{or} \quad x = \frac{-3 - \sqrt{73}}{4}$$

The solutions are $\dfrac{-3 + \sqrt{73}}{4}$ and $\dfrac{-3 - \sqrt{73}}{4}$.

18.
$$\frac{500 \text{ square feet}}{4 \text{ pounds fertilizer}} = \frac{3200 \text{ square feet}}{x \text{ pounds fertilizer}}$$
$$\frac{500}{4} = \frac{3200}{x}$$
$$500x = 4 \cdot 3200$$
$$500x = 12{,}800$$
$$x = 25.6$$

25.6 pounds of fertilizer are needed for 3200 square feet of lawn.

19. Let w = width of garden
Then $4w - 3$ = length of garden
$$P = 2l + 2w$$
$$64 = 2(4w - 3) + 2w$$
$$64 = 8w - 6 + 2w$$
$$70 = 10w$$
$$7 = w$$
The width is 7 feet and the length is $4(7) - 3 = 25$ feet.

20. Let w = walking speed
Then $w + 3$ = jogging speed

Time to walk 2 miles = $\dfrac{2}{w}$

Time to jog 2 miles = $\dfrac{2}{w + 3}$

Total time was 1 hour.

$$\frac{2}{w} + \frac{2}{w+3} = 1$$

$$w(w+3)\left[\frac{2}{w} + \frac{2}{w+3}\right] = 1(w+3)w$$

$$2(w+3) + 2w = w^2 + 3w$$

$$2w + 6 + 2w = w^2 + 3w$$

$$4w + 6 = w^2 + 3w$$

$$0 = w^2 - w - 6$$

$$0 = (w-3)(w+2)$$

$$(w-3)(w+2) = 0$$

$$w - 3 = 0 \quad \text{or} \quad w + 2 = 0$$

$$w = 3 \quad \text{or} \quad w = -2$$

Since w must be positive, his walking speed is 3 mph and his jogging speed is $3 + 3 = 6$ mph.